Lecture Notes in Artificial Intelligence 11658

Subseries of Lecture Notes in Computer Science

More information about this series at http://www.springer.com/series/1244

Albert Ali Salah · Alexey Karpov ·
Rodmonga Potapova (Eds.)

Speech and Computer

21st International Conference, SPECOM 2019
Istanbul, Turkey, August 20–25, 2019
Proceedings

 Springer

Editors
Albert Ali Salah
Utrecht University
Utrecht, The Netherlands

Boğaziçi University
Istanbul, Turkey

Rodmonga Potapova ⓘ
Moscow State Linguistic University
Moscow, Russia

Alexey Karpov ⓘ
St. Petersburg Institute for Informatics
and Automation of the Russian Academy
of Sciences
St. Petersburg, Russia

ISSN 0302-9743   ISSN 1611-3349   (electronic)
Lecture Notes in Artificial Intelligence
ISBN 978-3-030-26060-6   ISBN 978-3-030-26061-3   (eBook)
https://doi.org/10.1007/978-3-030-26061-3

LNCS Sublibrary: SL7 – Artificial Intelligence

This Springer imprint is published by the registered company Springer Nature Switzerland AG
The registered company address is: Gewerbestrasse 11, 6330 Cham, Switzerland

SPECOM 2019 Preface

The International Conference on Speech and Computer (SPECOM) was established by the St. Petersburg Institute for Informatics and Automation of the Russian Academy of Sciences (SPIIRAS) and the Herzen State Pedagogical University of Russia thanks to the efforts of Prof. Yuri Kosarev and Prof. Rajmund Piotrowski.

In its long history, the SPECOM conference was organized alternately by SPIIRAS and by the Moscow State Linguistic University (MSLU) in their home cities. SPECOM 2019 was the 21st event in the series, organized by Boğaziçi University (Istanbul, Turkey), in cooperation with SPIIRAS and MSLU. The conference was sponsored by ASM Solutions Ltd. (Moscow, Russia) and supported by the International Speech Communication Association. The conference was held jointly with the 4th International Conference on Interactive Collaborative Robotics (ICR) – where problems and modern solutions of human–robot interaction were discussed – during August 20–25, 2019 at Boğaziçi University, one of the top research universities in Turkey, established in 1863.

During the conferences three invited talks were given by Prof. Hynek Hermansky (Julian S. Smith Professor of Electrical Engineering and the Director of the Center for Language and Speech Processing at the Johns Hopkins University in Baltimore, Maryland, USA and Research Professor at the Brno University of Technology, Czech Republic), Prof. Odette Scharenborg (Delft University of Technology, The Netherlands), and Prof. Erol Şahin (Computer Engineering Dept., Middle East Technical University, Ankara, Turkey).

It is often argued that in in processing of sensory signals such as speech, engineering should apply knowledge of properties of human perception—both have the same goal of getting information from the signal. Prof. Hermansky's talk, entitled "If You Can't Beat Them, Join Them," showed examples from speech technology that perceptual research can also learn from advances in technology. Since speech evolved to be heard and properties of hearing are imprinted on speech, engineering optimizations of speech technology often yield human-like processing strategies. Prof. Hermansky presented a model of human speech communication which suggests that redundancies introduced in speech production in order to protect the message during its transmission through a realistic noisy acoustic environment are being used by human speech perception for a reliable decoding of the message. That led to a particular architecture of an automatic recognition (ASR) system in which longer temporal segments of spectrally smoothed temporal trajectories of spectral energies in individual frequency bands of speech are used to derive estimates of the posterior probabilities of speech sounds. Combinations of these estimates in reliable frequency bands were then adaptively fused to yield the final probability vectors, which best satisfy the adopted performance monitoring criteria.

Speech recognition is the mapping of a continuous, highly variable speech signal onto discrete, abstract representations. In both human and automatic speech processing, the phoneme is considered to play an important role. Abstractionist theories of human speech processing assume the presence of abstract, phoneme-like units that sequenced together constitute words, while many large vocabulary automatic speech recognition (ASR) systems use phoneme acoustic models. Prof. Scharenborg, in her talk entitled "The Representation of Speech in Human and Artificial Brain," argued that phonemes might not be the unit of speech representation during human speech processing and that comparisons between humans and dynamic neural networks and cross-fertilization of the two research fields can provide valuable insights into the way humans process speech and thereby improve ASR technology. The present volume includes an invited paper by Prof. Scharenborg that discusses these issues at length.

Prof. Şahin's talk, entitled "Animating Industrial Robots for Human–Robot Interaction," discussed interesting interaction research for robot-assisted assembly operations in the production lines of factories. Prof. Şahin argued that as platforms that require fast and fine manipulation of parts and tools remain beyond the capabilities of robotic systems in the near future, robotic systems are predicted not to replace, but to collaborate with the humans working on the assembly lines to increase their productivity. He briefly summarized the vision and goals of a recent TUBITAK project, titled CIRAK, which aims to develop a robotic manipulator system that will help humans in an assembly task by handing them the proper tools and parts at the right time in a correct manner. Toward this end, Prof. Şahin shared his group's recent studies on the creation of a commercial robotic manipulator platform, made more life-like by extensions and modifications to its look and behavior.

This volume contains a collection of submitted papers presented at the conference, which were thoroughly reviewed by members of the Program Committee consisting of more than 100 top specialists, as well as an invited paper by Prof. Scharenborg. Each paper was reviewed, single blind, by two to four committee members (three reviewers on the average) and then discussed by the program chairs. In total, 57 papers were selected by the Program Committee for presentation at the SPECOM Conference. A total of 126 submissions were received and evaluated for SPECOM/ICR. The conference sessions were thematically organized, into Audio Signal Processing, Automatic Speech Recognition, Speaker Recognition, Computational Paralinguistics, Speech Synthesis, Sign Language and Multimodal Processing, and Speech and Language Resources. An increasing number of papers used deep neural network-based approaches across these themes.

We would like to express our gratitude to all authors for providing their papers on time, to the members of the Program Committee for their careful reviews and paper selection, and to the editors and correctors for their hard work in preparing this volume. Special thanks are due to Alen Demirel, Cem Tunçel, Bilge Yüksel, Hasan Küçük of BROS Group, our Conference Office, for their excellent work during the conference organization.

August 2019

Albert Ali Salah
Alexey Karpov
Rodmonga Potapova

Organization

General Co-chairs

Albert Ali Salah Utrecht University and Boğaziçi University,
                  The Netherlands/Turkey
Alexey Karpov SPIIRAS Institute, Russia
Rodmonga Potapova Moscow State Linguistic University, Russia

Program Co-chairs

Heysem Kaya Namık Kemal University, Turkey
Murat Saraçlar Boğaziçi University, Turkey
Ebru Arisoy Saraçlar MEF University, Turkey

Program Committee

Shyam Agrawal, India
Lale Akarun, Turkey
Rafet Akdeniz, Turkey
Tanel Alumäe, Estonia
Levent M. Arslan, Turkey
Ebru Arisoy Saraçlar, Turkey
Elias Azarov, Belarus
Peter Beim Graben, Germany
Marie-Luce Bourguet, UK
Christian-Alexander Bunge, Germany
Eric Castelli, Vietnam
Vladimir Chuchupal, Russia
Nicholas Cummins, Germany
Vlado Delic, Serbia
Hasan Demir, Turkey
Olivier Deroo, Belgium
Anna Esposito, Italy
Keelan Evanini, USA
Vera Evdokimova, Russia
Nikos Fakotakis, Greece
Mauro Falcone, Italy
Vasiliki Foufi, Switzerland
Philip N. Garner, Switzerland
Gábor Gosztolya, Hungary
Tunga Gungor, Turkey
Ivan Himawan, Australia

Ruediger Hoffmann, Germany
Marek Hruz, Czech Republic
Kazuki Irie, Germany
Rainer Jaeckel, Germany
Oliver Jokisch, Germany
Denis Jouvet, France
Alexey Karpov, Russia
Heysem Kaya, Turkey
Andreas Kerren, Sweden
Tomi Kinnunen, Finland
Irina Kipyatkova, Russia
Daniil Kocharov, Russia
Liliya Komalova, Russia
Evgeny Kostyuchenko, Russia
Ivan Kraljevski, Germany
Galina Lavrentyeva, Russia
Benjamin Lecouteux, France
Boris Lobanov, Belarus
Elena Lyakso, Russia
Joseph Mariani, France
Maria De Marsico, Italy
Jindřich Matoušek, Czech Republic
Yuri Matveev, Russia
Li Meng, UK
Peter Mihajlik, Hungary
Iosif Mporas, UK

Bernd Möbius, Germany
Luděk Müller, Czech Republic
Satoshi Nakamura, Japan
Stavros Ntalampiras, Italy
Géza Németh, Hungary
Olga Perepelkina, Russia
Dimitar Popov, Bulgaria
Branislav Popović, Serbia
Rodmonga Potapova, Russia
Fabien Ringeval, France
Andrey Ronzhin, Russia
Paolo Rosso, Spain
Sakriani Sakti, Japan
Albert Ali Salah,
    The Netherlands/Turkey
Murat Saraçlar, Turkey
Maximilian Schmitt, Germany
Friedhelm Schwenker, Germany
Vidhyasaharan Sethu, Australia
Milan Sečujski, Serbia

Ingo Siegert, Germany
Vered Silber-Varod, Israel
Pavel Skrelin, Russia
Mikhail Stolbov, Russia
Tilo Strutz, Germany
György Szaszák, Hungary
Ivan Tashev, USA
Natalia Tomashenko, France
Laszlo Toth, Hungary
Isabel Trancoso, Portugal
Jan Trmal, USA
Liliya Tsirulnik, USA
Dirk Van Compernolle, Belgium
Vasilisa Verkhodanova, The Netherlands
Benjamin Weiss, Germany
Andreas Wendemuth, Germany
Matthias Wolff, Germany
Milos Zelezny, Czech Republic
Zixing Zhang, UK

Additional Reviewers

Cem Rıfkı Aydın
Somnath Banerjee
Branko Brkljač
Buse Buz
Koray Çiftçi
Gretel Liz De la Peña Sarracén
Ali Erkan
Nikša Jakovljević
Atul Kumar

Alexander Leipnitz
Michael Maruschke
Iris Ouyang
Sergey Rybin
Siniša Suzić
Juan Javier Sánchez Junquera
Oxana Verkholyak
Celaleddin Yeroglu

Contents

The Representation of Speech and Its Processing in the Human Brain and Deep Neural Networks

Odette Scharenborg[(✉)]

Multimedia Analysis Group, Delft University of Technology,
Van Mourik Broekmanweg 6, 2628 XE Delft, The Netherlands
o.e.scharenborg@tudelft.nl

Abstract. For most languages in the world and for speech that deviates from the standard pronunciation, not enough (annotated) speech data is available to train an automatic speech recognition (ASR) system. Moreover, human intervention is needed to adapt an ASR system to a new language or type of speech. Human listeners, on the other hand, are able to quickly adapt to nonstandard speech and can learn the sound categories of a new language without having been explicitly taught to do so. In this paper, I will present comparisons between human speech processing and deep neural network (DNN)-based ASR and will argue that the cross-fertilisation of the two research fields can provide valuable information for the development of ASR systems that can flexibly adapt to any type of speech in any language. Specifically, I present results of several experiments carried out on both human listeners and DNN-based ASR systems on the representation of speech and lexically-guided perceptual learning, i.e., the ability to adapt a sound category on the basis of new incoming information resulting in improved processing of subsequent speech. The results showed that DNNs appear to learn structures that humans use to process speech without being explicitly trained to do so, and that, similar to humans, DNN systems learn speaker-adapted phone category boundaries from a few labelled examples. These results are the first steps towards building human-speech processing inspired ASR systems that, similar to human listeners, can adjust flexibly and fast to all kinds of new speech.

Keywords: Speech representations · Adaptation · Non-standard speech · Deep neural networks · Human speech processing · Perceptual learning

1 Introduction

Automatic speech recognition (ASR) is the mapping of a continuous, highly variable speech signal onto discrete, abstract representations, typically phonemes or words. ASR works well in relatively restricted settings (e.g., speech without strong accents, quiet background) but tends to break down when the speech that needs to be recognised diverges from 'normal' speech, e.g., because of speech impediments or accents, or when no or only limited annotated training data is available for the type of speech or language for which the system is build (i.e., low-resource languages). In fact, for only

© Springer Nature Switzerland AG 2019
A. A. Salah et al. (Eds.): SPECOM 2019, LNAI 11658, pp. 1–8, 2019.
https://doi.org/10.1007/978-3-030-26061-3_1

about 1% of the world languages the minimum amount of training data that is needed to develop ASR technology is available [1]. This means that ASR technology is not available to all people in the world, including those people who would profit the most from it, i.e., people with disabilities or people whose native language does not have a common written form, because of which they need to rely on speech technology to communicate with people and/or computers. The Linguistic Rights as included in the Universal Declaration of Human Rights states that it is a human right to communicate in one's native language. This situation is obviously not yet reached.

Most ASR systems are phoneme-based systems which are based on the principle that a word is composed of a sequence of speech sounds called phonemes, and acoustic representations (i.e., acoustic models) are trained for context-dependent versions of each phoneme. In order to make ASR available for all types of speech in all the world's languages, simply recording and annotating enough speech material for training a phoneme-based ASR system is infeasible. First, because it is impossible to collect for every type of speech in every language of the world the hundreds of hours of speech with their textual transcriptions that are needed to train a system that works reasonably well. Second, because it is impossible for languages that do not have a common writing system. An obvious solution is to map an ASR system trained on a language and type of speech for which there is enough training data (e.g., English spoken by native speaker without a clear accent or speech impediment) to a language or type of speech for which there is little or no data [2–6]. This mapping of an ASR system from one type of speech or language to another requires explicit decisions by a human about which phoneme categories, or rather acoustic models, will need to be adapted or created in the ASR system.

In order to build ASR systems that can flexibly adapt to any type of speech in any language, we need: (1) invariant units of speech which transfer easily and accurately to other languages and different types of speech and lead to the best ASR recognition performance; (2) an ASR system that can flexibly adapt to new types of speech; (3) an ASR system that can decide when to create a new phoneme category, and do so.

Human listeners have been found to do exactly that. They are able to quickly adapt their phoneme categories on the basis of only a few examples to deviant speech, whether due to a speech impediment or an accent, using a process called lexically-guided perceptual learning [7]. Moreover, human listeners have been found to create new phoneme categories, e.g., when learning a new language [8].

So ideally, the search for invariant speech units and flexible adaptation processes in ASR are based on the speech representations and speech recognition processes in human speech processing as the best speech recogniser is a human who is a native speaker of the language [9]. Moreover, despite the differences in hardware between a human listener and an ASR system, they both carry out the same process: the recognition of speech [10]. There is ample evidence that knowledge about human speech processing has powerful potential for improving ASR ([9–14], for a review [15]). For instance, knowledge about human speech processing and human hearing has been used in the development of Mel-frequency cepstral coefficients (MFCCs, [16]) and Perceptual Linear Predictives (PLPs, [14]), while the episodic theory of human speech processing was the inspiration to the development of template-based approaches to ASR (e.g., [17]).

In this paper, I focus on the first two requisites for building an ASR system that can flexibly adapt to any type of speech in any language by comparing human speech processing and deep neural network (DNN)-based ASR. I will summarise experiments which compare the representation of speech and adaptation processes in the human brain and DNNs, with the ultimate aim to build human speech processing inspired ASR systems that can flexibly adapt to any speech style in any language, i.e., the third requisite. Recent advances in deep learning make DNNs currently the best-performing ASR systems [18]. DNNs are inspired by the human brain, which is often suggested to be the reason for their impressive abilities, e.g., [19]. Although both the human brain and DNNs consist of neurons and neural connections, little is known about whether DNNs actually use similar representations for speech and solve the task of speech recognition in the same way the human brain does.

Fig. 1. What features does a DNN use to distinguish between the plane in the blue sky on the left and the chair on the green lawn?

2 Speech Representations

When learning one's first language, human listeners learn to associate certain acoustic variability with certain phonological categories. The question I am interested in is whether a DNN also learns phonological categories similar to those used by human listeners. Using the visual example in Fig. 1 as an example: if a DNN is able to distinguish between a plane in a blue sky and a chair on a green lawn, has the DNN learned to distinguish the blue background from the green background or has it learned features that are associated with planes and features that are associated with chairs to distinguish the two objects as a human would do to distinguish these two objects in these pictures?

The question what speech representations a DNN learns during speech processing was investigated using a naïve, general feed-forward DNN which was trained on the task of vowel/consonant classification [20]. Vowel/consonant classification is a relatively simple, well-understood task, which allows us to investigate what a naïve, general DNN exactly learns when faced with the large variability of the speech sounds in the speech signal. Crucially, the speech representations in the different hidden layers of the DNN were investigated by visualising the activations of the speech representations in those hidden layers using different linguistic labels that are known to correspond to the underlying structures that human listeners use to process and understand speech.

The DNN consisted of 3 hidden layers with 1024 nodes each, and was trained on 64 h of read speech from the Corpus Spoken Dutch (CGN; [21]). Accuracy on the vowel/consonant classification task, averaged over five runs, was 85.5% (consonants: 85.2%; vowels: 86.7% correct). Subsequently, the input frames were labelled with:

- Phoneme labels: 39 in total.
- Manner of articulation: indicates the type of constriction in the vocal tract. For consonants, four categories were distinguished: plosive, fricative, nasal, approximant. For vowels, three categories were distinguished: short vowel, long vowel, diphthong.
- Place of articulation: indicates the location of the constriction in the vocal tract. For consonants, six categories were distinguished: bilabial, labiodental, velar, alveolar, palatal, glottal. For vowels, three tongue position categories were distinguished: front, central, back.

The clusters of speech representations at the different hidden layers were visualised using t-distributed neighbor embedding (t-SNE, [22]). The first visualisation investigated the clusters of consonants and vowels in the different hidden layers. The results showed that from earlier to later hidden layers, the vowel and consonant clusters become more compact and more separate, showing that the DNN is learning to create speech representations that are increasingly abstract.

In the second series of visualisations, the input frames were first labelled with the phoneme labels. This visualisation showed that the phoneme labels were not randomly distributed over the hidden layers. Rather, despite that the DNN was trained on a vowel/consonant classification task, the DNN implicitly learned to cluster frames with the same phoneme label to some extent. Subsequent analyses with labelling of the frames in terms of manner of articulation and place of articulation showed that the DNN learned to cluster sounds together that are produced in similar ways such that consonants with a similar manner of articulation and vowels with a similar place of articulation are clustered into clearly defined groups. The DNN thus appeared to learn structures that human listeners use to process speech without having been explicitly trained to do so.

3   Adaptation to Non-standard Speech

Adaptation to nonstandard speech is often referred to as 'perceptual learning' in the human speech processing literature. Perceptual learning is defined as the temporary or more permanent adaptation of sound categories after exposure to nonstandard speech such that the nonstandard sound is included into a pre-existing sound category, which leads to an improvement in the intelligibility of the speech (see for a review [23]). Perceptual learning is fast. Human listeners need only a few instances of the deviant sounds [24, 25] to adapt their sound category boundaries to include the nonstandard sound [7, 23–28]. ASR systems adapt to new speakers and listening conditions using both short-time adaptation algorithms (e.g., fMLLR [29]) and longer-term adaptation techniques (e.g., DNN weight training [30]). For both human listeners and ASR systems, lexical knowledge about the word in which the nonstandard sound occurs is crucial to correctly interpret the nonstandard sound [7, 23].

3.1   Does a DNN Show Human-Like Adaptation to Nonstandard Speech?

In recent work, we investigated the question whether DNNs are able to adapt to nonstandard speech as rapidly as human listeners, and whether DNNs use intermediate speech representations that correlate with those used in human perceptual learning [12]. Mimicking the set-up of a human lexically-guided perceptual learning study [28], which allows for the direct comparison between human listening behaviour and the behaviour of the DNN, we trained a feed-forward DNN on the read speech of CGN. The trained model was regarded as a 'native Dutch listener'. In the next step, the DNN was retrained with the acoustic stimuli from the original human perceptual learning study [28], i.e., speech from a new speaker who had an (artificially created) nonstandard pronunciation of a sound in between [l] and [ɹ], referred to as [l/ɹ]: One model was trained with the [l/ɹ] sound always occurring in /r/-final words; another model was trained with the [l/ɹ] sound always occurring in /l/-final words. A final, baseline model was trained on the same words but without nonstandard pronunciations.

The results showed that the DNNs retrained with the [l/ɹ] sounds indeed showed perceptual learning: The baseline model classified the nonstandard sound during a subsequent phase as both [l] and [ɹ], the model retrained with the [l/ɹ] sound in /r/-final words classified the sound as [ɹ] while the model retrained with the nonstandard sound in /l/-final words classified the sound as [l]. This difference between the two models trained with the nonstandard pronunciation is called the perceptual learning effect. Moreover, this perceptual learning effect did not only occur at the output level, but calculations of the distances between the average activations of the nonstandard sound and those of the natural sounds and the visualisations of the activations of the hidden layers showed that perceptual learning also occurred at the DNN's intermediate levels. Interestingly, the visualisations of the speech representations in the DNN's hidden layers showed that the phonetic space was warped to accommodate the nonstandard speech. This warping of the phonetic space seems to be at odds with theories of human speech processing, which assumes that the nonstandard sound is incorporated in the existing phoneme category by redrawing the phoneme category boundaries [26]. In follow-up research, I plan to test this prediction of the DNN about human speech processing in new human perceptual experiments.

3.2   Are Nonstandard Sounds Processed Similarly in Human Listeners and DNNs?

In subsequent work, this research was pushed further and we asked the questions whether nonstandard sounds are processed in the same way as natural sounds; and, how many examples of the nonstandard sound are needed before the DNN adapts? Again, the experimental design [24] and acoustic stimuli were taken from earlier research on lexically-guided perceptual learning in human listeners [28]. The same DNN as in the study described in Sect. 3.1, was retrained but this time using increasing amounts of nonstandard sounds (in 10 bins of 4 ambiguous items). Calculations of the distances between the average activations of the nonstandard sound and those of the natural sounds in the different hidden layers showed that the DNN showed perceptual learning after only four examples of the nonstandard sound, and little further adaptation for subsequent training examples.

Interestingly, human listeners have been found to show a similar type of step-like function after about 10–15 examples of the nonstandard sound. The difference in number of examples could be explained by the fact that the DNN sees each training example 30 times (30 epochs) whereas the human listener hears each token only once. In follow-up research, I plan to further investigate the step-like function in adaptation in human listening.

4   Concluding Remarks

In this paper, I summarised results from three studies comparing human speech processing and speech processing in deep neural networks. The results showed that:

- Similar to human listeners, the DNN progressively abstracted away variability in the speech signal in subsequent hidden layers;
- Without being explicitly trained to do so, the DNN captured the structure in speech by clustering the speech signal into linguistically-defined speech category representations, similar to those used during human speech processing;
- Similar to human listeners, the DNN adapted to nonstandard speech on the basis of only a few labelled examples by warping the phoneme space;
- This adaptation did not only occur in the output layer but instead occurred in the hidden layers of the DNN and showed a step-like function.

These detailed comparisons between human speech processing and DNN-based ASR highlight clear similarities between the speech representations and their processing in the human brain and in DNN-based ASR systems. Moreover, the DNNs made specific predictions about adaptation to nonstandard speech that will be investigated in experiments on human speech processing to further investigate the differences and similarities between adaptation to nonstandard speech in humans and DNN-based ASR systems. These experiments will lead to important new insights regarding the adaptation of human listeners to nonstandard speech.

Past research [9–17] has shown that knowledge of human speech processing can be used to improve ASRs. The observed similarities between human and DNN speech processing suggest that integrating the flexibility of the human adaptation processes into DNN-based ASRs is likely to lead to improved adaptation of DNN-based ASRs to nonstandard speech. Crucial for the development of human-speech processing inspired ASR systems that, similar to human listeners, can adjust flexibly and fast to all types of speech in all languages is understanding when and how human listeners decide to create a new phoneme category rather than adapting an existing phoneme category to include a nonstandard pronunciation. This is a crucial next step in this research.

Acknowledgments. I would like to thank Junrui Ni for carrying out the experiments described in Sect. 3.2 and Mark Hasegawa-Johnson for fruitful discussions on the experiments in Sect. 3.2.

References

1. Adda, G., et al.: Breaking the unwritten language barrier: the BULB project. In: Proceedings 5th Workshop on Spoken Language Technologies for Under-Resourced Languages (2016)
2. Waibel, A., Schultz, T.: Experiments on cross-language acoustic modelling. In: Proceedings of Interspeech (2001)
3. Vu, N.T., Metze, F., Schultz, T.: Multilingual bottleneck features and its application for under-resourced languages. In: Proceedings of the 3rd Workshop on Spoken Language Technologies for Under-Resourced Languages, Cape Town, South Africa (2012)
4. Xu, H., Do, V.H., Xiao, X., Chng, E.S.: A comparative study of BNF and DNN multilingual training on cross-lingual low-resource speech recognition. In: Proceedings of Interspeech, pp. 2132–2136 (2015)
5. Scharenborg, O., Ebel, P., Ciannella, F., Hasegawa-Johnson, M., Dehak, N.: Building an ASR system for Mboshi using a cross-language definition of acoustic units approach. In: Proceedings of the International Workshop on Spoken Language Technologies for Under-Resourced Languages, Gurugram, India (2018)
6. Scharenborg, O., et al.: Building an ASR system for a low-resource language through the adaptation of a high-resource language ASR system: preliminary results. In: Proceedings of the International Conference on Natural Language, Signal and Speech Processing, Casablanca, Morocco (2017)
7. Norris, D., McQueen, J.M., Cutler, A.: Perceptual learning in speech. Cogn. Psychol. **47**(2), 204–238 (2003)
8. Best, C.T., Tyler, M.C.: Nonnative and second-language speech perception. Commonalities and complementaries. In: Bohn, O.-S., Munro, M.J. (eds.) Language Experience in Second Language Speech Learning: In Honor of James Emil Flege, pp. 13–34. John Benjamins, Amsterdam (2007)
9. Davis, M.H., Scharenborg, O.: Speech perception by humans and machines. In: Gaskell, M.G., Mirkovic, J. (eds.) Speech Perception and Spoken Word Recognition, Part of the Series "Current Issues in the Psychology of Language", pp. 181–203. Routledge, London (2017)
10. Scharenborg, O., Norris, D., ten Bosch, L., McQueen, J.M.: How should a speech recognizer work? Cogn. Sci. **29**(6), 867–918 (2005)
11. Scharenborg, O.: Modeling the use of durational information in human spoken-word recognition. J. Acoust. Soc. Am. **127**(6), 3758–3770 (2010)
12. Scharenborg, O., Tiesmeyer, S., Hasegawa-Johnson, M., Dehak, N.: Visualizing phoneme category adaptation in deep neural networks. In: Proceedings of Interspeech (2018)
13. Dusan, S., Rabiner, L.R.: On integrating insights from human speech recognition into automatic speech recognition. In: Proceedings of Interspeech, pp. 1233–1236 (2005)
14. Hermansky, H.: Should recognizers have ears? Speech Commun. **25**, 3–27 (1998)
15. Scharenborg, O.: Reaching over the gap: a review of efforts to link human and automatic speech recognition research. Speech Commun. **49**, 336–347 (2007)
16. Davis, S., Mermelstein, P.: Comparison of the parametric representation for monosyllabic word recognition. IEEE Trans. Acoust. Speech Signal Process. **28**(4), 357–366 (1980)
17. De Wachter, M., Demuynck, K., van Compernolle, D., Wambaq, P.: Data driven example based continuous speech recognition. In: Proceedings of Eurospeech, Geneva, Switzerland, pp. 1133–1136 (2003)
18. Hinton, G., et al.: Deep neural networks for acoustic modeling in speech recognition: the shared views of four research groups. IEEE Sig. Process. Mag. **29**(6), 82–97 (2012)

19. Wan, J., et al.: Deep learning for content-based image retrieval: a comprehensive study. In: Proceedings of the 22nd ACM International conference on Multimedia (MM 2014), pp. 157–166 (2014)

20. Scharenborg, O., van der Gouw, N., Larson, M., Marchiori, E.: The representation of speech in deep neural networks. In: Kompatsiaris, I., Huet, B., Mezaris, V., Gurrin, C., Cheng, W.-H., Vrochidis, S. (eds.) MMM 2019. LNCS, vol. 11296, pp. 194–205. Springer, Cham (2019). https://doi.org/10.1007/978-3-030-05716-9_16

21. Oostdijk, N.H.J., et al.: Experiences from the spoken Dutch Corpus project. In: Proceedings of LREC, pp. 340–347 (2002)

22. Van der Maaten, L., Hinton, G.: Visualizing data using t-SNE. J. Mach. Learn. Res. **9**, 2579–2605 (2008)

23. Samuel, A.G., Kraljic, T.: Perceptual learning in speech perception. Atten. Percept. Psychophys. **71**, 1207–1218 (2009)

24. Drozdova, P., van Hout, R., Scharenborg, O.: Processing and adaptation to ambiguous sounds during the course of perceptual learning. In: Proceedings of Interspeech, pp. 2811–2815 (2016)

25. Poellmann, K., McQueen, J.M., Mitterer, H.: The time course of perceptual learning. In: Proceedings of ICPhS (2011)

26. Clarke-Davidson, C., Luce, P.A., Sawusch, J.R.: Does perceptual learning in speech reflect changes in phonetic category representation or decision bias? Percept. Psychophys. **70**, 604–618 (2008)

27. Drozdova, P., van Hout, R., Scharenborg, O.: Lexically-guided perceptual learning in non-native listening. Bilingualism: Lang. Cogn. **19**(5), 914–920 (2016). https://doi.org/10.1017/s136672891600002x

28. Scharenborg, O., Janse, E.: Comparing lexically-guided perceptual learning in younger and older listeners. Atten. Percept. Psychophys. **75**(3), 525–536 (2013). https://doi.org/10.3758/s13414-013-0422-4

29. Gales, M.J.: Maximum likelihood linear transformations for HMM-based speech recognition. Comput. Speech Lang. **12**(2), 75–98 (1998)

30. Liao, H.: Speaker adaptation of context dependent deep neural networks. In: Proceedings of ICASSP, pp. 7947–7951 (2013)

A Detailed Analysis and Improvement of Feature-Based Named Entity Recognition for Turkish

Arda Akdemir[1(✉)] and Tunga Güngör[2]

[1] University of Tokyo, Tokyo, Japan
aakdemir@hgc.jp
[2] Bogazici University, Istanbul, Turkey
gungort@boun.edu.tr

Abstract. Named Entity Recognition (NER) is an important task in Natural Language Processing (NLP) with a wide range of applications. Recently, word embedding based systems that does not rely on hand-crafted features dominate the task as in the case of many other sequence labeling tasks in NLP. However, we are also observing the emergence of hybrid models that make use of hand crafted features through data augmentation to improve performance of such NLP systems. Such hybrid systems are especially important for less resourced languages such as Turkish as deep learning models require a large dataset to achieve good performance. In this paper, we first give a detailed analysis of the effect of various syntactic, semantic and orthographic features on NER for Turkish. We also improve the performance of the best feature based models for Turkish using additional features. We believe that our results will guide the research in this area and help making use of the key features for data augmentation.

Keywords: Named Entity Recognition · Conditional Random Fields · Dependency Parsing · Turkish

1 Introduction

Named Entity Recognition was first defined officially as an NLP task in the Message Understanding Conference (MUC) in 1995. According to its first formal definition [2], NER consists of two main subtasks: Detection of named entities and categorizing each detected entity into predefined categories. Identification is an important step which enables information extraction over large texts. The second step can be considered as a more refined task where the aim is to use any kind of contextual or word-level, sub-word level information to distinguish between subcategories of entities. Ratinov et al. [15] show that this step is more challenging compared to detection. Detecting and properly categorizing the named entities is an important first step for analyzing a given text and is shown to improve the performance of many other NLP tasks such as machine translation [10] and

© Springer Nature Switzerland AG 2019
A. A. Salah et al. (Eds.): SPECOM 2019, LNAI 11658, pp. 9–19, 2019.
https://doi.org/10.1007/978-3-030-26061-3_2

question answering on speech data [13]. Named entities are also used to select a better language model to enhance the performance of speech-to-text systems [1].

Dependency Parsing (DP) is an important research topic in NLP. It is demonstrated to be highly useful for various NLP tasks. Dependency parsing is shown to be useful for machine translation, question answering and named entity recognition [3,18]. Following the previous work we used dependency parsing related features together with other features during our experiments to boost the NER performance in our feature based setting.

In this paper, we first give a detailed analysis of the effect of various morphological, syntactic and semantic level features on NER performance. Throughout our experiments we make use of a Conditional Random Fields (CRF) based model which makes use of hand crafted features. We also show improvements over the previous work on feature based NER for Turkish. Our final model which can be considered as an extension to the previous feature based models [4,19], makes use of dependency parsing related features which are not tested extensively in this setting before to the best of our knowledge. The main contributions of this paper can be considered as follows:

– A detailed analysis of each hand crafted feature on the NER performance.
– Showing an improvement over the previous work on feature based NER models for Turkish by using dependency related features in addition.

The paper is organized as follows: We start by giving the previous work done on NER and feature based models. Then we describe the dataset we have used in Sect. 3. This will be followed by the Methodology Section which describes the CRF model and the feature sets we have used in detail. Finally we give the results we have obtained and compare our results with related work.

2   Previous Work

Early work in this area is dominated by feature based statistical models. McCallum et al. [12] give the first results for using a CRF based model together with hand crafted features for the NER task. A more detailed overview of the feature based statistical models used for NER until 2007 can be found in the work of Nadeau et al. [14].

Recent work on NER is dominated by deep learning models and these models are consistently shown to outperform the previous work in this area. Using Convolutional Neural Networks (CNN), Bidirectional Long-short Term Memory (BiLSTM) Recurrent Neural Networks (RNN) is frequent as in the case for many other NLP tasks that can be formulated as a sequence labeling task [8,11]. The work done on less resourced languages is more limited but best results for NER are also obtained by using a similar deep learning architecture for the Turkish language [7].

Previous work on agglutinatively rich languages such as Turkish show that using morphological and syntactic features improves the performance of NER systems [4,7,19]. Yeniterzi et al. [23] exploit the morphological features of morphologically rich languages to gain improvement in NER for Turkish. They focus specifically on language specific morphological features and show that making use of them increase the performance. Şeker et al. [19] make use of various hand crafted features as well as gazetteers for the NER task for Turkish. Later they improve extend the same methodology to cover a wider variety of entity tags and to tackle the same task in a more challenging context where the input is user generated web content [20]. Demir et al. [4] make use of only language independent features along with word embeddings to gain improvement over the previous state of the art. The main contribution of their work is that the same feature set can easily be extended. Recently, Güngör et al. [7] showed that joint learning of morphological disambiguation and NER increases the performance of the NER model.

Using the surface form of the words causes the data sparsity problem as a single word can be extended in multiple ways in such agglutinative languages. Using stemming to solve this problem is often not a good idea as important semantic and syntactic information about the token is lost during this process. Specifically, morphological features are shown to be vital for such languages in several studies [4,23].

3 Datasets

During all our experiments we have made use of a dataset extracted from Turkish newspapers [22]. It is one of the most frequently used datasets for NER for Turkish and considered as the most important benchmark in this setting. As the dataset is relatively old and reannotated and refined many times by different researchers, it is difficult to keep the consistency of the exact version of this dataset being used in each paper. Table 1 gives some statistics about the training and test sets we have used during this paper.

Table 1. (A) Number of annotated entities in the Turkish NER dataset. (B) Number of annotated tokens.

A	LOC	ORG	PER	B	LOC	ORG	PER
Training	9,800	9,117	14,693	Training	11,137	15,470	21,641
Test	1,116	865	1,597	Test	1,315	1,680	2,394

The dataset is annotated in BIO scheme. The initial token of each entity sequence is tagged with 'B' followed by its entity type and the remaining token tags start with 'I'. In our setting we have used the following three entity types: Location (LOC), Person (PER) and Organization (ORG). So an example annotation for a two-token entity of type 'Person' will be tagged as follows: Akira (B-PER) Kurosawa (I-PER). Figure 1 gives an example sentence from the dataset that we have made use of which is additionally annotated with many hand crafted features. The dataset is structured in a token-per-line format where each line contains a single token followed by its feature values. Each annotation following a token will be explained in detail in the following section.

	Token	POS_tag	Capitalization	Stem_Form	Start_of_Sentence	Prop	Acro	Nom	Suff	Depind	Deprel	POShead	NER_label
429	Seçmen	Noun	1	seçmen	1	0	Notacro	Nom	None	0	root	ROOT	O
430	yaşı	Noun	0	yaş	0	0	Notacro	Notnom	SH	4	amod	Adj	O
431	18	Unkn	0	18	0	0	Notacro	Notnom	None	4	obj	Adj	O
432	olan	Adj	0	ol	0	0	Notacro	Notnom	None	8	acl	Noun	O
433	Almanya	Prop	1	Almanya	0	1	Notacro	Nom	None	8	nmod:poss	Noun	B-LOC
434	'da	Unkn	0	'da	0	0	Notacro	Notnom	None	5	flat	Prop	O
435	yarınki	Adj	0	yarın	0	0	Notacro	Notnom	None	8	nmod:poss	Noun	O
436	seçimlerde	Noun	0	seçim	0	0	Notacro	Notnom	DA	17	obl	Verb	O
437	3	Unkn	0	3	0	0	Notacro	Notnom	None	17	nummod	Verb	O
438	milyon	Adj	0	milyon	0	0	Notacro	Notnom	None	9	flat	Unkn	O
439	300	Unkn	0	300	0	0	Notacro	Notnom	None	9	flat	Unkn	O
440	bin	Adj	0	bin	0	0	Notacro	Notnom	None	9	flat	Unkn	O
441	kişi	Noun	0	kişi	0	0	Notacro	Notnom	None	17	nsubj	Verb	O
442	ilk	Adj	0	ilk	0	0	Notacro	Notnom	None	15	amod	Noun	O
443	kez	Noun	0	kez	0	0	Notacro	Notnom	None	17	obl	Verb	O
444	oy	Noun	0	oy	0	0	Notacro	Notnom	None	17	obj	Verb	O
445	kullanacak	Verb	0	kullan	0	0	Notacro	Notnom	YAcAk	1	conj	Noun	O

Fig. 1. Example sentence from the NER dataset.

4   Methodology

In this section we explain the undertaken methodology during this study to analyze and improve on using hand-crafted features for NER for Turkish. We begin by describing the model used during the experiments which will be followed by the explanation of each feature.

4.1   Model

During our experiments we have made use of the CRF based Wapiti toolkit implement by Lavergne et al. [9]. Wapiti is a sequence classifier toolkit which allows training models using various model types and optimization algorithms. The results achieved by this toolkit on the CoNLL-2003 English dataset is comparable to the state-of-the-art deep network based systems even though the training time is shorter and the memory requirement is significantly lower. The toolkit is chosen primarily because it enables fast configuration of various training models as well as fast configuration of the features that are being used by the model. Following subsections will describe the specific aspects of this toolkit.

The toolkit allows using various machine learning models for training as mentioned previously. The models and their brief description are as follows:

- **Maximum Entropy (MAXENT):** Maximum Entropy models are very general probabilistic methods that pick the output with the highest entropy by considering the observations and the prior knowledge. These models are frequently used in NLP tasks that can be formulated as sequence labeling tasks. A Maximum Entropy based model is used in [16] for the POS tagging task.
- **Maximum Entropy Markov Models (MEMM):** It is an extension of the Maximum Entropy models which consider the hidden features of Hidden Markov Models. It is also frequently used in NLP, especially for the sequence labeling tasks such as POS tagging and NER [6].
- **Conditional Random Fields (CRF):** This model calculates the transition probabilities from one prediction to another in addition to the Markovian assumption of the MEMM where the transition probabilities between tags are learned from the training dataset.

Our initial experiments showed that CRF based models consistently outperform others. Thus for the final models tested on the test set, the training is done using the CRF model. Sutton et al. [21] give a detailed formulation for CRF based models. Apart from the training model, we have trained the proposed models with several different optimization algorithms to be more confident about the results we have obtained. Below is the list of the optimization algorithms used together with a brief description:

- **l-bfgs:** Limited-memory Broyden-Fletcher-Goldfarb-Shanno algorithm [5]. It is a quasi-newton optimization algorithm with less memory requirements.
- **sgd-l1:** Stochastic gradient descent with l1 regularization. Our initial experiments showed that sgd-l1 is not suitable in our proposed setting so we have not included it in our grid search experiments.
- **rprop+/-:** Resilient backpropagation which only takes into account the sign of the partial derivative and acts independently on each weight. rprop- refers to the version of the algorithm without the backtracking step.

4.2 Features

We have analyzed many features in this study. Below we explain each feature briefly:

1. **Surface form** (Surf): The surface form of each word.
2. **Initial POS tag** (POS): The POS tag prediction for the stem form of the word by a third party morphological analyzer [17].
3. **Final POS tag** (POS): The POS tag for the complete surface form of the word. This feature is also referred to as POS as we never used both features at the same time and except for the initial experiment we consistently used the Final POS tag as the POS feature.
4. **Capitalization Feature** (Cap): A four valued feature giving information about the orthographic structure of a token. 0 for all lowercase, 1 for Only-firstletter, 2 for ALLUPPER and 3 for miXeD. Capitalization feature is a

fundamental feature for the NER task for Turkish as all named entities are expected to be capitalized. This feature significantly increases the performance in languages like Turkish.

5. **Stem of the word** (Stem): This feature is important to tackle the out-of-vocabulary problem in agglutinative languages like Turkish.

6. **Start of sentence** (SS): Binary feature to handle the ambiguity of capitalization at the beginning of each sentence.

7. **Proper noun** (Prop): This binary feature takes the value 1 if the morphological analyzer predicts the word to be a proper noun and 0 otherwise.

8. **Acronym feature** (Acro): Binary feature denoting whether the morphological analyzer predicts the word to be an acronym or not, e.g. ABD - Acro and Istanbul - Notacro. Acronym's are almost always in the form of ALLUPPER. Yet ALLUPPER is a purely orthographic feature whereas the Acro feature is the prediction made by the morphological analyzer. Also, arbitrary words that are not necessarily acronyms can be found in a dataset and ALLUPPER category detects such cases.

9. **Nominal feature** (Nom): This feature is a combination of three atomic features. Observing the morphological analyses of the labeled entities in the training set showed that, most of them share the following three features: They are capitalized, they are in their stem form and the analyzer predicts them to be Nominal. So we used a binary feature to check whether these three conditions are met or not.

10. **Final suffix** (Suf): The final suffix of the word is given in the morphological analysis format. If the word does not have any suffix 'None' value is given. In order to overcome the data sparsity of complete matching the surface form of the suffix is not used. For example the final suffix of the word 'kalitesinin' which means 'the quality of (something/someone)' is 'nin' but the feature value is 'NHn' where the uppercased letters denote the letters are subject to change in other words but the suffix itself is the same. By using this feature CRF based model can detect all the words that have the same suffix even though the surface form of them may differ as in the case of 'kalitesinin' - 'nin' and 'ormanın' - 'ın'.

11. **Regex Features**: Wapiti allows giving as input regular expressions which are converted either into binary features or the regex match itself is kept as the feature value. We used regular expressions to extract features such as all 1, 2, 3 and 4 character long suffixes and prefixes if they exist. We also used regular expression to create binary features to detect numericals and punctuations in a given token.

12. **Dependency Relation** (Deprel): The predicted relation between the word in question and its predicted head word by the dependency parser used.

13. **Dependency Index** (Depind): The index of the head word of the dependency relation. This can be considered as a positional feature.

14. **POS tag of the head word** (POShead): The POS tag of the head word of the dependency relation. In the case that the word itself is the root word a special POS tag "ROOT" is used.

All features are used with a window size two, i.e. two preceding and two succeeding words are taken into account for each token during calculating the conditional probabilities for the CRF-based model. Increasing the window size greatly increases the computational cost and we found that increasing the window size to more than two does not significantly improve the performance.

4.3 Evaluation Metrics

We used two evaluation metrics which are considered as the standard metrics for the NER task: F1 and MUC. For this task, F1 measures the systems performance of both detecting and categorizing an entity together. MUC metric considers detection and categorization as separate tasks and takes the average of the F1-measures obtained for each sub-task. Thus, MUC scores are higher compared to the F1 scores.

5 Results and Discussion

We performed various experiments with different subsets of the features given above. In this section we first give the results obtained on the 10% of the training set which is used as validation. We used the validation phase to find the best feature subset and then continued with a grid search over the learning algorithms and optimization methods explained in the previous section. Best performing model is tested on the test set to get the final results. We finish the section by comparing our results with the previous work on feature based NER for Turkish.

We started with analyzing the features by adding them cumulatively following the previous work [4]. We determined four core features as our baseline model (BM) and added the remaining features one-by-one. The core features are as follows: Surface form, POS tag, Capitalization and Stem form.

At each step we added each remaining feature, trained the model and observed the change in performance. According to the results we pick the feature that gave the highest improvement to be the next feature added to the current feature subset. The feature with the highest improvement can easily be identified from the order of appearance in Table 2(A) given below.

Table 2. (A)Initial results obtained for the first baseline (BM) together with the training times. (B) Results with the updated baseline (BM2).

A	MUC	F1-measure	Training time	B	F1-measure
BM	0.919	0.889	3,000 s	**BM2**	0.894
+SS	0.921	0.889	3,300 s	**+Cap+Stem+SS**	0.896
+Prop	0.924	0.896	3,400 s	**+Prop+Acro+Nom**	0.899
+Acro	0.924	0.897	3,900 s	**+Suf**	**0.900**
+Nom	0.925	0.896	4,800 s	**+Depind+Deprel**	0.899

At the last step of the experiments addition of the Nominal feature caused a decrease in the performance which is counter-intuitive. Following this, we changed the core feature set and started experiments from the baseline again to analyze in detail the effect of each feature better. The core features for the new baseline model (BM2) are as follows: Surface form, POS tag and all regex features with a window size of 2. Regex features are described in the previous section and includes all orthographic features except for the capitalization feature. Then again we added features in a cumulative manner but this time analyzed the effect of adding these features in groups rather than one-by-one. Table 2(B) gives the results obtained for these experiments.

Table 3. Exploration of combinations of all training models and optimization algorithms.

Model	Optimization algorithm	PER	LOC	ORG	Overall F1	MUC
CRF	l-bfgs	0.909	0.898	0.883	0.899	0.919
	rprop-	0.904	0.892	0.860	0.887	0.904
	rprop+	0.903	0.892	0.860	0.887	0.905
MAXENT	l-bfgs	0.910	0.890	0.865	0.892	0.915
	rprop-	0.913	0.887	0.847	0.887	0.908
	rprop+	0.913	0.887	0.847	0.887	0.908
MEMM	l-bfgs	0.910	0.879	0.845	0.883	0.909
	rprop-	0.911	0.883	0.826	0.879	0.901
	rprop+	0.911	0.883	0.826	0.879	0.901

At the final step we have observed a slight decrease in performance when we added the dependency related features together. Next we did a grid search over the training models and optimization algorithms, using the final feature set to be more confident about the results we have obtained. Table 3 gives the results for these experiments. After the grid search we have concluded that adding dependency relation and dependency index together does not improve the performance of the model, and the best model/optimization algorithm combination is the default combination of CRF/l-bfgs. This combination consistently outperforms all other combinations on both evaluation metrics (Overall F1 and MUC).

Next we trained a model by adding only the dependency relation feature and obtained the best results. The effect of this feature is given in Table 4. We restate the previous best result we have achieved which we call 'Previous Best' for readability.

We have successfully shown on the validation set that the addition of the dependency relation feature in our setting slightly improves the performance. Next we evaluated the true performance of our final proposed model which exploits the dependency relation information, on the test set. Table 5 gives the results obtained for these final experiments. 'Previous Best' denotes the feature

Table 4. Results for adding the dependency relation feature.

	PER	LOC	ORG	Overall F1
Previous Best	0.912	0.895	0.884	0.900
+Deprel	0.916	0.896	0.886	**0.902**

combination with the highest F1 score without taking into account the dependency related features. The feature combination is as follows: Surface form, POS tag, Stem form, Capitalization, Start of Sentence, Proper Noun, Acronym, Nominal, Final Suffix and all regex features explained in the previous section.

Table 5. Final results on the test set. "Previous Best" denotes the best combination observed during the experiments on the validation set without dependency related features.

Model	Entity type	Precision	Recall	F1
Previous Best+Deprel	PER	0.913	0.889	0.900
	LOC	0.921	0.899	0.910
	ORG	0.909	0.856	0.882
	Overall	0.915	**0.884**	**0.899**
+POShead	PER	0.917	0.880	0.898
	LOC	0.923	0.903	0.913
	ORG	0.917	0.850	0.882
	Overall	**0.919**	0.880	**0.899**

Table 6. Comparison with related work using F1 measure as the evaluation metric.

System	PER	ORG	LOC	Overall
Yeniterzi et al. [23]	89.32	83.50	92.15	88.94
Şeker et al. [19] without using gazetteers	90.65	86.12	90.74	89.59
Demir et al. [4] without using vector representations	92.26	83.53	90.73	89.73
Our Model	90.07	88.15	90.98	**89.89**

We did not observe a significant difference when we take into account the POS tag of the head word of the dependency relation.

Finally we compare our results with the previous work on feature based NER for Turkish. Table 6 shows the comparison of our model with the related work. Yeniterzi et al. [23] exploits the morphological features and analyzes the improvement obtained by using them. Following their work we have also made use of various morphological features as explained in the Methodology section.

As we have no access to the gazetteers used by Şeker et al. [19] and do not have access to the vector representations used by Demir et al. [4], we compare our results with their best versions that does not make use of gazetteers and vector representations.

6   Conclusion and Future Work

In this study we have given a detailed analysis of the effect of hand-crafted features on the performance of NER for Turkish language. We tried novel features such as dependency related features and analyzed their effect. We also compared our results with the previous work and showed improvement over them by using additional features. We hope that the findings stated in this work will guide the researchers working on this area. In future, we will be implementing deep learning models that make use of data augmentation by following the findings of this paper.

Acknowledgements. This work was partially supported by JST CREST Grant Number JPMJCR1402, JSPS KAKENHI Grant Numbers 17H01693, and 17K20023JST.

References

1. Bharadwaj, S.S., Medapati, S.B.: Named-entity based speech recognition. US Patent App. 14/035,845, 26 March 2015
2. Chinchor, N., Robinson, P.: MUC-7 named entity task definition. In: Proceedings of the 7th Conference on Message Understanding, vol. 29 (1997)
3. Chiu, J.P., Nichols, E.: Named entity recognition with bidirectional LSTM-CNNs. arXiv preprint arXiv:1511.08308 (2015)
4. Demir, H., Ozgur, A.: Improving named entity recognition for morphologically rich languages using word embeddings. In: ICMLA, pp. 117–122 (2014)
5. Fletcher, R.: Practical Methods of Optimization. Wiley, Hoboken (2013)
6. Fresko, M., Rosenfeld, B., Feldman, R.: A hybrid approach to NER by MEMM and manual rules. In: Proceedings of the 14th ACM International Conference on Information and Knowledge Management, pp. 361–362. ACM (2005)
7. Güngör, O., Üsküdarlı, S., Güngör, T.: Improving named entity recognition by jointly learning to disambiguate morphological tags. arXiv preprint arXiv:1807.06683 (2018)
8. Lample, G., Ballesteros, M., Subramanian, S., Kawakami, K., Dyer, C.: Neural architectures for named entity recognition. arXiv preprint arXiv:1603.01360 (2016)
9. Lavergne, T., Cappé, O., Yvon, F.: Practical very large scale CRFs. In: Proceedings the 48th Annual Meeting of the Association for Computational Linguistics (ACL), pp. 504–513. Association for Computational Linguistics, July 2010. http://www.aclweb.org/anthology/P10-1052
10. Li, Z., Wang, X., Aw, A., Chng, E.S., Li, H.: Named-entity tagging and domain adaptation for better customized translation. In: Proceedings of the Seventh Named Entities Workshop, pp. 41–46 (2018)
11. Ma, X., Hovy, E.: End-to-end sequence labeling via bi-directional LSTM-CNNs-CRF. arXiv preprint arXiv:1603.01354 (2016)

12. McCallum, A., Li, W.: Early results for named entity recognition with conditional random fields, feature induction and web-enhanced lexicons. In: Proceedings of the Seventh Conference on Natural Language Learning at HLT-NAACL 2003, CONLL 2003, vol. 4, pp. 188–191. Association for Computational Linguistics, Stroudsburg (2003). https://doi.org/10.3115/1119176.1119206

13. Mollá, D., Van Zaanen, M., Cassidy, S., et al.: Named entity recognition in question answering of speech data (2007)

14. Nadeau, D., Sekine, S.: A survey of named entity recognition and classification. Lingvisticae Investigationes **30**(1), 3–26 (2007)

15. Ratinov, L., Roth, D.: Design challenges and misconceptions in named entity recognition. In: Proceedings of the Thirteenth Conference on Computational Natural Language Learning, pp. 147–155. Association for Computational Linguistics (2009)

16. Ratnaparkhi, A.: A maximum entropy model for part-of-speech tagging. In: Conference on Empirical Methods in Natural Language Processing (1996)

17. Sak, H., Güngör, T., Saraçlar, M.: Morphological disambiguation of Turkish text with perceptron algorithm. In: Gelbukh, A. (ed.) CICLing 2007. LNCS, vol. 4394, pp. 107–118. Springer, Heidelberg (2007). https://doi.org/10.1007/978-3-540-70939-8_10

18. Sasano, R., Kurohashi, S.: Japanese named entity recognition using structural natural language processing. In: Proceedings of the Third International Joint Conference on Natural Language Processing, vol. II (2008)

19. Şeker, G.A., Eryiğit, G.: Initial explorations on using CRFs for Turkish named entity recognition. Proc. COLING **2012**, 2459–2474 (2012)

20. Şeker, G.A., Eryiğit, G.: Extending a CRF-based named entity recognition model for Turkish well formed text and user generated content 1. Semant. Web **8**(5), 625–642 (2017)

21. Sutton, C., McCallum, A., et al.: An introduction to conditional random fields. Found. Trends® Mach. Learn. **4**(4), 267–373 (2012)

22. Tür, G., Hakkani-Tür, D., Oflazer, K.: A statistical information extraction system for Turkish. Nat. Lang. Eng. **9**(2), 181–210 (2003)

23. Yeniterzi, R.: Exploiting morphology in Turkish named entity recognition system. In: Proceedings of the ACL 2011 Student Session, pp. 105–110. Association for Computational Linguistics (2011)

A Comparative Study of Classical and Deep Classifiers for Textual Addressee Detection in Human-Human-Machine Conversations

Oleg Akhtiamov[1,2]($\boxtimes$), Dmitrii Fedotov[1,2], and Wolfgang Minker[1]

[1] Institute of Communications Engineering, Ulm University, Ulm, Germany
oakhtiamov@gmail.com,
{dmitrii.fedotov,wolfgang.minker}@uni-ulm.de
[2] ITMO University, St. Petersburg, Russia

Abstract. The problem of addressee detection (AD) arises in multi-party conversations involving several dialogue agents. In order to maintain such conversations in a realistic manner, an automatic spoken dialogue system is supposed to distinguish between computer- and human-directed utterances since the latter utterances either need to be processed in a specific way or should be completely ignored by the system. In the present paper, we consider AD to be a text classification problem and model three aspects of users' speech (syntactical, lexical, and semantical) that are relevant to AD in German. We compare simple classifiers operating with supervised text representations learned from in-domain data and more advanced neural network-based models operating with unsupervised text representations learned from in- and out-of-domain data. The latter models provide a small yet significant AD performance improvement over the classical ones on the Smart Video Corpus. A neural network-based semantical model determines the context of the first four words of an utterance to be the most informative for AD, significantly surpasses syntactical and lexical text classifiers and keeps up with a baseline multimodal metaclassifier that utilises acoustical information in addition to textual data. We also propose an effective approach to building representations for out-of-vocabulary words.

Keywords: Text classification · Speaking style ·
Human-computer interaction · Spoken dialogue system

1 Introduction

The capabilities of modern automatic spoken dialogue systems (SDSs) are not confined only to the range of tasks that such systems can solve. Many research efforts are concentrated on improving the systems' adaptability to different environmental conditions and modelling human-like behaviour. People possess the ability to determine addressees within spoken conversations that allows them to

© Springer Nature Switzerland AG 2019
A. A. Salah et al. (Eds.): SPECOM 2019, LNAI 11658, pp. 20–30, 2019.
https://doi.org/10.1007/978-3-030-26061-3_3

maintain multiparty interactions involving several conversational agents. This capability is extremely useful for SDSs, such as personal assistants, social robots, and chat bots, and may essentially improve their performance alongside with users' perception of such systems.

Most modern SDSs handle the interaction between a human and the system as a pure human-machine (H-M) conversation, i.e, all the speech captured by the system is assumed to be system-directed [17], though this hypothesis does not take into consideration multiparty scenarios, in which several users solve collective tasks by addressing the SDS. In such scenarios, a user may also address another human while interacting with the system or even talk to him- or herself. E.g., interlocutors may be negotiating how they will spend this evening, asking the system to show information about cafes or cinema and discussing possible alternatives. As a result, a new type of interaction arises – human-human-machine (H-H-M) conversation – that is supposed to be handled by the SDS so that the system is able to maintain conversations in a realistic manner. Human-directed utterances either need to be processed in a specific way without a direct system response, e.g., the system may collect paralinguistic and contextual information to adapt to the users, or should be completely ignored in order not to confuse the system. This necessity leads to the problem of addressee detection (AD) in H-H-M conversations, i.e, the SDS is supposed to determine whether the user is addressing the artificial conversational agent or another human.

In human-human (H-H) conversations, people specify addressees in the following two ways: explicitly (addressees are specified directly in speech by their names) and implicitly (addressees are specified indirectly using some contextual markers). In both cases, the information required to make predictions regarding addressees is enclosed in the semantical content of users' utterances. Some other cues in terms of AD arise in H-M conversations. People tend to change their normal manner of speech, making it grammatically simpler and generally easier to understand as soon as they start talking to a modern SDS, since they do not perceive the system as an adequate conversational agent [22]. Another cue is related to the problem-oriented nature of H-M dialogues. People usually use some domain-related lexical units while addressing the system. Summarising all the observations mentioned above, we define the following textual aspects that should be taken into account for solving the AD problem in H-H-M conversations: lexical content (what has been said), structure of sentences (how it has been said) and semantical content (what it means).

The present paper has the following contributions. We demonstrate that modelling three aspects of users' speech (syntactical, lexical, and semantical) is sufficient for reliable AD in German. We also compare simple classifiers operating with supervised text representations learned from in-domain data and more advanced neural network-based models operating with unsupervised text representations learned from in- and out-of-domain data. The latter models provide a small yet significant AD performance improvement over the classical ones.

2   Related Work

As demonstrated in [1,5,24], multimodality brings a significant AD performance improvement in comparison with unimodal approaches. However, it is shown in [1] for the Smart Video Corpus (SVC) [5] being considered in the present paper that textual information provides the most significant contribution to the overall AD performance in comparison with the other modalities available. Therefore, we focus specifically on text analysis to improve existing textual baselines introduced in [3]. Most studies dedicated to textual AD analyse English speech, and therefore it seems interesting to obtain results for other languages, e.g., German. The authors of [15] tackled the problem of collecting realistic data from H-H-M conversations and demonstrated that the H-H-M scenario can be approximated combining data from H-M and H-H scenarios. In this approach, the data for the H-M scenario models machine-directed utterances and should be collected with a single user within the system domain, while the data for the H-H scenario being applied to modelling human-directed utterances may be collected from other domains. The authors of [20] compared classical n-gram and feedforward neural network-based language models (LMs) for the AD problem and found no improvement from simply replacing the standard n-gram LM with a neural network-based LM as class likelihood estimators. However, an improved classification accuracy was obtained by means of a modified neural network-based model that learned distributed word representations in the first training phase, and was trained on the utterance classification task in the second phase. The authors of [19] demonstrated advantages of applying recurrent neural networks over using simple feedforward networks for AD. Overall, the related studies motivate us to leverage advantages of both classical models operating with supervised text representations learned from in-domain data and recurrent neural network-based classifiers operating with unsupervised distributed word representations learned from in- and out-of-domain data.

3   Classifiers

We consider AD to be an utterance classification problem. Designing our models, we assume that simple classifiers and text representations for them may be trained on in-domain data exceptionally, while the usage of out-of-domain data is reasonable for training more complex architectures involving neural networks.

3.1   Classical Models

Lexical Model. We apply two classical models that carry out different stages of text analysis. The first classifier involving an n-gram LM utilising word tokens performs lexical analysis and gives us an utterance-level text representation. It is demonstrated in [3] that textual AD is not sensitive to various German word forms. Stemming thereby allows us to reduce the vocabulary size by around 20% with no influence on the classification performance. However, stop word filtering significantly decreases the performance, showing that stop words matter for AD in German [3]. The extracted n-grams are weighted with a supervised term weighting method that takes into account statistical information about class labels and therefore simplifies the classification problem for a classifier. The utterance-level text representation is calculated as the product of Term Frequency (TF – evaluates the statistics of term occurrences in a given document) and Inverse Document Frequency (IDF – estimates the statistics of term occurrences in an entire data set). Besides the well-known TF-IDF technique [21], six different supervised term weighting methods are applied to compute the IDF part of the product [8,9,13,14,23,25]. As a classifier, we apply the Support Vector Machine-based algorithm Fast Large Margin (SVM-FLM). The study [2] describes experiments with various term weighting methods and classification algorithms on the AD problem.

Syntactical Model. The only difference between this model and the lexical one is in their tokenisers: the syntactical model deals with Part-of-Speech (POS) and dependency tokens instead of real words and considers a longer context compared to the context fed to the lexical model.

We examine the following text representations for the two models described above: five tokenisers implemented using spaCy [11] (no filtering, stop word filtering, stemming, POS, and dependency parsing), five context lengths (from uni- to quintagram), and seven term weighting methods implemented in C++ (TF-IDF [21], Gain Ratio (GR) [8], Confident Weights (CW) [23], Term Second Moment (TM2) [25], Relevance Frequency (RF) [14], Term Relevance Ratio (TRR) [13], and Novel Term Weighting (NTW) [9]) that produce 175 feature configurations in total. For each model, the best feature configuration depicted in Fig. 1 was chosen in terms of both unweighted average recall (UAR) and macro F_1-score on a development set.

3.2   Deep Models

Originally, SVC has word-level labelling. Due to utterance segmentation errors and the absence of any requirements for the participants, some utterances contain words with different labels. In this case, a natural idea would be to use a word-level text representation and a sequential model that would allow us to track word label changes within each utterance. There were several attempts to apply such models to textual AD on various corpora [4,19].

Word Embeddings. For building word representations, we use the GloVe algorithm proposed in [18]. It is an unsupervised algorithm for learning global word representations based on word co-occurrences in a large amount of textual data, hence built word embeddings are domain-independent and may be used in a wide range of applications. Another interesting feature of this approach is its ability to form semantical linear substructures in the word vector space. The performance reached with GloVe word representations is very similar to the performance of Word2Vec embeddings in most applications, though the process of training GloVe representations can be easier parallelised since it is mostly based on matrix factorisation.

Besides SVC, we utilise two large out-of-domain textual corpora to train GloVe word embeddings: the TIGER [6] and the WikiNER Corpus [16]. We have chosen the resulting dimensionality of word embeddings to be equal to 300 in accordance with an existing model for German built in the spaCy toolkit being used for learning word representations.

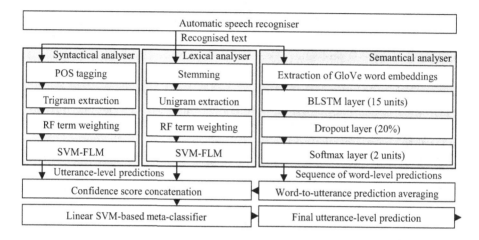

Fig. 1. Text metaclassifier involving syntactical, lexical, and semantical models.

Sequential Data Models. After extracting word embeddings, each utterance is represented as a sequence of word vectors. This sequence is processed with a sequential model. The study [19] considering applications of a simple Recurrent Neural Network (RNN) and a Long Short-Term Memory neural network (LSTM) to textual AD demonstrates that RNNs perform better on one data set with short utterances (utterance length mode is around 5 words), while LSTMs show a higher performance on another data set with long utterances (utterance length mode is around 10 words). Taking these results into account, we decide to apply a BLSTM network (bidirectional LSTM, though a regular LSTM may also be used) to our AD problem since SVC has an utterance length mode of roughly 10 words. In order to enable our network to process utterances of arbitrary length, we pad them with zero vectors at the end to the length of the longest utterance and add a masking operation before a recurrent layer so that the network ignores empty time steps. The recurrent layer is followed by a dropout and a softmax layer. As a result, the network receives an utterance and returns a sequence of addressee predictions (one for each word). To obtain an utterance-level addressee prediction for fusion with the other two models, we average word-level confidence scores over all words in the utterance. We use the following network parameters optimised on the development set: 15 BLSTM units, categorical cross-entropy as a loss function, RMSprop as a weight optimisation algorithm, a learning rate of 0.01, 50 epochs, 20% dropout, and a batch size of 32. The neural network was implemented applying Keras [7].

Handling Out-of-Vocabulary Words. It is noticed in [19] that sequential models are more sensitive to unknown words that may appear in test data than models utilising n-grams. A possible explanation for this is that such a word affects all the subsequent context perception of the utterance in case of sequential models, while in case of n-gram models the same unknown word influences only the neighbouring n-grams that include it. We faced this problem during our first experiments with the recurrent model on SVC that contains 20% of singleton words in its vocabulary. Using the large out-of-domain corpora (TIGER and WikiNER), we managed to reduce the number of unknown words, though they still affected the AD performance. Most of the words remaining unknown turned out to be either proper names, or numerals, or compounds. The latter category comprises 40% of all the words remaining unknown and appears due to the German habit to stack several simple words into long and complex constructions. To find representations for unknown words, we propose the following solution: according to the POS tags defined for each word prior to syntactical analysis, each found proper name and numeral is replaced by a word from the respective category in the out-of-domain corpora so that this word is already familiar to our system. For each word that remains unknown, we search for a match among the words contained in the training vocabulary, that covers the maximum number of characters starting from the end of the unknown word. This seems to be reasonable since the last sub-word of a German compound usually denotes its generic feature. If such a match is found, we represent it as a separate word that is already known to the system and continue the loop until no more matches are found, e.g., all sub-words in the compound Fußball+welt+meisterschaft (Football World Championship). For those words that remain unknown at the end, we apply a word hashing technique as described in [12]. We represent the unknown words as vectors of character trigrams, find the in-vocabulary word nearest to each out-of-vocabulary word in this space and associate its representation with this in-vocabulary word.

3.3 Fusion

The three models described above are fused at the decision level. Their resulting confidence scores are concatenated and fed to another SVM-based classifier returning the final confidence score for each utterance. A general scheme of this metaclassifier is depicted in Fig. 1. The SVM was implemented using RapidMiner [10] with default parameters.

4 Corpora

SVC was collected within large-scale Wizard-of-Oz experiments and consists of H-H-M conversations in German between a user, a confederate, and a multimodal

SDS [5]. The corpus contains users' queries in the context of a visit to a stadium of the Football World Cup 2006. A user was carrying a mobile phone, asking questions of certain categories (transport, sights, event schedule and statistics, and also open-domain questions) and discussing the obtained information with a confederate, who was always nearby but has never talked to the system directly. This experimental setup encouraged the interlocutors to use indirect addressing instead of calling each other by name. The data comprises 3.5 hours of audio and video, 99 dialogues (one unique speaker per dialogue), 2193 automatically segmented utterances with manual transcripts, and 25073 words in total. The labelling of addressees was carried out for each word; four word classes were specified: NOT, SOT, POT, and ROT. Their description is provided in Table 1. No requirements regarding Off-Talk were given to the users in order to obtain as realistic H-H-M conversations as possible.

Table 1. Examples of SVC utterances.

Category of human speech	#	Addressee	System action
On-Talk (NOT): system-directed utterances **Example:** "Wann wurde Berlin gegründet? Können Sie mir das sagen?" (When was Berlin founded? Can you tell me that?)	1 087	System	Explicit processing (response)
Read Off-Talk (ROT): reading the information aloud from the system display to another human **Example:** "Berlin wurde im Jahr 1237 gegründet." (Berlin was founded in 1237.)	309	Human	Implicit processing (adaptation)
Paraphrased Off-Talk (POT): retelling the information obtained from the system in arbitrary form to another human **Example:** "Oh, die Stadt ist ziemlich alt. Das Gründungsjahr ist 1237." (Oh, the city is quite old. The foundation year is 1237.)	323		
Spontaneous Off-Talk (SOT): any other human-directed utterances **Example:** "Toll! Das wusste ich nicht. Willst du noch den Name vom Gründer wissen?" (Cool! I didn't know that. Do you want to know the founder's name?)	474		

To provide those models, which utilise utterance-level features, with labels, we carry out a word-to-utterance label transformation: an utterance label is calculated as the mode of all word labels in the current utterance. Utterance examples are shown in Table 1. We consider a two-class task only (On-Talk vs the three Off-Talk classes) since it is equivalent to the AD problem. Experiments with a four-class task may be found in [5].

The TIGER Corpus [6] consists of around 50 000 sentences (900 000 tokens) of German newspaper text, taken from the Frankfurter Rundschau. The WikiNER Corpus [16] contains around 1 000 000 articles (400 000 000 tokens) from the German Wikipedia.

5   Experimental Results

It is shown in [3] that using the output of a state-of-the-art speech recogniser instead of the manual transcripts does not worsen the AD performance on SVC. Therefore, our system utilises the manual transcripts in the present study. For statistical analysis, we conduct an experimental scheme as specified in [3] - leave-one-speaker-group-out (LOSGO) cross-validation - splitting the entire speaker set into 14 folds so that the class proportion remains equal in each fold. The resulting AD performance calculated as UAR averaged over all folds is depicted in Fig. 2 (left). We use UAR since this metric is the gold standard for computational paralinguistic problems and all the previous studies on SVC [1,3–5] are also presented in terms of UAR. Our statistical comparisons are drawn applying a t-test with a significance level of 0.05. The metamodel (synt+lex) involving the syntactical (synt) and the lexical classifier (lex) significantly outperforms both standalone models included in it. However, the BLSTM-based model (sem) significantly surpasses this metamodel, thereby updating the current baseline for textual AD on SVC and reaching a performance at the level of the baseline multimodal metaclassifier (synt+lex+ac) introduced in [3] that utilises acoustical information (ac) in addition to textual data. The attempt to fuse the semantical, the lexical, and the syntactical model at the metalevel (synt+lex+sem) gives no significant AD performance improvement. We also examine our models on the fixed partition used in [1,3–5], splitting the entire SVC data into a training (48 speakers), a development (10 speakers), and a test set (41 speakers). These results alongside with the average LOSGO UAR are depicted in Fig. 2 (middle).

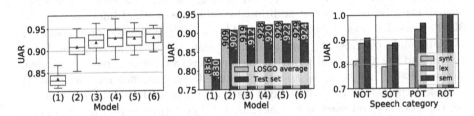

Fig. 2. LOSGO cross-validation (left), average LOSGO UAR and UAR on the single partition (middle), and AD performance on different speech categories (right). Models: (1) - synt, (2) - lex, (3) - synt+lex, (4) - sem, (5) - synt+lex+sem, (6) - synt+lex+ac.

The semantical classifier confirms the previous observation regarding textual AD that text-based models perform worse for spontaneous speech (spontaneous Off-Talk) than for constrained speech (paraphrased and particularly read Off-Talk) [3]. This trend is illustrated in Fig. 2 (right).

We wonder how early it is possible to predict addressees within one utterance. The SVC utterance length distribution depicted in Fig. 3 (left) has a mode of around 10 words. However, the trend illustrated in Fig. 3 (right) demonstrates that the main performance gain is reached with the context of the first four words and further context extensions contribute much less to the AD performance.

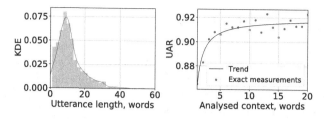

Fig. 3. Kernel density estimation (KDE) of the utterance length distribution (left) and AD performance for various context lengths (right).

6   Conclusions

The lexical and syntactical text representations have successfully been replaced by the single semantical one utilising GloVe word embeddings. Though the fine-tuned n-gram LMs perform well for the particular domain, they are likely to fail, particularly the lexical one, if the domain slightly changes. In combination with GloVe word embeddings, the semantical model demonstrates more effective results on the AD problem, although this classifier is sensitive to unknown words appearing in the test data. The problem of the lack of data for training word embeddings has been resolved utilising the two out-of-domain corpora alongside with SVC. As a solution for the problem of unknown words, we propose the data augmentation procedure replacing them by their nearest analogues from the training data vocabulary.

The semantical model keeps up with the baseline multimodal metaclassifier, even though the latter model additionally utilises acoustical information. The BLSTM-based model is able to make quite reliable addressee predictions by analysing only the first four words of an utterance. Fusing the semantical, the lexical, and the syntactical model at the metalevel would be a reasonable idea, however, it did not bring us any significant AD performance improvement. A possible explanation for this is that we have exhausted the potential of the textual modality and reached the maximum AD performance that it can provide on SVC. However, the potential of the acoustical modality has not been fully discovered yet.

Acknowledgements. This research is partially financially supported by DAAD jointly with the Ministry of Education and Science of Russia within the Michail Lomonosov Program (project No. 2.12779.2018/12.2), by RFBR (project No. 18-07-01407) and by the Government of Russia (grant No. 08-08).

References

1. Akhtiamov, O., Palkov, V.: Gaze, prosody and semantics: relevance of various multimodal signals to addressee detection in human-human-computer conversations. In: Karpov, A., Jokisch, O., Potapova, R. (eds.) SPECOM 2018. LNCS (LNAI), vol. 11096, pp. 1–10. Springer, Cham (2018). https://doi.org/10.1007/978-3-319-99579-3_1

2. Akhtiamov, O., Sergienko, R., Minker, W.: An approach to off-talk detection based on text classification within an automatic spoken dialogue system. In: 13th ICINCO, pp. 288–293 (2016)

3. Akhtiamov, O., Sidorov, M., Karpov, A., Minker, W.: Speech and text analysis for multimodal addressee detection in human-human-computer interaction. In: Interspeech, pp. 2521–2525. ISCA (2017)

4. Akhtiamov, O., Ubskii, D., Feldina, E., Pugachev, A., Karpov, A., Minker, W.: Are you addressing me? Multimodal addressee detection in human-human-computer conversations. In: Karpov, A., Potapova, R., Mporas, I. (eds.) SPECOM 2017. LNCS (LNAI), vol. 10458, pp. 152–161. Springer, Cham (2017). https://doi.org/10.1007/978-3-319-66429-3_14

5. Batliner, A., Hacker, C., Nöth, E.: To talk or not to talk with a computer. J. Multimodal User Interfaces **2**(3), 171–186 (2008)

6. Brants, S., et al.: TIGER: linguistic interpretation of a german corpus. Res. Lang. Comput. **2**(4), 597–620 (2004)

7. Chollet, F., et al.: Keras (2015). https://github.com/fchollet/keras

8. Debole, F., Sebastiani, F.: Supervised term weighting for automated text categorization. In: Sirmakessis, S. (ed.) Text Mining and Its Applications, pp. 81–97. Springer, Heidelberg (2004). https://doi.org/10.1007/978-3-540-45219-5_7

9. Gasanova, T., Sergienko, R., Akhmedova, S., Semenkin, E., Minker, W.: Opinion mining and topic categorization with novel term weighting. In: 5th WASSA, pp. 84–89. ACL (2014)

10. Hofmann, M., Klinkenberg, R.: RapidMiner: Data Mining Use Cases and Business Analytics Applications. CRC Press, Boca Raton (2013)

11. Honnibal, M., Montani, I.: spaCy (2017). https://github.com/explosion/spaCy

12. Huang, P.S., He, X., Gao, J., Deng, L., Acero, A., Heck, L.: Learning deep structured semantic models for web search using clickthrough data. In: 22nd CIKM, pp. 2333–2338. ACM (2013)

13. Ko, Y.: A study of term weighting schemes using class information for text classification. In: 35th SIGIR, pp. 1029–1030. ACM (2012)

14. Lan, M., Tan, C.L., Su, J., Lu, Y.: Supervised and traditional term weighting methods for automatic text categorization. IEEE TPAMI **31**(4), 721–735 (2009)

15. Lee, H., Stolcke, A., Shriberg, E.: Using out-of-domain data for lexical addressee detection in human-human-computer dialog. In: NAACL HLT, pp. 221–229 (2013)

16. Nothman, J., Ringland, N., Radford, W., Murphy, T., Curran, J.R.: Learning multilingual named entity recognition from Wikipedia. Artif. Intel. **194**, 151–175 (2013)

17. Paek, T., Horvitz, E., Ringger, E.: Continuous listening for unconstrained spoken dialog. In: 6th ICSLP (2000)

18. Pennington, J., Socher, R., Manning, C.: Glove: global vectors for word representation. In: EMNLP, pp. 1532–1543 (2014)

19. Ravuri, S., Stolcke, A.: Recurrent neural network and LSTM models for lexical utterance classification. In: Interspeech. ISCA (2015)

20. Ravuri, S.V., Stolcke, A.: Neural network models for lexical addressee detection. In: Interspeech. ISCA (2014)
21. Salton, G., Buckley, C.: Term-weighting approaches in automatic text retrieval. Inf. Process. Manag. **24**(5), 513–523 (1988)
22. Siegert, I., Krüger, J.: How do we speak with Alexa - subjective and objective assessments of changes in speaking style between HC and HH conversations. Kognitive Systeme **1** (2019). https://doi.org/10.17185/duepublico/48596
23. Soucy, P., Mineau, G.W.: Beyond TFIDF weighting for text categorization in the vector space model. IJCAI **5**, 1130–1135 (2005)
24. Tsai, T., Stolcke, A., Slaney, M.: A study of multimodal addressee detection in human-human-computer interaction. IEEE Trans. Multimedia **17**(9), 1550–1561 (2015)
25. Xu, H., Li, C.: A novel term weighting scheme for automated text categorization. In: 7th ISDA, pp. 759–764. IEEE (2007)

Acoustic Event Mixing to Multichannel AMI Data for Distant Speech Recognition and Acoustic Event Classification Benchmarking

Sergei Astapov[1]([✉]), Gleb Svirskiy[2], Aleksandr Lavrentyev[2], Tatyana Prisyach[2], Dmitriy Popov[2], Dmitriy Ubskiy[1,2], and Vladimir Kabarov[1]

[1] International Research Laboratory "Multimodal Biometric and Speech Systems", ITMO University, Kronverksky prospekt 49, St. Petersburg 197101, Russia
astapov@speechpro.com
[2] Speech Technology Center, Krasutskogo st. 4, St. Petersburg 196084, Russia
{svirskiy,lavrentyev,prisyach}@speechpro.com

Abstract. Currently, the quality of Distant Speech Recognition (DSR) systems cannot match the quality of speech recognition on clean speech acquired by close-talking microphones. The main problems behind DSR are situated with the far field nature of data, one of which is unpredictable occurrence of acoustic events and scenes, which distort the signal's speech component. Application of acoustic event detection and classification (AEC) in conjunction with DSR can benefit speech enhancement and improve DSR accuracy. However, no publicly available corpus for conjunctive AEC and DSR currently exists. This paper proposes a procedure of realistically mixing acoustic events and scenes with far field multi-channel recordings of the AMI meeting corpus, accounting for spatial reverberation and distinctive placement of sources of different kind. We evaluate the derived corpus for both DSR and AEC tasks and present replicative results, which can be used as a baseline for the corpus. The code for the proposed mixing procedure is made available online.

Keywords: Distant Speech Recognition · Acoustic event classification · Speech Enhancement · Synthetic mixing · AMI corpus

1 Introduction

Current achievements in the field of Automatic Speech Recognition (ASR) provide astonishing recognition quality, with accuracy even reaching the one of human listeners [24]. This is, however, true mostly for cases of clean speech acquired using close-talking microphones (i.e., lapel, headset microphones) and telephone conversations [16,24]. ASR of distant speakers is still struggling to reach human perception quality and suffers from the destructive influence of background noise. This is the reason behind Distant Speech Recognition (DSR)

© Springer Nature Switzerland AG 2019
A. A. Salah et al. (Eds.): SPECOM 2019, LNAI 11658, pp. 31–42, 2019.
https://doi.org/10.1007/978-3-030-26061-3_4

gaining ever rising popularity among researchers in the field of ASR. The late 5th CHiME challenge [2] has also addressed the problematic behind DSR of overlapping spontaneous speech in varying noise conditions.

The main problems situated with DSR arise from the far field nature of signal acquisition [22]. Firstly, the speech component is not necessarily dominant in the signal. Noise sources, arising in the speaker's environment distort and mask the speech component. Also, the noise sources arising in closer proximity to the acquisition point than the speaker may result in negative Signal to Noise Ratios (SNR) even if the noise power is relatively low. Secondly, speech acquired by a distant microphone cannot be considered a clean speech reference, as it is commonly done in ASR. Speech acquired in the far field is distorted due to wavefront decay; in enclosed spaces it is additionally distorted by the Room Impulse Response (RIR). Thirdly, the nature of noise is not predictable. In unconstrained environments noise is composed of acoustic events (AE) and acoustic scenes (AS), which possess varying dynamical properties and are also influenced by RIR distortions. We define AE as short-lasting (similar to an average utterance duration, not more than several seconds), usually transient sounds. AS is a long-lasting event which continuously alters mixture statistics, i.e., reoccurring AE with pauses in between cannot be considered an AS.

Acoustic event detection and classification (AEC) is currently a task mildly related to DSR. The application of AEC in conjunction with DSR has been previously shown to be beneficial for Speech Enhancement (SE) in terms of voice activity detection (VAD) [3], non-verbal sound separation [6], noise mask estimation and robust noise filtering [20]. The majority of such studies, however, is not systematized due to lack of common corpora. We argue that a speech corpus applied in such studies must satisfy certain requirements, which we address further. To our knowledge no such corpus for the English language is currently publicly available.

This paper proposes a method of synthetically producing a corpus, satisfying the conditions for proper application of both DSR and AEC. We attempt at creating a corpus simulating real life conditions of noisy office meetings containing typical office AE and several frequently encountered AS. As a base for the mixing procedure we employ the AMI meeting corpus [10] and AE/AS recordings from the Freesound database [5]. Our proposed procedure is composed of spatially reverberating AE recordings and mixing them with AMI multi-channel recordings, while maintaining a set of conditions, established to simulate natural noise emission. We further test the derived corpus for DSR and AEC tasks by applying an acoustic model for speech recognition trained on the AMI data with several SE pre-processing procedures, and a simple event classifier.

2   Preliminary Information

This section discusses currently available corpora partially applicable to conjunctive DSR and AEC tasks. Argumentation is provided as to why the available corpora do not satisfy the defined requirements and how the proposed corpus generation approach would benefit research in the field.

2.1   Revision of Available Corpora

Currently available corpora applicable for conjunctive DSR and AEC tasks can be divided into two major groups: real life far field recordings containing AE/AS with annotation of either utterance or AE/AS instances; synthetic corpora of mixed speech and AE, either reverberated from close-talking microphone recordings or re-recorded using multiple loudspeakers in enclosed environments.

The first kind of corpora would be the best choice for conjunctive DSR and AEC validation if they had annotation for both utterances and AE/AS. Annotation and transcription of speech does not pose a significant challenge because, in addition to far field recordings, close-talking microphones are almost always used to get clean speech references. Annotating AE/AS in far field recordings, however, is not as straightforward due to the unpredictability and ambiguity of third party sounds. Therefore, AE/AS annotation without solid reference information can result in an unacceptable human listener error.

The main disadvantage of the second kind of corpora is situated with their synthetic nature. In this regard the fully synthetic corpora are more beneficial as both speech and noise components are mixed with known and solid parameters. This aids in corpus reproduction if needed and provides a full list of mixture parameters, e.g., SNR, reverberation parameters (if applied), source position relative to the measurement point, convoluted transfer function parameters, etc. Re-recorded corpora can actually be less realistic than fully synthetic corpora if the frequency and phase responses of the loudspeakers are not considered, along with distortion produced by tweeter/mid-range/woofer cold start lags. Furthermore, directed speakers do not provide omnidirectional sound wave propagation, as most of real life AE would produce.

A revision of corpora partially suitable for conjunctive DSR and AEC studies is presented in Table 1 along with their respective drawbacks.

2.2   Problem Formulation

The corpus for conjunctive DSR/AEC testing should contain all the information necessary for both tasks. As publicly available corpora of real recordings do not contain AE/AS annotations and fully synthetic corpora cannot be considered sufficiently representative, we set to derive a corpus incorporating real life far field recordings and reverberated AE and AS. The corpus must satisfy the following conditions:

 - contain far field (preferably multi-channel) speech recordings;
 - contain a sufficient amount of AE and AS classes and instances of each class;
 - contain annotations for all speech utterances and AE/AS instances;
 - be publicly available free of cost.

For the base of the derived corpus we choose the AMI meeting corpus, as the speaker overlap ratio is lower compared to, e.g., the 5th CHiME corpus and, therefore, it is less cumbersome to analyze data. To simulate natural conditions of AE/AS occurrence we develop a mixing procedure with AMI room RIRs and AE/AS class-specific source spatial placement and occurrence probability.

Table 1. Corpora partially suitable for conjunctive DSR and AEC tasks.

Corpus	Description	Drawback
5th CHiME [2]	Contains 20 sessions and approximately 50 h of heavily overlapping noisy speech recorded on both multi-channel far field (six Microsoft Kinects) and binaural microphones in various living spaces	No AE/AS annotations
AMI [10]	100 h of meeting recordings, each performed by close-talking (headset and lapel) and far-field microphones (one or two circular arrays). Contains mildly overlapping speech with typical office noise	Too few AE/AS types
CHIL 2006 [11]	Contains multi-speaker fairly overlapping speech, recorded on a 64-microphone array, T-shaped omnidirectional microphone clusters and table microphones. Has speech and AE/AS annotations	Not publicly available
Noisy speech database [19]	56 speaker clean speech recordings mixed with various types of AE through convolution with RIRs of different spaces and at different SNR levels	Fully synthetic
SpEAR [21]	An ambitious recently started project. Contains noise corrupted speech with clean speech references, both synthetically mixed and physically re-recorded	In beta stage

3   Proposed Approach to Acoustic Event Mixing

The AMI corpus contains mild office noise and only a few non-human acoustic events, e.g., knocking door, keyboard typing. We add AE and AS (acquired from the Freesound database [5]), which are often encountered in office spaces, and several urban sounds of interest:

1. Babble noise—AS, which are encountered in vast office spaces or in meeting rooms if doors remain open;
2. Street—urban street noise AS, which are encountered if a window is open;
3. Alarm—AS of different kinds of office signalization;
4. Door—opening and closing doors;
5. Gunshot—specific sound of interest;
6. Computer—typing, clicking, various computer noise;
7. Drawer—opening and closing drawers of cabinets;
8. Knock—knocking on different surfaces;
9. Scissors—scissors snipping and cutting;
10. Squeak—squeaking of doors and mechanisms;
11. Telephone—different telephone rings and notification sounds;
12. Tool—sounds of hand, electric and power tools;
13. Writing—writing on paper with pens and pencils.

The proposed approach to acoustic event mixing is aimed at simultaneously satisfying two major conditions. Firstly, the synthetic mixture must be brought to real life conditions as much as possible in order to present an adequate challenge to SE, DSR and AEC procedures. Secondly, the amounts of included acoustic events must be chosen appropriately in order to present sufficient statistics for acoustic event detectors and classifiers. To achieve these goals we define the following requirements to the corpus as a whole:

1. There should be not less than κ percent of each individual session duration covered with added AE and AS.
2. AS types 1.–3. and AE types 4.–5. are added with source spatial placement corresponding to the coordinates on a room wall, i.e., simulating noise incoming from an open door or window.
3. AE types 6.–13. are added with source spatial placement inside the room, excluding the area of the microphone array itself.
4. Each AE and AS instance is added with a SNR value chosen from an appropriate distribution of SNR values for this specific type of event or scene.
5. Each AE or AS type appears (in the whole corpus) with a certain probability. Probabilities are specified empirically.
6. Acoustic event or scene overlap is not prohibited.

The procedure of AE/AS mixing consists of two major steps[1]: spatial reverberation of all AE/AS instances and mixing at randomly chosen SNR levels.

3.1 Acoustic Event Spatial Reverberation

Each AE and AS type has to be spatially distributed in the room of interest. This distribution should be type-specific, because events of different types occur more frequently in certain parts of the room then in others. Therefore, we specify three distribution types: normal $\mathcal{N}(\mu, \sigma)$, uniform $\mathcal{U}(a, b)$ and rectangular $\mathcal{R}()$. We define the rectangular distribution as the one, which situates the noise source strictly on one of the room walls. The distribution type and its parameters are defined for each AE/AS class.

To simulate RIR of the room of interest and convolve the AE/AS instance we employ the pyroomacoustics tool set [17], which requires: room length l_x, width l_y and height l_z in meters; coordinates of each microphone of the array; the absorption coefficient of the room surface K_{absorb}; and the number of sound wave reflections n_{refl}. The parameters K_{absorb} and n_{refl} are manually estimated per each room using the T_{60} reverberation time as a metric.

AE spatial reverberation is performed according to Algorithm 1. For each instance (sound file) from the database of AE/AS $w \in \{AE, AS\}$ the coordinates of sound emission are estimated depending on the specific distribution type $\mathcal{D}_w$ and its parameters (a_w, b_w). The set of RIR parameters $\mathfrak{r} = (l_x, l_y, l_z, \mathsf{c}, K_{absorb}, n_{refl})$ includes room dimensions; a subset c, which contains the coordinates of the microphone array center and the coordinates of all M microphones $\mathsf{c} = \{c_x, c_y, c_z, m_x^{(1)}, m_y^{(1)}, m_z^{(1)}, \ldots, m_z^{(M)}\}$; the absorption coefficient and the reflection number. During the procedure the source coordinates (x_w, y_w, z_w) are estimated along with the Direction of Arrival (DOA) relative to the array center (φ_w, θ_w), where φ_w and θ_w are the azimuth and elevation angles, accordingly. The coordinates for AE are constrained by 0.05 m from each wall, floor and ceiling;

---

[1] Corpus mixing scripts are available at https://github.com/sergeiastapov/nAMI.

Algorithm 1. AE and AS spatial reverberation

Require: $w \in \{AE, AS\}$, (a_w, b_w), $\mathcal{D}_w$, $\mathfrak{r} = \{l_x, l_y, l_z, \mathsf{c}, K_{absorb}, n_{refl}\}$

1: **if** $!\,(\mathcal{D}_w \sim \mathcal{R}())$ **then**
2:     **if** $\mathcal{D}_w \sim \mathcal{N}(\mu, \sigma)$ **then**
3:         $\mu_w \leftarrow a_w$, $\sigma_w \leftarrow b_w$
4:         $d_w \leftarrow \mathcal{N}(\mu_w, \sigma_w)$ ▷ distance to array center
5:     **else if** $\mathcal{D}_w \sim \mathcal{U}(a, b)$ **then**
6:         $d_w \leftarrow \mathcal{U}(a_w, b_w)$ ▷ distance to array center
7:     **end if**
8:     $\varphi_w \leftarrow \mathcal{U}(0, 360)$
9:     $z_w \leftarrow \min\left(|\mathcal{U}(0, 0.5)|, d_w - 0.05\right)$
10:    $\theta_w \leftarrow \arccos\left(z_w/(d_w + \epsilon)\right)$, $z_w \leftarrow z_w + c_z$ ▷ ϵ — double precision
11:    $x_w \leftarrow d_w \cos\theta\cos\varphi + c_x$, $y_w \leftarrow d_w \sin\theta\sin\varphi + c_y$
12:    $x_w \leftarrow \max\left(\min(l_x - 0.05, x_w), 0.05\right)$, $y_w \leftarrow \max\left(\min(l_y - 0.05, y_w), 0.05\right)$,
13:    $z_w \leftarrow \max\left(\min(l_z - 0.05, z_w), 0.05\right)$
14: **else if** $\mathcal{D}_w \sim \mathcal{R}()$ **then**
15:    $case \leftarrow [\mathcal{U}(1, 4)]$ ▷ round to nearest integer
16:    **if** $case = 1$ **then**   ▷ situate source on one of the walls
17:        $x_w \leftarrow 0$, $y_w \leftarrow \mathcal{U}(0, l_y)$
18:    **else if** $case = 2$ **then**
19:        $x_w \leftarrow l_x$, $y_w \leftarrow \mathcal{U}(0, l_y)$
20:    **else if** $case = 3$ **then**
21:        $y_w \leftarrow 0$, $x_w \leftarrow \mathcal{U}(0, l_x)$
22:    **else if** $case = 4$ **then**
23:        $y_w \leftarrow l_y$, $x_w \leftarrow \mathcal{U}(0, l_x)$
24:    **end if**
25:    $z_w \leftarrow \mathcal{U}(0.5, 1.5)$
26: **end if**
27: **return** $w^* \leftarrow \mathrm{RIR}(w, \mathfrak{r}, x_w, y_w, z_w)$

---

coordinates of AS are constrained by position on one of the walls. As a result, each AE/AS instance has its own coordinates with known distribution. The output w^* is a multi-channel recording of AE/AS received by every microphone in the array according to the DOA and RIR convolution.

3.2 Acoustic Event Mixing

Acoustic event mixing is performed for each corpus session separately. Input $\mathbf{X} = [x_1(t), \ldots, x_M(t)]$ contains the multi-channel recording of all M microphones. The parameters are as follows: lower bound for noise insertion κ in percent; noise instance $w \in \{AE, AS\}$—the result of Algorithm 1; its parameters for SNR value distribution μ_w, σ_w and its class occurrence probability $p(w)$.

The mixing procedure is performed according to Algorithm 2. Voiced segments are first established by applying VAD, which is performed according to the speaker annotations of AMI sessions. The speech signal mean power is estimated only on voiced segments. After choosing an AE/AS instance, the SNR is calculated between its power and the mean power of the whole voiced session. A

Algorithm 2. AE and AS mixing to corpus session

Require: $w \in \{AE, AS\}$, $(\mu_w, \sigma_w, p(w))$, κ, $n_w = 0$, $\mathbf{X}$, $\mathbf{Y} = \mathbf{X}$

1: $\mathbf{X}_v \leftarrow \text{VAD}(\mathbf{X})$ $\triangleright$ apply VAD according to annotation

2: $P_{\mathbf{X}_v} \leftarrow |\mathbf{X}_v|^2$ $\triangleright$ mean signal power

3: **while** $n_w < \kappa$ **do**

4:      Choose w with probability $p(w)$

5:      $P_w \leftarrow |w|^2$, $SNR(\mathbf{X}_v, w) \leftarrow 10 \log(P_{\mathbf{X}_v}/P_w)$

6:      $SNR_{req} \leftarrow \max(-1, \mathcal{N}(\mu_w, \sigma_w))$

7:      $w \leftarrow w \cdot 10^{(SNR(\mathbf{X}_v, w) - SNR_{req})/20}$

8:      Choose $t_{start} \leftarrow \mathcal{U}(0, len(\mathbf{Y}) - len(w))$, insert $\mathbf{Y} \leftarrow \mathbf{Y} + w|t_{start}$

9:      Increment $n_w \leftarrow n_w + len(w)/len(\mathbf{Y}) \cdot 100\%$

10: **end while**

11: **return** $\mathbf{Y}$

---

required SNR value is obtained from the distribution specific to this event class type and the power of the event instance is adjusted accordingly. The time interval for AE/AS insertion is randomly selected; the only constraint being that the whole event should be included in the mixture. The procedure continues until $\kappa\%$ of the session is mixed with noise.

As a result we derive noised corpus sessions, each containing not less than $\kappa\%$ of AE and AS, and annotation files per session, specifying: session ID; speaker ID; utterance transcription; utterance time interval; AE/AS ID (name of file); AE/AS time interval; AE/AS SNR value; AE/AS source coordinates (x_w, y_w, z_w); AE/AS DOA relative to the array center (φ_w, θ_w).

3.3 Parameter Specification for the AMI Corpus

From the AMI corpus we choose 168 sessions which have full recordings from all channels of the microphone array. For mixing we choose recordings of Array 1, situated on the table in the middle of the room. There are three rooms in total. We estimate each room acoustic parameters for RIR generation empirically, by convolving lapel microphone utterances of several speakers in their corresponding appropriate coordinates relative to the array and analyzing the T_{60} reverberation time and envelope of the resulting reverberated signal. For the Idiap Room the absorption coefficient and the number of reflections, which result in most similar response, are: $K_{absorb} = 0.13$, $n_{refl} = 20$; for Edinburgh Room these are $K_{absorb} = 0.15$, $n_{refl} = 16$; for TNO Room these are $K_{absorb} = 0.13$, $n_{refl} = 18$. The lower bound is set to $\kappa = 50\%$.

For the AE/AS database we employ Freesound [5] recordings. The parameters of each AE/AS class for the spatial reverberation Algorithm 1 are presented in Table 2. The mixing parameters for Algorithm 2 are presented in Table 3. These parameters satisfy the requirements stated in the beginning of Sect. 3.

Table 2. AE and AS reverberation parameters per class.

Class	Instances	Distribution	a_w	b_w
Babble	205	Rectangular	-	-
Street	167	Rectangular	-	-
Alarm	155	Rectangular	-	-
Door	5075	Rectangular	-	-
Gunshot	147	Rectangular	-	-
Computer	1284	Normal	0.35	0.10
Drawer	158	Normal	1.0	0.09
Knock	1935	Normal	3.0	1.0
Scissors	95	Normal	0.35	0.10
Squeak	300	Uniform	0.10	3.0
Telephone	833	Uniform	0.10	5.0
Tool	1658	Normal	3.0	0.64
Writing	270	Normal	0.35	0.10

Table 3. AE and AS mixing parameters per class.

Class	μ_w	σ_w	$p(w)$
Babble	10	3	0.060
Street	5	3	0.060
Alarm	7	4	0.060
Door	5	3	0.083
Gunshot	5	3	0.035
Computer	5	3	0.150
Drawer	7	3	0.067
Knock	7	3.5	0.083
Scissors	5	3	0.067
Squeak	7	3	0.083
Telephone	5	4	0.150
Tool	7	3	0.035
Writing	5	3	0.067

4   Evaluation and Results

This section discusses evaluation methods of the derived corpus and presents evaluation results of DSR and AEC.

4.1   Evaluation Methods and Metrics

To evaluate DSR on the derived noised AMI corpus (nAMI) we apply the model for speech recognition [14] implemented in Time Delay Neural Networks (TDNN). The model is trained using AMI Multi-channel Distant Microphone (MDM) data (at sampling frequency of 16000 Hz) with Individual Headset Microphone (IHM) targets. The Short Time Fourier Transform (STFT) window is set at 512 samples and 160 samples window overlap (step of 10 ms). The features used for TDNN input are: 40 Mel-frequency Cepstral Coefficients (MFCC) and an i-vector of length 100. The model is trained using cross-entropy and Lattice-free maximum mutual information (LFMMI) objectives. For SE prior to feature extraction the BeamformIt beamforming method is applied to MDM data. The train, dev and eval sets of the corpus are adopted according to AMI specification.

The nAMI corpus is evaluated using the TDNN model trained on AMI data. For evaluation we employ the Word Error Rate (WER) metric. nAMI is evaluated on the dev (18 sessions) and eval (16 sessions) sets with SE applied prior to feature extraction. Four SE approaches are applied: BeamformIt [1], Maximum Variance Distortionless Response (MVDR) with Ideal Ratio Mask (IRM) application; General Eigenvalue (GEV) beamforming with IRM mask application; Parameterized Multichannel Wiener Filter (PMWF) with IRM mask application. MVDR, GEV and PMWF are adopted from the setk tool kit [23]. The principle block diagram of DSR testing is presented in Fig. 1.

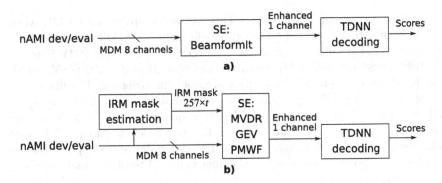

Fig. 1. Block diagram of DSR testing steps on nAMI. (a) SE with BeamformIt application; (b) SE with IRM mask and MVDR/GEV/PMWF.

IRM masks [9] are obtained by a CNN-TDNN-f [15] model trained on augmented data from Librespeech [12]. Room acoustics simulations are used to augment data [8]. This technology includes the addition of background noise to the training data and reverberation. Room acoustics simulation allows to generate a new training base using a relatively clean training base in a wide range of conditions such as reverberation time, room size, SNR, number of noise sources, localization of target speaker and noise sources. In our experiment we used 50,000 different rooms and noises from publicly accessible bases (TIMIT [4], MUSAN [18] and AURORA [13]). The CNN-TDNN-f is trained with an input of 80 Fbank features and generates a vector of 257 frequency bin mask coefficients per STFT frame. Each coefficient of the target IRM mask represents the ratio of the desired speech component in the corresponding STFT time-frequency bin:

$$\text{IRM}(t, f) = \sqrt{\frac{D(t, f)}{D(t, f) + R(t, f)}},$$

where $D(t, f)$ consists of both the direct path and early reflections of the target signal and the residual signal $R(t, f)$ is obtained by subtracting the desired signal from the noisy reverberant mixture.

For AEC of acoustic events, which were added to the original AMI corpus, a classifier based on the embeddings from VGGish [7] audio classification model is used. We used 128-dimensional embeddings as input features. After applying VGGish on the MDM data, output embeddings are scaled to the value range of $[0, 1]$ and forwarded to the classifier. The classifier itself is a multi-layer perceptron consisting of one input layer of 128 neurons with sigmoid activation and one output layer with the number of neurons equal to the number of classes and softmax activation.

4.2 Evaluation Results

The results of DSR testing are presented in Table 4. Applying a $\kappa = 50\%$ noising threshold we achieved a 9% increase of WER on both dev and eval sets of AMI for the best-performing BeamformIt. This can be compared to 14–15% WER increase on nAMI if no SE is performed (single channel recording as direct input for decoding). The application of IRM masks to MVDR and PMWF results in satisfying SE quality, but performs worse than BeamformIt. GEV, on the other hand, does not provide recognition accuracy improvement. Results of AEC testing on nAMI for 8 noise classes are presented in Fig. 2 in the form of a confusion matrix. The resulting classification quality equals to 38.3%, which indicates that AE/AS are sufficiently masked by speech at chosen SNR levels and, therefore, pose a challenge for AEC. The Computer and Telephone AE are classified best, possibly because the classifier is biased towards tonal sounds.

Table 4. Results of testing DSR on nAMI with reference to AMI corpus.

Corpus	SE method	WER dev (%)	WER eval (%)
AMI	BeamformIt	33.7	36.3
nAMI	BeamformIt	42.7	46.0
nAMI	IRM+MVDR	45.9	48.9
nAMI	IRM+GEV	50.6	53.2
nAMI	IRM+PMWF	44.9	48.8
nAMI	Single channel	47.9	51.4

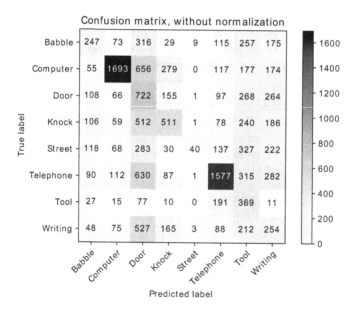

Fig. 2. Confusion matrix for the AEC test on nAMI. Total accuracy is equal to 38.3%

Generally it can be noted, that for the current settings of the mixing procedure the baseline for DSR is set too high with only 9% of available improvement against the best performing system. On the other hand, the baseline for AEC can be called sufficient, but may turn out to be too low for more sophisticated AEC systems. To establish a solid baseline for both DSR and AEC tasks a solution lies in establishing proper percent of noise inclusion κ and SNR distributions. Further development of the corpus will focus on establishing this balance.

5 Conclusion

The proposed event mixing procedure succeeds in providing a noised corpus applicable for conjunctive DSR and AEC benchmarking. Initial testing has shown, that the derived corpus is biased towards AEC benchmarking, as it does not provide as much room for DSR improvement against the best performing system, as it does for AEC. Fortunately, the procedure is highly tunable and can be balanced without additional development. The source code for the procedure and corpus replication is available online.

Acknowledgment. This research was financially supported by the Foundation NTI (Contract 20/18gr, ID 0000000007418QR20002) and by the Government of the Russian Federation (Grant 08-08).

References

1. Anguera, X., Wooters, C., Hernando, J.: Acoustic beamforming for speaker diarization of meetings. IEEE Trans. Audio Speech Lang. Process. **15**(7), 2011–2022 (2007)
2. Barker, J., Watanabe, S., Vincent, E., Trmal, J.: The fifth 'CHiME' speech separation and recognition challenge: dataset, task and baselines. In: Interspeech 2018–19th Annual Conference of the International Speech Communication Association, Hyderabad, India, September 2018
3. Cho, N., Kim, E.: Enhanced voice activity detection using acoustic event detection and classification. IEEE Trans. Consum. Electron. **57**(1), 196–202 (2011)
4. Dean, D.B., Sridharan, S., Vogt, R.J., Mason, M.W.: The QUT-NOISE-TIMIT corpus for the evaluation of voice activity detection algorithms. In: Interspeech 2010, September 2010
5. Font, F., Roma, G., Serra, X.: Freesound technical demo. In: ACM International Conference on Multimedia (MM 2013). Barcelona, Spain, pp. 411–412, October 2013
6. Fujimura, H., Nagao, M., Masuko, T.: Simultaneous speech recognition and acoustic event detection using an LSTM-CTC acoustic model and a WFST decoder. In: 2018 IEEE International Conference on Acoustics, Speech and Signal Processing (ICASSP), pp. 5834–5838, April 2018
7. Hershey, S., et al.: CNN architectures for large-scale audio classification. In: International Conference on Acoustics, Speech and Signal Processing, ICASSP (2017)
8. Kim, C., et al.: Generation of large-scale simulated utterances in virtual rooms to train deep-neural networks for far-field speech recognition in Google Home. In: INTERSPEECH 2017, pp. 379–383 (2017)

9. Li, X., Li, J., Yan, Y.: Ideal ratio mask estimation using deep neural networks for monaural speech segregation in noisy reverberant conditions. In: Proceedings of Interspeech 2017, pp. 1203–1207 (2017)

10. McCowan, I., et al.: The AMI meeting corpus. In: Proceedings of Measuring Behavior 2005, 5th International Conference on Methods and Techniques in Behavioral Research, pp. 137–140 (2005)

11. Mostefa, D., et al.: The CHIL audiovisual corpus for lecture and meeting analysis inside smart rooms. Lang. Resour. Eval. **41**(3), 389–407 (2007)

12. Panayotov, V., Chen, G., Povey, D., Khudanpur, S.: Librispeech: an ASR corpus based on public domain audio books. In: 2015 IEEE International Conference on Acoustics, Speech and Signal Processing (ICASSP), pp. 5206–5210, April 2015

13. Pearce, D., Hirsch, H.G., Gmbh, E.E.D.: The Aurora experimental framework for the performance evaluation of speech recognition systems under noisy conditions. In: ISCA ITRW ASR2000, pp. 29–32 (2000)

14. Povey, D.: AMI corpus Kaldi recipe s5b. https://github.com/kaldi-asr/kaldi/tree/master/egs/ami/s5b. Accessed Mar 2019

15. Povey, D., et al.: Semi-orthogonal low-rank matrix factorization for deep neural networks. In: Proceedings of Interspeech 2018, pp. 3743–3747 (2018)

16. Saon, G., et al.: English conversational telephone speech recognition by humans and machines. In: Interspeech 2017, pp. 132–136 (2017)

17. Scheibler, R., Bezzam, E., Dokmanic, I.: Pyroomacoustics: a Python package for audio room simulations and array processing algorithms. In: Proceedings of 2018 IEEE International Conference on Acoustics, Speech, and Signal Processing (ICASSP), pp. 351–355 (2017)

18. Snyder, D., Chen, G., Povey, D.: MUSAN: a music, speech, and noise corpus. CoRR (2015)

19. Valentini Botinhao, C., Wang, X., Takaki, S., Yamagishi, J.: Speech enhancement for a noise-robust text-to-speech synthesis system using deep recurrent neural networks. In: Interspeech 2016, pp. 352–356 (2016)

20. Vincent, E., Virtanen, T., Gannot, S.: Audio Source Separation and Speech Enhancement, 1st edn. Wiley, Hoboken (2018)

21. Wan, E., Nelson, A., Peterson, R.: Speech enhancement assessment resource (SpEAR) database. https://github.com/dingzeyuli/SpEAR-speech-database. Accessed Feb 2019

22. Woelfel, M., McDonough, J.: Distant Speech Recognition. Wiley, Hoboken (2009)

23. Wu, J.: SETK: Speech enhancement tools integrated with Kaldi. https://github.com/funcwj/setk. Accessed Mar 2019

24. Xiong, W., Wu, L., Alleva, F., Droppo, J., Huang, X., Stolcke, A.: The Microsoft 2017 conversational speech recognition system. Technical report MSR-TR-2017-39 (2017)

Speech-Based L2 Call System for English Foreign Speakers

Mohammad Ateeq and Abualsoud Hanani[(✉)]

Birzeit University, Birzeit, Palestine
mhmd.abed.ateeq@gmail.com, ahanani@birzeit.edu
http://www.birzeit.edu

Abstract. In this paper, we are presenting a language learning system which automatically evaluates English speech linguistically and grammatically. The system works by prompting the learner a question in his native language (text+figure) and waiting for his/her spoken response in English. Different types of features were extracted from the response to assess it in terms of language grammar and meaning errors. The universal sentence encoder was used to encode each sentence into 512-dimensional vector to represent the semantic of the response. Also, we propose a binary embedding approach to produce 438 binary features vectors from the student response. To assess the grammatical errors, different features were extracted using a grammar checker tool and part of speech analysis of the response. Finally, the best two DNN-based models have been fused together to enhance the system performance. The best result on the 2018 shared task test dataset is a D-score of 17.11.

Keywords: Speech recognition · Human-computer interaction · Linguistic assessment · CALL

1 Introduction

Over time, the introduction of Computer-Assisted Language Learning (CALL) models is a pioneer factor in development of speech and language technology especially after integrating Automatic Speech Recognition (ASR) as one of the components. CALL system can better help improve language skill of the L2 learners. To date, most of the common speech-based CALL systems focus on the pronunciation quality of the L2 language. A good and well-documented example of these systems is the EduSpeak system [9] which plays the student a recorded sentence, asks them to imitate it, and then rates them on the accuracy of their imitation, giving advice if appropriate on how to improve pronunciation or prosody. There is no doubt that this is useful, but does not give the student a real opportunity to practice spoken language skills.

Rayner et al. in [16] took this a further step by building a speech-based CALL system by which students can interact and respond to the system's prompts.

© Springer Nature Switzerland AG 2019
A. A. Salah et al. (Eds.): SPECOM 2019, LNAI 11658, pp. 43–53, 2019.
https://doi.org/10.1007/978-3-030-26061-3_5

This system prompts the student in his/her L1 language indicating in an indirect way what he/she is supposed to say in the L2 language. Then, the system automatically assesses the spoken response, based the grammar and linguistic, and provides a feedback. As an initiative to further develop related technologies, Baur et al. in 2016 [2] organized a shared task for the spoken CALL research. Participating systems were reported in the ISCA SLaTE 2017 workshop [2]. The task is to automatically assess prompt-based spoken responses by English learners in terms of grammar and language meaning. The system needs to accept the responses with no grammar nor linguistic errors, and reject others. Possibly giving some extra feedback. The shared task organizers provided participants by data consists of 52,222 training utterances and 966 testing utterances spoken by German-speaking Swiss teenagers as responses to prompts written in German [2]. The audio data was released together with accompanying metadata such as prompt in German, English transcription of each spoken response generated automatically by state-of-the-art English ASR, and judgments (correct/incorrect) for "language" and "meaning". Correct in the "language" means that the audio file was a fully correct response to the prompt. On the other hand, incorrect in the "language" means it was linguistically incorrect, but semantically correct. In addition to that, they provided a set of correct responses for each prompt that can be used a reference for the given response.

Following the success of the first shared task with 20 submissions from 9 participant teams, the second edition with new resources and updated training data was announced in October 2017 and the test data was released in February 2018 [3]. Similar to the first edition, the task organizers provide the audio data, ASR outputs, and reference response grammar. There are two tasks: the text task where the ASR outputs for the spoken responses are provided by the organizers, and the speech task where participants can use their own recognizes to process audio responses.

For the second edition, task organizers provided new subset of the corpus consisting of 6698 student utterances to serve as additional training data. This new data was selected in a similar way to the first training set, to be balanced and representative of the collected data, with the additional constraint that there should be no overlap of individual students between the first task and second task. Speech data were processed through the two best speech recognizer from the first shared task [13,14] after which the two sets of output transcriptions were merged and cleaned up by transcribers at the University of Geneva.

Five of the participants in the 2018 CALL shared task [1,8,10,12,15] presented their systems in the Interspeech 2018 conference which was held in 2–6 September 2018 in India. They introduced different ideas for improving to the baseline system at both the ASR and the text processing stages. In general, the worst entry from the second edition scored better than the best entry from the first edition, which served as the baseline here, and the best entry score was nearly four times higher than the baseline (D = 19.088 versus D = 5.343).

The best D score (19) among the participating teams in the 2018 shared task, was achieved by Nguyen et al. [12]. They improved the performance of the baseline speech recognition system provided by the shared task organizers. They developed a set of features to capture the linguistic and semantic meaning of the responses, and optimized the classification results for various factors (training set, n-best hypotheses of speech recognition, decision threshold, model ensemble).

Evanini et al. in [8] used additional features extracted by comparing the input response to language models trained on text written by English native speakers and L1-German English learners. In addition, they developed a set of sequence-to-label models using bidirectional LSTM-RNNs with an attention layer. The RNN model predictions were combined with the other feature sets using feature-level and score-level fusion approaches resulting in a best-performing system that achieved a D score of 7.397.

The team of the University of Birmingham [15] proposed improvements to the baseline system. They enhanced both components: automatic speech recognition and text processing units. Regarding to ASR component, Long short-term memory (LSTM) network was used instead of DNN network, where the LSTM network was trained using the alignments that were obtained from DNN-HMM system. Regarding to text processing, different methods were used to calculate the similarity between references and response. The Word Mover's Distance (WMD) [11] was used to calculate a sentence-level distance between response and its references. Also, a two-class classifier was used to take the decision.

A rule-based system was proposed in [10]. This system predicts the judgment for grammars and meaning of the responses based on pipe-lined rules. First Doc2Vec [6] was trained using the training set and all reference responses. Also, they enhanced the grammar by deleting any detected errors. They looked at meaning and grammar errors separately. Each response was judged in terms of grammar and meaning. Then, the final decision was taken based on a threshold value.

In our previous work [1], the text processing module is implemented as a rule-based, where its thresholds are optimized using genetic algorithm. This system achieved D score of 14.4 in the 2018 spoken call shared task. In this paper, a different approach was followed to evaluate the responses in this task. We used a deep learning model for predicting the assessment of the input response. To compute the semantic features, two sentence embedding methods were used and compared: The universal sentence encoder [7] and binary embedding method which was proposed in this paper. Finally, we proposed a fusion technique to exploit the output of the best two DNN models to improve the system performance.

The rest of the paper is organized as follows. In Sect. 2, we describe the dataset. Sects. 3 presents different types of features that used to train the model. Section 4 presents the experiments results and Sect. 5 gives conclusions.

2 Dataset Description

In all of the presented experiments, the dataset provided for the 2017 and 2018 spoken CALL shared tasks were used. As indicated earlier, this dataset is prompt-response pairs collected from an English course running CALL-SLT developed for German-speaking Swiss teenagers [3]. Prompts in the course are written texts in German associated with animation video clips each showing an English native speaker asking a question. Each response is labeled as "correct" or "incorrect" for its linguistic correctness (language) and its meaning, respectively. A student's response is accepted when it is correct in both grammar and meaning given the prompt. Otherwise, it is rejected. It is possible that a response is correct only in one aspect. The following shows an example of question, prompt in German (with English translation), and accepted student response: **Prompt**: Frag: Zimmer für 3 Nächte. (Ask: room for 3 nights) **ASR transcription of the student response**: I would like to stay for three nights. Table 1 shows the information of the data from the 2017 and 2018 tasks. In addition to training set, "grammar.xml" file is also available in [3] and includes some possible answers for each prompt.

Table 1. Numbers of accepts/rejects in different datasets.

Dataset	No. of accepts	No. of rejects	Total
2017 Training	3,880	1,342	5,222
2017 Test	716	279	995
2018 Training	4,418	2,281	6,698
2018 Test	750	250	1,000

3 Features Prediction

Our proposed system consists of two major components; English ASR followed by text processing unit. The ASR produces the transcription of the spoken response. The text processing unit extracts a set of features representing language and meaning from the transcription. Then, it evaluates the response by comparing these features with similar features extracted from a set of reference responses (set of possible responses provided in the grammar file) for each prompt provided in the dataset.

The proposed system is a machine learning based model which mainly depends on the extracted features from the student response and its references. In this paper, we investigate the effect of a set of extracted features on the overall system performance. First, we use a universal sentence encoder [7] to encode each sentence (student response and each possible reference) into a high-dimensional vector, and then we extract the features based on embedding vectors. A sentence encoder transforms the text into a 512-dimensional vector space, which can be further used to capture the semantic similarity.

Also, some other features were extracted to measure the grammatically correctness of the user response. These features were extracted from the output of two ASRs: Google ASR and SLaTE2018 ASR which was provided by the shared task organizers. This is to handle some of the errors caused by ASR system. Table 2 shows the transcriptions of two examples recognized by the two mentioned ASRs. It is clear that GOOGLE ASR is more accurate than the baseline ASR in the first example. On the other hand, the baseline ASR performs better in the second one.

Table 2. Examples for different recognized texts.

ASR	Recognized text	True transcription
GOOGLE	From Italy	From Italy
SLaTE2018	I'm from Italy	From Italy
GOOGLE	I want to leave on Tuesday	I want to leave at Tuesday
SLaTE2018	I want to leave at Tuesday	I want to leave at Tuesday

3.1 Features Produced by Universal Sentence Encoder

This encoder converts any sentence into a high dimensional vector which can be used for natural language processing tasks such as text classification and semantic similarity. The encoder is provided with a variable length English sentence as an input to construct 512-dimensional vector. We use this encoder to process the text from the student response and its all references. Formally, let $V_i = [F_1, F_2, ..., F_{512}]$ represents a feature vector for a student response. Also, let the set $PR = [R_1, R_2, R_3, ..., R_N]$ represents all possible references in the 'grammar.xml' file. Each element in PR is a possible reference and consists of 512 features $R_i = [F_1, F_2, ..., F_{512}]$. The universal sentence encoder is used to generate the feature set. Then, the cosine similarity measure is computed for each (V_i, R_i) pair. Finally, we take the R_i which has maximum cosine value (maximum similarity) to compute the difference between it and V_i. The difference vector was provided to a machine learning algorithm to predict the final decision.

3.2 Features Using Python English Grammar Checker Toolkit

We used a free available Python English grammar checker toolkit[1] to extract grammar errors from audio transcription given by the ASR. Two features were extracted using this tool:

- F1: The number of grammar errors produced when this tool was applied on the transcription given by SLaTE2018 ASR.
- F2: The number of grammar errors produced when this tool was applied on the transcription given by Google ASR.

---

[1] https://pypi.python.org/pypi/grammar-check/1.3.1.

3.3 Part-of-Speech (POS) Features

We used the POS tagger implemented in NLTK toolkit[2] to generate POS set for a given student response (the transcription given by the ASR) and each possible reference.

Formally, let the set $[t_1, t_2, t_3 \ldots, t_m]$ represents all terms that the transcription consists of. The set $[pos_1, pos_2, pos_3 \ldots, pos_m]$ is produced by NTLK POS tagger, where pos_i is the part of speech for the term t_i. Also, POS level set was generated for each reference. After that, we compute the similarity between the student response and each reference by Eq. 1.

$$\frac{POSs \bigcap POSr}{POS_s \bigcup POS_r} \qquad (1)$$

where $POSs$ represents the POS level set for the student response, and $POSr$ is the POS level set for a reference response. This equations was computed for each possible reference in 'grammar.xml' file. Tow features were extracted from this approach:

– F1: is the maximum similarity value between transcription given by SLaTE2018 ASR and each possible reference.
– F2: is the maximum similarity value between transcription given by Google ASR and each possible reference.

3.4 Response Embedding to Binary Features

In this feature extraction technique, each student response and all of its related references were embedded into 438 binary features vectors. Let the set $D = [t_1, t_2, t_3 \ldots, t_m]$ represents all terms in grammar file. Every term t_i was normalized by removing punctuation and stemming using Porter Stemmer. Then, the normalized term is added to the list B if it is not added before. The terms in the list B were used to extract the 438-dimensional vector for all responses, where the number 438 is the size of the list B.

Each student response is tokenized to find its terms. Then, each term is normalized and added to the list S_T. The same process is applied on each possible reference to find the list P_T. Let $SF = [F_1, F_2 \ldots, F_{438}]$ represents the 438-dimensional features vector for the student response. $F_i = 1$ if the i_{th} term in the list B exists in the list S_T. Otherwise $F_i = 0$. In the same way, we can find the 438-dimensional features vector RF_i for each possible reference.

Let the set $PF = [RF_1, RF_2, \ldots, RF_N]$ includes group of 438-dimensional vectors where each vector RF_i for a possible reference and N is the number of all possible references for a student response. The similarity between SF and RF_i can be computed by Eq. 2.

$$similarity = \sum_{i=1}^{438} SF_i * F_i \qquad (2)$$

---

[2] https://www.nltk.org/.

Where SF_i and F_i represent one item in SF and RF_i vectors respectively.

After computing the similarity measure between each (SF, RF_i) pair. We take the RF_i which has maximum similarity value to compute the difference between it and SF. The difference vector was provided to a machine learning algorithm to predict the final decision.

4   Evaluation

In this section, we present results of four DNN based systems. Feed-forward neural networks [5] were used in all of our presented experiments. The following four combinations of different feature sets were investigated:

- Feature Set1 includes: 512-dimensional feature vectors that described in Sect. 3.1.
- Feature Set2 includes: Two features which are described in Sect. 3.2, two features which are described in Sect. 3.3, and the 512 features that are described in Sect. 3.1.
- Feature Set3 includes: 438 features that described in Sect. 3.4.
- Feature Set4 includes: Two features which are described in Sect. 3.2, two features which are described in Sect. 3.3, and the 438 features that described in Sect. 3.4.

4.1   Evaluation Metric

To evaluate the overall system and to easily compare its performance with similar systems, D score is used as a performance measure for the overall system. D score metric was used in evaluating the performance of systems competing in this task. So, we use this score as an evaluation measure for our proposed system. D metric is computed by Eq. 3.

$$D = \frac{CR(FR + CA)}{FR(CR + FA)} \tag{3}$$

Where,

1. **Correct Reject (CR):** is the number of utterances where the system rejects student's response which is labeled as language incorrect one.
2. **Correct Accept (CA):** is the number of utterances where the system accepts student's response which is labeled as language correct one.
3. **False Reject (FR):** is the number of utterances where the system rejects student's response which is labeled as language correct one.
4. **False Accept (FA)** is defined by $FA = PFA + 3 * GFA$, where PFA is the number of utterances where the system accept student's response which is labeled as correct in meaning but has a grammar error. GFA is the number of utterances where the system accept student's response which is labeled as incorrect responses in terms of meaning.

4.2   Experiments and Results

A DNN based system is trained on each of the earlier mentioned four feature combinations, using the training dataset and evaluated on the test data of the 2018 CALL shared task, as shown in Table 1. The system performance is represented by the D score [4] which is mathematically defined in Eq. 3. In addition, the rejection rate on incorrect responses (IRej) and rejection rate on correct responses (CRej) are also presented. The results of each trained model is reported in Table 3.

Table 3. Results of four proposed systems, where IRej = rejections on incorrect responses and CRej = rejections on correct responses.

Model	IRej	CRej	D-score
Model-1	0.50	0.05	9.09
Model-2	0.55	0.05	10.0
Model-3	0.41	0.05	8.89
Model-4	0.58	0.06	10.2

Table 3 show the results of the four trained model. Feature Set1, Feature Set2, Feature Set3, and Feature Set4 were used to train Model-1, Model-2, Model-3, and Model-4, respectively. We can note that the grammar features played an essential role to increase the rejection rate (and to enhance the D-score) when are added to Feature Set1 and Feature Set3. This is because of its ability to detect some grammar errors in the incorrect utterances. Also, the results show that the Model-1 and Model3 are comparable in term of D-score. This proves that the two ways of embedding that were described in Sects. 3.1 and 3.4 are capable to represent the student response in this task.

4.3   Fusion of Multiple Models

In this section, we explore two fusion method to enhance the overall results:

– **Method-1:** As shown in the results above, Model-2 and Model-4 are achieved the best D-score of 10 and 10.2, respectively. In order to study the usefulness of combining these two models together, we fused Model-2 and Model-4 together, so that the final decision is 'reject' if the output of the two models is 'reject'. Otherwise, the final decision is 'accept'. The fused system was evaluated on the same test set (shared task 2018 test set), and achieved 35% improvement on the D-score of 13.87. This proof that the two features sets used in these two models are, to some extent, orthogonal and do the evaluation from different side. Therefore, by combining them together, we got a better performance.

- **Method-2:** In our previous work [1], the text processing module is implemented as a rule based, where optimized using genetic algorithm. We use this system to enhance the fusion results. The final decision is 'accept' if both of Model-2 and Model-4 agree on the response has no errors or the model in [1] accept that response. Otherwise, the final decision is 'reject'. In this way the target of the fused system is increasing the rejection rate on incorrect responses, and it also aims to reduce the rejection rate on correct responses. This fused system was evaluated on the same test set (shared task 2018 test set), and achieved improvement on the D-score of 17.11.

4.4   Comparison and Discussion

In this section, we compare our results with other five systems participated in the same shared task and used the same dataset, [1, 8, 10, 12, 15] and using the same measures. As shown in [12, 15], the improvement on the ASR component has a key factor of increasing the D-score. For this reason, we used Google ASR, in addition to that provided by the shared task organizers, as described in Sect. 3.3 and Sect. 3.2. This help use to reduce some of the errors caused by ASR system.

Further tuning for the model parameters to increase the D-score was proposed in [1, 12]. Also, in this paper, we proposed two fusion ideas to increase the D-score from 10.2 (best model) to 13.87 (method-1 in Sect. 4.3) and 17.11 (method-2 in Sect. 4.3).

In general, both rule-based approaches [1, 10] and machine learning based approaches [8, 12, 15] achieved good results. Table 4 reports the D-score of each system, where **Fusion-1** and **Fusion-2** represents our fused systems that described in Sect. 4.3.

Table 4. Comparison between results

System	D-score
Liulishuo's system [12]	19.088
Fusion-2	17.11
An optimization based approach [1]	14.4
Fusion-1	13.87
The University of Birmingham [15]	10.764
The CSU-K rule-based system [10]	10.08
Improvements to an automated content scoring system [8]	7.397

Table 4 shows the effect of combining the results from rule-based system and machine learning system. In this way we can achieve better D-score using low false rejection rate in [1] when the response is correct, and high rejection rate in Model-2 and Model-4 when the response is incorrect.

5 Conclusion and Future Work

The main objective of this research is developing a system which helps English learners to exercise and improve speaking skills in English conservation. Generally, different DNN models is trained on four combinations of different feature sets to evaluate the student responses in 2018 CALL shared task. Moreover, two fusion methods were proposed to enhance the D-score: The first one is fusing the two DNN models that achieved best results, and the second one uses our already implemented system to enhance the fusion results. The experiments showed that the D-score was increased to 13.87 and 17.11 respectively. In the future work, we intend to build a DNN model with D-score as a cost function of the optimizer.

References

1. Ateeq, M., Hanani, A., Qaroush, A.: An optimization based approach for solving spoken CALL shared task. In: Proceedings of Interspeech 2018, pp. 2369–2373 (2018)
2. Baur, C., et al.: Overview of the 2017 spoken CALL shared task (2017)
3. Baur, C., et al.: Overview of the 2017 spoken CALL shared task. In: Proceedings of Interspeech 2018 (2018)
4. Baur, C., Gerlach, J., Rayner, E., Russell, M., Strik, H.: A shared task for spoken CALL? (2016)
5. Bebis, G., Georgiopoulos, M.: Feed-forward neural networks. IEEE Potentials 13(4), 27–31 (1994)
6. Bojanowski, P., Grave, E., Joulin, A., Mikolov, T.: Enriching word vectors with subword information. Trans. Assoc. Comput. Linguistics 5, 135–146 (2017)
7. Cer, D., et al.: Universal sentence encoder. arXiv preprint arXiv:1803.11175 (2018)
8. Evanini, K., et al.: Improvements to an automated content scoring system for spoken CALL responses: the ETS submission to the second spoken CALL shared task. In: Proceedings of Interspeech 2018, pp. 2379–2383 (2018)
9. Franco, H., et al.: Eduspeak®: a speech recognition and pronunciation scoring toolkit for computer-aided language learning applications. Lang. Test. 27(3), 401–418 (2010)
10. Jülg, D., Kunstek, M., Freimoser, C., Berkling, K., Qian, M.: The CSU-K rule-based system for the 2nd edition spoken CALL shared task. In: Proceedings of Interspeech 2018, pp. 2359–2363 (2018)
11. Kusner, M., Sun, Y., Kolkin, N., Weinberger, K.: From word embeddings to document distances. In: International Conference on Machine Learning, pp. 957–966 (2015)
12. Nguyen, H., Chen, L., Prieto, R., Wang, C., Liu, Y.: Liulishuo's system for the spoken CALL shared task 2018. In: Proceedings of Interspeech 2018, pp. 2364–2368 (2018)
13. Oh, Y.R., et al.: Deep-learning based automatic spontaneous speech assessment in a data-driven approach for the 2017 slate CALL shared challenge. In: SLaTE, pp. 103–108 (2017)
14. Qian, M., Wei, X., Jancovic, P., Russell, M.: The University of Birmingham 2017 slate CALL shared task systems. In: Proceedings of the Seventh SLaTE Workshop, Stockholm, Sweden (2017)

15. Qian, M., Wei, X., Jančovič, P., Russell, M.: The University of Birmingham 2018 spoken CALL shared task systems. In: Proceedings of Interspeech 2018, pp. 2374–2378 (2018)
16. Rayner, E., Bouillon, P., Gerlach, J.: Evaluating appropriateness of system responses in a spoken CALL game (2012)

A Pattern Mining Approach in Feature Extraction for Emotion Recognition from Speech

Umut Avci[1](✉), Gamze Akkurt[2], and Devrim Unay[3]

[1] Faculty of Engineering, Department of Software Engineering,
Yasar University, Bornova, Izmir, Turkey
umut.avci@yasar.edu.tr
[2] Faculty of Engineering, Department of Computer Engineering,
Izmir University of Economics, Balcova, Izmir, Turkey
akkurtgamzee@gmail.com
[3] Faculty of Engineering, Department of Biomedical Engineering,
Izmir University of Economics, Balcova, Izmir, Turkey
devrim.unay@ieu.edu.tr

Abstract. We address the problem of recognizing emotions from speech using features derived from emotional patterns. Because much work in the field focuses on using low-level acoustic features, we explicitly study whether high-level features are useful for classifying emotions. For this purpose, we convert a continuous speech signal to a discretized signal and extract discriminative patterns that are capable of distinguishing distinct emotions from each other. Extracted patterns are then used to create a feature set to be fed into a classifier. Experimental results show that patterns alone are good predictors of emotions. When used to build a classifier, pattern features achieve accuracy gains up to 25% compared to state-of-the-art acoustic features.

Keywords: Emotion recognition · Speech processing · Pattern mining · Feature extraction

1 Introduction

Speech is the most natural communication channel. With recent advances, speech-based technologies have become an integral part of modern life. From basic mobile phones to advanced assistants such as Amazon's Alexa or from our cars to home automation, voice-controlled systems enable us to perform daily tasks using commands. Apart from personal use, speech recognition has its application in various domains: in businesses to cut costs and increase the productivity of customer services [18], in education to improve the quality of teaching [25], in healthcare to determine the state of patients [5]. Despite its widespread use, recognizing speech is only one part of the story. Chibelushi suggests that words are responsible for about 7% of the message perception while voice intonation for

© Springer Nature Switzerland AG 2019
A. A. Salah et al. (Eds.): SPECOM 2019, LNAI 11658, pp. 54–63, 2019.
https://doi.org/10.1007/978-3-030-26061-3_6

about 38% [3]. As intonation is directly affected by emotions, developing techniques to identify emotions from the speech is of great importance in conveying the full meaning of messages.

Recognizing emotions from speech have been addressed in many studies. These are generally distinguished from each other by the types of features and the methods of classification. Majority of the research focus on using prosody [1,16], voice quality [7,23] or spectral features [8,19]. Some of the researchers incorporate lexical information into acoustic features in order to improve emotion recognition. Linguistic cues are mainly captured with N-Grams [21], Bag-of-Words [20] or the language models [9]. Extracted features are used to build classifiers such as such as Support Vector Machines (SVMs) [26], Gaussian Mixture Models (GMMs) [13], Hidden Markov Models (HMMs) [15], Artificial Neural Networks (ANNs) [14] and Deep Neural Networks (DNNs) [4].

In this study, we propose an approach to produce a novel set of features for emotion recognition from speech. The method begins with transforming each continuous speech signal into discrete units. A pattern mining algorithm then takes as input the discretized signals and extracts patterns characterizing emotions. Finally, a feature is generated for each pattern of each emotion by counting how many times a pattern is observed on a converted signal. There are only a few studies available in the literature that use pattern mining in feature extraction. However, these works differ both in the domain of application, i.e. face [22] and EEG [24], and in the way that features are extracted. To our knowledge, this is the first study to suggest using pattern mining for emotion recognition from speech.

In the next section, we explain our approach. We describe the dataset used in this study and present experimental results in Sect. 3. We conclude the paper in Sect. 4.

2 Our Approach

It is a known fact that emotions affect the acoustic characteristics of speech. In most of the emotion recognition studies, these characteristics are captured by low-level prosodic or spectral features. In this study, we propose an approach that focuses on identifying acoustic patterns specific to different emotions as high-level features of vocal expressions. For this purpose, raw speech signals were transformed to strings via discretization. Discrete representations of signals were used to extract patterns of emotions in a discriminative manner. Emotion recognition was then performed with features elaborated from the patterns. The approach is summarized in Fig. 1 where the details are presented in the following sections.

2.1 Dimensionality Reduction

Given a speech signal of dimension t, $D = d_1, ..., d_t$, this step reduces the dimension of the original signal to t/w, $\bar{D} = \bar{d}_1, ..., \bar{d}_i$, by calculating the ith element as:

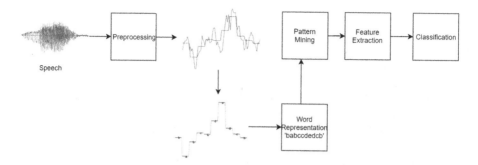

Fig. 1. Basic system diagram of speech emotion recognition.

$$\bar{d}_i = \frac{1}{w} \sum_{j=w\times(i-1)+1}^{w\times i} d_j \tag{1}$$

where w is the window size of arbitrary length and $i = 1, ..., t/w$.

In a nut shell, the speech signal consisting of t data points is divided into non-overlapping windows (partitions) of equal length, w (window size), where each window is represented by the average value of its data points (Fig. 2a). Before applying the Eq. 1 to a speech signal, we removed the silent parts of the speech and performed z-score normalization on each signal. In our study, we set w to 8.

2.2 Discretization

In discretization, we convert the scalar vector $\bar{D}$ into a string of characters $\bar{S}$. To this aim, we map each element of $\bar{D}, \bar{d}_i$ to each element of $\bar{S}, \bar{s}_i$. Mapping is done by fitting the Gaussian Distribution on $\bar{D}$ and dividing the distribution into equally probable regions. Here, breakpoints $B = b_1 \ldots b_n$ are defined as the values that divide the distribution into $n+1$ equiprobable regions. Each region is then tagged with a letter from the English alphabet in order, e.g. three regions are labeled as a, b and c for $n = 2$. Depending on the region that a $\bar{d}_i$ falls, $\bar{s}_i$ is assigned the label of the corresponding region. In our study, we set n to 4. Figure 2b. shows an example of discretization. By setting n to 4, we convert $\bar{D}$ into corresponding $\bar{S}$ as a sequence of characters **babccdedcb**.

2.3 Pattern Mining

Pattern mining provides a set of patterns that describe the characteristic of data in an informative manner. One of the well-known pattern mining techniques is contrast mining. The aim of contrast mining is to discover diverse patterns that have differences in the data set. Distinguishing pattern mining (DPS) is a specific type of contrast mining. The idea of DSP is to find a set of interesting patterns that are observed frequently in positive class and rarely in negative class. Data

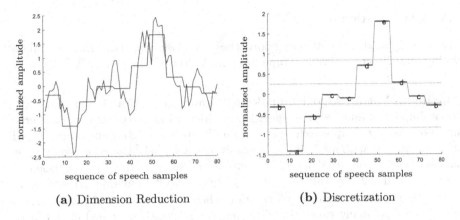

(a) Dimension Reduction   (b) Discretization

Fig. 2. (a) The dimension of a continuous speech signal of length t is reduced to t/w, w being the window size. (b) The signal is discretized based on the areas of the Gaussian distribution.

mining restrictions have an important part to determine a sequential pattern and provide scalability of the whole process. The specific restriction in DSP mining is gap constraint. Gap constraint set boundaries between two consecutive values in sequences.

In our research, we used KDSP-Miner (top-k distinguishing sequential patterns with gap constraint) [27]. We extracted top-1000 patterns with gap constraint of zero from each emotion using one against all strategy. As each pattern may be observed both in positive and negative classes at the same time, the algorithm provides two measures showing the extent to which a pattern appears in each class as positive support (PosSup) and negative support (NegSup). By dividing the PosSup to NegSup, a measure called C-ratio is obtained. We have created a set of discriminative patterns of each emotion by selecting them based on the highest C-ratio.

2.4 Feature Extraction

Patterns obtained in the previous step are used to extract acoustic descriptors. Let p_i^j be i^{th} pattern for j^{th} emotion where $i = 1, \ldots, n$ and $j = 1, \ldots, m$. Also let f_t be t^{th} element of the feature vector of size $n \times m$. Given a pattern specific to emotion, p_i^j, and a discretized speech signal, we compute f_t by counting the number of times that p_i^j is exactly matched on the discretized signal. In an exact match, we do not allow gaps between matches of individual pattern elements with the aim of retaining the motif that is represented by the pattern. Assume that **dceadceabdc** is a discrete representation of a speech signal and that there are two patterns: **cea** and **eadc**. The former is observed twice in the signal which makes its relative entry in the feature vector 2. The latter is matched once exactly and twice with a gap constraint of one, **b** being the gap in the substring **eabdc**. As our calculation is based only on exact matches, its feature value is set to 1.

2.5   Classification

We have applied two different approaches for classifying patterns: maximum voting and Directed Acyclic Graph Support Vector Machine (DAGSVM).

Maximum Voting Algorithm: Before learning a classification model, we utilize a simple maximum voting algorithm in order to explore the effect of patterns on emotions. In this approach, the emotion of a speech is determined solely based on the patterns without building a classification model. A speech signal to be labeled is first converted to its discretized version $\bar{S}$ with steps described in Sects. 2.1 and 2.2. We take a pattern p_i^j for a specific emotion j (note again that p_i^j is the ith pattern for j^{th} emotion where $i = 1, \ldots, n$ and $j = 1, \ldots, m$) and count how many times the given pattern is exactly matched on the $\bar{S}$ as performed in Sect. 2.4. This pattern matching phase is repeated for each pattern of an emotion type j. The number of matches for each pattern i is summed to obtain the cumulative number of matches for emotion j. The procedure is repeated for all the emotions resulting in j number of cumulative sums. The emotion for which the cumulative sum is the highest is assigned as the emotion label of the speech $\bar{S}$.

Here, although rare, there may be a case where the cumulative sums of distinct emotions are the same. In this situation, we randomly select one of the competing emotions and assign the chosen emotion as the emotion label of the speech.

DAGSVM: Support vector machines (SVM) is a popular classifier successfully applied to problems of pattern recognition, text classification, etc. Initially proposed for binary classification problems, SVM can be applied to multi-class problems by different strategies like one-versus-one and one-versus-all. One-against-all [10] builds m number of classes in SVM. The mth class of SVM is trained to separate the mth class from the other classes. One-against-one [12] method construct $m(m-1)/2$ SVM classifiers that are trained to differentiate samples of a class from other class samples. This method uses a pairwise coupling strategy for all class combinations.

Directed Acyclic Graph (DAG) SVM [17] can be used for multi-class classification as well. DAGSVM is closely related to one-versus-one SVM in the training phase. The graph has m number of multi-class classifier and it has $m(m-1)/2$ internal nodes where SVM classifier is included in each of them. In the testing phase, the classification begins at the root node and move on through the left or right node according to the output of SVM classification. The classification proceeds until a leaf node which determines predicted class. One of the advantages of DAGSVM is that the performance of testing time is lower than one-versus-one method of SVM. Also, experimental results [6] demonstrate that one-against-one and DAGSVM methods is more proper for practical uses. In classification, we adapted DAGSVM to SVM and used the implementation of LibSVM tool [2].

3   Dataset and Experimental Results

3.1   Dataset

We use Ryerson Audio Visual Database of Emotional Speech and Song [11]. RAVDESS is a multi-modal database containing audio-visual recordings of emotional speech and song from 24 actors (12 female and 12 male), and it is typically used by the research community to study acoustic and/or visual similarities. In the recordings, speech is restricted to two sentences: "kids are talking by the door" and "dogs are sitting by the door". Each actor expresses these sentences with 8 different emotions (neutral, calm, happy, sad, angry, fearful, disgust and surprise) in a North American accent. The song recordings contain first 6 emotions except for disgust and surprise. Each emotion is expressed at normal and strong intensities with two repetitions. Only the neutral emotion lacks the strong intensity. In the dataset, each actor performs distinct vocalizations of 60 spoken and 44 sung recordings. The total number of vocalizations is 2452 (24 actor × 60 recordings + 23 actor × 44 recordings) available in three modules: audio-only, video-only, and audio-visual.

In our research, we only used the speech signals with normal intensity from the RAVDESS database and omitted the song portion. Since the study that we use as the benchmark [28] focuses on recognizing emotions independent from the domain, i.e. speech and song, only common emotions to both domains are considered. To be aligned with this work, we excluded disgust and surprise emotions from the speech recordings. As a result of the pruning, the total number of audio recordings becomes 576 (1 domain × 24 actors × 2 sentences × 2 repetitions × 6 emotions).

3.2   Experimental Results

In this section, the performance of the proposed method was evaluated and compared with the results in [28]. In order to appraise the effect of pattern count on the performance, we created distinct sets with 5, 10, 15, 50, 100, 150, 250, 500 and 1000 patterns for each emotion based on the C-ratio criterion. The choice of the pattern count determines the size of the feature vector (see Sect. 2.4). For example, 5 patterns for each emotion results with a feature vector of size 30. Such a feature vector allows representing a speech signal independent from the type of emotion. Note that z-score normalization was performed on the feature vectors prior to their usage.

For the experiments where we model a classifier, leave-one-performer-and-sentence-out cross-validation is used. One sentence from one performer is evaluated in every round of testing data. The training data consists of other performers and other sentences. Optimization of model parameters is performed via 5-fold internal cross-validation on the folds of training data. The grid search determines the optimal hyper-parameters of SVM, i.e. C and γ where C is a regularization constant for the training error and γ is the kernel function to control

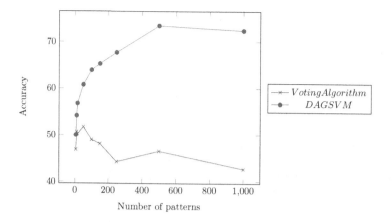

Fig. 3. Maximum voting algorithm and DAGSVM classification results.

the bandwidth of the radial basis function (RBF). In our experiments, we used the popular RBF kernel.

Figure 3 shows voting-based and model-based classification results as accuracies. From the figure, it can be seen that the voting approach provides results comparable to those provided with the state-of-the-art features (see Table 1). In this approach, classification accuracies decrease as the pattern count increases. As we sort patterns based on the C-ratio and select the pattern set from the list, the patterns that are up in the list have higher discriminative power than the followings. So, increasing the number of patterns decreases the overall discriminative power, hence results with a decrease in the accuracy. An important point worth noting is that a decrease in the number of patterns leads to an increase in the likelihood of having emotions with the same cumulative sums of pattern matches (see Sect. 2.5 - *Maximum Voting Algorithm*). Recall that, in cases where such emotions emerge, the emotion label of a speech is determined by a random selection process. This may cause a drop in classification accuracy, an example of which can be seen for 5 patterns in Fig. 3. As can be predicted, the model-based approach outperforms the voting-based approach in almost all cases. Besides, the model-based approach improves the results of the voting-based approach up to 30% for larger pattern counts. Contrary to the voting-based approach, classification results increase with the rise in the number of patterns. This is logical as the information embedded into the feature vectors increases proportionally to the pattern used.

Table 1 presents the classification accuracies of our approach for two different sets of patterns (5 and 500) and results given in [28]. The results are comparable as the cited study uses DAGSVM for classification and leave-one-performer-and-sentence-out cross-validation for the evaluation on the same dataset. In this benchmark paper, five sets of acoustic features are used, i.e. energy, spectral, MFCC, voicing and RASTA. Our approach with the smallest set of patterns outperforms the best of all the acoustic features, MFCC. Besides, the size of

Table 1. Classification results of acoustic and pattern-based features.

	Classification accuracy (%)
Energy [28]	34.78
Spectral [28]	48.01
MFCC [28]	48.73
Voicing [28]	38.41
Rasta [28]	30.43
5 Patterns (proposed)	50
500 Patterns (proposed)	73.44

the feature vector in the pattern-based approach is far less than the number of attributes in MFCC. This makes our approach much more efficient compared to known techniques. Moreover, in our approach, dramatic increases in the accuracies may be achieved by increasing the number of patterns with an additional cost of complexity.

4   Conclusion

This paper presents a new method for feature extraction using pattern mining in speech emotion recognition. Voting results show that patterns alone are moderately good predictors of emotion. Experiments demonstrate that the features extracted from even a small number of patterns outperform all state-of-the-art benchmark features. Important accuracy gains are provided with increasing pattern usage. Despite the growth in complexity due to both pattern mining and training, gains up to 25% could be achieved relative to the best prior art, i.e. MFCC features. We consider improving our work by using a standard set of features, e.g. INTERSPEECH 2013 acoustic feature configuration, under a fully subject independent cross-validation setting in the future.

References

1. Alex, S.B., Babu, B.P., Mary, L.: Utterance and syllable level prosodic features for automatic emotion recognition. In: 2018 (RAICS), pp. 31–35 (2018). https://doi.org/10.1109/RAICS.2018.8635059
2. Chang, C.C., Lin, C.J.: LIBSVM: a library for support vector machines. ACM Trans. Intell. Syst. Technol. (TIST) **2**(3), 27 (2011)
3. Chibelushi, C.C., Bourel, F.: Facial expression recognition: a brief tutorial overview. In: CVonline: (OLCCV), vol. 9 (2003)
4. Han, K., Yu, D., Tashev, I.: Speech emotion recognition using deep neural network and extreme learning machine. In: INTERSPEECH, pp. 223–227 (2014)
5. Hossain, M.S.: Patient state recognition system for healthcare using speech and facial expressions. J. Med. Syst. **40**(12), 1–8 (2016). https://doi.org/10.1007/s10916-016-0627-x

6. Hsu, C.W., Lin, C.J.: A comparison of methods for multiclass support vector machines. IEEE Trans. Neural Netw. **13**(2), 415–425 (2002)
7. Jacob, A.: Speech emotion recognition based on minimal voice quality features. In: 2016 (ICCSP), pp. 0886–0890 (2016). https://doi.org/10.1109/ICCSP.2016. 7754275
8. Khan, A., Roy, U.K.: Emotion recognition using prosodie and spectral features of speech and Naïve Bayes classifier. In: 2017(WiSPNET), pp. 1017–1021 (2017). https://doi.org/10.1109/WiSPNET.2017.8299916
9. Kim, W., Hansen, J.H.L.: Angry emotion detection from real-life conversational speech by leveraging content structure. In: 2010 IEEE (ICASSP), pp. 5166–5169 (2010). https://doi.org/10.1109/ICASSP.2010.5495021
10. Liu, Y., Zheng, Y.F.: One-against-all multi-class SVM classification using reliability measures. In: Proceedings of 2005 IEEE International Joint Conference on Neural Networks, vol. 2, pp. 849–854. IEEE (2005)
11. Livingstone, S.R., Russo, F.A.: The Ryerson audio-visual database of emotional speech and song (RAVDESS): a dynamic, multimodal set of facial and vocal expressions in north American English. PLoS ONE **13**(5), e0196391 (2018)
12. Milgram, J., Cheriet, M., Sabourin, R.: "one against one" or "one against all": Which one is better for handwriting recognition with SVMs? In: Tenth International Workshop on (FHR). Suvisoft (2006)
13. Neiberg, D., Elenius, K., Laskowski, K.: Emotion recognition in spontaneous speech using GMMs. In: INTERSPEECH, pp. 809–812 (2006)
14. Nicholson, J., Takahashi, K., Nakatsu, R.: Emotion recognition in speech using neural networks. Neural Comput. Appl. **9**(4), 290–296 (2000). https://doi.org/10. 1007/s005210070006
15. Nwe, T.L., Foo, S.W., Silva, L.C.D.: Speech emotion recognition using hidden Markov models. Speech Commun. **41**(4), 603–623 (2003). https://doi.org/10.1016/ S0167-6393(03)00099-2
16. Pervaiz, M., Khan, T.A.: Emotion recognition from speech using prosodic and linguistic features. Int. J. Adv. Comput. Sci. Appl. **7**(8), 84–90 (2016)
17. Platt, J.C., Cristianini, N., Shawe-Taylor, J.: Large margin DAGs for multiclass classification. In: ANIPS, pp. 547–553 (2000)
18. Rabiner, L.R.: Applications of speech recognition in the area of telecommunications. In: 1997 IEEE WASRUP, pp. 501–510 (1997). https://doi.org/10.1109/ ASRU.1997.659129
19. Rieger, S.A., Muraleedharan, R., Ramachandran, R.P.: Speech based emotion recognition using spectral feature extraction and an ensemble of KNN classifiers. In: The 9th International Symposium on Chinese Spoken Language Processing, pp. 589–593 (2014). https://doi.org/10.1109/ISCSLP.2014.6936711
20. Schmitt, M., Ringeval, F., Schuller, B.: At the border of acoustics and linguistics: bag-of-audio-words for the recognition of emotions in speech. In: Interspeech 2016, pp. 495–499 (2016). https://doi.org/10.21437/Interspeech.2016-1124
21. Schuller, B., Batliner, A., Steidl, S., Seppi, D.: Emotion recognition from speech: putting ASR in the loop. In: 2009 IEEE (ICASSP), pp. 4585–4588. IEEE (2009)
22. Shan, C., Gong, S., McOwan, P.W.: Robust facial expression recognition using local binary patterns. In: IEEE ICIP 2005, vol. 2, p. II-370 (2005). https://doi. org/10.1109/ICIP.2005.1530069
23. Sundberg, J., Patel, S., Björkner, E., Scherer, K.R.: Interdependencies among voice source parameters in emotional speech. IEEE Trans. Affect. Comput. **2**, 162–174 (2011)

24. Tiwari, A., Falk, T.H.: Fusion of Motif- and spectrum-related features for improved EEG-based emotion recognition. Comput. Intell. Neurosci. **2019**, 1–14 (2019). https://doi.org/10.1155/2019/3076324
25. Wald, M.: Using automatic speech recognition to enhance education for all students: turning a vision into reality. In: PFE 35th Annual Conference, p. S3G (2005). https://doi.org/10.1109/FIE.2005.1612286
26. Wongthanavasu, T.S.S.: Speech emotion recognition using support vector machines. In: 5th International Conference (KST), pp. 86–91 (2013). https://doi.org/10.1109/KST.2013.6512793
27. Yang, H., Duan, L., Hu, B., Deng, S., Wang, W., Qin, P.: Mining top-k distinguishing sequential patterns with gap constraint. J. Softw. **26**(11), 2994–3009 (2015)
28. Zhang, B., Essl, G., Provost, E.M.: Recognizing emotion from singing and speaking using shared models. In: 2015 International Conference on (ACII), pp. 139–145. IEEE (2015)

Towards a Dialect Classification in German Speech Samples

Johanna Dobbriner[1(✉)] and Oliver Jokisch[2]

[1] Institute of Applied Informatics, Universität Leipzig, 04107 Leipzig, Germany
`johanna@bioinf.uni-leipzig.de`
[2] Institute of Communications Engineering,
Leipzig University of Telecommunications (HfTL), 04277 Leipzig, Germany
`jokisch@hft-leipzig.de`

Abstract. The automatic classification of a speaker's dialect can enrich many applications, e.g. in the human-machine interaction (HMI) or natural language processing (NLP) but also in specific areas such as pronunciation tutoring, forensic analysis or personalization of call-center talks. Although a lot of HMI/NLP-related research has been dedicated to different tasks in affective computing, emotion recognition, semantic understanding and other advanced topics, there seems to be a lack of methods for an automated dialect analysis that is not based on transcriptions, in particular for some languages like German. For other languages such as English, Mandarin or Arabic, a multitude of feature combinations and classification methods has been tried already, which provides a starting point for our study. We describe selected experiments to train suitable classifiers on German dialect varieties in the corpus "Regional Variants of German 1" (RVG1). Our article starts with a systematic choice of appropriate spectral features. In a second step, these features are post-processed with different methods and used to train one Gaussian Mixture Model (GMM) per feature combination as a Universal Background Model (UBM). The resulting UBMs are then adapted to a varied selection of dialects by maximum-a-posteriori (MAP) adaptation. Our preliminary results on German show, that a dialect discrimination and classification is possible. The unweighted recognition accuracy ranges from 32.4 to 54.9% in a 3-dialects test and from 19.6 to 31.4% in a classification of 9-dialects. Some dialects are easier distinguishable, purely using spectral features, while others require a different feature set or more sophisticated classification methods, which we will explore in future experiments.

Keywords: Dialect recognition · Spectral features · MFCC · GMM

1 Introduction

Automatic Dialect Classification (ADC) is the process of automatically identifying a regional dialect of a given language from speech samples, which poses a challenge, since the dialects usually provide smaller distinguishable differences

© Springer Nature Switzerland AG 2019
A. A. Salah et al. (Eds.): SPECOM 2019, LNAI 11658, pp. 64–74, 2019.
https://doi.org/10.1007/978-3-030-26061-3_7

than languages in general. Beyond, the phonetic or prosodic borders between dialects are often diffuse and, since people move to different places over their lifetime, a speaker may exhibit a mixture of different dialects.

In spite of the limitations, it is useful for many applications to utilize ADC. A prominent example is Automatic Speech Recognition (ASR) where the variation within a language, individually or due to the speaker's regional dialect, can be challenging for the recognizer. By ADC the language model can be fitted to the dialect classified. Furthermore, dialect recognition can be useful in forensic analysis to match speech recordings to its region of origin or in the customer service, allocating the customer to an agent, who can speak the same dialect. In the described cases, it is unlikely to have transcripts of the speech that needs to be classified. Consequently, an automatic, text-independent dialect classification has been studied by several authors e.g. on English [1–4], Arabic [5–7] or Chinese [8–10].

The different approaches to ADC, which have been used for the aforementioned languages, are either acoustic/phonetic [11–13], phonotactic [6,7,14] or prosodic [5,15] with a number of variations and combinations in features, modeling and classification methods [16,17], but the base model to compare to is commonly a GMM-UBM system [1,4,18,19] that takes Mel-Frequency Cepstral Coefficients (MFCC) as features to create a Gaussian Mixture Model (GMM) as a Universal Background Model (UBM), followed by an UBM adaptation to the dialects, that need to be classified.

For German, however, no studies on text-independent ADC could be found. In this contribution, we attempt to establish a baseline ADC system for German dialects on a database of about 500 speakers (Regional Variants of German 1) using the GMM-UBM approach.

In this paper, at first, we describe the speech data and algorithms used in the methods section followed by the experimental setup, results and discussion, and our conclusions.

2   Methods

2.1   Speech Data

There are several corpora, which contain German speech samples – even some for dialect analysis in particular, including the "Regional Variants of German 1" (RVG1), a speech corpus within the BAS CLARIN Repository [20]. RVG1 contains recordings of about 500 speakers from 9 different dialect regions in Germany with samples of 1 min of spontaneous speech as well as single numbers, commands and phrases for each speaker, recorded by four microphones simultaneously. The 9 dialect regions of RVG1 are visualized in Fig. 1, a map from 1989 that shows the then current dialect regions of the German language. As RVG1 was recorded 1996–1997, the map corresponds well with the dialects in the corpus.

The speaker distribution over the 9 regions is shown in the Figs. 2 and 3, the first by birth place and the second by the current living place at the time of the recordings (1996–1997). Table 1 presents the number of speakers in the different regions and dialects.

Since spontaneous and read speech differ significantly in many ways (e.g. speed, clarity of pronunciation etc.), the two modes were not pooled for the same model. In this paper we decided to concentrate only on the spontaneous part of the corpus, which contains one sample per speaker of 1 min, each.

Table 1. Number of speakers per dialect

Region		Dialect	Speakers	Train	Test
North	A	Low Franconian	44	35	9
	B	West Low German	103	82	21
	C	East Low German	31	24	7
Center	D	West Central German	73	58	15
	E	East Central German	52	41	11
South	F	Alemannic	63	50	13
	G	East Franconian	19	15	4
	H	South Franconian	10	8	2
	I	Bavarian /Austrian	100	80	20

2.2   Models

To analyze, whether ADC is generally feasible for German, we started with the mentioned, basic GMM-UBM approach, which is comprised of the following steps:

1. Feature extraction
2. Processing of the features
3. Computing the UBM
4. Adapting the UBM to different dialects
5. Scoring each test sample in every dialect model
6. Classification

In Step 1, the Mel-Frequency Cepstral Coefficients (MFCC) were extracted at a sampling rate of 8kHz, frame length of 25ms, Hamming-windowing and 10ms shift between the frames, which are fairly standard conditions. The result were feature vectors consisting of 12 MFCC and the spectral energy per frame.

The feature vectors were then processed in Step 2 using Voice Activity Detection (VAD) through an energy threshold, RASTA-filtering to remove the spectral components, that changed at a rate different from human speech and Cepstral Mean and Variance Normalization (CMVN). Additionally, delta and double delta, as well as Shifted Delta Cepstra (SDC) were computed from the processed MFCC to incorporate temporal context for each frame. The speech data was then randomly divided into a training set and a test set.

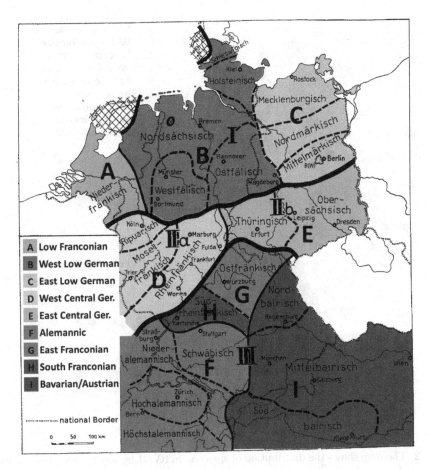

Fig. 1. The map, adapted from [21], shows the dialect regions as given in the corpus [20]. The dialect regions are colored according to the legend. (Color figure online)

For Step 3, the feature vectors of all training speakers were accumulated to train the UBM by Expectation-Maximization (EM) for 512 gaussians, a number which had proven to be successful in prior ADC-research.

Afterwards, the maximum-a-posteriori (MAP) algorithm was used, to adapt the means of the UBM to each dialect by using all speakers of this dialect in the training set. Then the log-likelihood score of each test sample was calculated in every adapted model, and the highest score per sample was determined as the corresponding dialect.

In the end, we determined the unweighted accuracy of the model by dividing all correctly classified test samples by the total number of test samples.

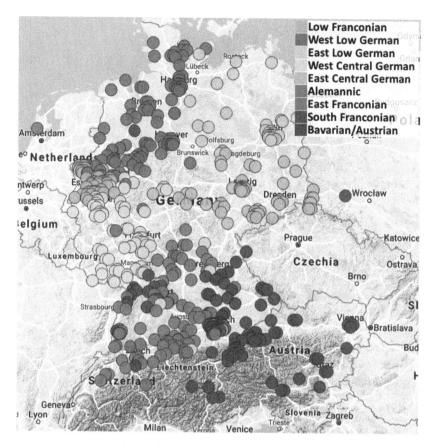

Fig. 2. The map shows the distribution of speakers in RVG1 by birth place – colored by their dialect as given in the corpus (created with: https://mapmakerapp.com/) (Color figure online)

3 Baseline Experiments

To determine, whether the GMM-UBM approach is suitable to identify German dialects too, we decided to experiment with several combinations of the potential feature processing. Always applying VAD, we varied the use of RASTA, CMVN, deltas and SDC. In addition, we switched between a coarse-grained dialect classification, which divided the speakers into just three main regions (low, central and high German) and the more fine-grained partition of the original corpus into 9 regions.

For the surveyed models we only used the spontaneous speech samples from the first microphone, which we divided randomly into a training set, containing 80% and a test set with 20% of the samples per dialect. The distribution of the speakers within each class on training and test set can be seen in Table 1. We used the full duration of 1 min for each sample and did not split any samples into smaller units. Since there is only one sample per speaker, the sets are speaker-disjunct by design. We processed all mentioned models for two such training/test combinations. Afterwards, we tried the same combinations on GMMs with less gaussians – 64, 128 and 256 respectively – to explore, whether similar accuracies can be achieved with smaller models that allow for lower calculation complexity (with regard to our trainings a few hours/days each).

To implement the setup, we used the Python toolkit "Sidekit" [22], which was written for the purpose of Speaker Identification and which enables the entire experimental process from the feature extraction to the classification.

4 Results and Discussion

Figure 4 summarizes our training and test results, in which the achieved unweighted accuracies are plotted per feature combination and model type. The

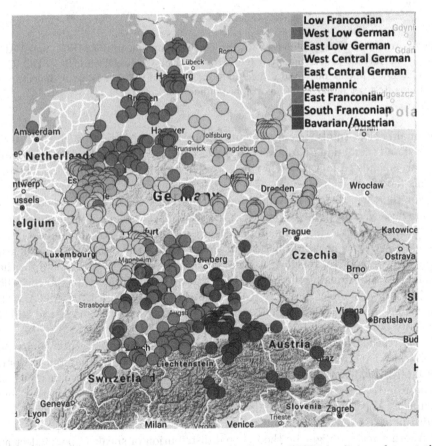

Fig. 3. The map shows the distribution of speakers in RVG1 by living place at the recording time – colored by their dialect as given in the corpus (created with: https:// mapmakerapp.com/) (Color figure online)

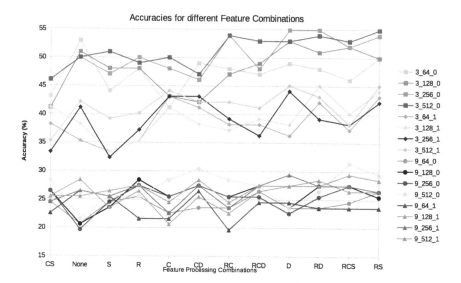

Fig. 4. Accuracies for the different feature combinations on top of MFCC and VAD: None – no further processing, R – RASTA, D – Delta/DoubleDelta, S – SDC, C – CMVN. Each line is one model combination, e.g. "9_64_0" refers to 9 dialects, 64 gaussians, test set number 0. (Color figure online)

four main colors (pink, green, blue and orange) show the training/test set (0 or 1) used and the number of dialects to be classified (3 or 9). Each of the main colors corresponds to four different lines, associated with the number of gaussians in this model.

For the three-dialects classification, the first test set mostly reached higher accuracies, even up to 54.9%, whereas the second set was apparently more difficult to classify, achieving a maximum accuracy of 45.1%. With nine dialects, the overall accuracy is naturally lower, but the impact of the test set used, was less than with the first set reaching a maximal accuracy of 31.4% and 29.4% for the second set. Additionally, the best-scoring feature combinations are shown to be (1) just Delta/DoubleDelta, (2) RASTA+CMVN+SDC, and (3) RASTA with either SDC or Delta/DoubleDelta, while the number of gaussians in the GMM is mostly best at 512 and 256.

Our reached accuracies were far from optimal but certainly above chance level, which is 11.1% for 9 dialects and 33.3% for 3 dialects. As a baseline system, the GMM-UBM approach seems effective for distinguishing German dialects. Aside from the chosen model, there may be other reasons for the rather low accuracies, e.g. there may be dialects that are very similar and therefore hard to distinguish, even for human listeners.

Another reason might be the unequal distribution of speakers per dialect as well as the unbalanced size of dialect regions. In the three-dialects classification, the variation of speech within one region might be too high, so that the models for each region are not specific enough to allow for a robust classification. As one can see in the confusion matrix of one of the best 3-way models in Table 2, both northern and southern German can be distinguished relatively well, but the middle region was confused with the northern region as frequently as it was correctly classified.

Table 2. Confusion matrix for 3 dialects

	North	Mid	South
North	23	10	6
Mid	9	10	10
South	5	6	23
Σ	37	26	39
Accuracy(%)	62.2	38.5	59.0

In Table 3, the confusion matrix for the best 9-dialects model is shown with the individual accuracies per dialect below. It is obvious, that some regions may be too small, or they have too few samples in both test and training sets, like G and H, which only included 4 and 2 test samples respectively, none of which were classified correctly. Likely the remaining samples of this dialect region that were assigned to the training set, 15 in G and 8 in H, were not sufficient to train a robust model for each dialect or the test speakers were outliers even within their own small dialect class.

On the other hand, the accuracies are not only affected by the size of the region, because region A is around the same size, but can be classified with 44.4% accuracy. The number of speakers, however, plays a role in the classification, since the models cannot be properly fitted with too little data.

Another area, that has been classified with a very low accuracy, is region E, which turns out to be surprising, as this region corresponds to eastern German dialects, that are usually quite easy to identify by human listeners. Instead, these speaker probes were mainly confused with the three northern dialects, which indicates test speakers without a strong dialect, since parts of northern German variations are colloquially called "High German" or "Standard German", and in bigger cities, that is usually the version of German spoken.

The further south one goes in Germany, the stronger the regional dialects usually get. Of the other six dialects, five are relatively well recognized (35.0% ...44.4% accuracy), with B being often wrongly recognized as D. An explanation for the confusion of B for D might again be a prevalence of "Standard German" in both regions, which may result in similar dialect models. Also, these regions are right next to each other. Therefore the speakers, who live near the border of B and D, might speak a mix of both dialects, which makes a classification more challenging.

While dialect I has been identified correctly for 35% of its test samples, it is also the dialect most frequently recognized as E, which ist interesting, when even E itself is not usually classified as E. Additionally, I and E represent two regions, that are usually known for people, who speak with a marked dialect. The dialects themselves (Bavarian in I and Saxon in E), however are perceived as quite distinguishable.

The dialect F is in between with 23.1% accuracy, being confused for D or G as frequently as it is recognized correctly. The reasons for this effect should be further explored, since both, the region and the number of speakers, are comparatively large and well-represented in the corpus.

Table 3. Confusion matrix for 9 dialects

	A	B	C	D	E	F	G	H	I
A	4	1	0	3	2	1	1	1	0
B	2	8	2	3	2	1	0	0	1
C	1	2	3	0	3	0	0	1	1
D	2	5	1	6	1	3	2	0	3
E	0	0	1	1	1	1	1	0	4
F	0	2	0	0	0	3	0	0	0
G	0	1	0	2	0	3	0	0	2
H	0	0	0	0	2	0	0	0	2
I	0	2	0	0	0	1	0	0	7
Σ	9	21	7	15	11	13	4	2	20
Accuracy(%)	44.4	38.1	42.9	40.0	9.1	23.1	0.0	0.0	35.0

5   Conclusions

In our experiments on ADC we have found, that German dialects can be classified by a GMM-UBM system, achieving accuracies significantly above chance. We were also able to identify five dialect regions out of nine, that appear to be quite distinguishable. We are expecting relevant improvements, when using more sophisticated classification methods, that combine our baseline results with e.g. prosodic features. A more reliable validation technique such as cross validation is also desirable, but in the current study it was too computationally demanding for all tested combinations.

Further experiments will include read speech (instead of spontaneous speech only) and further corpora with both, the baseline and advanced models aforementioned. The corpus choice needs to consider more speakers and samples of the regions, that were under-represented in our current study. In terms of the relatively high calculation complexity and processing time during the training, the further experiments will also require a more systematic schedule than our draft experiments.

References

1. Hanani, A., Russell, M.J., Carey, M.J.: Human and computer recognition of regional accents and ethnic groups from British English speech. Comput. Speech Lang. **27**, 59–74 (2013). https://doi.org/10.1016/j.csl.2012.01.003
2. Najafian, M., Khurana, S., Shon, S., Ali, A., Glass, J.R.: Exploiting convolutional neural networks for phonotactic based dialect identification. In: 2018 IEEE International Conference on Acoustics, Speech and Signal Processing, ICASSP 2018, Calgary, AB, Canada, 15–20 April 2018, pp. 5174–5178 (2018). https://doi.org/10.1109/ICASSP.2018.8461486
3. Wang, H., van Heuven, V.J.: Relative contribution of vowel quality and duration to native language identification in foreign-accented English. In: Proceedings of the 2nd International Conference on Cryptography, Security and Privacy, ICCSP 2018, Guiyang, China, 16–19 March 2018, pp. 16–20 (2018). https://doi.org/10.1145/3199478.3199507
4. Brown, G.: Automatic accent recognition systems and the effects of data on performance. In: Odyssey 2016: The Speaker and Language Recognition Workshop, Bilbao, Spain, 21–24 June 2016, pp. 94–100 (2016). https://doi.org/10.21437/Odyssey.2016-14
5. Bougrine, S., Cherroun, H., Ziadi, D.: Hierarchical classification for spoken Arabic dialect identification using prosody: Case of Algerian dialects. CoRR abs/1703.10065 (2017). http://arxiv.org/abs/1703.10065
6. Biadsy, F., Hirschberg, J., Habash, N.: Spoken Arabic dialect identification using phonotactic modeling. In: Proceedings of the Workshop on Computational Approaches to Semitic Languages, SEMITIC@EACL 2009, Athens, Greece, 31 March 2009, pp. 53–61 (2009). https://aclanthology.info/papers/W09-0807/w09-0807
7. Akbacak, M., Vergyri, D., Stolcke, A., Scheffer, N., Mandal, A.: Effective Arabic dialect classification using diverse phonotactic models. In: INTERSPEECH 2011, 12th Annual Conference of the International Speech Communication Association, Florence, Italy, 27–31 August 2011, pp. 737–740 (2011). http://www.isca-speech.org/archive/interspeech_2011/i11_0737.html
8. Zheng, Y., et al.: Accent detection and speech recognition for Shanghai-accented Mandarin. In: INTERSPEECH 2005 - Eurospeech, 9th European Conference on Speech Communication and Technology, Lisbon, Portugal, 4–8 September 2005, pp. 217–220 (2005). http://www.isca-speech.org/archive/interspeech_2005/i05_0217.html
9. Hou, J., Liu, Y., Zheng, T.F., Olsen, J.Ø., Tian, J.: Multi-layered features with SVM for Chinese accent identification. In: 2010 International Conference on Audio, Language and Image Processing, pp. 25–30 (2010). https://doi.org/10.1109/ICALIP.2010.5685023
10. Lei, Y., Hansen, J.H.L.: Dialect classification via text-independent training and testing for Arabic, Spanish, and Chinese. IEEE Trans. Audio Speech Lang. Process. **19**, 85–96 (2011). https://doi.org/10.1109/TASL.2010.2045184
11. Torres-Carrasquillo, P.A., Sturim, D.E., Reynolds, D.A., McCree, A.: Eigenchannel compensation and discriminatively trained Gaussian mixture models for dialect and accent recognition. In: INTERSPEECH 2008, 9th Annual Conference of the International Speech Communication Association, Brisbane, Australia, 22–26 September 2008, pp. 723–726 (2008). http://www.isca-speech.org/archive/interspeech_2008/i08_0723.html

12. Biadsy, F., Hirschberg, J., Collins, M.: Dialect recognition using a phone-GMM-supervector-based SVM kernel. In: INTERSPEECH 2010, 11th Annual Conference of the International Speech Communication Association, Makuhari, Chiba, Japan, 26–30 September 2010, pp. 753–756 (2010). http://www.isca-speech.org/archive/interspeech_2010/i10_0753.html

13. Biadsy, F.: Automatic dialect and accent recognition and its application to speech recognition. Ph.D. thesis, Columbia University (2011). https://doi.org/10.7916/D8M61S68

14. Zissman, M.A., Gleason, T.P., Rekart, D., Losiewicz, B.L.: Automatic dialect identification of extemporaneous conversational, Latin American Spanish speech. In: 1996 IEEE International Conference on Acoustics, Speech, and Signal Processing Conference Proceedings, ICASSP '96, Atlanta, Georgia, USA, 7–10 May 1996, pp. 777–780 (1996). https://doi.org/10.1109/ICASSP.1996.543236

15. Chittaragi, N.B., Prakash, A., Koolagudi, S.: Dialect identification using spectral and prosodic features on single and ensemble classifiers. Arab. J. Sci. Eng. **43**, 4289–4302 (2017). https://doi.org/10.1007/s13369-017-2941-0

16. Najafian, M., Safavi, S., Weber, P., Russell, M.J.: Identification of British English regional accents using fusion of i-vector and multi-accent phonotactic systems. In: Odyssey 2016: The Speaker and Language Recognition Workshop, Bilbao, Spain, 21–24 June 2016, pp. 132–139 (2016). https://doi.org/10.21437/Odyssey.2016-19

17. Zhang, Q., Boril, H., Hansen, J.H.L.: Supervector pre-processing for PRSVM-based Chinese and Arabic dialect identification. In: IEEE International Conference on Acoustics, Speech and Signal Processing, ICASSP 2013, Vancouver, BC, Canada, 26–31 May 2013, pp. 7363–7367 (2013). https://doi.org/10.1109/ICASSP.2013.6639093

18. Liu, G., Hansen, J.H.L.: A systematic strategy for robust automatic dialect identification. In: Proceedings of the 19th European Signal Processing Conference, EUSIPCO 2011, Barcelona, Spain, 29 August–2 September 2011, pp. 2138–2141 (2011). http://ieeexplore.ieee.org/document/7074191/

19. Lazaridis, A., el Khoury, E., Goldman, J., Avanzi, M., Marcel, S., Garner, P.N.: Swiss french regional accent identification. In: Odyssey 2014: The Speaker and Language Recognition Workshop, Joensuu, Finland, 16–19 June 2014 (2014). https://isca-speech.org/archive/odyssey_2014/abstracts.html#abs29

20. Burger, S., Schiel, F.: RVG 1 - a database for regional variants of contemporary German. In: Proceedings of the 1st International Conference on Language Resources and Evaluation, pp. 1083–1087. Granada, Spain (1998). https://www.phonetik.uni-muenchen.de/forschung/publikationen/Burger-98-RVG1.ps

21. Mettke, H.: Mittelhochdeutsche Grammatik. VEB Bibliographisches Institut, Leipzig, Germany (1989)

22. Larcher, A., Lee, K.A., Meignier, S.: An extensible speaker identification sidekit in Python. In: 2016 IEEE International Conference on Acoustics, Speech and Signal Processing, ICASSP 2016, Shanghai, China, 20–25 March 2016, pp. 5095–5099 (2016). https://doi.org/10.1109/ICASSP.2016.7472648

Classification of Regional Accent Using Speech Rhythm Metrics

Ghania Droua-Hamdani[(✉)]

Centre for Scientific and Technical Research on Arabic Language
Development (CRSTDLA), Algiers, Algeria
gh.drpoua@post.com, g.droua@crstdla.dz

Abstract. In this paper, MSA speech rhythm metrics were used to classify two
regional accent (northern vs. southern regions) using an MLP - neural network
classifier. Seven rhythm metrics vectors were computed from a speech dataset
taken from ALGerian Arabic Speech Database (ALGASD) using both Interval
Measures (IM) and Control/Compensation Index (CCI) algorithms. The classifier was trained and tested using different input vectors of speech rhythm
measurements. The best accuracy of the NN-classifier was achieved when a
combination of all metrics was used (88.6%).

Keywords: Rhythm metrics · Modern Standard Arabic · ALGASD corpus ·
MLP-NN-Classifier

1 Introduction

Nowadays, various tools of statistical measurement of durational variability in speech,
called rhythm metrics, were developed [1–4]. These metrics were used in different
research fields such as in: languages comparison and second language (L2) acquisition
[5–8] clinical applications [9] and in speech automatic recognition of emotion [10].

Many varieties of Artificial Neural Networks (ANNs) have appeared over the years,
with widely varying properties. The most widely used form, and the one we used in this
work, is the Multilayer perceptron MLP. Indeed, they have been successfully applied to
several speech tasks, i.e., phoneme recognition, out of vocabulary word detection,
confidence measure, etc. [11, 12].

The current research deals with speech rhythm data that were extracted from
recordings of speakers belonging to six Algerian regions [13]. An automatic classification system was built to recognize the location of speakers when rhythm values were
used as the input vectors. Therefore, the aim of the classifier is to identify speakers'
locality whether they belong to the north or to the south of the country. The classifier is
based on MLP Neural Network models.

The organization of the paper is as follows: Sect. 2 gives some proprieties of MSA
language. Section 3 presents an overview on rhythm algorithms. Section 4 exposes
speech material and speakers used for the purpose of the rhythm analysis. Section 5
carries out results of different rhythm experiments and classifier accuracies. Section 6
concludes this work.

© Springer Nature Switzerland AG 2019
A. A. Salah et al. (Eds.): SPECOM 2019, LNAI 11658, pp. 75–81, 2019.
https://doi.org/10.1007/978-3-030-26061-3_8

2 MSA Language

Modern Standard Arabic (MSA) is the official Arabic language in 22 countries. Written form of MSA is the language of literature and the media. Its phonetic system is composed of 28 consonants (C) and six vowels (three short vowels (v) vs. three long vowels (V). There are many allophones depending on the consonantal context. In addition, MSA has two diphthongs /ay/ and /aw/ such as in /laaylun/ (night) and /yaawm/ (day) respectively. Two distinctive consonant classes characterize MSA phonetic alphabet: pharyngeal and emphatic consonants. Likewise, Arabic language is endowed by two fundamental properties: long vowels and germination (consonant doubling). Arabic syllable structure has been subject to extensive studies. Researchers state that Arabic syllables can be open or closed such as -CV /CV:-or -CVC /CV:C/ CVCC- respectively. All Arabic syllables must contain at least one vowel.

3 Rhythm Modeling

It has often been asserted that languages exhibit regularity in the timing of successive units of speech, and that every language may be assigned one of three rhythmical types: stress-timed languages (Arabic, English, etc.); syllable-timed (French, Spanish, etc.) and mora-timed (Japanese, etc.). To categorize languages regarding to their speech rhythm scores, algorithms were performed such as: Interval Measures (IM), Pairwise Variability Indices (PVI) and Compensation and Control Index (CCI).

The IM approach involves computing of three separate measures from the segmentation of speech signals into vocalic (V) and consonantal (C) units [1]. These measures are:

- %V: the proportion of time devoted to vocalic intervals in the sentence
- ΔV: the standard deviation of vocalic intervals;
- ΔC: the standard deviation of consonantal intervals, the sections between vowel offset and vowel onset.

The time-normalized metric measures (VarcoV/C) are the normalized scores of the IM variables [3].

Basing on vowels and consonants durations, PVI model obeys to this formula [2]:

$$PVI = 100 \times \left[\sum_{k=1}^{m-1} \left| \frac{d_k - d_{k+1}}{(d_k + d_{k+1})/2} \right| / (m-1) \right] \qquad (1)$$

where m is the number of intervals in utterance, d is the duration of the kth interval.

CCI model was proposed to compute rhythm of languages when the basic unit of measurement focuses on syllable complexity model [4]. This algorithm, which is called Compensation and Control Index (CCI), was inspired by the syllable compensation. The CCI equation is:

$$cci = \frac{100}{(m-1)} \sum\nolimits_{k-1}^{m-1} \left| \frac{d_k}{n_k} - \frac{d_{k+1}}{n_{k+1}} \right| \quad (2)$$

where m is the number of intervals, d for duration, and n for number of segments within the relevant interval.

The rhythm metrics that are examined for the purpose are: three interval measures (%V, ΔV, and ΔC), two time-normalized indices (VarcoV, VarcoC) and two CCI metrics (CCI-C, CCI-V).

4 Participants

Speech material used in the rhythm analysis is a part of ALGASD corpus. This corpus composed about a set of 200 balanced sentences recorded from 300 speakers from 11 regions across Algeria. The database includes the main pronunciation variations of MSA due to regional differences in Algeria. Likewise, the distribution of inhabitants in these areas is proportional to the population in these regions. Thus, the regional coverage corresponds to the major dialect groups. Speakers come from different socioeconomic backgrounds and their mastery of Arabic is different. Each speaker read from 2 to 6 sentences from the whole text material. The whole database consists of 1080 wave files [12].

The present study used only a set of recording related to six regions. Three regions from the north of the country: Algiers – capital city - (R1), Tizi-Ouzou (R2) and Jijel (R3); and three regions from the south: (Bechar in the west - close to Morocco - (R4), El Oued is in the East -close to Tunisia - (R5) and Ghardaia in the center of Algeria' south – (R6)). 594 recordings from 166 speakers (82 males/84 females) were used in the study.

5 Experiments and Results

The experimentation deals with classification of the speakers, regarding speech rhythm cues, into two classes: southern vs. northern regions. Indeed, we attempted to build a classifier that can identify the accent of the speaker when speech rhythm measurements were used. The classifier is based on Neural Network - NN models.

5.1 Rhythm Metrics Dataset

To get the speech rhythm scores, an experimented annotator segmented manually all speech material i.e. 594 speech files of the dataset onto their different units (vowels and consonants) using WaveSurfer software. From these segments, we extracted by using program script all vowels and consonant durations (Fig. 1). Secondly, seven rhythm metrics were computed from the data using both algorithms quoted before -Interval Measures (%V, ΔV, and ΔC), two time-normalized indices (VarcoV, VarcoC), and Compensation and Control Index (CCI-C, CCI-V).

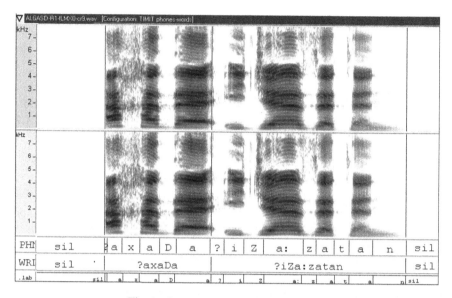

Fig. 1. Segmentation of speech sentence

5.2   Classifier Design

Neural networks have proven themselves as proficient classifiers. A multilayer perceptron (MLP) is a class of Artificial Neural Network. MLP has feed-forward architecture within input layer, a hidden layer, and an output layer. The input layer of this network has N units for an N dimensional input vector. The input units are fully connected to the hidden layer units, which are in turn, connected to the output layers units. Different feature vectors can be used as input vector. In our case, rhythm metrics values provide MLP input data. Feature vector is divided into three data sets: training, validation and testing data set. The rhythm MLP is based on a back propagation algorithm, a hyperbolic tangent and the logistic sigmoid. The nodes in this network are all sigmoid activated. The node weights are adjusted based on corrections that minimize the error in the entire output, given by:

$$\varepsilon(n) = \frac{1}{2} \sum_j e_j^2(n) \tag{3}$$

Using gradient descent, the change in each weight is

$$\Delta w_{ij} = -\eta \frac{\partial \varepsilon(n)}{\partial v_j(n)} y_i(n) \tag{4}$$

where y_i is the output of the previous neuron and η is the learning rate

5.3   Experiments

To build the speech rhythm classifier that can recognize speaker accent regarding speech rhythm measurements, we used all rhythm scores that were computed before from speakers' recordings. The rhythm samples were randomly divided into training (70%), validation (15%) and test (15%) sets. The training set was used to teach the network. The feed-forward algorithm assigned random weight value from input layer towards the output layer. The back-propagation algorithm goes through the network iteratively, updated the weight in each layer backwards from the output layer towards the input layer then. The size of the MLP is 20 neurons.

To attempt the best recognition rate that allows classifying speakers depending on their regional accent, the engine was trained and tested using different configurations of the input feature vectors. The aim is to get in the end, two different classes: speakers belonging to southern vs. northern regions. Therefore, the first configuration chosen consists on the assessment of the classifier using all seven rhythm metrics input vectors separately (IM and CCI). We tried by that to show the efficiency of each metric in classification experiments. Matrices of confusion show that the classifier gives different accuracies (Table 1). The best recognition rate (84.7%) is achieved when the input vector included the normalized interval measure – VarcoC - that were computed from durations of consonants

Table 1. Classifier's accuracies for different input vectors

Metrics	%V	ΔV	ΔC	VarcoV	VarcoC	CCI-V	CCI-C
Accuracy (%)	79.5	76.8	78.3	75.6	84.7	77.6	76.9

The second configuration considered that the input vector of the recognizer is composed by a combination of different rhythm vectors. Thus, we tried as a first step a mixture of all IM metric vectors (i.e. %V, ΔV and ΔC). Then we used the association of both time-normalized IM (i.e. VarcoV and VarcoC) followed by a combination of Compensation and Control Indices (CCI-V and CCI-C). In the last investigation, all input vectors were utilized at same time. Results of all experiments are displayed in Table 2. As it can be seen, the best accuracy was obtained when the input vector is included of the combination of all rhythm values: Interval Measures (IM), time-normalized metric measures (VarcoV/C), Compensation, and Control Index (CCI). The best confusion matrix accuracy is given when we used the whole of input vectors computed (88.6%). Therefore, the engine can categorize speakers' regional accent, considering their speech rhythm measurements, into two classes of speakers those belonging to northern regions from those of the southern ones. An improvement of ≈4% is obtained for the second configuration compared to the first one.

Table 2. Classifier's accuracies for combined input vectors

Vectors	IM	VarcoX	CCI	IM, VarcoX, CCI
Accuracy (%)	87,6	85.5	77.4	88.6

6 Conclusion

In this paper, speech rhythm metrics were used to classify six Algerian regions onto two big classes northern vs. southern localities. Each locality included three areas. Rhythm data were computed using Interval Measures (IM) and Compensation/Control Index (CCI) from 594 MSA recordings pronounced by 166 speakers.

The MLP - neural network classifier was trained and tested using different speech rhythm input vectors. The best accuracy was reached (88.6%) when we used a combination of all speech rhythm values. To improve the classifier's accuracy, we suggest adding in future works other rhythm scores as PVI (normalized Pairwise Variability Index).

References

1. Ramus, F., Nespor, M., Mehler, J.: Correlates of linguistic rhythm in the speech signal. Cognition **73**, 265–292 (1999)
2. Grabe, E., Low, E.L.: Durational variability in speech and the rhythm class hypothesis. In: Papers in Laboratory Phonology, no. 7, pp. 515–546 (2003)
3. Dellwo, V.: Rhythm and speech rate: a variation coefficient for deltaC. In: Karnowski, P., Szigeti, I. (eds.) Language and Language Processing, Paper presented at the 38th Linguistic Colloquium, 231241 (Peter Lang, Frankfurt (2006)
4. Bertinetto, P.M., Bertini, C.: On modelling the rhythm of natural languages. In: Proceedings of 4th International Conference on Speech Prosody, Campinas, pp. 427–430 (2008)
5. Vázquez, L.Q., Romero, J.: The improvement of Spanish/Catalan EFL students' prosody by means of explicit rhythm instruction. In: ISAPh 2018 International Symposium on Applied Phonetics, Aizuwakamatsu, Japan (2018)
6. Anh-Thư, T., Nguyễn, T.: L2 English rhythm by Vietnamese speakers: a rhythm metric study. Linguistics J. **12**(1), 22–44 (2018)
7. Droua-Hamdani, G., Selouani, S.A., Boudraa, M., Cichocki, W.: Algerian Arabic rhythm classification. ISCA International Speech Communication Association. In: Proceedings of the Third ISCA Tutorial and Research Workshop Experimental Linguistics, ExLing 2010, Greece, August 2010, pp. 37–41 (2010)
8. Droua-Hamdani, G., Boudraa, M.: Rhythm metrics in MSA spoken language of six Algerian regions. In: 15th International Conference on Intelligent Systems Design and Applications (IEEE-ISDA2015, Marrakech, Morocco, 14–16 December (2015)
9. Liss, J., et al.: Quantifying speech rhythm abnormalities in the dysarthrias. J. Speech Lang. Hear. Res. **52**, 1334–1352 (2009)
10. Ringeval, F., Chetouani, M., Schuller, B.: Novel metrics of speech rhythm for the assessment of emotion. In: Proceedings of Interspeech, Portland, OR, USA, pp. 2763–2766 (2008)
11. Zhu, Q., Stolcke, A., Chen, B.Y., Morgan, N.: Using MLP features in SRI's conversational speech recognition system. In: Interspeech 2005 – Eurospeech, Lisbon, Portugal, 4–8 September 2005

12. Park, J., Gales, M.J.F., Diehl, F., Tomalin, M., Woodland, P.C.: Training and adapting MLP features for Arabic speech recognition. In: IEEE International Conference on Acoustics, Speech and Signal Processing CASSP 2009, Taipei, Taiwan, 19–24 April 2009
13. Droua-Hamdani, G., Selouani, S.A., Boudraa, M.: Algerian Arabic Speech Database (ALGASD): corpus design and automatic speech recognition application. Arab. J. Sci. Eng. **35**(2C), 157–166 (2010)

PocketEAR: An Assistive Sound Classification System for Hearing-Impaired

Kamil Ekštein[(✉)]

Department of Computer Science and Engineering, Faculty of Applied Sciences,
University of West Bohemia, Plzeň, Czech Republic
kekstein@kiv.zcu.cz

Abstract. This paper describes the design and operation of an assistive system called *PocketEAR* which is primarily targeted towards hearing-impaired users. It helps them with orientation in acoustically active environments by continuously monitoring and classifying the incoming sounds and displaying the captured sound classes to the users. The environmental sound recognizer is designed as a two-stage deep convolutional neural network classifier (consists of the so-called superclassifier and a set of the so-called subclassifiers) fed with sequences of MFCC vectors. It is wrapped in a distributed client-server system where the sound capturing in terrain, (pre)processing and displaying of the classification results are performed by instances of a mobile client application, and the actual classification and maintenance are carried out by two co-operating servers. The paper discusses in details the architecture of the environmental sound classifier as well as the used task-specific sound processing.

Keywords: Environmental sound classification ·
Deep convolutional neural networks · Two-stage classifier ·
Client-server architecture

1 Introduction

Undisputable immense progress of the recognition and classification techniques based upon deep neural networks (DNN) in recent few years made it possible to not only think about but actually to build up effective assistive systems for humans with various disabilities or disadvantages.

As the accuracy and reliability of the DNN-based recognizers and classifiers rise, computer systems are more and more usable in the task of providing humans with the capabilities they lost or were born without. Furthermore, the computing power and network connectivity of current and future mobile devices

Supported by the university-specific research project SGS-2019-018.

(smartphones, tablets, etc.) allow running at least the client part of the application on portable equipment which does not restrict the respective users from normal activities.

This paper describes a year-long work on building up a distributed assistive system for hearing impaired persons named *PocketEAR* (EAR stands for Environmental Audio Recognition).

1.1 Motivation

Several years ago, an interdisciplinary team (speech recognition, natural language processing, and computer graphics) at our department was working on software for translating spoken Czech language into Czech Sign Language (CSL, ISO 639-3 code cse). The group had at its disposal 2 deaf persons, native speakers of CSL, to help with the proper implementation of the signs.

During informal talks with the deaf co-workers, they explained to the team members that their biggest problem is not to understand hearing people speaking (as they were trained in lip-reading). They pointed out that what complicated their lives most was the fact that they were not alerted to certain types of sounds and thus they didn't know they should use their practiced deaf skills to react properly.

They brought up the following example: When a deaf or hard-of-hearing person rings a doorbell by pressing the button at the entrance, he or she is then completely unaware whether somebody is speaking at them through an intercom or opens the door using a remote-controlled electromagnetic lock (buzzer).

At that moment, the key idea behind *PocketEAR* was born, i.e. to build up a system that would continuously scan the sound from the environment and try to identify sounds of specific importance for deaf or hard-of-hearing persons' orientation.

2 System Architecture

The general architecture of the *PocketEAR* system is depicted in Fig. 1. The central node is a server machine which runs two servers: (i) the **recognizer** server—it communicates with mobile clients, receives parametrized audio signal from them, launches the sound recognition routine on the received data, and sends back the results (i.e. recognized categories and types of sounds); and (ii) the **manager** server—it powers the operator's console (web application) and organizes the audio data for offline training of the sound classifier.

When designing the architecture of the system, it was considered important to limit the amount of data transferred over the network. Therefore, the audio signal preprocessing and parametrization is carried out on the client device. After parametrization, it requires only 26 KB to be transferred from the client to the server per each audio recording.

On the other hand, the computing power of mobile devices is nowadays still rather limited[1]. That is why the classification task is performed centrally on a high-performance computer hosting the **recognizer** server.

The overall design is optimized for real-time (or nearly real-time) operation of the whole system.

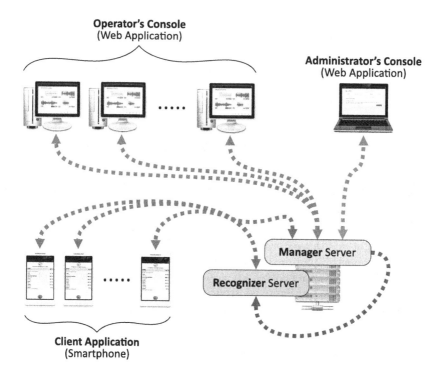

Fig. 1. Architecture of the *PocketEAR* system.

2.1   Client Application

The client application is targeted at mobile devices. It is written in C++ using the Qt 5 framework[2] and can be built for and run on Windows, Linux, MacOS X, Android, and iOS systems.

The main tasks of the client application are to (i) **interact** with a *PocketEAR* end user, to (ii) **record the sound** via the device audio interface and parametrize the recorded audio signal, and to (iii) **communicate** with both the recognizer server and the manager server (see Fig. 1).

---

[1] However, the recently introduced **TensorFlow Lite** framework (available from https://www.tensorflow.org/lite) makes it well possible to implement complex deep learning tasks on mobile and IoT devices.

[2] https://www.qt.io.

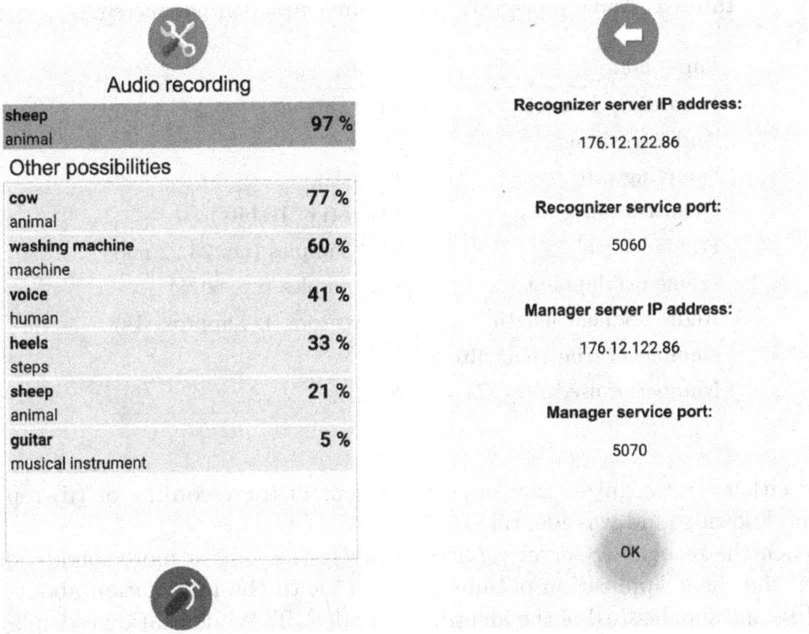

Fig. 2. The *PocketEAR* mobile client application screenshots: Main screen of the application in normal working mode, i.e. recording and recognizing sounds (left) and the settings screen (right).

Audio Signal Processing on Client. The client application (when switched to the active mode by a user) continuously records short segments (3 s) of the audio signal from client's environment using the mobile device audio subsystem: The signal is digitized using 16 bits per sample resolution and sampling frequency 44.1 kHz (i.e. the CD-DA standard settings). The digital audio signal is subsequently transformed into a sequence of MFCC coefficients. Each 1024-sample-long frame of the signal is windowed by the Hamming window. The frame overlapping is set experimentally to 50 %, accordingly to suggestions given in [3].

As a result, a sequence of vectors consisting of 26 MFCC coefficients (32-bit IEEE 754-1985 `floats`) is computed for each recorded audio chunk. The entire settings of the audio processing on client are summarised in Table 1. The computing power of common present-day mobile devices (smartphones, tablets) easily allows the signal processing to be performed in real time, specifically in approx. 0.3 RT. The original, unaltered recording in PCM format is, however, not discarded right at the moment the vector sequence is ready. It is kept in temporary storage of the device for prospective future use (explained in Sect. 2.1).

Client-Server Communication. Once the audio signal segment is recorded and processed, it is sent through TCP/IP socket to the **recognizer server**. The

Table 1. Audio processing and feature extraction parameters.

Parameter	Value
Recording channels	1 (i.e. mono)
Audio encoding	PCM
Sampling rate	44100 Hz
Quantization levels	65536 (i.e. 16 bits)
Frame length	1024 samples (i.e. 23.22 ms)
Frame overlapping	512 samples (i.e. 50 %)
Audio segment length	256 vectors (i.e. approx. 3 s)
Number of triangular filters	48
Number of used MFCCs	26

server either (i) recognizes the sound(s) present in the recording or (ii) replies that no known sound was identified.

When the recognizer server replies positively (i.e. one or more sounds identified), the client application obtains a packet[3] with the information about the class(es) and subclass(es) of the identified sound(s). This information is displayed to the user as shown in Fig. 2 (left).

If the recognizer server returns the code for unknown/unrecognized sound, the user is notified that there appeared a sound which cannot be identified. The application takes the previously saved, unaltered PCM recording of the unrecognized sound (see Sect. 2.1), compresses it into single-channel 192 kbps MP3 format and sends the MP3 to the manager server as an **unrecognized sound**.

2.2   Servers

The **Recognizer** server is *only* responsible for feeding the incoming parametrized audio signals into the classifier, launching the forward pass of the classifier, and sending the classifier result(s) back to the respective clients.

The **Manager** server powers the **Operator's Console** web application and manages the training dataset for the classifier: Every once the client obtains a negative reply (i.e. the sound was not recognized) from the recognizer server, it sends the original non-parametrized recording to the manager server which stores it into storage for unrecognized sounds.

2.3   Operator's Console

The **Operator's Console** is a web application powered by the manager server. Its main purpose is to work as a front-end (see Fig. 3) for specially trained

---

[3] The *PocketEAR* system defines its own character-oriented communication protocol. Each packet starts with 'PE' signature, then there goes a request/reply identification character (e.g. '0' means handshake); the message follows afterwards.

operators. It assists them with preparing and/or extending the training dataset for the recognizer: They use the application to edit and label the unrecognized recordings that were previously saved by the manager server (as explained in Sect. 2.1).

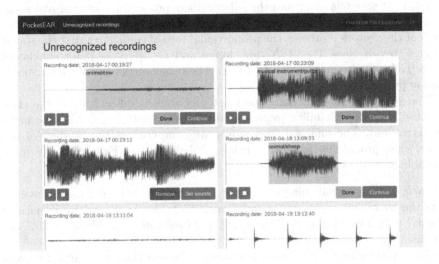

Fig. 3. The **Operator's Console** web application interface.

The administrator's console (as seen in Fig. 1) is just an operation mode of the operator's console with different authorization and user role. It is used to monitor the activities of operators, to enrol new operators, and to run other specific actions like e.g. batch training of the classifiers.

3   Environmental Sound Classification

The *PocketEAR* classifier of environmental sounds is based upon deep convolutional neural networks and built up using the *TensorFlow* framework [1].

Initially, a series of sound classification experiments was carried out with the model depicted in Fig. 4 only, as a single-stage classifier[4]. It is a moderate modification of the commonly used architecture for sound classification (as described in e.g. [2]). However, when using this model alone, the classification accuracy was not satisfactory (varied between 56 and 63 % depending on the model initialization).

Therefore, a **two-stage architecture** was designed and used: Each sound (i.e. the sequence of vectors of 26 MFCC coefficients) is at first classified by the so-called **superclassifier** which determines N most probable (super)classes the

---

[4] The same model was later on used in the final design of the classifier, too, however, as a two-stage classifier as described in details in Sect. 3.1.

analyzed sound might belong to (currently $N = 2$). Consecutively, the sound is classified parallelly by the N **subclassifiers** that correspond to the N most probable classes—each class has its own, specifically trained **subclassifier**. The **subclassifier** places the sound into one of $M + 1$ subclasses (the subclassifiers use one more class as a **garbage model**).

Both the superclassifier and the subclassifiers produce a vector of real numbers from the bounded interval $[0, 1]$, N- and M-long respectively. The components of the vectors represent the proportional rate of confidence that the sound belongs to i-th class, $i \in [1, N]$ for classes and $i \in [1, M + 1]$ for subclasses respectively. Their sum is equal to 1.0, i.e. the behaviour of the output layers is strictly probabilistic.

The subclassifers select only the most probable classification, i.e. the class with the highest probability (represented by the output neuron with the highest activation). The final subclass scores are computed as the product of the (super)class probability and the subclass probability (see Example 1), K most probable ones are sent to the client.

Example 1. The actual analyzed sound is "keyboard typing". Superclassifier puts the sound into "interior sounds" with 85% likelihood and into "natural sounds" with 14% likelihood (N = 2, other classes with joint likelihood 1 % are not taken into consideration).

The subclassifer of the "interior sounds" class sets the sound into the "keyboard typing" subclass with 48% likelihood, and the subclassifier of the "natural sounds" class sets the sound into the "crackling fire" subclass with 99% likelihood. As $0.85 \times 0.48 > 0.14 \times 0.99$, the sound is classified as "interior sounds/keyboard typing" with 40.8% likelihood.

If all subclassifiers put congruently the analyzed sound into the garbage class, it is marked as **unrecognized**.

3.1   Classifier Architecture

As mentioned above, the classifier is a two-stage Bayesian cascade consisting of one **superclassifier** and N **subclassifers**. Both the superclassifier and the subclassifers use *the same* deep convolutional neural network (DCNN) architecture shown in Fig. 4. Models for the superclassifier and the subclassifer differ only in the used final evaluation metric (see Sect. 3.2). The DCNN structure is summarized in Table 2. All network layers use $ReLU$[5] activation function except for the last dense layer which uses *softmax* function. Dropout value was set to 0.5. The used *cost function* was a modified *cross-entropy* to which a constant C_{mod} was added. The C_{mod} is computed as a sum of Euclidean norms of both convolutional and dense layers multiplied by 10^{-3} for superclassifier and subclassifers of the "human sounds" and the "interior sounds" classes, and by 0 for the other subclassifers. This modification provided the best results and was finetuned manually during a series of experiments.

---

[5] ReLU = **R**ectified **L**inear **U**nit, for details check [6].

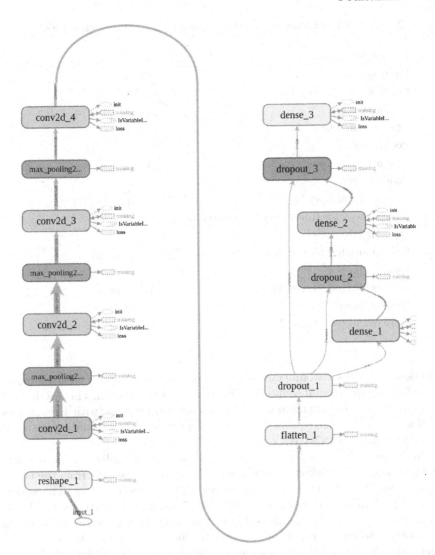

Fig. 4. The architecture of the deep convolutional network used as classifiers in the *PocketEAR* system.

The cost function was optimized using the *Adam* (adaptive moment estimation) method [4] implemented in the Keras library with initial learning rate set to 10^{-4}.

3.2 Classifier Training

For the initial evaluation purposes, the above-described classifier was trained on the **ESC-50: Dataset for Environmental Sound Classification**—a labeled

Table 2. The structure of the deep convolutional network classifiers.

Layer type	Size
Input layer	434×26
Convolutional layer	3×3
Pooling layer	4×1
Convolutional layer	3×3
Pooling layer	4×2
Convolutional layer	3×3
Pooling layer	4×1
Convolutional layer	3×3
Matrix-to-vector transformation (flatten layer)	
Dropout layer	
Fully connected (dense) layer	128 neurons
Dropout layer	
Fully connected (dense) layer	128 neurons
Dropout layer	
Fully connected (dense) layer	$\langle \# \text{ of classes} \rangle$ neurons

collection of 2000 environmental audio recordings suitable for benchmarking methods of environmental sound classification [5]. The recordings in this dataset are up to 5 s long and are organized into 50 semantical classes (with 40 examples per class) loosely arranged into 5 major categories [5]. Each recording is stored in an uncompressed PCM WAV file.

One training epoch of both super- and subclassifier is understood as one forward pass and error backpropagation per each sample–class pair from the training dataset. The evaluation stage, however, differs between them: The superclassifier performance is assessed by the `top_2_accuracy` metric (see Table 3) which defines the correct classification of the input MFCC vector sequence as the situation when the target label is among the 2 most probable classes. The subclassifier is assessed by the standard accuracy metric as implemented in the TensorFlow library.

However, the evaluation dataset for the subclassifier was adjusted so that it contained the same amount of samples for each class *including* the garbage class. The garbage class evaluation data was compiled by picking random samples from the rest of the dataset, i.e. from the samples *not used* for training of the respective subclassifier while for the training the whole class complement was used (thus, the accuracies for the garbage classes are significantly higher as they were trained with many more examples than the non-garbage classes).

The nature of the described classification problem implies that it is highly undesirable to let the classifier put an unrecognized sound into any class of which the score maximizes the above-outlined selection strategy even though the classifier confidence is extremely low. That is why the *garbage* model was

introduced. It makes it possible to detect the situation when the classified sound
is truly unknown with very high confidence (which is exactly the expected and
desired behaviour).

4   Results

Table 3 below summarizes the best performance obtained in a series of training-
evaluation passes. The **ESC-50** dataset was split into a training set (1800 examples) and an evaluation set (200 examples, 10 % of the whole dataset).

There were finally 50 subclasses defined for the purpose of the performance
evaluation according to the description given in Sect. 3. Thus, 4 testing samples
are available for each subclass (or alternatively 44 samples for each subclassifer).
As mentioned above, the garbage class of each subclassifier is understood (and
trained) as the complement of the training samples for the respective class.
Therefore, 160 evaluation samples ($200 - M \times 4, M = 10$, see Sect. 3) is available
for each of the N garbage classes. The evaluation would be skewed due to this
situation and that is why only 4 randomly picked (with uniform distribution)
samples are taken from the set of 160.

Table 3. Accuracies achieved during the classifier performance evaluation.

Classifier	Accuracy	Metric
Superclassifier	87.5 %	`top_2_accuracy`
Subclassifier (average)	74.1 %	std. `tf.metrics.accuracy`
Subclassifier (minimum)	70.5 %	std. `tf.metrics.accuracy`
Subclassifier (maximum)	79.5 %	std. `tf.metrics.accuracy`
Baseline (maximum)	63.0 %	std. `tf.metrics.accuracy`

The overall accuracy may seem unconvincing, however, it is necessary to take
into account the small size of the used training dataset. Considering that the
shown performance was achieved after training with 1800 examples (observation-
label pairs) only, it has to be judged as very promising. Figure 5 shows the
dependence of the number of training epochs and the overall performance of the
classifier. It indicates that the designed two-stage architecture works well in this
specific task and only needs larger training dataset.

Therefore, getting the large enough dataset by both compiling it from the
unrecognized recordings stored by the *PocketEAR* system running in an evaluation mode and seeking for a co-operation with research teams/facilities that are
involved in preparing environmental sounds corpora is the logical next step the
development team will take in near future.

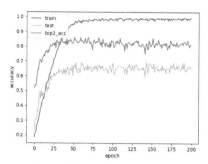

Fig. 5. The accuracies reached in training and evaluation stages depending on the number of training epochs.

Acknowledgements. The presented work was supported by the university-specific research project SGS-2019-018 "Processing of heterogeneous data and its specialized applications".

The author would like to thank deeply his graduate student František Pártl, and undergraduate students Jan Pašek and Michal Seják for implementing the software according to his design.

References

1. Abadi, M., et al.: TensorFlow: large-scale machine learning on heterogeneous systems (2015). https://www.tensorflow.org/. Software available from tensorflow.org
2. Abdoli, S., Cardinal, P., Koerich, A.L.: End-to-end environmental sound classification using a 1D convolutional neural network. arXiv preprint arXiv:1904.08990 (2019)
3. Almaadeed, N., Asim, M., Al-Maadeed, S., Bouridane, A., Beghdadi, A.: Automatic detection and classification of audio events for road surveillance applications. Sensors **18**(6) (2018). https://doi.org/10.3390/s18061858, http://www.mdpi.com/1424-8220/18/6/1858
4. Kingma, D.P., Ba, J.: Adam: a method for stochastic optimization. arXiv preprint arXiv:1412.6980 (2014)
5. Piczak, K.J.: ESC: dataset for environmental sound classification. In: Proceedings of the 23rd Annual ACM Conference on Multimedia, pp. 1015–1018. ACM Press (2015). https://doi.org/10.1145/2733373.2806390, http://dl.acm.org/citation.cfm?doid=2733373.2806390
6. Zeiler, M.D., et al.: On rectified linear units for speech processing. In: 2013 IEEE International Conference on Acoustics, Speech and Signal Processing, pp. 3517–3521, May 2013. https://doi.org/10.1109/ICASSP.2013.6638312

Time-Continuous Emotion Recognition Using Spectrogram Based CNN-RNN Modelling

Dmitrii Fedotov[1,2（✉）], Bobae Kim[1], Alexey Karpov[3], and Wolfgang Minker[1]

[1] Ulm University, Ulm, Germany
dmitrii.fedotov@uni-ulm.de
[2] ITMO University, Saint Petersburg, Russia
[3] SPIIRAS, Saint Petersburg, Russia

Abstract. In area of speech emotion recognition, hand-engineered features are traditionally used as an input. However, it requires an additional step to extract features before the prediction and prior knowledge to select feature set. Thus, recent research has been focused on approaches that predict emotions directly from speech signal to reduce the required efforts for the feature extraction and increase performance of emotion recognition system. Whereas this approach has been applied for prediction of categorical emotions, the study for prediction of continuous dimensional emotions is still rare. This paper presents a method for time-continuous prediction of emotions from speech using spectrogram. Proposed model comprises convolutional neural network (CNN) and Recurrent Neural Network with Long Short-Term Memory (RNN-LSTM). Hyperparameters of CNN are investigated to improve the performance of the our model. After finding the optimal hyperparameters, the performance of the system with waveform and spectrogram as input is compared in terms of concordance correlation coefficient (CCC). Proposed method outperforms the end-to-end emotion recognition system based on waveform and provides CCC of 0.722 predicting arousal on RECOLA database.

Keywords: Time-continuous affect recognition ·
End-to-end modelling · Spectrogram based emotion recognition

1 Introduction

Speech emotion recognition gained popularity over the last decade, as it has strong potential to improve the quality of understanding human and can find an application in different areas. For example, it can be applied to automotive navigation systems [20], movie recommendation systems or artificial tutor systems, where user's emotions affect responses of the system [4].

The traditional methodology of modern speech emotion recognition is to use acoustic features such as pitch, voice quality and mel-frequency cepstral coefficients as an input to a classification or regression model. However, it requires

© Springer Nature Switzerland AG 2019
A. A. Salah et al. (Eds.): SPECOM 2019, LNAI 11658, pp. 93–102, 2019.
https://doi.org/10.1007/978-3-030-26061-3_10

additional process of extracting the features. Furthermore, the feature set is not guaranteed to represent the emotional characteristics of speech signal because speaking styles and the way of expressing emotional state depend on culture, language and environment [1,12,16].

The recent studies have focused on representing an input directly from the waveform [18]. In this method, the raw waveform is fed to convolutional neural network (CNN) and the output of CNN is considered as an input of recurrent neural network with long short-term memory (RNN-LSTM). Such end-to-end approach does not require an a-priori knowledge to extract features, thus provides more flexibility to the model.

Recent research in area of emotion recognition focuses more on dimensional representing of emotions, i.e., arousal and valence, instead of discrete categories, e.g., anger, fear, happiness and sadness [6,11,13], hence increases systems flexibility [8].

In this paper, two different input types are investigated for speech emotion recognition using a deep neural network in end-to-end manner. The first input type is the raw waveform. The waveform is directly fed to the deep neural network which comprises CNN and RNN-LSTM. The second input type is the spectrogram, which is also fed to the deep neural network for time-continuous prediction of emotions. The performance of our models is evaluated with concordance correlation coefficient (CCC). The major contributions of this paper are as follows: (1) we introduce and test for the first time an approach to time-continuous dimensional speech emotion recognition in end-to-end manner using spectrogram as an input; (2) we evaluate the performance of our models with various lengths of segmenting window and demonstrate performance of our models on waveform and spectrogram in comparison with other existing models.

This paper has the following structure: Sect. 2 introduces related work on speech emotion recognition in time-continuous and end-to-end manner; Sect. 3 describes the database used in this paper and the preprocessing procedure of the data; Sect. 4 presents the methods and the results and Sect. 5 concludes the paper.

2   Related Work

The end-to-end approach has been explored in various learning tasks. Sainath et al. match the performance of raw waveform and log-mel cepstral features on a large-vocabulary speech recognition task by using convolutional long short-term memory deep neural network [15]. Dieleman et al. applied end-to-end learning on the waveform to solve a music information retrieval task [3].

Trigeorgis et al. proposed a convolutional recurrent model to perform a spontaneous emotion prediction on the waveform in end-to-end approach [18]. This model is evaluated in terms of CCC and achieves better performance than traditional designed features. This model is used as a comparison to proposed approach and discussed in Sect. 4.4.

Cai et al. proposed a methodology of applying spectrogram based end-to-end learning for paralinguistic information detection [2]. The authors used framework, that comprises CNN for feature maps extraction and gated recurrent units (GRU) for classification and proved its effectiveness in comparison with Gaussian mixture models trained (GMMs) on constant Q cepstral features (CQCC) [2]. Although spectrogram has been used as an input for speech emotion recognition in [1] and [10], these works represent emotions in discrete categories. As none of the works investigated continuous dimensional emotions on the spectrogram, it has motivated us to conduct this study.

3   Data and Preprocessing

In our research, the RECOLA database is employed for time-continuous emotion recognition from spontaneous interactions. Two different types of the audio signal are fed to models that comprise CNN and RNN-LSTM.

3.1   Database

The RECOLA database contains spontaneous interactions that were collected during solving a collaborative task [14]. The recorded audio signals of 23 participants are used for this paper, and the duration of each recording is 5 min. Although the spontaneous interactions recorded in the RECOLA database are spoken in French, participants have different mother tongues. Therefore, speakers are equally distributed into three sets on their mother tongue, gender and age to make results more comparable to previous research [18].

3.2   Labels

In modern research on affect recognition emotions are usually represented in two ways: either discrete categories or continuous dimensions. The latter provides more flexibility of affective states and has an ease of use for time-continuous labeling. Arousal and valence are commonly used as continuous dimensions of emotions. A high value of arousal indicates excitement, a low value – calmness or tiredness. Valence denotes how pleasured or displeasured a person is. Between arousal and valence, the former is selected as a label for this paper, since previous study has shown that audio has more impact on arousal than valence in the prediction of emotion [19].

In RECOLA database, arousal was annotated to have values ranging from -1 to 1 with a step of 0.01 at sample rate 25 Hz by six raters [14]. Six values of the arousal measured by six raters are averaged to produce only one label at each time step.

Fig. 1. Spectrograms generated by various Hamming window sizes. Left: 64 frames, middle: 256 frames, right: 1024 frames

3.3 The Spectrogram

The first input type investigated in this paper is spectrogram that represents an audio signal in the two-dimensional graph. Spectrograms generated by various Hamming windows are shown in Fig. 1. In our case, they show patterns of speech signal clearly when Hamming window with the size of 256 frames is used to produce the spectrogram. The spectrograms used in this paper are converted from the waveform at sample rate 6.4 kHz by Fast Fourier Transform (FFT) using Hamming window with the size of 256 frames since it provides a good resolution in the time domain and the frequency domain, that are easy to align with labels considering frame rate. As a result, the spectrogram has the sample rate of 100 Hz and the frequency ranges up to 3.4 kHz.

The spectrogram of each subject is normalized by z-score transformation. The mean and standard deviation of the train set is used to normalize not only the train set but also the validation and test sets. After the normalization, the spectrogram is segmented by an overlapping window with a shift step of 40 ms which corresponds to the sample rate of the label. Three different window sizes (2 s, 4 s, and 6 s) are investigated as quality of emotion recognition may depend on amount of context used [5].

3.4 The Waveform

The second input type used in our research is raw waveform. The recorded speech signal of the RECOLA database is down-sampled from 44.1 kHz to 6.4 kHz to comply with our previous experiment. After down-sampling, the waveform of each subject is normalized by z-score transformation with parameters obtained on the train set. After the normalization, the waveform is segmented by an overlapping window with a shift step of 40 ms.

4   Experiments and Results

Our experiments are conducted to investigate the performance of two different input types for time-continuous dimensional emotion recognition in the end-to-end manner. The performance of each model is measured in terms of concordance correlation coefficient (CCC, ρ_c) [9]. Since weights of a model are adjusted to minimize loss function during training, we used CCC-based loss:

$$\mathcal{L} = 1 - \rho_c = 1 - \frac{2\rho\sigma_y\sigma_{\hat{y}}}{\sigma_y^2 + \sigma_{\hat{y}}^2 + (\mu_y - \mu_{\hat{y}})^2} \tag{1}$$

where ρ is the Pearson correlation coefficient, σ_y and $\sigma_{\hat{y}}$ are the variances, σ_y^2 and $\sigma_{\hat{y}}^2$ are the standard deviations, and μ_y and $\mu_{\hat{y}}$ are the means of the predicted and gold-standard values, respectively.

Gaussian noise is added to the input and dropout with $p = 0.2$ is applied to two RNN-LSTM layers to avoid overfitting. Weights of RNN layers and biases are initialized by Glorot uniform [7] and zeros, respectively. RMSprop [17] with a mini-batch of 128 sequences is applied to optimize our models. Learning rates ranging from 0.0001 to 0.01 are applied to each experiment, and only one learning rate is chosen to show the best CCC at validation set at the end of experiments. The training of each model is stopped if the gap between CCC of train and validation sets is increasing. The optimal hyperparameters are chosen when the highest CCC of the validation set is achieved. In each table below we report the model performance in terms of total CCC (calculated on concatenation of all predictions).

4.1   The Spectrogram

The model for time-continuous prediction of emotions on the spectrogram includes CNN, RNN-LSTM and a fully connected layers. Since the spectrogram is represented in two dimensions, 2-d convolutional and 2-d max pooling layers are stacked. The optimal filter size of convolutional layers and pooling window sizes are chosen empirically.

Pooling Size. Pooling window size is chosen to match the rate of the input (100 Hz) with the rate of the labels (25 Hz). The various max pooling sizes are evaluated on the spectrogram segmented by 4 seconds window. To analyze an effect of pooling size on performance we fixed other hyperparameters. The results of analysis are shown in Table 1. The highest CCC of validation set is acquired when the first max pooling window has the size of 4×4 frames without the second pooling layer.

Table 1. Comparison of 2D max pooling size on the spectrogram

Pooling size	Train	Validation
4×4, no pooling	0.657	0.621
$2 \times 2, 2 \times 2$	0.657	0.615
no pooling, 4×4	0.667	0.591

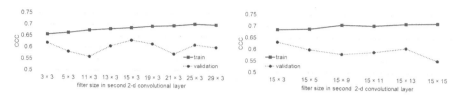

Fig. 2. Comparison of 2D filter size in the time domain (left) and frequency domain (rights) on the spectrogram

After the optimal max pooling window size is found, experiments are conducted to find the optimal filter size of convolutional layers. The filter size in the time domain and the frequency domain of the second convolutional layer are found separately with a fixed size of the first convolutional layer. CCC of train set is slightly increasing along with the filter size in the time domain. However, the highest CCC of validation set is found when the filter size in the time domain is 15 frames as seen in Fig. 2 (left). After the filter size is chosen for time domain, various filter sizes of frequency domain are investigated. The results show, that the highest CCC of validation set is obtained when the filter size of the second convolutional layer is 15 × 3 frames as seen in Fig. 2 (right).

The structure of our optimal model for the spectrogram is chosen based on results showed at Fig. 2 and in Table 1. The optimal model comprises two 2D convolutional layers, one 2D max pooling layer, two RNN-LSTM layers and a fully connected layer. Two convolutional layers contain 60 filters with the filter size of 3 × 3 frames and 15 × 3 frames, respectively. ReLU activation functions are used in both convolutional layers. The first convolutional layer is followed by the max pooling layer with the size of 4 × 4 frames. Gaussian noise with standard deviation of 0.1 is added to the output of CNN layers, and these are fed to RNN-LSTM layers and a fully connected layer. Two RNN-LSTM layers contain 80 neurons and 60 neurons, respectively. Sigmoid activation function and dropout with $p = 0.2$ are applied to both RNN-LSTM layers. The fully connected layer includes linear activation function. The number of output corresponds to the number of input that depends on the segmenting window length.

4.2   The Waveform

The model for the waveform also comprises CNN and RNN-LSTM and includes two 1D convolutional layers and two 1D max pooling layers, two RNN-LSTM layers and a fully connected layer. The optimal filter size of convolutional layers and pooling window size are chosen empirically.

Pooling Size. The pooling sizes of two max pooling layers are designed to match the sample rate of the waveform to the rate of the label. The input waveform for this experiment is segmented by 4 s overlapping window.

In Fig. 3, a significant difference is found on the validation set, although CCC of the train set is rarely changed with various sizes of max pooling layers. The

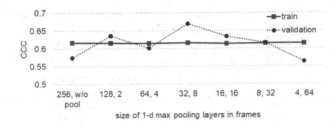

Fig. 3. Comparison of 1D max pooling size on the waveform

highest CCC of validation set is achieved when the size of first pooling window is 32 frames and the size of the second pooling window is 8 frames.

Filter Size. After the pooling window sizes are chosen, an effect of filter size is investigated. The size of the first filter is fixed to 3 frames and the size of the second filter is varied from 3 to 35 frames. The result shows the highest CCC of validation set when the filter of the first layer has the size of 3 frames and the filter of the second layer has the size of 21 frames.

Number of Filters. The number of filters for 1D CNN is investigated in range of $[20, 100]$. The results are shown in Table 2. The same number of filters is used in both 1D convolutional layers. As seen in Table 2, a significant difference is not found over the number of filters. Although CCC of train set is slightly increased along with the number of filters, the highest CCC is achieved when both convolutional layers contain 60 filters.

Table 2. Comparison of the number of filters in $1-d$ convolutional layer on the waveform

No. filters	Train	Validation
20	0.696	0.740
40	0.699	0.733
60	0.702	0.746
80	0.705	0.736
100	0.708	0.728

The optimal model for prediction of arousal on the waveform is acquired based on our results in Fig. 3, 4 and Table 2. Our optimal model comprises two 1D convolutional layers including 60 filters with the size of 3 frames and 21 frames, respectively. Both convolutional layers have ReLU activation function and are followed by 1D max pooling layer with the size of 32 frames and 8 frames, respectively. The rest part of the model contains two RNN-LSTM layers and the fully connected layer same as the optimal model for the spectrogram.

Table 3. Results over the segmenting window length from 2 s to 6 s

Model	Length	Train	Validation	Test
Waveform	2 s	0.5415	0.5454	0.4874
	4 s	0.648	0.690	0.636
	6 s	0.702	0.746	0.705
Spectrogram	2 seconds	0.587	0.493	0.4723
	4 s	0.664	0.623	0.650
	6 s	0.711	0.711	0.722

4.3 Comparison of Segmenting Window Length

The performance of our models is measured over the segmenting window size and the results are shown in Table 3. The model for waveform shows the best result when the waveform is segmented by the six second window that corresponds to 38400 frames, while shorter window length causes lower performance, which is in agreement with previous research [5]. The model for spectrogram also shows the best performance when the spectrogram is segmented by the six-second window that corresponds to 600 frames. In both models, two-second window leads to the lowest performance.

4.4 Comparison of the Proposed Approach to the Existing One

Both models are compared with the existing one that predicts arousal in the end-to-end manner. CCC of our models and the other existing model [18] are seen in Table 4. The model of Trigeorgis et al. comprises CNN and RNN-LSTM layers and predicts continuous dimensional emotions on the raw waveform. The results cannot be directly compared, as the authors used 46 subjects of the RECOLA database instead of 23 publicly available.

Our model for the waveform utilizes in general the same methodology and shows similar CCC of the validation set to this model despite of smaller amount of data. The model for the spectrogram performs comparably higher on a test set than for waveform in our experiments.

Table 4. Results in terms of CCC for our optimal models and the existing model on the validation set and test set

Method	Validation	Test
Waveform - CNN + RNN [18]	0.741	0.686
Waveform - CNN + RNN (ours)	0.746	0.705
Spectrogram - CNN + RNN (ours)	0.711	0.722

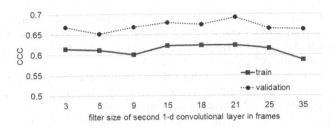

Fig. 4. Comparison of 1-d filter size in the second convolutional layer on the waveform

5   Conclusion

In this paper, two different input types were investigated for time-continuous prediction of dimensional emotion (arousal) in the end-to-end manner. We proposed CNN + RNN-LSTM model to make the time-continuous dimensional prediction of emotions with spectrogram taken as an input for the first time and compared it to existing end-to-end approaches. Furthermore, hyperparameters of the models are optimized and performance is measured in terms of concordance correlation coefficient. We have shown, that the model based on spectrogram achieves higher CCC than the waveform-based. Although different sizes of the RECOLA database were used in our experiments and the existing one, both models achieved compatible performance. The results of our study show that the spectrogram can lead to the excellent performance of the end-to-end time-continuous emotion recognition systems.

Acknowledgements. The results of this work were used in a master thesis of Bobae Kim. The research was partially financially supported by DAAD, the Government of the Russian Federation (Grant 08-08) and RFBR foundation (project No. 18-07-01407).

References

1. Badshah, A.M., Ahmad, J., Rahim, N., Baik, S.W.: Speech emotion recognition from spectrograms with deep convolutional neural network. In: 2017 International Conference on Platform Technology and Service (PlatCon), pp. 1–5. IEEE (2017)
2. Cai, D., Ni, Z., Liu, W., Cai, W., Li, G.: End-to-end deep learning framework for speech paralinguistics detection based on perception aware spectrum. In: Proceedings of Interspeech 2017, pp. 3452–3456 (2017)
3. Dieleman, S., Schrauwen, B.: End-to-end learning for music audio. In: 2014 IEEE International Conference on Acoustics, Speech and Signal Processing (ICASSP), pp. 6964–6968. IEEE (2014)
4. El Ayadi, M., Kamel, M.S., Karray, F.: Survey on speech emotion recognition: features, classification schemes, and databases. Pattern Recogn. **44**(3), 572–587 (2011)
5. Fedotov, D., Ivanko, D., Sidorov, M., Minker, W.: Contextual dependencies in time-continuous multidimensional affect recognition. In: Proceedings of the Tenth International Conference on Language Resources and Evaluation (LREC 2018) (2018). Accepted paper

6. Fedotov, D., Sidorov, M., Minker, W.: Context-awared models in time-continuous multidimensional affect recognition. In: Ronzhin, A., Rigoll, G., Meshcheryakov, R. (eds.) ICR 2017. LNCS (LNAI), vol. 10459, pp. 59–66. Springer, Cham (2017). https://doi.org/10.1007/978-3-319-66471-2_7

7. Glorot, X., Bengio, Y.: Understanding the difficulty of training deep feedforward neural networks. In: Proceedings of the Thirteenth International Conference on Artificial Intelligence and Statistics, pp. 249–256 (2010)

8. Khorrami, P., Le Paine, T., Brady, K., Dagli, C., Huang, T.S.: How deep neural networks can improve emotion recognition on video data. In: 2016 IEEE International Conference on Image Processing (ICIP), pp. 619–623. IEEE (2016)

9. Lawrence, I., Lin, K.: A concordance correlation coefficient to evaluate reproducibility. Biometrics **45**, 255–268 (1989)

10. Mao, Q., Dong, M., Huang, Z., Zhan, Y.: Learning salient features for speech emotion recognition using convolutional neural networks. IEEE Trans. Multimedia **16**(8), 2203–2213 (2014)

11. Mencattini, A., Martinelli, E., Ringeval, F., Schuller, B., Di Natale, C.: Continuous estimation of emotions in speech by dynamic cooperative speaker models. IEEE Trans. Affect. Comput. **8**(3), 314–327 (2017)

12. Miehle, J., Yoshino, K., Pragst, L., Ultes, S., Nakamura, S., Minker, W.: Cultural communication idiosyncrasies in human-computer interaction. In: Proceedings of the 17th Annual Meeting of the Special Interest Group on Discourse and Dialogue, pp. 74–79 (2016)

13. Ringeval, F., et al.: Prediction of asynchronous dimensional emotion ratings from audiovisual and physiological data. Pattern Recognit. Lett. **66**, 22–30 (2015)

14. Ringeval, F., Sonderegger, A., Sauer, J., Lalanne, D.: Introducing the Recola multimodal corpus of remote collaborative and affective interactions. In: 2013 10th IEEE International Conference and Workshops on Automatic Face and Gesture Recognition (FG), pp. 1–8. IEEE (2013)

15. Sainath, T.N., Weiss, R.J., Senior, A., Wilson, K.W., Vinyals, O.: Learning the speech front-end with raw waveform CLDNNs. In: Sixteenth Annual Conference of the International Speech Communication Association (2015)

16. Sidorov, M., Schmitt, A., Semenkin, E., Minker, W.: Could speaker, gender or age awareness be beneficial in speech-based emotion recognition? In: (Chair), N.C.C., Choukri, K. et al. (eds.) Proceedings of the Tenth International Conference on Language Resources and Evaluation (LREC 2016), Paris, France. European Language Resources Association (ELRA), May 2016

17. Tieleman, T., Hinton, G.: Lecture 6.5-rmsprop: Divide the gradient by a running average of its recent magnitude. COURSERA: Neural Netw. Mach. Learn. **4**(2), 26–31 (2012)

18. Trigeorgis, G., et al.: Adieu features? End-to-end speech emotion recognition using a deep convolutional recurrent network. In: 2016 IEEE International Conference on Acoustics, Speech and Signal Processing (ICASSP), pp. 5200–5204. IEEE (2016)

19. Valstar, M., et al.: Avec 2016: depression, mood, and emotion recognition workshop and challenge. In: Proceedings of the 6th International Workshop on Audio/Visual Emotion Challenge, pp. 3–10. ACM (2016)

20. Vogt, T.: Real-time automatic emotion recognition from speech (2010)

Developmental Disorders Manifestation in the Characteristics of the Child's Voice and Speech: Perceptual and Acoustic Study

Olga Frolova$^{(\boxtimes)}$ ⓘ, Viktor Gorodnyi ⓘ, Aleksandr Nikolaev ⓘ,
Aleksey Grigorev ⓘ, Severin Grechanyi ⓘ, and Elena Lyakso ⓘ

The Child Speech Research Group, St. Petersburg State University,
St. Petersburg, Russia
olchel@yandex.ru

Abstract. The paper presents the data of the perceptual experiment on recognition of the child's developmental disorders via speech. Participants of the study were 30 children aged 11–12 years: with autism spectrum disorders (ASD, n = 10), with Down syndrome (DS, n = 10), typically developing (TD, n = 10, control), and 50 Russian-speaking adults as listeners. The listeners were divided in 4 groups according to their professional experience: pediatric students, psychiatric students, psychiatrists, and researchers in the field of psychophysiology and child's speech development. Every group carried out the perception task separately. The speech material for the perceptual experiment was phrases and words from spontaneous speech. The results of the perceptual experiment showed that listeners could correctly recognize the child's state – disorders or typical development. Pediatric students classified the state of TD children better than the state of children with ASD and DS. Psychiatric students and psychiatrists recognized the state of children with ASD and DS better than pediatric students did. Acoustic features of speech samples correctly classified by listeners as uttered by children with disorders and TD children were described. High pitch values are specific for speech samples of children with ASD; long duration of stressed vowels is a feature of children with DS. The obtained data could be useful for specialists working with atypically developing children and for future studies of machine classification of the child's state – TD, ASD, and DS.

Keywords: Typically developing children · Autism spectrum disorders · Down syndrome · Perceptual experiment · Acoustic analysis

1 Introduction

To assess the speech and language skills of children appropriately, speech-language pathologists has to understand what effect their own biases may have on their clinical practices, including the very basic practice of perceiving and annotating productions of sounds and words [1]. The assessment of implicit attitudes of teachers and trained tutors towards individuals with autism vs. normally developing individuals has shown that participants produced more negative biases towards children with autism compared

© Springer Nature Switzerland AG 2019
A. A. Salah et al. (Eds.): SPECOM 2019, LNAI 11658, pp. 103–112, 2019.
https://doi.org/10.1007/978-3-030-26061-3_11

to children who were normally developing [2]. It was revealed that poor intelligibility of speech of children with autism spectrum disorders (ASD) contributes to college-aged adult listeners' negative social evaluation of children [3]. It is common practice to assess differences in the voice/speech of people with various diseases, based on speech-language therapists' opinions. Machine-learning-based voice analysis and human hearing judgments made by speech therapists for classifying children with ASD and typically developing (TD) are compared [4]. The question about effect of clinical training of the listeners taking part in the perceptual studies is considered. The special study examined whether trained speech-language pathologists and untrained listeners accommodate for presumed speaker dialects when rating children's productions of words. One surprising finding was that clinical training was not consistently associated with differences in ratings [5]. Speech-language therapists blind to patient's characteristics employed clinical rating scales to evaluate speech/voice in people with Parkinson's disease [6]. This approach is perspective and could be used for working with informants with different types of disorders.

To diagnose diseases by voice and speech, search of disease markers is necessary. A pause marker is proposed to distinguish early or persistent children's speech apraxia from speech delay [7]. A meta-analysis of 34 papers describing the acoustic markers of ASD was made [8]. Results of perceptual and acoustic studies of voice and speech sounds of children with Down syndrome (DS) are widely described [9]. Voice quality in DS is accepted as unusual, with altered nasal resonance. The voice of children with DS is presented by a lower pitch, the conjunction of frequencies of the first two formants providing a decreased distinction between the vowels reflecting the loss of articulatory processing [10]. Acoustic markers are considered as the significant characteristics for automatic recognition of baby's cry by the state and disease [11, 12]. The attempts of automatic diagnostics of ASD on the base of a complex assessment of crying and movements of infants [13] are made.

In our previous studies along with the assessment of acoustic characteristics of children with developmental disabilities [14, 15], the ability of adults to recognize the gender and age of children with atypical development [15], the emotional state of children with neurological disorders [16] was shown. Concerning the possibility of automatic recognition of the child's state, we conducted an experiment on the human recognition of children's disorders via speech. The presented study is the part of complex investigation of perceptual and acoustic features of typically developing children and children with atypical development (ASD, DS). The aim of the study is to explore the possibility of different groups of listeners to recognize the child's state – typical development or developmental disorders via speech.

2   Methods

Participants of the study were 30 children aged 11–12 years: 10 TD children, 10 children with ASD, 10 children with DS – five 11 year old children and five 12 year old children in each group; five girls and five boys in TD and DS groups; two girls and eight boys in ASD group (the frequency of ASD is higher in males). Speech material of children was taken from the speech database "AD-Child.Ru" containing audio and video records of atypically developing children and TD children (as control) [14]. We were guided by speech skills of children with atypical development when selecting the participants of certain age. Phrases in DS children appear later than in TD children and after the special training. Speech files are stored in the database in Windows PCM format WAV, 44.100 Hz, 16 bits per sample.

Three speech experts carried out express-analysis of audio records of dialogues of a child and an adult (experimenter or parents) in the model situation and the situation of spontaneous interaction. Words and phrases which meaning is recognized unambiguously by three experts were selected. Four words and three phrases of every child were selected for creating 4 test sequences (tests) for the perceptual study. Two tests contained the words of TD children, children with ASD and DS mixed randomly (one test was for 11 year old children, the other test – for 12 year old children, each test contained 60 words), two tests contained the phrases (for 60 phrases of 11 and 12 year old children). The speech signal (word or phrase) in the tests was presented once; the duration of pauses between speech signals was 5 s. The presentation of test sequences was carried out in an open field for groups of listeners. This approach was approved in our previous studies [15, 16], as this perceptual experiment is closed to natural conditions.

The listeners were 50 adults from groups: first year pediatric students (n = 20, 18.5 ± 1.2 years old); psychiatric students (n = 20, 24.7 ± 0.8 years old); psychiatrists (n = 5, 43.8 ± 8.8 years old); specialists - researchers in the field of psychophysiology and child speech development (n = 5, 28.8 ± 5.4 years old).

The main goal of the perceptual study was to reveal the possibility of listeners to recognize the child's state – developmental disorders or typical development via speech, but every group of listeners had their specific task.

The perceptual study included three experiments. Experiment 1: Pediatric students recognized the child's state, age, and gender, when listening to words and phrases (four test sequences). Experiment 2: Psychiatric students and psychiatrists recognized the state of the child and detected the severity of disorders – severe, moderate, and mild, when listening to the child's phrases (two test sequences). Results of the first and second perceptual experiments were compared to reveal the effect of the professional experience on the child's state recognition. Experiment 3: Specialists described the articulation clarity, intonation features, and utterance intelligibility when listening to the child's phrases (two test sequences).

Spectrographic analysis of the child's speech material from test sequences was carried out, based on the algorithms implemented in Cool Edit Pro sound editor. The prosodic features: the duration of phrases, words, stressed vowels, and pauses between words in the phrase, values of pitch - average, maximal, minimal pitch values of the phrase and stressed vowel in words were measured. The number of words in the phrases and syllables in the words were calculated. Acoustic features of TD children and children with ASD and DS were compared taking into account the perceptual data.

3 Results

3.1 Experiment 1. Recognition of the Child's State, Age, Gender by Pediatric Students

Pediatric students correctly recognized the state of children, when listening to the test sequences containing the child's words. The average recognition accuracy was 56% for 11 year old children and 57% for 12 year old children. 55% of words of 11 year old TD children and 35% of words of 12 year old TD children were correctly classified as typical development with perception rate 0.75–1.0. The agreement among the listeners in determining the state of children with ASD and DS was less vs. TD children. 10% of 11 year old ASD children's words, 25% of 12 year old ASD children's words, 15% of 11 year old DS children's words, and 35% of 12 year old DS children's words were correctly classified as disorders with perception rate 0.75–1.0.

The number of listeners' mistakes in the child's state classification decreased for tests containing the phrases (Table 1). Pediatric students correctly recognized the state of children by phrases with average recognition accuracy 75%. 93% of 11 year old TD children's phrases and 90% of 12 year old TD children's phrases were classified as typical development with perception rate 0.75–1.0. 80% of 11 year old DS children's phrases and 60% of 12 year old DS children's phrases were classified as disorders with perception rate 0.75–1.0. Recognition of the state of children with ASD was a more difficult task for pediatric students: 25% of ASD children's phrases were classified as developmental disorders with perception rate 0.75–1.0. Regression analysis revealed the correlation between a test type (words/phrases) and child's state recognition accuracy $F(1,100) = 13.105$ $p < 0.001$ $R^2 = 0.116$ (Beta = 0.34).

Table 1. Confusion matrices for child's state recognition by pediatric students.

Group of children	Words				Phrases			
	11 y		12 y		11 y		12 y	
	TD	Dis.	TD	Dis.	TD	Dis.	TD	Dis.
TD	**71**	29	**63**	37	**88**	12	**90**	10
ASD	55	**45**	49	**51**	45	**55**	44	**56**
DS	53	**57**	42	**58**	22	**78**	25	**75**

The second task for pediatric students was the child's age prediction. Students defined the age of children younger than in fact (Fig. 1).

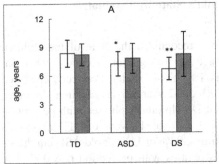 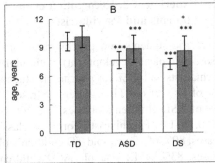

Fig. 1. Child's age prediction by listeners – pediatric students. A – tests containing child's words, B - tests containing child's phrases. White columns – 11 year old children, gray columns – 12 year old children. * p < 0.05, ** p < 0.01, *** p < 0.001, differences between TD and ASD, TD and DS children; + p < 0.05, differences between ASD and DS children - Mann-Whitney test.

Listeners noted that TD children are older than children with ASD; the age of children with DS was determined as the youngest (except one of tests containing the words of 12 year old children). The tendency was revealed that students noted the younger child's age for tests containing child's words than for tests containing child's phrases.

For gender prediction, the average recognition accuracy for tests containing words was lower than for tests containing phrases: 52% – 11 year old children, 47% – 12 year old children (words); 64% – 11 year old children, 61% – 12 year old children (phrases). Listeners recognized the male gender of all children better than the female gender (Table 2). Listeners classified most of speech samples of children with DS as the male gender.

Table 2. Confusion matrices for child's gender recognition by pediatric students.

Group of children	Gender	Words				Phrases			
		11 y		12 y		11 y		12 y	
		Male	Female	Male	Female	Male	Female	Male	Female
TD	M	**79**	21	**91**	9	**83**	17	**94**	6
	F	82	**17**	66	**45**	45	**55**	33	**67**
ASD	M	**63**	37	**67**	33	**68**	32	**56**	44
	F	79	**21**	86	**14**	55	**45**	35	**65**
DS	M	**82**	18	**87**	13	**95**	5	**95**	5
	F	92	**8**	84	**16**	96	**4**	85	**15**

3.2 Experiment 2. Recognition of the Child's State by Psychiatric Students and Psychiatrists

Psychiatric students and psychiatrists correctly recognized the state of the children (disorders/typical development) with high average recognition accuracy: 88% for psychiatrists and 83% for psychiatric students. Psychiatric students correctly classified 60% of 11 year old TD children's phrases, 40% of 12 year old TD children's phrases, 92% of ASD children's phrases, and 100% of DS children's phrases with perception rate 0.75–1.0. Psychiatrists correctly classified 73% of 11 year old TD children's phrases, 80% of 12 year old TD children's phrases, 92% of 11 year old ASD children's phrases, 83% of 12 year old ASD children's phrases with perception rate 0.75–1.0. Like psychiatric students, psychiatrists correctly classified 100% of DS children's phrases with perception rate 0.75–1.0.

Generally, in the state prediction task, psychiatric students and psychiatrists demonstrated less agreement in determining the state of TD children vs. determining the state of children with DS and ASD. Psychiatric students and psychiatrists more often determined the severity of disorders of ASD children as mild and moderate, DS children – as moderate and severe (Table 3).

The results of the Experiment 1 and 2 revealed that the professional experience affects the child's state classification via speech: group of listeners (pediatrician students/psychiatrist postgraduate students/psychiatrist doctors) correlates with recognition accuracy of the child's state $F(1,124) = 11.59$ $p < 0.001$ $R^2 = 0.085$ (Beta = 0.292) – Regression analysis.

Table 3. Confusion matrices for child's state recognition by psychiatric students and psychiatrists.

Psychiatric students								
Group	11 y				12 y			
	TD	Mild dis.	Moderate dis.	Severe dis.	TD	Mild dis.	Moderate dis.	Severe dis.
TD	**73**	18	6	3	**65**	27	6	2
ASD	16	36	31	17	10	40	38	12
DS	7	20	37	36	3	18	33	46
Psychiatrists								
Group	11 y				12 y			
	TD	Mild dis.	Moderate dis.	Severe dis.	TD	Mild dis.	Moderate dis.	Severe dis.
TD	**77**	16	7	0	**73**	25.5	1.5	0
ASD	10	50	22	18	8	45	35	12
DS	3	19	41	37	0	20	31	49

3.3 Acoustic Data

The comparison of acoustic features of child's speech samples correctly recognized by listeners as speech of TD children and children with developmental disorders with perception rate 0.75–1.0 was carried out. We revealed the correlations between child's state recognition and: phrases duration $F(1,49) = 7.178$ $p < 0.01$ $R^2 = 0.128$ (Beta = -0.357) – Regression analysis (phrases correctly recognized as uttered by TD children are longer than phrases recognized as uttered by children with disorders); the number of words in a child's phrase $F(1,51) = 19.929$ $p < 0.001$ $R^2 = 0.281$ (Beta = -0.53) – Regression analysis (phrases correctly recognized as uttered by TD children consist of more words vs. phrases uttered by children with disorders); stressed vowels duration $F(1,222) = 14.818$ $p < 0.001$ $R^2 = 0.063$ (Beta = 0.25) – Regression analysis (the duration values of stressed vowels in words from speech samples correctly recognized as uttered by TD children are lower than the corresponding parameter in speech samples uttered by children with disorders) (Fig. 2). The group of children (TD, ASD, DS) correlates with stressed vowels duration $F(1,222) = 18.563$ $p < 0.001$ $R^2 = 0.077$ (Beta = 0.278) – Regression analysis.

Pitch values of ASD children's speech – average pitch values (F0), maximal and minimal pitch values (F0 max, F0 min) of phrases and stressed vowels in words are significantly higher vs. corresponding pitch values in speech of TD children (Fig. 3) and children with DS. F0 max values of DS children's phrases are lower vs. the corresponding parameter of TD children.

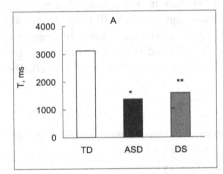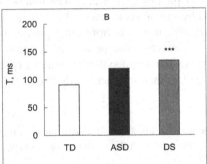

Fig. 2. The duration values of phrases (A) and stressed vowels in the words (B) of TD children and children with ASD and DS. Vertical axis - duration, ms; * $p < 0.05$, ** $p < 0.01$, *** $p < 0.001$ – Mann-Whitney test - differences between TD children and children with ASD and DS.

3.4 Experiment 3. Description of Child's Speech Material by Specialists (Researchers)

Specialists noted that TD children's articulation is clear, the speech is intelligible, the intonation is normal. 100% of TD children's phrases were classified by specialists as clearly articulated, with the normal intonation with perception rate 0.75–1.0.

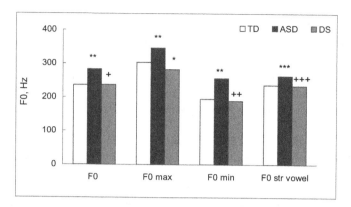

Fig. 3. Pitch values of phrases – F0, F0 max, F0 min, and pitch values of stressed vowels in words - F0 str vowel, of TD children, children with ASD and DS. Vertical axis – pitch values, Hz; * p < 0.05, ** p < 0.01, *** p < 0.001 – differences between TD children and children with ASD and DS; + p< 0.05, ++ p < 0.01, +++ p < 0.001 – differences between children with ASD and children with DS.

For children with ASD and DS, specialists revealed fuzzy articulation (mainly for DS children) and the abnormality of intonation (mainly for ASD children) (Table 4).

The phrases determined by specialists as intelligible (perception rate 0.75-1.0) were compared with other child's phrases. The number of words in phrases recognized by specialists as intelligible (5.2 ± 2.9) was higher (p < 0.05) than the number of words in other phrases (3.4 ± 2.2). The number of syllables in words from phrases recognized by specialists as intelligible (2.1 ± 1.1) was higher (p < 0.001) than the number of syllables in words from other phrases (1.6 ± 0.7). The comparison of intelligible and incomprehensible phrases of children with ASD and DS revealed the same patterns: the number of syllables is higher (p < 0.001) in words recognized as intelligible (2.2 ± 1.1) than in other words (1.6 ± 0.7).

Table 4. The number of child's phrases recognized by specialists as clearly articulated, intelligible, and with the normal intonation (perception rate 0.75–1.0).

Child's age	11 years			12 years		
Group of children	TD	ASD	DS	TD	ASD	DS
Clear articulation	100	42	7	100	67	13
Intelligible meaning	100	67	53	100	83	53
Normal intonation	100	50	47	100	17	53

4 Discussion

The perceptual study revealed the possibility of different groups of adults to recognize child's developmental disorders via speech. Recognition accuracy and the agreement among the listeners in determining the child's state were higher for speech material presented phrases vs. words. Our data correspond to the perceptual experiment, in which several words from spontaneous speech of children with ASD and TD were listened by college-aged adults who had no clinical training or experience. The results showed that lay listeners can distinguish atypical from typical children outside the social-interactional context based on speech intelligibility [3].

The professional experience of listeners impacts child's state classification via speech. Pediatric students (household experience of interaction with children) recognized the state of TD children better vs. the state of children with ASD and DS. Psychiatric students and psychiatrists recognized the state of children with ASD and DS better than pediatric students did. In our previous studies [15, 16], we compared experts in the field of child speech, students, older adults, and parents; it was revealed that the experience of interaction with children influences the speech recognition and emotions classification.

In our study, the specialists described lower articulation clarity and speech intelligibility, intonation abnormalities in the speech of children with ASD and DS that is in line with our previous findings [15]. The age of children with ASD and DS was detected by listeners as younger than the age of TD children. For all children (especially for DS children), the female gender was recognized worse than the male gender. Speech samples belonging to girls were attributed to boys. These results verify the findings in our former studies on TD children and children with ASD [15].

Acoustic features of speech samples correctly classified by listeners as uttered by children with disorders and TD children were described. According to our previous data [15], speech of children with ASD is characterized by high pitch values. High pitch values of phrases and stressed vowels in words of ASD children were revealed. Long duration of stressed vowels in words was detected in speech samples of children with DS.

In our future work we will combine the joint perception outputs: how well does a fusion of experts and non-experts (say three groups except the researchers) perform in terms of perception. The obtained data on recognition accuracy are the first step to future works on the machine state classification of child's speech. Our results could be useful for specialists working with atypically developing children and for training medical students.

5   Conclusions

The possibility of different groups of listeners to recognize the child's state – developmental disorders or typical development via speech was revealed. Pediatric students classified the state of children with ASD and DS worse than the state of TD children. Psychiatric students and psychiatrists recognized the state of children with ASD and DS better compared with pediatric students.

Predicting the age and gender of children with ASD and DS was a more difficult task for listeners than recognizing the age and gender of TD children.

High pitch values are specific for speech samples of children with ASD; long duration of stressed vowels is a feature of children with DS.

Acknowledgements. The study is financially supported by the Russian Science Foundation (project № 18-18-00063).

References

1. American Speech-Language-Hearing Association. Knowledge and skills needed by speech-language pathologists and audiologists to provide culturally and linguistically appropriate services. (2004). http://www.asha.org/policy. Accessed 15 Apr 2019
2. Kelly, A., Barnes-Holmes, D.: Implicit attitudes towards children with autism versus normally developing children as predictors of professional burnout and psychopathology. Res. Dev. Disabil. **34**(1), 17–28 (2013)
3. Redford, M.A., Kapatsinski, V., Cornell-Fabiano, J.: Lay listener classification and evaluation of typical and atypical children's speech. Lang. Speech **61**(2), 277–302 (2018)
4. Nakai, Y., Takiguchi, T., Matsui, G., Yamaoka, N., Takada, S.: Detecting abnormal word utterances in children with autism spectrum disorders: machine-learning-based voice analysis versus speech therapists. Percept. Mot. Ski. **124**(5), 961–973 (2017)
5. Evans, K.E., Munson, B., Edwards, J.: Does speaker race affect the assessment of children's speech accuracy? A comparison of speech-language pathologists and clinically untrained listeners. Lang. Speech Hear. Serv. Sch. **49**(4), 906–921 (2018)
6. Miller, N., Nath, U., Noble, E., Burn, D.: Utility and accuracy of perceptual voice and speech distinctions in the diagnosis of Parkinson's disease, PSP and MSA-P. Neurodegener. Dis. Manag. **7**(3), 191–203 (2017)
7. Shriberg, L.D., et al.: A diagnostic marker to discriminate childhood apraxia of speech from speech delay: I. Development and description of the pause marker. J. Speech Lang. Hear. Res. **60**(4), 1096–1117 (2017)
8. Fusaroli, R., Lambrechts, A., Bang, D., Bowler, D.M., Gaigg, S.B.: Is voice a marker for Autism spectrum disorder? A systematic review and meta-analysis. Autism Res. **10**(3), 384–407 (2017)
9. Kent, R.D., Vorperian, H.K.: Speech impairment in down syndrome: a review. J. Speech Lang. Hear. Res. **56**(1), 178–210 (2013)
10. Moura, C.P., et al.: Voice parameters in children with down syndrome. J. Voice **22**(1), 34–42 (2008)
11. Xie, Q., Ward, R.K., Laszlo, C.A.: Automatic assessment of infants' levels-of-distress from the cry signals. IEEE Trans. Speech Audio Process. **4**(4), 253–265 (1996)
12. Poel, M., Ekkel, T.: Analyzing infant cries using a committee of neural networks in order to detect hypoxia related disorder. Int. J. Artif. Intell. Tools **15**(3), 397–410 (2006)
13. Orlandi, S., Manfredi, C., Guzzetta, A., Belmonti, V., Barbagallo, S.D., Scattoni, M.L.: Advanced tools for clinical diagnosis of autism spectrum disorders. In: Zhang, Y.-T. (ed.) The International Conference on Health Informatics. IP, vol. 42, pp. 256–259. Springer, Cham (2014). https://doi.org/10.1007/978-3-319-03005-0_65
14. Lyakso, E., Frolova, O., Karpov, A.: A new method for collection and annotation of speech data of atypically developing children. In: Proceedings of 2018 International IEEE Conference on Sensor Networks and Signal Processing (SNSP 2018), Xi'an, China, pp. 175–180 (2018)
15. Lyakso, E., Frolova, O., Grigorev, A.: Perception and acoustic features of speech of children with autism spectrum disorders. In: Karpov, A., Potapova, R., Mporas, I. (eds.) SPECOM 2017. LNCS (LNAI), vol. 10458, pp. 602–612. Springer, Cham (2017). https://doi.org/10.1007/978-3-319-66429-3_60
16. Frolova, O., Lyakso, E.: Emotional speech of 3-years old children: norm-risk-deprivation. In: Ronzhin, A., Potapova, R., Németh, G. (eds.) SPECOM 2016. LNCS (LNAI), vol. 9811, pp. 262–270. Springer, Cham (2016). https://doi.org/10.1007/978-3-319-43958-7_31

RUSLAN: Russian Spoken Language Corpus for Speech Synthesis

Lenar Gabdrakhmanov, Rustem Garaev$^{(\boxtimes)}$, and Evgenii Razinkov

Institute of Computational Mathematics and Information Technologies,
Kazan Federal University, Kazan, Russia
rustem.garaev.personal@gmail.com, Evgenij.Razinkov@kpfu.ru

Abstract. We present RUSLAN – a new open Russian spoken language
corpus for the text-to-speech task. RUSLAN contains 22200 audio samples with text annotations – more than 31 h of high-quality speech of one
person – being the largest annotated Russian corpus in terms of speech
duration for a single speaker. We trained an end-to-end neural network
for the text-to-speech task on our corpus and evaluated the quality of the
synthesized speech using Mean Opinion Score test. Synthesized speech
achieves 4.05 score for naturalness and 3.78 score for intelligibility on a
5-point MOS scale.

Keywords: Russian speech corpus · End-to-end speech synthesis ·
Text-to-speech

1 Introduction

Spoken language is an essential tool for human communication. In a world of AI
systems and mobile computers, humans also communicate with machines. Ability to communicate with a machine using natural spoken language contributes
greatly to the user experience. Two tasks should be completed in order to make
it possible: speech synthesis and automatic speech recognition.

The main goal of text-to-speech systems is to generate an audio signal containing natural speech corresponding to the input text. There are several possible solutions. Speech synthesis systems based on concatenation and statistical parametrization might produce acceptable results in terms of quality but
they require deeply annotated speech corpora. Providing this level of speech
annotation is a time-consuming process that requires specific lexicology knowledge. Another possible drawback of this approach is language-dependent system
design [20].

Recent advances in deep learning resulted in significant improvements in
speech synthesis task [1,12,15,17,22,24]. Deep learning techniques excel at leveraging large amounts of training data. Thus, the quality of the synthesized speech

---

L. Gabdrakhmanov and R. Garaev—contributed equally to this work.

© Springer Nature Switzerland AG 2019
A. A. Salah et al. (Eds.): SPECOM 2019, LNAI 11658, pp. 113–121, 2019.
https://doi.org/10.1007/978-3-030-26061-3_12

for text-to-speech systems based on deep learning is heavily influenced by the quality and size of the speech corpus.

Depending on the text-to-speech neural network architecture various levels of corpus annotation might be required. While WaveNet [22] neural network relies on extensive annotation (linguistic features, fundamental frequency etc.), text-audio pairs are sufficient for more recent Tacotron [24] end-to-end architecture. It is much easier to collect text-audio pairs and it would lead to larger corpora and higher quality of synthesized speech in the future.

While large open speech corpora exist for some of the most widespread languages [4,6,10] this is not the case for many other languages.

Russian is the sixth most widespread language in the world by the number of native speakers being spoken by approximately 154 million people worldwide [5]. However, publicly available and annotated speech corpora in Russian are not sufficient. Availability of large amounts of annotated speech is crucial for the research community both in speech synthesis and recognition.

Amount of speech for a single speaker is an important factor for end-to-end neural speech synthesis. There are few Russian speech corpora: [3,23] are public and [7,16] are proprietary, but the amount of speech for a single speaker in these corpora is less than 7 h. Up until now, there was only one open-source Russian language speech corpus exceeding 7 h in audio duration for a single speaker namely M-AILABS [21], containing about 20 h of speech for a single speaker at most. In this work, we try to facilitate research in speech synthesis in Russian by providing large publicly available annotated speech corpus.

Our contributions are as follows:

- We collected the largest annotated speech corpus in the Russian language for a single speaker – RUSLAN (RUSsian spoken LANguage corpus) and made it publicly available. Our corpus is 50% larger in terms of audio duration in comparison with the second largest corpus in the Russian language for a single speaker to date [21].
  Speech corpus is publicly available under Creative Commons BY-NC-SA 4.0 license at https://ruslan-corpus.github.io.
- We trained text-to-speech neural network on RUSLAN and evaluated the quality of the synthesized speech using Mean Opinion Score with 50 participating native speakers as respondents[1].
- We propose several improvements for Tacotron text-to-speech end-to-end neural network that allow us to achieve comparable speech quality in fewer training iterations.

2   Speech Corpus

In this section, we describe RUSLAN speech corpus. The amount of annotated speech for a single speaker is a key feature of text-to-speech corpora. Therefore,

---

[1] Audio samples from corpus and examples of synthesized speech can be found at https://ruslan-corpus.github.io.

we focused on maximizing the amount of high-quality speech recording for a single speaker. Speaker is a 23 years old male who is a native Russian speaker. The pronunciation is clear and intelligible. The style of the text is narrative, the speech is neutral. Corpus contains 22200 training samples. Each training sample is a text-audio pair, where the text is a phrase or a sentence – an excerpt from works of Russian and American writer Sergei Dovlatov. The number of words in each training sample varies from 1 to 111 with an average of 12. The Russian language consists of 33 letters (10 vowels and 23 consonants). The frequency distribution for the phonemes are provided in Fig. 1. Phonemic transcription was performed as suggested in [25].

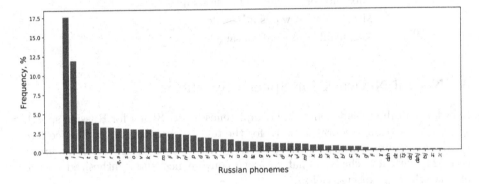

Fig. 1. Distribution of the Russian phonemes in the corpus.

2.1   Text Preprocessing

Text for each training sample was preprocessed in the following way:

- All numbers and dates were manually replaced by their textual representation.
- Acronyms were manually substituted with their expanded forms.
- All symbols except for Russian letters and punctuation marks were automatically deleted.

2.2   Recording Process

Audio samples were recorded in a quiet and noise-protected room using noise-reduction hardware. Each sample was recorded separately with a sampling frequency of 44.1 kHz and 16 bit linear PCM and saved in WAV format. Leading and trailing silent parts were deleted from each audio sample. All text-audio pairs were additionally verified in order to avoid annotation errors. The signal-to-noise ratio is approximately equal to 90 dB. Corpus statistics are presented in Table 1.

Figure 2 shows the ratio of the lengths and ratio of the number of symbols per sample for the whole corpus.

Table 1. RUSLAN corpus statistics

Total duration	31:32:55
Total number of samples	22200
Total symbols	1472377
Total words	267053
Unique words	52703
Min sample duration	0.61 s
Max sample duration	50.71 s
Min number of symbols in one sample	9
Max number of symbols in one sample	596
Min number of words in sample	1
Max number of words in sample	111

3 Neural Network for Speech Synthesis

In order to evaluate sufficiency and completeness of RUSLAN for Russian speech synthesis, we train a neural network for the text-to-speech task. In this section, we describe our neural network that is heavily based on Tacotron architecture [24] with few changes that improve convergence and synthesized speech quality which we discuss below.

We employ end-to-end trainable encoder-decoder deep neural network architecture that receives text as an input and produces a linear spectrogram. This spectrogram is later used for waveform reconstruction. Model architecture is illustrated in Fig. 3. We describe the encoder, decoder and audio reconstruction procedure below.

3.1 Neural Network Architecture

The input of the model is a text where each distinct character is represented as a trainable 256-dimensional character embedding vector. Thus, the lookup table has a shape of 78×256 since we use only 78 characters: Russian capital and lowercase letters, space and punctuation marks – $\{', -().:;!?\}$.

The model encoder consists of two parts: pre-net of two fully connected layers with dropout [18] and CBHL module which is a slight modification of Tacotron CBHG module. Our main and only modification here is a replacement of GRU with layer normalized LSTM (LN-LSTM) in bidirectional RNN for faster convergence [9].

Decoder consists of two parts to predict mel-frequency cepstral coefficients and linear spectrogram respectively. The first part includes pre-net, Attention RNN and Decoder RNN. We have replaced GRU with LN-LSTM in both Attention RNN [2] and Decoder RNN parts in contrast with the original Tacotron model. In Tacotron model the second part of the decoder is post-processing CBHG module, but we again replace it with our CBHL.

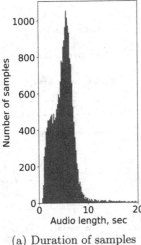

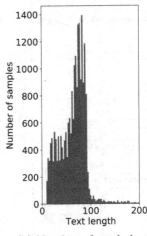

(a) Duration of samples   (b) Number of symbols

Fig. 2. Histograms (a) of the duration of samples, (b) of the number of symbols.

Loss Function. Since Decoder RNN predicts MFCCs and post-processing CBHL module predicts linear spectrogram, we employ two different loss functions.

Target values for Decoder RNN are 80-band MFCCs:

$$Loss_{mel} = \frac{1}{N} \sum_{i}^{N} |\mathbf{t}_i^{mel} - \mathbf{y}_{mel}(text_i)|_1, \tag{1}$$

where N is the number of samples in the training set, $text_i$ is the i-th text from the corpus, $\mathbf{t}_i^{mel}$ is ground truth mel-frequency cepstral coefficients for $text_i$, $\mathbf{y}^{mel}(text_i)$ is MFCCs predicted by Decoder RNN of the neural network given $text_i$ as an input.

Loss function for post-processing CBHL module:

$$Loss_{lin} = \frac{1}{N} \sum_{i}^{N} |\mathbf{t}_i^{lin} - \mathbf{y}_{lin}(text_i)|_1, \tag{2}$$

where t_j^{lin} is ground truth linear-spectral coefficients for $text_i$, $\mathbf{y}_{lin}(text_i)$ is linear-spectral coefficients predicted by post-processing CBHL module of the neural network given $text_i$ as an input.

The overall loss function of the neural network is computed as follows:

$$Loss = Loss_{mel} + Loss_{lin}. \tag{3}$$

Signal Reconstruction. In contrast to Tacotron we employ fast Griffin-Lim [11] algorithm to reconstruct an audio signal from magnitude-only values of the linear spectrogram.

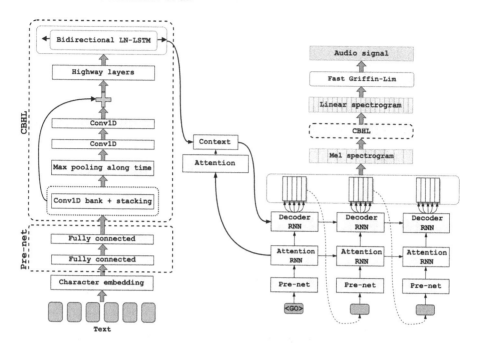

Fig. 3. Model architecture.

The signal is being recovered iteratively, we stop the process after 300 iterations. Optimization speed α was set to 0.99.

3.2 Training

Text from each text-audio pair from RUSLAN corpus was used as a training sample and corresponding audio was used to obtain target variables, MFCCs and a linear spectrogram.

Our model implementation had been training for 300 K iterations with a batch size of 8. The training was performed on a single GTX 1060 with 6 Gb of onboard memory. We used Adam optimizer [8] with exponential learning rate decay.

4   Evaluation

Synthesized speech is intelligible, natural and close to human speech. The described model shows good results even on a low amount of steps.

4.1   Mean Opinion Score

Mean Opinion Score (MOS) is the most frequently used method of a subjective measure of speech quality. MOS is used to evaluate methods of signal processing, including speech synthesis. The respondents rate the speech quality on a five-point scale. Score 1 corresponds to bad quality, score 5 corresponds to excellent quality. The final rating of the signal in question is calculated as the mean over rating scores from all respondents. This method is recommended by ITU and IEEE for the quality estimation of the synthesized speech [14,19]. The scale of MOS scores is presented in Table 2:

Table 2. MOS scale

Score	Quality	Distortions
5	Excellent	Imperceptible
4	Good	Tangible, but non-irritating
3	Fair	Sensible and slightly annoying
2	Poor	Annoying
1	Bad	Annoying and unpleasant

In our work, we rate speech intelligibility and naturalness. The respondents were allowed to listen to the samples on their own equipment in an uncontrolled environment. The scores produced by this method remain very close to those received in a controlled environment as it was mentioned in the work [13]. 50 respondents participated in the synthesis speech evaluation survey at the age of 20–40: 40% of them were female and 60% were male.

Twenty audio samples consisting of 11 samples of synthesized speech and 9 samples of recorded speech from the corpus were blindly presented to the respondents. Each respondent got acquainted with the survey rules in advance. Table 3 shows naturalness and intelligibility scores for the synthesized speech and original recordings from the corpus. In contrast to the similarity of scores achieved by real speech, the difference between naturalness and intelligibility scores for synthesized speech might be explained by the fact that respondents can understand all words clearly, although there are still some artefacts in audio due to use of the Fast Griffin-Lim algorithm.

Table 3. Naturalness and intelligibility scores

Type	Naturalness	Intelligibility
Real speech	4.83	4.87
Synthesized speech	3.78	4.05

We also evaluated the quality of the speech synthesized by our implementation of the reference Tacotron neural network that had been training on RUSLAN for 300 K iterations. Speech synthesized by Tacotron achieved 3.12 MOS score for intelligibility and 2.17 MOS score for naturalness. It should be noted, however, that in the original paper Tacotron neural network was trained for 2 million iterations [24].

5 Conclusion

We present RUSLAN spoken language corpus – the largest Russian open speech corpus for a single speaker for the text-to-speech task. It consists of 22200 text-audio pairs with the total audio duration being 31 h 32 min and exceeds the second largest Russian corpus for a single speaker by 50%. We evaluate the sufficiency and the completeness of our corpus by training an end-to-end text-to-speech neural network on RUSLAN. Our model achieves 4.05 for intelligibility and 3.78 for naturalness on a 5-point MOS scale.

References

1. Arik, S.O., et al.: Deep voice: real-time neural text-to-speech. arXiv preprint arXiv:1702.07825 (2017)
2. Bahdanau, D., Cho, K., Bengio, Y.: Neural machine translation by jointly learning to align and translate. arXiv preprint arXiv:1409.0473 (2014)
3. Festvox: Festvox project. http://festvox.org/festival/
4. Garofolo, J.S., Lamel, L.F., Fisher, W.M., Fiscus, J.G., Pallett, D.S.: DARPA TIMIT acoustic-phonetic continous speech corpus CD-ROM. NIST speech disc 1–1.1. NASA STI/Recon technical report n (1993)
5. Simons, G.F., Fennig, C.D.: Ethnologue: Languages of Africa and Europe, Twenty-First Edition. Summer Institute of Linguistics, Academic Publications (2018)
6. Honnet, P.E., Lazaridis, A., Garner, P.N., Yamagishi, J.: The SIWIS French speech synthesis database. Design and recording of a high quality French database for speech synthesis. Technical report, Idiap (2017)
7. Kachkovskaia, T., Kocharov, D., Skrelin, P.A., Volskaya, N.B.: CoRuSS-a new prosodically annotated corpus of Russian spontaneous speech. In: LREC (2016)
8. Kingma, D.P., Ba, J.: Adam: a method for stochastic optimization. arXiv preprint arXiv:1412.6980 (2014)
9. Lei Ba, J., Kiros, J.R., Hinton, G.E.: Layer normalization. arXiv preprint arXiv:1607.06450 (2016)
10. Panayotov, V., Chen, G., Povey, D., Khudanpur, S.: Librispeech: an ASR corpus based on public domain audio books. In: 2015 IEEE International Conference on Acoustics, Speech and Signal Processing (ICASSP), pp. 5206–5210. IEEE (2015)
11. Perraudin, N., Balazs, P., Søndergaard, P.L.: A fast Griffin-Lim algorithm. In: 2013 IEEE Workshop on Applications of Signal Processing to Audio and Acoustics (WASPAA), pp. 1–4. IEEE (2013)
12. Ping, W., et al.: Deep voice 3: scaling text-to-speech with convolutional sequence learning. arXiv preprint arXiv:1710.07654 (2017)
13. Ribeiro, F., Florêncio, D., Zhang, C., Seltzer, M.: CROWDMOS: an approach for crowdsourcing mean opinion score studies. In: 2011 IEEE International Conference on Acoustics, Speech and Signal Processing (ICASSP), pp. 2416–2419. IEEE (2011)
14. Rothauser, E.: IEEE recommended practice for speech quality measurements. IEEE Trans. Audio Electroacoust. **17**, 225–246 (1969)

15. Shen, J., et al.: Natural TTS synthesis by conditioning WaveNet on Mel spectrogram predictions. arXiv preprint arXiv:1712.05884 (2017)
16. Skrelin, P., Volskaya, N., Kocharov, D., Evgrafova, K., Glotova, O., Evdokimova, V.: CORPRES. In: Sojka, P., Horák, A., Kopeček, I., Pala, K. (eds.) TSD 2010. LNCS (LNAI), vol. 6231, pp. 392–399. Springer, Heidelberg (2010). https://doi.org/10.1007/978-3-642-15760-8_50
17. Sotelo, J., et al.: Char2Wav: end-to-end speech synthesis. In: Proceedings of International Conference on Learning Representations (ICLR) (2017)
18. Srivastava, N., Hinton, G., Krizhevsky, A., Sutskever, I., Salakhutdinov, R.: Dropout: a simple way to prevent neural networks from overfitting. J. Mach. Learn. Res. **15**(1), 1929–1958 (2014)
19. International Telecommunication Union - Radiocommunication Sector. Subjective assessment of sound quality (1990)
20. Taylor, P.: Text-to-Speech Synthesis. Cambridge University Press, Cambridge (2009)
21. The M-AILABS Speech Dataset. http://www.m-ailabs.bayern/en/the-mailabs-speech-dataset/
22. Van Den Oord, A., et al.: WaveNet: a generative model for raw audio. CoRR abs/1609.03499 (2016)
23. VoxForge: Voxforge.org website
24. Wang, Y., et al.: Tacotron: towards end-to-end speech synthesis. arXiv preprint arXiv:1703.10135 (2017)
25. Yakovenko, O., Bondarenko, I., Borovikova, M., Vodolazsky, D.: Algorithms for automatic accentuation and transcription of russian texts in speech recognition systems. In: Karpov, A., Jokisch, O., Potapova, R. (eds.) SPECOM 2018. LNCS (LNAI), vol. 11096, pp. 768–777. Springer, Cham (2018). https://doi.org/10.1007/978-3-319-99579-3_78

Differentiating Laughter Types via HMM/DNN and Probabilistic Sampling

Gábor Gosztolya[1,2(✉)], András Beke[3], and Tilda Neuberger[3]

[1] MTA-SZTE Research Group on Artificial Intelligence, Szeged, Hungary
ggabor@inf.u-szeged.hu
[2] Department of Informatics, University of Szeged, Szeged, Hungary
[3] Research Institute for Linguistics of the Hungarian Academy of Sciences, Budapest, Hungary

Abstract. In human speech, laughter has a special role as an important non-verbal element, signaling a general positive affect and cooperative intent. However, laughter occurrences may be categorized into several sub-groups, each having a slightly or significantly different role in human conversation. It means that, besides automatically locating laughter events in human speech, it would be beneficial if we could automatically categorize them as well. In this study, we focus on laughter events occurring in Hungarian spontaneous conversations. First we use the manually annotated occurrence time segments, and the task is to simply determine the correct laughter type via Deep Neural Networks (DNNs). Secondly we seek to localize the laughter events as well, for which we utilize Hidden Markov Models. Detecting different laughter types also poses a challenge to DNNs due to the low number of training examples for specific types, but this can be handled using the technique of probabilistic sampling during frame-level DNN training.

Keywords: Laughter events · Deep Neural Networks · Hidden Markov Models · Probabilistic sampling

1 Introduction

Laughter is one of the most interesting and important aspects of complex human behaviour [25]. But why do humans have an ability to laugh, what is the evolutional purpose of laughter, and how did it develop during our evolution? To answer these questions, the function of laughter has to be analyzed from the perspective of human behaviour. It has been shown that there are many types

This study was partially funded by the National Research, Development and Innovation Office of Hungary via contract NKFIH FK-124413. Gábor Gosztolya was also supported by the Ministry of Human Capacities, Hungary (grant 20391-3/2018/FEKUSTRAT). András Beke was supported by the János Bolyai Research Scholarship of the Hungarian Academy of Sciences.

A. A. Salah et al. (Eds.): SPECOM 2019, LNAI 11658, pp. 122–132, 2019.
https://doi.org/10.1007/978-3-030-26061-3_13

of laughter depending on the approach used in the analysis. Based on the vocal-production mode, laughter can be realized as voiced or unvoiced, and there are intervals where a participant both speaks and laughs, known as speech-laughs (see e.g. [18]). Unvoiced laughter is acoustically similar to breathing. Voiced laughter was found to be a more relevant predictor of emotional involvement in speech than general laughter. Other types of laughter may be voiced song-like, unvoiced grunt-like, unvoiced snort-like and mixed sounds [3,14]. The types of laughter may be differentiated by considering the emotion of the speaker as well; for example hearty, amused, satirical and social laughs [23]. At least 23 types of laughter have been identified (hilarious, anxious, embarrassed, etc.), where each laughter type has its own social function [21].

More recently, there has been more interest in creating automatic classifiers that are able to differentiate laughter types based on acoustics, facial expressions and body movement features (e.g. [2,15,31]). The laughter detector developed by Campbell et al. [6] can automatically recognize four laughter types based on the speaker's emotion in Japanese (the identification rate is greater than 75%). The results of Galvan et al. also supported the possibility of automatical discrimination among five types of acted laughter: happiness, giddiness, excitement, embarrassment and hurtful [7]. In their study, automatic recognition based only on the vocal features achieved higher accuracy scores (70% correct recognition) than by using both facial and vocal features (60%) or just facial features alone (40%).

In a previous study ([22]), we discriminated laughter based on the perceived sound according to the identity and/or number of participants (test person, other person(s), both), and according to the connection between laughter and speech. We distinguished five types of laughter, namely

(i) single laughter (**S**): only the speaker's laughter can be heard,
(ii) overlapping laughter (**O**): two or more speakers' laughter occur at the same time,
(iii) laughter during the speech of others (**D**): the test person's laughter is heard while another participant or participants are speaking,
(iv) laughed speech (**P**): the speaker's laughter co-occurs with their own speech,
(v) mixed (**M**): a mixture of the previous three categories (ii) + (iii) + (iv).

These five categories of laughter may be associated with various functions in conversations. Single laughter may be a sincere emotional expression or reaction to one's own message or the others' message. Overlapping laughter may indicate a cooperative act. Laughter during the speech of others may be a sign of attention or a feedback to their message as a backchannel. Laughed speech may express the fact that the speaker intends to refine or moderate the content of their message. A mixed type of laughter has diverse functions in conversation.

Laughter – due to its various functions – contributes to the organisation of conversation. We can get closer to understanding the structure of the conversation by analysing laughter types. However, to do this, first they have to be located and identified. In this study we seek to automatically classify laughter segments as one of these five pre-defined categories; to do this, we borrow

Table 1. Some important properties of the different laughter types in the dataset used.

	Laughter type					All laughter types	All utterances
	Single	Over-lapping	During other	Laughed speech	Mixed		
Total duration (m:ss)	2:12	2:13	4:17	1:52	1:27	12:01	147:36
% of duration	1.50%	1.50%	2.90%	1.26%	0.98%	8.14%	100.00%
Avg. duration (ms)	594	1087	937	1017	1887	930	—
Median duration (ms)	480	910	805	875	1620	740	—
No. of occurrences	223	122	274	110	46	775	—
% of occurrences	28.8%	15.7%	35.4%	14.2%	5.9%	100.0%	—
Frequency (1/s)	1.51	0.83	1.86	0.75	0.31	5.25	—

tools from Automatic Speech Recognition (ASR) such as acoustic feature sets and Deep Neural Networks (DNNs, [17]) for frame-level classification. To address both the *classification* and the *location* problems, in the second part of our study we combine the outputs of our frame-level DNNs with a Hidden Markov Model (HMM). However, as in laughter detection only a fraction of the training data corresponds to laughter, we shall use the sampling technique called *probabilistic sampling* [19] to assist frame-level DNN training.

2   The Recordings Used

Here, we used a part of the BEA Hungarian Spoken Language Database [9]. It is the largest speech database in Hungarian, which contains 260 h of material produced by 280 speakers (aged between 20 and 90 years), recorded in a sound-proof studio environment. In the present study we could use only the subset which had annotated laughter types at the time of writing, a total of 62 recordings of spontaneous conversations. The recordings lasted 148 min in total, from which we assigned 100 min (42 utterances) to the training set, while 20 and 27 min were assigned to the development set and the test set (10 recordings each). The segment boundaries of laughter segments were identified by human transcribers. Overall the total duration of laughter was 12 min, taking up 8.1% of all the utterances; of course, the different types of laughter were unevenly distributed.

Some main characteristics of the different laughter types in this dataset can be seen in Table 1. Unfortunately, the corpus we used is not very large, but it is typical in the area of laughter identification, especially if we can use only the utterances which have annotations about the types of laughter events. Surprisingly, the five types are roughly balanced when measured in total duration, the shortest sub-type (*Mixed*) taking up roughly 1% of the total playing time, and the most common one (*During others' speech*) comprised 2.9% of all the utterances. The main difference comes from the average duration and frequency of the types: the most frequently occurring laughter type was *Single*, but these laughter events were the shortest ones as well, while *Mixed* types occurred only once in three minutes of conversation, but then lasted for almost two seconds on average.

3   DNN Training by Probabilistic Sampling

For our experiments we borrowed techniques from Automatic Speech Recognition (ASR) such as Deep Neural Networks and Hidden Markov Models. Following standard ASR techniques, DNNs were used to provide a posterior probability estimate for each 10 ms for each utterance (i.e. for each *frame*). However, DNNs work best when they can be trained on hundreds or even thousands of hours of speech data (see e.g. [20]), and this amount is typically not available for laughter corpora. A further difference is that in ASR the classes are more-or-less uniformly present among the training frames, while in laughter detection only 4–8% of the duration corresponds to laughter, and the vast majority of training data belongs to the *non-laughter* class (i.e. other speech, silence and background noise). When we split the laughter class into several new classes, this class imbalance grows further.

The simplest solution for balancing the class distribution is to downsample the more frequent classes. This, however, results in data loss, hence it may also result in a drop in accuracy especially as our training set was quite small in the first place. A more refined solution is to *upsample* the rarer classes: we utilize the examples from these classes more frequently during training. A mathematically well-formulated upsampling strategy is the method called probabilistic sampling [19,29]. Probabilistic sampling selects the next training example following a two-step scheme. First we select a class according to some probability distribution, then we pick a training sample from the samples that belong to this class. For the first step, we assign the following probability to each class:

$$P(c_k) = \lambda \frac{1}{K} + (1 - \lambda)Prior(c_k), \tag{1}$$

where $Prior(c_k)$ is the prior probability of class c_k, K is the number of classes and $\lambda \in [0, 1]$ is a parameter. When $\lambda = 0$, the above formula returns the original class distribution, so probabilistic sampling will behave just as conventional sampling does. When $\lambda = 1$, we get a uniform distribution over the classes, so we get totally balanced samples with respect to class frequency. Selecting a value for λ between 0 and 1 allows us to linearly interpolate between the two distributions. According to our previous results, using probabilistic sampling can aid DNN training when the task is to detect laughter events [13] as well as other phenomena with rate occurrences such as filler events [12].

4   Classification Experiments

In the first series of experiments we just classify the laughter occurrences into one of the five types, relying on the manually annotated starting and ending points of the laughter segments. We simply trained our DNNs at the frame level and took the product of their output likelihoods, as in our previous studies we found that this approach worked quite well (see e.g. [11]). Following the results of preliminary tests, we divided the frame-level posterior estimates of the DNNs by the original class priors, which is common in HMM/DNN hybrids [4].

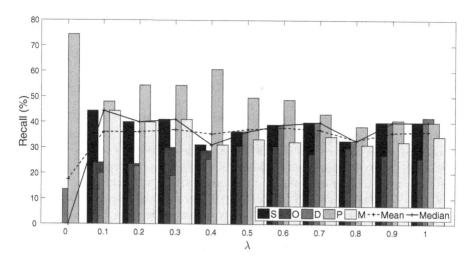

Fig. 1. Recall scores for the five laughter types on the development set as a function of λ.

Table 2. Some notable classification accuracy scores on the test set.

Classification method		Acc. (%)	Recalls (%)	
			Mean	Median
DNN with full sampling (baseline)		37.2	22.7	5.1
DNN + probabilistic sampling	$\lambda = 0.1$	35.3	**28.8**	**28.0**
	$\lambda = 0.6$	32.4	**27.2**	**26.1**
	$\lambda = 1.0$	30.1	**28.3**	**30.5**

4.1 DNN Parameters

We applied a DNN that had rectified linear units as hidden neurons [8,28] for frame-level classification. We used our custom DNN implementation [16], which achieved the best accuracy score published so far on the TIMIT database [27]. We employed DNNs with 5 hidden layers, each containing 256 rectified neurons. We applied the softmax function in the output layer. We used 40 mel filter bank energies as features along with first and second order derivatives, extracted using the HTK tool [30]. Training was performed on a sliding window containing 20 neighbouring frames from both sides, following the results of preliminary tests. Note that this sliding window size is quite large compared to ones used in speech recognition; but for laughter detection, using this many frames is clearly beneficial (see e.g. [5,11]).

4.2   Probabilistic Sampling

We evaluated the probabilistic sampling technique by varying the value of λ in the range $[0, 1]$ with a step size of 0.1. To reduce the effect of DNN random weight initialization, we trained five DNN models for each λ value; then we chose the value of λ based on the results obtained on the development set.

4.3   Evaluation

Since this was simply a classification task, we could have measured efficiency using the standard classification accuracy metric. However, it is well known that when class distribution is uneven, classification accuracy is biased towards the classes having more examples. Therefore we decided to calculate the recall of each laughter type. Afterwards, we aggregated the five recall values into one accuracy score via a simple arithmetic mean and median.

4.4   Results

Figure 1 shows the recall values got on the development set for all laughter types as a function of the λ parameter of probabilistic sampling. It is quite apparent that the values are not really consistent without applying probabilistic sampling (shown as $\lambda = 0$): actually no examples were classified as laughter types S, D and M. Using larger values for λ tends to balance the recall values of the five kinds of laughter, which is also reflected in the mean and median values. In our opinion, when the task is to identify the occurrences of distinct laughter sub-classes, the performance of an approach is more accurately described by the mean and even more so by the median of the recall values than traditional classification accuracy scores. Clearly, for values $\lambda \geq 0.5$ our approach works well for all laughter types, while it leads to a lower classification accuracy score.

Table 2 lists the accuracy, mean and median recall scores we got on the test set for some notable values of λ. (Values exceeding the baseline score are shown as **bold**.) Notice that the baseline case has the highest classification accuracy score (37.2%), but the low mean and especially the median recall value (5.1%) suggests a highly uneven behaviour. Overall, like that for the development set, all values of $\lambda \geq 0.1$ give a similar performance, which is significantly better than that for the baseline DNNs trained without probabilistic sampling.

5   Experiments with a Hidden Markov Model

Laughter (segment) classification is a simplified task in the sense that we rely on segment starting and ending points marked by human annotators. In the last part of our study we perform laughter *detection*, where, besides laughter types, we also have to find the *locations* of the different occurrences. We will do this by incorporating our likelihood values supported by DNNs into a Hidden Markov Model (HMM). In this set-up, the state transition probabilities of the HMM practically correspond to a state-level bi-gram language model. Following the study of Salamin et al. [26], we calculated the model from statistics of the training set; the weight of this language model was determined on the development set, individually for the five DNN models trained.

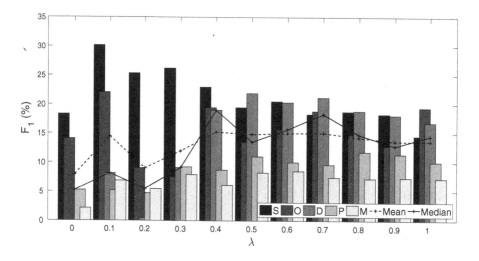

Fig. 2. Segment-level F_1 scores measured on the development set.

Table 3. Some notable segment-level F1 scores obtained on the test set.

Sampling approach	$F_1(\%)$						
	S	**O**	**D**	**P**	**M**	Mean	Median
DNN (baseline)	18.3	14.1	0.0	5.2	2.2	8.0	5.2
DNN + prob. sampling, $\lambda = 0.4$	**23.0**	**19.5**	**19.0**	**8.7**	**6.1**	**15.3**	**19.0**
DNN + prob. sampling, $\lambda = 1.0$	14.5	**19.4**	16.8	**10.1**	**7.3**	13.6	14.5

5.1   Evaluation Metrics

We opted for the information retrieval (IR) metrics of *precision, recall* and their harmonic mean, *F-measure* (or F_1). To decide whether two occurrences of events (i.e. a laughter occurrence hypothesis returned by the HMM and one labeled by an annotator) match, there is no de facto standard in the literature. In this study we required that the two occurrences intersect (as in [10] and [24]), while their centre also had to be close to each other (within 500 ms, as in [1]). Furthermore, following the work of Salamin et al. [26], we calculated these metrics at the frame level as well. Since the optimal meta-parameters (λ and language model weight) may differ in the two (evaluation) approaches used, we set them independently.

5.2   Results

Figures 2 and 3 show the averaged F_1 scores got on the development set at the segment level and frame level, respectively. It can be seen that the smaller λ values ($\lambda \leq 0.3$ and $\lambda \leq 0.4$, at the segment and frame level, respectively) led to quite low F_1 values for some laughter types, while for larger λ parameters we had a more balanced behaviour. This is also reflected in the mean and median F_1 scores. At the segment level, optimality is achieved with $\lambda = 0.4$, while at the frame level it is with $\lambda = 0.1$ (mean) and with $\lambda = 0.5$ (median).

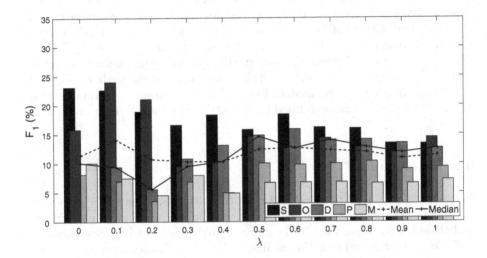

Fig. 3. Frame-level F_1 scores measured on the development set.

Table 4. Some notable frame-level F1 scores obtained on the test set.

Sampling approach	$F_1(\%)$						
	S	**O**	**D**	**P**	**M**	Mean	Median
DNN (baseline)	23.1	15.8	0.0	8.1	10.1	11.4	10.1
DNN + prob. sampling, $\lambda = 0.1$	22.6	**24.0**	9.4	6.9	7.4	**14.1**	9.4
DNN + prob. sampling, $\lambda = 0.5$	15.8	14.6	**14.8**	10.0	6.7	**12.4**	14.6
DNN + prob. sampling, $\lambda = 1.0$	13.4	14.4	**12.6**	9.4	7.2	**11.4**	12.6

Overall, the F_1 scores seem to be somewhat low, even after applying probabilistic sampling. In our opinion, however, these are quite realistic scores, for two reasons. Firstly, even when we treat laughter as one class, we get F_1 values between 40 and 60% (see e.g. [10,13,26]), which is likely to be reduced further when we split the laughter class into several sub-classes. Secondly, recall that the laughter sub-types were defined based on the relation between the laughter event and the other speaker's speech. This, combined with the large duration of laughter events, eventually leads to mixed laughter occurrences. For example, in an overlapping laughter event both the speakers are probably not laughing for the whole duration, but in some parts only one of them is (while the other speaks or remains silent). This, however, is quite hard to detect at the frame level.

Examining Tables 3 and 4 (containing the interesting F_1 scores obtained on the test set at the segment level and frame level, respectively), we see that the F_1 value of the Mixed laughter type is the lowest, which is probably due to the latter phenomenon. Overall, the F_1 values are more balanced for the different laughter types when using probabilistic sampling, and when we use the λ values found optimal on the development set, we get better results than either without probabilistic sampling or with uniform sampling (i.e. $\lambda = 1$). We got the highest frame-level mean F_1 value in the case where the mean was highest on the development set ($\lambda = 0.1$), and the same holds for the median ($\lambda = 0.5$). Overall, optimizing for the median led to a more balanced performance than optimizing for the mean, which led to a mixture or relatively high and low F_1 values.

6   Conclusions

In this study we sought to detect and identify multiple laughter types in Hungarian spontaneous conversations. We performed simple classification experiments and those where the location of laughter occurrences had to be determined as well. Overall, we found that the median of F_1 scores characterizes performance better than the arithmetic mean does, and the technique of probabilistic sampling aids the training of frame-level DNNs in the task of laughter sub-group classification, where the training data has a highly imbalanced class distribution.

References

1. NIST Spoken Term Detection 2006 Evaluation Plan (2006). http://www.nist.gov/speech/tests/std/docs/std06-evalplan-v10.pdf
2. Ayadi, M.E., Kamel, M.S., Karray, F.: Survey on speech emotion recognition: features, classification schemes, and databases. Pattern Recogn. **44**(3), 572–587 (2011)
3. Bachorowski, J.A., Smoski, M.J., Owren, M.J.: The acoustic features of human laughter. J. Acoust. Soc. Am. **110**(3), 1581–1597 (2001)
4. Bourlard, H., Morgan, N.: Connectionist Speech Recognition - A Hybrid Approach. Kluwer Academic (1994)
5. Brueckner, R., Schuller, B.: Hierarchical neural networks and enhanced class posteriors for social signal classification. In: Proceedings of ASRU, pp. 362–367 (2013)
6. Campbell, N., Kashioka, H., Ohara, R.: No laughing matter. In: Proceedings of Interspeech, pp. 465–468, Lisbon, Portugal (2005)
7. Galvan, C., Manangan, D., Sanchez, M., Wong, J., Cu, J.: Audiovisual affect recognition in spontaneous Filipino laughter. In: Proceedings of KSE, pp. 266–271 (2011)

8. Glorot, X., Bordes, A., Bengio, Y.: Deep sparse rectifier networks. In: Proceedings of AISTATS, pp. 315–323 (2011)

9. Gósy, M.: BEA: a multifunctional Hungarian spoken language database. Phonetician 105(106), 50–61 (2012)

10. Gosztolya, G.: On evaluation metrics for social signal detection. In: Proceedings of Interspeech, pp. 2504–2508, Dresden, Germany, September 2015

11. Gosztolya, G., Beke, A., Neuberger, T., Tóth, L.: Laughter classification using Deep Rectifier Neural Networks with a minimal feature subset. Arch. Acoust. 41(4), 669–682 (2016)

12. Gosztolya, G., Grósz, T., Tóth, L.: Social signal detection by probabilistic sampling DNN training. IEEE Trans. Affect. Comput. (2019, to appear)

13. Gosztolya, G., Grósz, T., Tóth, L., Beke, A., Neubergers, T.: Neurális hálók tanítása valószínűségi mintavételezéssel nevetések felismerésére. In: Proceedings of MSZNY, pp. 136–145, Szeged, Hungary (2017). (in Hungarian)

14. Grammer, K., Eibl-Eibesfeldt, I.: The ritualisation of laughter, Chapter 10. In: Natürlichkeit der Sprache und der Kultur: Acta colloquii, pp. 192–214, Brockmeyer (1990)

15. Griffin, H.J., et al.: Laughter type recognition from whole body motion. In: Proceedings of ACII, pp. 349–355 (2013)

16. Tóth, L., Grósz, T.: A comparison of deep neural network training methods for large vocabulary speech recognition. In: Habernal, I., Matoušek, V. (eds.) TSD 2013. LNCS (LNAI), vol. 8082, pp. 36–43. Springer, Heidelberg (2013). https://doi.org/10.1007/978-3-642-40585-3_6

17. Hinton, G., et al.: Deep neural networks for acoustic modeling in speech recognition: the shared views of four research groups. IEEE Signal Process. Mag. 29(6), 82–97 (2012)

18. Laskowski, K.: Contrasting emotion-bearing laughter types in multi participant vocal activity detection for meetings. In: Proceedings of ICASSP, pp. 4765–4768 (2009)

19. Lawrence, S., Burns, I., Back, A., Tsoi, A.C., Giles, C.L.: Neural network classification and prior class probabilities. In: Orr, G.B., Müller, K.-R. (eds.) Neural Networks: Tricks of the Trade. LNCS, vol. 1524, pp. 299–313. Springer, Heidelberg (1998). https://doi.org/10.1007/3-540-49430-8_15

20. McDermott, E., Heigold, G., Moreno, P., Senior, A., Bacchiani, M.: Asynchronous stochastic optimization for sequence training of Deep Neural Networks: towards big data. In: Proceedings of Interspeech, pp. 1224–1228, September 2014

21. McKeown, G., Cowie, R., Curran, W., Ruch, W., Douglas-Cowie, E.: Ilhaire laughter database. In: Proceedings of LREC, pp. 32–35 (2012)

22. Neuberger, T., Beke, A.: Automatic laughter detection in Hungarian spontaneous speech using GMM/ANN hybrid method. In: Proceedings of SJUSK Conference on Contemporary Speech Habits, pp. 1–13 (2013)

23. Ohara, R.: Analysis of a laughing voice and the method of laughter in dialogue speech. Master's thesis, Nara Institute of Science and Technology, Ikoma, Japan (2004)

24. Pokorny, F.B., et al.: Manual versus automated: the challenging routine of infant vocalisation segmentation in home videos to study neuro(mal)development. In: Proceedings of Interspeech, San Francisco, CA, USA, pp. 2997–3001, September 2016

25. Ross, M.D., Owren, M.J., Zimmermann, E.: The evolution of laughter in great apes and humans. Commun. Integr. Biol. 3(2), 191–194 (2010)

26. Salamin, H., Polychroniou, A., Vinciarelli, A.: Automatic detection of laughter and fillers in spontaneous mobile phone conversations. In: Proceedings of SMC, pp. 4282–4287 (2013)
27. Tóth, L.: Phone recognition with hierarchical Convolutional Deep Maxout Networks. EURASIP J. Audio Speech Music Process. **2015**(25), 1–13 (2015)
28. Tóth, L.: Phone recognition with deep sparse rectifier neural networks. In: Proceedings of ICASSP, pp. 6985–6989 (2013)
29. Tóth, L., Kocsor, A.: Training HMM/ANN hybrid speech recognizers by probabilistic sampling. In: Duch, W., Kacprzyk, J., Oja, E., Zadrożny, S. (eds.) ICANN 2005. LNCS, vol. 3696, pp. 597–603. Springer, Heidelberg (2005). https://doi.org/10.1007/11550822_93
30. Young, S., et al.: The HTK Book. Cambridge University Engineering Department, Cambridge (2006)
31. Zeng, Z., Pantic, M., Roisman, G., Huang, T.: A survey of affect recognition methods: audio, visual, and spontaneous expressions. IEEE Trans. Pattern Anal. Mach. Intell. **31**(1), 39–58 (2009)

Word Discovering in Low-Resources Languages Through Cross-Lingual Phonemes

Fernando García-Granada[✉], Emilio Sanchis[✉], Maria Jose Castro-Bleda[✉],
José Ángel González[✉], and Lluís-F. Hurtado[✉]

VRAIN Valencian Research Institute for Artificial Intelligence,
Universitat Politècnica de València, Camino de Vera s/n., 46022 Valencia, Spain
{fgarcia,esanchis,mcastro,jogonba2,lhurtado}@dsic.upv.es

Abstract. An approach for discovering word units in an unknown language under zero resources conditions is presented in this paper. The method is based only on acoustic similarity, combining a cross-lingual phoneme recognition, followed by an identification of consistent strings of phonemes. To this end, a 2-phases algorithm is proposed. The first phase consists of an acoustic-phonetic decoding process, considering a universal set of phonemes, not related with the target language. The goal is to reduce the search space of similar segments of speech, avoiding the quadratic search space if all-to-all speech files are compared. In the second phase, a further refinement of the founded segments is done by means of different approaches based on Dynamic Time Warping. In order to include more hypotheses than only those that correspond to perfect matching in terms of phonemes, an edit distance is calculated for the purpose to also incorporate hypotheses under a given threshold. Three frame representations are studied: raw acoustic features, autoencoders and phoneme posteriorgrams. This approach has been evaluated on the corpus used in Zero resources speech challenge 2017.

Keywords: Zero resources · Dynamic Time Warping · Autoencoders

1 Introduction

The zero resource speech task aims to automatically discover speech units without any linguistic knowledge. Most of the approaches to this problem are based on specific representations of the acoustic characteristics, and on the definition of a distance among segments to detect similarities [2,3,6,11,14–16,19–22]. The high computational complexity of a brute force approach (every speech file is compared against each other), forces to choose other methods, such as performing a previous analysis of the signal in order to detect some candidate segments. In our system, we have used a labeling process of the speech signal in terms of a set of universal phonetic units. This set is composed of phoneme models from a language which is different to the target language.

© Springer Nature Switzerland AG 2019
A. A. Salah et al. (Eds.): SPECOM 2019, LNAI 11658, pp. 133–141, 2019.
https://doi.org/10.1007/978-3-030-26061-3_14

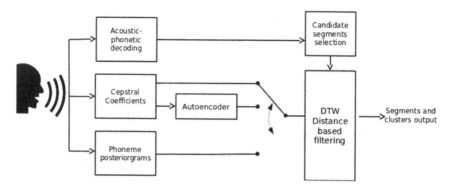

Fig. 1. Scheme of the system. One of three alternatives is chosen for the DTW filtering process: MFCC, autoenconder characteristics, or phoneme posteriorgrams.

Thus, the corpus can be labeled in linear time with the length of the data. In an ideal situation with no errors in the phonetic labeling, the segments that are labeled with the same sequence of phonemes would belong to the same class (each class representing a discovered word). But the acoustic-phonetic decoding errors make necessary to consider a larger number of hypotheses per class. This can be done by also including in the same class those segments with similar sequences of labels. We consider two sequences to be similar if their edit distance is lower than a given threshold. In a second phase, a pruning of the segments in each class is performed. This pruning is done by considering different Dynamic Time Warping (DTW) distances. These distances are based on three different speech representations: Mel-Frequency Cepstral Coefficients (MFCC), a compact representation of the MFCC using autoencoders, and phoneme posteriorgrams.

The remainder of this paper is organized as follows. Section 2 presents our system, Sect. 3 describes the autoencoder representation, Sect. 4 describes the corpus characteristics and the evaluation measures, and Sect. 5 describes the tuning process and the preliminary experiments done for tuning purposes. The experimental results are described and analyzed in Sect. 6, and finally some conclusions are exposed.

2   System Overview

The architecture of the system is illustrated in Fig. 1. The system is a combination of cross-lingual phoneme recognition, followed by identifying consistent strings of phonemes and doing some filtering based on the speech representations of candidate words. Our approach is composed of two phases. The first phase consists of an acoustic-phonetic decoding process that provides a sequence of phonetic labels associated to the sequence of speech frames. We have used a set of phonemes of a language not related with the target language because the goal is, precisely, to discover words without linguistic knowledge of the target language. The phoneme recognizer toolkit based on long temporal context, developed at Brno University of Technology, Faculty of Information Technology, was used for our experiments [18]. This decoder has four available systems, for Czech, English, Hungarian and Russian languages. The Hungarian decoder which uses 61 phonetic units (including three specialized units to represent noise or silence) was chosen [23].

Once the phonetic labeling is done, a process of selection of similar segments is performed. The criterion to group two segments is that they must have a distance smaller than a threshold between them. We have considered the distance zero (same sequence of phonetic units) and distance one (one phonetic unit of difference). Finally, only those classes that have more than three members are selected.

After the candidate segments for each class have been selected, a second phase to filter hypotheses is performed. To do this, three alternative speech signal representations are used:

- speech signal parametrized in terms of Cepstral coefficients plus derivatives, MFCC+Delta+Delta2,
- a compact representation of MFCC by means of an autoencoder (see Sect. 3) which generates 10-dimension vectors, and
- a representation of each frame composed by the phoneme posteriorgrams of the 61 considered phonemes from the Hungarian decoder.

Considering the previous representations, all-to-all distances among segments in each class are calculated. The distances are obtained by a DTW algorithm using cosine distance. These distances are used to eliminate the segments far from the centroid of the class.

Another heuristic refinement was to avoid overlaps among the candidates, that is, some segments corresponding to a sequence of n phonemes can contain subsegments of length $n-1$, $n-2$, ... corresponding to other selected segments. The discarding process consists of eliminating the candidates which overlapped more than 80% in the time, always leaving the longest segment and discarding the smallest one.

3 Autoencoders

An autoencoder is a neural network trained to learn efficient encodings in an unsupervised way. The aim of an autoencoder is to learn a more useful representation of data, by reconstructing the input at the output layer, in order to typically perform a dimensionality reduction that captures useful properties of the data [9] (similar to principal component analysis but using non-linear transformations). For this reason, this kind of systems was used in previous zero resources tasks, yielding large reductions on the error rate [1, 17].

The autoencoder used in our experiments consists of a single hidden layer ϕ with ReLU activation functions [13], which transform the input $x \in \mathbb{R}^d$ into an alternative lower dimensional representation space, $\mathbb{R}^{d'} : d' << d$; i.e. $\phi : \mathbb{R}^d \rightarrow$

$\mathbb{R}^{d'}$. Regarding to the reconstruction step, a linear layer ψ which transforms $z \in \mathbb{R}^{d'}$ to the original space $\mathbb{R}^d$ is used, then $\psi : \mathbb{R}^{d'} \to \mathbb{R}^d$. It should be noted that the training was done with the objective of minimizing the squared error of the reconstruction,

$$\phi, \psi = \underset{\phi, \psi}{\text{argmin}} \, \|X - \psi(\phi(X))\|^2 \,,$$

making use of the Adagrad optimization method [7] iterated during 60 epochs.

More concretely, given a sequence x of N cepstral vectors and derivatives, the autoencoder is independently applied to every vector $x_i \in \mathbb{R}^{39}$. The result is a new sequence y, also of N vectors, in which each element y_i is dimensionally reduced as $y_i \in \mathbb{R}^{10}$. Note that each vector is treated independently so the dimensionality reduction does not take into account context information of the sequence as other techniques do [4,5].

4   Corpus and Evaluation Measures

Three languages are available for training: English, French and Mandarin, and two unknown languages for test. The test languages turned out to be German and Wolof. Data are read speech and open source (either gathered from open source audio books, or open datasets). A forced alignment has been performed in order to build the corpus.

The training corpus consists of 64 wav files for English with a total amount of more than 38 h, 28 wav files for French (around 25 h) and finally 12 wav files for Mandarin (more than 2 h). All wav files are sampled at 16 KHz.

Three types of measures were defined for evaluation purposes: The first one mesures the phoneme similarity between the segments associated to words and the references. The second set measures the quality of groups of segments obtained, that is, if the segments represents the same word. And the third set measures the boundaries obtained [8]:

1. Evaluation as matching system. It consists of two scores:
   - **NED** is the average, over all matched pairs, of the Levenshtein distance between their phonemic transcriptions, with respect to the gold phonemic transcriptions of the fragments.
   - **Coverage (COV)** is the fraction of the corpus that is covered by all the discovered fragments. The discovered fragments are computed as the union of all of the intervals corresponding to all of the pairs of n-grams (with n between 3 and 20).
2. Evaluation as lexicon discovery system. Six scores were defined:
   - **Grouping Precision**, **Recall**, and **F-score**. These are defined in terms of the set of all pairs that are in the same cluster in the output of the system. The Grouping Recall is the set of all non-overlapping pairs of fragments which are both discovered by the system (not necessarily in the same cluster) and have exactly the same gold transcription.

Table 1. Results obtained from the spoken French sentences.

Method	Words	NED	COV	Grouping			Type			Token			Boundary		
				P	R	F	P	R	F	P	R	F	P	R	F
From9to3	205975	69.0	85.8	5.3	11.9	7.4	9.2	33.4	1.45	2.6	18.9	4.5	22.8	71.4	34.6
From7to4	85580	63.4	76.0	6.2	32.9	10.3	6.1	17.5	9.1	2.4	7.4	3.6	23.8	61.5	34.3
7grams	517	15.6	1.1	76.3	100.0	84.4	4.5	0.1	0.2	3.5	0.0	0.1	28.5	0.5	0.9
6grams	4603	38.1	8.0	26.3	96.9	39.9	2.6	0.5	0.8	1.9	0.2	0.3	27.3	3.8	6.6
5grams	28486	55.2	38.3	9.8	88.8	17.4	3.4	4.0	3.7	2.1	1.4	1.7	25.5	25.0	25.2
4grams	45453	63.0	69.7	6.1	36.6	10.4	4.8	12.1	6.9	2.6	5.0	3.4	24.2	56.2	33.9

- **Type Precision, Recall**, and **F-score**. Type Precision is the probability that discovered types belong to the gold set whereas Type Recall is the probability that gold types are discovered.

3. Evaluation as word segmentation system. Six scores were defined:
   - **Token Precision, Recall**, and **F-score**. Token Precision is the probability that discovered fragment tokens that are in the gold set. Token Recall is the probability that the gold fragments are discovered.
   - **Boundary Precision, Recall**, and **F-score**. They are defined with respect to the set of discovered and gold word boundaries.

5 Tuning Process

We have done some tests using the French data in order to tune the parameters of the system. These experiments are shown in Table 1. The first experiment consisted of looking for the phoneme sequences found by the acoustic-phonetic decoder of different sizes: 9, 8, 7, 6, 5, 4, and 3 phonemes (From9to3) in order to verify if the coverage of the acoustic phonetic decoding has been correct. We obtained a coverage up to 85.5%. Other experiments were performed taking into account only the sequences of 7, 6, 5, and 4 phonemes (7grams, 6grams...), in order to see their influence in the result. We concluded that using sequences of sizes from 7 to 4 phonemes (From7to4) was the most appropriate, reaching a high coverage, 76%, with a moderate NED of 63.4%.

In addition, experiments were carried out to test the best configuration for the second part of our system, which consists of filtering the candidates within the classes using DTW with the cosine distance. Results are shown in Table 2. To do this filtering all the acoustic segments corresponding to the phonetic sequences into a class are compared among them. This comparison is performed by means of a DTW algorithm that supplies a normalized distance between each two acoustic segments. These distances were calculated by using the three studied representations for the frames: MFCC (Filcepstrals), the autoencoder representation (Filautoenc), and the phoneme posteriorgrams (Filposterior). Using these distances a threshold is used to discard segments that are far from the centroid. The more restricted threshold, the more precision, but at the cost of coverage. It

Table 2. Results obtained from the spoken French sentences using sequences of phonemes from length 7 to 4.

Method	Words	NED	COV	Grouping			Type			Token			Boundary		
				P	R	F	P	R	F	P	R	F	P	R	F
Filcepstrals	81104	62.4	72.3	6.6	36.6	11.2	5.9	16.0	8.6	2.4	6.7	3.5	24.1	58.4	34.1
Filautoenc	79052	62.2	71.1	6.7	37.3	11.3	5.9	15.6	8.5	2.4	6.5	3.5	24.2	57.2	34.0
Filposterior	83623	61.2	72.3	7.1	38.7	12.0	5.9	15.9	8.6	2.4	6.7	3.5	24.1	58.0	34.0

Table 3. Baseline results from [8].

Language	Words	Pairs	NED	COV	Grouping			Type			Token			Boundary		
					P	R	F	P	R	F	P	R	F	P	R	F
English	12886	15730	33.9	7.9	34.7	96.6	47.9	5.0	0.7	1.2	3.9	0.3	0.5	33.9	3.1	5.7
French	1803	1636	25.4	1.6	81.1	66.4	64.2	6.9	0.2	0.3	5.2	0.1	0.1	30.9	0.6	1.1
Mandarin	156	160	30.7	2.9	30.2	96.7	44.7	4.5	0.1	0.2	4.0	0.1	0.1	37.5	0.9	1.8
German	2973	3315	30.5	3.0	54.8	94.6	64.9	5.5	0.3	0.6	4.0	0.1	0.2	28.2	1.2	2.3
Wolof	462	545	33.5	3.2	39.1	72.1	32.8	2.3	0.1	0.2	1.6	0.0	0.1	25.3	1.0	2.0

should be noted that this process is strongly conditioned by the previous selection of segments based on phonetic similarity. Therefore it is not possible in this phase to add new segments, only the refinement in terms of precision is possible.

Different values were experimentally tested and it was concluded that a value of 1.2 times the mean of distances among all of them was the most suitable threshold. Similar performance for the three data sources (MFCC, autoencoder representation and phoneme posteriorgrams) was obtained, choosing the autoencoder representation due to the fact that it can be more independent of the phonetic characteristics of the new target languages, such as oriental languages.

6   Experiments

Table 3 shows the baseline results given by the Zero Resource Speech Challenge 2017, organized by Dunbar et al. [8]. The baseline system was computed using PLP features [10] and obtaining groups of pairs using graph clustering. The parameters of the system stayed the same across all languages, except for Mandarin, in order to obtain a NED value similar to that of other languages [8].

Results of our first system are shown in Table 4. It uses a supervised Automatic Speech Recognition system for Hungarian to decode the speech. Chunks of (transcribed) speech match if they have the same transcription. These matches are then filtered: a representation of the speech is obtained by training an autoencoder, and only pairs with DTW sufficiently low in this representational space (below a threshold) are retained.

We also analyzed the idea of joining classes whose difference of edit distance between their associated phoneme sequence was equal to one. A Longest Common Subsequence between the sequences of phonemes algorithm was implemented to this end. Table 5 shows the results of this second system.

Table 4. Results obtained from the first system.

Language	Words	Pairs	NED	COV	Grouping			Type			Token			Boundary		
					P	R	F	P	R	F	P	R	F	P	R	F
English	92544	864639	71.4	71.0	3.3	76.2	6.2	3.9	8.6	5.4	3.2	3.5	3.3	27.1	29.4	32.1
French	58701	515507	62.8	67.0	6.1	82.3	11.3	3.3	6.4	4.4	2.6	2.7	2.7	26.1	37.4	30.7
Mandarin	2887	17845	80.2	45.4	2.4	45.0	4.6	4.5	2.9	3.5	3.6	2.0	2.6	22.8	18.6	20.5
German	60658	582009	59.9	71.8	5.7	63.8	10.4	3.2	6.8	4.3	2.4	3.1	2.7	20.6	37.2	26.6
Wolof	5468	37191	56.8	47.8	7.6	43.3	12.8	5.9	8.2	6.9	6.1	4.2	4.9	29.6	29.6	29.6

Table 5. Results obtained from the second system.

Language	Words	Pairs	NED	COV	Grouping			Type			Token			Boundary		
					P	R	F	P	R	F	P	R	F	P	R	F
English	92466	866170	71.4	71.0	3.2	75.8	6.2	3.9	8.6	5.4	3.2	3.5	3.3	27.0	39.4	32.1
French	58716	518113	62.7	67.0	6.3	81.7	11.6	3.3	6.4	4.4	2.6	2.7	2.7	26.0	37.4	30.7
Mandarin	2882	17824	80.0	43.3	2.5	45.3	4.7	4.4	2.9	3.5	3.6	2.0	2.5	22.7	18.5	20.4
German	60498	588162	59.9	71.8	5.8	64.0	10.7	3.2	6.8	4.3	2.4	3.1	2.7	20.6	37.2	26.5
Wolof	5460	37273	56.8	47.8	7.7	44.0	13.0	6.0	8.3	7.0	6.1	4.2	4.9	29.7	29.6	29.6

As the results show, there are not significative differences between both systems. This can be explained by the fact that the selecting phase is very determinant for the posterior processes. On the other hand, results are logically better for occidental languages that for Mandarin, probably because the set of phonemes chosen is more related to these languages.

As seen from the Tables, results are very sensible to the thresholds to accept or discard hypotheses.

Comparing to the baseline, our systems generate much more hypotheses, and therefore our precision in terms of NED (that is, the Levenshtein distance of our word pairs hypotheses) is lower, but the coverage is much more higher. It should be noted that the baseline is very restricted for generation hypotheses, because (in German, for example) for more than 2 millions of words they propose only 3315 pairs, and our system more that 500000 pairs.

Other systems, from Kamper et al. [12], uses k-means to discover acoustic patterns, jointly optimized with an exhaustive segmentation. On the other hand, our grouping results clearly works better than the baseline k-means clustering, and better recall than the system Kamper et al. [12].

7   Conclusions

In this paper we have presented our approach to word discovering in raw speech. Our runs are based in a previous phase of selection of candidate segments considering a generic transcription of the speech, in order to avoid the computational complexity of a brute force approach. Once the candidate segments are selected, a filtering of the results is done by means of DTW distances. Results show that the approach is reasonable even with the strong simplification of the first phase. As future works we want to explore other ways to select segment candidates.

Acknowledgments. This work was funded by the Spanish MINECO and FEDER founds under contract TIN2017-85854-C4-2-R. Work of José-Ángel González is also financed by Universitat Politècnica de València under grant PAID-01-17.

References

1. Badino, L., Canevari, C., Fadiga, L., Metta, G.: An auto-encoder based approach to unsupervised learning of subword units. In: 2014 IEEE International Conference on Acoustics, Speech and Signal Processing (ICASSP), pp. 7634–7638, May 2014. https://doi.org/10.1109/ICASSP.2014.6855085
2. Badino, L., Mereta, A., Rosasco, L.: Discovering discrete subword units with binarized autoencoders and hidden-Markov-model encoders. In: INTERSPEECH (2015)
3. Baljekar, P., Sitaram, S., Muthukumar, P.K., Black, A.W.: Using articulatory features and inferred phonological segments in zero resource speech processing. In: Sixteenth Annual Conference of the International Speech Communication Association (2015)
4. Bowman, S.R., Vilnis, L., Vinyals, O., Dai, A.M., Józefowicz, R., Bengio, S.: Generating sentences from a continuous space. CoRR abs/1511.06349 (2015). http://arxiv.org/abs/1511.06349
5. Dai, A.M., Le, Q.V.: Semi-supervised sequence learning. In: Cortes, C., Lawrence, N.D., Lee, D.D., Sugiyama, M., Garnett, R. (eds.) Advances in Neural Information Processing Systems, vol. 28, pp. 3079–3087. Curran Associates, Inc. (2015). http://papers.nips.cc/paper/5949-semi-supervised-sequence-learning.pdf
6. Driesen, J., ten Bosch, L., hamme, H.V.: Adaptive non-negative matrix factorization in a computational model of language acquisition. In: INTERSPEECH (2009)
7. Duchi, J., Hazan, E., Singer, Y.: Adaptive subgradient methods for online learning and stochastic optimization. J. Mach. Learn. Res. **12**, 2121–2159 (2011). http://dl.acm.org/citation.cfm?id=1953048.2021068
8. Dunbar, E., et al.: The zero resource speech challenge 2017. In: 2017 IEEE Automatic Speech Recognition and Understanding Workshop (ASRU), pp. 323–330, December 2017. https://doi.org/10.1109/ASRU.2017.8268953
9. Hinton, G.E., Zemel, R.S.: Autoencoders, minimum description length and Helmholtz free energy. In: Cowan, J.D., Tesauro, G., Alspector, J. (eds.) Advances in Neural Information Processing Systems, vol. 6, pp. 3–10. Morgan-Kaufmann (1994). http://papers.nips.cc/paper/798-autoencoders-minimum-description-length-and-helmholtz-free-energy.pdf
10. Jansen, A., Durme, B.V.: Efficient spoken term discovery using randomized algorithms. In: 2011 IEEE Workshop on Automatic Speech Recognition Understanding, pp. 401–406, December 2011. https://doi.org/10.1109/ASRU.2011.6163965
11. Jansen, A., Church, K.: Towards unsupervised training of speaker independent acoustic models. In: INTERSPEECH 2011, 12th Annual Conference of the International Speech Communication Association, Florence, Italy, 27–31 August 2011, pp. 1693–1692 (2011). http://www.isca-speech.org/archive/interspeech_2011/i11_1693.html

12. Kamper, H., Livescu, K., Goldwater, S.: An embedded segmental k-means model for unsupervised segmentation and clustering of speech. CoRR abs/1703.08135 (2017). http://arxiv.org/abs/1703.08135

13. Nair, V., Hinton, G.E.: Rectified linear units improve restricted Boltzmann machines. In: Fürnkranz, J., Joachims, T. (eds.) Proceedings of the 27th International Conference on Machine Learning (ICML 2010), pp. 807–814. Omnipress (2010). http://www.icml2010.org/papers/432.pdf

14. Park, A.S., Glass, J.R.: Unsupervised pattern discovery in speech. IEEE Trans. Audio Speech Lang. Process. **16**(1), 186–197 (2008). https://doi.org/10.1109/TASL.2007.909282

15. Qin, L., Rudnicky, A.I.: OOV word detection using hybrid models with mixed types of fragments. In: INTERSPEECH (2012)

16. Räsänen, O.: A computational model of word segmentation from continuous speech using transitional probabilities of atomic acoustic events. Cognition **120**(2), 149–176 (2011)

17. Renshaw, D., Kamper, H., Jansen, A., Goldwater, S.: A comparison of neural network methods for unsupervised representation learning on the zero resource speech challenge. In: Sixteenth Annual Conference of the International Speech Communication Association (2015)

18. Schwarz, P., Matejka, P., Burget, L., Glembek, O.: Phoneme recognizer based on long temporal context. http://speech.fit.vutbr.cz/software/phoneme-recognizer-based-long-temporal-context

19. Siu, M.H., Gish, H., Chan, A., Belfield, W., Lowe, S.: Unsupervised training of an HMM-based self-organizing unit recognizer with applications to topic classification and keyword discovery. Comput. Speech Lang. **28**(1), 210–223 (2014). https://doi.org/10.1016/j.csl.2013.05.002

20. Vanhainen, N., Salvi, G.: Word discovery with beta process factor analysis. In: Thirteenth Annual Conference of the International Speech Communication Association (2012)

21. Vanhainen, N., Salvi, G.: Pattern discovery in continuous speech using block diagonal infinite hmm. In: 2014 IEEE International Conference on Acoustics, Speech and Signal Processing (ICASSP), pp. 3719–3723. IEEE (2014)

22. Zhang, Y., Glass, J.R.: Unsupervised spoken keyword spotting via segmental DTW on Gaussian posteriorgrams. In: 2009 IEEE Workshop on Automatic Speech Recognition Understanding, pp. 398–403, November 2009. https://doi.org/10.1109/ASRU.2009.5372931

23. Zhang, Y., Glass, J.R.: Unsupervised spoken keyword spotting via segmental DTW on Gaussian posteriorgrams. In: IEEE Workshop on Automatic Speech Recognition & Understanding, ASRU 2009, pp. 398–403. IEEE (2009)

Semantic Segmentation of Historical Documents via Fully-Convolutional Neural Network

Ivan Gruber[1,2,3(✉)], Miroslav Hlaváč[1,2,3], Marek Hrúz[1,2], and Miloš Železný[1]

[1] Faculty of Applied Sciences, DEPT of Cybernetics, UWB, Pilsen, Czech Republic
{mhlavac,zelezny}@kky.zcu.cz
[2] Faculty of Applied Sciences, NTIS, UWB, Pilsen, Czech Republic
{grubiv,mhruz}@ntis.zcu.cz
[3] ITMO University, St. Petersburg, Russia

Abstract. This paper presents a method for character semantic segmentation in full-text documents from post World War II Czechoslovakia. Unfortunately, standard optical character recognition algorithms have problems to accurately read these documents due to their noisy nature. Therefore we were looking for some ways to improve these unsatisfactory results. Our approach is based on fully-convolutional neural network inspired by U-Net architecture. We are utilizing a synthetic image generator for obtaining a training set for our method. We reached 99.53% recognition accuracy for synthetic data. For real data, we are providing qualitative results.

Keywords: Character recognition · Segmentation · OCR · Machine learning · Generating images · Computer vision

1 Introduction

Optical character recognition (OCR) is an important field of computer vision. Data digitization is very demanded by doctors, police, or historians because it enables indexing and searching for specific documents, information retrieval, or full-text search. Standard OCR algorithms are based on a rule-driven system often divided into detection and recognition parts. Probably the most popular example is Tesseract [6]. Novel methods are usually based on neural networks (NNs) and try to detect and read texts at once in an end-to-end fashion [7,8].

However, these networks are generally designed only for sparse text detection in real-world environments. In this paper, we also would like to use a machine learning approach, but with a focus on digitalized full-text historical document. Semantic segmentation (classification on pixel-wise level) is a very attractive topic of research in the last few years [2–4] and we believe that this approach offers great potential for an end-to-end OCR algorithm. We use fully convolutional network with Encoder-Decoder structure. For training data generation,

© Springer Nature Switzerland AG 2019
A. A. Salah et al. (Eds.): SPECOM 2019, LNAI 11658, pp. 142–149, 2019.
https://doi.org/10.1007/978-3-030-26061-3_15

we utilize our generator of synthetic texts [1]. Using this setup, we performed two types of experiments: (1) semantic segmentation into two classes: text, and background; (2) semantic segmentation when each character of Czech language has its own class and moreover there was one class for a background. Both experiments showed great potential and very promising results.

This paper is organized as follows: in Sect. 2 we briefly describe our synthetic data generator, used training dataset and real historical documents we are working with; in Sect. 3 we discuss our approach to semantic text segmentation; in Sect. 4 we describe our experimental settings and show obtained results, while we draw conclusions and discuss future research in Sect. 5.

2 Data

To produce a synthetic version of an old typewritten document we needed two parts. The first part is a background generator which creates a synthetic image of a paper typically used in the typewriters of the given era. We already developed a method based on the Variational Auto-Encoder (VAE) [9] in our previous article [1]. Our VAE was trained on the images of real backgrounds that were extracted from the actual documents. The text is removed using Otsu's method of brightness thresholding followed by dilatation of the detected region. The empty areas are then replaced by a mean value of the remaining background pixels. The incurred discontinuities in the replaced areas are smoothed out by blurring the affected areas with local averages. The remaining noise and other artifacts are then handled by the VAE during training because it produces blurred versions of the original images by design.

As previously published in [1], 685 old paper images were used to train the VAE background generator. The images were first processed by the method described above. Then they were resized to a resolution of 128. The structure of the VAE is described in Table 1. Parameters for the training can be found in the original paper [1]. The output images are then resized to the original resolution of 2480 using linear interpolation.

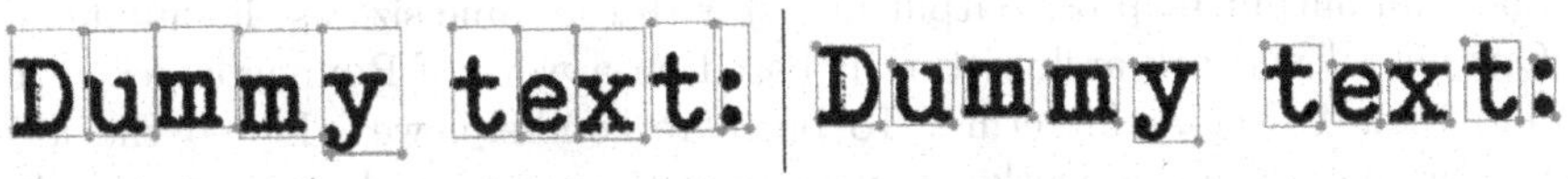

Fig. 1. The example of bounding boxes for each character (left). The example of fine-tuned bounding boxes (right).

A text generator is used to fill the generated backgrounds with a synthetic text. The font named Bohemian typewriter is used to add authenticity. The text is loaded from a predefined dictionary or file and filled into selected areas of the background. A random offset of ±3 in both axes is added to each character to simulate the effect of a real typewriter. The text is also blurred by a Gaussian to add noise caused by the age of the original paper. The benefit of the synthetic text includes the exact locations of each character bounding box, as can be seen in Fig. 1, and the exact pixels for each printed character.

Table 1. Structure of VAE background generator. The encoder is composed of four convolutional layers with 64 kernels with ReLU activation function, every even one is moreover followed by batch normalization. The intermediate layer is represented by fully-connected layer with 500 neurons with *tanh* activation function. The decoder mirrors this structure. Furthermore, the latent space is represented by two fully connected layers with 250 neurons and linear activation function [1].

Encoder	Decoder
Conv(64, 2 × 2), ReLU	Deconv(64, 3 × 3), ReLU
Conv(64, 2 × 2), BN, ReLU	Deconv(64, 3 × 3), ReLU
Conv(64, 3 × 3), ReLU	Deconv(64, 3 × 3), ReLU
Conv(64, 3 × 3), BN, ReLU	Conv(3, 2 × 2), sigmoid
Fully-connected (500)	

With this setup, we generated 150 thousand synthetic documents, whereas we split these documents into three subsets - training (100 thousand), development (20 thousand), and testing (30 thousand) set.

3   Method

Our method is built upon a Fully-Convolutional network with Encoder-Decoder structure, which proved itself to be perfectly suitable for semantic segmentation tasks [2–4]. The Encoder-Decoder structure is a type of feed-forward NN. The main idea of this structure is, firstly, in the Encoder part compressing the data from input raw image pixels into a feature vector representation (i.e. latent space representation). Secondly, the Decoder takes these features and via upsampling produces an output map (or output maps) with the same size as the input.

Our neural network architecture is based on a work of Ronnenberger et al. [3] and their U-Net architecture. To be more concrete, we adopted the idea that for each class our network produces one output map with segmentation for this specific class. The final semantic segmentation map can be constructed by combining the results from all output maps in a simple manner.

Before designing network architecture, we calculated the average height of the text lines. We use this knowledge to decide the size of the receptive field we should work with in the hidden convolutional layers. In our opinion, NN should be able to handle the lines independently, because the information in individual lines is more-or-less independent on each other. Therefore, the ideal receptive field will be high enough to see the whole line, however, not much higher, so it can focus on this single line. With original resolution 2480 × 3504 pixels, the average line is 36 pixels high, however, for purposes of training the resolution of all images was decreased to 620×876 pixels. That means the average line is 9 pixels high.

With this finding in mind, we firstly designed a very simple baseline architecture. The exact network configuration we used is shown in Table 2. We would like to point out the total max-pooling layer omission because of the line average weight. All the convolutions and deconvolutions in this paper are used with stride 1.

Table 2. Structure of our baseline architecture. The encoder is composed of three convolutional layers with 16, 32, and 64 kernels, followed by batch normalization and ReLU activation function. The decoder mirrors this structure. N in the last convolutional layer of the decoder is the number of classes.

Encoder	Decoder
Conv(16, 3×3), BN, ReLU	Deconv(64, 5×5), BN, ReLU
Conv(32, 3×3), BN, ReLU	Deconv(32, 3×3), BN, ReLU
Conv(64, 5×5), BN, ReLU	Deconv(16, 3×3), BN, ReLU
	Conv(N, 1×1), Softmax

Second architecture, we are using in our work is inspired by Badrinarayanan et al. [4] and their usage of skip-connections. Skip-connections are implemented as element-wise summation between each mirrored part of the encoder-decoder structure (Table 3).

Table 3. Structure of our improved architecture. The encoder is composed of four convolutional layers with 16, 32, 64, and 64 kernels, followed by batch normalization and ReLU activation function again. The decoder mirrors this structure. N in the last convolutional layer ConvF of the decoder is the number of classes. Skip-connections are implemented for outputs of layers Conv1-Deconv4, Conv2-Deconv3, and Conv3-Deconv2.

Encoder	Decoder
Conv1(16, 3×3), BN, ReLU	Deconv1(64, 5×5), BN, ReLU
Conv2(32, 3×3), BN, ReLU	Deconv2(32, 3×3), BN, ReLU
Conv3(32, 3×3), BN, ReLU	Deconv3(32, 3×3), BN, ReLU
Conv4(64, 3×3), BN, ReLU	Deconv4(16, 3×3), BN, ReLU
	ConvF(N, 1×1), Softmax

All tested NN architectures were implemented in Python using Chainer deep learning framework [10,11].

4   Experiments and Results

In this section, we present experimental settings and results of two experiments. For both of them, we are providing quantitative results for testing synthetic data and qualitative results for real data.

4.1   Two-Class Classification

In the first experiment, we teach our network semantic segmentation of input image into one of the following two classes: text, and background. We train baseline network architecture described in Subsect. 3 with mini-batch size 2 (due to memory limitations). For updating NN parameters we use standard SGD optimization with a starting learning rate $l=0.01$ and step decay $d=0.1$ every 10 epochs. We use the cross-entropy loss for the network training. We stop the training after 30 epochs and reach 99.28% recognition accuracy on synthetic data on the testing set.

The numeral results look very promising, however, our network did not learn to segment only the text. On the real documents, the network learned to filter out unwanted background spots and paper inaccuracies, but leaves other unwanted text elements (for example text underlining, line margins, etc.) intact, see Fig. 2. This phenomenon occurs because these types of anomalies aren't present in our synthetic data. Nevertheless, we believe that this approach can be used as a part of a preprocessing pipeline for the standard OCR algorithms.

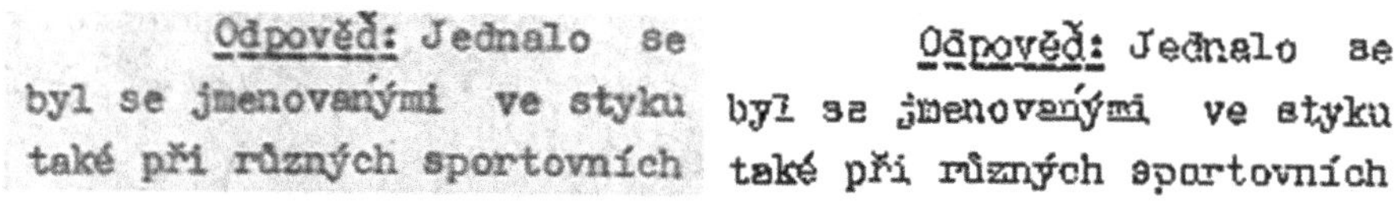

Fig. 2. A result (on the right) of the semantic segmentation for the text class of the real historical document (on the left).

According to Hajic et al. [5], for NN it should be easier not to segment characters directly, but to segment their convex hulls. Inspired by this idea, we regenerate our synthetic data labels to obtain convex-hull maps. Then we train the same NN architecture to convex hull prediction with the same settings as in the previous experiment. This step decreased error by 0.27% absolute error on the test set (which is a relative improvement by 37.50%), see Table 4, but still did not solve the problem with unwanted text elements.

4.2   Single-Character Classification

In our second experiment, we train NN to semantic segmentation of an input image into one of 107 classes (one class for each text character of Czech language and one for the background), i.e. we train NN to perform single-character

Table 4. Results of per pixel recognition accuracy of two-class segmentation on the real document.

NN architecture	Development set	Test set
Direct-char	99.32%	99.28%
Convex-hull	99.60%	99.55%

segmentation. This approach should solve the problem from the previous sub-section. All experiments in this subsection have the same training settings as the ones in the previous subsection. We firstly train two baseline NN architectures for both direct-character segmentation, and convex-hull segmentation. We reach recognition accuracy of 97.75%, 97.58% respectively. Qualitatively these results look good, however, we find out that the network provides an almost flawless prediction for frequent characters like a or e, but completely ignore the rare ones like F or G. This phenomenon stems from their unbalanced frequency in the training data as our training data preserve the nature of the Czech language.

To overcome this flaw we need to motivate our network to stop ignoring the rare classes. Therefore, we decided to weight the loss from individual classes w.r.t. their frequency, i.e. the loss from less frequent classes has a bigger weight than from the more frequent ones. The frequencies of individual characters needed for calculating the weight matrix were obtained from 10 thousand synthetically generated documents. With weighted categorical cross entropy we reached slightly better results, see Table 5.

Table 5. Results of per pixel recognition accuracy of single-character segmentation on the test set.

NN architecture	Direct-char	Convex-hull
Baseline	97.75%	97.58%
Baseline_weighted	97.83%	97.75%
Improved	99.14%	99.17%
Improved_weighted	99.53%	99.52%

After this experiment, we test a few modifications to our baseline NN architecture. The results from the best one (Improved) and the same one with weighted categorical cross entropy are listed in Table 5. For a detailed description of the architecture see Sect. 3. We also provide qualitative results on Fig. 3.

Overall, the final settings provide very good results, which, as we believe, can be utilized as a part of a novel OCR algorithm for historical documents in the future. The algorithm still has some problems to correctly segment rare characters, especially in case of real documents. Moreover, in the segmentation of the real documents there is still some noise present. In the future, we would like to address these problems by employing more complex architecture and

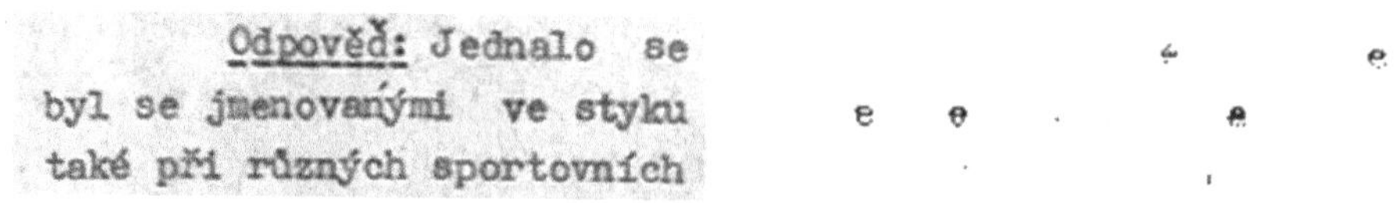

Fig. 3. A result (on the right) of the semantic segmentation for letter *e* of the real historical document (on the left).

by extending our training data with more augmentations simulating other real document features.

Finally, we would like to point out to one interesting finding during our testing, that with our experimental settings convex-hull prediction reach only comparable results. We believe, it is caused by the relative similarity of characters' convex hulls and the characters themselves as opposed to the findings in work [5] with convex hulls of musical symbols.

5   Conclusion and Future Work

Optical character recognition of full-text historical documents is a very challenging task, which, however, shows great importance in real-world applications. We presented a method for semantic segmentation of this type of documents into two classes: characters, and background. In the future, we are planning to utilize this approach in a preprocessing pipeline for a standard OCR algorithm. With a small modification of this method, we obtained semantic single-character segmentation, which reached very promising results.

In our future research, we would like to focus on an extension of our training dataset and testing more complex architecture with residual skip connections. We believe, that with these changes we will solve the problem of rare character segmentation and therefore will have a reliable tool to easily digitize typewriter documents of all different kinds.

Acknowledgments. This research was supported by the Ministry of Culture of the Czech Republic, project No. DG16P02B048. Access to computing and storage facilities owned by parties and projects contributing to the National Grid Infrastructure Meta-Centrum provided under the programme "Projects of Large Research, Development, and Innovations Infrastructures" (CESNET LM2015042), is greatly appreciated.

References

1. Bureš, L., Neduchal, P., Hlaváč, M., Hrúz, M.: Generation of synthetic images of full-text documents. In: Proceedings Speech and Computer, pp. 68–75 (2018)
2. Noh, H., Hong, S., Han, B.: Learning deconvolution network for semantic segmentation. In: Proceedings of the IEEE International Conference on Computer Vision, pp. 1520–1528 (2015)

3. Ronneberger, O., Fischer, P., Brox, T.: U-net: convolutional networks for biomedical image segmentation. In: International Conference on Medical Image Computing and Computer-Assisted Intervention, pp. 234–341 (2015)
4. Badrinarayanan, V., Kendall, A., Cipolla, R.: SegNet: a deep convolutional encoder-decoder architecture for image segmentation. IEEE Trans. Pattern Anal. Mach. Intell. **39**, 2481–2495 (2017)
5. Hajic, J., Dorfer, M., Widmer, G., Pecina, P.: Towards full-pipeline handwritten OMR with musical symbol detection by U-Nets. In: Proceedings of the 19th International Society for Music Information Retrieval Conference, pp. 23–27 (2018)
6. Smith, R.: An overview of the Tesseract OCR engine. In: Ninth International Conference on Document Analysis and Recognition (ICDAR 2007), vol. 2, pp. 629–633 (2007)
7. Jaderberg, M., Vedaldi, A., Zisserman, A.: Deep features for text spotting. In: Fleet, D., Pajdla, T., Schiele, B., Tuytelaars, T. (eds.) ECCV 2014. LNCS, vol. 8692, pp. 512–528. Springer, Cham (2014). https://doi.org/10.1007/978-3-319-10593-2_34
8. Jaderberg, M., Simonyan, K., Vedaldi, A., Zisserman, A.: Reading text in the wild with convolutional neural networks. Int. J. Comput. Vision **116**(1), 1–20 (2016)
9. Larsen, A.B.L., Sønderby, S.K., Larochelle, H., Winther, O.: Autoencoding beyond pixels using a learned similarity metric. In: Proceedings of the 33rd International Conference on International Conference on Machine Learning, ICML vol. 48, pp. 1558–1566 (2016)
10. Tokui, S., Oono, K., Hido, S., Clayton, J.: Chainer: a next-generation open source framework for deep learning. In: Proceedings of Workshop on Machine Learning Systems(LearningSys) in The Twenty-Ninth Annual Conference on Neural Information Processing Systems (NIPS) (2015)
11. Akiba, T., Fukuda, K., Suzuki, S.: ChainerMN: scalable distributed deep learning framework. In: Proceedings of Workshop on ML Systems in The Thirty-First Annual Conference on Neural Information Processing Systems (NIPS) (2017)

A New Approach of Adaptive Filtering Updating for Acoustic Echo Cancellation

Mahfoud Hamidia$^{(\boxtimes)}$ and Abderrahmane Amrouche

USTHB, Faculty of Electronics and Computer Science, LCPTS,
Speech Communication and Signal Processing Laboratory,
P.O. Box 32, 16111 Bab Ezzouar, Algiers, Algeria
{mhamidia, namrouche}@usthb.dz

Abstract. This paper addresses the acoustic echo issue in communication systems which affects the quality of the transmitted speech. This echo occurs due to the acoustic coupling between the loudspeaker and the microphone of the voice terminals. Acoustic echo cancellation (AEC) based on adaptive filtering is generally used to remove this undesirable echo where an adaptive algorithm updates the filter coefficients iteratively until the convergence occurred. In this paper, we propose a new approach of the filter coefficients updating for improving the performance of the adaptive filtering algorithms. The proposed approach is evaluated using the normalized least mean squares (NLMS) algorithm with stationary and non-stationary input signals. The simulation results demonstrate that the proposed approach outperforms the original NLMS algorithm in terms of steady-state error reduction and echo return loss enhancement (ERLE) improvement.

Keywords: Acoustic echo cancellation (AEC) · Adaptive filtering ·
Filter coefficients update · Normalized least mean squares (NLMS) ·
Steady-state error · Echo return loss enhancement (ERLE)

1 Introduction

The speech quality is one of the major performance indexes in communication systems. In fact, the presence of background noise and acoustic echo effect the listener's perception where the voice communication would became difficult or even impossible [1]. The acoustic echo is caused by the reflection of sound waves and acoustics coupling between the loudspeaker and the microphone on the teleconference and the hands-free communication systems. Hence, acoustic echo cancellation (AEC) techniques are generally used to remove this undesired echo and improve the speech intelligibility [2]. Moreover, adaptive filtering is considered as the most effective solution of this problem. The adaptive filter contains two blocks: digital filter and adaptive algorithm. Also, a finite impulse response (FIR) structure of the digital filter is an attractive choice because of the ease in design and stability considerations. Several adaptive filtering algorithms are proposed to update the filter coefficients, including least mean squares (LMS) [3], recursive least squares (RLS) [4], affine projection (AP) [5] algorithms, etc. The filter coefficients updating is the corner stone of the adaptive filtering algorithm.

© Springer Nature Switzerland AG 2019
A. A. Salah et al. (Eds.): SPECOM 2019, LNAI 11658, pp. 150–159, 2019.
https://doi.org/10.1007/978-3-030-26061-3_16

It allows to achieve an optimum coefficients values able to reduce the effect of the echo signal. In addition, a step-size value should be well selected to achieve a good behavior of the adaptive algorithm.

In this paper, we investigate in the step-size parameter of the adaptive filtering algorithm for acoustic echo cancellation. Many works have been proposed in this task to improve the adaptive filtering algorithms like variable step-size versions [6–10] and partial update [11–15].

The rest of this paper is organized as follow. Section 2 provides the principle of AEC based on adaptive filtering with discussion of the NLMS algorithm. In Sect. 3, the proposed approach of the filter coefficients updating is presented. Section 4 illustrates the simulation results obtained by the proposed approach, and Sect. 5 presents some conclusions.

2 Adaptive Filtering Based Acoustic Echo Cancellation

Acoustic echo cancellation is considered as a system identification issue, when the main role of the adaptive filter is to estimate the echo path between the loudspeaker an the microphone. This echo path is modeled by the impulse response of the loudspeaker-enclosure-microphone (LEM) system [16]. In addition, the adaptive filtering choice for acoustic echo cancellation assures a simultaneous full-duplex communication and keeps the speakers more comfortable.

The principle of AEC is shown in Fig. 1, where the basic steps of the AEC can be summarized as follow:

1. Estimate the characteristics of echo path (impulse response $\mathbf{h}$).
2. Create a replica of the echo signal (estimated echo $\hat{y}(n)$).
3. The estimated echo signal $\hat{y}(n)$ is then subtracted from microphone signal $d(n)$ to remove the undesirable echo $y(n)$. Adaptive filter $\mathbf{w}(n)$ is a good supplement to achieve a good replica because of the echo path is usually unknown and time-varying.

The acoustic echo signal $y(n)$ is the filter resulting from the far-end signal $x(n)$ through the LEM system impulse response $\mathbf{h}$ as is depicted in Fig. 1.

At each sample time n, the echo signal is modeled by the following equation:

$$y(n) = \mathbf{x}^T(n)\mathbf{h} \tag{1}$$

where

$$\mathbf{h} = [h_0 \quad h_1, \ldots h_{L-1}]^T \tag{2}$$

L is the length of the echo path, the superscript $(\cdot)^T$ denotes transpose of a vector.

$$\mathbf{x}(n) = [x(n)x(n-1), \ldots x(n-L+1)]^T \tag{3}$$

is the length-L history of the received signal, or far-end signal $x(n)$.

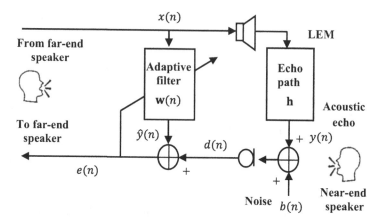

Fig. 1. A basic structure of AEC system.

The desired signal $d(n)$ of the microphone input includes the echo signal $y(n)$, and the background noise signal $y(n)$ as:

$$d(n) = y(n) + b(n) \tag{4}$$

In this paper we consider that the near-end signal is absent (single-talk scenario) for evaluating the adaptive algorithm performance without the perturbation of the near-end signal.

The adaptive filter generates an estimate of echo $\hat{y}(n)$ which is a linear combination of several inputs at time n. This signal represents the echo replica which is expressed as:

$$\hat{y}(n) = \mathbf{x}^T(n)\mathbf{w}(n) \tag{5}$$

where

$$\mathbf{w}(n) = [w_0(n)\ w_1(n), \ldots w_{L-1}(n)]^T \tag{6}$$

is the weight vector of the adaptive filter.

The error signal $e(n)$ corresponds to the residual echo signal and it is obtained by subtracting this estimate $\hat{y}(n)$ from the microphone signal $d(n)$ [8]. This error signal is given by:

$$e(n) = d(n) - \hat{y}(n) \tag{7}$$

The NLMS algorithm is the most popular adaptive filtering algorithms, due to its low complexity and its robustness to finite precision errors. It's used for updating the filter coefficients in AEC context, which is defined as [4]:

$$\mathbf{w}(n+1) = \mathbf{w}(n) + \frac{\mu}{\mathbf{x}^T(n)\mathbf{x}(n) + \varepsilon} e(n)\mathbf{x}(n) \tag{8}$$

where $\mathbf{w}(n)$ is the present tap weight value of the adaptive filter. μ is the step-size parameter which is used in the weight vector updating with $0 < \mu < 2$, and $\varepsilon > 0$ is a regularization constant that prevents division by a very small number of the data norm.

3 Proposed Approach of Adaptive Filtering Updating

Two main characteristics of the acoustic echo are: reverberation and latency. Reverberation is the persistence of sound after stopping of the original sound. Impulse response is the pressure-time response function at the receiver position inside a room as a result of an impulse excitation. The impulse response contains three main parts: the direct sound, early reflections and late reverberation as is depicted in Fig. 2 [17]. Various types of reverberation formulae are derived. Most of those formulae feature exponentially decay of reverberation in a room [18].

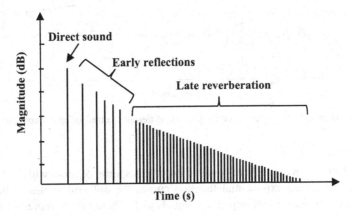

Fig. 2. Room impulse response.

The sound level decays exponentially over time in the room, so generally the evolution of the acoustic impulse response represents an exponential decay. Moreover, to estimate the impulse response, the update of non-significant coefficients (late reverberation) and significant coefficients (early reflections) by the same step-size value slow-down the global convergence of the filter coefficients.

For this reason, we propose a new strategy of adaptive filtering update based on a weighted updating. In this proposition, the filter coefficients are not updated by the same step-size value when the step-size parameter μ is replaced by a vector $\boldsymbol{\mu}$. This new vector contains step-size values which vary according to the exponential function over the length of the adaptive filter which is defined as:

$$\boldsymbol{\mu} = \mu \exp(-\lambda t) \tag{9}$$

where μ is the step-size parameter, $t = 1, \ldots, L$ and λ is the exponential decay constant with $0 < \lambda < 1$, $\min(\boldsymbol{\mu}) > 0$ and $\max(\boldsymbol{\mu}) < 2$. Generally, the length of the adaptive filter L is chosen to be equal to the length of the impulse response.

The update of the filter coefficients by the new approach for NLMS algorithm can be expressed as follow:

$$\mathbf{w}(n+1) = \mathbf{w}(n) + \frac{e(n)}{\mathbf{x}^T(n)\mathbf{x}(n) + \varepsilon}\boldsymbol{\mu}\mathbf{x}(n) \tag{10}$$

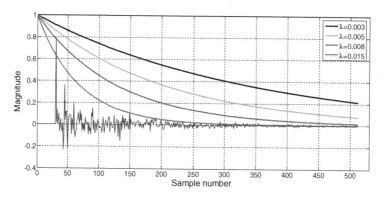

Fig. 3. The proposed step-size function $\boldsymbol{\mu}$ with different values of the exponential decay constant λ.

Figure 3 shows an example of acoustic impulse response of room with 512 samples of length in blue, also exponential function curves for different values of the exponential decay constant λ with step-size μ equals to 1. These curves represent the step-size values distribution for the filter coefficients update where the non-significant coefficients have small values of the step-size compared to the significant coefficients.

4   Simulation Results and Discussions

In the evaluation task, we have used two types of inputs signals: stationary and non-stationary signals. The stationary signal is presented by a white Gaussian noise (WGN). On the other hand, speech signal taken from the TIMIT database [19] is used to evaluate the proposed approach for the non-stationary input signal and simulate AEC scenario. This signal represents the far-end speaker signal. These input signals are sampled at 16 kHz and they are plotted in Fig. 4.

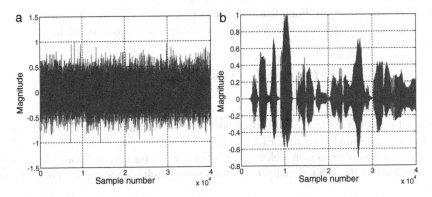

Fig. 4. The input signals. (a) the stationary signal, (b) the non-stationary signal.

Two measured impulse responses are used to model the echo paths: the first one consists of 1024 samples [20] and the second 512 samples [21] as shown in Fig. 5.

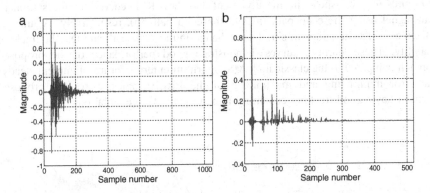

Fig. 5. Two acoustic echo paths.

The AEC system based on adaptive filter uses NLMS algorithm to update their coefficients with, $\mu = 0.9$ and $\varepsilon = 2.2204 \times 10^{-16}$. The length of this filter L is equal to the length of the echo path. Hence, the acoustic echo signal $y(n)$ is resulting from the linear convolution between the input signal and the measured impulse response (echo path).

In order to evaluate the proposed approach, we have used two criteria measures: a normalized misalignment (system mismatch) and echo return loss enhancement (ERLE) with a total number of iterations N = 40000. These criteria are defined as:

$$\text{Misalignment (dB)} = 10 \log_{10} \left[\frac{\|\mathbf{w}(n) - \mathbf{h}\|^2}{\|\mathbf{h}\|^2} \right] \tag{11}$$

where $\|\mathbf{w}(n) - \mathbf{h}\|$ is the Euclidian distance between the adaptive coefficients vector $\mathbf{w}(n)$ and the real echo path vector $\mathbf{h}$, and $\|\mathbf{h}\|$ is the Euclidian norm of $\mathbf{h}$.

$$\text{ERLE(dB)} = 10 \log_{10} \left\{ \frac{E\left[|y(n)|^2\right]}{E\left[|e(n)|^2\right]} \right\} \tag{12}$$

where $E[.]$ denotes mathematical expectation. The role of AEC system is to minimize the misalignment and maximize ERLE.

The real environment is modeled by a white Gaussian background noise signal $b(n)$ that is added to the echo signal $y(n)$ at different signal-to-noise ratio (SNR) values, where

$$\text{SNR(dB)} = 10 \log_{10} \left\{ \frac{E\left[|y(n)|^2\right]}{E\left[|b(n)|^2\right]} \right\} \tag{13}$$

Figures 6 and 7 show the misalignment and the ERLE curves for the stationary input signal using the echo path (a) and the echo path (b), respectively. A jump is realized at 20000 iterations to simulate a change in the echo path and test the tracking capability. These learning curves demonstrate good performance of the proposed approach compared to the classical NLMS algorithm in terms for misalignment steady-state error minimizing and maximizing of the ERLE values. Also, the proposed approach has a good tracking capability in echo path change situations.

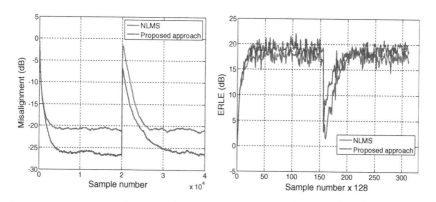

Fig. 6. Evaluation curves of the NLMS and the proposed approach for WGN input signal with the acoustic echo path (a) of 1024 taps, $\mu = 0.9$, $\lambda = 0.0025$, SNR = 20 dB. Left: misalignment curves, right: ERLE curves.

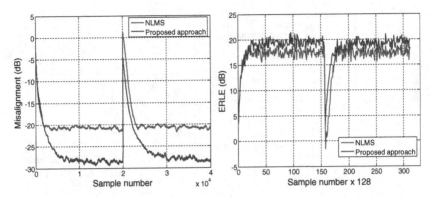

Fig. 7. Evaluation curves of the NLMS and the proposed approach for WGN input signal with the acoustic echo path (b) of 512 taps, $\mu = 0.9$, $\lambda = 0.008$, SNR $= 20$ dB. Left: misalignment curves, right: ERLE curves.

The obtained results in Figs. 8 and 9 confirm that the proposed approach has a better performance in terms of small steady-state error and large values of the ERLE for the non-stationary input signal using the two echo paths. These results denote that the proposed approach can reduce the effect of the acoustic echo and enhance the communication quality.

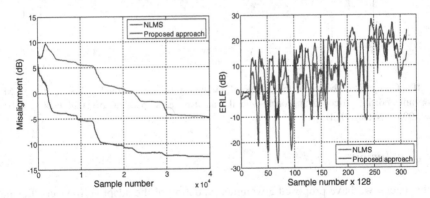

Fig. 8. Evaluation curves of the NLMS and the proposed approach for speech input signal with the acoustic echo path (a) of 1024 taps, $\mu = 0.9$, $\lambda = 0.005$, SNR $= 30$ dB. Left: misalignment curves, right: ERLE curves.

The temporal evolution of the error signal $e(n)$ (residual echo) for the NLMS and the proposed approach is plotted in Fig. 10. From this result we can note that the proposed approach performs well in acoustic echo cancellation scenario compared to the original NLMS in terms of residual echo reduction. Therefore, it can improve the speech quality in the communication systems.

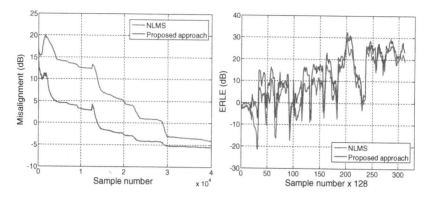

Fig. 9. Evaluation curves of the NLMS and the proposed approach for speech input signal with the acoustic echo path (b) of 512 taps, $\mu = 0.9$, $\lambda = 0.008$, SNR $= 30$ dB. Left: misalignment curves, right: ERLE curves.

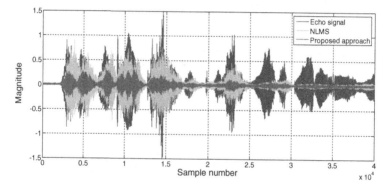

Fig. 10. Comparison between the temporal evolution of the residual echo of the NLMS algorithm and the proposed approach with the acoustic echo path (a) of 1024 taps, $\mu = 0.9$, $\lambda = 0.005$, SNR $= 30$ dB.

5   Conclusion

In this paper, we have proposed a weighted updating of the adaptive filter coefficients for acoustic echo cancellation. The basic idea behind this work is the use of the significant degree to update the filter coefficients where a small step-size is used to update a non-significant coefficient and vice versa. The performance of the proposed approach is verified using stationary and non-stationary input signals. This proposed approach provides better performance than the original NLMS algorithm in terms of steady-state error reduction, echo return loss enhancement maximization and has a good tracking capability. Also, it shows robustness against background noise.

References

1. Benesty, J., Chen, J., Huang, Y., Cohen, I.: Noise Reduction in Speech Processing, vol. 2. Springer, Heidelberg (2009). https://doi.org/10.1007/978-3-642-00296-0
2. Hamidia, M., Amrouche, A.: A new robust double-talk detector based on the Stockwell transform for acoustic echo cancellation. Digit. Sig. Process. **60**, 99–112 (2017)
3. Widrow, B., Stearns, S.D.: Adaptive Signal Processing, 1st edn. Prentice-Hall, Inc., Englewood Cliffs (1985)
4. Haykin, S.S.: Adaptive Filter Theory, 4th edn. Prentice-Hall, Englewood Cliffs (2002)
5. Ozeki, K., Umeda, T.: An adaptive filtering algorithm using an orthogonal projection to an affine subspace and its properties. Electron. Commun. Jpn. Part I: Commun. **67**(5), 19–27 (1984)
6. Cho, J., Baek, H.J., Park, B.Y., Shin, J.: Variable step-size sign subband adaptive filter with subband filter selection. Sig. Process. **152**, 141–147 (2018)
7. Huang, F., Zhang, J., Zhang, S.: Combined-step-size normalized subband adaptive filter with a variable-parametric step-size scaler against impulsive interferences. IEEE Trans. Circuits Syst. II Express Briefs **65**(11), 1803–1807 (2018)
8. Hamidia, M., Amrouche, A.: Improved variable step-size NLMS adaptive filtering algorithm for acoustic echo cancellation. Digit. Sig. Process. **49**, 44–55 (2016)
9. Huang, H.C., Lee, J.: A new variable step-size NLMS algorithm and its performance analysis. IEEE Trans. Sig. Process. **60**(4), 2055–2060 (2012)
10. Vega, L.R., Rey, H., Benesty, J., Tressens, S.: A new robust variable step-size NLMS algorithm. IEEE Trans. Sig. Process. **56**(5), 1878–1893 (2008)
11. Godavarti, M., Hero, A.O.: Partial update LMS algorithms. IEEE Trans. Sig. Process. **53**(7), 2382–2399 (2005)
12. Werner, S., De Campos, M.L., Diniz, P.S.: Partial-update NLMS algorithms with data-selective updating. IEEE Trans. Sig. Process. **52**(4), 938–949 (2004)
13. Dogancay, K., Tanrikulu, O.: Adaptive filtering algorithms with selective partial updates. IEEE Trans. Circuits Syst. II: Analog. Digit. Sig. Process. **48**(8), 762–769 (2001)
14. Douglas, S.C.: Adaptive filters employing partial updates. IEEE Trans. Circuits Syst. II: Analog. Digit. Sig. Process. **44**(3), 209–216 (1997)
15. Dogancay, K.: Partial-Update Adaptive Signal Processing: Design Analysis and Implementation. Academic Press, Cambridge (2008)
16. Hamidia, M., Amrouche, A.: Effect of a signal decorrelation on adaptive filtering algorithms for acoustic echo cancellation. In: the 5th International Conference on Electrical Engineering-Boumerdes (ICEE-B), pp. 1–4 (2017)
17. Badeau, R.: Unified stochastic reverberation modeling. In: the 26th European Signal Processing Conference (EUSIPCO), pp. 2175–2179 (2018)
18. Tohyama, M.: Sound in the Time Domain. Springer, Singapore (2018). https://doi.org/10.1007/978-981-10-5889-9
19. Fisher, W.M., Zue, V., Bernstein, J., Pallett, D.S.: An acoustic-phonetic data base. J. Acoust. Soc. Am. **81**(S1), S92–S93 (1987)
20. Djendi, M., Bouchard, M., Guessoum, A., Benallal, A., Berkani, D.: Improvement of the convergence speed and the tracking ability of the fast Newton type adaptive filtering (FNTF) algorithm. Signal Process. **86**(7), 1704–1719 (2006)
21. Yu, Y., Zhao, H.: Novel sign subband adaptive filter algorithms with individual weighting factors. Sig. Process. **122**, 14–23 (2016)

Code-Switching Language Modeling with Bilingual Word Embeddings: A Case Study for Egyptian Arabic-English

Injy Hamed[1(✉)], Moritz Zhu[2], Mohamed Elmahdy[3], Slim Abdennadher[1], and Ngoc Thang Vu[2]

[1] Computer Science Department, The German University in Cairo, Cairo, Egypt
{injy.hamed,slim.abdennadher}@guc.edu.eg
[2] Institute for Natural Language Processing, University of Stuttgart, Stuttgart, Germany
{moritz.zhu,thang.vu}@ims.uni-stuttgart.de
[3] Data Science Department, Raisa Energy LLC, Cairo, Egypt
melmahdy@raisaenergy.com

Abstract. Code-switching (CS) is a widespread phenomenon among bilingual and multilingual societies. The lack of CS resources hinders the performance of many NLP tasks. In this work, we explore the potential use of bilingual word embeddings for code-switching (CS) language modeling (LM) in the low resource Egyptian Arabic-English language. We evaluate different state-of-the-art bilingual word embeddings approaches that require cross-lingual resources at different levels and propose an innovative but simple approach that jointly learns bilingual word representations without the use of any parallel data, relying only on monolingual and a small amount of CS data. While all representations improve CS LM, ours performs the best and improves perplexity 33.5% relative over the baseline.

1 Introduction

Code-switching is a common phenomenon in multilingual communities where people use more than one language in a conversation [22]. Due to several factors such as colonization, the rise in education levels and international business and communication, code-switching is seen in several Arab countries, such as Arabic-French in Morocco, Tunisia, Algeria, and Lebanon and Arabic-English in Egypt, Jordon and Saudi Arabia. CS is becoming widely used in Egypt, especially among urban youth, which has motivated research in the NLP field in that direction [14,25]. As shown in [15], Egyptians mix the three languages: Modern Standard Arabic, Dialectal Arabic and English, thus posing challenges to NLP tasks. With the widespread of CS due to globalization, more attention from the speech and language research community has been given towards building NLP applications that can handle such mixed-language input. However, given the scarcity of CS data, NLP tools often fail or need to be extensively adapted to perform well on CS data [4], including the LM task. Language modeling (LM) is a widely-used

© Springer Nature Switzerland AG 2019
A. A. Salah et al. (Eds.): SPECOM 2019, LNAI 11658, pp. 160–170, 2019.
https://doi.org/10.1007/978-3-030-26061-3_17

technique in many NLP applications, including Automatic Speech Recognition (ASR) systems. The performance of language models on code-switched data are greatly hindered by data sparsity problem. The problem of data sparseness affects the performance of traditional n-grams and neural-based LMs, as many word sequences can occur in the testing data without being present in the training data.

Previous work proposed several techniques such as artificial CS text generation using statistical machine translation-based methods [29] and integrating linguistic knowledge in recurrent neural networks and factored LMs [1] or to pose constraints on CS boundaries [36]. Another option is leveraging multi-task learning, where the model jointly predicts the next word and POS tagging on CS text. Recently, [10] proposed dual LMs, where two complementary monolingual LMs are trained separately and then a probabilistic model is used to switch between them. This approach overcame the problem of limited CS data by relying on the large amounts of monolingual data.

In this paper, we address the data sparseness problem in CS LM from a different perspective, leveraging the advantages of representing words using continuous vectors [3,21,24]. We explore the use of bilingual word embeddings[1] as shared latent space to bridge the gap between languages in CS LM for Egyptian Arabic-English. Compared to other previous work, our proposed method does not require any external knowledge, e.g. generated from a part-of-speech tagger or a syntax parser which is not a trivial task in the CS context [4]. To the best of our knowledge, this work is the first research towards this direction. We compare different bilingual embeddings using state-of-the-art approaches that rely on different levels of cross-lingual supervision; word-aligned [19] and sentence-aligned [16] parallel corpora, and a bilingual lexicon [9]. Moreover, we propose two new approaches, where the first approach only relies on monolingual and small CS corpora (Bi-CS) and the second approach combines two of the existing approaches [9,19]. We investigate their impact on LM as well as evaluate them intrinsically on monolingual and bilingual tasks. Our results reveal that bilingual embeddings improve LM, with our proposed bilingual embeddings (Bi-CS) performing best, achieving 33.5% relative improvement in perplexity (PPL) over the baseline.

2   Related Work

Bilingual word embeddings have proven to be a valuable resource to various NLP tasks, such as machine translation [34], cross-lingual entity linking [27], document classification [12], cross-lingual information retrieval [32], part-of-speech tagging [13] and sentiment analysis [35]. Several approaches have been proposed for building bilingual word embeddings, where the bilingual word representations across multiple languages can be jointly learned, or where independently-learned monolingual representations can be mapped to one vector space. For both tasks,

---

[1] The bilingual word embeddings and the compiled Egyptian Arabic-English dictionary and thesaurus can be obtained by contacting the authors.

different forms of cross-lingual supervision are leveraged, including alignments at word level [16], sentence level [12,16], both word and sentence level [19], or document level [32,33], in addition to bilingual lexicons [9,13,30,35] and comparable un-aligned data [33]. A comprehensive survey on crosslingual word embedding models is provided by Ruder et al. [23]. The survey presents a comparison between the models regarding their data requirements and objective functions, as well as a discussion covering the different evaluation methods used for cross-lingual word embeddings.

In [28], Upadhyay et al. present an extensive evaluation of four popular cross-lingual embedding methods [9,16,19,31] that all require parallel training data, but differ in the degree of data parallelism required. In this work, we propose a new approach (Bi-CS) for training bilingual word embeddings that requires no level of cross-lingual supervision and compare it against the first three models compared in [28] on two tasks: language modeling and concept categorization. While the existing approaches require different levels of cross-lingual supervision (word-aligned [19] and sentence-aligned [16] parallel corpora as well as bilingual lexicon [9]), Bi-CS only uses monolingual data in addition to a small amount of CS data. We also investigate integrating two of the existing approaches [9,19].

3   Data

CS Data For language modeling evaluation, we further extend the Egyptian Arabic speech transcriptions obtained in [15]. The corpus contains a total of 14,191 Arabic and 7,758 English words, which shows high usage of the embedded English language in the conversations. Out of the total 2,407 sentences, there are 573 (23.8%) monolingual Arabic, 239 (9.9%) monolingual English and 1,595 (66.3%) CS sentences, which also shows a high rate of code-mixing. A sample of the the corpus is given in Table 1.

Table 1. Samples from the Egyptian Arabic-English CS speech corpus. The * marks the start of the sentence.

Sentences
* Actually هتبقى experience ت انت ان حلوة do research في مصر
Translation: *Actually* it will be a nice *experience* that you *do research* in Egypt.
* لو انت عندك object that you need to track in a fish-eye camera اصعب علشان ال بتبقى الّي في الجناب ok ? distortion
Translation: If you have an *object that you need to track in a fish-eye camera* it becomes harder due to the *distortion* in the edges *ok*?
convert visual information into sounds for visually impaired ن بنحاول احنا ان عن كانت * people.
Translation: It was about that we were trying to *convert visual information into sounds for visually impaired people.*

Resources for Bilingual Embeddings For word embeddings training, we gathered text from Facebook pages that are related to Egypt and tweets obtained from Twitter with the location restricted to Cairo. The corpus contains a total of 1,521,818 monolingual Arabic, 270,741 monolingual English and 123,445 CS sentences, as further detailed in Table 2. We obtain parallel sentences from LDC's BBN Arabic-Dialect/English Parallel Text [37], containing 38,154 Egyptian Arabic-English aligned sentences. All the embeddings were trained using the text corpus and the parallel corpus. For BiCCA, we obtain 41,777 Egyptian Arabic-English translation pairs from *Lisaan Masy*[2] dictionary, out of which 14,812 translation pairs were found in our text corpus. We extracted the text from the available PDF format and parsed it into a machine-readable format. We also extracted an Egyptian Arabic-English thesaurus provided in the *Lisaan Masry* dictionary for the intrinsic evaluation. The extracted thesaurus contains a total of 43 general categories, divided into 356 sub-categories, each having an average of 35 Arabic and 29 English words. After pruning to words available in the text corpus, we end up with 40 general categories, 343 sub-categories, with an average of 25 Arabic and 10 English words in each sub-category.

Table 2. The number of sentences gathered from Facebook and Twitter per language.

	Monolingual Arabic	Monolingual English	Arabic-English CS	Total
Facebook	634,914	140,954	61,210	837,078
Twitter	886,904	129,787	62,235	1,078,926
Facebook + Twitter	1,521,818	270,741	123,445	1,916,004

4 Bilingual Word Embeddings

We train bilingual word embeddings using three of the models compared in [28] and propose two other simple extensions (BiCCAonBiSkip and Bi-CS). In order to conduct a fair comparison between all algorithms, the same data is used for training all word embeddings. Across all models, both corpora are used: the set of Egyptian Arabic parallel sentences in [37] as well as the text corpus that was gathered from the social media platforms.

Bilingual Compositional Vector Model (BiCVM) Hermann and Blunsom [16] proposed to use sentence-aligned parallel data to train bilingual word embeddings. Their model is motivated by the fact that aligned sentences express the same meaning and therefore have similar sentence representation. We train the models using the parallel corpus, as well as the text corpus, where each sentence in the text corpus acts as its own equivalent sentence. The models are trained using both proposed composition functions used for summarizing a sentence;

---

[2] http://eg.lisaanmasry.com/intro_en/index.html.

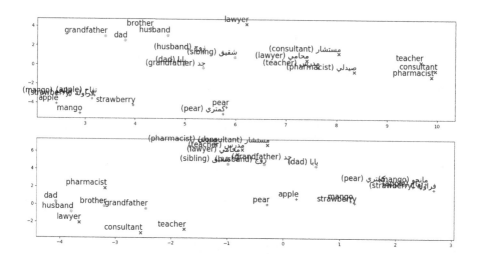

Fig. 1. t-SNE [20] visualization of BiCCAonBiSkip and Bi-CS for words in 3 clusters: fruits (+), family (o) and professions (x).

additive (BiCVM_add) and bigram (BiCVM_bi) models. We train the models using a hinge loss margin set to the embeddings dimension ($m = d$, as set in [16]), noise parameter of 10, batch size of 50, L2 regularization with $\lambda = 1$, a step-size of 0.05 and *AdaGrad* as the adaptive gradient method [6]. All models are trained over 20 iterations.

Bilingual Correlation-Based Embeddings (BiCCA) Faruqui and Dyer [9] proposed to project two (independently trained) vector spaces into a single space, with the use of a translation lexicon. We investigate the use of continuous bag-of-words (CBOW) and Skip-gram models [21] for the vector spaces before projection. The Arabic vector space is trained using the subset of Arabic and CS sentences in the text corpus as well as the parallel corpus, while the English vector space is trained using the subset of English and CS sentences in both corpora. CBOW models are trained with Negative Sampling, while Skip-gram models are trained with Hierarchical Softmax. All models are trained with a window of size 5. For BiCCA projection, we set the number of canonical components $k = 0.8$.

Bilingual Skip-Gram Model (BiSkip) Luong et al. [19] proposed BiSkip to train bilingual embeddings using parallel corpora with word alignments. Given a word alignment link from w_1 in language l_1 to w_2 in language l_2, the model predicts the context words of w_1 using w_2 and vice-versa. The model aims at creating high-quality monolingual and bilingual embeddings by learning the context concurrence information from the monolingual text, and the meaning equivalent signals from the parallel corpus. As in BiCVM, the parallel and text corpora provide the sentence-aligned data used for training the word embedding models. We use cdec [7] to lowercase, tokenize and generate word alignments for the parallel corpus. For the sentences obtained from the text corpus, we use fake alignments, where each word is aligned with itself. The models are trained with the same hyperparameters as given in [28]. We use a window of size 10, cross-lingual weight of 4, 30 negative samples, and 5 training iterations.

BiCCAonBiSkip We observed that BiSkip model outperforms BiCCA and BiCVM in monolingual and bilingual intrinsic evaluations. However, BiCCA provides a vector space where similar words from both languages were most closely represented. Therefore, we combine both best-performing approaches by applying BiCCA on the output embeddings of BiSkip to draw the Arabic and English word embeddings closer, while maintaining the high monolingual and bilingual quality of BiSkip embeddings.

Bilingual CS Embeddings (Bi-CS) It is not always possible to find parallel corpora or bilingual lexicons, especially for low-resource languages. In this work, CS data is available for free which could be used as glue forcing the monolingual embeddings being closer together in the shared vector space. Therefore, we propose Bi-CS that jointly learns word representations of both languages by training the Skip-gram and CBOW models on monolingual data of both languages in combination with a small amount of CS data. The models are trained using the concatenation of all sentences in the text and parallel corpora. The parallel corpus was used as a text corpus added to the training data in order to unify the data used across algorithms to insure a fair comparison. However, the Bi-CS approach does not require any parallel data. CBOW models are trained with Negative Sampling, while Skip-gram models are trained with Hierarchical Softmax. All models are trained with a window of size 5.

5 Language Modeling

Neural-Based LM We use TheanoLM[3] (TLM) to train our recurrent neural network (RNN) LMs [8]. As TLM does not allow the use of pretrained word embeddings, we extend the implementation accordingly by adding an embedding layer that is initialized with pre-trained embeddings and replaces the projection layer in the small default architecture in [8]. The embedding layer weights are then updated with the other layers. A neural language model with an LSTM layer, followed by a softmax output layer is used. The embedding layer is of size 100 or 200, the LSTM layer has 300 LSTM cells and the softmax layer has the vocabulary size. We use this network architecture in all experiments. All the bilingual embeddings are filtered to only include words from the training data to ensure an identical vocabulary across all experiments and comparable PPLs. For all experiments, we fix the random seed, and optimize with *AdaGrad* [6]. We set the mini-batch size to 16 and train until no improvement is observed on the development set.

---

[3] https://github.com/senarvi/theanolm

Experiment 1 In the first setting, the models are trained using the extended speech transcriptions [15]. The corpus was divided into training, development and testing sets as follows: 2040, 187 and 180 sentences. The division was made taking into consideration having balanced sets in terms of speakers and genders. The bilingual embeddings are filtered to only include words from the training set.

Results In Table 3, we compare the PPLs obtained using the bilingual word embeddings for the first experiment. We only show the results obtained using embedding dimension of 200, as they are superior over the dimension of 100. The baseline LM with randomly initialized embeddings has a PPL of 300.2 on the development set and 291.5 on the evaluation set. All bilingual word embeddings outperform the baseline with a large margin. Despite the simplicity of the Bi-CS approach, it achieves best results, giving a relative improvement of 33.5% in PPL on the test set.

Experiment 2 In experiment 1, the substantial improvements in PPLs show great potential in the integration of bilingual word embedding for improving CS speech recognition. However, under this setting, the improvements in the PPLs cannot be traced back exclusively to the incorporation of the pre-trained word embeddings, as the LMs using the pre-trained word embeddings were given access to more CS data over the baseline. Therefore, we conduct a second experiment where all models are trained using the CS sentences obtained in our social media text corpus. The word embeddings are also filtered to only contain the words in that subset of the corpus. The Egyptian Arabic speech transcriptions obtained in [15] are used in development and testing, where the corpus was divided evenly into two sets.

Table 3. Experiment 1 - PPLs on the development and the test set

	Experiment 1		Experiment 2	
	Dev	Test	Dev	Test
Baseline	300.2	291.5	2146.7	2188.0
BiCVM_add	226.3	228.1	1890.9	1994.1
BiCVM_bi	225.3	217.7	1977.4	2102.9
BiSkip	224.9	220.9	1712.1	1851.5
BiCCA_skip	249.5	241.4	2033.6	2156.6
BiCCA_cbow	247.8	241.4	1956.8	2145.2
BiCCAonBiSkip	257.5	248.9	1988.9	2117.8
Bi-CS_skip	223.2	214.5	1895.2	2016.6
Bi-CS_cbow	**204.7**	**193.6**	**1588.3**	**1697.0**

Results In Table 3, we compare the PPLs obtained using the bilingual word embeddings for the second experiment. The results are similar to those of the first experiment, where all bilingual word embeddings outperform the baseline, and Bi-CS gives the lowest PPL. The best-performing (Bi-CS) model achieves a relative improvement of 22.4% in PPL on the test set. It is to be noted that in this setting, the PPLs are very high since the models are trained on text gathered from social media platforms, while it is tested on speech text. This setting is only used to confirm the effectiveness of using bilingual word embeddings in low-resourced CS language modeling.

6   Intrinsic Evaluations

In this Section, we present intrinsic evaluations on the word embeddings. The goal of bilingual word embeddings is to obtain distributed word representations that are of high quality monolingually and bilingually; such that similar words in each language and across different languages end up close to each other in the embedding space. We evaluate both intrinsic objectives: (a) monolingual objective using *concept categorization* task on Arabic and English words separately and (b) bilingual objective using *concept categorization* on words from both languages.

Concept Categorization The task of *concept categorization*, also known as *word clustering*, is to divide a set of words into n subsets. (e.g., correctly categorizing the words in the set {*teacher,apple,mango,scientist*} into two subsets) The word vectors are clustered into n groups (where n is determined by the gold standard partition) using the CLUTO toolkit [17]. Clustering is done with the *repeated bisections* with *global optimization* method and CLUTO's default settings otherwise, as outlined in [2]. Performance is evaluated in terms of *purity*, which measures the extent to which each cluster contains words from primarily one category, as defined by the gold standard partition. We created our own gold standard partition using 12 concept categories from the compiled thesaurus. The dataset consists of 211 Egyptian Arabic and 205 English words (or "concepts"). In order to evaluate the word embeddings in terms of monolingual quality, we report the clustering *purity* of the Arabic words and English words separately. The overall monolingual *purity* is calculated as the average of both. For the bilingual evaluation, we report the *purity* of clusters on all words from both languages. The results are shown in Table 4.

Table 4. Intrinsic evaluations of bilingual word embeddings (Mono. = monolingual and Bi. = bilingual)

	ARB	EN	Mono.	Bi.
BiCVM_add	32.2%	24.9%	28.6%	27.2%
BiCVM_bi	26.5%	23.9%	25.2%	23.1%
BiSkip	64.5%	38.0%	51.3%	41.6%
BiCCA_skip	42.2%	**57.6%**	49.9%	**43.0%**
BiCCA_cbow	36.0%	52.7%	44.4%	38.2%
BiCCAonBiSkip	**70.6%**	46.8%	**58.7%**	**43.0%**
Bi-CS_skip	56.4%	48.8%	52.6%	42.3%
Bi-CS_cbow	57.8%	46.8%	52.3%	**43.0%**

Results The performance of the three models (BiCVM, BiSkip and BiCCA) shows that BiSkip and BiCCA outperform BiCVM on all tasks. The ordering of BiSkip and BiCCA is task-dependent: BiSkip achieves better results on Arabic monolingual task, while BiCCA performs better on the English monolingual task as well as the bilingual task. By combining both approaches, the BiCCAonBiSkip model outperforms all other models for both monolingual and cross-lingual categorization tasks. This shows that BiCCAonBiSkip is able to bring the crosslingual word vectors closer without compromising the high-quality embeddings provided by BiSkip. Figure 1 presents a t-SNE [20] visualization of word embeddings obtained by BiCCAonBiSkip for words in three clusters: fruits, family and professions, in which words from both languages can be observed within clusters. Surprisingly, Bi-CS, which is trained in a completely unsupervised manner, displays good performance, outperforming BiSkip, BiCCA and BiCVM which rely on richer resources. This is an interesting observation, as it is usually the case that models trained with weaker supervision show lower performance on semantic tasks [28].

7   Discussion

While all models show varying performance across tasks, Bi-CS achieves good performance consistently, outperforming all models in LM, and performing second best on the categorization task. This highlights the effectiveness of the Bi-CS model, especially that it requires the least data and supervision requirements. When comparing the performances of the other models, we find that the their ordering is inconsistent within categorization, as well as across categorization and LM tasks. This observation is in-line prior work [11, 26, 28] reporting that performances are task-dependent. It is interesting to note that the models show almost opposite ordering of performances (excluding Bi-CS). The performance mismatch is most obvious for BiCCAonBiSkip (achieving highest performance in categorization and least in LM) and BiCVM (ranking last in categorization and second best in LM). The mismatch can also be seen in the additive and bigram composition functions used by BiCVM, where the former performs better in the categorization tasks, while the latter shows better results in LM. Furthermore, when comparing CBOW and Skip-gram models, we find that Skip-gram models (mostly) outperform CBOW models in the categorization task, while CBOW models are superior in LM. It is also to be noted that word embeddings fuse multiple word senses (or meanings) into one representation. Given that sense embeddings have shown improvements in NLP tasks [5,18], it would be interesting to further improve our embeddings to incorporate the different word senses and investigate its effect on the categorization and CS LM tasks.

8   Conclusion

We investigated the use of various state-of-the-art bilingual word embeddings for improving CS LM. We explored various state-of-the-art approaches that require different levels of cross-lingual supervision for training the embeddings. In order to relax the need for parallel corpora and bilingual lexicons, which are usually scarce, we proposed Bi-CS, a simple, yet effective model. Bi-CS only requires monolingual corpora along with a small amount of CS data, and can thus be more easily applied to low-resource languages. All LMs using bilingual word embeddings outperformed the baseline trained with randomly initialized word embeddings. Bi-CS gives the best performance, achieving a relative improvement of 33.5% over the baseline. It also outperforms the existing approaches on the intrinsic evaluation. In future work, we plan to investigate the effectiveness of incorporating the bilingual word embeddings into language modeling on the task of automatic speech recognition.

References

1. Adel, H., Vu, N.T., Schultz, T.: Combination of recurrent neural networks and factored language models for code-switching language modeling. In: ACL, vol. 2, pp. 206–211 (2013)
2. Baroni, M., Dinu, G., Kruszewski, G.: Don't count, predict! a systematic comparison of context-counting vs. context-predicting semantic vectors. In: ACL, vol. 1, pp. 238–247, Long Papers (2014)
3. Bengio, Y., Ducharme, R., Vincent, P., Jauvin, C.: A neural probabilistic language model. JMLR **3**, 1137–1155 (2003)
4. Çetinoğlu, Ö., Schulz, S., Vu, N.T.: Challenges of computational processing of code-switching. In: Proceedings of the Second Workshop on Computational Approaches to Code Switching, pp. 1–11. Association for Computational Linguistics (2016)
5. Cocos, A., Apidianaki, M., Callison-Burch, C.: Word sense filtering improves embedding-based lexical substitution. In: Proceedings of the 1st Workshop on Sense, Concept and Entity Representations and their Applications, pp. 110–119 (2017)
6. Duchi, J., Hazan, E., Singer, Y.: Adaptive subgradient methods for online learning and stochastic optimization. JMLR **12**, 2121–2159 (2011)
7. Dyer, C., et al.: cdec: a decoder, alignment, and learning framework for finite-state and context-free translation models. In: ACL, pp. 7–12 (2010)
8. Enarvi, S., Kurimo, M.: TheanoLM-an extensible toolkit for neural network language modeling. In: Interspeech, pp. 3052–3056 (2016)
9. Faruqui, M., Dyer, C.: Improving vector space word representations using multilingual correlation. In: EACL, pp. 462–471 (2014)
10. Garg, S., Parekh, T., Jyothi, P.: Dual language models for code switched speech recognition. In: Interspeech (2018)
11. Glavas, G., Litschko, R., Ruder, S., Vulic, I.: How to (properly) evaluate cross-lingual word embeddings: on strong baselines, comparative analyses, and some misconceptions. CoRR abs/1902.00508 (2019)
12. Gouws, S., Bengio, Y., Corrado, G.: Bilbowa: fast bilingual distributed representations without word alignments. In: ICML, pp. 748–756 (2015)
13. Gouws, S., Søgaard, A.: Simple task-specific bilingual word embeddings. In: NAACL, pp. 1386–1390 (2015)
14. Hamed, I., Elmahdy, M., Abdennadher, S.: Building a first language model for code-switch Arabic-English. Proc. Comput. Sci. **117**, 208–216 (2017)
15. Hamed, I., Elmahdy, M., Abdennadher, S.: Collection and analysis of code-switch egyptian Arabic-English speech corpus. In: LREC, vol. 117, 208–216 (2018)

16. Hermann, K.M., Blunsom, P.: Multilingual models for compositional distributed semantics. In: ACL, vol. 1, pp. 58–68, Long Papers (2014)
17. Karypis, G.: Cluto: A clustering toolkit. University of Minnesota Department of Computer Science, Technical report (2003)
18. Li, J., Jurafsky, D.: Do multi-sense embeddings improve natural language understanding? arXiv preprint arXiv:1506.01070 (2015)
19. Luong, T., Pham, H., Manning, C.D.: Bilingual word representations with monolingual quality in mind. In: NAACL Workshop on Vector Space Modeling for NLP, pp. 151–159 (2015)
20. Maaten, L.V.D., Hinton, G.: Visualizing data using t-SNE. JMLR **9**, 2579–2605 (2008)
21. Mikolov, T., Sutskever, I., Chen, K., Corrado, G.S., Dean, J.: Distributed representations of words and phrases and their compositionality. In: Advances in Neural Information Processing Systems, pp. 3111–3119 (2013)
22. Poplack, S.: Syntactic structure and social function of code-switching, vol. 2. Centro de Estudios Puertorriqueños, City University of New York (1978)
23. Ruder, S., Vulić, I., Søgaard, A.: A survey of cross-lingual word embedding models. arXiv preprint arXiv:1706.04902 (2017)
24. Rumelhart, D.E., Hinton, G.E., Williams, R.J.: Learning representations by back-propagating errors. Nature **323**, 533–536 (1986)
25. Sabty, C., Elmahdy, M., Abdennadher, S.: Named entity recognition on Arabic-English code-mixed data. In: 2019 IEEE 13th International Conference on Semantic Computing (ICSC), pp. 93–97. IEEE (2019)
26. Schnabel, T., Labutov, I., Mimno, D., Joachims, T.: Evaluation methods for unsupervised word embeddings. In: EMNLP (2015)
27. Tsai, C.T., Roth, D.: Cross-lingual wikification using multilingual embeddings. In: NAACL, pp. 589–598 (2016)
28. Upadhyay, S., Faruqui, M., Dyer, C., Roth, D.: Cross-lingual models of word embeddings: an empirical comparison. In: ACL, pp. 1661–1670 (2016)
29. Vu, N.T., et al.: A first speech recognition system for Mandarin-English code-switch conversational speech. In: ICASSP, pp. 4889–4892 (2012)
30. Vulić, I., Moens, M.F.: A study on bootstrapping bilingual vector spaces from non-parallel data (and nothing else). In: EMNLP, pp. 1613–1624 (2013)
31. Vulić, I., Moens, M.F.: Bilingual word embeddings from non-parallel document-aligned data applied to bilingual lexicon induction. In: Proceedings of the 53rd Annual Meeting of the Association for Computational Linguistics and the 7th International Joint Conference on Natural Language Processing (Volume 2: Short Papers), vol. 2, pp. 719–725 (2015)
32. Vulić, I., Moens, M.F.: Monolingual and cross-lingual information retrieval models based on (bilingual) word embeddings. In: ACM SIGIR, pp. 363–372 (2015)
33. Vulić, I., Moens, M.F.: Bilingual distributed word representations from document-aligned comparable data. JAIR **55**, 953–994 (2016)
34. Wang, R., Zhao, H., Ploux, S., Lu, B.L., Utiyama, M., Sumita, E.: Graph-based bilingual word embedding for statistical machine translation. TALLIP **17**, 31 (2018)
35. Wick, M., Kanani, P., Pocock, A.C.: Minimally-constrained multilingual embeddings via artificial code-switching. In: AAAI, pp. 2849–2855 (2016)
36. Ying, L., Fung, P.: Language modeling with functional head constraint for code switching speech recognition. In: EMNLP, pp. 907–916 (2014)
37. Zbib, R., et al.: Machine translation of Arabic dialects. In: NAACL, pp. 49–59 (2012)

Identity Extraction from Clusters of Multi-modal Observations

Marek Hrúz[1,2(✉)], Petr Salajka[1,2], Ivan Gruber[1,2,3], and Miroslav Hlaváč[1,2,3]

[1] Faculty of Applied Sciences, UWB, NTIS, Pilsen, Czech Republic
{mhruz,salajka,grubiv}@ntis.zcu.cz
[2] Faculty of Applied Sciences, Department of Cybernetics, UWB,
Pilsen, Czech Republic
mhlavac@kky.zcu.cz
[3] ITMO University, St. Petersburg, Russia

Abstract. In this paper, we present a method for identity extraction from TV News Broadcasts. We define the identity as a set of multi-modal observations. In our case it is the face of a person and a name of a person. The method is based on agglomerative clustering of observations. The resulting clusters represent individual identities, that appeared in the broadcasts. To evaluate the accuracy of our system, we hand labelled approximately one year worth of TV News broadcasts. This resulted in total of 10 301 multi-modal observations and 2563 unique identities. Our method achieved a coverage measure of 90.69 % and precision measure of 94.69 %. Given the simplicity of the proposed algorithm, these results are very satisfactory. Furthermore, the designed system is modular and new modalities can be easily added.

Keywords: Identity extraction · Agglomerative clustering ·
Face recognition · Text reading

1 Introduction

Identity is a complex concept and is defined in many domains suiting the needs for theoretical description and/or discrimination of phenomena in the given fields. In this work, we are interested in identity of humans based on the perception of events directly or indirectly resulting from their physical manifestation, via possible different electronic receptors. This definition of identity includes abstract concepts such as name, address, passport number and so on, which are not direct physical manifestations of people, but nevertheless bear the information about their identity. Using observations of different attributes of people, we want to automatically extract identities - groups of observations produced by a single person. An important attribute of such autonomous system should be its scalability according to the different types of observations. If we want to add an observation (modality) into the description of the identity, the system should enable it with little effort. Furthermore, an identity as naturally understood,

© Springer Nature Switzerland AG 2019
A. A. Salah et al. (Eds.): SPECOM 2019, LNAI 11658, pp. 171–179, 2019.
https://doi.org/10.1007/978-3-030-26061-3_18

does not change with time, or location, or other seemingly marginal conditions. This is difficult from our perspective, since the appearance and thus observations of different modalities can be strongly conditioned by above-mentioned circumstances (people grow in time, their voice changes, they dress differently in different environments, change names or appearance using surgery and so on). That is why we need to define another term – Persona as a subset of Identity. To test the usefulness of such definition of identity, we will test an algorithm of agglomerative clustering for automatic extraction of identities. We will demonstrate the effectiveness of the algorithm on a data-set of TV News Broadcasting.

2   Definitions and Methods

In this section we provide formal definitions of terms used in this paper and describe the methods used in the algorithm.

2.1   Identity

Identity Ω is a set of personae Π_i representing the same person.

$$\Omega = \{\Pi_i\}_{i=0}^{N}, \tag{1}$$

where N is the number of personae clusters in the dataset under consideration. The concept of persona is explained in the next Section.

2.2   Persona

Persona Π is a set of multi-modal observations O_i of the same person in similar circumstances - appearance, age, same name, and so on.

$$\Pi = \{O_j\}_{j=0}^{M}, \tag{2}$$

where M is the number of observations. The similar circumstances are implicitly defined by the quality of the uni-modal detectors/descriptors. A poor descriptor will generate more personae than a good one. The better the descriptors, the better personae representation we obtain.

2.3   Multi-modal Observation

A multi-modal observation O is a set of multiple uni-modal observations z^X.

$$O = \left\{z_{i_X}^{X}\right\}_{X=0}^{K}, \tag{3}$$

where X is the type of modality (face, age, gender, name, ...) , i_X is the ith observation in modality X. The observation O does not necessary need to describe one person. It is just a hypothetical description of a person and another algorithm will decide whether it describes one person or not. The observations $z_{i_X}^{X}$ that form one multi-modal observation, must be time correlated. The time correlation is dependent on the nature of the relationship between individual modalities and needs to be designed for each pair of modalities.

In this paper we are focusing on two modalities - face of a person and a name of a person. The observations from the modality X = face are feature vectors representing the appearance of faces in a face-track extracted from a video sequence.

$$z_i^{\text{face}} = \left\{ x_0^t, y_0^t, x_1^t, y_1^t, f \right\}_{t=t_0}^{t_1}, \tag{4}$$

where t_0, and t_1 are the start, and the end time of the observation, $x_0^t, y_0^t, x_1^t, y_1^t$ are the top-left and the bottom-right corners of the bounding box of the detected faces in individual time instances, f is a median feature vector computed from individual feature vectors in different time instances. The faces are detected and described using a commercial software Eyedea[1]. The facial description is created by a deep convolutional network outputting a 256-dimensional feature vector of unit length. The network was trained so that it produces an embedding where similar faces lie close and different faces are far apart. First experiments with similar approach using Siamese neural networks were published in [1]. A direct estimation of the embedding was introduced in [5] in a form of computing a triplet loss. This approach was further developed in [2,3,6]. The Eyedea software is based on the concepts developed in these papers. The face-tracks are obtained by merging faces regions that have a large overlap in consecutive frames and have similar feature vectors. The bounding boxes of individual detections are stored for later usage.

The observations from the modality X = name are textual hypotheses of first and last name of a person as appeared in a video sequence.

$$z_i^{\text{name}} = \left\{ x_0^t, y_0^t, x_1^t, y_1^t, s_{fn}, s_{ln} \right\}_{t=t_0}^{t_1}, \tag{5}$$

where t_0, and t_1 are the start, and the end time of the observation, $x_0^t, y_0^t, x_1^t, y_1^t$ are the top-left and the bottom-right corners of the bounding box of the detected text in individual time instances, s_{fn}, and s_{ln} are the textual representations of first name, and last name respectively. They are often in a form of hypotheses, because of the ambiguity of the result of the text reader. The texts are obtained by a two-stage algorithm. In the first stage the texts are detected using methods from [7]. The results are regions in images in the form of rotated rectangles. In the next stage, these regions are normalized and inputted into a reading Convolutional Neural Network as in the work [4]. To obtain the text-tracks we apply similar algorithm as for the faces. If we detect similar regions in consecutive frames with similar textual representation, we merge the detections into one track. To differentiate between a text representing a name and normal text we compare the texts to a lists of first and last names. We have lists containing thousands of names covering nationalities all over the world. We match the recognized words to this list and if the Levenshtein distance is lower or equal

---

[1] http://www.eyedea.cz.

to one, we assume the recognized word is either a first or last name. Next, we assume that the first name must be written before the last name, and on the same line, which is typical for the data under consideration.

In this paper the multi-modal observations O_i are pairs of uni-modal observations $O_i = \left\{ z_a^{\text{face}}, z_b^{\text{name}} \right\}$. For simplicity we will denote z^{face} as z_a^{f} and z^{name} as z_a^{n}. An example of how the multi-modal observations are obtained is visualized in Fig. 1.

2.4 Time Correlation Functions

To obtain the mutli-modal observations, we need to know which uni-modal observations correspond together. For this, we design a special function which takes pairs of uni-modal observations and outputs either 1 if the observations are corresponding, otherwise zero. In our case of facial and textual modalities we are interested whether they appeared in a video stream at the same time.

$$f(z_a^{\text{f}}, z_b^{\text{n}}) = \begin{cases} 1, \text{ if } \left[z_a^{\text{f}}(t_0), z_a^{\text{f}}(t_1) \right] \cap \left[z_b^{\text{n}}(t_0), z_b^{\text{n}}(t_1) \right] \neq \emptyset \\ 0, \text{ otherwise} \end{cases} \tag{6}$$

This means that the function in Eq. 6 outputs 1 if the uni-modal observations have a non-empty overlap in time. Furthermore, one can set a minimal desired duration of the overlap to obtain more probable mutli-modal observations. Also, we want to make it clear that this function is specially tailored for the pair of uni-modal observations at hand and for different types of modalities needs to be designed in another way. Some modalities do not need to have an overlap in time. For example, in TV News broadcasting the reporter can mention a name of a person whose face appears after the utterance. In the case of text from speech modality and face modality the function should reflect this in its design. Important part is to find a common ground for the individual modalities, in this case it is the time.

2.5 Multi-modal Distances

Since we use clustering for identity extraction, we need to define distances between the multi-modal observations. We define the multi-modal distances as a linear combination of uni-modal distances defined over the individual metrics.

$$d(O_i, O_j) = \lambda_1 d^{\text{n}}\left(z_i^{\text{n}}, z_j^{\text{n}} \right) + \lambda_2 d^{\text{f}}\left(z_i^{\text{f}}, z_j^{\text{f}} \right), \tag{7}$$

where $\lambda_1 + \lambda_2 = 1$. For the distances in the text modality we use the well established Levenshtein distance:

$$d^{\text{n}}\left(z_i^{\text{n}}, z_j^{\text{n}} \right) = d^{\text{fn}}\left(z_i^{\text{fn}}, z_j^{\text{fn}} \right) + d^{\text{ln}}\left(z_i^{\text{ln}}, z_j^{\text{ln}} \right), \tag{8}$$

where

$$d^{\text{fn}}\left(z_i^{\text{fn}} \right) = \min_{a,b} levenshtein\left(z_i^{\text{n}}\left[s_{fn}(a) \right], z_j^{\text{n}}\left[s_{fn}(b) \right] \right) \tag{9}$$

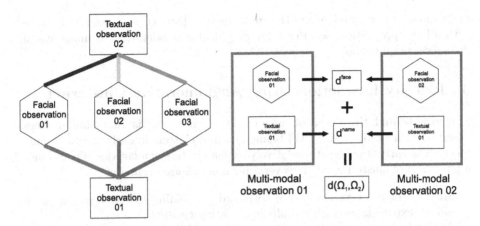

Fig. 1. Example of multi-modal observations when in correlated time instances there were three faces detected and two names were detected. This would produce total of six multi-modal observations. On the right, there is a representation of multi-modal distances computation for two of the multi-modal observations. Note, that the multi-modal observation share the same textual observation.

$$d^{ln}\left(z_i^{ln}\right) = \min_{a,b} levenshtein\left(z_i^{n}\left[s_{ln}\left(a\right)\right], z_j^{n}\left[s_{ln}\left(b\right)\right]\right) \tag{10}$$

The minimum in the equations is carried out through the possible different hypotheses of first and last names in the individual textual observations.

In the facial modality, we take advantages of modern approaches for face recognition. Using a deep neural network, we obtain a robust representation of the face in the form of a feature vector. In our case, the feature vectors lie on a unit hyper-sphere and the distance between faces is computed as cosine distance:

$$d^{f}\left(z_i^{f}, z_j^{f}\right) = \frac{1}{2}\left(1 - \cos\left(\angle z_i^{f}\left[f\right], z_j^{f}\left[f\right]\right)\right) \tag{11}$$

To make the distances in individual modalities comparable, we need to normalize them. Cosine distance, and hence the facial distance d^f, is normalized by definition to interval $\langle 0, 1 \rangle$. To normalize the textual distance d^n we define the maximum Levenshtein distance for the first and last name to be 2. Any distance larger than this is clipped to the value of 3. This means that any two names that differ by more than 2 character operations in respectively first and last name are considered to be maximally different. Then we can assume the individual distances will be in interval $\langle 0, 3 \rangle$ and a simple normalization can be performed: $d^n_{norm} = d^n/6$. For future reference, we will denote the normalized distance as d^n.

As can be seen from Eq. 7, the multi-modal distance can be easily extended by other modalities. The only requirement is that the individual uni-modal distances are comparable, meaning they are normalized (a maximum distance exists). Neither the normalization nor linear combination of uni-modal distances break the multi-modal metric and hence the multi-modal distance is a proper distance with all the properties. See Fig. 1 for graphical representation of multi-modal distances computation.

3   Identity Extraction Using Agglomerative Clustering

The idea behind the usage of agglomerative clustering is that similar faces observed with similar names will be merged into clusters in early stages of clustering. The early stage creates relatively robust clusters of identities. Then comes a late stage of clustering where several phenomena are occurring.

– Mistakes of the text reader are corrected, by joining the observations with minor text mistakes with the already existing clusters.
– Atypical appearances of a person are being added to existing clusters thanks to the similarity of observed names.
– Observations with non-corresponding name and face are being rejected.

The late stage ends, when the algorithm tries to merge observations with different face and name into one cluster. The clustering algorithm is straightforward:

Result: Clusters representing individual identities.
All clusters are initialized as individual multi-modal observations
$\Pi_i = \{O_i\}$;
while *any hard condition is **True*** **do**
    find the closest clusters Π_i and Π_j;
    compute hard conditions for each uni-modal distance;
    if *all hard conditions are **True*** **then**
        | merge clusters Π_i and Π_j;
    end
    if *any (but not all) hard condition is **False*** **then**
        | put smaller cluster into **left-over** clusters;
    end
end

Algorithm 1. Algorithm for agglomerative clustering.

In Algorithm 1, to find the closest clusters we use a pre-computed distance matrix. The distance between clusters is defined as the minimal distance between the elements of the clusters $d(\Pi_i, \Pi_j) = \min_{a,b} d(O_a, O_b), a \in \Pi_i, b \in \Pi_j$. When clusters are being merged, the distance matrix is updated and the process continues until the algorithm tries to merge clusters presumably representing other identities.

3.1   Hard Conditions

The hard conditions are implemented for several reasons, the main one being the stopping criterion for the clustering. They are evaluated for individual modalities. When a hard condition is **True**, it means that it was passed and the considered clusters represent the same identity w.r.t. the analyzed uni-modal observation. We define the conditions as thresholds imposed on the uni-modal distances. When the distance is above the threshold it means that the uni-modal observations are representing different identities w.r.t. the modality. The values of the thresholds are set experimentally. In our case the threshold for the facial modality is 0.3 and for the textual modality 0.5. These thresholds are also useful for setting the values of weights $\lambda_{1,2}$. We simply set $\lambda_1 = \frac{0.3}{0.3+0.5} = 0.375$ and $\lambda_2 = 0.625$. This recipe can be used when adding modalities. One would use formula

$$\lambda_i = \frac{\sum_{k \in \{1..N\} \setminus \{i\}} \tau_k}{(N-1) \sum_{l \in \{1..N\}} \tau_l}, \tag{12}$$

where τ_i is a threshold belonging to the ith modality. This is supported by the idea that the values of the thresholds represent the same condition but in different modalities.

3.2 Leftover Clusters

If the closest clusters about to be merged broke at least one hard condition, it is considered a conflict and needs to be resolved before proceeding. The most frequent situation when this happens is when a fake identity tries to be merged with a real identity. A fake identity is a set of multi-modal observations that are not representing only one person. It will happen, for example, in the case when in an image a name appears, but with several faces. The algorithm joins all the faces with the name into individual multi-modal observations (since they are time correlated), but only one (or none) are true, other are fake. Another case is when the algorithm tries to merge two different people with the same name, or two very similar looking individuals (e.g. twins) with different names. The conflict is resolved by putting the smaller cluster into the set of leftover clusters. Then the clustering continues. It is obvious that this process will yield some errors, but in much more cases it will work correctly.

4   Experiments

To evaluate the efficiency of the approach, we prepared a data-set of multi-modal observations. The data-set was obtained from approximately one year of TV News Broadcast of the Czech National Television. A typical example of the data under consideration can be seen in Fig. 2. Using the methods described in Sect. 2.3 we obtained 10 301 multi-modal observations. These were manually labeled using our own annotation tool. We recovered 2563 unique identities. The chosen evaluation metrics are coverage and purity of the clusters.

$$\text{coverage}(R, H) = \frac{\sum_{r \in R} \max_{h \in H} |r \cap h|}{\sum_{r \in R} |r|}, \tag{13}$$

Fig. 2. An example image from Czech TV News Broadcasting data-set. There are two face observations and two name observations resulting in total of four multi-modal observations.

where R, and H are the sets of reference respectively hypothesized clusters. Purity measurement is a dual representation, where the role of R and H is interchanged. The values of purity and coverage fall into the interval $\langle 0, 1 \rangle$, where 1 is the best possible value. A pure cluster (purity = 1) is one that contains only one identity. The best coverage is achieved, when one identity is represented by just one cluster and not more.

Our presented method without any further modification achieved value of coverage = 0.9069 and the value of purity = 0.9469. Although these results are very satisfactory, they could be improved. When we observed the errors, we noticed the problems arise mostly from non-definitive data. Many of the identities appear in the data only once (1778 out of 2563). If more faces appear simultaneously with one name, the algorithm has a random chance to fail. But in some cases even an expert cannot be sure to which face the name belongs. Another typical error is that the host of the News broadcast appears with a name more times than the person whose name it is. This could be addressed by modelling all the hosts beforehand and use this knowledge in the clustering process. Another open question is how to handle the leftover clusters. In small percentage of cases there will be some proper clusters left in these leftover clusters. This is already discussed in Sect. 3.2.

5 Conclusion

In this paper, we presented a method of identity extraction from TV News Broadcast using unsupervised agglomerative clustering. The output of this algorithm can be used for statistics computing, coverage computing, indexing and searching for people, and much more. We measure the quality of the results using coverage-purity measurement and achieve coverage of 0.9069 and purity of 0.9469. The designed system is modular and can be easily extended by using other modalities. The condition is that it must be possible to measure distances in the newly added modality. Since we compute the distance of clusters as the minimal distance of points of these clusters, the modality does not need to be represented in a vector space. Only the computation of distance must be provided (e.g. Levenshtein distance). Also, it should be noted that in the data under consideration almost all identities were composed only by one persona. But in future, this issue should be addressed and an approach of persona merging should be implemented. Final remark is, that the practical intention with this algorithm is to use it in a Human-in-the-loop scenario, when an expert would supervise the clustering process to obtain errorless identities so that they can be modeled.

Acknowledgment. This paper was supported by Ministry of Education, Youth and Sports of the Czech Republic project No. LO150 and by the Ministry of Education of the Czech Republic, project No. LTARF18017. The work has also been supported by the grant of the University of West Bohemia, project No. SGS-2016-039. This research is also partially supported by the Government of Russia (grant No. 08-08). Access to computing and storage facilities owned by parties and projects contributing to the National Grid Infrastructure MetaCentrum provided under the programme "Projects of Large Research, Development, and Innovations Infrastructures" (CESNET LM2015042), is greatly appreciated.

References

1. Chopra, S., Hadsell, R., LeCun, Y.: Learning a similarity metric discriminatively, with application to face verification. In: 2005 IEEE Computer Society Conference on Computer Vision and Pattern Recognition (CVPR 2005), San Diego, CA, USA, 20–26 June 2005, pp. 539–546 (2005). https://doi.org/10.1109/CVPR.2005.202,
2. Deng, J., Guo, J., Zafeiriou, S.: ArcFace: additive angular margin loss for deep face recognition. CoRR abs/1801.07698 (2018), http://arxiv.org/abs/1801.07698
3. Liu, W., Wen, Y., Yu, Z., Li, M., Raj, B., Song, L.: SphereFace: deep hypersphere embedding for face recognition. In: The IEEE Conference on Computer Vision and Pattern Recognition (CVPR), July 2017
4. Patel, Y., Busta, M., Matas, J.: E2E-MLT - an unconstrained end-to-end method for multi-language scene text. CoRR abs/1801.09919 (2018). http://arxiv.org/abs/1801.09919
5. Schroff, F., Kalenichenko, D., Philbin, J.: FaceNet: a unified embedding for face recognition and clustering (2015). https://doi.org/10.1109/CVPR.2015.7298682, http://arxiv.org/abs/1503.03832. Also published. In: Proceedings of the IEEE Computer Society Conference on Computer Vision and Pattern Recognition (2015)
6. Wang, F., Cheng, J., Liu, W., Liu, H.: Additive margin softmax for face verification. IEEE Signal Process. Lett. **25**(7), 926–930 (2018). https://doi.org/10.1109/LSP.2018.2822810
7. Zhou, X., et al.: East: an efficient and accurate scene text detector. In: 2017 IEEE Conference on Computer Vision and Pattern Recognition (CVPR), pp. 2642–2651 (2017)

Don't Talk to Noisy Drones – Acoustic Interaction with Unmanned Aerial Vehicles

Oliver Jokisch[1]([✉]), Ingo Siegert[2], Michael Maruschke[1], Tilo Strutz[1], and Andrey Ronzhin[3]

[1] Institute of Communications Engineering,
Leipzig University of Telecommunications (HfTL), 04277 Leipzig, Germany
{jokisch,maruschke,strutz}@hft-leipzig.de
[2] Institute of Information and Communication Engineering,
Otto von Guericke University, 39016 Magdeburg, Germany
ingo.siegert@ovgu.de
[3] St. Petersburg Institute for Informatics and Automation of the Russian Academy of Sciences (SPIIRAS), 199178 St. Petersburg, Russia
ronzhin@iias.spb.su

Abstract. Common applications of an unmanned aerial vehicle (UAV, aerial drone) utilize the capabilities of mobile image or video capturing, whereas our article deals with acoustic-related scenarios. Especially for surveillance tasks, e.g. in disaster management or measurement of artificial environmental noise in large industrial areas, an UAV-based acoustic interaction or measurement can be important tasks. A sound and speech signal processing at UAVs is complex because of rotor and maneuver-related noise components. The signal processing has to consider various sound sources, and the wanted signals (e.g. artificial environmental noise or speech signals) have to be separated from the UAVs' own flight and wind noise. The contribution discusses the acoustic scenarios and some acoustic characteristics of a sample UAV, including the effect of flight maneuvers. We recorded speech signals in best practice with regard to the outcome of our preliminary analyses and then conducted objective speech quality measurements and speech recognition experiments with a state-of-the-art recognizer. Aside, the measurability of environmental noise signals is analyzed exemplarily. The article concludes with lessons learned for acoustic UAV interactions or measurements and preliminary thoughts with regard to a novel category of 'low-noise' UAVs.

Keywords: UAV sound · Speech control · Speech quality · Intelligibility

1 Introduction

So far, the fairly limited research on UAV-related acoustics was directed to the sound immission in humans – e.g. involving measurements of the sound pressure level [1–3] and spectral analyses of overflight noise [4]. A few studies on

© Springer Nature Switzerland AG 2019
A. A. Salah et al. (Eds.): SPECOM 2019, LNAI 11658, pp. 180–190, 2019.
https://doi.org/10.1007/978-3-030-26061-3_19

influencing factors dealt with the number and type of rotor blades [5], the motor rotation speed [1] and the differences between quad, tri or hexcopters [4].

While UAV-related image processing in civil and military environments was intensively studied, a targeted sound processing turns out to be challenging due to rotor and other noise at flying UAVs [4,5]. Also the processing of environmental information was focused on electromagnetic signals or image processing, including object recognition with a variety of camera techniques. Consequently, the potential of sound or speech analysis directly at an UAV or in the near field was not systematically analyzed, although the additional acoustic or speech event analyses have some advantages over video-only analyses, including a lower transmission bandwidth of acoustic signals with typically 6.6 ... 23.85 kbps (AMR-WB VoLTE) or 1,411 kbps (Wav uncompressed) in comparison to video streaming, requiring 1.6 Mbps (720P HD, low quality H.264) ... 16 Mbps (5MP, high quality H.264) but also the possibility of intuitive interaction, as speech is the most natural way for humans to interact [6].

For our acoustic study, it is necessary to distinguish between different sound sources, e.g. noise which disturbs the analysis and the classification of external signals such as speech commands, acoustic events (characterizing environmental objects) or other useful signals that even allow a characterization of UAV operations or failures [3]. Except for the ultrasonic sensors, small consumer UAVs do not provide acoustic recording facilities. Nevertheless, possible applications of audio processing at the flying UAV include interesting use cases, such as the recognition of speech commands or the classification of environmental sounds.

In this article, we summarize the conceptualization and some experiments for a small sample UAV from [7–11], which include the acoustic characterization of the sample UAV as well as speech command and environmental noise recordings at the operating UAV. Afterwards, the speech commands were assessed by a speech recognizer and via the perceptual objective listening quality analysis (POLQA) [12] to roughly estimate the communication quality or perceptibility of environmental sounds. After all, we revisit the sketched communication scenarios and try some conclusions regarding an acoustic optimization of UAVs.

2   UAV-Based Communication Scenarios and Challenges

UAVs up to 25 kg are primarily used as airborne sensor platforms for surveillance, monitoring, documentation tasks and disaster management [13,14]. The transmission of the control and and mission data in almost all of these systems is realized via a digital radio-data link. However, this connection can be affected by topographic and electromagnetic interferences or might be not available. Furthermore, the humans located within areas under surveillance are generally not linked to the UAV and thus cannot establish contact with the UAV or its operator, as no interaction interface is available. A possible solution for trained rescue teams is a visual UAV control, e.g. by a gesture alphabet for operations management [15,16]. Nevertheless, gesture-based solutions are not applicable for untrained humans in a disaster scenario, since the team members are usually not familiar with the gesture set. Therefore, we are aiming at a speech-based interaction interface for UAVs as visualized in Fig. 1a.

(a) UAVs in disaster management – direct communication support and cloud-computing supported operators

(b) UAVs in industrial noise measurement at unapproachable
locations, e.g. at wind turbines or chimneys

Fig. 1. Illustrations of speech/acoustic-enabled UAV operations.

Another field of application, which appeared recently, is the acoustic measurement of environmental noise in impassable areas as demonstrated in Fig. 1b.
Two types of measures are distinguished: (a) the noise measurement directly at
the source of generation or (b) the noise measurement at areas under surveillance
(e.g. nearby living residents). Hereby, it is highly important to measure according
to pre-defined and comprehensible standards, cf. EU Directive 2000/14/EC [17].
The EU directive requires longer measurements at defined positions, and UAVs
are a good choice for impassable areas or measurements at big heights.

3   Sound and Communication Experiments

In this section, we describe some acoustic experiments utilizing the small quadcopter DJI Mavic Pro as our sample UAV platform. Beyond systematic sound recordings in different microphone positions, the induced environmental noise and some speech commands under extremely noisy conditions in the near field were recorded. The most popular UAVs are designed to gather visual recordings and to have a stable flight avoiding movement blur. The flight noise does not matter in camera UAVs, which results in loud UAVs. Table 1 summarizes the sound pressure levels (SPL) of different UAVs, reported using similar measurement conditions. It can be seen for various UAVs, that the SPL is high in general, which is the main reason for challenging acoustic recordings.

Table 1. Sound pressure level (SPL) measurements for typical commercial UAVs, sorted by SPL. The sample UAV is highlighted with gray.

UAV	Weight [kg]	Diameter [cm]	SPL [dB]	Reference
DJI Mavic Air	0.430	21.3	98	[18]
DJI Mavic Pro	0.734	33.5	98	[18]
DJI Mavic Pro Platinum	0.734	33.5	98	[18]
Syma X5C	0.907	31.0	~82	[1]
DJI Inspire 1 Pro	3.400	56.0	81	[19]
SwellPro Splashdron	2.300	50.0	80	[19]
RC Eye One Xtreme	0.157	18.0	~66	[1]
Quad-rotor MUAS	2.100	65.0	~64	[20]

3.1   Acoustic Characteristics of the Sample UAV

The studied quadcopter (DJI Mavic Pro) weighs 734 g and has a thrust-to-weight ratio (TTWR) of about 2.5 [10]. Figure 2 shows the UAV and the recording

Fig. 2. Measurement setup, microphone and recording phone [8].

equipment including the mounting material (in total 102 g) – an omnidirectional micro Rode smartLav+ (frequency range 20 Hz ... 20 kHz) connected to a hanging Jelly Pro smartphone. The additional UAV weight of 13.9 % reduces the TTWR to ≈2.2, which slightly degrades the flight quality. To analyze the influence of the recording positions onto different flight maneuvers, use cases and environments, we placed the microphone at different positions on the UAV. The smartphone as recording device was mounted in the UAV center to ensure an appropriate weight distribution. Acoustic measurements at a flying UAV pose some challenges, which affect the reducibility of the signal analysis and also the potential of noise filtering. The flight control together with micro movements, varying rotor speeds and other dynamic factors, such as turbulent flow or reflections, can hardly be synchronized with a harmonic or other analysis. All sound samples were recorded at 44.1 kHz, 16 bit, WAV format (linear PCM).

For our acoustic analyses, five basic flight maneuvers have been considered (hovering, climb, dive, directional flight and rotation). Both, sensor technology and semi-automatic control of a commercial UAV limit the environmental test scenarios: e.g., the crash protector prevents a close side-approach to walls, and the barrier detection starts to intervene already ≈30 cm over ground. Hence, we only recorded simple indoor and outdoor maneuvers like hovering under a concrete ceiling or hovering over a wood plate, carpet, grassland or reed.

3.2   Speech Command and POLQA Tests

Beside gestures, a speech control represents a potential task in a close-by human-UAV interaction. For this purpose we played random sequences of the seven German commands "Halt", "Stopp", "Start", "Fliege", "Eins", "Zwei" and "Drei", prerecorded at 44.1 kHz, linear 16 bit (mono) from a male voice aged 22. To test different effects of rotor noise, microphone position and turbulent flow, we simulated three (loud) speaker positions with two speaker-microphone distances (SMD) of 0.5 and 1.0 m respectively, while the UAV was hovering.

To assess the possible improvement by automatic noise reduction (ANR), we tested a single-channel ANR and a notch-filter method respectively [10] as well as low-pass filtering with a cut-off frequency of 4 kHz. The UAV-recorded command samples, including real-world noise and certain noise-reduced versions of each command, were fed in random order to the Google Cloud Speech-to-Text API without additional training or adaptation to the specific noise conditions. In total, 735 command realizations were tested – in average 14 samples per command, including the original and up to four noise-reduced versions.

Additionally, a POLQA test was targeting on the potential of a UAV-based human-to-human interaction e.g. during rescuing activities. POLQA is an objective method to predict the overall speech quality as perceived by humans in an ITU-T P.800 absolute category rating (ACR) listening-only test, [12,21] without performing real human listening tests. We utilized POLQA in super-wideband mode using SwissQual's SQuadAnalyzer. The prediction algorithm reaches a saturation level at a certain mean opinon score (listening quality objective, MOS-

LQO) value. For clean high-quality super-wideband (SWB) samples this level is considered 4.75.

3.3   Environmental Noise Measurement Setup

The decisive question for the use of an UAV-based environmental noise-measurement scenario (Fig. 1b) is the chance of analyzing ambient signals with UAVs. Exemplarily, we have examined three quite different environmental signals: (a) a quiet vehicle at 80 km/h on a country road – limousine BMW 5 series, (b) a loud vehicle at 30 km/h on a field – motocross motorcycle Yamaha JZF 250, and (c) a loud and recurrent, tonal sound – a ringing bell in the church tower. The signals were recorded at different microphone positions, in short distances of 1...5 m to the measured objects, at which the vehicles passed under the UAV.

4   Results and Discussion

This section presents the acoustic characteristics of UAVs at different flight maneuvers. Furthermore, the recognition rate of the speech-commands is given, supplemented by a POLQA measurement to get a preliminary impression of speech communication capabilities nearby an UAV, that need to be extended by elaborate communication tests including humans in the loop. Finally, the perceptibility of different environmental noise is analysed.

4.1   Generic Acoustic Characteristics

A representative rotation speed in the *hovering mode* is about $6,000\,\text{min}^{-1}$. Considering two blades, the associated blade passing frequency (BPF) results in $f_{BPF} = 2 \cdot f_{engine} = 2 \cdot 6,000/60$ s $= 200$ Hz. In Fig. 3a, the BPF and its dominant harmonics can be observed in the frequency range up to $\approx$3kHz. The additional, characteristic peaks in the frequency ranges 3.9...4.4 kHz and 6.5...7.5 kHz are related to the engine sound, as an affixed-UAV measurement campaign showed. The overall decline of the curve characterizes the frequency response of the microphone.

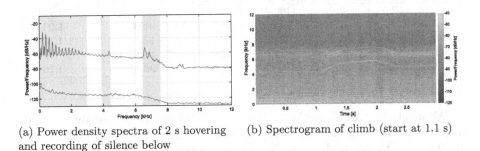

(a) Power density spectra of 2 s hovering and recording of silence below

(b) Spectrogram of climb (start at 1.1 s)

Fig. 3. Acoustic measurement and analysis of different flight maneuvers.

At the beginning of a *climb maneuver*, the rotation speeds are shortly increased for UAV acceleration, before they turn back to the previous level, as demonstrated in Fig. 3b within the time interval 1.1...2.5 s. The *dive maneuver* (negative frequency shift at the beginning) results in analog spectral effects. As the speed of *directional flight* is mainly controlled by the orientation angle of the UAV, caused by slight modifications in the rotation differences only, the power density spectra at lower UAV speeds like 10 or 30 km/h are quite similar [8]. For higher speeds like 60 km/h (sport mode), the power density in the range till 2 kHz is rising considerably. As a result, according to our experimental setup, we can not find reproducible spectral patterns related to the tested indoor and outdoor flight environments – even in short distances of 30...60 cm over ground or under ceiling. Although the recorded signals are affected by sound reflections and absorption, the spectra are presumably dominated by the influences of micro position and flight maneuver.

4.2   Speech Command Analyses

In line with our previous acoustic characterization of the sample UAV, the harmonic components of both, speech and rotor sounds, overlap to a large extent, in particular in the frequency range till 2 kHz. Even for a short microphone distance of 0.5 m, the signal-to-noise ratio (SNR) averages at 0 dB only. Hence, a command recognition without noise reduction is impossible, and a BPF-related filtering of the rotor harmonics shows a limited success, as already described in [10]. The perceptive assessment of the same commands via POLQA shows that, regardless of the filtering method, the resulting MOS-LQO values are only slightly varied and improved (1.18...1.21), which is still considered as "bad" quality, cf. Table 2, whereas the MOS-LQO of the original speech samples scores 4.73, which is practically the reachable maximum in super-wideband speech (4.75).

Table 2. Overall recognition rate (RR), rejections and MOS-LQO values of 343 signals recorded with SMD ≈0.5m

Noise reduction	SNR [dB]	Rejections [%]	RR [%]	RR w/o rejections [%]	MOS-LQO
–	0	(100.0)	–	–	1.18
ANR	20	**89.80**	10.20	100.00	**1.21**
Notch & low pass	5	69.39	28.57	93.33	1.17
Notch & ANR	25	53.06	32.65	69.57	1.17
Notch-filtering	3	46.94	**51.02**	**96.15**	1.20

Although the "ANR" method achieves an SNR improvement of about 20 dB, it can not provide adequate input signals for the speech recognizer (rejection rate of 89.8 %). The notch-filtering tries a targeted suppression of rotor harmonics with only 3 dB improvement but it seems to work in narrow limits for ASR and

POLQA. Regardless of the unacceptable rejection rate of still 46.9 %, the over-all recognition rate (exclusive rejections) achieves 96.2 %, while the MOS-LQO values are slightly improving from 1.18 to 1.20, see also Fig. 4. Unfortunately, a correlation between the psychoacoustic modelling via POLQA, the noise-level improvements (Fig. 4) as well as the recognition results cannot be revealed for our samples.

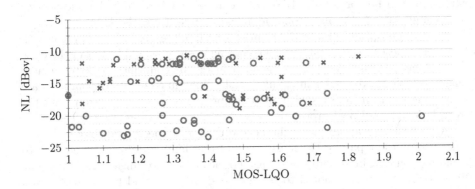

Fig. 4. Illustration of MOS-LQO values against Noise Level of the Probe (NL) in dBov for the noisy (×) and filtered signal (○).

4.3 Environmental Noise Measurement Analyses

Regarding the also investigated induced environmental noise, we have made different observations. The *car sound* is almost completely masked by the UAV noise (Fig. 5a), i.e., it is not clearly audible or detectable in the spectrogram, apart from a short level reduction, which is presumably caused by the air blast in the moment of passing. In contrast, the UAV-masked *motocross sound* (Fig. 5b) and also the masked *bell-ringing* can be still detected at close distances.

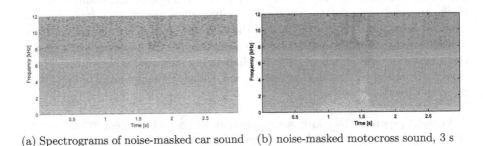

(a) Spectrograms of noise-masked car sound   (b) noise-masked motocross sound, 3 s

Fig. 5. Acoustic measurement of different induced environmental noise.

5   Lessons Learned for the UAV Research in Progress

Acoustic interaction with UAVs and acoustic measurements at/nearby UAVs are quite challenging. The quickly varying frequencies of blade passing and motor sound can not be easily filtered and require the design of advanced filters, which consider the known sound characteristics and flight maneuvers. Also moving the sound recording from the UAV to a nearby location (e.g. using an arm extension) can be considered. Hereby, it can be imagined that the microphone hangs under the UAV on a rope or inflexible pole from the UAV's center to ensure an appropriate weight distribution. Such an "external" microphone can be lowered closer to the human. The recording position would be out of the close UAV range, and the noises are lowered. It has to be confirmed by experiments, whether such approaches can ensure stable flight maneuvers. Beyond, we are examining sound recordings with an 8-channel microphone array, supplemented by a decided signal post-processing.

An alternative approach might be the design of specific 'low-noise' UAVs, since a significant part of the noise results from flight-stabilizing maneuvers to avoid motion blur in camera recordings. For acoustic recordings, highly-dynamic flight stability can be ignored to some extend, which would reduce motor and rotor noise. An acoustically improved UAV might provide lower velocity, thrust and mobility but a significantly improved SNR. Furthermore, a successful design of 'low-noise' UAVs might also serve strict acoustic demands, as e.g. in wildlife monitoring [22,23], in which the currently available UAVs can stress wild animals to a large extent [24].

6   Conclusions

Sound analyses at a small UAV are highly affected by the blade passing frequencies and their harmonics, at which the recorded signals significantly vary with the microphone position and the flight maneuver. With the best proposed noise reduction method, unfortunately half of the commands are rejected but the rest is correctly recognized. Thus, a conventional single or two-channel microphone approach does not allow a proper analysis of sounds or speech commands. And the command control is thus at the moment limited to non-time-critical scenarios. Also the perception of wanted environmental noise, not to mention the appropriate measurement, is quite challenging. Some possible solutions have been indicated in the lessons-learned section, showing the potential of our future research directions.

Acknowledgment. This work was supported by the EU project "Collaborative strategies of heterogeneous robot activity at solving agriculture missions controlled via intuitive human-robot interfaces (HARMONIC)" within the "ERA.Net RUS Plus/Robotics" program 2018–2020 (project ID 99) co-funded by the German Federal Ministry of Education and Research (BMBF) under Grant No. 01 DJ18011 and the Russian Foundation for Basic Research under Grant No. 18-58-76001_ERA.Net.

Special thanks goes to Dominik Fischer and Franziska Wolf for their valuable experiments, enabling our study. We also thank Rohde & Schwarz SwissQual, in particular Jens Berger, for supplying the POLQA testbed.

References

1. Papa, U., Iannace, G., Core, G.D., Giordano, G.: Determination of sound power levels of a small UAS during flight operations. In: Proceedings of the INTER-NOISE, vol. 45, pp. 216–226 (2016)
2. Miesikowska, M.: Analysis of signal of X8 unmanned aerial vehicle. In: Proceedings of the IEEE Conference on Signal Processing: Algorithms, Architectures, Arrangements and Applications (SPA), pp. 69–72, September 2017
3. Kloet, N., Watkins, S., Clothier, R.: Acoustic signature measurement of small multi-rotor unmanned aircraft systems. Int. J. Micro Air Veh. 9(1), 3–14 (2017). https://doi.org/10.1177/1756829316681868
4. Cabell, R., Grosveld, F., McSwain, R.: Measured noise from small unmanned aerial vehicles. In: Proceedings of the INTER-NOISE/NOISE-CON, vol. 252, pp. 345–354 (2016)
5. Intaratep, N., Alexander, W., Devenport, W., Grace, S., Dropkin, A.: Experimental study of quadcopter acoustics and performance at static thrust conditions. In: Proceedings of the Aeroacoustics Conference (AIAA/CEAS), vol. 22, June 2016
6. Carroll, J.M.: Human Computer Interaction - Brief Intro, 2nd edn. The Interaction Design Foundation, Aarhus (2013)
7. Vu, Q., Raković, M., Delic, V., Ronzhin, A.: Trends in development of UAV-UGV cooperation approaches in precision agriculture. In: Ronzhin, A., Rigoll, G., Meshcheryakov, R. (eds.) ICR 2018. LNCS (LNAI), vol. 11097, pp. 213–221. Springer, Cham (2018). https://doi.org/10.1007/978-3-319-99582-3_22
8. Jokisch, O., Fischer, D.: Drone sounds and environmental signals - a first review. In: Birkholz, P., Stone, S. (eds.) Proceedings of the ESSV Conference (Studientexte zur Sprachkommunikation) vol. 93, pp. 212–220, Dresden, March 2019
9. Jokisch, O.: A pilot study on the acoustic signal processing at a small aerial drone. In: Antokhina, Y. (ed.) Proceedings of the 14th International Conference on Electromechanics and Robotics "Zavalishin's Readings" ER(ZR), Kursk, April 2019
10. Fischer, D.: Untersuchung von Geräusch-und Sprachsignalen beim Einsatz von Flugdrohnen (UAV) [in German]. Bachelor's thesis, HfT Leipzig, November 2018
11. Wolf, F.: Untersuchung von Methoden zur Störgeräuschunterdrückung beim Einsatz von Flugdrohnen (in German). Master's thesis, HfT Leipzig, March 2019
12. ITU-T: Methods for objective and subjective assessment of speech quality (POLQA): perceptual objective listening quality assessment. REC P.863, September 2014. http://www.itu.int/rec/T-REC-P.863-201409-I/en
13. Erdelj, M., Natalizio, E.: UAV-assisted disaster management: applications and open issues. In: 2016 International Conference on Computing, Networking and Communications (ICNC), pp. 1–5, February 2016
14. Restas, A.: Drone applications for supporting disaster management. World J. Eng. Technol. 3, 316–321 (2015)
15. Schelle, A., Stütz, P.: Modelling visual communication with UAS. In: Hodicky, J. (ed.) MESAS 2016. LNCS, vol. 9991, pp. 81–98. Springer, Cham (2016). https://doi.org/10.1007/978-3-319-47605-6_7

16. Schelle, A., Stütz, P.: Gestural transmission of tasking information to an airborne UAV. In: Yamamoto, S., Mori, H. (eds.) HIMI 2018. LNCS, vol. 10904, pp. 318–335. Springer, Cham (2018). https://doi.org/10.1007/978-3-319-92043-6_27
17. EC: European Communities (Noise Emission by Equipment For Use Outdoors) Regulations, Directive 632 (2001)
18. Miljković, D.: Methods for attenuation of unmanned aerial vehicle noise. In: 41st International Convention on Information and Communication Technology, Electronics and Microelectronics (MIPRO), pp. 0914–0919, May 2018
19. Christiansen, F., Rojano-Doñate, L., Madsen, P.T., Bejder, L.: Noise levels of multi-rotor unmanned aerial vehicles with implications for potential underwater impacts on marine mammals. Front. Mar. Sci. **3**, 277 (2016)
20. Kloet, N., Watkins, S., Clothier, R.: Acoustic signature measurement of small multi-rotor unmanned aircraft systems. Int. J. Micro Air Veh. **9**, 3–14 (2017)
21. ITU-T: Methods for subjective determination of transmission quality. REC P.800 (1996). https://www.itu.int/rec/T-REC-P.800-199608-I/en
22. Simek, P., Pavlík, J., Jarolimek, J., Ocenásek, V., Stoces, M.: Use of unmanned aerial vehicles for wildlife monitoring. In: Proceedings of the 8th Conference on Information and Communication Technologies in agriculture, Food and Environment (HAICTA 2017), pp. 795–804, Chania (2017)
23. Hodgson, J.C., Baylis, S.M., Mott, R., Herrod, A., Clarke, R.H.: Precision wildlife monitoring using unmanned aerial vehicles. Sci. Rep. **6**, 22574 (2016)
24. Hodgson, J.C., Koh, L.P.: Best practice for minimising unmanned aerial vehicle disturbance to wildlife in biological field research. Curr. Biol. **26**(10), R404–R405 (2016)

Method for Multimodal Recognition of One-Handed Sign Language Gestures Through 3D Convolution and LSTM Neural Networks

Ildar Kagirov$^{(\boxtimes)}$![ORCID], Dmitry Ryumin ![ORCID], and Alexandr Axyonov ![ORCID]

St. Petersburg Institute for Informatics and Automation of the Russian Academy of Sciences, St. Petersburg, Russia
kagirov@iias.spb.su,
{dl_03.03.1991,a.aksenov95}@mail.ru

Abstract. The paper presents an approach to the multimodal recognition of dynamic and static gestures of Russian sign language through 3D convolutional and LSTM neural networks. A set of data in color format and a depth map, consisting of 48 one-handed gestures of Russian sign language, is presented as well. The set of data was obtained with the use of the Kinect sensor v2 and contains records of 13 different native signers of Russian sign language. The obtained results are compared with these of other methods. The experiment on classification showed a great potential of neural networks in solving this problem. Achieved recognition accuracy was of 73.25%, and, compared to other approaches to the problem, this turns out to be the best result.

Keywords: Gesture recognition · Sign language · 3D CNN · Convolution LSTM · Human-Machine interaction

1 Introduction

Gestures as a form of nonverbal communication are of great importance in everyday life and constitute different language systems and sub-systems: from the « body language » to sign languages [1, 2]. Nowadays gesture recognition increasingly finds applications in various domains associated with computer vision tasks, such as human-machine interaction (HMI) [3] or virtual reality [4]. In a general sense, the gesture recognition aims at comprehension of any meaningful movement of a person's hand, or hands, or other body parts. The problem of gesture recognition has not been resolved so far due to variations between the sign languages of the world, noisy signing environment, small size of articulators (hands, fingers).

The gesture recognition, in most cases, comes down to processing of a video sequence, which provides the viewer with information about a part of the human body and its coordinates in space and time [5]. The exceptions are the so-called static gestures, involving no constant, dynamic articulator movements, and the time-space coordinates are mostly one and the same for all the gesture time [6]. Complex gestures involving different articulators and localizations also contribute to difficulties of gesture recognition due to challenges of spatial feature extraction, where it finds out that the

A. A. Salah et al. (Eds.): SPECOM 2019, LNAI 11658, pp. 191–200, 2019.
https://doi.org/10.1007/978-3-030-26061-3_20

articulators are relatively small if compared to the whole picture. It seems reasonable, therefore, that the process of gesture recognition should be based on processing of a video sequence, not a single video picture, so that not only spatial coordinates, but also time features could be extracted.

The rest of this paper is structured in the following way: in Sect. 2, current approaches to sign language recognition are considered; in Sect. 3, a multimodal 3D database of one-handed gestures of Russian sign language is presented, and the 4th section depicts the proposed algorithm for a multi-modal recognition of specific gestures of Russian sign language. The subject of Sect. 5 is a discussion of the results of experiments, and the conclusions and perspectives of this investigation are drawn.

2   Related Work

Most of widely used methods and approaches, that have been applied by other researchers to the gesture recognition task, are briefly outlined in this section.

The first method to be mentioned involves using of two-stream convolutional networks [7] to extract space-time features of a gesture from integrated color (RGB) and 3D frames (depth map) separately. The second way presupposes first applying long-term recurrent convolutional networks (LRCN) [8] in order to extract spatial features of each individual area, and then obtaining temporary gesture features with the use of a recurrent neural network, based on the previously obtained spatial information. Another method makes use of the VideoLSTM [9] architecture to use long short-term memory (LSTM) [10] and extract the space-time features of gestures from a chain of previously annotated 2D areas.

These methods are based on extraction of the spatial and temporal information at different stages, or independently. Extracting both the spatial and temporal components of a gesture would be an effective solution, considering the possibility of having a complex background component on the scene. For example, 3D convolutional neural networks [11] are used for simultaneous extraction of short-term space-time features. However, it is LSTM networks that are best suited for storing temporary features. As one could see above, it is reasonable to use a 3D convolutional neural network to extract short-term spatial-temporal features and then use LSTM to extract spatial-temporal dependencies from a long duration chain of frames. Such a 3D convolutional LSTM network, due to its ability to store 3D spatial information, forms more efficient spatial-temporal characteristics of a gesture.

Traditional approaches to gesture recognition usually involve handcrafted algorithms [12], such as the support vector machine method [13], or machine learning methods, e.g. Monte Carlo algorithms [14], hidden Markov models [15], neural networks of various design [8, 10, 16]. In paper [17], it is suggested to recognize the trajectory of gestures (drawing letters with fingers in space) through the method of structured dynamic time deformation (SDTW). The authors of another work [18] use the hidden Markov models and the naive Bayes model to analyze the recognition of dynamic gestures recorded via Kinect sensor. In [19], a system of static gesture recognition is presented, based on geometric normalization of the hand regions and the 2D Krawtchouk moments. In paper [20], an adaptive space-time function is applied to represent information of external and temporal features of gestures using data from a color camera and a depth sensor (RGB-D).

The aforementioned handcrafted algorithms are not very efficient because they do not meet the requirements of practice-oriented gesture recognition systems being unable to process simultaneously many factors during signing (noise of various nature or occlusion on a video stream). Moreover, current methods that belong to the set of "handcrafted" functions did not cope with the tasks that were set during the large ChaLearn Looking at People (LAP) [21] Competition on static and dynamic gestures recognition, held in 2016 within the framework of the International Conference on Pattern Recognition (ICPR). On the contrary, machine learning methods based on deep neural networks demonstrate fairly good results in image segmentation and classification [22], recognition of both static and dynamic objects [23], face recognition [24], gesture [25], actions of a person [26].

Nowadays, many models based on deep neural networks (DNN) are used in various interactive systems, medicine, military robotics, etc. 3D convolutional neural network-based approaches [11] to gesture recognition tasks showed quite good results [27], as it was shown during ChaLearn LAP Competition within ICPR. The authors of [28] presented a pyramid 3D design of ultra-precise neural network aimed at static gestures recognition. 3D convolutional neural networks are used to extract space-time features, while the pyramid representation allows to save contextual information about the gesture during the scaling process. The best results of the ChaLearn LAP on the ICPR were obtained by the authors of [29]. Their approach implies combining the convolutional two stream consensus voting network (2SCVN) for the RGB and the ConvNet 3D convolutional network (3DDSN), in order to determine more reliable features of gestures. An updated and improved version of this approach was published in [30].

Based on the experiments that have been carried out by other authors, it can be concluded that the problem of relatively small size of articulators, i.e. hands, and various conditions of signing can be partially solved through a simultaneous extraction of the space-time component of a gesture. The 3D convolutional LSTM neural network seems to be good suited for this task.

Hence, an approach to multimodal (color video stream and depth map) recognition of both dynamic and static one-handed gestures from Russian sign language based on the use of a 3D convolutional LSTM neural network is proposed within the present paper. All the video sequences are brought to a fixed length through a normalization procedure. The 3D convolutional neural network extracts short-term spatial-temporal features from the video stream, and the LSTM network extracts long-term spatial-temporal features. A spatial pyramid pooling [28] is also used, and is aimed at normalizing the obtained spatial-temporal features for the subsequent hypothesis about the following gesture. The modalities obtained from the color camera and the depth sensor are trained separately and are further combined only at the level of hypothesis for decision making.

Summarizing, one can list the following features of the proposed approach for recognizing some of the Russian sign language gestures: (a) ability to customize the learning process and the prediction algorithm through the process of extracting 3D features of gestures; (b) suitability of the approach, both for static and dynamic gestures; (c) possibility to teach recognition models for other sign languages of the world, for example [31] and [32], with available multimodal databases, for example, such as [33].

3   Database

This section describes a multimedia database of 3D one-handed gestures of Russian sign language (TheRuSLan).

At the current stage of the research, the TheRuSLan data set consists of video recordings of Russian sign language in the formats of RGB and depth map (48 one-handed gestures in total). Examples of frames showing a gesture are shown in Fig. 1.

Fig. 1. Examples of frames presenting a gesture in FullHD format (left), and in the depth map mode (right)

The subject area of the data set is the food, namely, food available in supermarkets. There were 13 signers that took part in the recordings, each signer demonstrated each gesture 5 times at a distance of 1.5–2 m from the Kinect 2.0 sensor. The main characteristics of the database (TheRuSLan) are presented in Table 1.

Both static and dynamic gestures are included into the database. By static gestures we mean such gestures that include no significant change of hand location or the number of active fingers. On the contrary, dynamic gestures do imply some significant change of the number of articulators or their location.

The second cluster, communicant data, covers information regarding the number and peculiarities of the communicants (Fig. 2).

Table 1. Characteristics of the TheRuSLan database

Characteristics	Values
Number of signers	13
Total number of gestures	48
Iterations of each gesture by the signer	5
Resolution (color frames)	FullHD (1920 × 1080)
Resolution (depth map)	512 × 424
Distance from the recorder to the signers	1.2–2 m.
Average age of the signers	24
Total size of the output data	≈798 Gb.

4 Method

This section presents the process of multi-modal recognition of one-handed static and dynamic gestures of Russian sign language evaluated by the authors (Fig. 2).

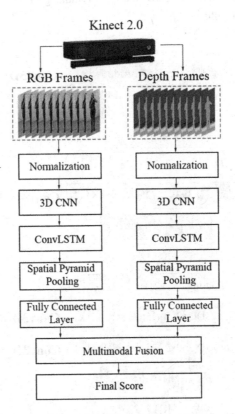

Fig. 2. The process of multimodal recognition of one-handed gestures

In most cases, a gesture demonstration involves the following stages: preparation for a gesture, functional component of a gesture (the core), and retraction [34]. The preparation may consist of an initial movement with the hands to the starting location, a neutral movement with the hands, or a residual movement from the previous gesture. The functional core of the gesture includes a context-independent movement with the arms. Retraction is the movement of the hands to the position of preparation for the next gesture. However, the problem is that each signer demonstrates gestures at different speeds. Thus, any gesture consists of various sequences of video frames (the length of the gesture), and it is necessary to input data of the same dimensionality to the neural network all the time. Therefore, it is first necessary to normalize the video sequences. There are two ways to perform the normalization, either dividing all video sequences with gestures into sequences of frames of fixed length, or using an approach based on lowering the frequency of all marked sequences with gestures to a constant length.

The first method is bad because it is impossible to pick out video sequences of equal length, in order to get rid of any preparation and retraction stages. The second approach is free of this disadvantage, and this was the reason for the authors of this paper for using it. Normalized samples are video sequences of 30 frames.

The 3D CNN designed for recognizing individual gestures of Russian sign language is presented in Fig. 3.

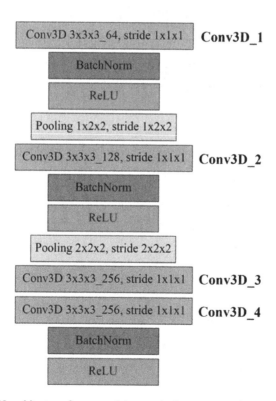

Fig. 3. 3D CNN architecture for recognizing particular gestures of Russian sign language

Four 3D convolutional layers are used with 64, 128, 256, and 256 filters correspondingly. Each 3D convolutional layer has a core size of $3 \times 3 \times 3$, while stride and padding of each layer are all size of $1 \times 1 \times 1$. Each 3D convolutional layer (except the 3rd one) is followed by a normalization procedure, in order to solve the problem of internal covariant displacement and the activation function of the ReLU. The first layer has only the function of spatial unification due to a downsampling layer with a core size of $1 \times 2 \times 2$ and the same stride and padding. The second layer performs a space-time association procedure, with the core size and padding and stride of $2 \times 2 \times 2$. These layers make it possible to reduce the spatial size of the output layer of the 3D CNN 4 times, and to reduce the temporary size of the output layer 2 times. Thus, using 3D CNN network, only short-term time-space features are extracted.

Next, a two-level convolutional LSTM network is used, which allows both input-state and state-state convolutions. The size of the convolution core is 3×3, with padding and stride of 1×1. The first convolutional layer contains 256 filters, while the second one contains 384 filters. This allows to extract space-time features of the gesture. As a result, for each gesture, the convolutional LSTM network extracts a long-term time-space feature. The output features of the convolutional LSTM network have the same spatial size as the features from the 3D CNN.

A spatial pyramid pooling [12] is used before fully connected layers, which allows to reduce the spatial dimension of the signs of gestures.

Before classification, modalities are combined by averaging the estimates from the two obtained neural networks.

5   Experiment

This section provides test results for the proposed approach, based on TheRuSLan database.

For training, 4 iterations of each one-handed gesture were used, and one iteration by each signer for testing. Thus, 2496 iterations of gestures were used for training, and 624 iterations for testing. A relatively small number of testing iterations is due to the small size of the database.

All the neural networks described within the present paper were implemented using the TensorFlow [35] and Keras [36] tools, which simplify creation, training, and deployment of deep learning models. The best results were obtained in the following case: Training was made from zero level. The initial learning rate was 0.1 and decreased every 10 thousand iterations. After 50 thousand iterations, the learning rate was 0.01 and decreased every 2000 iterations. The total number of iterations was 80.000. All the models were trained with NVIDIA GeForce GTX 1080 GPU graphics device. The proposed approach showed the following accuracy: 68.31% for color video sequences only, 64.93% for data obtained from the depth map only, and 73.25% for the multimodal data set with two combined modalities.

A comparative table of the proposed approach and other methods is presented in Table 2. The results, i.e. accuracy, are taken directly from the cited works and were obtained for different testing material.

Table 2. Experimental results

Methods	Modalities	Accuracy, %
Liu and Shao [37]	RGB + depth	61.53
Proposed method	Depth	64.93
Proposed method	RGB	68.31
Tung and Ngoc [38]	RGB + depth	69.57
Molchanov et al. [39]	RGB + depth	72.04
Zheng et al. [40]	RGB + depth	72.97
Proposed method	RGB + depth	73.25

6 Conclusion

This article proposes an approach to the recognition of both dynamic and static one-handed gestures of Russian sign language with the use of a 3D LSTM convolutional neural network. From the results, it can be concluded that the space-time features extracted from the gesture are quite stable under complex background components on the scene. CNN 3D is well suited for obtaining short-term spatial and temporal features, and super-precise LSTM networks for long-term spatial and temporal features. The best accuracy was achieved on a multimodal data set, being 73.25%.

In the future studies, attempts will be made to improve recognition accuracy by increasing the data set, as well as to expand the data for recognition with two-handed gestures.

Acknowledgments. This research is financially supported by the Ministry of Science and Higher Education of the Russian Federation, agreement No. 14.616.21.0095 (reference RFMEFI61618X0095).

References

1. Ryumin, D., Karpov, A.A.: Towards automatic recognition of sign language gestures using kinect 2.0. In: Antona, M., Stephanidis, C. (eds.) UAHCI 2017. LNCS, vol. 10278, pp. 89–101. Springer, Cham (2017). https://doi.org/10.1007/978-3-319-58703-5_7
2. Karpov, A., Krnoul, Z., Zelezny, M., Ronzhin, A.: Multimodal synthesizer for Russian and Czech sign languages and audio-visual speech. In: Stephanidis, C., Antona, M. (eds.) UAHCI 2013. LNCS, vol. 8009, pp. 520–529. Springer, Heidelberg (2013). https://doi.org/10.1007/978-3-642-39188-0_56
3. Ryumin, D., Ivanko, D., Axyonov, A., Kagirov, I., Karpov, A., Zelezny, M.: Human-robot interaction with smart shopping trolley using sign language: data collection. In: Proceedings of IEEE International Conference on Pervasive Computing and Communications, PerCom-2019, Kyoto, Japan (2019, in press)
4. Lin, W., Du, L., Harris-Adamson, C., Barr, A., Rempel, D.: Design of hand gestures for manipulating objects in virtual reality. In: Kurosu, M. (ed.) HCI 2017. LNCS, vol. 10271, pp. 584–592. Springer, Cham (2017). https://doi.org/10.1007/978-3-319-58071-5_44

5. Cao, Z., Hidalgo, G., Simon, T., Wei, S.-E., Sheikh, Y.: OpenPose: realtime multi-person 2D pose estimation using part affinity fields. In: IEEE Conference on Computer Vision and Pattern Recognition, CVPR-2018, arXiv preprint arXiv:1812.08008 (2018)
6. Oyedotun, O., Khashman, A.: Deep learning in vision-based static hand gesture recognition. Neural Comput. Appl. **28**(12), 3941–3951 (2017)
7. Zhu, Y., Lan, Z., Newsam, S., Hauptmann, A.G.: Hidden two-stream convolutional networks for action recognition. arXiv preprint arXiv:1704.00389 (2017)
8. Ouyang, D., Zhang, Y., Shao, J.: Video-based person re-identification via spatio-temporal attentional and two-stream fusion convolutional networks. Pattern Recogn. Lett. **117**, 153–160 (2019)
9. Li, Z., Gavves, E., Jain, M., Snoek, C.G.: VideoLSTM convolves, attends and flows for action recognition. arXiv preprint arXiv:1607.01794 (2016)
10. Hochreiter, S., Schmidhuber, J.: Long short-term memory. Neural Comput. **9**(8), 1735–1780 (1997)
11. Ji, S., Xu, W., Yang, M., Yu, K.: 3D convolutional neural networks for human action recognition. IEEE Trans. Pattern Anal. Mach. Intell. **35**, 221–231 (2010)
12. Nanni, L., Ghidoni, S., Brahnam, S.: Handcrafted vs non-handcrafted features for computer vision classification. Pattern Recogn. **71**, 158–172 (2017)
13. Chang, C., Lin, C.: LIBSVM: a library for support vector machines. ACM Trans. Intell. Syst. Technol. TIST **2**(3), 27 (2011)
14. Remilekun Basaru, R., Slabaugh, G., Alonso, E., Child, C.: Hand pose estimation using deep stereovision and markov-chain monte carlo. In Proceedings of the IEEE International Conference on Computer Vision, pp. 595–603 (2017)
15. Sinha, K., Kumari, R., Priya, A., Paul, P.: A computer vision-based gesture recognition using hidden markov model. In: Chattopadhyay, J., Singh, R., Bhattacherjee, V. (eds.) Innovations in Soft Computing and Information Technology, pp. 55–67. Springer, Singapore (2019). https://doi.org/10.1007/978-981-13-3185-5_6
16. Krizhevsky, A., Sutskever, I., Hinton, G.: ImageNet classification with deep convolutional neural networks. In: Advances in Neural Information Processing Systems, pp. 1097–1105 (2012)
17. Tang, J., Cheng, H., Zhao, Y., Guo, H.: Structured dynamic time warping for continuous hand trajectory gesture recognition. Pattern Recogn. **80**, 21–31 (2018)
18. Li, G., Wu, H., Jiang, G., Xu, S., Liu, H.: Dynamic gesture recognition in the Internet of Things. IEEE Access **7**, 23713–23724 (2019)
19. Priyal, S., Bora, P.: A robust static hand gesture recognition system using geometry based normalizations and Krawtchouk moments. Pattern Recogn. **46**(8), 2202–2219 (2013)
20. Lin, J., Ruan, X., Yu, N., Yang, Y.: Adaptive local spatiotemporal features from RGB-D data for one-shot learning gesture recognition. Sensors **16**(12), 2171 (2016)
21. Wan, J., Zhao, Y., Zhou, S., Guyon, I., Escalera, S., Li, S.: Chalearn looking at people RGB-D isolated and continuous datasets for gesture recognition. In: Proceedings of the IEEE Conference on Computer Vision and Pattern Recognition Workshops, pp. 56–64 (2016)
22. Girshick, R.: Fast R-CNN. In: Proceedings of the IEEE International Conference on Computer Vision, pp. 1440–1448 (2015)
23. Huang, J., et al.: Speed/accuracy trade-offs for modern convolutional object detectors. In: Proceedings of 30th IEEE Conference on Computer Vision and Pattern Recognition, CVPR-2017, pp. 3296–3297 (2017)
24. Ranjan, R., Patel, V., Chellappa, R.: Hyperface: a deep multi-task learning framework for face detection, landmark localization, pose estimation, and gender recognition. IEEE Trans. Pattern Anal. Mach. Intell. **41**(1), 121–135 (2019)

25. Pigou, L., Van Den Oord, A., Dieleman, S., Van Herreweghe, M., Dambre, J.: Beyond temporal pooling: recurrence and temporal convolutions for gesture recognition in video. Int. J. Comput. Vis. **126**, 430–439 (2018)
26. Redmon, J., Divvala, S., Girshick, R., Farhadi, A.: You only look once: unified, real-time object detection. In: Proceedings of the IEEE Conference on Computer Vision and Pattern Recognition, pp. 779–788 (2016)
27. Escalante, H., et al.: ChaLearn joint contest on multimedia challenges beyond visual analysis: an overview. In: 23rd International Conference on Pattern Recognition, ICPR-2016, pp. 67–73 (2016)
28. Zhu, G., Zhang, L., Mei, L., Shao, J., Song, J., Shen, P.: Large-scale isolated gesture recognition using pyramidal 3D convolutional networks. In 23rd International Conference on Pattern Recognition, ICPR-2016, pp. 19–24 (2016)
29. Duan, J., Zhou, S., Wan, J., Guo, X., Li, S.: Multi-modality fusion based on consensus-voting and 3D convolution for isolated gesture recognition. arXiv preprint arXiv:1611.06689 (2016)
30. Duan, J., Wan, J., Zhou, S., Guo, X., Li, S.: A unified framework for multi-modal isolated gesture recognition. ACM Trans. Multimedia Comput. Commun. Appl. (TOMM) **14**(1), 21 (2018)
31. Kudubayeva, S., Ryumin, D., Kalghanov, M.: The influence of the kazakh language semantic peculiarities on computer sign language. In: International Conferences on Information and Communication Technology, Society, and Human Beings, ICT-2016, Madeira, Portugal, pp. 221–226 (2016)
32. Karpov, A., Kipyatkova, I., Zelezny, M.: Automatic technologies for processing spoken sign languages. In: 5th Workshop on Spoken Language Technologies for Under-Resourced Languages, SLTU-2016, vol. 81, pp. 201–207 (2016)
33. Wang, P., Li, W., Liu, S., Gao, Z., Tang, C., Ogunbona, P.: Large-scale isolated gesture recognition using convolutional neural networks. In: Proceedings of the 23rd International Conference on Pattern Recognition, ICPR-2016, pp. 7–12 (2016)
34. Gavrila, D.: The visual analysis of human movement: a survey. Comput. vis. Image Underst. **73**(1), 2–98 (1999)
35. Abadi, M., et al.: TensorFlow: a system for large-scale machine learning. In: 12th Symposium on Operating Systems Design and Implementation, pp. 265–283 (2016)
36. Gulli, A., Pal, S.: Deep Learning with Keras. Packt Publishing Ltd (2017)
37. Liu, L., Shao, L.: Learning discriminative representations from RGB-D video data. In: Twenty-Third International Joint Conference on Artificial Intelligence (2013)
38. Tung, P., Ngoc, L.: Elliptical density shape model for hand gesture recognition. In: International Proceedings of the ICTD (2014)
39. Molchanov, P., Yang, X., Gupta, S., Kim, K., Tyree, S., Kautz, J.: Online detection and classification of dynamic hand gestures with recurrent 3D convolutional neural network. In: Proceedings of the IEEE Conference on Computer Vision and Pattern Recognition, pp. 4207–4215 (2016)
40. Zheng, J., Feng, Z., Xu, C., Hu, J., Ge, W.: Fusing shape and spatiotemporal features for depth-based dynamic hand gesture recognition. In: Zheng, J., Feng, Z., Xu, C., Hu, J., Ge, W. (eds.) Multimedia Tools and Applications, vol. 76, pp. 1–20. Springer, New York (2016). https://doi.org/10.1007/s11042-016-3988-8

LSTM-Based Kazakh Speech Synthesis

Arman Kaliyev$^{(\boxtimes)}$ iD

ITMO University, St. Petersburg, Russia
kaliyev.arman@yandex.kz
https://en.ifmo.ru

Abstract. Currently, the level of penetration of speech technology in modern life begins to vary greatly by country and by language environment. This is especially noticeable in the services developed in leading technology companies, where high-resource languages such as English, Russian, etc. have become the main service languages. Whereas, the speech technologies for under-resourced languages lag in their development. The article presents the first speech synthesis system based on the long-term short-term memory (LSTM) neural network architecture for the Kazakh language. The presented text-to-speech (TTS) system includes previously developed methods of prosodic processing for under-resourced languages and an acoustic model based on LSTM. The system receives the linguistic features of the text, including phonetic transcription, and it generates Kazakh speech with an acceptable quality of perception. Briefly summing up, this work describes the method of developing a speech synthesis for the Kazakh language, which has limited resources in terms of natural language processing. This approach can also be applied to other under-resourced languages.

Keywords: Statistical parametric speech synthesis ·
Speech synthesis · LSTM · Kazakh language ·
Under-resourced languages

1 Introduction

At the present time, we can note the high penetration of speech technologies into modern systems of human-machine interfaces. Unfortunately, it became apparent that the level of penetration of such technologies is varied by countries and language environments. The systems, operating in high resourced languages such as English and French, are provided with high quality speech services. Whereas, their analogs for under-resourced languages are provided with poorly developed speech services or with their complete absence. Accordingly, in societies where the main languages of communication are under-resourced languages, there is a demand for such technologies. Developing a speech synthesis system for under-resourced languages is a crucial task. This article presents the statistical parametric speech synthesis (SPSS) based on LSTM for the Kazakh language.

At the moment there are two approaches of neural network application for speech synthesis:

© Springer Nature Switzerland AG 2019
A. A. Salah et al. (Eds.): SPECOM 2019, LNAI 11658, pp. 201–208, 2019.
https://doi.org/10.1007/978-3-030-26061-3_21

1. End-to-end models, when a neural network is trained to directly identify the relationship between linguistic and speech features, examples of this approach are VoiceLoop [19], Char2Wav [17], and Tacotron [16];
2. Conventional pipeline processing, when the main task is divided into separate subtasks, and neural networks are used to solve some tasks.

Despite the fact that the first method is capable of producing high-quality speech signal, it is expensive in term of computational costs, as it requires high computational capabilities for operating. In the second method, the neural network acoustic model is trained, where the inputs are prosodic and linguistic features (including phonetic transcription) and the outputs are acoustic features. Neural networks can also be used to detect some prosodic features, for example, the duration of phonemes.

The main distinguishing feature of the SPSS is that it allows controlling and changing the acoustic features of the speech. Thus, researchers can better understand the influence of certain features on speech perception. The LSTM acoustic model were successfully applied in [1,4,20], thanks to the long-term memory LSTM can more successfully identify the long-term phonetic dependencies than, for example, the feed forward deep neural networks (DNN).

As far as we know, so far there was only one TTS system for the Kazakh language, developed by the Speech Technology Center Ltd. in 2014 based on the Unit Selection technology. Unfortunately, at the end of the development, the evaluation results of the system performance were not published.

In modern concepts of natural language processing, the Kazakh language is an under-resourced (the term was proposed by Krauwer [10] and Berment [2]) and poorly studied language [8]. A particular problem is the identification of all prosodic parameters affecting the sound of speech. Despite this, we were able to develop a number of methods [5–7] of prosodic processing for the Kazakh language, which can also be applied to other under-resourced languages.

Summing up, we present a new SPSS for the Kazakh language, where LSTM was used to train the acoustic model. As far as the author knows, this is the first SPSS system for the Kazakh language.

The paper is organized as follows: Sect. 2 describes the corpus and the selected language, Sect. 3 presents the methods of prosodic processing, Sect. 4 introduces the acoustic model, Sect. 5 discusses the architecture of the TTS, Sect. 6 presents the evaluation method, Sect. 7 talks about the results of the evaluation, and Sect. 8 gives conclusion.

2   Corpus and Language

This SPSS was created for the Kazakh language and it is the first such system for this language. And, the methods used here can also be applied to other languages, especially for under-resourced languages.

2.1 Language

The Kazakh language belongs to the Kypchak group of Turkic languages. According to A.Z. Salmenova, agglutinative nature of Turkic languages (postpositive suffixation, fixed order of words, special auxiliary words) is reflected in the fact that the functional load of melodic, temporal and dynamic characteristics in the Kazakh non-finite syntagma turned out to be of little importance compared to Russian and English. Thus, not only the morphological and syntactic factors influence the prosody of the Kazakh phrase, but also phonetic features at the segment level. We are talking about the phenomenon of the vowel harmony, which is able to create a special segmental and prosodic organization of words, syntagms and sentences for these languages [14].

2.2 Corpus

We used the speech corpus "Assel" [9] of the Kazakh language, which was created in 2014 by the Speech Technology Center Ltd. in partnership with the Kostanay State University. The speech corpora consists of 5.6 h of neutral female speech or 6 thousand separate phrases and sentences.

3   Prosodic Processing

Since the Kazakh language is an under-resourced language, there is a limited set of extractable features for conducting experiments. For example, when solving the problem of predicting pause placements, traditionally, the parameters of the input data are POS tags, punctuation and emphases [13,15]. However, so far, the semantic analyzer has not been developed for the Kazakh language, there are not classifier of named entities, the analyzer of the dependence tree, etc. Therefore, the authors have developed methods of predicting prosodic parameters based on distributional semantics.

We introduce the following notation.

i – sentence number.
m_i – number of phonemes in the i-th sentence.
$\{v_{i,j}\}, j = 1, 2, ..., m_i$ – phoneme sequence in the i-th sentence.
$w_{i,k}$ – k-th word in the i-th sentence.

3.1 Pause Place Prediction

Pause place prediction was carried out according to the method proposed in [5]. In this study, we used the parameters of the lexical representations obtained from the cluster model of Brown et al. [3] and word embedding obtained by the algorithm of Stratos et al. [18].

The prediction of the pause places was carried out at the level of bigrams, where the input parameters of the bigram $w_{i,k}$ and $w_{i,k+1}$ were the vector representations of both of its tokens, their bit string representation in the Brown cluster model, and the words themselves. For the classification of bigrams, the support vector machine was used.

3.2   Phoneme Duration Prediction

The method of phoneme duration prediction for the Kazakh language was presented in [6], where to predict the duration of $v_{i,j}$ phoneme in i-th sentence, the $v_{i,j}$ phoneme and its four neighboring phonemes were selected. In addition, we extracted $w_{i,k}$ word in which the phoneme was located, and four its neighboring words. Thus, 5-gram phonemes and 5-gram words are used. DNN with 6 layers of 1024 nodes each has also been applied for the prediction of the phoneme duration (Fig. 1). To activate hidden nodes of DNN, the rectifier linear activation function was used.

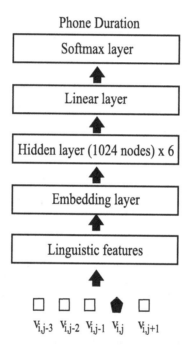

Fig. 1. The scheme of phoneme duration prediction.

4   Acoustic Model

4.1   Acoustic Model Based on LSTM

LSTM allows to process a sequence of events where each event can have an impact on other events. During the prediction of local events, LSTM takes into account the results of previous events calculations. Therefore, it can detect and simulate events that are influenced by other events and vice versa.

At the same time, it is obvious that during the speech, the sound of each phoneme has an impact on other phonemes and vice versa. This is largely caused by natural physical processes that change the vocal tract from one position to another. Thus, LSTM is an appropriate architecture for prediction of sequences of acoustic features.

4.2   Training Acoustic Model

For training the acoustic model, 50 sentences for the test set and 50 sentences for the validation set were randomly selected from the corpus. The acoustic features were extracted with a frequency of 200 Hz (5 ms) from a 22 kHz sound signal. Acoustic parameters were extracted using WORLD [12] vocoder (D4C edition [11]), so 60 Mel-generalized coefficients (MGC), 5 band aperiodicity coefficients (BAP) and the F0 feature were extracted. For each sample, 97 linguistic features were calculated.

The acoustic model was trained by the 3-layer LSTM, where each layer had 256 memory blocks. The tanh (hyperbolic tangent) activation function was used in each layer.

5   TTS

The scheme of the TTS system is presented in Fig. 2. The system consists of four modules. These are the text-processing module, the prosodic processing module, the acoustic prediction module, and the speech generation module.

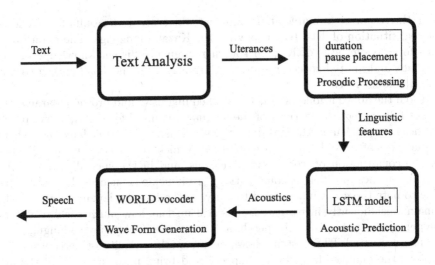

Fig. 2. The architecture of TTS.

The text-processing module preprocesses the text: selects sentences and splits them into separate words, decodes abbreviations, numerals and other non-standard entries, defines the morpho-grammatical characteristics of words, obtains phonetic transcription (grapheme-to-phoneme conversion). In the module of prosodic processing, pause place prediction and phoneme duration prediction are made. At this stage, the durations of the pauses are also determined, by considering the pause as another phoneme. Further, the collected linguistic and prosodic features are transfered to the acoustic module, in which the acoustic features are predicted for each 5 ms interval: 60 MGC, 5 BAP, F0. Then in the speech generation module, the speech is generated from the acoustic parameters using the WORLD vocoder.

6   Evaluation

MOS evaluation on a 5-point scale was carried out to assess the quality of the generated speech. 11 speakers of the Kazakh language participated in the survey, who were asked to assess 6 sets of the records. For each set, a separate screen was prepared, where the listeners were asked to listen to and evaluate each recording separately. It was allowed to give a fractional number score. Each set consisted of two recordings. Listeners were allowed to listen to an unlimited number of times each audio recording but we recommended to limit to 2–3 auditions.

Upon completion of the survey, the average MOS score was equal to 3.1. The standard deviation was 0.18 points.

7   Discussion

With the resources available at the moment, the evaluation results fully reflects the real situation of TTS technology for the Kazakh language. The main problems for the synthesis of Kazakh speech remain insufficient knowledge of the language and limited speech resources. Currently only one small speech corpus is available for research.

From the above it follows that the applied linguistic and prosodic parameters do not fully reflect the features of the language required for high-quality speech synthesis. In particular, the Kazakh language is an agglutinative language, where special rules of vowel harmony are observed. Which are reflected in special rules for the construction of words and phonemes, and in the special sound of the same phonemes in different combinations of phoneme sequences. It is also possible to note the great influence of tonality on the Kazakh language, which still remains insufficiently investigated. It is still unclear how much tonality affects the perception of the Kazakh speech, and what role it plays in the language.

The presented TTS system shows an acceptable quality of perception. To improve the quality of synthesized speech and bring it to the state of the art results, it is sufficient to increase the amount of training data and improve its representativeness.

8 Conclusion

In this paper, the first LSTM-based SPSS for the Kazakh language was presented. A number of prosodic processing methods were applied that were developed purposefully for under resourced languages. Obtained MOS score shows a sufficiently good level of speech synthesis.

Despite the fact that training and testing was carried out on the Kazakh speech corpus, this approach can also be acceptable to other under resourced languages. In the near future, we plan to expand the Kazakh speech corpus, and continue to work on the development of the proposed TTS system.

Acknowledgements. This work was partially financially supported by the Government of the Russian Federation (Grant 08-08).

References

1. An, S., Ling, Z., Dai, L.: Emotional statistical parametric speech synthesis using LSTM-RNNS. In: 2017 Asia-Pacific Signal and Information Processing Association Annual Summit and Conference (APSIPA ASC), pp. 1613–1616, December 2017. https://doi.org/10.1109/APSIPA.2017.8282282
2. Berment, V.: Methods to computerize "little equipped" languages and groups of languages. Theses, Université Joseph-Fourier - Grenoble I, May 2004. https://tel.archives-ouvertes.fr/tel-00006313
3. Brown, P.F., Pietra, V.J.D., de Souza, P.V., Lai, J.C., Mercer, R.L.: Class-based n-gram models of natural language. Comput. Linguist. **18**(4), 467–479 (1992)
4. Fan, Y., Qian, Y., Xie, F., Soong, F.K.: TTS synthesis with bidirectional LSTM based recurrent neural networks. In: INTERSPEECH 2014, 15th Annual Conference of the International Speech Communication Association, Singapore, 14–18 September 2014, pp. 1964–1968 (2014). http://www.isca-speech.org/archive/interspeech_2014/i14_1964.html
5. Kaliyev, A., Rybin, S.V., Matveev, Y.: The pausing method based on brown clustering and word embedding. In: Karpov, A., Potapova, R., Mporas, I. (eds.) SPECOM 2017. LNCS (LNAI), vol. 10458, pp. 741–747. Springer, Cham (2017). https://doi.org/10.1007/978-3-319-66429-3_74
6. Kaliyev, A., Rybin, S.V., Matveev, Y.N.: Phoneme duration prediction for Kazakh language. In: Karpov, A., Jokisch, O., Potapova, R. (eds.) SPECOM 2018. LNCS (LNAI), vol. 11096, pp. 274–280. Springer, Cham (2018). https://doi.org/10.1007/978-3-319-99579-3_29
7. Kaliyev, A., Rybin, S.V., Matveev, Y.N., Kaziyeva, N., Burambayeva, N.: Modeling pause for the synthesis of kazakh speech. In: Proceedings of the Fourth International Conference on Engineering & MIS 2018, ICEMIS 2018, pp. 1:1–1:4. ACM, New York (2018). https://doi.org/10.1145/3234698.3234699
8. Karpov, A., Verkhodanova, V.: Speech technologies for under-resourced languages of the world. Voprosy Jazykoznanija 2015, pp. 117–135, January 2015
9. Khomitsevich, O., Mendelev, V., Tomashenko, N., Rybin, S., Medennikov, I., Kudubayeva, S.: A bilingual Kazakh-Russian system for automatic speech recognition and synthesis. In: Ronzhin, A., Potapova, R., Fakotakis, N. (eds.) SPECOM 2015. LNCS (LNAI), vol. 9319, pp. 25–33. Springer, Cham (2015). https://doi.org/10.1007/978-3-319-23132-7_3

10. Krauwer, S.: The basic language resource kit (BLARK) as the first milestone for the language resources roadmap. In: Proceedings of SPECOM 2003, pp. 8–15 (2003)
11. Morise, M.: D4C, a band-aperiodicity estimator for high-quality speech synthesis. Speech Commun. **84**, 57–65 (2016). https://doi.org/10.1016/j.specom.2016.09.001. http://www.sciencedirect.com/science/article/pii/S0167639316300413
12. Morise, M., Yokomori, F., Ozawa, K.: World: a vocoder-based high-quality speech synthesis system for real-time applications. IEICE Trans. Inf. Syst. **99**(7), 1877–1884 (2016). https://doi.org/10.1587/transinf.2015EDP7457
13. Parlikar, A., Black, A.W.: A grammar based approach to style specific phrase prediction. In: Interspeech 2011, 12th Annual Conference of the International Speech Communication Association, Florence, Italy, 27–31 August 2011, pp. 2149–2152 (2011). http://www.isca-speech.org/archive/interspeech_2011/i11_2149.html
14. Salmenova, A.: Prosodic design of syntagmas and phonetic correlates of excretion. Ph.D. thesis, Saint Petersburg State University, Saint Petersburg, Russia, December 1984. (in Russian)
15. Sarkar, P., Rao, K.S.: Data-driven pause prediction for speech synthesis in storytelling style speech. In: Twenty First National Conference on Communications, NCC 2015, Mumbai, India, 27 February 1 March 2015, pp. 1–5 (2015). https://doi.org/10.1109/NCC.2015.7084924
16. Skerry-Ryan, R.J., et al.: Towards end-to-end prosody transfer for expressive speech synthesis with tacotron. CoRR abs/1803.09047 (2018). http://arxiv.org/abs/1803.09047
17. Sotelo, J., et al.: Char2Wav: end-to-end speech synthesis. In: International Conference on Learning Representations (Workshop Track), April 2017
18. Stratos, K., Kim, D., Collins, M., Hsu, D.: A spectral algorithm for learning class-based n-gram models of natural language. In: Proceedings of the Thirtieth Conference on Uncertainty in Artificial Intelligence, UAI 2014, pp. 762–771. AUAI Press, Arlington (2014). http://dl.acm.org/citation.cfm?id=3020751.3020830
19. Taigman, Y., Wolf, L., Polyak, A., Nachmani, E.: Voice synthesis for in-the-wild speakers via a phonological loop. CoRR abs/1707.06588 (2017). http://arxiv.org/abs/1707.06588
20. Zen, H., Sak, H.: Unidirectional long short-term memory recurrent neural network with recurrent output layer for low-latency speech synthesis. In: 2015 IEEE International Conference on Acoustics, Speech and Signal Processing, ICASSP 2015, South Brisbane, Queensland, Australia, 19–24 April 2015, pp. 4470–4474 (2015). https://doi.org/10.1109/ICASSP.2015.7178816

Combination of Positions and Angles for Hand Pose Estimation

Jakub Kanis[✉], Zdeněk Krňoul, and Marek Hrúz

Faculty of Applied Sciences, NTIS - New Technologies for the Information Society, University of West Bohemia, Univerzitní 8, 306 14 Pilsen, Czech Republic
{jkanis,zdkrnoul,mhruz}@ntis.zcu.cz

Abstract. This paper deals with the estimation of hand pose from a single depth image. We present a method that is based on a description of the hand pose via local rotations of bones trained discriminatively in an end-to-end fashion using a convolutional neural network. We compare our method with existing approach of hand pose estimation of 3D locations of hand joints. For this purpose, we collected precise ground-truth data with a passive marker-based optical motion capture technology. The results show, that the estimation of the hand pose formulated as a combination of local rotations of bones and relative locations of joints outperforms the direct estimation of 3D global joints locations.

Keywords: Hand pose estimation · Sign language processing · Shadow speaker

1 Introduction

Hand gestures are a very important part of human communication. It is natural to extend the usage into human-machine interaction. The problem of hand pose estimation in real-time from visual data is being addressed in many fields - robotics [2], medicine, automotive, virtual/augmented reality [7], gesture and sign language processing [18]. The human hand has a large number of degrees of freedom with frequent self-occlusions of fingers and the hand pose estimation leads to nonlinear regression. Despite this, there is a huge demand for such technologies that would perform well with consumer quality sensors. In our case with a depth sensor, where there are two main challenges: how to obtain precise ground-truth data and how to recover the hand pose.

This work was supported by the European Regional Development Fund under the project AI&Reasoning (reg. no. CZ.02.1.01/0.0/0.0/15 003/0000466). This work was supported by the Ministry of Education of the Czech Republic, project No. LTARF18017. Access to computing and storage facilities owned by parties and projects contributing to the National Grid Infrastructure MetaCentrum provided under the programme "Projects of Large Research, Development, and Innovations Infrastructures" (CESNET LM2015042), is greatly appreciated.

© Springer Nature Switzerland AG 2019
A. A. Salah et al. (Eds.): SPECOM 2019, LNAI 11658, pp. 209–218, 2019.
https://doi.org/10.1007/978-3-030-26061-3_22

Machine learning methods based on convolutional neural networks (CNNs) currently outperform earlier approaches, most often based on random decision forest classification and/or regression techniques [9]. In scope of machine learning methods the task of hand pose estimation from individual depth images is performed either in a supervised [3,6,12] or in a semi-supervised manner from unlabeled data [11,13]. In general, a large volume of training data and the capturing of all possible states of 3D hand pose impose a condition on a robust hand pose estimator [15]. In this work, they used 6 degrees of freedom (DoF) magnetic sensors and obtain a large labeled hand pose dataset. In [14] the authors introduce a per frame detection of 2D fingertip positions from depth images by a CNN combined with the prediction of wrist joint angle with 3 DoFs of hand orientation. Later in [15] the authors predict 3D positions of hand joints obtained with kinematic constraints. The positions of joints are also estimated in an end-to-end fashion with the effort to model the prior of the hand pose in a bottleneck of a CNN modeled by Principal Component Analysis (PCA) [4,5]. Currently the prediction of joints angles on a per-frame basis is defined as hierarchical classification [7] or geometrically informed responses together with the discriminative depth features to regularize the hand angle parameters [1].

We are interested in the task of per-frame hand pose estimation of a known subject from single depth maps capturing his/her upper body by non-invasive and commonly used capturing device (e.g. "shadow speaker"[1] of the sign language who is captured by MS Kinect v2). This real-word scenario is challenging due to very low resolution of the hand in depth maps caused by a larger distance of the sensor from the subject. Such estimated hand poses can be used for e.g. sign language recognition, or sign language synthesis where intelligibility of hand gesture during processing of hand poses is a crucial factor. The idea behind the ground-truth acquisition is to get a very precise description of hand pose independently on quality of the input depth map. Our approach differs from other current benchmark datasets [10,12] that provide target hand pose as set of isolated, noisy and topologically incorrect 3D joints positions. For example NYU dataset [12], the joint angle poses that are optimized via forward kinematic function from 14 of all 36 original annotated joints positions produce average error of 5.68 mm [17].

The main contribution of our work is a novel method based on a direct (end-to-end) regression of a 3D hand pose described by a combination of local rotations and relative locations of joints that outperforms state-of-the-art method of a prediction based on the direct regression of 3D joints locations. We are extending recent works [7,14] where only the orientation of hand is predicted in the angular form. We consider the whole hand pose as a vector of local joints' angles. Thus the optimization process can directly benefit from the angular form and the trained estimator can predict hand pose vector that is straightforwardly integrated to a target model; e.g. an avatar's hand or a controller of virtual environments.

---

[1] The sign language speaker who interprets the spoken language to be used for signing avatar broadcasting.

A second significant contribution of this paper is an accompanying novel acquisition approach that enables to collect a large amount of precise annotated depth images of full human body poses. The 3D pose description is based on a skeleton, it is anatomically valid and its precision is close to annotations of artificially generated depth maps. Our approach combines a passive marker-based optical motion capturing with depth sensor recording to obtain a hand and/or a body pose ground-truth.

2 Methods

The hand pose is defined by a 3D skeleton of a hand. The hand pose estimation method is based on several CNNs by the formula: $\hat{\Theta}_t = \{\hat{\theta}_t = f_t(D_{crop})\}$, where $\hat{\theta}_t$ is the estimation of a subset of the ground-truth values of hand pose parameters $\Theta = \{\theta_i\}, i = 1 \ldots N$, θ_i is a vector of the target data, f_t is one of the CNN per-frame estimators and D_{crop} is the hand crop in the depth map.

Acquisition Approach: The hand pose is measured by a VICON motion capture system. We use standard representation of a 3D hand skeleton, commonly used in computer graphics. Our model is composed of 17 joints of the right hand and includes the forearm, wrist, and 5×3 finger bones. In general, the palm is considered to be one rigid object as in most cases. We integrated the forearm joint into the capturing setup because pose of the forearm is a part of entire hand in cropped depth data and this information may be useful in future training scenarios.

We use 20 different sized retro-reflective markers in total - so that every bone is constrained by at least one marker (see Fig. 1, on the left); 5 of them are spherical with a radius of 14 and 6.5 mm and 15 are hemispherical with a radius of 4 mm. The placement of the markers on the forearm, wrist, and palm follows common fashion. The placement of the markers on the fingers in the middle of the dorsal side of the phalanges was experimentally determined to preserve the free finger articulation. The movement of the markers is tracked by 8 cameras with 2 Mpix resolutions and 120 Hz frame rate.

The root of the skeleton is the elbow joint with 6 DoF. There are three DoF for the wrist and for the thumb ball joint, proximal phalanges have two DoF and the other phalanges have one DoF. This enables proper solving of the full hand articulation. We calibrate the skeletal model on the subject by capturing the full range of motion (ROM) of fingers, palm and forearm. In this stage, we determine unknown and constant parameters: length of bones, marker-bone constrain offsets, a maximal range of rotations and stiffness of the joints. This calibrated mocap model is then used for solving hand poses of all ground-truth data. The solving is strongly influenced by human annotator doing careful visual check of marker's swaps arising due to occluded markers in the mocap cameras. The used combination of spherical and hemispherical markers, the given placement of mocap cameras around the hand, and also the optimal settings of the 3D marker position reconstruction reduces the amount of lost and false marker reconstructions, which minimizes the amount of the visual checking.

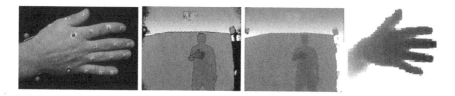

Fig. 1. First: marker setup omitting elbow marker, second: input depth image, third: depth image after depth hole filling, last: result of the hand tracking = training data.

In contrast to [16] we produce much less missing data (only 2.2% of missing marker positions in our training data). After the checking phase, the rotations of joints are automatically computed against a rest pose - a hand with stretched fingers pressed against each other, the fingers pointing away from the performer and the palm faces the ground.

Ground-truth Data: We assume a hand pose defined by local rotations of bones, i.e. the rotation of one bone is computed relative to its parent bone. The quaternions are a convenient mathematical notation representing a rotation θ around a rotation axis $\mathbf{v}$ well known in 3D computer graphics for proper spherical linear interpolation. For this purpose, the quaternions provide us with compact solution and avoid the possible singular states of the Euler angles form (i.e. Gimbal lock). All 17 joints angles are represented in quaternion form $\mathbf{q} = (q_w, q_x, q_y, q_z) = (\cos(\theta/2); \mathbf{v} \cdot \sin(\theta/2))$ in half-space, $q_w > 0$, where $\mathbf{v}$ is the vector representing the rotation axis.

We compute forward kinematics (FK) to derive 15 3D joints positions as precise geometrical rotation centers of the skeletal model. In addition, 5 fingertip positions are defined from offsets of distal joints and end of the fingers. They are determined from a 3D scan of the performer's hand. For this purpose, we consider the 3D scan of subject's hand in the rest pose to get a polygonal mesh. The 3D mesh naturally corresponds to the bones of the calibrated skeleton model. In total 20 (x, y, z) positions form the global position features. Next, similarly with the idea of canonical coordinate frame in [8], we derive the local joints positions describing only the finger articulation independently on the global orientation of the whole hand as the global hand pose derived from the solving skeleton with zero rotation in the wrist and the forearm.

Depth Data: The depth data are recorded simultaneously with the mocap recordings. We assume a common depth sensor based on ToF - Kinect v2. The recording rate is 30 Hz and the image resolution is 512×424 pixels. The sensor is positioned in 3rd person's point of view in front of the performer approximately 1.8 meters away and captures the whole upper body (see Fig. 1). In this setup, the average size of the hand region is only 92×92 pixels in contrast to 250×250 pixels for NYU dataset and 201×201 pixels for ICVL dataset [10].

A straightforward synchronization of the mocap Vicon system and the depth sensor is not available by default. We synchronize the data manually by saving time stamps of the depth maps and performing synchronizing hand gesture as fast snapping of fingers at the beginning of every capturing. The resulting synchronization error is less than 10 ms.

ToF technology does not measure highly reflective surfaces (like mocap markers) and we get missing data (holes) in places where the markers are being projected. This differs from the magnetic motion sensors in a recently published dataset [15] where projections of the sensors are measured. In [15] this is not handled explicitly since the visibility of the sensors is considered to be limited. The missing data are actually better than faulty depth data because we can detect and repair them easily. For a given distance of the sensor and the subject, the finger markers (4 mm) are projected as small holes ($\approx$3 pixels) and can be automatically fixed. We repair the depth map as a whole in every pixel via standard linear nearest neighbor grid data interpolation. This process removes other unmeasured pixels which arose due to noise or high depth gradient as an effect of the capture technology, see Fig. 1.

Hand Detection: The localization of the hand is a necessary step that produces a region (the crop) of the depth map that contains just the hand. This region determines the neural networks' input D_{crop}. For the reference data, the region could be obtained by known geometrical and projective relations but this is not possible for unseen test data. We follow the idea of the algorithm in [5] and consider simple localization based on the nearest object detection.

The convex hull of the smoothed thresholded depth map defines the most probable region of the hand. We use the center of this location as a mean distance M of the detected hand to the sensor. M is used for (1) adaptive computation of the size of hand region (in pixels) and (2) normalization of the depth for the CNN input. By (1) we rescale and interpolate depth map crop to uniform size rather than transform the depth data into sparse volumetric space [9]. Similar to [5], the resized size of the hand region ensures the relative size of the hand in the region to be constant, independent on the distance from the sensor. We use the formula: $R = f \cdot \frac{r}{M}$, where R is the size of the region, f is the focal length in the image axis and r defines the relative size of the hand in the region. The region of size $R \times R$ is put on top of the center of the convex hull of the hand and it is resized to the desired input shape of the CNN. Next, the depth data are normalized so that they lie in the interval of $\langle -1; 1 \rangle$ by the formula: $D_{norm} = s \cdot (D_{raw} - M) + d$, where D_{raw} is the original depth of the pixel in mm, s is a constant representing the range of the farthest and the nearest possible depth and $d > 0$ defines the constant shift of the range relative to the depth M. The parameter d controls the "amount of forearm" that will be visible by the CNN. The results of the depth data acquisition are in Fig. 1, on the right.

Data Augmentation: We use two types of augmentation; (1) random shifts and (2) rotation of the depth data [10]. For (1) we obtain a new depth map by applying a small random translation of all the depth pixels. We consider such augmentation to be label preserving and thus the target does not need to change. The aim of (1) is for the CNN to be independent on performance of the hand detection phase. By applying the type (2) augmentation the target needs to be changed to get new training data for unseen rotations of the hand. We apply

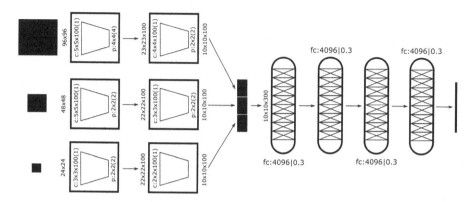

Fig. 2. Network architecture: c = convolutional: kernel × kernel × #kernels(stride), p = maxpool: kernel × kernel(stride), fc = full_connected: size|dropout, all layers perform batch normalization before maxout (Actually, we are using the maxout activation function as is defined in the Chainer framework with pool size 2.) activation function

the random angle of the planar rotation as an addition to the joint angle of the skeleton root (forearm). We use only anatomically plausible rotations from pre-defined ranges.

3   Experiments

The training data was created by the process described in previous Sect. 2. The training set contains 21 076 depth images of the right hand from one recording session. There was one subject, who performed 52 different hand poses used in Czech sign language, in different rotations and positions relative to the depth sensor. The hand localization in depth maps was performed by the algorithm described in Sect. 2. The relative size of the hand parameter r was set to 241, the relative depth parameter d to 0.6 of normalized depth and the scaling parameter s to 15. The detected hand region R is resized to the final size of 96×96 pixels. All training frames were augmented using the methods described in Sect. 2 and randomly shuffled to remove any time correlation between consecutive frames. The shifts in augmentation (1) were sampled from normal distributions $\mathcal{N}(0, 5)$ for planar translations in pixels and $\mathcal{N}(0, 0.1)$ for normalized depth translations and we generate 10 augmented images for each training image. The angles used in augmentation (2) were chosen uniformly from the interval $\langle -45, 45 \rangle$ degrees with the step of 22.5 degrees. The resulting size of the dataset was increased to 1 074k frames .

The evaluation and testing data were performed by the same subject in compliance with the task of shadow speaker. The evaluation set is composed of 643 frames of calibrating ROM and 658 frames with arbitrary free hand pose/movement. The test set contains 634 frames of arbitrary free hand pose/movement. When CNN predicts the quaternion features they are only normalized to unit length. The hand pose is then obtained by using forward kinematics (FK). Euclidean distances of the 15 3D joints positions represent the mean global position error (MGPE). By applying the above-mentioned procedure we are able to compare the poses defined by quaternions and also by 3D locations of joints with the ground-truth data. For the given dataset, we provide established error metric as the percentage of good frames that have an error less than a threshold. Also, we are able to visualize the 3D model of the predicted values which enables a qualitative comparison with the ground-truth data.

4   Results and Discussion

Currently, there is no benchmark dataset available that consists of both joints positions and anatomically correct joints rotations. In contrast to rotation predictions, it is possible to use our dataset to compare results of current methods using just the joint global position estimation. For this comparison, we chose a freely available framework DeepPrior++ [4] achieving state-of-the-art results on the established benchmark datasets and train it on our dataset (denoted D in Table 1). The hand detection in the depth maps was performed by an original algorithm based on the detection of the center-of-mass (CoM) [4]. The detected hand region is resized to the default size of 128×128 pixels. To be able to use this framework with our data, we converted its annotation to the format of the ICVL dataset[2]. All training frames were augmented using the Deepprior++ default methods and randomly shuffled to remove any time correlation between consecutive frames. A CNN with the topology described in [5] (Fig. 1, type (d)) was used because we empirically found out that on our dataset this topology is superior to the later one based on ResNet (Residual Network) architecture [4]. Adam optimizer is used for optimization on batches of size 128 with the default hyper-parameters and the learning rate of $1 \cdot 10^{-4}$, which was progressively adjusted with the number of the training epochs, and trained for 100 epochs.

For our estimator we used a multi-scale CNN with the topology described in Fig. 2, which was trained for a fixed amount of time (24 h) resulting in more then 70 epochs. For all experiments, we used the same training data. The difference was the dimensionality of the ground-truth data and thus the size of the output layer of the CNN. In the case of global positions (denoted GP), the estimation has the dimensionality of the ground-truth data equal to 60 (20 global joints locations $\times$ 3). In the case of joints angles estimation (denoted QP) we train separate CNNs for the wrist and each finger (6 CNNs in total). Information about the local joints positions is added to the angular representation. This results in 13 dimensions for the wrist (one joint quaternion + 3×3 joints locations of the index, little and thumb root joint) and 24 dimensions for each finger (3×4 joints quaternions + 4×3 relevant joints locations) of the ground-truth data. The estimation for the whole hand is then composed of the estimations of the particular fingers and the wrist.

---

[2] https://labicvl.github.io/hand.html.

Table 1. Results for MGPE on the evaluation and the test data.

Methods	MGPE [mm]	
	Eval	Test
D	12.5	12.8
GP	11.2	12.3
QP	**11.0**	**10.9**

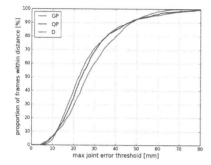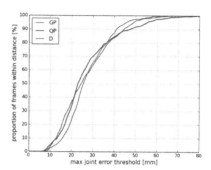

Fig. 3. Max joints error thresholds for MGPE, left: evaluation data, right: test data

For each setup we trained our networks with different starting learning rates $(0.001, 1 \cdot 10^{-4}$ and $1 \cdot 10^{-5})$. The results reported in the Table 1 are for the network and epoch that achieved the best performance on the evaluation data. For optimization, we used Adam on mini-batches of size 100, with beta1 (0.9), beta2 (0.999) and weight decay $(5 \cdot 10^{-4})$. In the case when mixing rotations and 3D locations (QP) only the predicted rotations are used for evaluation.

The results are reported only for 15 joints; the wrist joint and the fingertips are omitted from the final comparison. From Table 1 it can be seen that using the QP predictor achieves the best results both on the evaluation and the test data. Interestingly, also the GP predictor surpasses the DeepPrior++ framework. This may be due to a different training protocol and approach to data augmentation. Furthermore, we can observe that while D and GP predictors have worse results for test data than eval data, the QP predictor performs slightly better. This may lead to the conclusion that the QP predictor is able to better generalize to unseen data.

When observing the curves in Fig. 3 the picture is less clear. For lower threshold of the max joints error both the GP and QP predictors exceed the D predictor. The GP and QP predictors themselves are very competitive in these lower bounds and a clear winner cannot be established. For the higher thresholds the D predictor overcomes the GP and QP predictors. This may be due to the optimization of the D predictor with respect to the max joint error. The qualitative results can be seen in Fig. 4.

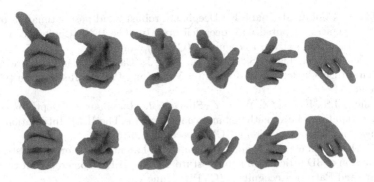

Fig. 4. Hand pose estimation: line1 = rendered ground-truth, line2 = QP estimations.

5   Conclusion

A novel approach for the per-frame prediction of hand pose from single depth image is presented as a high-dimensional and non-linear regression problem. The approach is based on a description of the hand pose via combination of local joints angles and positions. We compare it with the state-of-the-art approach using the description via global 3D joints positions. For this purpose, we recorded and released a new dataset providing the ground-truth data consisting of accurate annotations including both 3D joints locations and all relevant joints angles. We report results for the regression of combination of angular and position representations of hand pose having better prediction precision then regression of 3D joints positions.

References

1. Choi, C., Kim, S., Ramani, K.: Learning hand articulations by hallucinating heat distribution. In: 2017 IEEE International Conference on Computer Vision (ICCV), pp. 3123–3132, October 2017. https://doi.org/10.1109/ICCV.2017.337
2. Feix, T., Romero, J., Ek, C.H., Schmiedmayer, H.B., Kragic, D.: A metric for comparing the anthropomorphic motion capability of artificial hands. IEEE Trans. Rob. **29**(1), 82–93 (2013). https://doi.org/10.1109/TRO.2012.2217675
3. Ge, Y., Liang, H., Yuan, J., Thalmann, D.: Robust 3D hand pose estimation in single depth images: from single-view CNN to multi-view CNNS. In: Proceedings of IEEE International Conference on Computer Vision and Pattern Recognition (CVPR 2016), June 2016
4. Oberweger, M., Lepetit, V.: Deepprior++: Improving fast and accurate 3D hand pose estimation. In: 2017 IEEE International Conference on Computer Vision Workshops, ICCV Workshops 2017, Venice, Italy, 22–29 October 2017, pp. 585–594 (2017). https://doi.org/10.1109/ICCVW.2017.75
5. Oberweger, M., Wohlhart, P., Lepetit, V.: Hands deep in deep learning for hand pose estimation. In: CVWW, February 2015
6. Simon, T., Joo, H., Matthews, I., Sheikh, Y.: Hand keypoint detection in single images using multiview bootstrapping. In: The IEEE Conference on Computer Vision and Pattern Recognition (CVPR), July 2017

7. Sinha, A., Choi, C., Ramani, K.: Deephand: robust hand pose estimation by completing a matrix imputed with deep features. In: The IEEE Conference on Computer Vision and Pattern Recognition (CVPR), June 2016
8. Sun, X., Wei, Y., Liang, S., Tang, X., Sun, J.: Cascaded hand pose regression. In: The IEEE Conference on Computer Vision and Pattern Recognition (CVPR), June 2015
9. Supancic, J.S., Rogez, G., Yang, Y., Shotton, J., Ramanan, D.: Depth-based hand pose estimation: data, methods, and challenges. In: The IEEE International Conference on Computer Vision (ICCV), December 2015
10. Tang, D., Jin Chang, H., Tejani, A., Kim, T.K.: Latent regression forest: structured estimation of 3D articulated hand posture. In: The IEEE Conference on Computer Vision and Pattern Recognition (CVPR), June 2014
11. Tang, D., Yu, T.H., Kim, T.K.: Real-time articulated hand pose estimation using semi-supervised transductive regression forests. In: Proceedings of the 2013 IEEE International Conference on Computer Vision, pp. 3224–3231. ICCV 2013. IEEE Computer Society, Washington (2013). https://doi.org/10.1109/ICCV.2013.400
12. Tompson, J., Stein, M., Lecun, Y., Perlin, K.: Real-time continuous pose recovery of human hands using convolutional networks. ACM Trans. Graph. **33**(5), 169:1–169:10 (2014). https://doi.org/10.1145/2629500
13. Wan, C., Probst, T., Van Gool, L., Yao, A.: Crossing nets: combining GANs and VAEs with a shared latent space for hand pose estimation. In: The IEEE Conference on Computer Vision and Pattern Recognition (CVPR), July 2017
14. Wetzler, A., Slossberg, R., Kimmel, R.: Rule of thumb: deep derotation for improved fingertip detection. In: BMVC (2015)
15. Yuan, S., Ye, Q., Stenger, B., Jain, S., Kim, T.K.: BigHand2. 2M benchmark: hand pose data set and state of the art analysis. In: CVPR, July 2017
16. Zhao, W., Chai, J., Xu, Y.Q.: Combining marker-based mocap and RGB-D camera for acquiring high-fidelity hand motion data. In: Lee, J., Kry, P. (eds.) Eurographics/ACM SIGGRAPH Symposium on Computer Animation. The Eurographics Association (2012). https://doi.org/10.2312/SCA/SCA12/033-042
17. Zhou, X., Wan, Q., Zhang, W., Xue, X., Wei, Y.: Model-based deep hand pose estimation. In: Proceedings of the Twenty-Fifth International Joint Conference on Artificial Intelligence, IJCAI 2016, pp. 2421–2427. AAAI Press (2016). http://dl.acm.org/citation.cfm?id=3060832.3060960
18. Zimmermann, C., Brox, T.: Learning to estimate 3D hand pose from single RGB images. In: The IEEE International Conference on Computer Vision (ICCV), October 2017

LSTM-Based Language Models for Very Large Vocabulary Continuous Russian Speech Recognition System

Irina Kipyatkova[✉]

St. Petersburg Institute for Informatics and Automation of the Russian Academy
of Sciences (SPIIRAS), St. Petersburg, Russia
kipyatkova@iias.spb.su

Abstract. This paper presents language models based on Long Short-Term
Memory (LSTM) neural networks for very large vocabulary continuous Russian
speech recognition. We created neural networks with various numbers of units
in hidden and projection layers using different optimization methods. Obtained
LSTM-based language models were used for N-best list rescoring. As well we
tested a linear interpolation of LSTM language model with the baseline 3-gram
language model and achieved 22% relative reduction of the word error rate with
respect to the baseline 3-gram model.

Keywords: Speech recognition · Recurrent Neural Networks ·
Long Short-Term Memory · Language models · Russian speech

1 Introduction

A language model (LM) is one of the main parts of a speech recognition system.
Nowadays, neural networks (NNs) are widely used for language modeling. As it was
shown in many papers, NN-based LMs outperform standard n-gram models [1, 2]. For
language modeling, the usage of recurrent NNs (RNNs) is preferable because this type
of NN can store the whole context preceding the given word in contrast to feedforward
NNs which store a context of restricted length.

A long short-term memory (LSTM) network is RNN, which contains special units
called memory blocks. Each memory block is composed of a memory cell, which
stores the temporal state of the network, and multiplicative units named gates (an input
gate, an output gate, and a forget gate) controlling the information flow [3].

In our research we used a LSTM-based LM for N-best list rescoring for automatic
speech recognition (ASR) system. The paper is organized as follows: in Sect. 2 we give
a survey of application of LSTMs for language modeling, in Sect. 3 we give a
description of our LSTM-based LMs, experimental results of N-best list rescoring
using LSTM-based LMs are presented in Sect. 4.

A. A. Salah et al. (Eds.): SPECOM 2019, LNAI 11658, pp. 219–226, 2019.
https://doi.org/10.1007/978-3-030-26061-3_23

2 Related Works

LSTMs are widely used in speech recognition systems at N-best or lattice rescoring stage. In [4] comparison of LMs based on n-grams, feedforward, recurrent, and LSTM NNs in terms of perplexity and word error rate (WER) is presented. LMs were created for English and French. In the paper, it was shown that application of LSTM-based LMs for lattice rescoring outperforms other type of LMs. In addition, experimental analysis of relationship between perplexity of NN-based LMs and WER was performed. It showed that WER decreases with decreasing perplexity that is analogous to correlation between perplexity and WER for n-gram LMs.

In [5] LSTM-based LM was used for lattice rescoring for a YouTube speech recognition task. The proposed model decreased WER by 8% as compared with the result obtained with the n-gram model.

Automatic speech recognition for conversational Finnish and Estonian speech with LSTM LM is described in [6]. The authors tried subword-based and fullword-based language modeling and investigated the usage of classes for language modeling. LSTM LM was used for lattice rescoring. On both languages, the best results were obtained from class-based subword models.

Czech language modeling using LSTM is represented in [7]. As the baseline, 5-gram Knesser-Ney statistical model with 120 K vocabulary was used. The LSTM LMs were trained with limited vocabulary consisted of 10 K most frequent words. LSTM LM interpolated with the baseline model was used for rescoring of 1000-best list. Experiments were performed on the corpus of Czech spontaneous speech which was recorded from phone calls. Application of LSTM LM allowed increasing speech recognition accuracy by 3.7% in relative comparing to the result obtained with the baseline model.

A comparison of LMs based on LSTM and gated recurrent units (GRU) is presented in [8]. In experiments of lattice rescoring for English speech recognition task, LSTM-based LM outperformed GRU-based LM in terms of both perplexity and WER. Also experiments with Highway network based on GRU were performed that showed WER improvement, but similar investigation on the base of LSTM was not conducted.

In [9] a system which uses LSTM for both acoustic and language modeling is presented. The system uses CNN-BLSTM acoustic models and 4-gram LM for decoding and lattice rescoring. LSTM-based LM was applied for 500-best list rescoring. Relative WER reduction obtained after rescoring was about 20%.

Russian language modeling with the use of LSTM is described in [10]. The baseline 3-gram LM was trained on transcriptions of telephone conversations (390 h of speech) as well as on text corpus (about 200 M words) containes materials from Internet forum discussions, books etc. Vocabulary for the baseline model contains 214 K words. NN-based LMs were trained only with a part of the test corpus, and for this corpus the vocabulary of 45 K most frequent words was used. LSTM-based LM was used for rescoring of 100-best list. Relative WER reduction was equal to 8%.

In our previous researches on Russian language modeling [11, 12] we have experimented with LMs created on the base of RNN with one hidden layer using RNNLM toolkit [13]. We have obtained relative WER reduction of 14% as compared to the result obtained with our 3-gram model. The current research is aimed to investigation of another type of RNN for language modeling.

3 LSTM Language Models for Russian

For training of LSTM language models, we used TheanoLM toolkit [14]. We trained LMs on a text corpus composed with the use of on-line Russian newspapers [15]. The vocabulary size was 150 K word-forms. We created NN LMs consisting of a projection layer, which maps words to specified dimensional embeddings, one hidden LSTM layer, and a hierarchical softmax layer. Hierarchical softmax factors the output probabilities into the product of multiple softmax functions [16]. Thus, the output layer is factorized into two levels, both performing normalization over an equal number of choices [6], it allows using of very large vocabulary for language modeling. NN LM architecture is presented on Fig. 1, where w_t is an input word at time t; h_t is the hidden layer state, c_t is LSTM cell state.

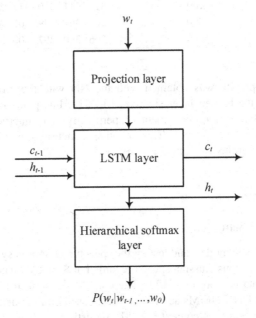

Fig. 1. LSTM-based LM architecture

We tried NNs with LSTM layer sizes equal to 256 and 512, and projection layer sizes equal to 100, 500, and 1000. LSTM-based LMs were trained using stochastic gradient descent (SGD) optimization method. The stopping criteria was *"no-improvement"* which means that learning rate is halved when validation set perplexity stops improving, and training is stopped when the perplexity does not improve at all with the current learning rate [14]. The maximum number of training epoch was 15. The initial learning rate was equal to 1.

As well, we made a linear interpolation of the LSTM-based LM and baseline LM. As a baseline, we used 3-gram LM with Kneser-Ney discounting trained on the same text corpus using the SRI Language Modeling Toolkit (SRILM) [17]. Perplexities of the obtained LMs computed on held-out text data are presented in Table 1. The interpolation coefficient of 1.0 means that only LSTM-based LM was used. The perplexity of the baseline model was 553.

Table 1. Perplexities of LSTM LMs

Hidden layer size	Projection layer size	Interpolation coefficient					
		0.5	0.6	0.7	0.8	0.9	1.0
256	100	339	336	336	343	359	431
	500	330	325	325	330	345	407
	1000	328	323	323	328	342	405
512	100	317	311	310	313	325	383
	500	308	301	299	302	311	363
	1000	306	300	**297**	300	309	361

The lowest perplexity was obtained with the NN with the projection layer size equal to 1000 and the hidden layer size equal to 512. Interpolation with the 3-gram model gave the additional improvement of perplexity. The interpolation coefficient equal to 0.7 provided the best result. Thus, relative reduction of perplexity was 46% as compared with the perplexity of the baseline model.

4   Experiments

4.1   Experimental Setup

For training the acoustic models and testing the speech recognition system, we used our own corpora of continuous Russian speech recorded at SPIIRAS. The total duration of the entire speech data is more than 30 h. The corpus is described in detail in [18].

We used hybrid DNN/HMMs acoustic models based on time-delay neural network with 5 hidden layers and time context [−8, 8]. Acoustic models were trained using the open-source Kaldi toolkit [19]. Mel-frequency cepstral coefficients (MFCCs) were used as input to the NNs. For speaker adaptation, 100-dimensional i-Vector [20] was appended to the 40-dimensional MFCC input. Detail description of our acoustic models is presented in [12]. We have obtained WER equal to 17.62% with our baseline 3-gram model, and WER equal to 15.13 was obtained after rescoring 500-best list with the help of RNN LM with one hidden layer interpolated with the 3-gram model.

LSTM-based LM was applied for rescoring of 500-best list of hypotheses and for selection of the best recognition hypothesis for the pronounced phrase. Interpolated LMs were used for rescoring as well. Obtained speech recognition results are presented in Table 2.

Table 2. WER after 500-best list rescoring (%)

Hidden layer size	Projection layer size	Interpolation coefficient						
		0.4	0.5	0.6	0.7	0.8	0.9	1.0
256	100	15.36	15.09	15.15	15.37	15.73	16.20	16.44
	500	15.54	15.39	15.41	16.62	15.86	16.09	16.52
	1000	15.21	15.06	14.94	14.79	14.94	15.22	15.67
512	100	15.17	14.83	14.59	14.74	14.85	15.02	15.39
	500	14.51	14.36	14.21	**14.06**	14.19	14.64	14.96
	1000	15.32	15.21	15.04	15.13	15.15	15.36	15.52

As one can see from the table, application of LSTM-based LMs allows to improve speech recognition results. Additional improvement was achieved with interpolated LSTM-based LM with baseline LM. The lowest WER (14.06%) was obtained using NN with projection layer size equal to 500 and hidden layer size equal to 512 interpolated with the baseline model with interpolation coefficient equal to 0.7, though this model was not the best in terms of perplexity. This may be connected with the fact that we used different texts material for estimation of perplexity and for speech corpora recordings.

Then we experimented with optimization method for NN training. We tried Nesterov Momentum [21], AdaGrad [22], and Adam [23] optimization methods, and compared them with SGD method in terms of perplexity and WER of the created models. We trained models with 512 units in the hidden layer and 512 units in the projection layer because LSTM with these parameters gave us the best results in terms of WER in our previous experiments with models with SGD optimization method. Initial learning rates were chosen according to recommendations of TheanoLM toolkit. Results of experiments on comparing optimization methods in term of perplexity and WER are presented in Tables 3 and 4 respectively.

Table 3. Results of experiments with LMs trained using different optimization methods in terms of perplexity

Optimization method	Initial learning rate	Interpolation coefficient					
		0.5	0.6	0.7	0.8	0.9	1.0
SGD	1.00	308	301	299	302	311	363
Nesterov momentum	1.00	299	292	**289**	291	300	346
AdaGrad	1.00	308	302	300	303	313	375
Adam	0.01	321	316	314	317	327	386

Table 4. Results of experiments with LMs trained using different optimization methods in terms of WER (%)

Optimization method	Initial learning rate	Interpolation coefficient					
		0.5	0.6	0.7	0.8	0.9	1.0
SGD	1.00	14.36	14.21	14.06	14.19	14.64	14.96
Nesterov Momentum	1.00	14.33	14.08	**14.01**	14.16	14.34	14.55
AdaGrad	1.00	15.00	14.93	14.91	14.81	14.89	15.36
Adam	0.01	14.78	14.63	14.53	14.48	14.68	14.78

Only Nesterov Momentum method slightly outperform SGD in terms of both perplexity and WER of the obtained models. Thus, the best results (perplexity equals 289; WER equals 14.01) were obtained after interpolation of LSTM LM trained using Nesterov Momentum optimization method interpolated with the baseline LM with interpolation coefficient equal to 0.7.

Then we trained NNs with 2 and 3 LSTM layers using the parameters of the best 1-layer LSTM. In these NNs we applied dropout at rate 0.3 between LSTM layers. Obtained results are presented in Table 4.

Table 5. Results of experiments with LMs with different number of LSTM layers

Number of LSTM layers	Interpolation coefficient							
	0.7		0.8		0.9		1.0	
	Perplexity	WER, %	Perplexity	WER, %	Perplexity	WER, %	Perplexity	WER, %
1	289	14.01	291	14.16	300	14.34	346	14.55
2	286	13.88	279	13.80	292	13.90	323	13.93
3	294	14.05	301	14.23	327	14.35	357	14.62

Thus, the best result was obtained using NN LM with 2 LSTM layers interpolated with the baseline LM with interpolation coefficient of 0.8, in this case WER equaled 13.80%. Further increasing the number of the hidden layers led to increasing WER that may be caused by overtraining (Table 5).

5   Conclusions and Future Work

In the paper, we have investigated LSTM-based LMs for Russian speech recognition task. We have tried NNs with different hidden layer sized, projection layer sizes, optimization methods, and number of hidden layers. LSTM-based LMs were applied for N-best list rescoring. The lowest WER was achieved with the NN with 2 hidden layers, 512 units in hidden layer and projection layer of 500 trained with Nesterov Momentum optimization method. We have achieved 22% relative reduction of WER using LSTM LM with respect to the baseline 3-gram model. In further research, we are going to investigate other topologies of RNNs for language modeling.

Acknowledgements. This research is financially supported by the Ministry of Science and Higher Education of the Russian Federation, agreement No. 14.616.21.0095 (reference RFMEFI61618X0095).

References

1. Mikolov, T., Karafiat, M., Burget, L., Cernocky, J., Khudanpur, S.: Recurrent neural network based language model. In: INTERSPEECH'2010, Makuhari, Chiba, Japan, pp. 1045–1048 (2010)
2. Sundermeyer, M., Oparin, I., Gauvain, J.-L., Freiberg, B., Schluter, R., Ney, H.: Comparison of feedforward and recurrent neural network language models. In: Proceedings of International Conference on Acoustics, Speech and Signal Processing (ICASSP), Vancouver, B.C., Canada, pp. 8430–8434 (2013)
3. Hochreiter, S., Schmidhuber, J.: Long short-term memory. Neural Comput. **9**(8), 1735–1780 (1997)
4. Sundermeyer, M., Ney, H., Schlüter, R.: From feedforward to recurrent LSTM neural networks for language modeling. IEEE/ACM Trans. Audio, Speech, Lang. Process. **23**(3), 517–529 (2015)
5. Kumar, S., Nirschl, M., Holtmann-Rice, D., Liao, H., Suresh, A.T., Yu, F.: Lattice rescoring strategies for long short term memory language models in speech recognition. In: IEEE Automatic Speech Recognition and Understanding Workshop (ASRU), pp. 165–172 (2017)
6. Enarvi, S., Smit, P., Virpioja, S., Kurimo, M.: Automatic speech recognition with very large conversational finnish and estonian vocabularies. IEEE Trans. Audio, Speech, Lang. Process. **25**(11), 2085–2097 (2017)
7. Soutner, D., Müller, L.: Application of LSTM neural networks in language modelling. In: Habernal, I., Matoušek, V. (eds.) TSD 2013. LNCS (LNAI), vol. 8082, pp. 105–112. Springer, Heidelberg (2013). https://doi.org/10.1007/978-3-642-40585-3_14
8. Irie, K., Tüske, Z., Alkhouli, T., Schlüter, R., Ney, H.: LSTM, GRU, highway and a bit of attention: an empirical overview for language modeling in speech recognition. In: INTERSPEECH-2016, pp. 3519–3523 (2016)
9. Xiong, W., Wu, L., Alleva, F., Droppo, J., Huang, X., Stolcke, A.: The Microsoft 2017 Conversational Speech Recognition System. Preprint arXiv:1708.06073, https://arxiv.org/abs/1708.06073 (2017)
10. Medennikov, I., Bulusheva, A.: LSTM-based language models for spontaneous speech recognition. In: Ronzhin, A., Potapova, R., Németh, G. (eds.) SPECOM 2016. LNCS (LNAI), vol. 9811, pp. 469–475. Springer, Cham (2016). https://doi.org/10.1007/978-3-319-43958-7_56
11. Kipyatkova, I., Karpov, A.: Language models with RNNs for rescoring hypotheses of Russian ASR. In: Cheng, L., Liu, Q., Ronzhin, A. (eds.) ISNN 2016. LNCS, vol. 9719, pp. 418–425. Springer, Cham (2016). https://doi.org/10.1007/978-3-319-40663-3_48
12. Kipyatkova, I.: Improving Russian LVCSR using deep neural networks for acoustic and language modeling. In: Karpov, A., Jokisch, O., Potapova, R. (eds.) SPECOM 2018. LNCS (LNAI), vol. 11096, pp. 291–300. Springer, Cham (2018). https://doi.org/10.1007/978-3-319-99579-3_31

13. Mikolov, T., Kombrink, S., Deoras, A., Burget, L., Černocký, J.: RNNLM - recurrent neural network language modeling toolkit. In: ASRU 2011 Demo Session (2011)
14. Enarvi, S., Kurimo, M.: TheanoLM—an extensible toolkit for neural network language modeling. In: INTERSPEECH-2016, pp. 3052–3056 (2016)
15. Kipyatkova, I., Karpov, A.: Lexicon size and language model order optimization for Russian LVCSR. In: Železný, M., Habernal, I., Ronzhin, A. (eds.) SPECOM 2013. LNCS (LNAI), vol. 8113, pp. 219–226. Springer, Cham (2013). https://doi.org/10.1007/978-3-319-01931-4_29
16. Morin, F., Bengio, Y.: Hierarchical probabilistic neural network language model. In: Cowell, R.G., Ghahramani, Z. (eds.) Proceedings of International Workshop on Artificial Intelligence and Statistics (AISTATS), New Jersey, USA, pp. 246–252. Society for Artificial Intelligence and Statistics (2005)
17. Stolcke, A., Zheng, J., Wang, W., Abrash, V.: SRILM at sixteen: update and outlook. In: Proceedings of IEEE Automatic Speech Recognition and Understanding Workshop ASRU 2011, Waikoloa, Hawaii, USA (2011)
18. Kipyatkova, I.: Experimenting with hybrid TDNN/HMM acoustic models for Russian speech recognition. In: Karpov, A., Potapova, R., Mporas, I. (eds.) SPECOM 2017. LNCS (LNAI), vol. 10458, pp. 362–369. Springer, Cham (2017). https://doi.org/10.1007/978-3-319-66429-3_35
19. Povey, D., et al.: The Kaldi speech recognition toolkit. In: IEEE Workshop on Automatic Speech Recognition and Understanding ASRU (2011)
20. Saon, G., Soltau, H., Nahamoo, D., Picheny, M.: Speaker adaptation of neural network acoustic models using i-vectors. In: IEEE Automatic Speech Recognition and Understanding Workshop (ASRU), pp. 55–59 (2013)
21. Nesterov, Y.: Introductory Lectures on Convex Optimization: A Basic Course, vol. 87. Springer, Heidelberg (2013)
22. Duchi, J., Hazan, E., Singer, Y.: Adaptive subgradient methods for online learning and stochastic optimization. J. Mach. Learn. Res. 12, 2121–2159 (2011)
23. Kingma, D.P., Ba, J.: Adam: a method for stochastic optimization. In: International Conference on Learning Representations, pp. 1–13 (2015)

Svarabhakti Vowel Occurrence and Duration in Rhotic Clusters in French Lyric Singing

Uliana Kochetkova[✉]

Saint Petersburg State University,
Universitetskaya nab. 11, Saint Petersburg, Russia
ukochetkova@phonetics.pu.ru

Abstract. The aim of the current study was to analyze the occurrence and duration of the epenthetic (svarabhakti) vowel in consonant clusters containing the uvular /R/ in French lyric singing. It was of special interest to consider this phenomenon in vocal speech of the worldwide renowned French opera singers. Firstly, because the uvular /R/ has been traditionally considered as an obstacle to the airflow projection and was supposed to be replaced by the alveolar /r/. Secondly, because consonant clusters present a problem for singers in any language, for they interrupt the airflow and hinder a good legato in singing. Rhotic clusters present both challenges combined. Svarabhakti vowel can be helpful in this case, aiming at the simplification of syllable structures in singing. The current study considered various factors, which may have an impact on the occurrence and duration of the svarabhakti vowel: cluster structure (CR or RC), sonority, voicing, manner and place of articulation of the adjacent consonant, musical tempo and neighboring vowel duration. Performances of two distinguished French singers with high voices and with the same repertoire were analyzed. The results of the study showed that in singing of both artists the svarabhakti vowel occurred in all cluster types and in all musical tempi. In RC clusters it was longer than in CR clusters (at the p-level < 0,05). Other correlations between the above-mentioned factors and the svarabhakti frequency and duration occurred to be singer-dependent.

Keywords: French rhotic clusters · Lyric singing analysis · Epenthetic vowel

1 Introduction

1.1 Rhotics in French Lyric Singing

Vocal speech analysis is of special interest today because it allows considering interplay between linguistics and music. At the same time there is still some lack of information about its characteristics, notably, about consonant articulation and acoustics in singers' performances. This information is particularly important for the French language, especially for its rhotic sounds pronunciation, because their interpretation in formal singing is ambiguous. As the uvular consonant is supposed to disturb and destroy the airflow projection in singing, only the alveolar /r/ should be performed. This tradition takes its origins in 17th century. It coincided together with the appearance of the Italian Bel Canto style of singing in France. Bertrand de Bassilly was

© Springer Nature Switzerland AG 2019
A. A. Salah et al. (Eds.): SPECOM 2019, LNAI 11658, pp. 227–236, 2019.
https://doi.org/10.1007/978-3-030-26061-3_24

one of the first authors who in 1679 described the /r/ quality in singing [1]. From this time onwards the alveolar /r/ remained obligatory for formal singers in both operatic and lyric genres [2–9]. At the same time, the recent analysis demonstrated that many modern singers prefer to pronounce the uvular /R/ in art songs as well as in operatic arias [10, 11]. They show much more consistency than the previous generations and can seemingly be divided into two groups. While 50% of them pronounce the alveolar variant in more than 90% of cases, the other half of performers produce the uvular variant with the same high rate of occurrence [11].

How can the singers manage to articulate the inconvenient uvular consonant and produce a good airflow at a time? The hypothesis would be the appearance of an epenthetic vowel [12], for which K. Pike suggested the term vocoid [13, 14] because of its undecided phonemic status. In the current study this epenthetic vowel or vocoid will be considered in various clusters with the uvular /R/. Therefore the term svarabhakti, originating from Sanskrit, is used, because it is a precise term designating an epenthesis in consonant clusters with liquids.

1.2   Consonant Clusters vs. Syllable Structure

In the current analysis the term cluster designates any sequence of consonants in the word-internal and cross-word-boundary positions. Although this term is often used for the group of consonants only within the syllable [15–19], there are many examples of its interpretation in more general sense [20–23]. In this case, they are divided into tauto- and heterosyllabic clusters. In the following text the dot indicates the syllable boundary.

The French language phonotactic rules provide constraints on consonant clustering depending on its position [18, 21]. For instance, RC clusters are impossible in syllable- or word-initial (onset) position. This sequence is always heterosyllabic. The syllabification in French seems to follow the sonority sequencing principle (SSP), so that the more sonorant consonant is, the closer to the syllable nucleus (vowel) it appears. Therefore in the sequence CR (Obstruent + /R/) the syllable boundary will always pass before the obstruent consonant after a vowel or another consonant. It means that the sequences VCRV or VCCRV will be divided into syllables as following: V.CRV and VC.CRV, neither *VC.RV nor *VC.CRV. Only if the first consonant is a glide, the boundary will appear before the /R/, due to the above-mentioned SSP. However, there were no such sequences in the studied material.

1.3   Svarabhakti Vowel in Singing

Any consonants, and especially the consonant clusters, present a difficulty for singer, as in singing "one must think hard about where and how the legato line is interrupted by the consonants and then sick to minimize that interruption in every way possible" [24]. The author of this quotation, though emphasizing the difficulty of the technique, advises to sing the consonant clusters without splitting them. The svarabhakti vowel is therefore forbidden and considered as destroying the legato line in Italian, as well as in French and other languages. The author criticizes the use of epenthetic vowels that create new syllables and make vowels unaligned [24]. The same advice can be found in the work concerning the lyric diction in Polish [25]. This language is well known for its highly difficult consonant clusters, especially the onset clusters. Even in this case, epenthesis is recommended only as an exercise. In performance it must be omitted [25].

The suggested technique of consonant cluster singing is slightly different in French and Italian. In French, one can find recommendation never to shorten the preceding vowel, but to move through the cluster to the following syllable, i.e. to the next vowel [5]. In Italian, inversely, the first consonant of the cluster may be lengthened and the preceding vowel shortened, especially if the latter is set to a long note [26]. Thus, no recommendations to use an epenthetic vowel were observed in the studied treatises on classical lyric diction.

At the same time, an epenthetic vowel occurrence seems to be the most natural and easiest way to overcome the described difficulty, for it helps creating additional vowels maintaining the airflow. This phenomenon was observed even in the early ecclesiastic practices. The insertion of parasitic vowels in the singing of antiphones caused some anaptyctic forms (i.e. forms with an epenthetic vowel) found in medieval manuscripts [27]. Studies in ethnomusicology also prove the insertion of such vowels in various styles of singing [28–30].

In regard to the cited recommendations and observations, the study of rhotic cluster pronunciation by the high-level professional native opera singers will be of special interest and importance. Thus the two main questions were formulated: how often will the svarabhakti appear in their singing, and what factors may influence its occurrence and duration?

2 Material and Method

2.1 Performers and Repertoire

According to the results of the previous analysis [10], nowadays, the highest rate of uvular /R/'s was observed in art songs performances of three famous operatic singers: two sopranos (Natalie Dessay and Isabelle Druet) and one countertenor (Phillipe Jaroussky). However, only Ph. Jaroussky and N. Dessay have a wide-ranging comparable recorded French repertoire, while I. Druet's accessible recordings represent only few art songs by French composers. Therefore the following study analyzes rhotic cluster pronunciation by two worldwide renowned singers: the countertenor Ph. Jaroussky and the soprano Natalie Dessay. Despite gender differences, both of them sing in high register. Natalie Dessay is supposed to be the champion among coloratura sopranos attending the highest notes. At the same time, Phillippe Jaroussky is a unique countertenor with a large voice diapason whose recorded repertoire embraces not only the baroque music, but also a wide range of composers.

For the analysis of rhotic clusters 17 interpretations of art songs by French composers of the late 19th –early 20th century were chosen. Six art songs were interpreted by both of singers. Two art songs were added in Ph. Jaroussky's interpretation; three were interpreted by N. Dessay (Table 1).

Table 1. List of the selected art songs by French composers.

Art Songs	Countertenor (PhJ)	Soprano (ND)
Mandoline (G. Fauré)	+	+
Clair de lune (G. Fauré)	+	+
Spleen (G. Fauré)	+	+
En sourdine (G. Fauré)	+	+
Colibri (E. Chausson)	+	+
Romance (C. Debussy)	+	+
Automne (G. Fauré)	+	−
Après un rêve (G. Fauré)	−	+
Nuits d'Espagne (J. Massenet)	+	−
Invitation au voyage (H. Duparc)	−	+
Les filles de Cadix (L. Délibes)	−	+

2.2 Acoustic and Statistic Analysis

As the audio processing provided some challenges due to the file format and to the accompaniment noise, all the acoustic analysis, i.e. segmentation and transcription, was done manually using Praat software. The duration of svarabhakti vowel was measured, its relative frequency and duration were calculated in two types of clusters (CR and RC clusters). Then the statistic analysis was accomplished to verify the difference of svarabhakti occurrence in various environment and types of clusters: the chi-squared test was done with the Yates correction coefficient when needed, i.e. when the anticipated values in the fourfold table were less than 9. The Fisher's exact test was used when the anticipated values in the fourfold table were less than 5. For the duration analysis the Student t-test was used. The Pearson correlation coefficient was calculated for the comparison of the svarabhakti vowel occurrence and duration with the musical tempo indication, as well as with the neighboring vowels mean duration.

3 Results

487 contexts with /R/s in chosen art songs were observed. 310 samples contained consonant clusters, both tauto-and heterosyllabic. They were divided into two groups: CR and RC clusters, i.e. clusters with a consonant preceding or following /R/, no matter how long was the cluster. In French connected speech, as well as in singing, the word chain is divided into syllables, causing in some cases the resyllabification [21]. Thus word-internal and cross-word-boundary clusters were considered together. The clusters R + Glide + V were excluded from the current analysis, because glides do not present such an obstacle for the airflow as other sonorant consonants or obstruent consonants. The frequency of the svarabhakti vowel occurrence and its duration were calculated in two types of clusters for each singer.

3.1 CR vs. RC Clusters

Mostly single clusters, i.e. V.CRV contexts, in which the CR sequence was preceded and followed by vowels word-internally or across word boundaries, represented the group of CR clusters. All these clusters are tautosyllabic in French. Examples are the word-internal cluster in *navrant* /na.vrã/ and the cross-boundary cluster in the group *votre âme* /vɔ.tra(mᵊ)/. The last consonant is given in parenthesis, for it belongs to the following syllable.

Only two single CR clusters were observed in the onset position in the phrase (after a pause): in *brilliant* /# bri.jã/ and in *brune* /# bry(nᵊ)/. Few double clusters VC.CRV occurred in both singers' performances. Although these clusters are heterosyllabic in French, the sequence CR always belongs to the same syllable, due to French phonotactic rules and sonority sequencing principle (SSP) as in *ciels brouillés* /siɛl.bru.je/ or in *esprit* /ɛs.pri/. Double tautosyllabic clusters # CRGliV and V.CRGliV with glides /w, j, ɥ/ appeared in the onset position after a pause, i.e. phrase-, word- and syllable-initially, as in *croise* /# krwa(zᵊ)/, or in intervocalic position word-internally or across word boundaries, as in *le bruit* /lə.brɥi/.

All RC clusters are heterosyllabic in Standard French. The single clusters in intervocalic position, i.e. the VR.CV contexts (except for V.RGliV sequences), were the most frequent. These clusters appeared word-internally, as in *parmi* /paR.mi/, and across word boundaries, as in the group *leur bonheur* /lœR.bɔ.nœr/. Double clusters with glides VR.CGliV also occurred, as in *leur joie* /lœR.ʒwa/. Double clusters including two /R/'s were observed only in three examples: *arbres* /aR.bRə/, *marbres* / maR.bRə/ and *ordre* /ɔR.dRə/. As such contexts were rare in the studied material, the first /R/ of the VR.CRV cluster was considered as a part of RC type and the second as a part of CR type of cluster. A triple RC cluster VR.CCCV occurred only once, at the word boundaries in *leur splendeur* /lœR.splã.dœR/.

The comparison of the occurrence of the svarabhakti vowel in two types of contexts showed that the epenthetic vowel was more frequent in RC clusters in both singers's performances, though significant difference (83% and 35% respectively) was observed only in the countertenor's singing (at the $p < 0{,}001$). In the soprano's singing this difference was insignificant (89% and 70%).

The comparison of the mean duration of the epenthetic vowel in CR and RC clusters showed statistically relevant results for both singers (at the $p < 0{,}05$). In countertenor's singing the svarabhakti mean durations were 84 ms in CR clusters and 124 ms in RC clusters. In soprano's performances mean durations were 83 ms and 119 ms respectively.

3.2 Consonantal Environment Impact

Comparison of the svarabhakti occurrence and duration after and before concrete consonants would be of interest. Nevertheless, such an analysis necessitates much larger material. Thus in the current study the possible impact of consonant classes was considered. In CR clusters the only voiced consonants were /b, v, g/ in countertenor's singing and /b, v, g, d/ in soprano's singing. Voiceless consonants for both performers were /f, k, t, p/. In RC clusters /j, ɲ, r/ were absent in both singers' performances, while in countertenor's singing there was also a lack of /p/ and /g/.

Voicing. In countertenor's performances an epenthetic vowel occurred more often in the voiced environment both in CR (50% vs. 22%) and RC (93% vs. 69%) clusters with the significance at the p < 0,05 and p < 0,005 respectively. For soprano's performances the opposite relationship was observed in CR clusters: epenthetic vowels after voiceless consonant were more frequent (88% vs. 54%) with the significance at the p < 0,005. In RC clusters there was the same proportion as in countertenor's singing (92% vs. 83%), though statistically insignificant. In soprano's interpretations of the art songs the svarabhakti vowel was significantly longer (at the p < 0,05) before voiced consonants, i.e. in RC clusters. Its mean duration was 132 ms in voiced environment vs. 91 ms in voiceless one. In countertenor's performances the difference (130 ms vs. 112 ms) was not significant.

Manner of Articulation. The countertenor produced more epenthesis after fricatives than after plosives (71% vs. 30%) with the significance at the p < 0,05. In RC contexts, there is an opposite proportion: 70% before fricatives and 89% before plosives (with the significance at the p < 0,05). Svarabhakti mean duration is significantly longer after plosives in CR clusters (87 ms vs. 64 ms) in soprano's singing (at the p < 0,05), while in countertenor's performance epenthetic vowel duration increases before plosives (at the p < 0,05) in RC clusters (132 ms vs. 103 ms).

Place of Articulation and Sonority. Neither place of articulation nor sonority showed statistically reliable results for svarabhakti occurrence and duration. It should also be mentioned that in CR clusters no groups with sonorant consonants were observed.

3.3 Svarabhakti Occurrence vs. Duration vs. Musical Tempo

Correlation between svarabhakti occurrence and duration was observed in soprano's singing with the Pearson correlation coefficient > 0,7 (approved by the t-test at the p < 0,05), which shows a high correlation. It means that in N. Dessay's performances the more epenthesis occurred, the longer they were. This correlates well with tempo indications given by composers as well. To analyze the tempo, art songs were ranged; tempo indications were designated by numbers. This correlation appears only in soprano's singing and is high (r > 0,7 at the p < 0,05).

Another way to analyze the musical tempo impact was to compare mean duration of neighboring vowels with the svarabhakti vowel duration. This correlation again appears only in N. Dessay's singing and is very high (r > 0,9 at the p < 0,05). It means that for this singer the slower the musical piece is, the more frequently an epenthesis occurs. At the same time, there is no compensatory effect in Dessay's singing, it doesn't become shorter when the number of epenthesis increases. An interesting fact is that in Ph. Jaroussky's singing no correlation between these parameters was observed (Tables 2 and 3).

Table 2. Statistically significant differences in svarabhakti vowel occurrence.

Clusters	Countertenor (PhJ)	Soprano (ND)
Type of cluster	RC > CR	–
Voicing in CR	Voiced > voiceless	Voiceless > voiced
Voicing in RC	Voiced > voiceless	–
Articulation manner in CR	Fricatives > plosives	–
Articulation manner in RC	Fricatives > plosives	–
Place of articulation in CR	–	–
Place of articulation in RC	–	–
Sonority in CR	–	–
Sonority in RC	–	–

Table 3. Statistically significant differences in svarabhakti vowel duration.

Clusters	Countertenor (PhJ)	Soprano (ND)
Type of cluster	RC > CR	RC > CR
Voicing in CR	–	–
Voicing in RC	–	Voiced > voiceless
Articulation manner in CR	–	Plosives > fricatives
Articulation manner in RC	Plosives > fricatives	–
Place of articulation in CR	–	–
Place of articulation in RC	–	–
Sonority in CR	–	–
Sonority in RC	–	–

4 Discussion

Some results of the current study can be related to those obtained by other authors [16, 17, 19]. This is the case of the more frequent svarabhakti after voiced consonants in countertenor's singing. It corresponds well to the fact that in CR clusters the beginning of /R/ is most often represented by an open phase of articulation. This phase is considered as an intrinsic part of the consonant by some of the authors [23], while others consider it as a separate epenthetic vowel [16]. It should however be mentioned, that in the current analysis the phonological status of this vowel (or vocoid, following K. Pike definition [13, 14]) is not discussed. In this relation the opposite proportion of epenthesis number after voiced and voiceless consonants in soprano's singing seems to be of special interest. Is it an individual peculiarity or can it be used by other sopranos as well? What are the factors that led to such proportion? Will it occur only in sung speech? Although the comparison of the two singers' performances cannot give answers to these questions, one can observe that in vocal speech the mechanisms of the svarabhakti vowel appearance differ from those described for the ordinary speech.

Another important observation, which can be made, is the difference in singers' strategies. Comparing Tables 2 and 3, one can remark that the singers' decisions coincided only for one parameter: both singers made longer epenthesis in RC clusters. The other characteristic differed. The countertenor's epenthetic vowel occurrence seems to be influenced more by the consonant environment, while soprano's epenthesis, and especially its duration, correlates more with the temporal features. Thus, we may suppose that singers "use" different characteristics of the svarabhakti vowel in different ways. Some singers may produce them more often and others may make them longer in order to facilitate the uvular /R/ pronunciation.

5 Conclusion

In the current paper the impact of various factors on svarabhakti vowel occurrence and duration was analyzed. The choice of the material is based on the previous studies' results. Performances of the two distinguished opera singers (Ph. Jaroussky and N. Dessay) were compared, firstly, because they pronounce uvular /R/'s in singing in more than 90% of cases. Secondly, they are both renowned French native artists with a wide-ranging repertoire. This fact allowed making a comparison using a well-balanced material. Thirdly, both of singers have high voices. At the same time, Ph. Jaroussky's interpretations of French art songs cannot be compared to any other countertenor's performances at this moment, because of the rarity of this voice and differences in singers's repertoire. N. Dessay's art songs performances cannot be compared to other soprano's recordings either, for the number of accessible commercial recordings of other singers pronouncing uvular /R/'s in singing is much lower.

This analysis showed the significant prevalence of svarabhakti vowel duration in RC clusters vs. CR clusters for both singers. At the same time, other parameters seem to depend on individual preferences of singers and may represent their individual techniques, which aim at achieving a good airflow projection. One may suppose that svarabhakti occurrence, especially in RC clusters, may facilitate not only the articulation, but also the perception of the sung speech by listeners.

Another challenge concerns svarabhakti duration measurements. One can suppose that the svarabhakti sung in different registers with different duration may have the same number of pitch periods. Although this question was not considered in the current study, it presents an important interest for the future research.

The results of the current analysis may be useful for the theory of opera singing and of the French diction for singers, as they provide new data about rhotic cluster pronunciation in formal singing. On the one hand, this information corresponds to the results of the previous and recent studies in ethnomusicology. On the other hand, it totally contradicts what has been recommended in various treatises on vocal technique. However, the high professional level and competence of the considered artists makes no doubt about the suitability of svarabhakti in their performances. Indeed, it seems to be an individual strategy that helps maintaining an appropriate airflow projection when pronouncing uncomfortable uvular consonants in the high register. In future, the comparison with other singers with the same or lower registers, singing with the uvular /R/ or alveolar /r/ seems to be of importance. The obtained results may also be applied in singing voice synthesis and recognition, which are the most challenging and up-to-date questions in this field. Thus, a higher rate of the svarabhakti vowels and of the open syllables may be one of the signals of the vocal speech.

References

1. Bacilly, B.: L'Art de bien chanter de M. Bacilly, Bacilly, Paris (1679)
2. Lavoix, H., Lemaire, T.: Le Chant. Ses Principes et son Histoire. Heugel et fils, Paris (1881)
3. Grubb, T.: Singing in French: A Manual of French Diction and French Vocal Repertoire. Schirmer Books, Belmont (1979)
4. Vennard, W.: Singing: The Mecanism and the Technic. Karl Fisher, New York (1967)
5. Nedecky, J.: French Diction for Singers: A Handbook of Pronunciation for French Opera and Melodie. Book POD, Toronto (2015)
6. Yarbrough, J.: Modern Languages for Musicians. Pendragon Press, Stuyvesan (1991)
7. Miller, R.: On the Art of Singing. Oxford University Press, Oxford (1996)
8. Miller, R.: Solutions for Singers: Tools for Performers and Teachers. Oxford University Press, Oxford (2004)
9. Montgomery, J.: The Advanced French Lyric Diction Workbook. S.T.M. Publications, Nashviller (2015)
10. Kochetkova, U.: Some aspects of /r/ articulation in French vocal speech. In: Botinis, A. (ed.) Proceedings of the 7th Tutorial and Research Workshop on Experimental Linguistics, pp. 87–90, Saint Petersburg (2016)
11. Kochetkova, U.: Phonetic environment effect on /r/ articulation in French sung speech. In: Androsova, S. (ed.) Theoretical and Applied Linguistics, vol. 3, no. 1, pp. 16–27. Amur State University, Blagoveshensk (2017)
12. Kochetkova, U.: Manners of rhotic articulation in French lyric singing. In: Botinis, A. (ed.) Proceedings of the 9th Tutorial and Research Workshop on Experimental Linguistics, pp. 69–72, Paris (2018)
13. Pike, K.L.: Language in Relations to a Unified Theory of Human Behavior, 2nd edn. Mouton & Co., The Hague (1967)
14. Pike, K.L.: Phonetics: A Critical Analysis of Phonetic Theory and a Technique for the Practical Description of Sounds. University of Michigan Press, Ann Arbor (1943)
15. Bartkova, K., Jouvet, D.: Analysis of prosodic correlates of emotional speech data. In: Botinis, A. (ed.) Proceedings of the 9th Tutorial and Research Workshop on Experimental Linguistics, pp. 21–24, Paris (2018)
16. Chow, I., Poiré, F.: Consonant-rhotic clusters in southwestern Ontario French: a study of rhotic variation and schwa epenthesis. In: LACUS, vol. 33, pp. 93–103, Toronto (2007)
17. Colantoni, L., Steele, J.: Liquid asymmetries in French and Spanish. In: Toronto Working Papers in Linguistics, vol. 24, pp. 1–14, Toronto (2005)
18. Gendrot, C., Kuhnert, B., Demolin, D.: Aerodynamic, articulatory and acoustic realization of French /ʁ/. In: Proceedings of ICPhS 2015, Glasgow (2015)
19. Schmeiser, B.: On the durational variability of svarabhakti vowels in Spanish complex onsets. In: Alcazar, A., Hernández, R.M., Temkin-Martínez, M. (eds.) Proceedings of WECOL 2004. University of Southern California, Los Angeles (2004)
20. Celata, C., Vietti, A., Spreafico, L.: An articulatory account of rhotic variation in Tuscan Italian: Synchronized UTI and EPG data. In: Gibson, M., Gil, J. (eds.) Romance Phonetics and Phonology. Oxford University Press, London (2019
21. Dell, F.: Consonant clusters and phonological syllables in French. In: Lingua 1995, pp. 5–26 (1995)

22. Meunier, C.: Voicing assimilation as a cue for cluster identification. In: Proceedings of EUROSPEECH 1997, pp. 935–938, Rhodes (1997)
23. Meunier, C.: Phonétique acoustique. In: Auzou, P. (ed.) Les Dysarthries, pp. 164–173, Solal (2007)
24. Smith, W.S., Chipman, M.: The Naked Voice: A Wholistic Approach to Singing. Oxford University Press, New York (2007)
25. Schultz, B.: Singing in Polish: A Guide to Polish Lyric Diction and Vocal Repertoire (Guides to Lyric Diction). Rowman & Littlefield, Lanham (2016)
26. Adams, D.: A Handbook of Diction for Singers: Italian, German, French, 2nd edn. Oxford University Press, Oxford (2008)
27. Boyce, B.: The Language of the Freedmen in Petronius' Cena Trimalchionis (Mnemosyne Supplement CXVII). Brill, Leiden (1991)
28. Dell, F.: Singing in Tashlhiyt Berber, a language that allows vowel-less syllables. In: Cairn, C.E., Raimy, E. (eds.) Handbook of the Syllable. Brill, Leiden (2010)
29. Shaw, J.: Language, music and local esthetics: views from Gaeldom and beyond. Scott. Lang. 11(12), 37–64 (1992)
30. Wilson, G.: The Sociolinguistics of Singing: Dialect and Style in Classical Choral Singing in Trinidad. MV Wissenschaft, Münster (2014)

The Evaluation Process Automation of Phrase and Word Intelligibility Using Speech Recognition Systems

Evgeny Kostuchenko[1](✉) , Dariya Novokhrestova[1] ,
Marina Tirskaya[1], Alexander Shelupanov[1] ,
Mikhail Nemirovich-Danchenko[1] , Evgeny Choynzonov[1,2] ,
and Lidiya Balatskaya[1,2]

[1] Tomsk State University of Control, Systems and Radioelectronics,
Lenina Str. 40, 634050 Tomsk, Russia
key@keva.tusur.ru
[2] Tomsk Cancer Research Institute, Kooperativniy Av. 5, 634050 Tomsk, Russia
nii@oncology.tomsk.ru
http://www.tusur.ru, http://www.oncology.tomsk.ru/

Abstract. The article proposes the application of the assessment of phrase and word intelligibility through speech recognition approach in the framework of solving the problems of speech rehabilitation after the combined treatment of oncological diseases. Speech intelligibility assessments were obtained using three speech recognition systems (Google, Yandex, Voco) and compared with expert assessments of intelligibility. Experimental results show a positive opinion about the proposed approach and they are agreed with expert assessments. Based on the processed data from rehabilitation for the Russian language, a recommendation is formulated on using the Google recognition system in the first version of the being developed product. The statistical significance of the differences in the obtained estimates of intelligibility between patient sessions and the coincidence of the sign of these differences with expert estimates and theoretical expectations are shown.

Keywords: Speech recognition · Cancer of the oral cavity and oropharynx · Speech quality criteria

1 Introduction

According to statistics [1, 2], the prevalence of oncological diseases of the organs of the speech apparatus increased in 2017 in Russia, in particular, the prevalence of oncological diseases of the oral cavity became 27.2 per 100,000 population against 26.6 in 2016. The proportion of newly diagnosed diseases in I and II stages increased, the mortality decreased with such localization (except for lungs, trachea and bronchus diseases), the number of patients admitted for treatment increased. The average age of patients is 60–63 years with such localization of oncology. Therefore, there is an urgent need for speech rehabilitation after surgical treatment of cancer. The relevance of this area of research is confirmed by the appearance of similar works abroad, although they cannot be directly applied to the processing of Russian-speaking speech [3]. As part of rehabilitation, it is necessary to assess both the patient's speech and the dynamics of speech recovery. Currently, speech rehabilitation is carried out at Cancer Research Institute, Tomsk National Research Medical Center of the Russian Academy of Sciences is based on GOST R 50840-95 "Speech transmission over varies communication channels. Techniques for measurements of speech quality, intelligibility and voice identification" [4]. In the process of rehabilitation, assessment methods of syllable and phrase intelligibility are used, the bases of which are taken from the standard. The main disadvantage of these methods is the subjectivity of the resulting estimates. Therefore, automated systems are being developed to obtain objective quantitative assessments of the quality and intelligibility of speech, namely, syllable and phrase intelligibility. The proposed systems and algorithms for assessing syllable intelligibility are described in [5–7]. Concerning phrase intelligibility approach is offered to use, based on speech recognition algorithms and the subsequent evaluation of the recognized text - whether the recognized text matched what was or had to be pronounced. This article describes the attempt to apply various speech recognition systems to the existing database of phrase records according to GOST R 50840-95, formed on the basis of session records of patients who were treated at Cancer Research Institute. The estimates obtained by the results of recognition are compared with the estimates obtained by the method currently used, namely, listening to the record base by experts. A comparison of both phrase and word intelligibility is proposed. Phrase intelligibility is understood as an assessment of the phrase pronunciation correctness. Word intelligibility is understood as the proportion of correctly pronounced words in a phrase.

2   Proposed Approach

2.1   Applied Assessment Method

GOST R 50840-95 proposes an assessment of phrasal and verbal intelligibility in two ways. The first of these is the speaker's paired comparison of the recordings of phrases in the test and control transmission paths by grading on a 5-point scale in 0.1 increments for each record. Then the average values are calculated for the test and control paths. The final assessment is the ratio of these average values multiplied by 5. In accordance with the obtained assessment, the quality class is assigned, the description of which is given in Table 1 in GOST R 50840-95. For recording, 7 basic and 2 additional phrases from Appendix G GOST R 50840-95 are suggested. It is also proposed an evaluation of phrase intelligibility at an accelerated pace of pronunciation. The measurement is carried out by transferring phrases through the subject channel at the normal and accelerated rate of pronunciation. A couple of operators participate in the reception: an auditor and a controller. The auditor says out loud the received phrase, and the controller detects the correctness of its reception (binary score - 0 or 1). In this case, measurements are carried out at the normal and accelerated rate of pronouncing two tables of phrases with the participation of a brigade consisting of at least 3 announcers and 4–5 pairs of operators. Tables of phrases are given in Appendix D

GOST R 50840-95, which contains 100 tables of 50 phrases in each. Direct use of the above techniques in the task of assessing the speech quality in the rehabilitation process is not possible. Therefore, now phrase intelligibility is carried out as follows: a set of phrases is recorded and a score of 0 or 1 is set for these records, where 1 is the phrase spoken completely legibly and 0 otherwise. For recording, phrases from Appendix D GOST R 50840-95 are used. Evaluation of word intelligibility is not performed. Also, one of the drawbacks of the existing methodology is that the auditor knows in advance what should be pronounced, which leads to a distortion of the resulting assessment.

2.2   Description of Speech Recognition Systems

In the framework of automating the process of evaluating phrase and word speech intelligibility, it was proposed to use three speech recognition systems (converting sound files into text). The first is Google Cloud Speech-to-Text API [8]. It allows converting audio to text using deep-learning neural network algorithms. The API recognizes 120 languages and variants. Speech-to-Text has three main methods to perform speech recognition: Synchronous Recognition (audio data of 1 min or less in duration), Asynchronous Recognition (audio data of any duration up to 480 min) and Streaming Recognition. Both off-line (i.e. providing already pre-recorded audio) and on-line recording (i.e. streaming the audio as it comes) modes are supported. All audio file formats are permissible, but FLAC and WAV are recommended for best results. This system uses the most basic recognition algorithms, however, due to the large amounts of computing power, high recognition accuracy is achieved. Also, a possible disadvantage of the system can be considered the fact that it was originally developed not for the Russian language.

The second system is Yandex SpeechKit [9]. This system is designed for both recognition and speech synthesis. Currently, the system supports three languages: Russian, English and Turkish. Initially, the system was developed specifically for the peculiarities of the Russian language. In the system, the recognition problem is solved in two stages. The first is the selection of sets of sounds that can be interpreted as words, and for each set there are several variants of words. At the second stage, a language model is added, which determines the best of the variants due to the analysis of consistency with the previously recognized words. The language model is based on machine learning of neural networks. For each of the languages there are their own models, for the Russian language currently there are 5 models: short queries (general), addresses (maps), dates (dates), names (names), numbers (numbers). Both off-line (i.e. providing already pre-recorded audio) and on-line recording (i.e. streaming the audio as it comes) modes are supported. The following restrictions are imposed on audio files: size no more than 1 MB, duration no more than 1 min, 1 audio channel.

The third system is Voco [10], a speech-to-text application developed by the Speech Technology Center. The recognition language is Russian, the volume of the dictionary is 334750 words and word forms. The claimed audio recognition time is approximately $1 \times$ real-time. Recognition accuracy is 86% for prepared dictated speech and up to 77% for audio recording from the media channel (news channel). The general vocabulary and colloquial vocabulary are included in the basic vocabulary, there are also special subject dictionaries: legal and financial. Recognition is possible both dictation of speech from a microphone and downloadable audio recordings. The program supports most existing audio formats, however, for best results, it is suggested to use WAV and FLAC. This is the only one of the three systems presented that works in offline mode.

2.3 Description of the Database and Experiment Methodology

To test the proposed approach to the assessment of phrasal and verbal intelligibility, a database from the Tomsk Oncology Research Institute was used. Records of only those patients who had 2 or more sessions were selected. This is due to the need to check the efficiency of the approach, not only on the records before the operation, where speech is close to normal, but also on the sessions after surgical treatment. There are 21 patients in the record database used, totally 60 sessions of 25 records each (totally 1500 records). Of these 21 patients, 12 are women and 9 are men. 12 speakers have 3 sessions, 6 speakers have 2 sessions each, the remaining 3 speakers have 4 sessions. For the recording of phrases, a list of the first 25 phrases of the table D3 of Appendix D GOST R 50840-95 is used.

Table 1. The assessment table for a session.

Pronounced	Recognized	Phrase is right	How many words
Белая пелена лежала на полях (bʲ'eləjə pʰɪlʲɪn'a lʲɪʐ̵'alə nə pɐlʲ'æx White shroud lies on fields)	Белая пелена лежала на полях (bʲ'eləjə pʰɪlʲɪn'a lʲɪʐ̵'alə nə pɐlʲ'æx White shroud lies on fields)	1	5
В школу приезжали герои фронта (f‿ ʂk'olʊ prʲɪjɪʐ̵'alʲɪ gʲɪr'oɪ fr'ontə In school front heroes came)	Школу приезжали герои фронта (ʂk'olʊ prʲɪjɪʐ̵'alʲɪ gʲɪr'oɪ fr'ontə School front heroes came)	0	4
Белый пар расстилается над лужами (bʲ'elɨj p'ar rəs:tʲɪl'ajɪtsə nəd‿ l'uʐ̵əmʲɪ White steam spreads over puddles)	Белый зал высылается на дружбе (bʲ'elɨj z'al vɪsɨl'ajɪtsə nə dr'uʐ̵bʲɪ White hall sends on friend-ship)	0	1
Экипаж танка понял задачу (ɪkʲɪp'aʂ t'ankə p'onʲɪl zɐd'atɕʊ Tank crew understood task)	Экипаж танка понял задачу (ɪkʲɪp'aʂ t'ankə p'onʲɪl zɐd'atɕʊ Tank crew understood task)	1	4
Этот блок работает хорошо ('ɛtət blʲok rɐb'otəjɪt xɐrɐʂ'o This block works well)	Блок работает хорошо (blʲok rɐb'otəjɪt xɐrɐʂ'o Block works well)	0	3

As part of the experiment, each of the sessions was evaluated by an expert, as well as by each of the three systems described above. In the case of an expert assessment, the assessment was made as follows: the expert listens to a record, writes down what he heard, and assesses how much what he heard coincides with what was supposed to be pronounced. In the case of a recognition system, a record is made at the system input, the system issues a recognition result, and the expert evaluates how much what the system issued coincides with what was supposed to be pronounced. For each session record, phrase intelligibility (0 or 1) and word intelligibility (the number of words that were correctly recognized) are set. An example of the assessment table for a session is presented in Table 1. The Table shows the pronounced and recognized phrases in Russian, their phonetic transcription according to [11] and the translation into English. The evaluation of the phrase intelligibility of a session is obtained as the ratio of the number of correctly recognized phrases to the total number of phrases in the session. The assessment of the word intelligibility of the session is obtained as the ratio of the total number of correctly recognized words in all records to the total number of words.

3   Results

The first thing that was calculated as the average phrase and word intelligibility for each type of assessment. Hereinafter, we will use the following notation: expert assessment - Expert, Google Cloud Speech-to-Text API recognition system - Google, Yandex SpeechKit - Yandex recognition system, Voco recognition system from the Speech Technology Center - Voco. The mean values of intelligibility were compared for three types of sessions (before the operation - the first session of the patient, immediately after the operation and before rehabilitation - the second session, after rehabilitation - the third session). Some patients also have a fourth session (usually several months after the completion of rehabilitation), but since there are only 3 such patients, therefore the average for them was not considered. The results for phrase intelligibility, namely average values and standard deviations, are presented in Fig. 2. Additionally, the significance of differences between the average values was calculated. The significance is assessed based on testing the null hypothesis of equality of averages with the alternative hypothesis of their inequality. The t-test was used [12]. The levels of significance for each of the pairs are presented in Tables 2 and 3. The differences between the obtained average values are statistically significant. From the presented data it is clear that Google produces more quality recognition than other recognition systems. And this advantage takes place both for records before the operation, and after. Also, by average values, it can be seen that the best speech intelligibility is observed in sessions before surgery, after surgery the lowest values, after rehabilitation the scores improve, but do not reach the level before the operation. The results are consistent with the data on rehabilitation provided by Cancer Research Institute.

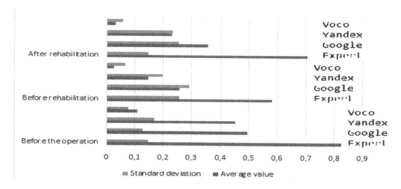

Fig. 1. Average values and standard deviations of word intelligibility.

Table 2. The significance for the null hypothesis of equality of averages with the alternative hypothesis of their inequality.

	Before the operation			Before rehabilitation			After rehabilitation		
	Google	Yandex	Voco	Google	Yandex	Voco	Google	Yandex	Voco
Google	1	0.358	0	1	0.166	0	1	0.164	0
Yandex		1	0		1	0		1	0
Voco			1			1			1

Table 3. The significance for the null hypothesis of equality of averages with the alternative hypothesis of their inequality.

Expert			Google		
Before the operation	Before rehabilitation	After rehabilitation	Before the operation	Before rehabilitation	After rehabilitation
1	0.002	0.038	1	0.004	0.068
	1	0.094		1	0.294
		1			1
Yandex			Voco		
Before the operation	Before rehabilitation	After rehabilitation	Before the operation	Before rehabilitation	After rehabilitation
1	0	0.004	1	0	0.002
	1	0.276		1	0.832
		1			1

By analogy with phrase intelligibility, results are obtained for word intelligibility. Average values and standard deviations are presented in Fig. 1. The significance for average values of word intelligibility are presented in Tables 4 and 5. As with phrase intelligibility, Google produces more quality recognition than others regarding word intelligibility among the recognition systems. Also, by evaluating phrase and word intelligibility, it can be concluded that in most cases it is impossible after rehabilitation to achieve the same level of intelligibility that was before the operation.

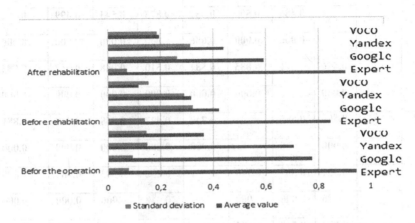

Fig. 2. Average values and standard deviations of word intelligibility.

Table 4. The significance for the null hypothesis of equality of averages with the alternative hypothesis of their inequality.

	Before the operation			Before rehabilitation			After rehabilitation		
	Google	Yandex	Voco	Google	Yandex	Voco	Google	Yandex	Voco
Google	1	0.09	0	1	0.282	0	1	0.162	0
Yandex		1	0		1	0		1	0
Voco			1			1			1

Table 5. The significance for the null hypothesis of equality of averages with the alternative hypothesis of their inequality.

Expert			Google		
Before the operation	Before rehabilitation	After rehabilitation	Before the operation	Before rehabilitation	After rehabilitation
1	0.016	0.174	1	0	0.022
	1	0.144		1	0.099
		1			1
Yandex			Voco		
Before the operation	Before rehabilitation	After rehabilitation	Before the operation	Before rehabilitation	After rehabilitation
1	0	0.008	1	0	0.008
	1	0.25		1	0.176
		1			1

Table 6. Correlation values and their significance.

		EP	GP	YP	VP	EW	GW	YW	VW
					Correlation				
EP	r	1	0.486	0.500	0.331	0.873	0.543	0.499	0.462
	t		0.000	0.000	0.006	.000	0.000	0.000	0.000
GP	r	0.486	1	0.885	0.582	0.510	0.948	0.917	0.784
	t	0.000		0.000	0.000	0.000	0.000	0.000	0.000
YP	r	0.500	0.885	1	0.740	0.422	0.868	0.948	0.881
	t	0.000	0.000		0.000	0.000	0.000	0.000	0.000
VP	r	0.331	0.582	0.740	1	0.232	0.583	0.684	0.895
	t	0.006	0.000	0.000		0.040	0.000	0.000	0.000
EW	r	0.873	0.510	0.422	0.232	1	0.586	0.491	0.386
	T	0.000	0.000	0.000	0.040		0.000	0.000	0.001
GW	r	0.543	0.948	0.868	0.583	0.586	1	0.949	0.797
	t	0.000	0.000	0.000	0.000	0.000		0.000	0.000
YW	r	0.499	0.917	0.948	0.684	0.491	0.949	1	0.884
	t	0.000	0.000	0.000	0.000	0.000	0.000		0.000
VW	r	0.462	0.784	0.881	0.895	0.386	0.797	0.884	1
	t	0.000	0.000	0.000	0.000	0.001	0.000	0.000	

Bold Font, light grey background - The correlation is significant at the level of 0.01 (one-sided).
Dark grey background - The correlation is significant at the level of 0.05 (one-sided).

We also calculated the values of the Pearson correlation coefficient between all obtained sets of estimates of sessions and their significance. The results are presented in Table 6. The following notation is used in the table: EP - phrase intelligibility, assessed by an expert, GP - phrase intelligibility through Google, YP - phrase intelligibility through Yandex, VP - phrase intelligibility through Voco, EW - word intelligibility, assessed by an expert, GW - word intelligibility through Google, YW - word intelligibility through Yandex, VW - word intelligibility through Voco, r - Pearson correlation coefficient, t - significance (one-sided). For a conclusion about the applicability of the proposed approach and the choice of the optimal recognition system for use, it is necessary to look at the correlation between expert evaluation and the evaluations of each of the systems. From the presented data it can be concluded that if we talk about phrase intelligibility, the correlation coefficient between Expert and Yandex estimates is the highest, but it is only slightly more correlation coefficient between Expert and Google (0.486 vs. 0.5). If we talk about word intelligibility, then Google is closest to Expert. All scores obtained through recognition systems are consistent, but the consistency between Google and Yandex is higher than between them and Voco.

4 Conclusion

As a result of the analysis of the obtained data on the word and phrase intelligibility assessment, it can be concluded that the approach to assessing the pronunciation of phrases and words in phrases based on the use of speech recognition systems is applicable. The results obtained based on the application of the described approach are consistent with the results obtained using the methodology currently used. A comparison of the three speech recognition systems (Google, Yandex, Voco) showed that Google's system is best at recognizing. Therefore, this system is proposed for use in the first version of the module for the assessment of phrase intelligibility in a program for assessing speech quality in the process of speech rehabilitation. The resulting estimates can be used to assess the dynamics of speech recovery from the point of view of phrase and word intelligibility.

The values obtained for healthy speakers and the speech of patients before the operation are comparable in terms of word intelligibility to the results presented in [13].

However, the results obtained through the selected system are not close (although they are consistent) with the results obtained by the expert. Therefore, one of the areas for further research is the development of a recognition system that will be designed specifically for solving a specific local task of assessing patients' speech in the process of speech rehabilitation after surgical treatment of oncological diseases. It is possible to attempt the use of existing speech recognition algorithms designed for the Russian language [14], with a refinement to the task. It is assumed that in this system there will be a setting for specific patients, a model for non-standard speakers (considering the peculiarity of surgical intervention), as well as methods for setting up the system, in particular using optimization methods [15].

Additionally, in the course of the experiment, an auditor significant "addiction" to the phrases was revealed, which makes it impossible to obtain an assessment on the same speech material. This effect will be investigated further by comparing with the results obtained by individual selection of an auditor for each session. However, now the identification of such a problem increases the relevance of using the developed objective assessment method.

Acknowledgments. The study was performed by a grant from the Russian Science Foundation (project 16-15-00038).

References

1. Kaprin, A.D., Starinskiy, V.V., Petrova, G.V.: Malignancies in Russia in 2017 (Morbidity and mortality), 250 p. MNIOI name of P.A. Herzen, Moscow (2018)
2. Kaprin, A.D., Starinskiy, V.V., Petrova, G.V.: Status of cancer care the population of Russia in 2017, 236 p. Moscow, MNIOI name of P.A. Herzen, Moscow (2018)
3. Laaridh, I., Meunier, C., Fredouille, C.: Dysarthric speech evaluation: automatic and perceptual approaches. In: Proceedings of the 11th Language Resources and Evaluation Conference, Miyazaki, Japan. European Language Resource Association (2018)
4. Standard GOST R 50840-95 Voice over paths of communication. Methods for assessing the quality, legibility and recognition, 234 p. Publishing Standards, Moscow (1995)
5. Kostyuchenko, E., Meshcheryakov, R., Ignatieva, D., Pyatkov, A., Choynzonov, E., Balatskaya, L.: Correlation normalization of syllables and comparative evaluation of pronunciation quality in speech rehabilitation. In: Karpov, A., Potapova, R., Mporas, I. (eds.) SPECOM 2017. LNCS (LNAI), vol. 10458, pp. 262–271. Springer, Cham (2017). https://doi.org/10.1007/978-3-319-66429-3_25
6. Kostyuchenko, E., Roman, M., Ignatieva, D., Pyatkov, A., Choynzonov, E., Balatskaya, L.: Evaluation of the speech quality during rehabilitation after surgical treatment of the cancer of oral cavity and oropharynx based on a comparison of the fourier spectra. In: Ronzhin, A., Potapova, R., Németh, G. (eds.) SPECOM 2016. LNCS (LNAI), vol. 9811, pp. 287–295. Springer, Cham (2016). https://doi.org/10.1007/978-3-319-43958-7_34
7. Kostyuchenko, E., Ignatieva, D., Mescheryakov, R., Pyatkov, A., Choynzonov, E., Balatskaya, L.: Model of system quality assessment pronouncing phonemes. In: 2016 Dynamics of Systems, Mechanisms and Machines (Dynamics), pp. 1–5 (2016). https://doi.org/10.1109/Dynamics.2016.7819016
8. Cloud Speech-to-Text documentation. https://cloud.google.com/speech-to-text/docs/
9. Yandex SpeechKit. https://cloud.yandex.ru/docs/speechkit/
10. Programs for speech recognition into text VOCO. https://www.speechpro.ru/product/programmy-dlya-raspoznavaniya-rechi-v-tekst/voco/specification
11. Translator of Russian words in phonetic transcription. https://easypronunciation.com/ru/russian-phonetic-transcription-converter#phonetic_transcription
12. Kanji, G.K.: 100 Statistical Tests, 3rd edn. SAGE Publications Ltd., Thousand Oaks (2006)
13. Markovnikov, N.M., Kipyatkova, I.S.: An analytic survey of end-to-end speech recognition systems. SP **3**, 77–110 (2018). https://doi.org/10.15622/sp.58.4
14. Karpov, A.: An automatic multimodal speech recognition system with audio and video information. Autom. Remote Control **75**, 2190–2200 (2014). https://doi.org/10.1134/S000511791412008X
15. Evsutin, O., Shelupanov, A., Meshcheryakov, R., Bondarenko, D., Rashchupkina, A.: The algorithm of continuous optimization based on the modified cellular automaton. Symmetry **8**, 84 (2016). https://doi.org/10.3390/sym8090084

Detection of Overlapping Speech for the Purposes of Speaker Diarization

Marie Kunešová[1,2]([✉]) [ID], Marek Hrúz[1] [ID], Zbyněk Zajíc[1] [ID],
and Vlasta Radová[1,2] [ID]

[1] Faculty of Applied Sciences, NTIS - New Technologies for the Information Society,
University of West Bohemia, Univerzitní 8, 306 14 Pilsen, Czech Republic
{mkunes,mhruz,zzajic}@ntis.zcu.cz, radova@kky.zcu.cz
[2] Faculty of Applied Sciences, Department of Cybernetics,
University of West Bohemia, Univerzitní 8, 306 14 Pilsen, Czech Republic

Abstract. The presence of overlapping speech has a significant negative impact on the performance of speaker diarization systems. In this paper, we employ a convolutional neural network for the detection of such speech intervals and evaluate it in terms of the potential improvements to speaker diarization. We train the network on specifically-created synthetic data, while the evaluation is performed on the AMI Corpus and the SSPNet Conflict Corpus.

Keywords: Overlapping speech · Speaker diarization ·
Convolutional neural network

1 Introduction

In natural human conversations, there are often instances where multiple individuals speak at the same time – this includes interruptions, backchannel responses (e.g. "yeah", "uh-huh"), or simply brief natural overlaps during rapid turn-taking. Such overlapping speech can prove problematic for automatic speech processing, particularly for speech recognition and for speaker diarization.

Specifically, in our recent paper [17], we found that accurate detection of overlapping speech would have improved the results of our diarization system by a significant margin: on the development set of the DIHARD II corpus, the use of ground-truth overlap labeling decreased the Diarization Error Rate (DER) from 20.78 to 16.16% (22% relative improvement). Similar observations have previously been made by other authors, e.g. in [8]. This potential for improvement is what motivated our work on overlap detection.

The research of this topic has evolved over the last decade with only mild success: The more traditional approaches rely on a careful selection of hand-crafted features, to be fed into a HMM decoder [2,16] or a neural network [1,3]. A more recent alternative is to let a neural network extract the relevant information form "raw" input, such as a spectrogram of acoustic signal [10,14]. Our work is also based on this latter approach.

A. A. Salah et al. (Eds.): SPECOM 2019, LNAI 11658, pp. 247–257, 2019.
https://doi.org/10.1007/978-3-030-26061-3_26

1.1 Problems with Data

During our work on the overlap detector, we have encountered some difficulties, particularly with the lack of suitable data.

Training and evaluating an overlap detector generally requires a large amount of well-annotated data with frequent overlaps. Unfortunately, there do not appear to be any publicly available datasets made specifically for this purpose, and other corpora often lack sufficiently precise labels.

Like some other authors (e.g. [1,10,14]), we resorted to creating our own synthetic training data – we describe this in Sect. 3.1. However, the same problem with inadequate labels also applies to subsequent evaluation of the overlap detector on real corpora, and its use in a speaker diarization system.

It is difficult, as well as very time-consuming, to precisely annotate overlapping speech. For this reason, reference annotations often tend to exclude very short occurrences (<0.5 s), especially those at the boundaries between speakers. This can be a problem if the overlap detector is more sensitive, as such detected overlaps will be incorrectly evaluated as false alarms.

A similar issue is also with the classification of overlaps with voiced non-speech sounds such as laughter or humming. On the one hand, these sounds can often be identified as a specific speaker and can negatively affect speaker diarization. On the other hand, these events are often not included in speech transcripts, especially when they happen in the background of another speakers' speech, so such regions may be (in this case incorrectly) marked as non-overlap in the reference. This may again lead to a seemingly high false alarm rate of an overlap detector evaluated on such data.

When evaluating overlap detection, various authors deal with these issues in different ways, such as by ignoring very short intervals, applying generous tolerance windows, or, if they can be identified by other means, excluding intervals with non-speech from evaluation.

2 Overlap Detector

We have previously [6,7] used a Convolutional Neural Network (CNN) for the detection of speaker changes in an audio stream. In this paper, we employ the same general approach for the detection of overlapping speech.

A summary of the network architecture can be found in Table 1. The input of the network is a spectrogram of a short window of the acoustic signal. The output of the last layer is a value between 0 and 1, indicating the probability of overlapping speech in the middle of the window. Training references use a fuzzy labeling function, with a linear slope (width 0.4 s) at the boundaries between overlap and non-overlap (see the lower two plots of Fig. 3 for an example). The sliding window has a length of 1 s and is shifted with a step of 0.05 s.

We use a median filter with a window length of 5 samples to smooth the raw network output, then apply a threshold to obtain overlap/non-overlap classification. Additionally, we fill in any gaps (non-overlaps within a longer overlap) which are shorter than 0.1 s, and then discard overlaps under 0.5 s, as these are unlikely to be included in the reference labeling (as discussed in Sect. 1.1).

Table 1. Summary of the network architecture.

Layer	Kernels	Size	Shift
Convolution	128	8×16	2×2
Max pooling		2×2	2×2
Batch normalisation			
Convolution	256	4×4	1×1
Max pooling		2×2	2×2
Batch normalisation			
Convolution	512	3×3	1×1
Max pooling		2×2	2×2
Batch normalisation			
Fully connected	1024		
Fully connected	256		
Fully connected	1		

3   Data

3.1   Synthetic Training Data

Given the lack of sufficient real data (as mentioned in Sect. 1.1), we resorted to artificially creating training data from two corpora of read English speech, LibriSpeech [13] and TIMIT [5], using an automated and randomized process. In the creation of this synthetic dataset, we used some of the ideas previously described in [4,14].

TIMIT - The TIMIT corpus consists of the recordings of single English sentences, approx. 2–5 s long. We used the data from 320 speakers for training.

To obtain overlapped data, we first concatenated all utterances from a single speaker into one file of approx. 30 s, with random-length pauses (up to 2 s) in-between. In order to avoid noticeable seams, the silence at the beginning and end of each utterance is linearly tapered. Then, files from two random speakers are combined at different volumes and augmented with added background noise (office, hallway, meeting) from the DEMAND database [15] and, for 50% of the files, reverberation (via convolution with room impulse response from the AIR database [9]). The result is illustrated in Fig. 1.

Reference labels were created with the use of the original phone-level transcripts - so that only the intervals where both speakers are truly active are labeled as overlap.

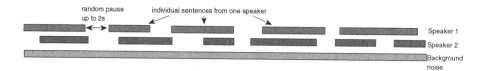

Fig. 1. Creation of artificial overlap data from the TIMIT corpus.

LibriSpeech - We also used data from the "train-other-500" set of the LibriSpeech corpus - this consists of approx. 500 hours of speech from over 1000 speakers, in the form of 10–15 s long recordings derived from audiobooks.

Given the very large amount of available LibriSpeech data, we were able to create several different types of overlaps, to better represent the possibilities which may occur in real data (see Fig. 2):

(a) Two full length (approx. 10–15 s) utterances, with an overlap of 1/2 length
(b) Two utterances with a short overlap (up to 2 s) or pause (up to 1 s) in-between
(c) A single utterance with an inserted word or phrase from another speaker: Utterance 1 is split on pauses and a randomly selected speech interval (0.25–2 s) is placed over utterance 2, either: fully overlapping speech, fully inside a pause, or randomly placed.

In the case of (b) and (c), the resulting file is shortened to 5 s of non-overlap data on each side of the overlap or pause, as seen in Fig. 2. The is done to keep a better ratio between non-overlaps and overlaps.

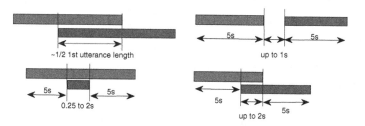

Fig. 2. Different types of synthetic overlap created from the LibriSpeech corpus. (Additive noise not shown.)

As with TIMIT, we added noise and reverberation. Speech/non-speech labelling was obtained using a voice activity detector (VAD) on the original single speaker data without added noise.

3.2 Test Data

We evaluated our overlap detector on three different sets of data: one artificially created dataset and two corpora of real conversations.

LibriSpeech Test Data - We created synthetic test data from the "test-other" subset of the LibriSpeech corpus, in a very similar way to the TIMIT training data - but with 5–10 s pauses between a single speaker's utterances, and without the added noise or reverberation.

SSPNet Conflict Corpus [1] [11] - This is a dataset of French-language political debates, consisting of 1430 clips of exactly 30 s each, cut from 45 separate debates. Each clip usually involves between 2–5 people and, as these are spontaneous discussions, there are frequent instances of overlapping speech. The same corpus was also used for overlap detection in [10].

We selected 5 debates (06-05-31, 06-09-20, 06-10-11, 07-05-16, and 08-01-15; 161 files total = 80.5 min of audio data) as development data for tuning the decision threshold, the remainder (1269 files = 10.6 h) was used for evaluation.

As the corpus hadn't been created with overlaps in mind, the original reference labels are relatively rough in this regard - they do not include very short overlaps at speaker changes or during isolated backchannel responses (e.g. "Oui, ... oui."), nor shorter non-overlap intervals within a longer overlap region (e.g. pauses in the speech of one speaker). However, our network proved capable of detecting all of the above. For this reason, we also selected a small number of audio clips (30 files = 15 min) and manually corrected the labels [2] to better correspond to the audio data (example shown in Fig. 3). These 30 files were then evaluated separately, using both the original and corrected labels, to illustrate how labelling quality affects the reported results (see Table 2).

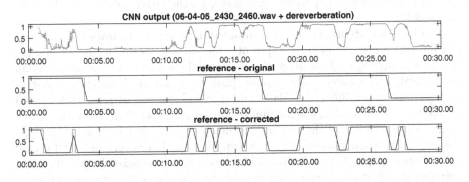

Fig. 3. Example output (raw + median filter) for dereverberated SSPNet data and the corresponding reference labels - original (middle) and manually corrected (bottom).

---

[1] http://www.dcs.gla.ac.uk/vincia/?p=270.

[2] The corrected labels and the code used in this paper can be found at https://github.com/mkunes/CNN-overlap-detection.

AMI Meeting Corpus[3] - A set of recordings from meetings between 3–6 people. We tested the overlap detector on the "headset mix" data, using the same train/validation/test split as Sajjan et al. [14]. We used the original transcripts as ground truth, rather than Sajjan et al.'s force-aligned labels[4], as we found the latter to be less accurate in some regards, but both versions have errors – in particular, there are many instances where overlaps with non-speech such as laughter are not labeled.

The corpus consists of several subsets of meetings which were recorded at different sites and vary in audio and transcription quality. We particularly found the Idiap scenario meetings (IS) to have very different optimal settings from the rest of the test set, so we also evaluate them separately.

4   Evaluation

Previous works on overlap detection use a variety of different evaluation metrics, including frame-level precision and recall or F-score [1], or per-overlap miss and false alarm rate [10] (see Table 3). However, as our main motivation is the improvement of speaker diarization, we decided to primarily evaluate the overlap detector in terms of the potential gains in diarization performance.

There are two main ways in which overlap information can be used in a diarization system: First, by excluding such intervals from any clustering process, we can avoid "polluting" the clusters and negatively influencing the clustering decisions. Secondly, in the final output, we assign multiple labels to each overlap region. The exact benefits of the first point depend on the diarization system in question. Thus, in this paper, we concentrate on the latter point, which is easier to quantify.

Diarization systems are usually evaluated in terms of Diarization Error Rate (DER), which consists of three types of error: *missed speech* (including missing speakers in overlaps), *false alarm* (silence mislabelled as speech or non-overlap as overlap), and *speaker error* (wrong speaker). In an ideal diarization system with no overlap handling, false alarm and speaker error will be zero, while missed speech will correspond to the amount of overlapping speech in the data.

In our evaluation of the potential benefits of overlap detection, we assume that the diarization system assigns two speaker labels to every detected region of overlapping speech (regardless of the true number speakers), and that (for correctly detected overlap) it does so perfectly – the *speaker error* is still zero.

In such a scenario, correctly detected overlaps will directly decrease the amount of *missed speech* compared to the baseline system, while false overlaps will increase the *false alarm*. Thus, we can obtain the potential improvement as the difference between the two values.

Note: By the correct definition, DER is calculated as a ratio of total speech (excluding silence), with overlaps being counted multiple times – once for each

---

[3] http://groups.inf.ed.ac.uk/ami/corpus/.
[4] https://github.com/BornInWater/Overlap-Detection.

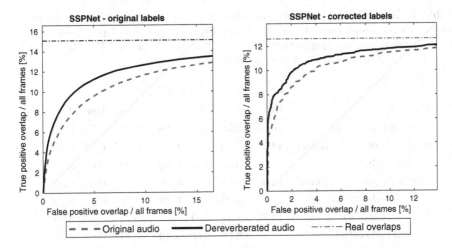

Fig. 4. False Positive vs True Positive for SSPNet data (frame-level percentage of all audio). Original labels (all 1269 test files) on the left, corrected labels (30 files, 15 min total) on the right. "Real overlaps" denotes the overlap percentage in the ground truth.

speaker. However, for simplicity, we calculate the potential improvements here as relative to the total length of the audio data.

4.1 Results

The results we achieved on the different corpora are shown in Table 2 and in Figs. 4 and 5.

The overlap detector appears to work very well on clean audio, such as the synthetic LibriSpeech data and the SSPNet Conflict Corpus. The network also seems to be very sensitive and capable of detecting even very short overlaps and non-overlaps, down to the level of individual words – a much greater precision than typically found in the reference annotations (as illustrated by the example output in Fig. 3).

On the other hand, the detector had issues with the AMI corpus. This may be in part due to errors in the reference labels – we have found instances of missing speech, or long unlabeled intervals where multiple people are laughing, which our network also considers to be overlaps. However, the lower performance is likely also caused by the higher level of noise in the these recordings, as well as the sometimes very large differences in the voice volumes of individual speakers. This is evidenced by the fact that we were able to improve the results to some extent by including the training set of the AMI corpus in the training data – this suggests that we may need to improve the synthetic dataset.

Initial experiments also suggested that the network had problems with reverberant speech, which was often incorrectly labeled as overlap. We have partly mitigated this effect by adding reverberation to the training data (as described in Sect. 3.1). However, we have also experimented with dereverberation of the

Table 2. Results of overlap detection on evaluation data. Overlap percentages are relative to total audio length, precision and recall are calculated per frame. (Ref. = Real overlap ratio according to the reference, TP = True Positive, FP = False Positive, Δ = TP−FP $\simeq$ potential DER improvement).

Dataset	Overlaps [% of all frames]				Prec.	Rec.	Thresh.
	Ref.	TP	FP	Δ			
LibriSpeech test mix	16.32	11.99	2.82	**9.18**	0.81	0.73	0.25
SSPNet - original (10.6 h)	14.77	7.86	2.94	4.92	0.73	0.52	0.80
+ dereverberation		9.58	2.68	**6.90**	0.78	0.63	0.70
SSPNet - precise (15 min)	12.62	8.05	1.42	6.63	0.85	0.65	0.80
+ dereverberation		8.90	1.41	**7.49**	0.86	0.71	0.70
SSPNet - original (15 min)	12.86	7.47	2.00	5.47	0.79	0.59	0.80
+ dereverberation		8.60	1.71	**6.89**	0.83	0.68	0.70
AMI test (all subsets)	12.21	2.25	0.96	1.30	0.70	0.19	0.50
+ dereverberation		2.38	1.03	**1.34**	0.70	0.20	0.25
AMI test (only "IS")	7.82	2.75	1.34	1.41	0.67	0.36	0.80
+ dereverberation		3.71	1.76	**1.95**	0.68	0.48	0.60
Retrained network - with added AMI training data:							
AMI test (all subsets)	12.21	5.73	2.35	**3.38**	0.71	0.48	0.50
+ dereverberation		4.92	1.61	3.31	0.75	0.41	0.25
AMI test (only "IS")	7.82	3.28	1.24	2.04	0.73	0.43	0.90
+ dereverberation		3.73	1.61	**2.12**	0.70	0.48	0.80

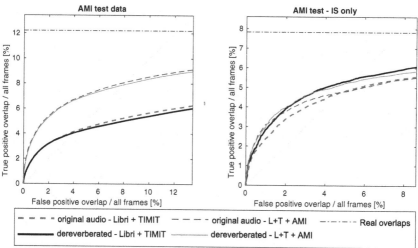

Fig. 5. False Positive vs True Positive for AMI data (frame-level percentage of all audio), with overlap detector trained only on synthetic LibriSpeech + TIMIT data or with the addition of AMI training data. Results are for all test files (left) and only for the Idiap scenario meetings (right).

test data - to evaluate the potential benefits, we used the WPE Dereverberation package[5] created by Nakatani et al. [12]. Even with the default settings without any adjustments, this has proven to be clearly beneficial for SSPNet data, but for AMI the difference is negligible (with the exception of the Idiap scenario (IS) meetings).

Finally, in Table 3 we present a comparison of our overlap detector with some other works on the topic. This comparison is somewhat complicated by the fact that other authors have used many different combinations of datasets (or their parts) and metrics to evaluate their systems. For instance, while 3 other systems in the table used the AMI corpus, each of them selected different files. Similarly, the results of [10] on the SSPNet Conflict Corpus are not directly comparable with ours, as their system was evaluated only on voiced frames.

Table 3. Comparison of the proposed system (selected results from Table 2, without added AMI training data) with prior works. With the exception of our "all subsets" and [14]'s "original labels" AMI results, no two systems used identical test data and ground-truth labelling.

System	Dataset	Prec.	Rec.	F-score	Accuracy
Proposed	LibriSpeech test mix	0.81	0.73	0.77	0.93
	SSPNet (original labels)	0.73	0.52	0.61	0.90
	+ dereverberation	0.78	0.63	0.70	0.92
	AMI (16 files - all subsets)	0.70	0.19	0.30	0.89
	+ dereverberation	0.70	0.20	0.31	0.89
	AMI (4 files - only "IS" subset)	0.67	0.36	0.47	0.94
	+ dereverberation	0.68	0.48	0.56	0.94
[1]	Custom dataset	0.81	0.78	0.8	0.802
[10]	SSPNet (voiced frames only)	0.71	0.78	0.75	0.92
[2]	AMI (12 "IS" files, force aligned)	0.67	0.26	0.38	-
[14]	AMI (16 files, original labels)	-	-	-	76.0/60.6*
-	AMI (16 files, force aligned labels)	-	-	-	87.9/71.0*
[16]	AMI (25 files)	-	-	0.51	-

(*overlap-detection accuracy/single-speaker detection accuracy)

5 Conclusion

In a previous paper [17], we measured the improvement achievable with a ground-truth overlap labelling in a real diarization system. Here, we looked at the problem from the opposite angle - evaluating an overlap detector under the assumption that the diarization system otherwise functions without error.

The results we achieved here appear to be very promising, particularly those on relatively clean and noise-free data, although some more work will be required

---

[5] http://www.kecl.ntt.co.jp/icl/signal/wpe/index.html.

in order to improve the performance on data with higher levels of noise. The next step in our research will be to connect the two systems and to evaluate the full effects of the overlap detector on the entire diarization pipeline.

Acknowledgements. This research was supported by the Ministry of Culture Czech Republic, project No. DG16P02B048. Access to computing and storage facilities owned by parties and projects contributing to the National Grid Infrastructure MetaCentrum, provided under the programme "Projects of Large Research, Development, and Innovations Infrastructures" (CESNET LM2015042), is greatly appreciated.

References

1. Andrei, V., Cucu, H., Burileanu, C.: Detecting overlapped speech on short time-frames using deep learning. In: Proceedings of Interspeech, pp. 1198–1202 (2017)
2. Boakye, K., Vinyals, O., Friedland, G.: Two's a crowd: improving speaker diarization by automatically identifying and excluding overlapped speech. In: Proceedings of Interspeech, pp. 32–35 (2008)
3. Diez, M., et al.: BUT system for DIHARD speech diarization challenge 2018. In: Proceedings of Interspeech, pp. 2798–2802 (2018)
4. Edwards, E., et al.: A free synthetic corpus for speaker diarization research. In: Karpov, A., Jokisch, O., Potapova, R. (eds.) SPECOM 2018. LNCS (LNAI), vol. 11096, pp. 113–122. Springer, Cham (2018). https://doi.org/10.1007/978-3-319-99579-3_13
5. Garofolo, J.S., et al.: TIMIT acoustic-phonetic continuous speech corpus, LDC93S1 (1993)
6. Hrúz, M., Kunešová, M.: Convolutional neural network in the task of speaker change detection. In: Ronzhin, A., Potapova, R., Németh, G. (eds.) SPECOM 2016. LNCS (LNAI), vol. 9811, pp. 191–198. Springer, Cham (2016). https://doi.org/10.1007/978-3-319-43958-7_22
7. Hrúz, M., Zajíc, Z.: Convolutional neural network for speaker change detection in telephone speaker diarization system. In: Proceedings of ICASSP, pp. 4945–4949 (2017)
8. Huijbregts, M., Wooters, C.: The blame game: performance analysis of speaker diarization system components. In: Eighth Annual Conference of the International Speech Communication Association (2007)
9. Jeub, M., Schafer, M., Vary, P.: A binaural room impulse response database for the evaluation of dereverberation algorithms. In: 16th International Conference on Digital Signal Processing, pp. 1–5 (2009)
10. Kazimirova, E., Belyaev, A.: Automatic detection of multi-speaker fragments with high time resolution. In: Proceedings of Interspeech, pp. 1388–1392 (2018)
11. Kim, S., Valente, F., Filippone, M., Vinciarelli, A.: Predicting continuous conflict perception with Bayesian Gaussian processes. IEEE Trans. Affect. Comput. **5**(2), 187–200 (2014)
12. Nakatani, T., Yoshioka, T., Kinoshita, K., Miyoshi, M., Juang, B.: Speech dereverberation based on variance-normalized delayed linear prediction. IEEE Trans. Audio Speech Lang. Process. **18**(7), 1717–1731 (2010)
13. Panayotov, V., Chen, G., Povey, D., Khudanpur, S.: LibriSpeech: an ASR corpus based on public domain audio books. In: 2015 IEEE International Conference on Acoustics, Speech and Signal Processing (ICASSP), pp. 5206–5210 (2015)

14. Sajjan, N., Ganesh, S., Sharma, N., Ganapathy, S., Ryant, N.: Leveraging LSTM models for overlap detection in multi-party meetings. In: Proceedings of ICASSP, pp. 5249–5253 (2018)
15. Thiemann, J., Ito, N., Vincent, E.: The diverse environments multi-channel acoustic noise database: a database of multichannel environmental noise recordings. J. Acoust. Soc. Am. **133**(5), 3591–3591 (2013)
16. Yella, S.H., Bourlard, H.: Overlapping speech detection using long-term conversational features for speaker diarization in meeting room conversations. IEEE/ACM Trans. Audio Speech Lang. Process. (TASLP) **22**(12), 1688–1700 (2014)
17. Zajíc, Z., Kunešová, M., Hrúz, M., Vaněk, J.: UWB-NTIS speaker diarization system for the DIHARD II 2019 challenge. In: Submitted to Interspeech (2019). https://arxiv.org/abs/1905.11276

Exploring Hybrid CTC/Attention End-to-End Speech Recognition with Gaussian Processes

Ludwig Kürzinger$^{(\boxtimes)}$![ORCID], Tobias Watzel ![ORCID], Lujun Li ![ORCID], Robert Baumgartner, and Gerhard Rigoll ![ORCID]

Institute for Human-Machine Communication, Technische Universität München, Munich, Germany
ludwig.kuerzinger@tum.de

Abstract. Hybrid CTC/attention end-to-end speech recognition combines two powerful concepts. Given a speech feature sequence, the attention mechanism directly outputs a sequence of letters. Connectionist Temporal Classification (CTC) helps to bind the attention mechanism to sequential alignments. This hybrid architecture also gives more degrees of freedom in choosing parameter configurations. We applied Gaussian process optimization to estimate the impact of network parameters and language model weight in decoding towards Character Error Rate (CER), as well as attention accuracy. In total, we trained 70 hybrid CTC/attention networks and performed 590 beam search runs with an RNNLM as language model on the TEDlium v2 test set. To our surprise, the results challenge the assumption that CTC primarily regularizes the attention mechanism. We argue in an evidence-based manner that CTC instead regularizes the impact of language model feedback in a one-pass beam search, as letter hypotheses are fed back into the attention mechanism. Attention-only models without RNNLM already achieved 10.9% CER, or 22.4% Word Error Rate (WER), on the TEDlium v2 test set. Combined decoding of same attention-only networks with RNNLM strongly underperformed, with at best 40.2% CER, or, 49.3% WER. A combined hybrid CTC/attention model with RNNLM performed best, with 8.9% CER, or 17.6% WER.

Keywords: Connectionist Temporal Classification ·
Attention-based neural networks · End-to-end speech recognition ·
Gaussian process optimization · Multi-objective training ·
Hybrid CTC/attention

1 Introduction

Conventional hybrid DNN/HMM models for automatic speech recognition (ASR) rely on handcrafted linguistic information, and the training process requires multiple refinement steps [18]. The training labels of a DNN are only

© Springer Nature Switzerland AG 2019
A. A. Salah et al. (Eds.): SPECOM 2019, LNAI 11658, pp. 258–269, 2019.
https://doi.org/10.1007/978-3-030-26061-3_27

obtained after estimating phoneme or state alignments through a Gaussian mixture model. The decoding process requires a global search over many possible word sequences using weighted finite-state transducers.

End-to-end ASR aims to simplify the training and decoding procedure by directly inferring sequential letter probabilities given a speech signal [6,18]. Such systems usually transcribe speech features to letters or word fragments without any intermediate representations. It is also possible to train these networks in an end-to-end manner without previous refinement steps.

There are two major techniques for end-to-end speech recognition: (1) Frame-based classification using Connectionist Temporal Classification (CTC [9]), where the HMM-like structure of CTC loss gives strong temporal dependencies on decoding. (2) Sequence generation using attention-based encoder-decoder architectures [6], as attention models are very flexible but also require additional information about the sequential arrangement of the input features.

The hybrid CTC/attention architecture combines these two traits. However, combining those two techniques in one architecture also introduces complexities, as there are now more sub-networks. The structural shape of each network as well as its priority in a multi-objective framework is controlled by parameters. We use Gaussian processes to assess these parameter configurations. Gaussian process optimization provides a method to systematically estimate good parameter configurations based on an *expected improvement* criterion, providing a trade-off between space exploration and convergent optimization. This technique enables to optimize parameters towards an arbitrary metric, for example CER, instead of optimizing towards sub-goals, such as frame-based classification.

In our work, we use the ESPnet speech recognition toolkit [17] and the TEDlium v2 corpus [13]. Gaussian process optimization was applied in two separate stages, to the training of the hybrid model, as well as to joint beam search. Based on the results, we discuss properties of multi-objective training and inference in hybrid CTC/attention models.

Our contributions are:

- We give an overview over results obtained with sequential Gaussian process optimization, in total 70 different hybrid CTC/attention models and 590 beam search iterations. Based on obtained results, we assess the performance of individual parameter groups.
- We identify a feedback loop in the hybrid CTC/attention architecture that causes deteriorated performance in a certain parameter configuration, and revisit one key assumption of the hybrid CTC/attention approach stating that CTC provides alignments to the attention mechanism.
- Compared with the baseline model that achieved 10.1% CER on the TEDlium v2 test set [17], our best model achieved 8.9% CER, an absolute improvement of 1.2% CER.

2 Background

The main goal of a speech recognition system is to find the most probable letter sequence $\hat{Y}$ given a speech feature sequence X.

End-to-end speech recognition systems directly infer letter and sequence probabilities and do not require any pretraining steps; the model parameters of a network are tuned based on training examples consisting of audio feature vectors and letter sequences. As the number of speech training samples contains a limited number of words, inference is supported by a language model that has been trained on a larger text corpus.

End-to-end speech recognition systems fall into two categories. First, frame-based estimation of letter probabilities $p(y_t)$ using Connectionist Temporal Classification (CTC [9]). Second, recursive sequence generation using sequential letter probabilities $p(y_l|y_1,\ldots,y_{l-1})$ obtained from attention-based encoder-decoder architectures [6]. When introducing both techniques in the following paragraphs, as part of the hybrid CTC/attention architecture, frame-based values are indicated with the indices $t \in [1;T]$ and sequential indices with $l \in [1;L]$.

2.1 Location-Aware Attention-Based Encoder and Decoder

The attention-based encoder-decoder sequence transformation was proposed as a method for machine language translation in [1]. Location-aware attention for speech recognition is shown in [7]. An in-depth description of the hybrid CTC/attention mechanism can be found in [18]. The following paragraphs outline its architecture and network parts: the encoder f_{enc} (Fig. 1), the attention network f_{att}, and the decoder network f_{dec} (Fig. 2).

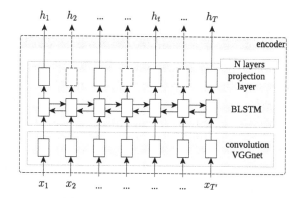

Fig. 1. Encoder of the hybrid CTC/attention architecture.

We start with an input sequence X that consists of feature vectors. The *encoder* transforms the input sequence to a hidden representation denominated by $h_1, \cdots, h_T$. The encoder network f_{enc} contains a convolutional VGGnet [14], followed by a multiple-layer stack of long short term memory (BLSTM) cells combined with a fully connected layer of projection neurons denoted by $\mathrm{Lin}(\cdot)$.

$$h_t = f_{\mathrm{enc}}(X) = [\mathrm{Lin}(\mathrm{BLSTM})]^{N_{\mathrm{elayers}}}(\mathrm{VGG}(X)) \qquad (1)$$

Based on the hidden values from the encoder, the attention network and the decoder network generate a sequence in a recurrent manner that is depicted in Fig. 2 and described in the following paragraphs.

Analogous to an alignment model in conventional ASR, the *location-aware attention network* f_{att} attends the hidden values in a recurrent manner. It carries over information from the previous step contained in the decoder state vector q_{l-1} and its previous attention weights $a_{l-1,t}$ in order to calculate the attention weights $a_{l,t}$ for l-th decoding step.

$$a_{l,t} = f_{\text{att}}(q_{l-1}, h_t, a_{l-1,t}) \qquad (2)$$
$$= \text{Softmax}(g^T \cdot \tanh(\ \text{Lin}(q_{l-1}) + \text{Lin}(h_t) + \text{Lin}(K * a_{l-1,t})\ )) \qquad (3)$$

Here, $*$ denotes the convolution operator and K the convolution kernel. A scalar product with the learnable vector g reduces the activations of the inner linear layers of the attention network to a single scalar. Attended sequence parts are then merged into the *context vector* c_l in a weighted sum, i.e., $c_l = \sum_{t \in T} a_{l,t} h_t$.

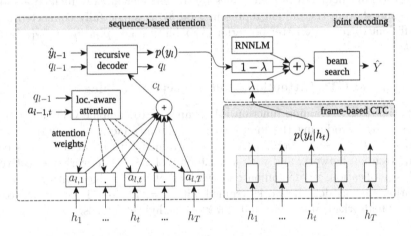

Fig. 2. Decoder of the hybrid CTC/attention architecture.

Given the context vector, the *decoder network* f_{dec} finally produces posterior probabilities of letters, including an additional label indicating the end of the sequence. It consists of multiple LSTM layers, without intermediate projection layers or subsampling. Decoding is done in a recursive manner, based on its previous internal *state vector* q_{l-1}, and the beam search hypothesis of the previous letter $\hat{y}_{l-1}$.

$$q_l = f_{dec}(c_t, \hat{y}_{l-1}) = [\text{LSTM}]^{N_{\text{dlayers}}}(c_t, q_{l-1}, \hat{y}_{l-1}) \qquad (4)$$
$$p(y_l) = \text{Softmax}(\text{Lin}(q_l)) \qquad (5)$$

Based on the letter posteriors $p(y_l)$, the beam search chooses a probable letter hypothesis $\hat{y}_l$, and the recursion jumps back to the attention network; until the decoding process reaches the label for the end of the sequence.

2.2   Frame-Discriminative CTC Network

Frame-discriminative CTC loss [9] is often combined with bidirectional recurrent neural networks, that provide a short-time context for each frame and give strong temporal dependencies on decoding. CTC was modeled with HMMs in mind; in training, the CTC-HMM is constructed using a modified letter sequence. The target letter sequence $C = \{y_l \in \mathcal{U} | l = 1, \cdots, L\}$ is extended with a blank label and rewritten as the letter sequence $C' = \{-, y_1, -, \cdots, -, y_L, -\}$. The CTC loss function estimates the most probable path through the label sequence: the probability of a certain target sequence is calculated by summing up the frame-based letter probabilities in all possible paths through the modified letter sequence using the forward-backward algorithm. As this step is computationally tractable, neural network training with the CTC loss function trims the network to maximize the correct frame-based letter posteriors w.r.t. the target letter sequence.

Our CTC network setup is shown in Fig. 2 alongside the attention mechanism. Here, the pre-calculated hidden values by the encoder already include a short-time context from the hidden representation h_t. A single fully connected layer is sufficient to generate letter posterior probabilities, i.e., $p(y_t | h_t) = f_{\mathrm{CTC}}(h_t) = \mathrm{Lin}(h_t)$.

2.3   Hybrid CTC/Attention Multi-objective Training

A multi-objective training function [11] is applied to combine CTC and attention loss by introducing the multi-objective training factor $\kappa \in [0; 1]$, so that $\mathcal{L}_{\mathrm{hybrid}} = \kappa \mathcal{L}_{CTC} + (1 - \kappa) \mathcal{L}_{att}$. A network trained with $\kappa = 0.0$ consists only of an attention network, and with $\kappa = 1.0$ only of a CTC network, respectively. In this publication, we denominate networks that were trained with $\kappa = 0.0$ as attention-only models, networks trained with $\kappa = 1.0$ as CTC-only networks, whereas networks trained with $0.0 < \kappa < 1.0$ as hybrid models.

2.4   Joint One-Pass Beam Search Decoding

Beam search concatenates letters according to their posterior probabilities to a reconstructed letter sequence [8]. Attention networks apply beam search decoding by iteratively building up a list of letter sequences, i.e., partial hypotheses Y' ordered by their probability [6], until the end of the sequence is detected. It searches for the most probable letter sequence hypothesis $\hat{Y} = \arg\max_Y p(Y|X)$.

Hybrid CTC/attention architecture uses joint one-pass decoding beam search [18], combining frame-based as well as sequential letter probabilities. The probability of a partial hypothesis Y' in the attention network is estimated by using the probabilistic chain rule. In the CTC network, this probability is estimated based on the forward function of the forward-backward algorithm. The algorithm integrates the language model using *shallow fusion* [10]. The hybrid probability is then calculated in a multi-objective manner with weight parameter λ, together with β as the weight of the RNNLM language model, as described in [17], to

$$p_{\text{hybrid}}(Y'|X) = \lambda p_{\text{CTC}}(Y'|X) + (1 - \lambda)p_{\text{att}}(Y'|X) + \beta p_{\text{LM}}(Y'|X). \quad (6)$$

2.5 Gaussian Processes Optimization

Gaussian processes are a highly effective tool for parameter optimization [15]. It was shown in [3] that for hyper-parameter optimization problems with few influential parameters, sequential model-based optimization methods are able to surpass the performance of random search, as these techniques offer an approach to weight the importance of each dimension. Furthermore, given the choice of a suitable kernel and acquisition function [15], it has been shown that Gaussian process optimization outperforms random brute-force search and human performance for many algorithms. In our work, a sequential model-based approach is applied to optimize hyper-parameters using Gaussian processes [4].

Gaussian processes provide an estimate of an unknown function, denoted by $f : \mathcal{X} \rightarrow \mathbb{R}$. A Gaussian process is a set of random variables, where any finite set of points $\{X^{(n)} \in \mathcal{X}\}$, induces a joint Gaussian distribution in $\mathbb{R}^N$, and is described by two functions, the mean-function $\mu : \mathcal{X} \rightarrow \mathbb{R}$ and the kernel $k : \mathcal{X} \times \mathcal{X} \rightarrow \mathbb{R}$.

We use the Matérn-kernel [12] defined by

$$k_{\text{Matérn}}(r^{(n)}) = \frac{2^{1-\nu}}{\Gamma(\nu)}\left(\frac{\sqrt{2\nu}r^{(n)}}{l}\right)^\nu K_\nu\left(\frac{\sqrt{2\nu}r^{(n)}}{l}\right). \quad (7)$$

Here, ν and l are positive parameters, K_ν is a modified Bessel function and $\Gamma(\nu)$ is the Gamma-function, with $r^{(n)} = ||X^{(n)} - X'^{(n)}||$ as Euclidean distance. Gaussian noise in the target value $f(X^{(n)})$ is modeled by adding a small noise constant ϵ onto the kernel in all sample points.

Based on a set of hypothesized models of the target function as a Gaussian process $f_{GP} \propto GP(\mu, k)$, the mean-function and the kernel are weighted to find the next optimal point $X^{(n+1)}$. This is done by maximizing an acquisition function [15], such as the Expected Improvement (EI). Given the so far minimum observed value f_{min}, the EI is described as

$$f_{\text{EI}}(X^{(n+1)}) = \mathbb{E}[max(0, f_{min} - f_{GP}(X^{(n+1)}))|X^{(n+1)}, D], \quad (8)$$

given point $X^{(n+1)}$ and the set of our previous observations $D = \{(X^{(i)}, Y^{(i)})\}$, $i = \{1, 2, ..., n\}$. The EI function is usually optimized by performing a grid search over its input space [3]. Starting from several randomly sampled points, L-BFGS-B optimization [5], a quasi-Newton method, is applied to maximize the EI to avoid local optima.

3 Experiment Setup

In our experiment, we use the location-aware hybrid CTC/attention network in ESPnet[1]. The ESPnet framework already provides a receipt for the TEDlium corpus and previous benchmark results.

---

[1] To be precise, ESPnet version 0.3.0, on git commit hash `716ff54`.

The first stage optimized the parameter configuration of the hybrid CTC/attention architecture. Network parameters of the attention mechanism, described in Subsect. 2.1, and the multi-objective training parameter κ from Subsect. 2.3, along with their upper and lower bounds were passed to the Gaussian process optimizer.[2] We kickstarted the optimization in this stage with 20 initial parameter configurations. The optimization routine calculated then 40 iterations on the CER of the model without a language model, followed by 10 iterations over the accuracy of the attention network as target parameter.

In a parallel second stage, Gaussian process optimization was applied on beam search parameters as in Subsect. 2.4. The target value for this stage was the CER on the TEDlium dev set. We prepared four different RNNLM language models, consisting of 2-layers to each 650 LSTM units, that the optimizer could choose from. Hybrid models from the previous experiment were added to the optimizer in an adaptive list. In a first pass, all initial hybrid CTC/attention models were decoded with and without language models; additionally to a beam search run that carried over the multi-objective training parameter κ to the beam search parameter λ.[3]

4 Results and Evaluation

In the course of the experiment, Gaussian process optimization showed preference for certain hybrid parameter configurations. Table 1 lists the best results of selected categories, with and without RNNLM, as well as CTC-only and attention-only networks. The columns of attention-only or CTC-only models still contain parameter configurations that were handpicked in the first stage of the experiment. While most results gravitate between 10% and 20% CER, they show a wide difference in terms of WER and CER, as depicted in Fig. 3a[4]. Manual investigation did not find supporting evidence of a significant correlation between single parameters and CER. In general, hybrid models with deeper networks exhibit a tendency to perform better, as shown in Fig. 3b, as EI shifted towards deep encoder and decoder networks.

4.1 Observations on Certain Parameter Groups

Some groups of parameter configurations in Fig. 3a stand out that led to degraded performance. We further analyze these observations by partitioning

---

[2] Bounds on architecture parameters: Number of encoder/decoder layers $\in [1;6]$; number of cells in a fully connected decoder/attention layer $\in [25;400]$, in the encoder layer $\in [25;500]$; $\kappa \in [0;1]$; channels in conv. network $K \in [1;20]$; filters in $K \in [30;150]$. Subsampling was applied to the second and third layer of the encoder, i.e., only every second hidden value is forwarded in these projection layers to the subsequent layer.

[3] Bounds on beam search decoding parameters: $\lambda \in [0;1]$; $\kappa \in [0;1]$, $\beta \in [0;1]$. Beam search was configured with a beam size of 20. Initial RNNLM weight $\lambda \in \{0.0, 1.0\}$.

[4] Parameter groups in Fig. 3a: Attention-only beam search with RNNLM $\rightarrow \lambda < 0.05; \beta > 0.3$. CTC-only beam search without RNNLM $\rightarrow \lambda > 0.8; \beta < 0.1$.

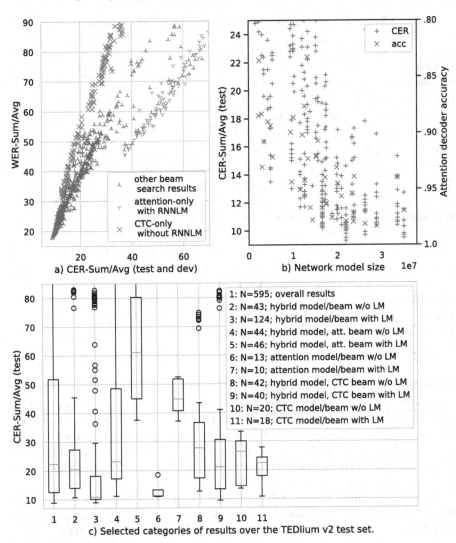

Fig. 3. TEDlium v2 results overview as discussed in Sect. 4.

overall results, as shown in Fig. 3c item (1), into categories[5]. Note that the y-axis scale of Fig. 3c is set to CER, which introduces a certain framing on distributions with different CER-to-WER ratios.

Attention-only beam search in combination with an RNNLM yields a high CER but a low WER, e.g., with word loops and dropped sentence parts but few misspellings. We state following observations: Attention-only beam search on

---

[5] Figure 3c: Hybrid models $\rightarrow \kappa \in\ ]0.0; 1.0[$; att.-only models$\rightarrow \kappa = 0.0$; att.-only beam search $\rightarrow \lambda = 0.0$; CTC-only model$\rightarrow \kappa = 1.0$; CTC-only beam search$\rightarrow \lambda = 1.0$; 'w/o LM' $\rightarrow \lambda = 0.0$; 'with LM' $\rightarrow \lambda = 1.0$.

Table 1. Comparison of best results in selected categories.

Parameter	Baseline [17]	With LM			Without LM		
		Hybrid	Att.-only	CTC-only	Hybrid	Att.-only	CTC-only
Encoder layers	6	6	6	6	4	6	6
Encoder BLSTM cells	320	485	400	400	497	400	400
Projection units	320	292	320	320	377	320	320
Decoder Layers	1	5	2	2	3	2	2
Decoder LSTM cells	300	352	100	400	364	100	400
Attention neurons	320	379	100	350	172	100	350
Att. channels in K	10	2	10	10	10	10	10
Att. filters in K	100	122	100	100	128	100	100
Multi-obj. (training) κ	0.5	0.69	0.00	1.00	0.15	0.00	1.00
Model size (1e6)	18.7	35.1	23.6	26.6	28.8	23.6	26.6
RNNLM weight β	1.0	0.73	0.41	1.00	0.00	0.00	0.00
Multi-obj. (beam) λ	0.3	0.62	*0.08*	1.00	0.15	0.00	1.00
TEDlium dev/CER	10.8	**9.2**	37.1	11.3	10.4	10.4	13.7
TEDlium dev/WER	19.8	**18.5**	47.1	23.3	22.5	22.4	36.5
TEDlium test/CER	10.1	**8.9**	40.2	11.3	10.6	10.9	14.4
TEDlium test/WER	18.6	**17.6**	49.3	22.6	22.1	22.4	36.9

hybrid models performs better without RNNLM (4) than with it (5). Using networks that were only trained with attention mechanism, beam search performs significantly better without RNNLM (6) than with it (7). By intuition, adding an RNNLM to an attention network in beam search is expected to improve results, as it is trained on far more text data, but evidence indicates that adding the RNNLM in the beam search deteriorates results. Sect. 4.2 discusses this observation in more detail.

Next, we examine the second parameter group, as *CTC-only beam search without the support of a language model* yields a high WER but a comparatively low CER, e.g., with shifted word boundaries and intra-word misspellings. CTC-only beam search on hybrid models performs better with RNNLM (8) than without it (9). CTC-only models in combination with CTC-only beam search perform also worse without RNNLM (10) than with it (11). The CTC network provides primarily temporal alignments, but is partially agnostic of short-term letter orderings, so combining it with a sequence-based RNNLM is beneficial.

4.2 Feedback Loops Caused by Unexpected Letter Hypotheses

As observed, adding a language model to an attention-only model using the joint beam search deteriorates results. This stands in contrast to previous publications that combined attention-only models with a language model using shallow fusion, but with improved results [6,16]. In comparison to these models, two notable differences stand out.

During training, the hybrid CTC/attention architecture uses teacher forcing [19], i.e., feeding ground-truth letters as previous letter hypothesis y_{l-1} to the attention network during training[6]. The *listen-attend-spell* architecture presented in [6] applies scheduled sampling [2], which samples from a probability distribution to choose y_{l-1}. Scheduled sampling is motivated by the observation that training letter sequence is the ground truth sequence, but beam search during inference exposes the model to state sequences that were not seen during training. This discrepancy between training and inference distributions leads to an accumulation of errors [2]. In a joint attention/RNNLM beam search, integrating the language model into the beam search introduces such discrepancies in the form of unexpected letter hypotheses. While this notion explains an amplification of small errors in the beginning of the generated sequence, it does not yet fully explain why word loops are generated.

The second notable difference lies within the location-aware attention mechanism that, additional to the previous state vector q_{l-1}, also takes previous attention weights $a_{l-1,t}$ into account. The indication to change the attention focus originates from the decoder and arrives at the attention network with an additional delay. In other words, after an unexpected letter hypothesis y_{l-1} was fed in, the network should readjust its attention focus. However, at the time of computing the context vector c_l by the attention network, the information of the previous letter y_{l-1} is not considered. Only at step $l + 1$, this information propagates into the attention network through q_l, and through the attention weights with a delay of two steps, i.e., at $l + 2$.

In some cases, these delays of information propagation of letter hypothesis feedback accumulate and lead to greater adjustments in the attention focus, either backwards or forwards, leading to repeated or dropped sentence parts. There is no penalty during beam search to detect these misaligned sequences, as the attention decoder calculates the posterior probabilities $p(y_l)$ mainly based on c_l and the previous letter hypotheses, and therefore will classify a wrong letter based on a misaligned attention focus with a high decision confidence.

4.3   CTC as Aligning Regularizer

We revisit the hypothesis that CTC regulates the attention mechanism by binding it to alignments [18]. For this, we compare the observed performance without RNNLM of the hybrid model with joint beam search, as in Fig. 3c item (2), and an attention-only approach (6). Both transcriptions consist of mostly correctly aligned sentences but wrongly detected words. Lost alignments in the transcriptions of attention-only beam search were rare with only a few deletion error outliers, and the rate of insertion errors was approximately equal in both scenarios. Additionally, hybrid models used for attention-only beam search (4) did not perform better than attention-only models (6). From this perspective, there is no clear advantage of combining CTC and attention for multi-objective

---

[6] As mentioned in ESPnet Github issues #706 and #224.

training. Evidence shows that, without the RNNLM, hybrid training and inference underperforms, whereas attention-only models already achieve acceptable performance.

However, misspellings and similar-word substitutions in the transcription are a sign of the lack of a language model. As discussed beforehand, attention-only beam search underperforms when combined with the RNNLM, resulting in lost alignments and word loops. Here, adding CTC provides temporal alignments, adding a penalty on misaligned sequences, and therefore regularizes the joint beam search. The combination of attention and CTC in a hybrid model with the RNNLM as language model yields the best performance. This parameter group is depicted in Fig. 3c item (3).

5 Conclusion

We investigate parameter configurations of the hybrid CTC/attention architecture, in particular multi-objective configurations. For this, we trained 70 networks and performed 590 beam search runs with different parameters over the TEDlium data set, guided by an expected improvement criterion derived from Gaussian process optimization. Observations indicate that CTC-only networks perform best in combination with a sequential language model. Attention-only beam search without RNNLM already has a good performance, however, in combination with an RNNLM language model, it transcribes word loops and drops sentence parts. We argue that this is the result of a feedback loop caused by teacher forcing during training in combination with an architectural trait of the location-aware attention mechanism. As CTC adds a penalty on misaligned sentences, the combined hybrid CTC/attention model together with an RNNLM achieves the best performance.

References

1. Bahdanau, D., Cho, K., Bengio, Y.: Neural machine translation by jointly learning to align and translate. arXiv preprint arXiv:1409.0473 (2014)
2. Bengio, S., Vinyals, O., Jaitly, N., Shazeer, N.: Scheduled sampling for sequence prediction with recurrent neural networks. In: Advances in Neural Information Processing Systems, pp. 1171–1179 (2015)
3. Bergstra, J., Bengio, Y.: Random search for hyper-parameter optimization. J. Mach. Learn. Res. **13**(Feb), 281–305 (2012)
4. Bergstra, J.S., Bardenet, R., Bengio, Y., Kégl, B.: Algorithms for hyper-parameter optimization. In: Advances in Neural Information Processing Systems, pp. 2546–2554 (2011)
5. Byrd, R.H., Lu, P., Nocedal, J., Zhu, C.: A limited memory algorithm for bound constrained optimization. SIAM J. Sci. Comput. **16**(5), 1190–1208 (1995). https://doi.org/10/bpjm24
6. Chan, W., Jaitly, N., Le, Q., Vinyals, O.: Listen, attend and spell: a neural network for large vocabulary conversational speech recognition. In: 2016 IEEE International Conference on Acoustics, Speech and Signal Processing (ICASSP), pp. 4960–4964. IEEE (2016)

7. Chorowski, J.K., Bahdanau, D., Serdyuk, D., Cho, K., Bengio, Y.: Attention-based models for speech recognition. In: Neural Information Processing Systems, pp. 577–585 (2015)
8. Graves, A.: Sequence transduction with recurrent neural networks. arXiv preprint arXiv:1211.3711 (2012)
9. Graves, A., Fernández, S., Gomez, F., Schmidhuber, J.: Connectionist temporal classification: labelling unsegmented sequence data with recurrent neural networks. In: Proceedings of the 23rd International Conference on Machine Learning, pp. 369–376. ACM (2006)
10. Gulcehre, C., et al.: On using monolingual corpora in neural machine translation. arXiv preprint arXiv:1503.03535 (2015)
11. Lu, L., Kong, L., Dyer, C., Smith, N.A.: Multitask learning with CTC and segmental CRF for speech recognition (2017). https://doi.org/10/gf3hs6
12. Rasmussen, C.E.: Gaussian processes in machine learning. In: Bousquet, O., von Luxburg, U., Rätsch, G. (eds.) ML -2003. LNCS (LNAI), vol. 3176, pp. 63–71. Springer, Heidelberg (2004). https://doi.org/10.1007/978-3-540-28650-9_4
13. Rousseau, A., Deléglise, P., Estève, Y.: Enhancing the TED-LIUM corpus with selected data for language modeling and more TED talks. In: LREC, pp. 3935–3939 (2014)
14. Simonyan, K., Zisserman, A.: Very deep convolutional networks for large-scale image recognition. arXiv preprint arXiv:1409.1556 (2014)
15. Snoek, J., Larochelle, H., Adams, R.P.: Practical Bayesian optimization of machine learning algorithms. In: Advances in Neural Information Processing Systems, pp. 2951–2959 (2012)
16. Toshniwal, S., Kannan, A., Chiu, C.C., Wu, Y., Sainath, T.N., Livescu, K.: A comparison of techniques for language model integration in encoder-decoder speech recognition. In: 2018 IEEE Spoken Language Technology Workshop (SLT), pp. 369–375. IEEE (2018)
17. Watanabe, S., et al.: ESPnet: end-to-end speech processing toolkit. arXiv preprint arXiv:1804.00015 (2018)
18. Watanabe, S., Hori, T., Kim, S., Hershey, J.R., Hayashi, T.: Hybrid CTC/attention architecture for end-to-end speech recognition. IEEE J. Sel. Top. Signal Process. 11(8), 1240–1253 (2017). https://doi.org/10/gcm8hv
19. Williams, R.J., Zipser, D.: A learning algorithm for continually running fully recurrent neural networks. Neural Comput. 1(2), 270–280 (1989). https://doi.org/10/chwnmt

Estimating Aggressiveness of Russian Texts by Means of Machine Learning

Dmitriy Levonevskiy$^{(\boxtimes)}$ (ID), Dmitrii Malov (ID),
and Irina Vatamaniuk (ID)

St. Petersburg Institute for Informatics and Automation of the Russian Academy
of Sciences (SPIIRAS), 14th Line, 39, 199178 St. Petersburg, Russia
DLewonewski.8781@gmail.com

Abstract. This paper considers emotional assessment of texts in Russian using machine learning on the example of aggression detection. It summarizes the related work, methods, models and datasets, describes actual problems, proposes a text processing pipeline and a software system for training neural networks on heterogeneous datasets. The experiments show that neural networks trained on the annotated corpora both in Russian and English, allow to determine whether a text item in Russian contains an aggressive message. Authors thoroughly compare different assessment methods, particularly corpus-based approaches, machine learning solutions and hybrid variants. Results, obtained here, can be used to estimate the aggressiveness probability, for example, to rank messages for subsequent manual verification. They also enable feasibility studies on the possibilities of detecting a particular type of emotion in a text using corpora in other languages. The paper highlights further research directions, where different Python toolkits (NLTK, Keras) could be used for better model performance.

Keywords: Emotion detection · Sentiment Analysis ·
Natural language processing · Text analysis · Aggressive text detection ·
Neural networks · Machine learning

1 Introduction

The problem of emotion detection in text is of current interest, as it can be applied in various domains: network discussion moderation, analysis of public opinion on companies, goods, events; text classification [1, 2]. At the same time this problem causes a lot of difficulties. The problems associated with the task of automating of emotion detection in text content are related to ambiguity and subjectivity of the natural language. It should be considered that the methods of identifying emotions are practically limited and, as a rule, are suitable primarily for detection of explicit emotions [2]. A more difficult task consists, for example, in identification of implicit aggression and, more generally, in correct processing of the content that can be either aggressive or neutral when taken out of context.

Moreover, it is necessary to pay attention to the peculiarities of the environment. In particular, discussions in social media and forums may contain heterogeneous textual and audiovisual content in different languages [21]. Depending on the analyzed media,

© Springer Nature Switzerland AG 2019
A. A. Salah et al. (Eds.): SPECOM 2019, LNAI 11658, pp. 270–279, 2019.
https://doi.org/10.1007/978-3-030-26061-3_28

the common terms, jargon, memes, lexicon and cultural canons of social groups may differ significantly. The techniques used by intruders to bypass auto-moderation in social media complicate technical text processing. The content is also characterized by the presence of messages with spelling errors, typos, punctuation quirks, emoticons. Poor grammatical correctness and vague syntactic structure of social media posts complicates the usage of natural language processing tools [8]. The task turns out to be challenging even for human annotators, although they could refer to context of each message [9].

Another feature of the social media content is a large number of short messages: such messages can be classified well only provided, they contain explicitly expressed emotions. Another problem consists in detecting sarcasm and irony in text messages as there is no agreement on formal description of these concepts. The results in [17] are satisfactory but have a limited practical applicability.

Large amount and heterogeneous structure of the content require its preprocessing, before the methods described here could be applied. The preprocessing is performed by reducing the text dimension for further consumption by neural networks and other classifiers. The diversity of the social network content complicates the research: it should be noticed that working on domain-specific corpus gives better results than working on the domain-independent corpus [5].

2 Related Work

2.1 Methods and Systems

Considering the aggression as a kind of sentiment expressed in text, we can use Sentiment Analysis (SA) as a method of data mining [13] for its detection. SA identifies the sentiment expressed in a text and then analyzes it. The datasets used in SA are of high importance in this field. The social network sites and micro-blogging sites are considered a very good data source because people share and discuss their opinions about a certain topic freely there [5]. Fields in SA include emotion detection (ED) that aims to extract and analyze emotions, both explicit and implicit, present in the sentences. It was argued in [15] that there are eight basic and prototypical emotions, specifically: joy, sadness, anger, fear, trust, disgust, surprise, and anticipation; there are also more approaches as well [27]. The problem is either handled as a binary classification case, where only positive and negative sentiments are considered, or as a multiclass classification problem when a fine-grained list of sentiments is used (e.g., anger, disgust, fear, guilt, interest, joy, sadness, shame, surprise) [4].

The difference between SA and ED consists in following: SA is concerned mainly in specifying positive or negative opinions, whereas ED is concerned with detecting various emotions from text. As a SA task, ED can be implemented using ML approach or Lexicon-based approach, but Lexicon-based approach is more common one [5].

In order to implement SA or ED, feature selection (FS) should be carried out first of all. FS may be performed by lexicon-based methods that require human annotation, and statistical methods which are automatic methods that are more frequently used; statistical methods may ignore or retain the information on the word sequence [5].

Key features mostly used for ED are terms presence and frequency [16], parts of speech (POS), opinion words and phrases, negations.

As an example of such features we can consider activity markers, psycholinguistic, lexical and semantic markers described in [14]. Natural language markers allow evaluating possibly aggressive or other harmful text aspects (presence of manipulative techniques, negative emotional background), reveal "hot" news characteristic of tabloid press, fake news, etc. Psycholinguistic markers (number of personal pronouns, POS frequency ratios, etc.), lexical markers (injective lexicon, destructive semantics) can be measured and used for text analysis.

Various methods for emotional text classification and, in particular, for aggressive text detection, are discussed in review articles [5, 12] and in the article [10]. Some web services for solving SA tasks are analyzed in [11]. At the same time, a lot of sources deal with a binary classification problem of single messages, without analyzing entire threads; they often employ a very similar text preprocessing pipeline comprising stop-word removal, tokenization, POS tagging, emoticon detection, stemming, etc., and a typical text feature extraction step which resulted in bag-of-words, or, bag-of-stems representations [4]. Some methods that deal with the problems specified in the previous section are summarized in Table 1.

Table 1. Methods for emotion detection.

Method	Classes	Features	Advantages	Application
Hybrid (lexicon-based + super-vised machine learning) [1]	Anger, disgust, fear, happiness, sadness, surprise, trust, neutral; bullying and neutral posts and threads	Sentiment uni- and bi-grams (occurrences of sentiment changes in consecutive posts); personal pronouns; bullying bi- and tri-grams (using BullyTracer lexicon)	Performs sentiment analysis at message level, but considers the whole threads as the context; building "sentiment n-grams" for threads	Web forums, discussions (tested on MySpace)
Machine learning (random forest) [3]	Bully/aggressive/spam/normal messages	User-based: post frequency, account existence time, etc.; text-based: number of hashtags, emoticons, upper cases, emotional scores, etc.; network-based: follower and friend lists, etc.	Deals with short and imperfect messages, takes the context (chains of tweets) into account, tries to detect sarcasm and trolling	Social media (Twitter)

(continued)

Table 1. (*continued*)

Method	Classes	Features	Advantages	Application
Corpus-based approach [4]	Types of bullying (threat/blackmail; insult; curse/exclusion; defamation; sexual talk), victim defense, encouragement to the harasser, other	Word and character n-grams in bag of words; term lists (for example, "allness" indicators, intensifiers, etc.); subjectivity lexicon features	Deals with short and distorted messages. Robustness to spelling variations	Social media (ASK.fm, etc.)
Support vector machine + recurrent neural network [5]	Openly aggressive/covertly aggressive/not aggressive	GloVe features; sentiment scores according to SentiWordNet features; N-gram TF-IDF features	Detecting messages with covert aggression	Social media (Facebook, Twitter, etc.)
Traditional and deep machine learning [6]	Openly aggressive/covertly aggressive/not aggressive	Bad words; POS tags; text length; capitalization; numerical tokens; named entities; sentiment polarity	Deals with short messages and their context. Detecting messages with covert aggression	Social media (Facebook, Twitter)
Hybrid classifier (Naïve Bayes, random forest, support vector machine, logistic regression) [7]	Positive/negative polarity	Vector representation of the "Bag of words"	Classifies short messages	Social media (Twitter)
Profile-based representations (TF-IDF, NN) [8]	Aggressive texts, including sexual aggression	Word and character n-grams	Early recognition for sexual predator detection and aggressive text identification. Possible application for irony/sarcasm detection, opinion mining, etc.	Social media
NB, SVM, and DT [14]	Ironic and sarcastic texts	N-grams, POS n-grams, funny, positive/negative, affective, pleasantness profiling	Irony and sarcasm detection	Amazon reviews

Among the considered approaches, neural networks show the most robust and high performance [9, 10]. While applying the methods described above, some problems still remain. In particular, the overwhelming majority of methods require that corpora of labeled texts exist. Beside the tasks of constructing such a corpus for the Russian language, the problem is that the social media lexicon is volatile, so the corpus becomes obsolete.

The language problem is also significant: the majority of methods are optimized for English language; some other languages under research are Germanic and Latin languages, some languages of South-Eastern Asia and the Near East.

The text analysis services mentioned in [11] are shown in Table 2. It should be noted that some services described there are not available now, though they are said to be able to provide a wide range of possibilities, including evaluating not only the message polarity, but also the separate emotional constituents like fear, gratitude, shame (Lymbix).

Table 2. Services for text analysis.

Service	Possibilities	Methods
SentiStrength http://sentistrength.wlv.ac.uk/	Estimating the polarity of short messages	Text Mining – detecting "good" and "bad" words, their relations
OpinionCrawl http://www.opinioncrawl.com/	Estimating the polarity of relation to a certain subject in the web (news, analytics) Languages: EN, FR, DE, SP	Text mining and multidocument Summarization
OpenDover http://demo.opendover.nl/	Extracts semantic features from the text, calculates the text rating	Ontologies on applied areas (law, education, etc.)
Semantria http://semantria.com/	Languages: EN, FR, DE, SP, PT Good accuracy (about 74% в [9])	Connotative lexicon, calculating frequency of such words in text and their proximity to the object in question
Sentiment140 http://www.sentiment140.com/	Tweets classification (positive/negative/neutral)	Naive Bayes, Maximum Entropy, Support Vector Machines (SVM)
uClassify https://uclassify.com/browse https://uclassify.com/browse/uclassify/sentiment	Provides a set of classifiers for language, sentiment detection, text gender and age recognition Languages: EN, SP, FR, SE Good accuracy (about 76% in [9])	ML: trained on 2.8 million documents with data from Twitter, Amazon product reviews and movie reviews

2.2   Datasets

The data problem arises most pronounced when analyzing non-English texts. For example, there is an annotated corpus of messages from more than 200 000 units [19] in Russian, but those messages are classified just as negative and positive, without any detailed description of the emotions expressed. Datasets in English are much more diverse. Some of them are analyzed in [18]. These datasets are characterized by a large variety in emotion handling: classification by Ekman [20], Plutchik [15], and also some other approaches are present. Datasets of tweets in Russian [19], "The Emotion in Text, published by CrowdFlower" (39 740 tweets, Ekman) [22], TEC (Twitter Emotion Corpus, Ekman) [23], Emobank (Valence - Arousal - Dominance) [24] were used as well as some smaller corpora. In this work they were processed separately to determine which corpora provide the most accurate results.

One of the options for the use of English-language datasets for the classification of Russian-language text is the use of machine translation. Currently, machine translation systems show quite good results when using English as source or target language. Translation causes accuracy loss, but it can be assumed that the features discussed in Sect. 2.1 are preserved to a large extent.

3 Processing Scheme

To handle various datasets in uniform manner, they were supplied by JSON metadata files containing descriptions of the dataset format and structure. Such file pairs were used as the input data. Firstly, a cleanup operation is performed on the datasets, particularly, removal of irrelevant and special characters, hyperlinks, identifiers. Then comes standardization of whitespace characters, converting all characters to uniform case. In addition, the converted versions (translated and normalized) are created for the datasets.

Emotion estimates were converted into a numerical form. For datasets providing binary classification [19], the estimate was normalized. For the datasets annotated with a variety of emotions, transformed datasets were created with score values in the range [0; 1] for each considered emotion. In the context of identifying aggression, the classes "hate", "anger", "aggression", etc. were assigned the value 1.0; all classes that do not carry any negative constituent ("happiness", "fun", "trust") were characterized by the value 0.0; neutral classes with 0.5; classes with negative properties that do not characterize aggression explicitly ("fear", "worry", "boredom") were described with values from the range (0.5; 1).

For the datasets, n-gram dictionaries are built. In this paper, n-grams of characters and words with different values of n were used. The approach with n = 1 for words is identical to the "bag of words" concept. The n-gram occurrence is used to build vectors for neural network training.

Summarizing the aforementioned concerns, the pipeline of data preprocessing can be represented in Fig. 1.

Fig. 1. Dataset preprocessing pipeline

To organize the full processing pipeline, the following class model was developed (Fig. 2):

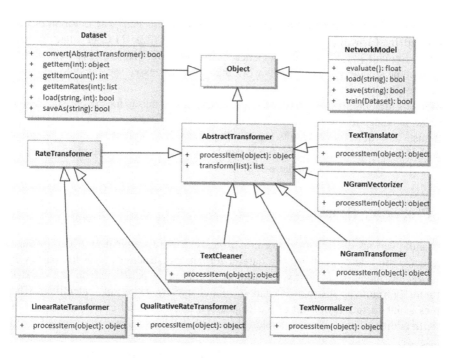

Fig. 2. Classes for data processing

For data processing, as well for creating and training neural networks Python 3.6 was used. The train and test datasets comprise 67% and 33% of the original datasets, respectively. Libraries NLTK and Keras were applied to process text data and train neural networks, respectively, to predict the text aggressiveness using a regression predictive model.

4 Experiments

The modelling results are shown in Figs. 3 and 4. Experiments show that the highest accuracy is achieved for binary classification using the original Russian corpus. Text normalization does not positively influence the result, which can be explained by the semantic loss caused by converting word forms. The considered neural network architectures contained 1 or 2 hidden layers and up to k neurons, where k is the vector size. The maximum accuracy 83% was achieved with the configuration of a neural network with 2 hidden layers consisting of 50 neurons each. The achieved accuracy is lower than in the work [26], but it deals with domain-specific texts (film, customer reviews) which simplifies the classification task.

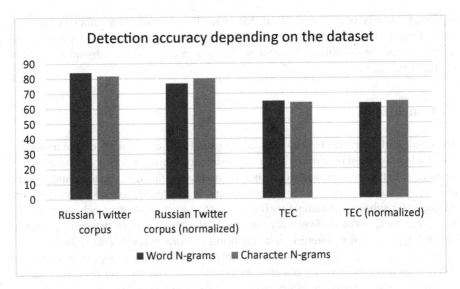

Fig. 3. Accuracy of aggression detection depending on the input data

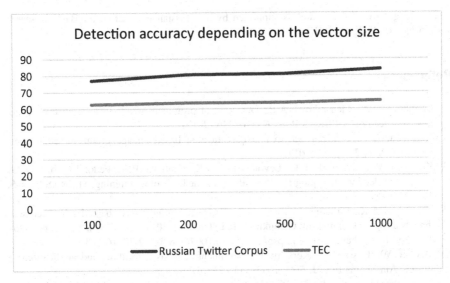

Fig. 4. Accuracy of aggression detection depending on the vector size

The use of machine translation enables distinguishing particular emotions, but the accuracy is much lower in this case. The best results were achieved when using the TEC dataset (65%) for recognizing aggressive messages. Approximately the same accuracy was obtained in [25], and the authors are also able to distinguish overtly and covertly aggressive messages, but that work deals with English texts, so the authors could use English corpora directly.

Using datasets smaller than of 10 000 items did not result in a sufficient accuracy level. Despite the high error rate, such an approach can be used to estimate the aggressiveness probability, for example, to rank messages for subsequent manual verification.

5   Conclusions

The conducted experiments show that, using neural networks trained on the annotated corpora both in Russian and English it is possible to determine with a certain accuracy whether a text item in Russian contains an aggressive message. Such results can be used to estimate the aggressiveness probability, for example, to rank social network messages for subsequent manual verification or to adjust the chatbot behavior models. These results also enable feasibility studies on the possibility of detecting particular emotion types, i.e. fear, interest, in a text using corpora in another languages.

Further research directions include comparison of different approaches to build dictionaries and reduce vector dimensions, comparative analysis and feasibility studies of detecting particular types of emotions, complex analysis of multimodal content on the basis of the technique proposed in [21].

Acknowledgment. This research is supported by the Russian Foundation for Basic Research (project No. 18-29-22061_MK).

References

1. Kocharov, D.A., Menshikova, A.P.: Detection of prominent words in Russian texts using linguistic features. SPIIRAS Proc. **6**, 216–236 (2017)
2. Glazkova, A.V.: An approach to text classification based on age groups of addressees. SPIIRAS Proc. **3**, 51–69 (2017)
3. Vorobiev, V.I., Evnevich, E.L., Levonevskiy, D.K., Fatkieva, R.R., Fedorchenko, L.N.: A study and selection of cryptographic standards on the basis of text mining. SPIIRAS Proc. **5**, 69–87 (2016)
4. Ventirozos, F.K., Varlamis, I., Tsatsaronis, G.: Detecting aggressive behavior in discussion threads using text mining. In: Gelbukh, A. (ed.) CICLing 2017. LNCS, vol. 10762, pp. 420–431. Springer, Cham (2018). https://doi.org/10.1007/978-3-319-77116-8_31
5. Medhat, W., Hassan, A., Korashy, H.: Sentiment analysis algorithms and applications: a survey. Ain Shams Eng. J. **5**(4), 1093–1113 (2014)
6. Chatzakou, D., Kourtellis, N., Blackburn, J., De Cristofaro, E., Stringhini, G., Vakali, A..: Mean birds: detecting aggression and bullying on twitter. In Proceedings of the 2017 ACM on Web Science Conference, pp. 13–22. ACM (2017)
7. Van Hee, C., et al.: Automatic detection of cyberbullying in social media text. PLoS One **13**(10), e0203794 (2018)
8. Tommasel, A., Rodriguez, J.M., Godoy, D.: Textual aggression detection through deep learning. In: Proceedings of the First Workshop on Trolling, Aggression and Cyberbullying, TRAC-2018, pp. 177–187 (2018)

9. Golem, V., Karan, M., Šnajder, J.: Combining shallow and deep learning for aggressive text detection. In: Proceedings of the First Workshop on Trolling, Aggression and Cyberbullying, TRAC-2018, pp. 188–198 (2018)

10. Escalante, H.J., Villatoro-Tello, E., Garza, S.E., López-Monroy, A.P., Montes-y-Gómez, M., Villaseñor-Pineda, L.: Early detection of deception and aggressiveness using profile-based representations. Expert Syst. Appl. **89**, 99–111 (2017)

11. Serrano-Guerrero, J., Olivas, J.A., Romero, F.P., Herrera-Viedma, E.: Sentiment analysis: a review and comparative analysis of web services. Inf. Sci. **311**, 18–38 (2015)

12. Mäntylä, M.V., Graziotin, D., Kuutila, M.: The evolution of sentiment analysis—a review of research topics, venues, and top cited papers. Comput. Sci. Rev. **27**, 16–32 (2018)

13. Jo, H., Kim, S.M., Ryu, J.: What we really want to find by sentiment analysis: the relationship between computational models and psychological state. arXiv preprint arXiv: 1704.03407 (2017)

14. Smirnov, I.V., SHelmanov, A.O., Kuznecova, E.S., Hramoin, I.V.: Semantiko-sintaksicheskij analiz estestvennykh yazykov. CHast' II. Metod semantiko-sintaksicheskogo analiza tekstov (Semantic-syntactic analysis of natural languages. Part II. Method of semantic-syntactic analysis of texts). Iskusstvennyj intellekt i prinyatie reshenij, vol. 1, pp. 11–24. ISA RAS, Moscow (2014)

15. Plutchik, R.: A general psychoevolutionary theory of emotion. In: Theories of Emotion, pp. 3–33. Academic Press (1980)

16. Mejova, Y., Srinivasan, P.: Exploring feature definition and selection for sentiment classifiers. In: Fifth International AAAI Conference on Weblogs and Social Media (2011)

17. Reyes, A., Rosso, P.: Making objective decisions from subjective data: detecting irony in customer reviews. Decis. Support Syst. **53**(4), 754–760 (2012)

18. Bostan, L.A.M., Klinger, R.: An analysis of annotated corpora for emotion classification in text. In: Proceedings of the 27th International Conference on Computational Linguistics, pp. 2104–2119 (2018)

19. Rubtsova, Y.: Constricting a corpus for sentiment classification training. Softw. Syst. **1**(109), 72–79 (2015)

20. Ekman, P.: An argument for basic emotions. Cogn. Emot. **6**(3–4), 169–200 (1992)

21. Levonevskii, D., SHumskaya, O., Velichko, Uzdyaev, M., Malov, D.: Methods for determination of psychophysiological condition of user within smart environment based on complex analysis of heterogeneous data. Paper presented at the 14th International Conference on Electromechanics and Robotics "Zavalishin's Readings", ER(ZR)-2019 (2019)

22. Sentiment Analysis in Text. https://data.world/crowdflower/sentiment-analysis-in-text. Accessed 15 Feb 2019

23. Emotion, Sentiment, and Stance Labeled Data. http://saifmohammad.com/WebPages/SentimentEmotionLabeledData.html. Accessed 21 Jan 2019

24. Buechel, S., Hahn, U.: EMOBANK: studying the impact of annotation perspective and representation format on dimensional emotion analysis. In: Proceedings of the 15th Conference of the European Chapter of the Association for Computational Linguistics, vol. 2, pp. 578–585 (2017)

25. Risch, J., Krestel, R.: Aggression identification using deep learning and data augmentation. In: Proceedings of the First Workshop on Trolling, Aggression and Cyberbullying (co-located with COLING), pp. 150–158 (2018)

26. Yussupova, N., Bogdanova, D., Boyko, M.: Applying of sentiment analysis for texts in Russian based on machine learning approach. In: IMMM 2012: The Second International Conference on Advances in Information Mining and Management, pp. 8–14 (2012)

27. Neidenthal, P.M., Kranth-Gruber, S., Ric, F.: Psychology of Emotions: Interpersonal, Experiential, and Cognitive Approach. Psychology Press, New York (2006)

Software Subsystem Analysis of Prosodic Signs of Emotional Intonation

Boris Lobanov[(✉)] and Vladimir Zhitko

The United Institute of Informatics Problems of National Academy of Sciences
of Belarus, Minsk, Belarus
lobanov@newman.bas-net.by, zhitko.vladimir@gmail.com

Abstract. The main results of the update of the "IntonTrainer" system are the purposes of analyzing and studying the prosodic signs of emotional intonation are described. A distinctive functional feature of the updated system is the creation of an expanded set of prosodic signs of emotional intonation. The paper presents preliminary assessments of their effectiveness using the RAVDESS database of emotional phrases of English speech.

Keywords: Speech intonation · Basic emotions ·
Emotional intonation · Melodic portrait · Intonation analysis ·
Software model

1 Introduction

Well known that human speech conveys not only semantic but also emotional information. There are many different discrete sets of emotions. However, most studies are limited to analyzing the prosodic characteristics of the following 6 emotional states: "Neutrality", "Joy", "Sadness", "Anger", "Fear", "Surprise". There are also a number of emotions attributed quite often to the main ones, such as "Suffering", "Aversion", "Contempt", "Shame", and in addition, numerous shades of the above emotions.

Today, there is not enough knowledge about the details of acoustic models that describe certain emotions of the human voice. Typical acoustic characteristics that are believed to be involved in this process include the following [1,2]:

- Level, range and shape of the pitch contour;
- Level of vocal energy and speech rate.

Recently, some important new speech characteristics have been investigated, such as formant frequencies, linear prediction coefficients (LPC), and the Mel-frequency cepstral coefficients (MFCC) [3–5].

In one of the recent works devoted to the analysis of prosodic characteristics of emotions [6], it is proposed to use the following description of the pitch contour:

© Springer Nature Switzerland AG 2019
A. A. Salah et al. (Eds.): SPECOM 2019, LNAI 11658, pp. 280–288, 2019.
https://doi.org/10.1007/978-3-030-26061-3_29

- The number of maxima in the contour of the main tone in the voiced segment;
- Average value and peak variance;
- Medium tilt;
- Average gradient between two sample points on the pitch curve;
- Variance of pitch gradients.

Our previous work [7] was devoted to the analysis and comparison of the pitch contours of various intonation patterns with the help of software system "IntonTrainer". It aimed to for study, training, and analysis of speech intonation. The software system "IntonTrainer" contains subsystems that include sets of reference phrases that represent the basic intonation models of Russian, English (British and American versions), German and Chinese speech.

The purpose of this work is to update the existing system by supplementing it with a subsystem for analyzing the prosodic signs of emotional intonation. Such a subsystem should provide analysis and visualization of an effective set of prosodic signs of emotional intonation using the available databases of emotional speech. In this work, for testing purposes, we use the Ryerson Audio-Visual Database of Emotional Speech and Song (RAVDESS) [8].

2 Visual Representation of Emotional Intonation Features

To create a subsystem that allows for detailed analysis and visualization of emotional intonation we add to the "IntonTrainer" system some new functions described below (see: folder name "English Emotions" at the site https://intontrainer.by).

The initial Application window is shown in Fig. 1.

Fig. 1. Initial window

After clicking the "Start" button, the main window opens, containing a structured list of reference phrases indicating the name of the announcer, the name of the emotion and the text of the phrase in which it is reflected (see Fig. 2). The numbers 0 or 1 indicated two levels of emotional intensity.

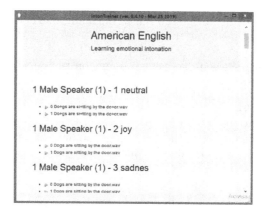

Fig. 2. Main window

By selecting the desired directory with the cursor, for example: "1 Male Speaker (1) - 1 neutral _1 Dogs are sitting by the door" opens a window (Fig. 3) in which are displayed the results of the intonation analysis of this phrase in a graphic view. The continuous curve in Fig. 3 displays the trajectory of F0 change on the voice sections of the phrase and is presented in the form of the Normalized Melodic Portrait (NMP).

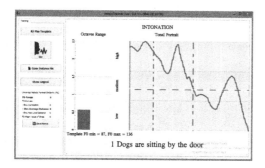

Fig. 3. Window displaying the NMP curve of the phrase "Dogs are sitting by the door" (Neutral emotion)

Segmentation of speech signal into voice regions is carried out automatically (by selecting the Auto Marking mode). Segmentation is based on the information about periodicity in the signal (voice presence), while the presence of a sufficiently high signal amplitude - A0 (t). The construction of the NMP curve, in contrast to the Universal Melodic Portrait of the UMP [7], does not require "manual" marking of the phrase on the "pre-core", "core" and "post-core" sections. The horizontal dashed line on the screen shows the average value of the

NMP curve. Two vertical lines show the information on the position of the center of the NMP curve and its width on the normalized time axis.

It is also possible to calculate and display the derivative of the NMP in a similar way (see Fig. 4). The height of the column (to the left of the NMP) shows the range of variation of the F0 in octaves.

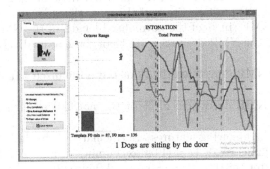

Fig. 4. Displaying of the NMP and its derivative

In the left part in Figs. 3, 4 control buttons are shown with which the following functions are available:

- "Play Template" - listening to reference phrases.
- "Rec" - quick recording of user phrases through a microphone,
- "Open Instance File" - call test phrases from the "TEST" folder.

For individual training of emotional intonation, the user can apply an extended or built-in microphone by pressing button "Rec".

The user has also the ability to visually compare melodic portraits of various emotions using test phrases from the "TEST" folder by pressing the button "Open Instance File". In Fig. 5 there are presented for comparison 2 curves of NMP (neutral emotion and emotion of anger) for the same speaker and phrase.

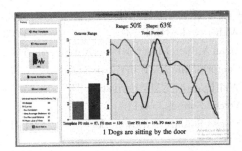

Fig. 5. NMPs of neutral (red line) and anger (dark line) emotions (Color figure online)

3   Numerical Evaluation of Signs of Emotional Intonation

The numerical estimates of the signs of emotional intonation are based mainly on the results of measuring various parameters of the NMP presented in Figs. 3, 4, 5. Based on the NMP, the following set of features is calculated:

- Mean Value of the NMP (in % of the maximal value of the NMP);
- Center of the NMP position (in % of the normalized length of the NMP);
- Width of the NMP (in % of the normalized length of the NMP);
- Mean Value of the NMP derivative (in % of the maximal value of the NMP derivative);
- Center of the NMP derivative (in % of the normalized length of the NMP derivative);
- Width of the NMP derivative in % of the normalized length of the NMP derivative).
- Additionally, the following features are calculated from the source signal:
- F0-Diapason (in octaves): $D = (F0max/F0min) - 1$;
- F0-Mean Register (in Hz): $R = (F0max - F0min)/2$;
- Voiced Sounds Level (in %, as the average value of the signal amplitudes relative to the maximum value;
- Voiced Sounds Duration [in seconds], as the total duration of voice sections.

In the left part at the bottom of Figs. 3, 4, 5 control buttons are shown for "Save Metrics" functions. When you click the "Save Metrics" button appears and a page opens in EXCEL, on which a complete set of 10 prosodic features of the reference phrase is written (see Table 1). The obtained data is stored in the same folder where the reference phrase being studied is stored.

Table 1. Prosodic features of the phrase "Dogs are sitting by the door" (Neutral emotion)

#	Names of prosodic features	Results
1	F0-Diapason [Octaves]	0,56
2	F0-Register [Hz]	111,50
3	Mean Value of the NMP [%]	46,14
4	Center of the NMP [%]	42
5	Width of the NMP [%]	33,03
6	Mean Value of the NMP derivative [%]	54,65
7	Center of the NMP derivative [%]	5,77
8	Width of the NMP derivative [%]	54,71
9	Voiced Sounds Level [%]	24
10	Voiced Sounds Duration [Sec]	1,71

Table 2 shows an example of the results of calculating the numerical values of the prosodic signs of a phrase expressing the emotion "Anger".

Table 2. Prosodic features of the phrase "Dogs are sitting by the door" (Anger emotion)

#	Names of prosodic features	Results
1	F0-Diapason [Octaves]	1,17
2	F0-Register [Hz]	258,5
3	Mean Value of the NMP [%]	36,94
4	Center of the NMP [%]	42,69
5	Width of the NMP [%]	36,91
6	Mean Value of the NMP derivative [%]	44,26
7	Center of the NMP derivative [%]	44,92
8	Width of the NMP derivative [%]	47,34
9	Voiced Sounds Level [%]	34
10	Voiced Sounds Duration [Sec]	2,43

At the time, when the user makes a visual comparison of NMPs of reference and tests phrases (see Fig. 5), it is also possible to calculate and to click the "Save Metrics" button to store values of ratios for each prosodic signs of this couple of phrases in dB scale. The results of a calculation based on the data given in Tables 1 and 2 (a pair of phrases with "Anger/Neutrality" emotions) is shown in Table 3.

The use of ratios in dB scale allows the comparison of a pair of phrases with different emotions, using prosodic signs of different nature and in various units of measurement.

Table 3. Relative values for the prosodic features of a pair "Anger/Neutrality" emotions

#	Names of prosodic features	Results
1	F0-Diapason	1,33
2	F0-Register	3,66
3	Mean Value of the NMP	−1,22
4	Center of the NMP	0,21
5	Width of the NMP	−0,11
6	Mean Value of the NMP derivative	−2,69
7	Center of the NMP derivative	0,30
8	Width of the NMP derivative	−0,16
9	Voiced Sounds Level	2,06
10	Voiced Sounds Duration	1,27

4   Preliminary Testing of the Developed Signs of Emotional Intonation

For testing of the developed signs, we used the RAVDESS emotion database [8]. It is a validated multimodal database of emotional speech. The database is gender balanced consisting of 24 professional actors and actresses, vocalizing lexically-matched statements in a neutral North American accent. Speech includes Neutral, Happy, Sad, Angry, Fearful, Surprise, and Disgust expressions of emotions. The common number of emotional speech samples available for testing is 1534. The testing and analysis of such a big database become possible only with the involvement of special programs for processing big data, for example, using neural network algorithms that we are planning to realize in the future.

Below on Fig. 6 we present comparative graphs of the NMP and the tables with data in the logarithmic ratio for each of the 10 signs (see: Table 3) for three pairs of emotions expressed by one of the male and female actors.

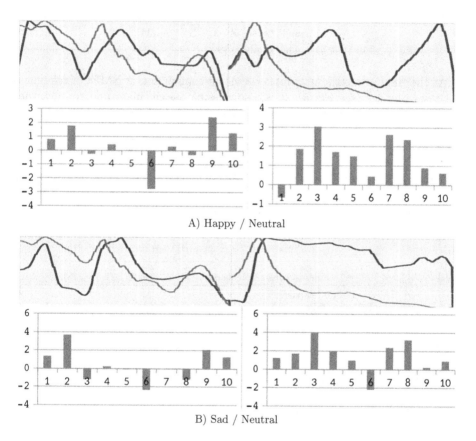

A) Happy / Neutral

B) Sad / Neutral

Fig. 6. Graphs of the NMP (top rows) and the tables (bottom rows) for three pairs of emotions expressed by one of male (left column) and female (right column) actors.

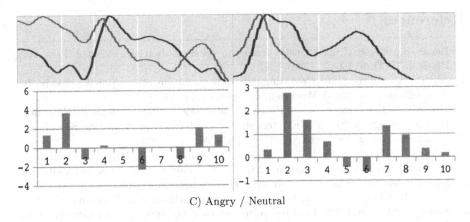

C) Angry / Neutral

Fig. 6. (*continued*)

The present study of the effectiveness of the developed signs of emotional intonation showed their significant distinctive power when comparing different pairs of emotions. It should be noted that one group of signs can play a large role in distinguishing the emotions of one speaker and be poorly informative for another speaker. So, for example, from Fig. 6 it is clear that signs 1, 2, 9, 10, calculated from the source signal, play the most significant role in distinguishing emotions in a male speaker. To distinguish the emotions of a female speaker, the most significant role is played by signs of 3, 4, 5, 6 calculated from NMPs.

5 Conclusions

The task of upgrading the "IntonTrainer" system wasn't including the creation of a valid speech emotion recognition model. The ultimate goal of refinement was limited to the creation of such a software tool that would provide analysis and visualization of an extended set of prosodic signs of emotional intonation, and which could be used as a new tool for phonetic studies of speech.

We do not exclude also some applied aspects of the application, for example, in the tasks of teaching the required emotional intonation of actors, as well as people of various professions who are striving to enhance their so-called "emotional intelligence (EQ)". For this, in the Similarity Measure section (see the Main settings window of the "IntonTrainer") it is possible choose a method for assessing the intonation proximity of the spoken phrase to the reference one, using various similarity measures. The chosen method of calculating the intonational similarity is then used in calculating the digital or verbal evaluation assessment of the intonation quality of the spoken phrase.

References

1. Banse, R., Sherer, K.R.: Acoustic profiles in vocal emotion expression. J. Pers. Soc. Psychol. **70**(3), 614–636 (1996)
2. Abelin, A., Allwood, J.: Cross-linguistic interpretation of emotional prosody. In: Proceedings of the ISCA Workshop on Speech and Emotion (2000)
3. Ververidis, D., Kotropoulos, C., Pitas, I.: Automatic emotional speech classification. In: Proceedings of 2004 IEEE International Conference on Acoustics, Speech and Signal Processing, Montreal, vol. 1, pp. 593–596, May 2004
4. Xiao, Z., Dellandrea, E., Dou, W., Chen, L.: Features extraction and selection for emotional speech classification. In: 2005 IEEE Conference on Advanced Video and Signal Based Surveillance (AVSS), pp. 411–416, September 2005
5. Pao, T.-L., Chen, Y.-T., Yeh, J.-H., Li, P.-J.: Mandarin emotional speech recognition based on SVM and NN. In: Proceedings of the 18th International Conference on Pattern Recognition (ICPR 2006), vol. 1, pp. 1096–1100, September 2006
6. Sbattella, L., Colombo, L., Rinaldi, C., Tedesco, R., Matteucci, M., Trivilini, A.: Extracting emotions and communication styles from prosody. Physiological Computing Systems. LNCS, vol. 8908, pp. 21–42. Springer, Heidelberg (2014). https://doi.org/10.1007/978-3-662-45686-6_2
7. Lobanov, B., Zhitko, V., Zahariev, V.: A prototype of the software system for study, training and analysis of speech intonation. In: Karpov, A., Jokisch, O., Potapova, R. (eds.) SPECOM 2018. LNCS (LNAI), vol. 11096, pp. 337–346. Springer, Cham (2018). https://doi.org/10.1007/978-3-319-99579-3_36
8. Livingstone, S.R., Russo, F.A.: The Ryerson Audio-visual Database of Emotional Speech and Song (RAVDESS): a dynamic, multimodal set of facial and vocal expressions in North American English (2018). https://doi.org/10.1371/journal.pone.0196391

Assessing Alzheimer's Disease from Speech Using the i-vector Approach

José Vicente Egas López[1(✉)], László Tóth[1], Ildikó Hoffmann[2,3],
János Kálmán[4], Magdolna Pákáski[4], and Gábor Gosztolya[1,5]

[1] Institute of Informatics, University of Szeged, Szeged, Hungary
egasj@inf.u-szeged.hu
[2] Department of Linguistics, University of Szeged, Szeged, Hungary
[3] Research Institute for Linguistics, Hungarian Academy of Sciences,
Budapest, Hungary
[4] Department of Psychiatry, University of Szeged, Szeged, Hungary
[5] MTA-SZTE Research Group on Artificial Intelligence, Szeged, Hungary

Abstract. One of the world's chronic neuro-degenerative diseases, Alzheimer's Disease (AD), leads its sufferers, among other symptoms, to suffer from speech difficulties. In particular, the inability to recall vocabulary which makes patients' speech different. Furthermore, Mild Cognitive Impairment (MCI) is usually considered as a prodromal neuro-degenerative state of AD. The key to abate the progress of both disorders is their early diagnosis. However, actual ways of diagnosis are costly and quite time-consuming. In this study, we propose the extraction of features from speech through the use of the i-vector approach, by which we seek to model the speech pattern of the three mental conditions from the subjects. To the best of our knowledge, no previous studies have utilized i-vector features to assess Alzheimer's before. These i-vectors are extracted from Mel-Frequency Cepstral Coefficients (MFCCs), then they are given to a SVM classifier in order to identify the speech in one of the following manners: AD - Alzheimer Disease, MCI - Mild Cognitive Impairment, HC - Healthy Control. We tested these i-vector features by performing a 5-fold cross-validation and we achieved an F1-score of 79.2%.

Keywords: i-vectors · Alzheimer's · SVM · Speech recognition

1 Introduction

Speech difficulties among patients suffering from Alzheimer's Disease (AD) become palpable from the moderate stage of the disease and such adversities are often characterized by the incapacity to recall vocabulary, leading to constant incorrect word substitutions, also known as paraphasias [8]. The language of the AD patient is diminished to simple phrases or single words; progressively, the patient may entirely lose their speech, resulting in a substantial decrease in

© Springer Nature Switzerland AG 2019
A. A. Salah et al. (Eds.): SPECOM 2019, LNAI 11658, pp. 289–298, 2019.
https://doi.org/10.1007/978-3-030-26061-3_30

the quality of life [8,9]. In most cases, these factors create the structure of speech of a patient suffering from Alzheimer's, which is generally formed by syntactic complexity, insufficient speech fluency, and vocabulary limitation.

Insufficient screening techniques have made Alzheimer's too complex to diagnose. The early diagnosis of the disease could lead to a more effective confrontation of the AD in order to slow down its development; this stage of diagnosis is difficult to achieve [14,24]. Generally speaking, patients arrive at the clinic when Alzheimer's is already in an advanced state, which lowers the ratio of early AD detection cases. MCI (Mild Cognitive Impairment), as part of the process of dementia, is prone to start around the age of 40. Screening tests to detect MCI take a long time, they shortage of pre-clinical state diagnosis and require a high budget to fund them [18].

Speech recognition tools are widely used for similar tasks within this branch of medicine. Fraser et al. [10–12] utilized speech recognition to detect aphasia. Lehr et al. [22] applied speech recognition in order to diagnose MCI. Other groups [1,26] diagnosed Alzheimer's through the use of speech recognition tools. To detect and assess other neuro-degenerative diseases such as Parkinson's (PD), the i-vector approach has been successfully applied to model the speech of PD patients by extracting i-vectors from it and performing classification through the comparison with those of the test speakers by means of cosine distance scoring [16]; likewise, classifying them using of Support Vector Machines (SVM) [17]. Also, i-vectors have been used to perform classification and regression of the speaker's age. To be precise, Grzybowska et al. [19] carry out an examination of the use of i-vectors both for age regression and for age classification based on the speech of the subjects.

To the best of our knowledge, no previous studies exist that classify Alzheimer's Disease based on utterances by applying the i-vector approach. Here, we fit a (linear) Support Vector Machines (SVM) classifier which is given i-vectors features extracted from the Mel-Frequency Cepstral Coefficients (MFCCs) of the utterances. The diagnosis is predicted as one of the following three states: HC (Healthy Control), MCI (Mild Cognitive Impairment), and AD (Alzheimer's Disease).

2   Data

The data for the experiments in this study is defined as follows: 225 speech signals recorded from 75 subjects (*dementia dataset*), and 44 recordings taken from generic speakers (*BEA dataset*). The speech utterances used are the same as those employed in [18], which were recorded at the Memory Clinic, University of Szeged, Hungary. Three categories of utterances were recorded, namely, subjects suffering from MCI, subjects affected by the early-stage of AD, and subjects having no cognitive impairment at the time of recording. Such categories were matched for age, gender and education. We worked with the utterances of 25 speakers for each speaker group, resulting in a total of 75 speakers and 225 recordings.

Table 1. The characteristics of the three groups of the study participants. Groups: MCI = mild cognitive impairment; mAD = mild Alzheimer's Disease. Tests: MMSE = Mini-Mental State Examination; CDT = Clock Drawing Test; ADAS-Cog = Alzheimer's Disease Assessment Scale. Values are given as mean ± standard deviation.

	Subject groups			Statistics	
	Control (n = 25)	MCI (n = 25)	mAD (n = 25)	$F(2;74)$	p
Age	70.72 ± 5.004	72.4 ± 3.594	73.96 ± 6.846	2.321	$p = 0.105$
Years of education	12.08 ± 2.326	10.84 ± 2.304	10.76 ± 2.818	2.202	$p = 0.118$
MMSE score	29.24 ± 0.523	27.16 ± 0.898	23.92 ± 2.488	76.213	$p < 0.001$
CDT score	8.88 ± 2.007	6.44 ± 3.429	5.88 ± 3.244	7.254	$p = 0.001$
Adas-COG score	8.575 ± 2.374	12.044 ± 3.205	18.675 ± 5.818	38.35	$p < 0.001$

Mini-Mental State Examination (MMSE, [7]), Clock Drawing Test (CDT; [13]) and the Alzheimer's Disease Assessment Scale (ADAS-Cog, [25]) were the clinical tests employed in order to assess the cognitive states of the subjects. From the MMSE test, one can get a maximum of 30 points in the following manner: 29–30 points for healthy elderly, 27–28 points for mild neurocognitive impairment, 20–26 points for mild dementia, 10–19 points for moderate dementia, and 0–9 points for severe dementia [7]. The CDT test is up to a total of 10 points, where a score below 7 corresponds to a cognitive decline [13]. The ADAS-Cog test, which employs an inverse scoring (i.e. errors are counted rather than right answers), has the following scoring system: 0–8 points for normal cognitive abilities, 9–15 points for mild neurocognitive impairment, and 16–70 points for severe neurocognitive impairment [25].

The Geriatric Depression Scale (GDS) was used to assess the state of depression. The three groups ($F(2;74) = 2.202$; p = 0.118) were aligned with regard to gender ($X2(2) = 1.389$; p = 0.499), age ($F(2;74) = 2.321$; p = 0.105) and years of education ($F(2;74) = 2.202$; p = 0.118). Table 1 lists the clinical characteristics of the control, the MCI and the mAD group. The recordings reflect a spontaneous speech of the subjects and the experimental setup for them was as follows: (1) *Immediate recall*, after the presentation of a specially designed one-minute-long film, the subjects were asked to talk about details seen on the film. (2) *Previous day*, the subjects were asked to talk in detail about their previous day. (3) *Delayed recall*, in the end, a second film was played, and after having one minute pause, the subjects were asked to speak about what they saw. The structure of the data became a set of 3 spontaneous-speech recordings per speaker, where each was edited in such a manner that we cropped parts before the subject starts to speak and after the subject's last phoneme.

3   Methods

The study was achieved by performing the extraction of the i-vectors in the following manner: (1) MFCCs features were extracted separately from 225 (i.e.

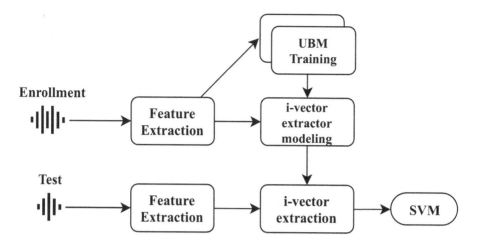

Fig. 1. The generic methodology applied in our work.

dementia dataset) and 44 speech recordings (i.e. BEA dataset) (2) the UBM was trained using the MFCCs obtained from the BEA dataset (3) the i-vector extractor model was trained using the UBM of the previous step, and MFCCs from the dementia dataset (4) MFCCs from the dementia dataset were processed to extract a set of 225 i-vectors, and lastly, (5) a Support Vector Machines (SVM) performed the classification process. These stages are outlined in Fig. 1.

3.1 Feature Extraction

Among the most popular short-term acoustic features are the MFCCs (Mel-Frequency Cepstral Coefficients), which are obtained by implementing the following operations on the utterances: power spectrum, logarithm, and Discrete Cosine Transform (DCT), these deliver the first coefficients plus one more coefficient associated with the energy of the frame. Velocity and acceleration (first and second derivatives) are affixed to the MFCCs together with their energy's coefficients. In this study, we will use MFCCs because this technique has proved to be one of the most effective when it comes to creating a speaker model [15, 20].

3.2 The i-vector Approach

GMM (Gaussian Mixture Model) supervectors [2] and JFA (Joint Factor Analysis) [21] are successful approaches that were once the state-of-the-art systems for robust speaker recognition. In an attempt to combine of both techniques, JFA speaker factors were used as features for SVM classifiers [5]. It found that the channel factors estimated with JFA not only contain channel effects but speaker-dependent information as well; hence, speaker and channel factors were combined into a single space. Factor Analysis (FA), which is used as a feature extractor, defines a new low-dimensional *total variability space* in which a speech utterance is defined by a new vector called *i-vector* [6] that contains the estimates of the *total factors*:

$$M = m + Tw, \qquad (1)$$

where M is the Gaussian Mixture Model (GMM) speaker supervector for a given signal; m is the speaker/channel-independent component, namely, the UBM supervector; T is the Total Variability matrix (TV); and w is a standard normal distributed hidden variable, i.e. the i-vector. This vector can be thought of as a representation of a given recording in a lower-dimension space.

In contrast to JFA, i-vectors do not make any distinction between speaker and channel; here, each utterance is assumed to be acquired from a different speaker. The i-vector approach is, in plain words, a dimensionality reduction technique of the GMM supervector.

To the best of our knowledge, no previous studies described in the literature used i-vector features specifically to predict AD from speech. We think that, owing to the nature of factor analysis, which is used to obtain information about speaker and channel variabilities, i-vector features are able to capture efficiently the information needed in order to model an AD subject's speech in a proper way.

4 Experiments and Results

Here, we describe the experiments carried out using the i-vectors as features obtained from the speech of 225 bio-signals (i.e. utterances). Moreover, we will analyze the classification results given by the Support Vector Machines algorithm which utilized the k-fold cross-validation technique.

4.1 i-vectors Extraction

Bob Kaldi [3] was used to perform the i-vectors extraction process, it being a python wrapper for the Kaldi speech recognition toolkit [23]. In our work, 20 MFCCs features are extracted from the audio signals, which were 25 ms in duration and had a 10 ms time-shift.

Our UBM was trained relying on the BEA Hungarian Spoken Language Database that consists of spontaneous speech similar to the recordings collected from the patients. We worked with a 120 min-long set of recordings from the BEA corpus, mostly utilizing utterances from elderly subjects so as to match the age group targeted audience. The UBM was supplied with the MFCCs related to the BEA dataset in order to get a universal model of the speakers. The values of the following parameters were adjusted in order to train the UBM: the number of Gaussian components, C, from 2 to 256; and the number of Gaussians to keep per frame, C_f, was given by $log_2(C)$.

MFCC features extracted from the utterances of the MCI, HC, and AD subjects (i.e dementia dataset), were used both to model the i-vector extractor, for which we used training utterances only, and to extract i-vectors from each

Table 2. Scores obtained when SVM classifies with i-vectors.

Used recording(s)	UBM size	Performance (%)			
		Acc.	Prec.	Rec.	F_1
Immediate recall	32	42.7%	82.6%	76.0%	79.2%
Previous day	32	41.3%	72.2%	78.0%	75.0%
Delayed recall	4	46.7%	78.7%	74.0%	76.3%
All utterances	16	56.0%	80.9%	76.0%	78.4%

MFCC feature vector (i.e. using train, development and test utterances, respectively). The i-vector extractor model was fitted using the UBM as well as the MFCC features extracted from the *dementia* dataset. Then, the i-vector extractor makes use of the i-vector extractor model together with the UBM to extract the i-vector features from each utterance.

4.2   Evaluation

We performed our classification with the use of Support-Vector Machines [27] and we relied on the libSVM implementation [4]. To avoid overfitting due to having a large number of meta-parameters, we applied a linear kernel; the value of complexity (C) was set in the range $10^{\{-5, -4, ..., 0, 1\}}$. The subjects were classified using 5-fold cross-validation. Each fold contained the utterances of 5 healthy controls, 5 speakers having AD, and 5 speakers suffering from MCI. Each SVM model was trained on the utterances of 60 subjects.

The evaluation was carried out in 4 ways, where we measured the performance of the recordings: immediate recall, previous day, delayed recall, and all utterances together, respectively. Table 2 lists the results got in terms of F1-scoring and accuracy. The best F1-score outcome belongs to the immediate recall measurement. However, the best accuracy score was obtained when using all the utterances. It can be seen that Immediate Recall and Previous Day recordings performed the best with 32 Gaussian components in the UBM; but this is not true for Delayed recall, and All utterances evaluations, they performed the best when the size of the UBM was 4 and 16, respectively.

Figure 2 shows a big difference between the values of accuracy related to the set 'All tasks' and the accuracy scores from the other set of tasks (i.e. Immediate recall, Previous day, and Delayed recall). This happens because the accuracy score was measured as a 3-wise set, that is, it was obtained in terms of the AD, MCI, and HC classifications. This means that SVM had a 3-class classification with an accuracy score of 56%. In contrast, a 2-wise set used in the rest of the scores, that is, AD and MCI were treated as one class, while HC was the other class, which allowed the classifier to perform better. Thus here the evaluation was basically whether the subject has dementia (AD or MCI) or the subject is healthy (HC). The same figure describes the number of Gaussian components required to get the best results in terms of accuracy, it turns out that the best configurations

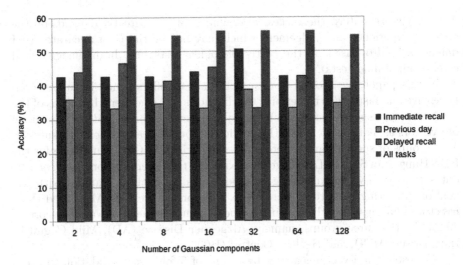

Fig. 2. Achieved accuracy scores in terms of the number of Gaussian components.

were obtained when using the number of Gaussian components was less than 32 in the case of Immediate Recall and Previous Day tasks. For Delayed Recall just 4 components were needed. When all the utterances were combined, it was enough to use 16 Gaussian components so as to achieve the best accuracy scores with less computation time. Thus, i-vector features in these experiments performed better when using smaller number of Gaussian components.

It should be mentioned that the best configuration of the number of components C in the SVM classifier differed in relation to the type of recordings used, i.e. for the best F1-score (Immediate recall) $C = 10^{-2}$, while for the best accuracy (All utterances) $C = 10^{-3}$. A complexity constant value that is too large may lead to overfit the model; on the other hand, a value that is too small may result in over-generalization. Here, the best SVM complexity constant values, which set the tolerance for misclassification, were low in the two best cases, which means that C just needed 'hard' boundaries of tolerance to perform the best, and over-fitting was controlled by the cross-validation.

5   Conclusions and Future Work

Alzheimer's Disease is currently very difficult to diagnose accurately, and the methods of diagnosis generally comprise several costly and time-consuming tasks that the patient may be asked to repeat more than once. A successful and precise diagnosis might be relative due to the fact that it is strongly dependent of the expertise of the physician. Mild Cognitive Impairment is commonly viewed as a prodromal stage of Alzheimer's, it causes a gentle-yet-noticeable decline in cognitive abilities (i.e. memory and thinking). Generally speaking, a person with MCI has a relatively high risk of developing AD or another type of dementia disease. Unfortunately, the successful diagnosis of MCI greatly depends on the doctor's experience and judgement which may not be the most accurate. MCI diagnosis is also based on the costly biomaker tests (e.g. brain imaging and cerebrospinal fluid tests).

In this paper, we showed how speech analysis offers a non-intrusive, non-expensive and faster way to perform the diagnosis of Alzheimer's by means of the utterances (i.e. speech recordings) of subjects. Here, we presented the advantage of i-vectors as features to model the particular speech of an Alzheimer's sufferer. Two groups of speech signals were represented via MFFCs features, one for the BEA Hungarian Spoken Language Database and the other got from the *dementia* dataset. Next, i-vector modeling was performed over these features with the goal of extracting their total factors (i.e. i-vector features). SVM utilized these i-vectors and classified them using a linear kernel. It achieved an F1 score of 79.2% for the three groups, namely, Alzheimer Disease (AD), Mild Cognitive Impairment (MCI), and Healthy Control (HC).

We tested the i-vector features by means of 5-fold cross-validation to avoid overfitting. Evaluation took place over three types of recordings (Immediate recall, Previous day, Delayed recall) from each of the 75 speakers, plus one more evaluation over all these together.

In a future study, we intend to perform a standard i-vector preprocessing before classifying them with the SVM. LDA (Linear Discriminant Analysis) and WCCN (Within-class Covariance Normalization) are commonly used on i-vector features in order to achieve the compensation for the intersession problem. We expect that, with the use of LDA, undesired information may be removed from the total factors (i.e. i-vectors) and that the variance between speakers can be maximized (discrimination of multiple classes); on the other hand, WCCN can be utilized to compensate the intersession variability. Such processes on i-vectors may lead to a dimension reduction in the features which should cut CPU time and make it easier to classify them.

Acknowledgments. This study was partially funded by the National Research, Development and Innovation Office of Hungary via contract NKFIH FK-124413 and by the Ministry of Human Capacities, Hungary (grant 20391-3/2018/FEKUSTRAT). László Tóth was supported by the János Bolyai Research Scholarship of the Hungarian Academy of Sciences.

References

1. Baldas, V., Lampiris, C., Capsalis, C., Koutsouris, D.: Early diagnosis of Alzheimer's type dementia using continuous speech recognition. In: Lin, J.C., Nikita, K.S. (eds.) MobiHealth 2010. LNICST, vol. 55, pp. 105–110. Springer, Heidelberg (2011). https://doi.org/10.1007/978-3-642-20865-2_14
2. Campbell, W.M., Sturim, D.E., Reynolds, D.A.: Support vector machines using GMM supervectors for speaker verification. IEEE Signal Process. Lett. **13**(5), 308–311 (2006)
3. Cernak, M., Komaty, A., Mohammadi, A., Anjos, A., Marcel, S.: Bob speaks Kaldi. In: Proceedings of Interspeech, August 2017

4. Chang, C.C., Lin, C.J.: LIBSVM: a library for support vector machines. ACM Trans. Intell. Syst. Technol. **2**, 1–27 (2011)
5. Dehak, N., et al.: Support vector machines and joint factor analysis for speaker verification. In: 2009 IEEE International Conference on Acoustics, Speech and Signal Processing, pp. 4237–4240. IEEE (2009)
6. Dehak, N., Kenny, P.J., Dehak, R., Dumouchel, P., Ouellet, P.: Front-end factor analysis for speaker verification. IEEE Trans. Audio Speech Lang. Process. **19**(4), 788–798 (2011)
7. Folstein, M., Folstein, S., McHugh, P.: Mini-mental state: a practical method for grading the cognitive state of patients for the clinician. J. Psychiatr. Res. **12**(3), 189–198 (1975)
8. Förstl, H., Kurz, A.: Clinical features of Alzheimer's disease. Eur. Arch. Psychiatry Clin. Neurosci. **249**(6), 288–290 (1999). https://doi.org/10.1007/s004060050101
9. Frank, E.: Effect of Alzheimer's disease on communication function. J. S. C. Med. Assoc. **9**(90), 417–23 (1994)
10. Fraser, K., Rudzicz, F., Graham, N., Rochon, E.: Automatic speech recognition in the diagnosis of primary progressive aphasia. In: Proceedings of SLPAT, Grenoble, France, pp. 47–54 (2013)
11. Fraser, K.C., et al.: Automated classification of primary progressive aphasia subtypes from narrative speech transcripts. Cortex **55**, 43–60 (2014)
12. Fraser, K.C., Rudzicz, F., Rochon, E.: Using text and acoustic features to diagnose progressive aphasia and its subtypes. In: Proceedings of Interspeech, Lyon, France, pp. 25–29 (2013)
13. Freedman, M., Leach, L., Kaplan, E., Winocur, G., Shulman, K., Delis, D.: Clock Drawing: A Neuropsychological Analysis. Oxford University Press, New York (1994)
14. Galvin, J.E., Sadowsky, C.H.: Practical guidelines for the recognition and diagnosis of dementia. J. Am. Board Fam. Med. **25**(3), 367–382 (2012)
15. Ganchev, T., Fakotakis, N., Kokkinakis, G.: Comparative evaluation of various MFCC implementations on the speaker verification task. In: Proceedings of the SPECOM, vol. 1, pp. 191–194 (2005)
16. García, N., Orozco-Arroyave, J.R., D'Haro, L.F., Dehak, N., Nöth, E.: Evaluation of the neurological state of people with Parkinson's Disease using i-vectors. In: INTERSPEECH (2017)
17. García, N., Vásquez-Correa, J., Orozco-Arroyave, J.R., Nöth, E.: Multimodal i-vectors to detect and evaluate Parkinson's disease. In: Proceedings of Interspeech 2018, pp. 2349–2353 (2018)
18. Gosztolya, G., Vincze, V., Tóth, L., Pákáski, M., Kálmán, J., Hoffmann, I.: Identifying mild cognitive impairment and mild Alzheimer's disease based on spontaneous speech using ASR and linguistic features. Comput. Speech Lang. **53**, 181–197 (2019). http://www.sciencedirect.com/science/article/pii/S088523081730342X
19. Grzybowska, J., Kacprzak, S.: Speaker age classification and regression using i-vectors. In: INTERSPEECH, pp. 1402–1406 (2016)
20. Hansen, J.H.L., Hasan, T.: Speaker recognition by machines and humans: a tutorial review. IEEE Signal Process. Mag. **32**(6), 74–99 (2015). https://doi.org/10.1109/MSP.2015.2462851
21. Kenny, P.: Joint factor analysis of speaker and session variability: theory and algorithms. CRIM, Montreal, (Report) CRIM-06/08-13, vol. 14, pp. 28–29 (2005)
22. Lehr, M., Prud'hommeaux, E., Shafran, I., Roark, B.: Fully automated neuropsychological assessment for detecting mild cognitive impairment. In: Proceedings of Interspeech, Portland, OR, USA, pp. 1039–1042 (2012)

23. Madikeri, S., Dey, S., Motlicek, P., Ferras, M.: Implementation of the standard i-vector system for the Kaldi speech recognition toolkit. Idiap-RR Idiap-RR-26-2016, Idiap, October 2016

24. Nelson, L., Tabet, N.: Slowing the progression of Alzheimer's disease; what works? Ageing Res. Rev. **23**(B), 193–209 (2015)

25. Rosen, W., Mohs, R., Davis, K.: A new rating scale for Alzheimer's disease. J. Psychiatry Res. **141**(11), 1356–1364 (1984)

26. Satt, A., Hoory, R., König, A., Aalten, P., Robert, P.H.: Speech-based automatic and robust detection of very early dementia. In: Proceedings of Interspeech, Singapore, pp. 2538–2542 (2014)

27. Schölkopf, B., Platt, J.C., Shawe-Taylor, J., Smola, A.J., Williamson, R.C.: Estimating the support of a high-dimensional distribution. Neural Comput. **13**(7), 1443–1471 (2001)

AD-Child.Ru: Speech Corpus for Russian Children with Atypical Development

Elena Lyakso[(✉)] [ID], Olga Frolova [ID], Arman Kaliyev [ID],
Viktor Gorodnyi [ID], Aleksey Grigorev [ID], and Yuri Matveev [ID]

The Child Speech Research Group, St. Petersburg State University,
St. Petersburg, Russia
lyakso@gmail.com

Abstract. The paper presents the speech database "AD-Child.Ru" that contains speech materials of 4–16 year old children with atypical development. The choice of informants with certain diagnoses is due to speech disorders or lagging speech development as one of the leading symptoms of each of these diseases. At the present time the database includes 1.1 Tb of audio and video records collected from children (n = 278) and adults aged 20–46 years (n = 20) with mental retardation (with a mental age of 12 years). Audio recordings were carried out in a model situation and spontaneous interaction with adults. This database is designed to study the speech development in dysontogenesis. The paper reports two experiments on the speech material included in the database "AD-Child.Ru": (i) recognition by listeners of the words meaning of preschool typically developing (TD) children, children with autism spectrum disorders (ASD), and Down syndrome (DS); (ii) determination by the listeners of the child state "typical development – disorder". Our database can be the basis for scientific projects on the Russian language mastering in case of atypical development and can be used in the studies of automated child speech recognition system.

Keywords: Speech database · Atypically developing children ·
Perceptual analysis · Spectrographic analysis

1 Introduction

In recent years, one of the priority directions of the development of modern society has been the improvement of the quality of life of people with developmental disabilities and atypical development. The creation of alternative communication systems, human-computer interfaces, and training programs is associated with the need to obtain data on the peculiarities of speech development and communication skills of adults and, especially, children.

A prerequisite to the creation of such systems is the mastering of speech bases of children with atypical development and developmental disabilities. Automatic systems can provide complementary information that may be helpful for a clinician in the early screening of a voice disorder [1]. When creating child's speech databases, it is necessary to take into account the specificity of children's speech determined by the age of

© Springer Nature Switzerland AG 2019
A. A. Salah et al. (Eds.): SPECOM 2019, LNAI 11658, pp. 299–308, 2019.
https://doi.org/10.1007/978-3-030-26061-3_31

the child, the formation of articulatory patterns and the methods of annotating and analysis of speech [2, 3]. Such databases are usually compiled for specific purposes. These databases contain speech material of children specific for a single disease and the database is collected for a specific goal, as a rule. There are speech databases of children with Specific Language Impairment (SLI) [4], 5–12 year old Chinese children with cleft palate [5]. There are two databases created in 2016 on Czech language material and containing the speech of typically developing children (TD) and children with SLI [6]. The database [7] on American English material contains the speech of 19 patients with cerebral palsy. "TalkBank" includes records of the speech of children with speech pathology. They are presented by the speech of patients with autism spectrum disorders (ASD) (20 records of patients with Asperger syndrome in Spanish) and the speech of patients with Down syndrome (DS) (in English and Danish). "Autism Spectrum Database, UK" [8] collects the information about ASD people living in Great Britain and includes their speech materials. These databases vary depending on availability. Such speech bases are absent in Russian children with various specific diagnoses, accompanied by speech disorders.

The goals of our current work are the collection of speech material of 4–16 year old Russian children with atypical development and developmental disabilities, the formation of database and an analysis of these data for studies of speech development in dysontogenesis.

2 Speech Database for Children with Atypical Development

2.1 Data Collection

The database "AD-Child.Ru" contains speech material of children and adults with atypical development: ASD, DS, Cerebral palsy (CP), developmental disorders (DD), Light neurological violations (LNV), Intellectual disabilities, mental retardation (ID), and TD (control) (Table 1). The choice of informants with certain diagnoses is due to speech disorders at different levels of the organization or lagging speech development as one of the leading symptoms of each of these diseases. The diagnoses for children were established by specialists – psychiatrists, neuropathologists, and pediatricians. When the leading diagnosis was in doubt, an additional examination was conducted with the involvement of interdisciplinary team. The children selected for the study were tested using standardized scales and questionnaires. The recordings of informants' speech material were made in kindergarten, at school, in the laboratory, orphanage, at home, day care center, and Child center. The situation of spontaneous interaction between children and the researcher, model situations applied early were used: dialogue with the researcher or parents (the child answered to the set of questions), repetition of the words pronounced by an adult, play with the set of toys, picture description, retelling of the story (monologue), reading a book (Table 2). The difficulties of the collection of speech materials are described in our previous paper [9]. The total duration of recording was 20–40 min each, duration of model situation was 5-15 min.

The recording for every child was made from three to ten times. Speech of adults with intellectual disabilities (mental age up to 12 years) was recorded using the model situations of interaction with the researcher used for children. The records were made by the digital recorder "Marantz PMD660" with external microphone "SENNHEIZER e835S" and video camera "SONY HDR-CX560E". Speech files were stored in Windows PCM format WAV, 44.100 Hz, 16 bits per sample; video files were in AVI format. Every record is accompanied by a detailed protocol and video recording of child's behavior in parallel.

Table 1. Diagnosis, gender, and age of informants.

Diagnosis*	Place of speech record	Age, year	Number of children	Gender	
				m	f
Autism spectrum disorders (F 84)	Laboratory	4–16	39**	31	8
	Special school	8–11	13	11	2
	Kindergarten	4–7	20	18	2
	Medical center	3–11	21	16	5
	Home	6–12	3	3	
Down syndrome (Q 90)	Orphanage	5–7	4	4	
	Child Center	4–16	20	9	11
Cerebral palsy (G 80)	Laboratory	4–7	6	3	3
Developmental disorders (F 83)	Orphanage	4–9	25	19	6
	Kindergarten	6–7	10	7	3
	Medical Center	3–11	5	5	
Intellectual disabilities, mental retardation (F 70, 71)	Orphanage	4–11	20	11	9
	Day care center	20–46	20	11	9
Light neurological violations (F80, 90)	Orphanage	4–10	12	6	6
Typical development (control)	School	15–16	46	18	28
	Kindergarten	5–6	34	17	17

* Diagnosis according ICD-10
** Longitudinal data

At the present time the database "AD-Child.Ru" includes 1.1 Tb of audio and video records collected from 4–16 year old children (n = 198) with atypical development, 5–16 year old TD children (n = 80, control), and adults (n = 20) with mental retardation. The database "AD-Child.Ru" contains speech material for children living not only in St. Petersburg, but also from other regions of the Russian Federation who speak

Russian. This is a specificity of the new speech database from our previous databases [10]. This will allow to analyze the features of pronunciation and to identify speech signs that are specific for the disease. Another specificity of the new database is the inclusion of long original files (10–15 min), which contain the speech of the experimenter, parents, and sometimes other children.

All long original speech files are annotated by age, gender and the type of disorders of the child. So far, about 10% of the data are annotated for emotional states "comfort – neutral – discomfort".

All procedures were approved by the Health and Human Research Ethics Committee (St. Petersburg State University). The informed consent was written by the parents of the child participant and by the adult informants.

2.2 Database Structure

The "AD-Child.Ru" database is an organizational tool that provides streamlined access to storing and searching the child's audio recordings and the documentation of the audio recording. The database consists of aggregated binary files which managed by Microsoft SQL Server. Data can be added, modified, and deleted by the user only through the application interface. The database structure is presented in Fig. 1.

Database Management Access Application. The interface of application contains two blocks. The interface of the block-1 has access to the management of the following audio recordings:

The main catalog includes audio records of child's speech in accordance with the leading diagnosis of the child (ASD, Down syndrome, neurological disorders, mental retardation, mixed specific developmental disorders, norm, etc.) Subdirectories of the main catalog are data for each child, which include age, record situation (dialogue, playing with a standard set of toys, repetition, talking about the picture, picture description, the natural interaction of the child with the parents). For each child, there is information about the child's name, gender, date of birth, birth number in the family, place of birth, diagnosis, and information about parents. For each record, there is information about the place of recording and the equipment used.

The interface of block-2 has access to the management of audio and video recordings of child's articulatory movements during utterance special speech samples (repeated words). The interface of the block 2 is similar to the interface of the block 1.

The repeated words were chosen taking into account: (a) the minimum effect of co-articulation (vowels /a/, /i/ and /u/ after the following consonants: /k/ and /d/ for /a/, /b/ and /g/ for /u/, /t'/ for /i/); (b) words with stressed cardinal vowels /a/, /i/ and /u/.

The application contains search fields and filters that allow the user to extract data based on the type of the disease, the age of the child, the recording situation. Additional filters make it possible to select data based on all available metadata: the child's family number, the information about parents, the equipment used during recordings, etc. The application is written in C # language.

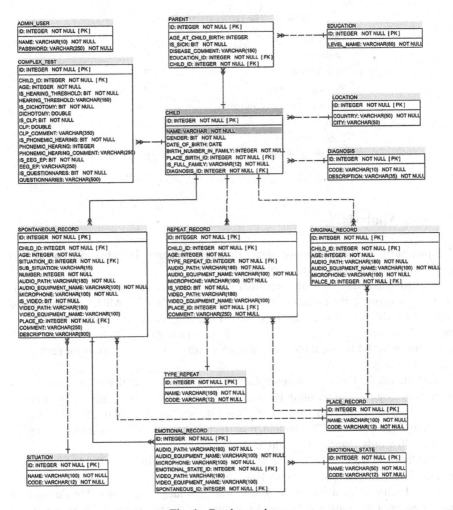

Fig. 1. Database schema.

Audio and video files are stored separately in the computer's file system and their file names are generated by the application. The following designation is used to indicate the recording situation (Table 2), type of disease, the gender of the child, and the emotional state. Identification of child's gender: m – male, f – female. In annotating the emotional state into three categories, abbreviations were used: comfort – C, neutral – N, discomfort – D. At this stage of work, the annotation on a greater number of emotional states was not made.

The file name contains next information about the child <type of disorders> <name or ID number> <age> <gender> <the recording situation> <emotional state>.

Table 2. The recording situations.

Original file (long)	L
Dialogue	D
Play with toys	P
Picture description	PD
Retelling (story or movie)	SR
Reading	BR
Spontaneous speech	S
Repetition words	R
Interactions with parents (experimenter)	IP (IE)

3   Data Analysis

We presented two experimental data. Both experiments included perceptual and spectrographic analysis of preschool child's speech.

Experiment-1: The aim of perceptual study-1 was to reveal the listeners' possibilities to recognize the meaning of 6–7 year old child's (TD, ASD, DS) words and presence or absence of disease via speech. Four test sequences were made: three – include 25 words in each test for TD (n = 5), ASD (n = 5) and DS (n = 5) children (5 words for each child); one mixed test (n = 45 words) contained 3 words for each child from the three tests.

Experiment-2: The aim of perceptual study-2 was to reveal the listeners' possibilities to recognize the meaning of child's (TD and ASD) words, age and gender via speech. Two test sequences were formed from the speech material of 20 children aged from 4 to 7 years (n = 10 TD children, n = 10 children with ASD). Every test sequence includes 30 words uttered by children.

The listeners were 90 adults (age 18.8 ± 1.6 y) in experiment-1. The test sequences in experiment-2 were presented to 100 adults (age – 19.7 ± 4.2 y) for perceptual analysis. Each speech signal in the 5 tests was presented three times. The duration of pauses between the same words was 3 s, between different words – 5 s. In the mixed test, the words were presented once with an interval of 3 s. We calculated the percentage of listeners' answers correctly recognized the meaning of child's words (with the perception rate 0–0.25 meaning not recognized; with rate 0.75–1.0 recognized) and recognition accuracy of the child's state via speech.

Spectrographic analysis of speech samples from two perceptual experiments was carried out in "Cool Edit Pro" sound editor. Pitch and duration of words and vowels were automatically calculated, based on the algorithms implemented in "Cool Edit Pro" sound editor. The waveform view was used to calculate duration of words, stressed and unstressed vowels in the word, and the spectral view was used to measure the pitch and formants.

4   Experimental Results

4.1   Experiment 1. Word's Meaning and State (Normally Development or Disorder) Recognition by Listeners via Speech of TD Children and Children with ASD and DS

Listeners correctly recognized the meaning of words of TD children (the recognition accuracy was 40%), of children with ASD (32%) and children with DS (24%).

The words of TD children whose meaning is recognized by listeners (range 0.75–1.0) have a longer duration ($p < 0.05$ – Mann – Whitney U test) than unrecognized words (range 0–0.25), the words of children with ASD have a longer duration ($p < 0.05$) than the words of children with DS. Words, stressed vowels (and their stationary parts) in the words of children with ASD and DS, the meaning of which is recognized correctly (0.75–1.0), are characterized by higher pitch values ($p < 0.05$) than the words of TD children. Unrecognized words (0–0.25) are characterized by a longer duration of stressed vowels ($p < 0.001$ for children with ASD, $p < 0.01$ for children with DS) in words compared to the corresponding features of TD child's words.

Listeners better recognized the state (norm) of TD children by speech samples (92%) and disorder for children with DS (70%). Only 54% of speech samples of children with ASD were correctly classified as speech signals belonging to children with disorder (Table 3).

Table 3. Confusion matrices for TD children, ASD children and children with DS state prediction – typical development or disorder.

Groups	State	
	Typical development	Disorder
TD	**92**	8
ASD	46	**54**
DS	30	**70**

The words of children with DS correctly defined as belonging to children with developmental disorder are characterized by a longer duration of stressed vowels ($p < 0.05$), the words of children with ASD – by higher pitch ($p < 0.05$) vs. the corresponding features of the words incorrectly classified as belonging to TD children.

4.2   Experiment 2. Word's Meaning, Age, and Gender of TD and ASD Children Recognition by Listeners

Listeners correctly recognized the meaning of 65.8% words of TD children and 44.8% words of ASD children. The listeners' experience of interaction with children is a predictor of the correct recognition of the meaning of words of ASD children $F(3,34) = 1.763$ $p < 0.02$ ($R^2 = 0.128$ Beta = 0.431) – Multiple regression analysis. Children with ASD, the meaning of which words was recognized by listeners, had 31 ± 4 points on the Child Autism Rating Scale (CARS) [11], children whose words were not recognized −34.4 ± 5.3 points. Words recognized by listeners with a range of 0.75–1.0 are characterized by a longer duration (p < 0.05) – for TD children and (p < 0.01) – for ASD children vs. words with an unrecognized meaning (range 0–0.25) (Fig. 2 A). The pitch values of stressed vowels and stationary parts of stressed vowels in the unrecognized words are higher (p < 0.001 – for ASD children, p < 0.05 – for TD children) vs. corresponding parameters in the recognized words (Fig. 2B).

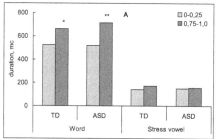 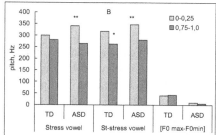

Fig. 2. The duration of words and stressed vowels (A), pitch values of stressed vowels, pitch values of stressed vowels in the stationary part and variation of pitch (B) in words recognized by listeners with range 0–0.25 and 0.75–1.0. Vertical axis – duration, ms (A), pitch values, Hz (B); * p < 0.05, ** p < 0.01 – Mann-Whitney U test.

The age of 6–7 years of TD children was defined by the listeners as real, the age of 4 and 5 years was higher for TD children than real, for children with ASD – the age was determined lower than real. Listeners attributed more voices of girls to boys' voices (Fig. 3).

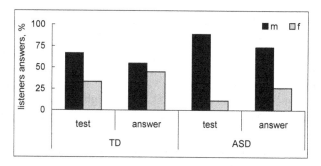

Fig. 3. Boy's and girl's speech samples in test sequences and speech samples perceived by listeners as male and female. Vertical axis – listeners' answers, %.

5 Discussion

Creating the database "AD-Child.Ru" is the main result of our work. Database structure is traditional for speech bases. Original approach is collection and presentation of speech material of children with various diagnoses, accompanied by speech disorders.

We select speech of children with different types of psychiatric or neurological diagnosis: ASD, DS, mixed specific developmental disorders, mental retardation – intellectual disabilities, cerebral palsy. ASD is characterized by impairments in language and emotional cognition. Multiple symptomatology of disorders, combined into an "autistic triad", include a violation of social behavior and speech, limited forms of behavior and stereotypes [12]. DS is one of chromosomal abnormalities. Children with DS have specificity of the vocal tract structure - a smaller volume of the oral and nasal cavities, lowering of the lower jaw, a narrow palate, and shorter length of the vocal tract vs. TD children. The specificity of children and adults with DS is a large folded tongue and muscular hypotonia [13]. It is shown that in children with DS the deficit of verbal skills is maintained and strengthened with child's age [14]. Mild and moderate mental retardation is intellectual disabilities that caused lower level of language development. Cerebral palsy is a group of neurological disorders affecting the development of movement and posture, often accompanied by disturbances of sensation, perception, cognition, behavior, and speech disorders are a consequence of motor disruption and fine motor skills. Light neurological violations include behavior, speech and emotional disorders. By analogy with the database [6] which contains speech material of informants with SLI given the severity of symptoms, we also take into account the severity of developmental disability according medical conclusion and the points of CARS for ASD children. However, we used a greater variety of recording situations than it is used to create specialized bases [for example, 4, 6], which allowed us to get a variety of speech material, including emotional speech. An analysis of the available literature in free access has shown the absence of speech databases for the emotional speech of informants with atypical development.

The paper presents the results of two experiments on the recognition by adults of information containing in child speech. The ability of listeners to determine the words meaning of TD children, children with DS, and children with ASD aged 6–7 years and the state of children "typical development – disorder" is shown. When recognizing the gender and age of TD children and children with ASD aged 4–7 years, listeners defined the age of children with ASD lower than real. Listeners attributed more voices of girls to boys' voices. The results of presented experiments correspond to our previous data [9].

The presented examples of using the database material to determine the meaning of words of children, gender, age, presence or absence of the disease by speech make it possible to widely use the created base "AD-Child.Ru" in psychophysiological research, clinical practice, at the research of automated child speech recognition system.

6   Conclusions

We introduced the "AD-Child.Ru" database containing speech material of children with atypical development and developmental disorders, designed to study the speech and Russian language mastering in dysontogenesis. The particularities of database are as follows: it includes child's speech material in a wide age range of 4–16 year old, with various diagnoses, accompanied by impaired speech. The results of the perceptual study of the speech of preschool TD children and children with ASD and DS are presented as the example of using of speech material annotation by age and disease.

Acknowledgements. The study is being performed with the financial support from the Russian Science Foundation (project № 18-18-00063).

References

1. Ali, Z., et al.: Intra- and inter-database study for Arabic, English, and German databases: do conventional speech features detect voice pathology? J. Voice **31**(1), 386.e1–386.e8 (2017)
2. Beckman, M.E., Plummer, A.R., Munson, B., Reidy, P.F.: Methods for eliciting, annotating, and analyzing databases for child speech development. Comput. Speech Lang. **45**, 278–299 (2017)
3. Lyakso, E., Frolova, O., Grigorev, A., Gorodnyi, V., Nikolaev, A., Matveev, Y.N.: Speech features of adults with autism spectrum disorders and mental retardation. In: Karpov, A., Jokisch, O., Potapova, R. (eds.) SPECOM 2018. LNCS (LNAI), vol. 11096, pp. 357–366. Springer, Cham (2018). https://doi.org/10.1007/978-3-319-99579-3_38
4. Tomblin, J.B.: The EpiSLI database: a publicly available database on speech and language. Lang. Speech Hear. Serv. Sch. **41**(1), 108–117 (2010)
5. He, L., Zhang, J., Liu, Q., Yin, H., Lech, M., Huang, Y.: Automatic evaluation of hypernasality based on a cleft palate speech database. J. Med. Syst. **39**(5), 61 (2015)
6. Grill, P., Tučková, J.: Speech databases of typical children and children with SLI. PLoS One **11**(3), e0150365 (2016)
7. Kim, H., et al.: Dysarthric speech database for universal access research. In: INTERSPEECH-2008, Brisbane, Australia, pp. 1741–1744 (2008)
8. Autism Spectrum Database – UK. http://www.asd-uk.com. Accessed 12 Apr 2019
9. Lyakso, E., Frolova, O., Karpov, A.: A new method for collection and annotation of speech data of atypically developing children. In: Proceedings of 2018 International IEEE Conference on Sensor Networks and Signal Processing (SNSP 2018), Xi'an, China, pp. 175–180 (2018)
10. Lyakso, E., Frolova, O., Kurazhova, A., Gaikova, J.: Russian infants and children's sounds and speech corpora for language acquisition studies. In: INTERSPEECH-2010, Makuhari, Japan, pp. 1981–1988 (2010)
11. Schopler, E., Reichler, R.J., De Vellis, R.F., Daly, K.: Toward objective classification of childhood autism: Childhood Autism Rating Scale (CARS). J. Autism Dev. Disord. **10**(1), 91–103 (1980)
12. Kanner, L.: Autistic disturbances of affective contact. Nerv. Child **2**, 217–250 (1943)
13. Markaki, M., Stylianou, Y.: Voice pathology detection and discrimination based on modulation spectral features. IEEE Trans. Audio Speech Lang. Process. **19**(7), 1938–1948 (2011)
14. Dodd, B., Thompson, L.: Speech disorder in children with Down's syndrome. J. Intellect. Disabil. Res. **45**(4), 308–316 (2001)

Building a Pronunciation Dictionary
for the Kabyle Language

Demri Lyes$^{(\boxtimes)}$ ⓘ, Falek Leila ⓘ, and Teffahi Hocine ⓘ

Laboratoire de Communication Parlée et de Traitement du Signal,
Faculté d'Electronique et d'Informatique,
Université des Sciences et de la Technologie Houari Boumediene,
El Alia 32, 16111 Algiers, Algeria
ldemri1987@hotmail.fr, lfalek@hotmail.fr,
hteffahi@gmail.com

Abstract. This paper presents the methods used and results obtained for the creation of a Festival-compatible pronunciation dictionary of above 10k words for the kabyle language. Kabyle is a berber dialect spoken in Northern Algeria. This dictionary will be useful in the design of text-to-speech and automatic speech recognition systems for the kabyle language. It was built using a bootstrapping method in which we incrementally build rules to predict word pronunciations while correcting wrong predictions. We thus obtain a large pronunciation dictionary as well as a set of rules to predict pronunciations for unknown words. The rules are embedded in Classification and Regression Trees and achieve 91,62% of correct prediction rate for entire words and 97,85% for phonemes.

Keywords: Text-to-speech synthesis · Automatic speech recognition · Pronunciation lexicon · Bootstrapping · Classification and Regression Trees · Letter-to-sound rules

1 Introduction

Kabyle is a berber dialect spoken in the North of Algeria by approximately 5 to 7 million people. It is the most spoken berber dialect after Tashelhit which is spoken in Morocco [1]. Kabyle texts can be found in latin or tifinagh characters. The use of latin characters to transcribe Kabyle was originated by M. Mammeri and is thus also called "Tammammerit", whereas Tifinagh is the original alphabet for the Berber language but its inclusion in the Unicode system is relatively recent [2].

Speech synthesis and recognition have been growing and improving since the second half of the 20th century. Current trends are now shifting to the use of deep learning, specifically deep neural networks for the development of speech synthesis and recognition systems. The introduction of deep learning has allowed an improvement in recognition rates for speech recognition and naturalness in speech synthesis. Both technologies however are dependent upon the availability of linguistic resources such as pronunciation dictionaries, part-of-speech taggers and morphological analyzers.

© Springer Nature Switzerland AG 2019
A. A. Salah et al. (Eds.): SPECOM 2019, LNAI 11658, pp. 309–316, 2019.
https://doi.org/10.1007/978-3-030-26061-3_32

The challenge in building speech synthesizers and recognizers for under-resourced languages is therefore to provide such resources to allow the alignment of acoustic features from a given speech audio file to the corresponding phonemes, syllables, and parts of speech.

Methods to assist the construction of such resources have been investigated since the advent of computers with sufficient processing power. One such method is known as bootstrapping and consists in incrementally adding words into an originally small set of manually annotated words. It was originally presented in [3], based on [4], as a method to rapidly provide pronunciation dictionaries for new languages.

Recent trends in the field of Grapheme to Phoneme conversion have introduced newer methods in the learning and prediction scheme [5–7]. However, these approaches focus on predicting pronunciations for unseen words without developing a new lexicon. In [8] and [9], HMMs are used in order to derive phonemes automatically from audio speech data before aligning these phonemes to the corresponding graphemes in the orthographic words. The method is ultimately used to develop a lexicon, however it requires more resources (acoustic speech), has higher complexity, and the integration of the lexicon in the Festival speech synthesis system is not straightforward. For all these reasons, we preferred the use of the bootstrapping approach described in [3], which is well documented [10] and leads us closer to our objectives.

The aim of this work is threefold: (a) to provide a new pronunciation lexicon for the Kabyle language in order to help TTS and ASR research for the kabyle language; (b) to evaluate the efficacy of the bootstrapping approach in terms of efficacy and precision for the Kabyle language; and (c) to enrich the Festival speech synthesis system with an under-resourced language.

2 Methodology

Figure 1 shows the various steps in building the pronunciation lexicon. In this section we will present the text corpus used for the study and detail each of these steps.

2.1 Text Corpus

The text was gathered from various websites on the internet. It consists of kabyle song lyrics, wikipedia articles, and a kabyle translation of the New Testament in the latin writing system. This choice was made because texts in the Tifinagh alphabet are less common. Audio recordings of the kabyle New Testament can be found online, and the same can be said for the songs. We have benefited from this in order to disambiguate difficult words. Foreign words were suppressed from the corpus as much as possible. All of the text was copied into a single text file which consisted of approximately 200000 tokens.

2.2 Phone Set

In order for the bootstrapping method to work, it is necessary to define the possible combinations of letters and phonemes in the language for which the lexicon is to be

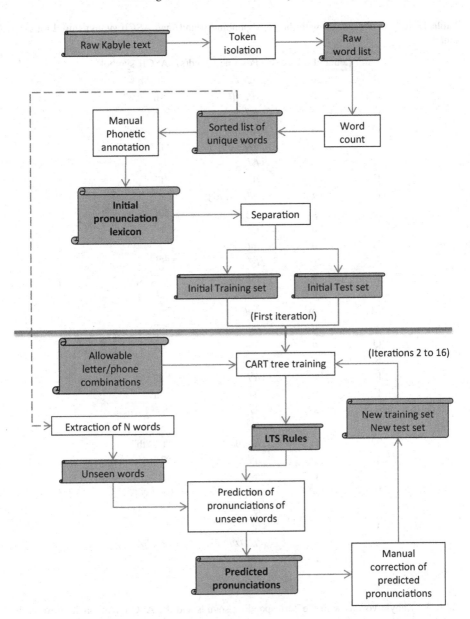

Fig. 1. Lexicon building steps. Steps above the bold red line are performed only for the first iteration. The new training and test sets comprise all the previous sets plus a number of new unseen words. Bold letters indicate an output (result) of the algorithm.

built. Tables 1 and 2 give the possible phonemes in IPA notation as well as in the ASCII notation we used for each letter found in the Kabyle alphabet. Table 1 is for consonants and Table 2 is for vowels. For words which contained letters not found in these tables, either the non-existent letter was replaced, or the entire word was discarded.

Table 1. Kabyle consonants with the corresponding sounds and ASCII symbols used for each sound

Latin Letter	Lowercase	Possible sound(s)	ASCII symbols
B	b	/b//β/	"b" "b~"
C	c	/ʃ/, /tʃ/	"sh" "ch"
Č	č	/tʃ/	"ch"
D	d	/d/, /ð/	"d", "dh"
Ḍ	ḍ	/dˤ/, /ðˤ/	"D", "DH"
Ɛ	ɛ	/ʕ/	"3"
F	f	/f/	"f"
G	g	/g/, /ʒ/, /dʒ/	"g", "j", "dj"
Ǧ	ǧ	/dʒ/	"dj"
H	h	/h/	"h"
Ḥ	ḥ	/ħ/	"7"
J	j	/ʒ/	"j"
K	k	/k/, /q/	"k", "q"
L	l	/l/	"l"
M	m	/m/	"m"
N	n	/n/	"n"
Q	q	/q/	"q"
R	r	/r/	"r"
Ṛ	ṛ	/rˤ/	"R"
Γ	γ	/ʁ/	"gh"
S	s	/s/	"s"
Ṣ	ṣ	/sˤ/	"S"
T	t	/t/, /θ/	"t", "th"
Ṭ	ṭ	/tˤ/	"T"
Ŧ	ŧ	/ts/	"ts"
W	w	/w/	"w"
X	x	/χ/	"x"
Y	y	/j/	"y"
Z	z	/z/, /zˤ/	"z", "Z"
Ẓ	ẓ	/zˤ/	"Z"

Table 2. Kabyle vowels with the corresponding sounds and the ASCII symbols used for each sound

Latin letter	Lowercase	Possible sound(s)	ASCII symbols
A	a	/a/, /ə/	"a" "e"
E	e	/ə/, /a/, /u/	"e" "a" "u"
I	i	/i/	"i"
O	o	/u/	"u"
U	u	/u/, /ə/	"u" "e"

2.3   Algorithm

Step 1: Corpus Cleaning. This step was performed to remove all punctuation signs, numbers, and other symbols. The goal was to leave only words into the lexicon and to train the letter to sound rules.

Step 2: Word Isolation, Counting and Sorting. The words in the "cleaned" corpus were then isolated to constitute a (redundant) list of all the words in the corpus. Each word might appear several times in this first list. The appearance of each word in the list was then counted and the words were sorted in descending order of appearance to form a list of approximately 10000 unique words.

Step 3: Annotation. We then manually annotate (i.e. provide pronunciations for) the first 350 words of the list of unique words (i.e. the 350 most frequent words in the text corpus). The pronunciation of uncertain words was disambiguated by listening to the audio recording of that word from the source to which it belonged.

Step 4: CART Tree Building. The list of annotated words is then used to build letter-to-sound rules based on CART trees. The words are first separated into a set of 90% words for training and 10% words for testing. As suggested in [10] every tenth word in the test list is taken for the test set instead of taking the last 10% of words in the list because the unique words list is sorted in frequency order. The percentage of correctly predicted phonemes and correctly predicted words at this step is sampled.

Step 5: Generation of Pronunciations for a New Set of Unseen Words. We then extract a number N of new unseen words from the list of unique words and use the letter-to-sound rules embedded into the trained CART trees to predict pronunciations from them for these words.

Step 6: Manual Verification and Lexicon Enrichment. The pronunciations generated by the CART trees are then verified to correct potential errors in predicted phonemes and the correctly annotated words are added to the previous set of words in order to build better letter-to-sound rules. It was suggested that an algorithm based on n-grams should automatically compute confidence scores for the predicted pronunciations in order to save time and effort during this process. We therefore implemented the algorithms for the computation as described in [11] and [12] (based on [13]), however it seemed that the confidences scores were often high for erroneous pronunciations and low for correct pronunciations. We therefore preferred to manually verify every single word regardless of the confidence score. This choice was also made in [14], probably for similar reasons.

The process hereby described (steps 4 to 6) was repeated until iteration 16 after which the lexicon comprises 11250 words. For the first 10 iterations, the number N of unseen words was equal to 100. Afterwards, we increased the value of N to 250, 500, 750, 1000, and the 5000.

3 Results

Figure 2 shows the rates of correctly predicted phonemes and words. The overall shape is similar to that in [3], but the correct prediction rates are slightly lower.

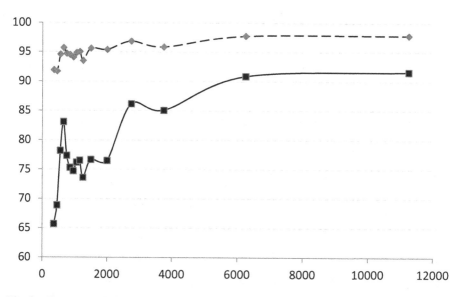

Fig. 2. Correct prediction rates in function of the number of words. Dashed line: Correct phones. Solid line: Correct words.

It can be seen that the final rate of correct prediction for entire words is above 90% (precisely 91,62%). This corresponds to a training set of 10125 words and a testing set of 1125 words. The LTS rules are embedded in a tree with 668 nodes.

It is interesting that although the global shape is about the same as the one in [3], there is a large peak in at the 4th iteration, but the rate drops back to about 75% for the next few iterations. This might be explained by the relative low frequency of occurrence of certain letters relative to others. For the first few iterations, some letters might not have appeared enough times for rules to be generated for them. After these few iterations, the system might be presented with new letters for which it doesn't have any rule, and therefore the rate drops back down for a few iterations. After enough examples are added, the system can correctly form rules for every word in the Kabyle script.

Analysis of the errors made by the system shows that the majority of errors are due to spirantization, which is the development of stops into fricatives (cf. [1], p. 466). Another kind of error consists in phoneme doubling, i.e. when there is a pair of the same letters, only the first should generate a phoneme. For example, the correct pronunciation for the word "beccer" is /b e sh e r/ and not /b e sh sh e r/. These errors are not too consequential phonetically speaking and most often do not alter the meaning of the words.

About 15% of the other errors consist of omissions of phonemes. Depending on the omitted phoneme, the error can have rather severe phonetic consequences. However, this ultimately happens about 1% of the time.

4   Conclusion

This work has provided a new phonetic lexicon of more than 10k words for the kabyle language. The lexicon is accompanied with letter-to-sound rules for words not existing in the lexicon. The letter-to-sound rules achieve above 90% accuracy for unseen words, with most errors having little phonetic impact. Efforts will be made to provide this lexicon as a readily available Festival module.

The use of a biblical text as a major part of our text corpus means that a lot of modern words and names might be lacking. This can be improved by including more words from news articles.

It might also be interesting to compare the bootstrapping algorithm with other approaches for pronunciation prediction. It has been shown that the approach provides reasonable results, provided that we manually check every predicted pronunciation at each step, which is time consuming and tiresome. Unfortunately, the use of a confidence metric hasn't proven reliable enough.

For a speech synthesis system to effectively use this lexicon, it is also necessary to know the stress patterns in the kabyle words. There doesn't seem to be a consensus on the question of whether berber languages exhibit lexical stress, as can be seen by comparing [15] and [16].

Finally, it is tempting to produce a similar lexicon and rules for the Tifinagh alphabet, which is becoming more commonly used as time goes on.

References

1. Kossmann, M.G., Stroomer, H.J.: Phonologies of Asia and Africa, 1st edn. Eisenbrauns, Winona Lake (1997)
2. The Unicode Consortium: The Unicode Standard, Version 4.1.0, defined by: The Unicode Standard, Version 4.0, as amended by Unicode 4.0.1 and by Unicode 4.1.0. Addison-Wesley, Boston (2003)
3. Maskey, S.R., Black, A.W., Tomokiyo, L.M.: Bootstrapping phonetic lexicons for new languages. In: International Conference on Speech and Language Processing 2004, pp. 69–72. ISCA, Jeju Island (2004)
4. Black, A., Lenzi, K., Pagel, V.: Issues in building general letter to sound rules. In: 3rd ESCA Workshop on Speech Synthesis, pp. 77–80. Jenolan Caves, Australia (2004)
5. Davel, M., Barnard, E.: Pronunciation prediction with default&refine. Comput. Speech Lang. 22(4), 374–393 (2008)
6. Bisani, M., Hermann, N.: Joint-sequence models for grapheme-to-phoneme conversion. Speech Commun. 50(5), 434–451 (2008)
7. Jyothi, P., Hasegawa-Johnson, M.: Low-resource grapheme-to-phoneme conversion using recurrent neural networks. In: 2017 IEEE International Conference on Acoustics, Speech and Signal Processing (ICASSP). IEEE, New Orleans (2017)

8. Razavi, M., Rasipuram, R., Doss, M.M.: Pronunciation lexicon development for under-resourced languages using automatically derived subword units: a case study on Scottish Gaelic. In: Proceedings of 4th Biennial Workshop on Less-Resourced Languages, pp. 1–2. Society for Language Resources and Technology, Poznan (2015)

9. Razavi, M., Rasipuram, R., Doss, M.M.: Towards weakly supervised acoustic subword unit discovery and lexicon development using hidden Markov models. Speech Commun. **96**, 168–183 (2018)

10. The Festival Speech Synthesis System System Documentation. http://www.festvox.org/docs/manual-2.4.0/festival_toc.html. Accessed 31 Mar 2019

11. Inkpen, D., Frunza, O., Kondrak, G: Automatic identification of cognates and false friends in French and English. In: Proceedings of the International Conference Recent Advances in Natural Language Processing, pp. 251–257. Bulgarian Academy of Sciences, Borovets (2005)

12. Montalvo, S., Pardo, E.G., Martinez, R., Fresno, V..: Automatic cognate identification based on a fuzzy combination of string similarity measures. In: 2012 IEEE International Conference on Fuzzy Systems. IEEE, Brisbane (2012)

13. Brew, C., McKelvie, D.: Word-pair extraction for lexicography. In: Oflazer, K., Somers, H. (eds.) Proceedings of the 2nd International Conference on New Methods in Language Processing, Ankara, Bilkent University, pp. 45–55 (1996)

14. Davel Marelie, H.: Pronunciation Modelling and Bootstrapping. (Thesis), University of Pretoria, p. 99 (2005)

15. Faizi, R.: Stress systems in Amazigh: a comparative study. Revue Asinag **6**, 115–127 (2011)

16. Roettger, T.B., Bruggeman, A., Grice, M.: Word stress in Tashlhiyt-Post lexical prominence in disguise? In: Proceedings of 18th International Congress on Phonetic Sciences. International Phonetic Association, London/Glasgow (2015)

Speech-Based Automatic Assessment of Question Making Skill in L2 Language

Eman Mansour, Rand Sandouka, Dima Jaber, and Abualsoud Hanani[✉]

Birzeit University, Birzeit, Palestine
ahanani@birzeit.edu
http://www.birzeit.edu

Abstract. In this paper, we present a spoken educational system to automatically assess Arabic-native children's skill in forming English questions for different presented prompts. These prompts consist of images with a sentence that includes the answer to the required question. The answer key is colored to indicate what to ask. The main methodology of the proposed system is to record the spoken response of the child and pass it through state-of-the-art ASR to convert it into text. The output transcription is passed through three pipelined subsystems; Wh-question word checker, English grammar checker, which returns the number of grammar errors in the given question, and machine learning based grammar/language checker. The student response is accepted only if it is accepted by the three subsystems. The system was trained on 650 recorded responses made by 60 students (5th to 8th grades) as response to 75 different prompts. The number of grammar errors produced by the English grammar checker, best cosine similarity, best edit distance and best Jaccard distance between student response and the corresponding reference possible responses, are used to train KNN and SVM models with different parameters. The best precision, recall, f-measure and accuracy were achieved by SVM with linear kernel and degree of 2, 91%, 88%, 89% and 89%, respectively.

Keywords: Speech recognition · Human-computer interaction · Computational paralinguistics

1 Introduction

Information technology is entwined in almost every part of our culture. It affects how we live, work, play and most importantly learn. It has been widely used in education. Using information technology in education facilitates learning to improve the productivity and performance. Language processing is a very vital field in these days for learning and education in general and particularly, for language learning. Language processing can be divided into natural language processing which concerns in processing languages in text form, and speech processing which concerns in processing spoken languages. Our graduation project

© Springer Nature Switzerland AG 2019
A. A. Salah et al. (Eds.): SPECOM 2019, LNAI 11658, pp. 317–326, 2019.
https://doi.org/10.1007/978-3-030-26061-3_33

uses both natural language processing and spoken language processing for building a computer system, which can assess the skills of making questions in foreign language correctly in terms of grammar and language meaning. In our case, we target Arabic native students who learn English as a second language. We focus on children aged from 11–14 years (i.e. 5th grade to 8th grade). In this paper, students get a prompt for asking a question verbally in English. The prompt compromises of text sentence, pictures, drawings, or combinations of all of them. Student should make a suitable question, in English, as a response to the given prompt. Student should pronounce the question loudly to the system. The system records the student response and assesses it grammatically and linguistically, then provide him/her with a feedback about the correctness of the made question. In addition to correct/incorrect, the feedback may include the mistake and the correct question forms. This system can be implemented as a mobile phone application or a web application, which is accessible from everywhere and at any time.

2   Related Works

Many studies have been published on the topic of Automatic Speech Recognition (ASR) for children and use it in building learning systems, such as questions and reading assessments. The ASR is considered the core of any speech processing application and it is used in many applications [8]. The ASR is usually trained on a huge speech data, mainly adult speakers. Since children voice is quite different than adults voice, the state-of-the-art ASR works better for adults and quite poor for children [10]. This makes it challenging for developing speech-based application dedicated for children. A study in [1] targeted this and proposed a methodology for improving the performance of speech recognition for children speakers and reducing acoustic mismatch between children and adult acoustic spaces. The ASR feature extraction stage is difficult for children voices since the fundamental frequency and the formants bandwidths are of comparable magnitude. However, children are shown to be less skilled in coarticulation, display longer duration and they tend to exaggerate newly mastered skills. This signifies that simpler acoustic models can be used for certain ASR tasks. The normalization procedures and age-dependent acoustic models were used to reduce variability (that was a major hurdle in building high performance ASR applications for children), mismatch and increase resolution between classes. Various experiments have been made showing word accuracy vs. speaker's age using HMMs trained from children and adult speakers before and after the speaker normalization algorithm is applied [9]. The techniques of normalization and age-dependent (linear, bi-parametric and phoneme-dependent frequency wrapping functions) improved recognition performance up to 55% for children speakers [9]. Wilson in [14] focused on the skills needed for making question correctly by children, Particularly, in foreign language. She developed communicative competence in questions assessment. Forming questions in the correct form is a difficult skill for children specially in foreign language where semantic and syntactic subtleties are the key of learning this skill. QuestionQuest curriculum

[13] was designed to improve children's ability to comprehend, ask, and answer questions. It focuses on receptive language intervention that provides the essential input required to develop a lexicon, set parameters, and establish syntactic competence. The QuestionQuest curriculum is divided into three levels, each containing seven modules. Each module trains one to four question forms using 10 stimulus sets. The grammar of a language is composed of the lexicon (words) and the syntactic computational system (forms sentences from lexical items). The representation of a word in the lexicon includes phonological and semantic properties (i.e., sound and meaning), in addition to syntactic features such as categorical membership (e.g., whether it is a noun, verb, adjective, etc.). The lexicon is divided into two categories that are essential to the comprehension and production of sentences: 1. Lexical category that includes nouns, verbs and adjectives. 2. Functional category that consists of determiners (associated with nouns e.g., the), complementizers (are associated with clause e.g., if and whether) and tense (associated with verbs e.g., will and is). Wh-questions can be formed by subject questions that has no auxiliary verb and the word order is not changed, or object questions that involve overt Wh-movement and auxiliary inversion. According to a study in [3], children formed subject questions 63% of the time, whereas they correctly formed object questions just 49% of the time. The main conclusion is that using computer technology in learning offers many advantages to children who enjoy working with properly designed educational software whether in classrooms or at home. Research has shown that language intervention software improved language development and communication skills [7]. Recently, Magooda et al. in [5] used machine learning and syntactic and semantic features for building a computer system that assists language learning. It provides learners with informative feedback on their spoken response that helps them improving their language skills. It uses speech recognition system to generate a text transcription from spoken response. The designed system accepts or rejects the response based on the meaning and the language quality. Hence, some features were adopted, such as language and meaning related features in order to detect similarities between sentences. Where, n-gram model was used to accomplish the feature extraction.

A more recent work was published in children readings assessment [12]. This system supports teachers in children reading assessment process, by replacing the classical way (writing down the errors) with an automatic system that detects errors and measures the needed parameters in children reading.

For the assessment of reading speed, the time information provided by the ASR system was used, based on KALDI toolkit[1]. Furthermore, tri-phone acoustic Hidden Markov Model (HMM) was used for building acoustic models. According to this study, training dataset was gathered from 115 children. Each one reads 58 to 65 sentences. Different Language models (LM) were used to detect correctness assessment; pronunciation errors, truncation and substitutions of words). Data set was collected from 20 children to compute the performance of the system. The system score of the correctness of children's reading was compared the

---

[1] http://kaldi-asr.org.

one given by the teacher. The correlation between system scores and teacher's scores were used as a performance measure. Thus, two different references were used, the Ideal Reference Text (IRT) and the Manual Transcription Reference (MTR).

As we have seen in the literature, most of the related works are based on using ASR for converting speech into text. Therefore, the ASR accuracy has a significant impact on the systems accuracy. What makes this more challenging for our system is that users are young children (11–14 years old). Open source and commercial ASRs are usually trained on adult speech, therefore, they works better for adult speakers and poor for children. Researchers have targeted this issue. Gray et al. in [2], demonstrated a child ASR system using less amount of data in adapting linguistic and acoustic models of adult centric speech recognition. The obstacles that were presented about automatic speech recognition for children and the techniques for adapting a better ASR, such as normalization and age-dependent acoustic models. The child-adapted ASR was evaluated on 6.8 h of child's speech. It provided an average of 27.2% relative Word Error Rate (WER) improvement. The adult-centric models can be adapted to improve language and acoustic models' accuracy of children's ASR. It's also observed that the system performance is age-dependent (the older the child, the better the results).

3   System Description

This section describes our overall system. The block diagram in Fig. 1 illustrates the main components of our system, and how they are connected to each other. As shown in the diagram, the system takes the spoken response (question) made by children, and passes it to an English ASR to convert it to a text (transcription). The output text is feed into three pipelined blocks to evaluate the given text question in term of grammar and language. The first block is question tool checker, followed by an English grammar checker and language/grammar checker. Each one of that blocks checks if the child response has errors in term of grammar and language or not. If a block cannot detect any errors in the given question, the response passes to the next block. The response is accepted (i.e. identified as correct in terms of grammar and language meaning) if and only if none of these blocks detects any errors. The subsequent subsections includes more details about each component.

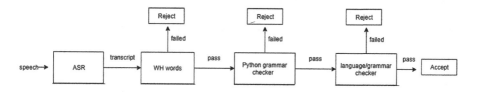

Fig. 1. Block diagram of the overall system

3.1   Speech Recognition System

The major component of the proposed system is the automatic speech recognizer (ASR) which takes the children spoken question and converts it into text. In our case, the system assesses the question making skills in English as a foreign language. Therefore, English ASR is needed. since there is no available children English ASR, general Google cloud English ASR[2] was used in all of our experiments. Google ASR incorporates the state-of-the-art system based on the powerful deep learning technology.

3.2   WH-Question Word Rule-Based Component

This component is a rule-based assessment subsystem. It simply checks the wh-question word in the given children response. If the used Wh-question word is correct and matches with the provided prompt, then the response is passed to the following component. On the other hand, if the wh-question word is wrong and doesn't match with the provided prompt, then the response is rejected and the provided question is counted as a wrong response. In order to do this, for each prompt, we defined a list of possible wh-question words that can be successfully used with that particular prompt. The wh-question word is extracted from the user response and then compared with all defined words for that prompt. If no one word matches the extracted word from the user response, then the provided response is rejected. In the case of yes/no question, the wh-question word is replaced by the auxiliary verbs which can be used for that particular prompt. By applying this rule only, the system accuracy is 83%.

3.3   Python English Grammar Checker

The user response enters an English grammar checker component. A free available Python implementation of English grammar checker[3] was used in our system. This toolkit returns the number of grammar errors. If the returned number is zero, it means that the input question does not have errors, hence, passes to the next stage. If the number is greater than zero, then the process is terminated and the system indicates that the given response contains errors, hence, rejected. By applying only this grammar checker toolkit, the system accuracy is 75%.

3.4   Machine Learning Based Grammar/Language Checker

The third component in our system is a machine learning based system which mainly depends on the extracted features from the user response of specific prompt and all of its corresponding possible responses provided for each prompt. The following four different features are extracted for each user response and used in the machine learning subsystem.

---

[2] https://cloud.google.com/speech-to-text/.
[3] https://pypi.python.org/pypi/grammar-check/1.3.1.

- feature extracted from the grammar checker: The number of grammar errors produced by the English grammar checker toolkit, described earlier, is used as a feature for the machine learning system.
- Cosine similarity feature: Cosine Similarity (CS) [4] is a commonly used app-roach to compute the similarities between two vectors of an inner product space. It is measured by the cosine of the angle between two vectors and determines whether they are pointing to the same direction or not. The user response (UR) and each of the reference responses are converted into a high dimensional vectors using bag-of-words model of all distinct terms occurred in the set of all possible responses (PR). Then, each vector is multiplied by a weighting vector $Tw = [Tw1, Tw2, ..., Twm]$, where m is the number of distinct terms and Twi is the weight of corresponding term Ti calculated as:

$$Twi = TFi * \frac{ni}{N} \qquad (1)$$

where, TFi is the frequency of a term Ti in response $ri \in UR$, PRi. N is the number of all reference responses, and ni is the number of possible responses containing term Ti. The Weighting vector in equation above puts more weight on the term that occurs more frequently in the corresponding possible responses. The maximum weighted cosine between the user response and each of the reference responses is used as a feature for the machine learn-ing system.
- Edit distance feature: Edit Distance (ED) [11] is a measure to qualify the simi-larity between two strings (user response and each of the reference responses) by counting the minimum number of operations required to transform the user response into each reference response, with the allowable edit operations: insertion, deletion, or substitution of a single word. The lower ED distance, the more similar the two strings. The minimum ED distance is used as a feature for the machine learning system.
- Jacard distance feature: Jaccard Distance (JD) [6] is a used to measure the dissimilarities between two strings or sets. It is calculated by subtracting the Jaccard index from 100%. Jaccard similarity index (JI) or the Jaccard similarity coefficient compares members of two sets to find out which members are shared and which are not. JI is calculated using the following equation:

$$J(A, B) = \frac{|A \cap B|}{|A \cup B|} \qquad (2)$$

$|A \cap B|$ refers to the number of shared terms between the two strings, and $|A \cup B|$ refers to the number of un-shared terms between the two responses. The higher the percentage, the more similar the two strings. After that, in order to find the JD distance, we subtract J(A, B) from 1, as in the following formula:

$$D(A, B) = 1 - J(A, B) \qquad (3)$$

The lower the Jaccard distance, the more similar the two strings. The mini-mum Jaccard distance is used as a feature for the machine learning system.

By this, each user response is represented by a 4-dimensional feature vector, as explained above. The feature vectors extracted from a set of correct (grammar and language) labeled responses and a set of incorrect labeled responses (training dataset) are used to train K Nearest Neighbor (KNN) and Support Vector Machines (SVM). Resulted models are used to evaluate new user responses (testing data set) by predicting the class label (correct vs. incorrect) of the testing responses. By applying the machine learning component only, the system accuracy is 86%.

4   Data Collection and Description

In order to build and evaluate our system, a data set of sufficient number of prompts and responses is needed. For this purpose, 65 prompts are carefully designed and verified by two English experts (English instructors at Birzeit university). In this study, we target children of age from 11 to 14 years old (i.e. 5th to 8th grade), whose native language is Arabic. Therefore, each prompt contains a graphic or a photo with English sentence and one word/phrase colored in red. Student needs to look at the prompt and response by asking a question verbally with the colored word/phrase is its answer. A sample of these prompts is shown in Fig. 2.

Tweety is my favorite cartoon character

Fig. 2. Sample of the prompts used in the data collection

In addition to the prompts, a set of reference possible responses (i.e. a set of correct questions forms) have been made and verified by the two English experts. Each prompt has different number of reference responses. The list below shows a set of ten possible responses for the prompt shown in Fig. 2.

1. Who is your favorite cartoon character?
2. Who is your favorite cartoon?
3. Which cartoon character is your favorite?
4. Which is your favorite cartoon character?
5. Which is your favorite cartoon?
6. Which cartoon is your favorite?

7. What is your favorite cartoon character?
8. What is your favorite cartoon?
9. What cartoon character is your favorite?
10. What cartoon is your favorite?

The designed prompts are displayed on a laptop screen to around 70 primary school students (5th grade to 8th grade) from four primary schools. Their spoken responses are recorded with a smart mobile phone in a quiet environment. By the end of this process, around 864 different responses were recorded (on average 12 responses for each student). All of the resulted responses are listened and evaluated by the two English experts and labeled as correct/incorrect grammatically and correct/incorrect in terms of language meaning. It is worth to mention here, that the experts discussed and agreed on one evaluation (correct/incorrect label) for the responses with disagreement. Our proposed system considers student response as correct if and only if it is correct in terms of both grammar and language meaning. The collected dataset is divided into two subsets; training set and testing set, as shown in Table 1.

Table 1. Collected data description.

subset	No of students	No of recordings	Percentage
Training	60	650	75.2
Testing	10	214	24.8

Some of the prompts were displayed to more than one student. Therefore, each prompt in the dataset has a unique id, recorded student response, user response evaluation (correct/incorrect) in terms of grammar and language meaning, and a set of reference possible responses.

5   Experiments and Results

As described earlier, the overall system consists of ASR followed by three components (or subsystems); wh-question word rule-based subsystem, English grammar checker rule-based sub-systems, and the grammar/language machine learning based subsystems. The response is considered as a correct if and only if passed the three subsystems. Any subsystem rejects the response, it is considered as incorrect response. Training data subset was used to extract four features for each response (recordings); number of grammar errors, best cosine similarity, edit distance and Jaccard distance between user response and the corresponding reference possible responses. These feature vectors with their correct/incorrect labels are used to train KNN and SVM binary classifiers, with different parameters, as shown in Table 2. The 214 recorded responses of the testing data subset was used to evaluate the overall system. The system performance is represented

Table 2. Results of the overall system.

Machine learning algorithm	Precision	Recall	F-measure	Accuracy
KNN, K neighbors = 3	0.76	0.50	0.38	0.50
KNN, K neighbors = 3	0.72	0.52	0.41	0.52
Svm kernel = 'linear' degree = 2	0.91	0.88	0.89	0.89
Svm kernel = 'poly' degree = 2	0.77	0.53	0.43	0.53
Svm kernel = 'rbf' degree = 2	0.87	0.81	0.81	0.81
Svm kernel = 'rbf' degree = 4	0.87	0.81	0.81	0.81

by four measures; precision, recall, accuracy and F-measure. The results of the overall system are presented in Table 2.

From the results shown in Table 2, we can notice that the SVM outperforms KNN for this task. The best precision, recall, f-measure and accuracy were achieved by SVM with linear kernel and degree of 2, 91%, 88%, 89% and 89%, respectively.

6   Conclusion

In this paper, we present a system that automatically assesses children skills in making English questions. We used Google ASR for converting spoken response to text transcription. The system consists of three piplelined subsystems; Wh-question word rule-based subsystem, English grammar checker, and machine learning based grammar/language checker. The student response is accepted only if it accepted by the three subsystems. This system was trained on 650 recorded responses made by 60 students (5th to 8th grades) as response to 75 different prompts. The number of grammar errors produced by the English grammar checker, best cosine similarity, best edit distance and best Jaccard distance between student response and the corresponding reference possible responses, are used to train KNN and SVM models with different parameters. The best precision, recall, f-measure and accuracy were achieved by SVM with linear kernel and degree of 2, 91%, 88%, 89% and 89%, respectively.

References

1. D'Mello, S., Graesser, A., Schuller, B., Martin, J.-C. (eds.): ACII 2011. LNCS, vol. 6975. Springer, Heidelberg (2011). https://doi.org/10.1007/978-3-642-24571-8
2. Gray, S.S., Willett, D., Lu, J., Pinto, J., Maergner, P., Bodenstab, N.: Child automatic speech recognition for US English: child interaction with living-room-electronic-devices. In: WOCCI, pp. 21–26 (2014)
3. Haser, V., et al.: I English language. Year's Work Engl. Stud. **90**(1), 1–154 (2011)
4. Huang, A.: Similarity measures for text document clustering. In: Proceedings of the Sixth New Zealand Computer Science Research Student Conference (NZCSRSC 2008), Christchurch, New Zealand, vol. 4, pp. 9–56 (2008)

5. Magooda, A., Litman, D.J.: Syntactic and semantic features for human like judgement in spoken CALL. In: SLaTE, pp. 109–114 (2017)
6. Niwattanakul, S., Singthongchai, J., Naenudorn, E., Wanapu, S.: Using of Jaccard coefficient for keywords similarity. In: Proceedings of the International Multiconference of Engineers and Computer Scientists, vol. 1, pp. 380–384 (2013)
7. Paul, R.: Interventions to improve communication in autism. Child Adolesc. Psychiatr. Clin. North Am. **17**(4), 835–856 (2008)
8. Perez-Meana, H.: Advances in Audio and Speech Signal Processing: Technologies and Applications: Technologies and Applications. IGI Global (2007)
9. Potamianos, A., Narayanan, S.: Robust recognition of children's speech. IEEE Trans. Speech Audio Process. **11**(6), 603–616 (2003)
10. Potamianos, A., Narayanan, S., Lee, S.: Automatic speech recognition for children. In: Fifth European Conference on Speech Communication and Technology (1997)
11. Ristad, E.S., Yianilos, P.N.: Learning string-edit distance. IEEE Trans. Pattern Anal. Mach. Intell. **20**(5), 522–532 (1998)
12. Taddei, S., Contena, B., Caria, M., Venturini, E., Venditti, F.: Evaluation of children with attention deficit hyperactivity disorder and specific learning disability on the wisc and cognitive assessment system (CAS). Proc.-Soc. Behav. Sci. **29**, 574–582 (2011)
13. Weber, P.: Question Quest: Discovering Ways to Ask Worthwhile Questions. Hawker Brownlow Education (1993)
14. Wilson, M.S., Fox, B.J., Pascoe, J.P.: Asking and answering questions; theory & research based intervention (2012)

Automatic Recognition of Speaker Age and Gender Based on Deep Neural Networks

Maxim Markitantov[✉] and Oxana Verkholyak

St. Petersburg Institute for Informatics and Automation of the Russian Academy of Sciences (SPIIRAS), St. Petersburg, Russia
m.markitantov@yandex.ru, overkholyak@gmail.com

Abstract. In the given article, we present a novel approach in the paralinguistic field of age and gender recognition by speaker voice based on deep neural networks. The training and testing of proposed models were implemented on the German speech corpus aGender. We conducted experiments using different network topologies, including neural networks with fully-connected and convolutional layers. In a joint recognition of speaker age and gender, our system reached the recognition performance measured as unweighted accuracy of 48.41%. In a separate age and gender recognition setup, the obtained performance was 57.53% and 88.80%, respectively. Applied deep neural networks provide the best result of speaker age recognition in comparison to existing traditional classification methods.

Keywords: Age and gender recognition · Computational Paralinguistics · Deep neural networks · Convolutional neural networks · Machine learning

1 Introduction

In a daily communication, people use not only verbal (speech, text, etc.), but also non-verbal (paralinguistic, gesture, etc.) sources of information. The later may contain such speaker characteristics as his/her psycho-emotional state, age, gender, presence of a disease condition and other personal parameters reflecting current speaker state. Without a direct contact with a client (user), paralinguistic information may turn out useful for rendering certain services over the Internet.

Automatic speaker age recognition is necessary for various applications, such as speaker identification and verification systems, call-centers, healthcare, target marketing, and in particular, human-computer interaction. Also, automatic speaker age recognition system may prove useful for medico-legal purposes, for example, to narrow down the list of suspects when speech samples are available. Other commercial use cases for speaker age recognition include smart rooms and houses, vehicle assistants capable of adaptation to target user needs.

Various researches have been done on extracting acoustic features and developing classifiers for automatic speaker age recognition, but none achieves a satisfactory performance. Extracting age information from speech signal is complicated by such

© Springer Nature Switzerland AG 2019
A. A. Salah et al. (Eds.): SPECOM 2019, LNAI 11658, pp. 327–336, 2019.
https://doi.org/10.1007/978-3-030-26061-3_34

factors as background noise and voice variation. Thus, the key problem in detection of speaker age lies in extracting reliable features and building an effective classification method.

For these purposes most popular methods nowadays include Deep Neural Networks (DNN), and in particular, Convolutional Neural Networks (CNN), since they serve as powerful machine learning algorithms and may be used in various tasks. In recent years DNNs are effectively employed for feature extraction and classification in the field of computer vision [1, 2], image processing [3] as well as in automatic speech recognition systems [4, 5].

In this work we have used feed-forward artificial neural networks with various topologies (including CNNs) for determining age and gender of the speaker by his/her voice. As a baseline method for comparison we used Support Vector Machine (SVM) classifier. This method is one of the most popular for classification and it is simple for implementation.

The rest of the article is organized as following: Sect. 2 presents analysis of existing approaches in the field of speaker age recognition by speech signal, Sect. 3 gives a description of the used speech corpus (aGender), Sect. 4 describes the novel approach proposed for speaker age recognition by voice, Sect. 5 shows the results of conducted experiments, and Sect. 6 contains the discussion, conclusions and future work directions.

2   Related Work

The 2nd Computational Paralinguistics Challenge (ComParE, http://www.compare. openaudio.eu/tasks), held in the framework of the International conference INTERSPEECH-2010 in Japan, included two sub-challenges: speaker age (4 classes) and gender (3 classes) recognition [6]. The competitors were given audio files from aGender corpus [7], as well as a set of 450 features, acquired with the open-source platform openSMILE [8]. Unweighted Accuracy (UA) was a baseline performance measure. The organizers provided the results obtained via baseline system based on SVM with a linear kernel, which reached a test set performance of 49.91% and 81.21% for speaker age and gender recognition, respectively. These values became the lowest level for the competition [6]. The validation set accuracies for classifying speaker age and gender were 47.11% and 77.28%.

The best result among competitors for detection of speaker age in ComParE-2010 was 52.88% [9]. The presented system consisted of several parts. In their work, the authors used both acoustic and prosodic features. The system used Gaussian Mixture Models (GMM) and SVM as a classifier. For one of the sub-systems the improvement relative to the baseline system reached 2%. The result of sub-systems fusion for speaker age and gender detection was 52.88% and 81.82% on the validation dataset, 52.35% and 83.14% on the test set.

The best system for speaker gender detection [10] was also comprised of several sub-systems. The features consisted of 26 Perceptual Linear Prediction (PLP) coefficients and Static Modulation Spectrogram (MSG). The classifiers included Gaussian Mixture Models - Universal Background Model (GMM-UBM), Multi-Layer Perceptrons (MLP) and SVM. As a result of fusion of mentioned systems, the validation set accuracy was 51.20% and 83.10%, and the test set accuracy 48.70% and 84.30% for speaker age and gender recognition.

After ComParE-2010 the interest in the research in this field kept growing. In [11], a complex system made of several constituents was proposed along with using acoustic and prosodic features, as well as GMM and SVM as classifiers. The accuracy performance reached 52.80% and 81.70% for speaker age and gender recognition. In [12], a system with 7 sub-modules was proposed, with the best aGender corpus accuracies reaching 54.10% and 90.39% for speaker age and gender recognition. The system used spectral and prosodic features, and GMM and SVM classification methods. The work [13] used i-vectors as features, which were extracted from 19 Mel-Frequency Cepstral Coefficients (MFCC) with the first and second order derivatives using Matlab MSR Identity Toolbox [14]. With the SVM classifier, the accuracy for joint recognition of age and gender showed 62.90%.

DNN was also used both for feature extraction [15, 16] and classification [15–18]. The features used were MFCCs and i-vectors. The average accuracy for such systems comprised 57.40%.

In [17], authors proposed an end-to-end recognition approach based on DNN trained on x-vectors that are known for good performance in speaker verification tasks [18]. The system was trained and tested on the NIST SRE2008-10 corpus. The method for evaluating the system was Mean Absolute Error (MAE), which showed a value of 4.92. An attempt to combine x-vectors with i-vectors on the feature level resulted in MAE of 5.20.

3   Speech Corpus

For training and testing our recognition systems we used aGender corpus that was introduced in the ComParE-2010 Challenge. It consists of 49 h of telephone speech, which was recorded from 945 speakers. The corpus was divided into a training (23 h, 471 speakers), validation (14 h, 299 speakers), and test (12 h, 175 speakers) datasets. The total number of utterances, recorded in 6 sessions, is 65364. The length of the utterances varies: for command words, month names and dates, time, telephone number, names and surnames, the duration falls in the range of 1 to 6 s. Every utterance is annotated in accordance with the speaker's age and gender. The data is stored as sound files with the sample rate of 8000 Hz, 8 bit encoding per sample. Seven groups of speakers (classes) used for annotation in the corpus are presented in Table 1.

Table 1. Age and gender classes of the aGender corpus [6].

Class	Group	Age	Gender	Speakers/Instances
1	Child	7–14	X (F&M)	106/6802
2	Youth	15–24	F	99/7360
3	Youth	15–24	M	88/6189
4	Adult	25–54	F	113/7934
5	Adult	25–54	M	107/6929
6	Senior	55–80	F	123/8485
7	Senior	55–80	M	134/9375

4 Proposed System for Age and Gender Recognition

The architecture of our proposed system for recognition of speaker age and gender is depicted in Fig. 1.

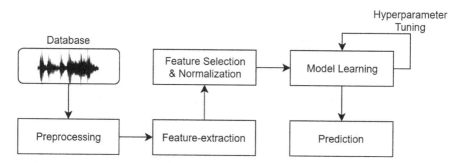

Fig. 1. Pipeline of the proposed system for speaker's age and gender recognition

We used open-source platform openSMILE and Python library librosa [20] for extracting features.

With the help of openSMILE we extracted 4 sets of features, using 4 different configuration files that are distributed in the original package. For dimensionality reduction we used Principle Component Analysis (PCA) method. The classifier for these features was chosen to be the SVM, with the hyperparameter tuning done via grid search, and DNN with varying number of fully connected and dropout layers. We will call these methods "FullyConn" for simplicity of presenting the results.

Using librosa we extracted Mel-Spectrogram (MEL) and MFCC features with first and second order derivatives (deltas) with the window size of 32 ms and 10 ms step. The classifiers used for these features are three CNNs with different architectures. All of them were implemented with the PyTorch programming platform [21].

The first network comprises one convolutional layer with a batch normalization and Rectified Linear Unit (ReLU) activation function. After that, an attention mechanism is applied, followed by a statistical pooling operation, which computes mean and standard deviation in time axes. These statistics are later combined and propagated to the last softmax layer. We call this network "SimpleCNN".

In the second system there are three convolutional layers with kernel sizes of 1, 2 and 3. Different kernel sizes allow extracting different features from the same sequence. Global max pooling is applied to every obtained filter; the results are concatenated and propagated through a fully connected layer. We call this network "3xCNN". The architecture of this network is shown in Fig. 2.

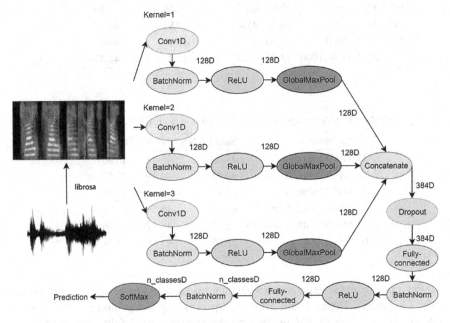

Fig. 2. CNN architecture with 3 layers (3xCNN)

The third neural network is different from the second in that an additional convolutional layer is added resulting in kernel sizes of 1, 2, 3, and 4. We call this network "4xCNN" for simplicity.

For all of the networks the loss function used was cross entropy. The batch size was equal 128. We used Adam optimizer with 0.0001 initial learning rate. The learning rate was decreased by the order of 2, when the loss function was no longer declining during the two consecutive epochs on the validation dataset. The training of DNN and CNN was conducted for the 30 and 60 epochs, respectively.

5   Experimental Results

The proposed system was tested on the validation dataset of aGender corpus (the same as at ComParE-2010). In the first place, we conducted experiments on the joint recognition of age and gender (7 classes) using methods described above. Table 2 contains the results of the systems trained on openSMILE features. The best result (UA = 48.41%) was obtained via DNN with 4 fully-connected layers. Table 3 presents the results of the systems train on MEL and MFCC features. The best result (UA = 48.13%) was achieved by CNN with 3 convolutional layers.

Table 2. UA for age & gender recognition with SVM and fully-connected DNN models (%)

Audio features	SVM	1xFullyConn	2xFullyConn	4xFullyConn
IS10_PCA_600	42.90	45.51	46.50	47.15
IS11_PCA_1200	46.50	47.46	47.81	46.77
IS13_PCA_2000	46.80	47.45	47.96	46.07
Avec2013_PCA_1000	43.90	46.88	47.32	**48.41**

Table 3. UA for age & gender recognition with CNN models (%)

Audio features	SimpleCNN	3xCNN	4xCNN
23 MFCC without Δ	43.52	46.27	46.90
23 MFCC with Δ	40.75	40.19	40.57
23 MFCC with $\Delta\Delta$	37.87	36.86	37.53
23 MFCC with Δ and $\Delta\Delta$	42.76	46.58	47.87
13 MFCC with Δ and $\Delta\Delta$	31.73	**48.12**	43.76
64 MEL	38.06	43.85	44.34

After that we made separate experiments on recognition of age (4 classes) and gender (3 classes). Tables 4 and 5 list the speaker age recognition results. The best accuracy (UA = 57.53%) was reached by the system with 2 fully-connected layers. With the number of fully-connected layers increasing, overfitting does not allow improving the performance.

Table 4. UA of age recognition with SVM and fully-connected DNN models (%)

Audio features	SVM	1xFullyConn	2xFullyConn	4xFullyConn
IS10_PCA_600	51.40	49.39	56.61	48.83
IS11_PCA_1200	54.10	51.39	**57.53**	51.40
IS13_PCA_2000	54.40	50.40	53.26	51.11
Avec2013_PCA_1000	52.90	49.90	57.41	49.95

Table 5. UA of age recognition with CNN models (%)

Audio features	SimpleCNN	3xCNN	4xCNN
23 MFCC without Δ	46.90	50.40	50.75
23 MFCC with Δ	44.75	47.55	46.62
23 MFCC with ΔΔ	40.52	44.53	45.13
23 MFCC with Δ and ΔΔ	47.37	50.69	**51.21**
13 MFCC with Δ and ΔΔ	40.48	50.41	47.98
64 MEL	48.86	49.45	48.79

The ternary speaker gender classification results are presented in Tables 6 and 7. The best performance (UA = 88.80%) was shown by CNN with 1 convolutional layer and statistical pooling layer. For DNN with 1 fully-connected layer, UA reached 88.10%. Similar results were obtained via SVM, however only 2 classes out of 3 were predicted.

Table 6. UA of gender recognition with SVM and fully-connected DNN models (%)

Audio features	SVM	1xFullyConn	2xFullyConn	4xFullyConn
IS10_PCA_600	**88.10**	**88.10**	83.14	83.28
IS11_PCA_1200	87.50	85.57	82.38	85.37
IS13_PCA_2000	88.00	84.49	85.12	87.00
Avec2013_PCA_1000	85.60	87.32	82.03	85.15

Table 7. UA of gender recognition with CNN models (%)

Audio features	SimpleCNN	3xCNN	4xCNN
23 MFCC without Δ	86.62	86.35	86.62
23 MFCC with Δ	84.83	85.72	84.93
23 MFCC with ΔΔ	86.92	79.39	81.32
23 MFCC with Δ and ΔΔ	86.01	87.26	87.32
13 MFCC with Δ and ΔΔ	77.11	84.80	85.75
64 MEL	**88.80**	87.37	87.28

Table 8 shows a comparison of our best systems with other solutions proposed in the recent literature. As can be seen from the table, our system is the first among all others in the age classification task and is second one in the gender recognition task. In the join speaker age and gender recognition setup, our system reached UA = 48.12%, that beats some of the systems recently proposed by other authors.

Table 8. Comparison of the proposed system with existing ones on development set of aGender corpus, UA (%)

Methods	Age & Gender (7 classes)	Age (4 classes)	Gender (3 classes)
ComParE-2010 baseline [6]	44.24	47.11	77.28
Bocklet et al. [22]	47.80	–	–
Nguyen et al. [23]	45.19	47.68	78.99
Gajšek et al. [24]	–	–	80.32
Kockmann et al. [9]	53.86	52.88	81.82
Meinedo and Trancoso [10]	–	51.20	83.10
Li et al. [11]	50.30	52.80	81.70
Yücesoy and Nabiyev [12]	53.50	54.10	**90.39**
Qawaqneh et al. [15]	58.98	–	–
Równicka and Kacprzak [13]	**62.90**	–	–
Abumallouh et al. [16]	57.63	–	–
Proposed System	48.12	**57.53**	88.80

6   Conclusions and Future Work

In this article, we studied different deep neural network topologies based on fully-connected and convolutional layers in the task and speaker age and gender recognition. The training and testing were done on aGender corpus. The best classification accuracy obtained for joint speaker age and gender recognition was 48.12%. In age classification, DNN with 2 fully-connected layers reached UA = 57.53%. In gender classification, the best performance (UA = 88.80%) was shown by CNN with 1 convolutional layer and statistical pooling layer. Our age recognition result beats state-of-the-art results known in literature to date.

In the follow-up work, our aim is to investigate different kinds of neural network topologies, as well as feature representations based on i-vectors and x-vectors.

Acknowledgements. This research is supported by the Russian Science Foundation (project No. 18-11-00145).

References

1. Ranzato, M., Hinton, G.: Modeling pixel means and covariances using factorized third-order Boltzmann machines. In: Proceedings of IEEE Conference on Computer Vision and Pattern Recognition (CVPR), pp. 2551–2558 (2010)
2. Lee, H., Ekanadham, C., Ng, A.: Sparse deep belief net model for visual area V2. In: Proceedings of the 20th International Conference on Neural Information Processing Systems, pp. 873–880 (2007)
3. Dahl, G., Yu, D., Deng, L., Acero, A.: Context-dependent pre-trained deep neural networks for large-vocabulary speech recognition. IEEE Trans. Audio Speech Lang. Process. **20**, 30–42 (2012)

4. Deselaers, T., Hasan, S., Bender, O., Ney, H.: A deep learning approach to machine transliteration. In: Proceedings of the Fourth Workshop on Statistical Machine Translation, pp. 233–241 (2009)

5. Yu, D., Wang, S., Karam, Z., Deng, L.: Language recognition using deep-structured conditional random fields. In: Proceedings of IEEE International Conference on Acoustics Speech and Signal Processing (ICASSP), pp. 5030–5033 (2010)

6. Schuller, B., et al.: The INTERSPEECH 2010 paralinguistic challenge. In: Proceedings of the 11th Annual Conference of the International Speech Communication Association, INTERSPEECH 2010, pp. 2794–2797 (2010)

7. Burkhardt, F., Eckert, M., Johannsen, W., Stegmann, J.: A database of age and gender annotated telephone speech. In: Proceedings of 7th International Conference on Language Resources and Evaluation (LREC 2010) (2010)

8. Eyben, F., Wöllmer, M., Schuller, B.: openSMILE - the Munich versatile and fast open-source audio feature extractor. In: Proceedings of the ACM Multimedia 2010 International Conference, pp. 1459–1462 (2010)

9. Kockmann, M., Burget, L., Cernocký, J.: Brno University of Technology system for Interspeech 2010 paralinguistic challenge. In: Proceedings of the 11th Annual Conference of the International Speech Communication Association, INTERSPEECH 2010, pp. 2822–2825 (2010)

10. Meinedo, H., Trancoso, I.: Age and gender classification using fusion of acoustic and prosodic features. In: Proceedings of the 11th Annual Conference of the International Speech Communication Association, INTERSPEECH 2010, pp. 2818–2821 (2010)

11. Li, M., Han, K., Narayanan, S.: Automatic speaker age and gender recognition using acoustic and prosodic level information fusion. Comput. Speech Lang. **27**(1), 151–167 (2013)

12. Yücesoy, E., Nabiyev, V.: A new approach with score-level fusion for the classification of a speaker age and gender. Comput. Electr. Eng. **53**, 29–39 (2016)

13. Równicka, J., Kacprzak, S.: Speaker age classification and regression using i-vectors. In: Proceedings of the 17th Annual Conference of the International Speech Communication Association (INTERSPEECH 2016): Understanding Speech Processing in Humans and Machines, pp. 1402–1406 (2016)

14. Sadjadi, S., Slaney, M., Heck, L.: MSR identity toolbox v1.0: a Matlab toolbox for speaker-recognition research. Speech Lang. Process. Tech. Committee Newsl. **1**, 1–32 (2013)

15. Qawaqneh, Z., Abumallouh, A., Barkana, B.: Deep neural network framework and transformed MFCCs for speaker's age and gender classification. Knowl.-Based Syst. **115**, 5–14 (2016)

16. Abumallouh, A., Qawaqneh, Z., Barkana, B.: New transformed features generated by deep bottleneck extractor and a GMM-UBM classifier for speaker age and gender classification. In: Neural Computing and Applications, vol. 30, no. 8, pp. 2581–2593 (2017)

17. Ghahremani, P., et al.: End-to-end deep neural network age estimation. In: Proceedings of the 19th Annual Conference of the International Speech Communication Association, INTERSPEECH 2018, pp. 277–281 (2018)

18. Snyder, D., Garcia-Romero, D., Sell, G., Povey, D., Khudanpur, S.: X-Vectors: robust DNN embeddings for speaker recognition. In: Proceedings of the IEEE International Conference on Acoustics, Speech and Signal Processing (ICASSP), pp. 5329–5333 (2018)

19. Abumallouh, A., Qawaqneh, Z., Barkana, B.: Deep neural network combined posteriors for speakers' age and gender classification. In: Annual Connecticut Conference on Industrial Electronics, Technology & Automation (CT-IETA), pp. 1–5 (2016)

20. McFee, B., et al.: librosa: audio and music signal analysis in Python. In: Proceedings of the 14th python in science conference, pp. 18–24 (2015)

21. Paszke, A., et al.: Automatic differentiation in PyTorch (2017)
22. Bocklet, T., Stemmer, G., Zeißler, V., Noeth, E.: Age and gender recognition based on multiple systems - early vs. late fusion. In: Proceedings of the 11th Annual Conference of the International Speech Communication Association, INTERSPEECH 2010, pp. 2830–2833 (2010)
23. Nguyen, P., Le, T., Tran, D., Huang, X., Sharma, D.: Fuzzy support vector machines for age and gender classification. In: Proceedings of the 11th Annual Conference of the International Speech Communication Association, INTERSPEECH 2010, pp. 2806–2809 (2010)
24. Gajsek, R., Žibert, J., Justin, T., Štruc, V., Vesnicer, B., Mihelic, F.: Gender and affect recognition based on GMM and GMM-UBM modeling with relevance MAP estimation. In: Proceedings of the 11th Annual Conference of the International Speech Communication Association, INTERSPEECH 2010, pp. 2810–2813 (2010)

Investigating Joint CTC-Attention Models for End-to-End Russian Speech Recognition

Nikita Markovnikov[1,2(✉)] and Irina Kipyatkova[1,3]

[1] St. Petersburg Institute for Informatics and Automation of the Russian Academy of Sciences (SPIIRAS), Saint-Petersburg, Russia
niklemark@gmail.com
[2] ITMO University, Saint-Petersburg, Russia
[3] St. Petersburg State University of Aerospace Instrumentation (SUAI), St. Petersburg, Russia
kipyatkova@iias.spb.su

Abstract. We propose an application of attention-based models for automatic recognition of continuous Russian speech. We experimented with three types of attention mechanism, data augmentation based on a tempo and pitch perturbations, and a beam search pruning method. Moreover we propose a using of sparsemax function for our task as a probability distribution generator for an attention mechanism. We experimented with a joint CTC-Attention encoder-decoders using deep convolutional networks to compress input features or waveform spectrograms. Also we experimented with Highway LSTM model as an encoder. We performed experiments with a small dataset of Russian speech with total duration of more than 60 h. We got the recognition accuracy improvement by using proposed methods and showed better performance in terms of speech decoding speed using the beam search optimization method.

Keywords: End-to-end models · Attention mechanism ·
Deep learning · Russian speech · Speech recognition

1 Introduction

Automatic speech recognition (ASR) systems have been traditionally built with the use of an acoustic model (AM) with application of Hidden Markov Models (HMM), the Gaussian Mixture Model (GMM), and a language model (LM). Such models show good recognition accuracy, but they are made up of multiple parts that are tuned independently. This can cause failures, with errors in one part involving errors in the others. Thus, standard recognition scenarios need a large amount of memory and capacity that does not allow to use such systems locally at some devices and need remote computations at servers.

© Springer Nature Switzerland AG 2019
A. A. Salah et al. (Eds.): SPECOM 2019, LNAI 11658, pp. 337–347, 2019.
https://doi.org/10.1007/978-3-030-26061-3_35

Another approach, called end-to-end approach, has recently been adopted with use of deep neural networks (DNN). This approach allows to implement models easily using only one neural network that is tuned with gradient descent and one loss function. End-to-end models often demonstrate better performance in terms of both recognition speed and accuracy. Potentially these models require less amount of memory that allows using them at mobile devices locally. However, they need more training data to be learned properly.

The goal of our research was to explore end-to-end models for recognition of continuous Russian speech, to tune and compare them in terms of recognition accuracy and computing characteristics as training and decoding speed. To our best knowledge it is the first research of using attention-based encoder-decoder models for Russian speech recognition task.

The performance of the models was evaluated in terms of character error rate (CER), word error rate (WER) and real-time factor (RTF). In our previous research we explored models with Connectional Temporal Classification (CTC). But it is rather interesting to get some results with using of encoder-decoder models for low-resource language as Russian.

The rest of the paper is organized as follows. In Sect. 2, we survey related works. In Sect. 3, we describe architectures of attention-based encoder-decoder models. In Sect. 4, we describe the experimental setup and some methods that we used to improve learning. In Sect. 5 we present results that we got using trained models and provide a short analysis of the results. Finally, we conclude and discuss future work in Sect. 6.

2   Main Related Works

In paper [2], an attention-based model integrated with LM was proposed. Weighted finite state transducer (WFST) was used to merge an end-to-end model with the language model. At the decoding stage, a launched output search was performed that minimised encoder-decoder model and LM. Thus the authors got WER = 11.3% and CER = 4.8%.

Independently, a similar attention-based end-to-end model called Listen, Attend and Spell (LAS) was proposed in [4]. An encoder was pyramidal-shaped bidirectional long short-term memory (BLSTM) and a decoder used stack of LSTMs. The model was recomputed using LM after a decoding step, and WER for a Google Voice Search was 10.3%.

In paper [22], an attention-based encoder-decoder model using sub-words units was introduced. According to the scheme, pretraining starts with a high time reduction factor which is lowering during training. Using of sub-words units partly solves out-of-vocabulary problem. But it strongly increases number of labels and requires a lot of training data. However the authors could achieve state-of-the-art result (WER = 3.54%) using 1000 h audio data from LibriSpeech corpus.

As we can see, end-to-end models are able to work well both with and without LM for languages with strict word order (e.g. English). Also these models give good results with huge speech datasets. The Russian language is characterised by a higher degree of syntactical freedom and complex morphological word formation [3]. Also it has more complex phonetics. Thus, we need to use external LMs in order to increase accuracy. One can state that usage of encoder-decoder models for Russian speech recognition is a challenging task in that aspect.

3 Model Architecture

3.1 Attention-Based Encoder-Decoder Model

Encoder-Decoder networks are used for tasks, in which lengths of input and output sequences are variable [5,17]. The term "encoder" refers to a neural network that transforms input $x = (x_1, \ldots, x_{L'})$ into the intermediate state $h = (h_1, \ldots, h_L)$ and extracts features. The term "decoder" is usually applied to refer to a recurrent neural network (RNN) that uses an intermediate state for generating output sequences. Decoder generates output sequence $(y_1, \ldots, y_T)$ using h as input. Also decoder uses a subnetwork called attention mechanism. Attention mechanism chooses a subsequence of the input and then uses it for updating hidden states of RNN and predicting an output.

On the i-th step decoder generates an output y_i focusing on separate components of h as follows [6]:

$$\alpha_i = \text{Attend}(s_{i-1}, \alpha_{i-1}, h) \quad \text{and} \quad g_i = \sum_{j=1}^{L} \alpha_{i,j} h_j$$

where s_{i-1} is the $(i-1)$-th state of RNN called *Generator*, $\alpha_i \in \mathbb{R}^L$ denotes attention weights, vector g_i called glimpse and Attend denotes some function that calculates attention weights. The step comes to an end with computing a new generator state as $s_i = \text{Recurrency}(s_{i-1}, g_i, y_i)$. Attention mechanism can be divided into three types. The following equations represent how to compute them:

– dot:
$$e_{i,j} = w^\top \tanh(W s_{i-1} + b)$$

– content-based:
$$e_{i,j} = w^\top \tanh(W s_{i-1} + V h_j + b)$$

– location-based:
$$f_i = F * \alpha_{i-1}$$
$$e_{i,j} = w^\top \tanh(W s_{i-1} + V h_j + U f_{i,j} + b)$$

where $w \in \mathbb{R}^m$ and $b \in \mathbb{R}^n$ denote weight vectors, $W \in \mathbb{R}^{m \times n}$, $V \in \mathbb{R}^{m \times 2n}$ and $U \in \mathbb{R}^{m \times k}$ are weight matrices, n and m are numbers of hidden units in the encoder and in the decoder, respectively, vectors $f_{i,j} \in \mathbb{R}^k$ are convolutional features. Eventually, an attention weights matrix is calculated as $\alpha_i = \text{softmax}_i(e)$.

In this work we compare all three types of attention mechanism for the Russian speech recognition task. In [11] a joint CTC-Attention model was presented. The model optimises multitask objective function during training as follows:

$$\mathcal{L}_{\mathrm{MTL}} = \lambda \mathcal{L}_{\mathrm{CTC}} + (1 - \lambda)\mathcal{L}_{\mathrm{Attention}}$$

where a $\lambda \in [0; 1]$ is a hyperparameter, $\mathcal{L}_{\mathrm{CTC}}$ denotes an objective for CTC [8] and $\mathcal{L}_{\mathrm{Attention}}$ is an objective for attention-based model. As soon as we have a few amount of training speech data using of CTC objective can be helpful. So we decided to study this idea too.

3.2 Proposed Recognition Model

The model presented in this work was obtained for the recognition of continuous Russian speech. We trained some our models using filter banks (fBank) with deltas features. As well we experimented with the usage of a raw spectrogram waveform data to learn models. Spectrogram contains a lot of noise information, hence we need to filter the data. So, firstly a convolutional neural network (CNN) was used in order to extract compressed information from a spectrogram data. CNN had 4 convolutional layers with kernel 3×3, 2 maxpooling layers with window 2×2 and stride 2. Also we used ReLU activation function and batch normalization [9] in between layers that showed a great stabilization effect on a performance.

A regular LSTM network was used as the decoder, and a BLSTM network was used as the encoder. After each layer in the encoder, a subsampling layer along the time axis was used to reduce the length of the encoder's network. We skipped every second frame in the middle part of the encoder's network. The encoder's network contained 5 BLSTM layers with 512 cells in each. The decoder's network contained 2 LSTM layers. In general, our model was similar to the model proposed in [11].

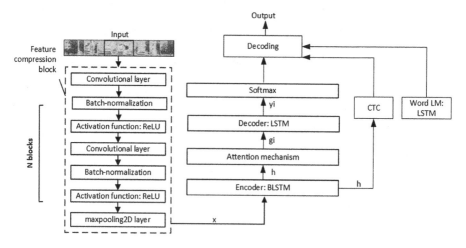

Fig. 1. Proposed recognition model. Number of convolutional blocks N equals 2.

A multilayer perceptron (MLP) was used as a mechanism of attention [1]. Also, we used all three types of attention mechanism and compared their efficiency for Russian speech recognition. Additionaly, we learned LSTM LM based on words. It had 1 LSTM layer with 256 cells. A proposed recognition model scheme is presented on Fig. 1.

3.3 Beam Search Prunning Method

We proposed a pruning method at a decoding stage in the encoder-decoder. In common, our method was similar to the approach described in [7]. Usually beam search builds the output sequence keeping a sorted query of a fixed size (beam size). For each iteration it selects the best hypothesis from the query and reduces the query size. Query size becomes equal $2 \times$ beam at worst. Every new iteration is started with a full query (except the first and the last iterations). So, the idea was to filter query with some condition to remove too bad hypotheses. We used the following filter condition:

$$\left| \max_{h \in H}(\text{score}(h)) - \text{score}(h^*) \right| < \theta$$

where H denotes hypothesises query, h^* is a candidate to be removed, θ is a threshold that is hyperparameter being tuned. If this condition is met, the hypothesis remains in the query, and otherwise it is deleted. To tune θ we greedily increased it while the recognition error stopped to increase.

3.4 Using of Sparsemax Function

In [14] a sparsemax function was proposed. This function has similar properties as a softmax. But sparsemax has a distinctive feature. It can return sparse posterior distributions. In other words it may assign exactly zero probability to some of its output variables. Sparsemax is defined as follows:

$$\text{sparsemax}(z) = \arg \min_{p \in \Delta} \|p - z^2\|$$

where Δ is a set of probability distributions, p denotes a probability distribution from Δ and z is a vector to be mapped.

In [14] it was found to be useful in a classification and translation tasks. So, we decided to apply it to a speech recognition task where input and output are in the different domains. The key idea is that an attention mechanism can make an attention on some useless parts of a hidden representation of an original audio input like noises, hezitations, etc. Sparsemax tries to solve this problem. In this case an attention weights matrix is calculated as $\alpha_i = \text{sparsemax}(e)$.

3.5 Highway BLSTM Encoder

In the end we propose the usage of Highway BLSTM network as the encoder. We used a network similar to model from [13]. We used the following variant of Highway LSTM:

$$g_T = \sigma(W_T x + b_T)$$

$$g_C = \sigma(W_C x + b_C)$$

$$y = x \cdot (1 - g_C) + \tanh(Wx + b) \cdot g_T$$

where W_T, W_C, W are weight matrices and b_T, b_C, b are biases. x in this case denotes LSTM cell's output. This LSTM type shows a good performance for language modeling tasks. It was interesting to know if these models can show some improvement in case of a speech recognition task with a small training dataset. To our knowledge the highway networks strengthen the LSTM capability of handling long-range dependencies in audio frames sequences.

4   Experimental Setup

4.1   Training Dataset

We used the training speech corpus collected by SPIIRAS [10]. The corpus consists of three parts with the total duration of more than 30 h. Additionally, we union our dataset with free speech corpuses Voxforge[1] and M-AILABS[2]. All data was preprocessed to have 16000 Hz sample rate and a similar volume level. Audio was truncated at the begging and at the end using voice activity detection methods. Also we removed examples with a non-alphabet symbols to have only 33 letters of Russian alphabet and a dash symbol in the lexicon. As a result we had 60.6 hours of speech data. This speech dataset was splitted into validation and trains parts with sizes of 5% and 95%.

To test the system we used another speech database of 500 phrases pronounced by 5 speakers.

Our language model was learned using data from Russian news sites [12]. The dataset for the training of the language model contains approximately 300 millions words and a vocabulary size was 150000 words.

4.2   Data Augmentation

In our work, we perform tempo and pitch perturbation-based data augmentation, because we have a few amount of training data.

The WSOLA [19] based implementation in the tempo command of the SoX[3] tool was used to perform tempo augmentation. Two additional copies of the original training data were created by modifying the speed with a factor value taken from uniform distribution $U(0.7; 1.3)$. To modify the pitch we also used the SoX tool. Pitch was modified with a semitone values taken from uniform distribution $U(-5; 5)$. After performing two data augmentation methods, dataset size increased to approximately 180 h.

---

[1] http://www.voxforge.org/.

[2] https://www.caito.de/2019/01/the-m-ailabs-speech-dataset/.

[3] http://sox.sourceforge.net/sox.html.

5   Results of the Proposed Model

We used ESPnet [20] framework to conduct experiments with attention-based models with a PyTorch as a back-end part.

The batch size was equal to 10. The AdaDelta algorithm [21] was used for the optimization with $\rho = 0.95$ $\epsilon = 10^{-6}$ and initial learning rate equal to 1.0. We initialized the weights randomly from the uniform distribution in interval $[-1; 1]$ without a scaling variance. At the training time $\lambda = 0.5$ was used. Also, we compared recognition accuracy depending on the CTC weight parameter at the beam search during decoding. Parameters with values in range $[0; 1]$ with step 0.1 were used. The best result was obtained using CTC weight equal to 0.4 at a decoding stage. The weight of word LM was equal to 0.7.

In order to prevent our model from making over-confident predictions, we used label smoothing [18] as a regularization mechanism with a smoothing factor of 0.01. We used dropout [16] in LSTM layers at every timestep in the encoder's network. A dropout probability was equal to 0.2. Moreover we used gradient clipping [15] to control training process and convergence.

RTF was measured on a laptop with Intel Core i7, 8 Gb RAM, CPU 2.70 GHz. Training was performed on Nvidia GeForce GTX 1080 GPU with CUDA.

Results of our proposed models are shown in Table 1. As a baseline we used regular encoder-decoder model with BLSTM as an encoder with a location-based attention. The best result was 14.1% and 39.8% in terms of CER and WER respectively, it was obtained with using spectrograms as input. The nearest results were given by using of sparsemax. The best RTF value was 1.34 by using of beam search pruning method. To our surprise the model used sparsemax and spectrograms evaluated worse than the model used spectrograms only. We suggest that it could happen because of too small training dataset.

Table 1. Experimental results. Beam size was equal to 10. 'Tempo' denotes a tempo-perturbation augmentation, 'pitch' means a pitch perturbation.

Model	Features	Attention	CER, %	WER, %	RTF
BLSTM (baseline)	fBank+Δ	Location	20.8	54.5	1.68
Proposed model	fBank+Δ	Dot	23.1	56.2	1.48
Proposed model	fBank+Δ	Content	18.0	52.2	1.46
Proposed model	fBank+Δ	Location	17.4	47.5	1.55
Proposed model + tempo	fBank+Δ	Location	16.9	44.6	1.56
Proposed model + tempo + pitch	fBank+Δ	Location	16.7	44.3	1.55
Proposed model + sparsemax	fBank+Δ	Location	15.8	44.6	1.57
Proposed model	**spectrogram**	**Location**	**14.1**	**39.8**	**1.62**
Proposed model + prunning	fBank+Δ	Location	17.4	47.6	1.34
Proposed model + Highway LSTM	fBank+Δ	Location	17.1	48.5	1.59
Proposed model + sparsemax	spectrogram	Location	14.3	44.5	1.61

Tuning of an absolute pruning method is shown in Fig. 2 applying to a base proposed model. Selected value of θ was equal to 7. Starting from this point, recognition error stops increasing. The total RTF's improvement was approximately 15% comparing with an initial model.

Highway LSTM network did not give us a significant accuracy improvement but we found that model converges much faster. In Fig. 3 loss on a validation corpus is shown. In future work we are going to continue research of this model.

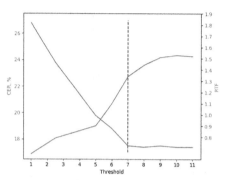

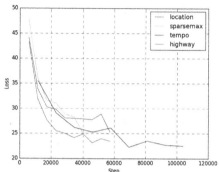

Fig. 2. Tuning of an absolute pruning method. Beam size was equal to 10. The dotted line is a selected threshold Θ value.

Fig. 3. Loss function on validation data of the speech corpus for training steps.

We see that location-based attention mechanism gives the best accuracy. Augmentation allows to improve accuracy too, when we have a few amount of training data. Sparsemax gives significant improvement in terms of CER. And we are going to explore this method in the future by combining it with the others. We could not achieve RTF = 1 with beam size of 10. But we showed that pruning approach gives a good speed up without any accuracy loss. Supposedly, if we collect much more training data models performance can be better in terms of CER and WER.

In Fig. 4 an attention mechanism alignment between the input and the output sequences for a test example is shown. We can see that alignment was learned properly. But in the middle there is a gap. In this place an ending of the word was missed. Also, we analysed some results of recognition. We can see that character substitutions (50.4%) and deletions (34.1%) give the most error contribution. By the way sparsemax and spectrograms give a noticeable reduction of deletions.

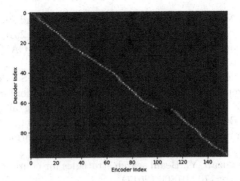

Fig. 4. An inference alignment of a test example.

6 Conclusion

In this work, we focused on the Russian speech recognition task using a joint CTC-Attention encoder-decoder model. We compared three types of attention mechanisms. Also we proposed using of a pruning at a decoding stage and a sparsemax function in the attention mechanism. The usage of Highway LSTM networks as an encoder was explored. Moreover, we used deep CNN with a batch-normalization to extract compressed features from spectrograms and fBank with deltas features.

We achieved a recognition accuracy higher than that achieved with use of baseline encoder-decoder models. Sparsemax and spectrogram approaches gave a significant improvement. Also, we noticed that it is rather important to use word-based language models for a such small dataset of Russian speech. In the nearest future we are going to carry out experiments with another neural networks models, coverage mechanism and the usage of purely raw data.

Acknowledgements. This research was supported by he Russian Foundation for Basic Research (project No. 18-07-01216).

References

1. Bahdanau, D., Cho, K., Bengio, Y.: Neural machine translation by jointly learning to align and translate. arXiv preprint arXiv:1409.0473 (2014)
2. Bahdanau, D., et al.: End-to-end attention-based large vocabulary speech recognition. In: 2016 IEEE International Conference on Acoustics, Speech and Signal Processing (ICASSP), pp. 4945–4949 (2016)
3. Besacier, L., Barnard, E., Karpov, A., Schultz, T.: Automatic speech recognition for under-resourced languages: a survey. Speech Commun. **56**, 85–100 (2014). https://doi.org/10.1016/j.specom.2013.07.008

4. Chan, W., Jaitly, N., Le, Q., Vinyals, O.: Listen, attend and spell: a neural network for large vocabulary conversational speech recognition. In: 2016 IEEE International Conference on Acoustics, Speech and Signal Processing (ICASSP), pp. 4960–4964. IEEE (2016)

5. Cho, K., van Merrienboer, B., Gülçehre, Ç., Bougares, F., Schwenk, H., Bengio, Y.: Learning phrase representations using RNN encoder-decoder for statistical machine translation. CoRR abs/1406.1078 (2014). http://arxiv.org/abs/1406.1078

6. Chorowski, J.K., Bahdanau, D., Serdyuk, D., Cho, K., Bengio, Y.: Attention-based models for speech recognition. In: Advances in Neural Information Processing Systems, pp. 577–585 (2015)

7. Freitag, M., Al-Onaizan, Y.: Beam search strategies for neural machine translation. arXiv preprint arXiv:1702.01806 (2017)

8. Graves, A., Fernández, S., Gomez, F., Schmidhuber, J.: Connectionist temporal classification: labelling unsegmented sequence data with recurrent neural networks. In: Proceedings of the 23rd International Conference on Machine Learning, pp. 369–376. ACM (2006)

9. Ioffe, S., Szegedy, C.: Batch normalization: accelerating deep network training by reducing internal covariate shift. CoRR abs/1502.03167 (2015). http://arxiv.org/abs/1502.03167

10. Karpov, A., Markov, K., Kipyatkova, I., Vazhenina, D., Ronzhin, A.: Large vocabulary Russian speech recognition using syntactico-statistical language modeling. Speech Commun. **56**, 213–228 (2014). https://doi.org/10.1016/j.specom.2013.07.004

11. Kim, S., Hori, T., Watanabe, S.: Joint CTC-attention based end-to-end speech recognition using multi-task learning. CoRR abs/1609.06773 (2016). http://arxiv.org/abs/1609.06773

12. Kipyatkova, I., Karpov, A.: Lexicon size and language model order optimization for Russian LVCSR. In: Železný, M., Habernal, I., Ronzhin, A. (eds.) SPECOM 2013. LNCS (LNAI), vol. 8113, pp. 219–226. Springer, Cham (2013). https://doi.org/10.1007/978-3-319-01931-4_29

13. Kurata, G., Ramabhadran, B., Saon, G., Sethy, A.: Language modeling with highway LSTM. CoRR abs/1709.06436 (2017). http://arxiv.org/abs/1709.06436

14. Martins, A.F.T., Astudillo, R.F.: From softmax to sparsemax: a sparse model of attention and multi-label classification. CoRR abs/1602.02068 (2016). http://arxiv.org/abs/1602.02068

15. Pascanu, R., Mikolov, T., Bengio, Y.: Understanding the exploding gradient problem. CoRR abs/1211.5063 (2012). http://arxiv.org/abs/1211.5063

16. Srivastava, N., Hinton, G.E., Krizhevsky, A., Sutskever, I., Salakhutdinov, R.: Dropout: a simple way to prevent neural networks from overfitting. J. Mach. Learn. Res. **15**(1), 1929–1958 (2014)

17. Sutskever, I., Vinyals, O., Le, Q.V.: Sequence to sequence learning with neural networks. In: Advances in Neural Information Processing Systems, pp. 3104–3112 (2014)

18. Szegedy, C., Vanhoucke, V., Ioffe, S., Shlens, J., Wojna, Z.: Rethinking the inception architecture for computer vision. In: Proceedings of the IEEE Conference on Computer Vision and Pattern Recognition, pp. 2818–2826 (2016)

19. Verhelst, W., Roelands, M.: An overlap-add technique based on waveform similarity (WSOLA) for high quality time-scale modification of speech. In: 1993 IEEE International Conference on Acoustics, Speech, and Signal Processing, ICASSP-1993, vol. 2, pp. 554–557. IEEE (1993)

20. Watanabe, S., et al.: ESPnet: end-to-end speech processing toolkit. In: Interspeech, pp. 2207–2211 (2018). http://dx.doi.org/10.21437/Interspeech.2018-1456
21. Zeiler, M.D.: ADADELTA: an adaptive learning rate method. arXiv preprint arXiv:1212.5701 (2012)
22. Zeyer, A., Irie, K., Schlüter, R., Ney, H.: Improved training of end-to-end attention models for speech recognition. CoRR abs/1805.03294 (2018). http://arxiv.org/abs/1805.03294

Author Clustering with and Without Topical Features

Polina Panicheva[1,2] , Olga Litvinova[2] ,
and Tatiana Litvinova[2,3(✉)]

[1] National Research University Higher School of Economics,
16 Soyuza Pechatnikov st., St. Petersburg 190121, Russia
ppanicheva@hse.ru
[2] RusProfiling Lab, Voronezh State Pedagogical University,
86 Lenina st., Voronezh 394043, Russia
centr_rus_yaz@mail.ru
[3] Plekhanov Russian University of Economics, Stremyanny lane 36,
Moscow 117997, Russia

Abstract. Typically, the task of authorship attribution has been solved using supervised machine learning methods. It is only recently that unsupervised methods have been applied to authorship attribution, namely author clustering. Clustering could be useful in realistic scenario as it represents natural grouping of documents without *a priori* authorship information, although the problem of feature selection remains unsolved. That is particularly true for a cross-domain scenario. Studies have shown that in cross-domain settings some domain-specific text features cause noise in authorship attribution. In the current work we introduce a modification of unmasking technique aimed at selecting and removing the features most influenced by topic change. We apply the proposed technique to identify topical features and assess the quality of author clustering with different feature sets in a real-world dataset of forum texts in Russian. The main assumption is that the topical features result in topic-based text instead authorship-based clustering, and removing them could increase the performance of document clustering against authorship ground truth. We test this consideration by first clustering cross-topic documents with state-of-the-art authorship attribution features. Second, we remove the most significant topical features, and cluster texts with resulting feature set. Both clustering results are evaluated against ground truth authorship. The results demonstrate that the described approach of removing some topical features increases author clustering performance, however one should be cautious with the number of removed features.

Keywords: Author clustering · Unmasking · Topic classification ·
Cross-domain authorship attribution

1 Introduction

Authorship attribution (AA), which entails determining the author of an anonymous text from either a closed or an open set of possible authors is the task which has attracted both scholars and forensic experts' attention. Different approaches to solving

© Springer Nature Switzerland AG 2019
A. A. Salah et al. (Eds.): SPECOM 2019, LNAI 11658, pp. 348–358, 2019.
https://doi.org/10.1007/978-3-030-26061-3_36

this problem have been tested, including sophisticated ones such as complex network approach [3]. In the recent years researchers working in the field of authorship attribution have begun to employ unsupervised techniques aimed at automatic grouping of texts according to their authorship in addition to the widely used supervised machine learning techniques [11]. The task of AA currently involves training and testing samples containing documents which differ in modes, genres, topics, etc. (cross-domain AA) [7], which is a more realistic scenario comparing to single-domain AA. Author clustering (also called author-based clustering, authorship clustering, or authorial clustering) is a very important task as it represents real-world setting, where the ground truth on document authorship may be unavailable *a priori*, however work on author clustering is still limited. Author clustering also seems daunting [14, 15], especially in a cross-domain scenario, as the latter has been shown to affect the number of features needed for authorship-based document clustering [7].

In the current study we address the problem of authorship-based clustering of real-world documents belonging to different topics. We apply modified unmasking technique [6] in order to remove highly topic-dependent textual features and evaluate the result with natural groups of texts formed by hierarchical clustering.

The goal of the current work is to analyze the performance of authorship-based text clustering after removing significant topical features from the feature set. The research hypothesis is that various features, including topical ones, are useful in author clustering, but the most significant topical features will result in clusters representing topics, not authors. Thus removing a number of significant topical features could result in more effective authorship-based text clustering. We set out to test the hypothesis by performing topic classification of forum posts and iteratively removing a different number of features most significant for topic classification. At each iteration we cluster the documents with the resulting feature space and evaluate the clustering performance in terms of ground truth authorship.

2 Related Work

2.1 Unmasking for Cross-Domain Authorship Attribution

Cross-domain AA is a demanding sort of AA, where training and test sets contain texts which differ in topic, genre and even mode (written/oral) [7, 12, 13]. Several techniques have been developed to tackle this problem. One the well-known technique which was originally designed for author verification but useful for cross-domain AA is unmasking. Unmasking was introduced in [6]. It is a technique aimed at removing the features most useful at discriminating between two collections of texts and looking at the speed with which classification performance between the two collections degrades as more features are removed.

The general idea behind unmasking is that if two text collections are produced by the same author, the differences between them will be reflected in a very small number of features, and as the features are removed, the classification performance degrades in a sudden and dramatic manner. As the most informative features are removed, so is the impact of genre and other domain-specific characteristics. Originally, unmasking was employed as a technique for authorship verification for 21 English books by 10 authors. By analyzing the performance degradation curve in a leave-one-book-out experiment 95.7% accuracy was achieved in authorship verification, although the dataset spanned a variety of genres [6].

Unmasking was further investigated in [5] where it was applied to cross-genre authorship verification. Although the results in the cross-genre setting were modest, the technique still proved to be very interesting in terms of the results interpretation.

The idea behind unmasking, which is that there are specific features informative in domain classification to be accounted for in cross-domain AA, has recently gained research interest. While character n-grams are widely used and reported to be the most effective type of features in AA [11, 12], the authors [8, 12] investigate whether different character n-grams account for single- and cross-domain settings. Indeed, word n-grams are useful in single-domain settings, mostly capturing topic-related information, whereas punctuation and affix n-grams are more useful in cross-domain settings capturing author-specific information irrespective of topic change.

In [13], the idea of excluding topic-related features from text is taken one step further by using text distortion techniques to mask information associated with topic preferences. After choosing the k most frequent words in the language, all the other words and digits are replaced with asterisks. The results have shown that the masking technique improves the performance of cross-domain AA: namely, cross-topic AA benefits from masking all but the most frequent 300 words, i.e. mainly function words.

2.2 Author Clustering

Document-level author clustering was introduced in the 2016 PAN competition [14].

In author clustering, given a document collection the task is to group documents written by a single author in a single cluster. The number of authors is not known to the participants, so it has to be chosen based on the data.

The extrinsic evaluation metrics for author clustering in the PAN competitions are BCubed F-score, Precision and Recall, which have been shown to perform well compared to other extrinsic clustering evaluation metrics [1]. The BCubed precision of a document d is the proportion of documents in the cluster of d by the same author of d. The BCubed recall of d is the proportion of documents by the author of d that are found in the cluster of d. The BCubed F-score is the harmonic mean of BCubed precision and recall.

The evaluation results of the participants ranged from 0.23 to 0.82 BCubed F-score. The two best approaches to author clustering both include bottom-up clustering with character-based features and most frequent terms.

The PAN 2017 author clustering competition included the same texts chunked into very short paragraphs between 100 and 500 characters [15]. Despite the difficulty in processing very short documents, most of the approaches beat the baselines and ranged from 0.53 to 0.57. The top-performing method made use of agglomerative hierarchical clustering with character and word n-grams and a number of text-length, orthographic and lexical statistics features with TF-IDF and Log-Entropy weighting schemes [15].

2.3   Unmasking for Author Clustering in Russian

Stability of authorship features against change of mode, topic and time of text production in the Russian language has been investigated in [7] concluding that some features are highly affected by topic, especially mode change, whereas other features remain stable for an individual author.

While author clustering is a difficult task, it is beneficial in evaluating different feature sets. Clustering performs natural grouping of the data based on the features, whereas modern text classification techniques automatically assign weights to features in terms of their significance in a classification task. In the current cross-topic scenario, author clustering allows us to evaluate natural groups for different feature sets and determine whether the groups (clusters) represent topic or authorship.

To the best of our knowledge, this is the first work to use a document clustering task in order to evaluate topical features unmasking. Moreover, to identify topical features noisy for author clustering, we have introduced a modification to the original unmasking technique [6] enabling us to investigate the influence of the significant topical features on author clustering. Finally, we perform our experiments on a real-world noisy dataset in Russian, which is an understudied language in terms of authorship attribution.

3   Experiment

3.1   Dataset Description

The dataset for the experiment consists of postings from the KavkazChat dataset which contains post from forums in Russian dedicated to jihad in the North Caucasus. This dataset was collected under the Dark Web Project conducted by the University of Arizona's Artificial Intelligence Lab [2].

KavkazChat dataset contains 699,981 posts written by 7,125 members in the period 3/21/2003-5/21/2012. These posts in dataset are organized into 16,854 "threads", or topics. Each post contains information on topic, authorship and time of posting. For the purpose of current study, 10 productive authors were chosen from the KavkazChat dataset, so that there are 10 posts written by each author. All the texts are more than 1,000 characters long and are written in Russian as identified by the *langid* library [9]. The 10 posts by each author belong to one topic. As a result, our dataset includes 100 documents by 10 authors, with documents by each author belonging to one of three topics. The dataset organization is illustrated in Table 1.

Table 1. Dataset characteristics

Author	Topic	Number of texts	Average text length (tokens)
Шариат>правда	Более подробно о	10	575.6
Инал_Нохчий	Чеченских тейпах…	10	1216.3
Polevoj Buketik	*In detail on the Chechen teips*	10	895.1
Белг1то		10	750.7
musulmexx	33 повода принять Ислам	10	1339.3
Maga77	*33 reasons to convert to Islam*	10	449.4
Jasmin		10	370.2
at_tawbah	Садитесь с нами, укрепим	10	2304.4
Salah ad-Din	нашу веру	10	1140.8
Аль-Фаляк	*Sit with us, let's strengthen our faith*	10	1364.7

3.2 Methods

The current research goal is to perform topic classification of forum posts and iteratively remove a number of the most significant features in the topic classification, while evaluating author clustering with the resulting feature space in each iteration.

Feature Space. The initial feature space contains features proven to be useful in the previous work on AA. First, we employ the typed character n-gram features described in [12]. Second, we add a number of generalized features representing discourse and punctuation patterns described in [8]. Finally, we add word and part-of-speech n-grams with n ranging from 1 to 3, which have been shown to be instrumental in some previous works [4, 7, 15]. We only include frequent features occurring in at least 10 documents. TF-IDF weighting was applied. The resulting feature space contains 8,497 features.

Unmasking Topical Features. To perform topic classification, we apply Linear Support Vector Classification as developed in the *sci-kit learn* package [10], with two-fold cross-validation, l2 penalty and otherwise default parameters. We apply recursive feature elimination to remove 10 least informative features iteratively and evaluate the topic classification performance with F1-micro. Thus we get a ranking for every feature, ranging from 1 to 849 according to its importance in the topic classification.

Author Clustering. Given the ranking of the most significant topical features, the goal of the experiment is to identify a group of topical features which introduce noise in author clustering. In order to test this, we have performed clustering experiments with different feature sets. First, the full feature set is applied to text clustering. Then, the significant topical features are removed from the feature set iteratively: first, the 7 most significant topical features ranked 1 are removed; after that, the 10 topical features of rank 2 are removed, etc. with the 10 highest rank features removed at every step. Clustering is performed with the resulting feature set at every step so that a feature set is 10 features smaller at each iteration. If the research hypothesis is true, there is a feature set smaller than the full one for which author clustering performs higher than for the full feature set. For document clustering, we use agglomerative clustering as it was the top-performing author clustering approach in the 2017 PAN competition [4]. Our preliminary experiments have shown that only *Ward* linkage with *Euclidean* metric result in evenly distributed clusters, while the other strategies tend to form one very large cluster with the rest of the clusters containing single documents. We set the desired number of clusters equal to 10, which is the ground-truth number of authors. Clustering is evaluated against authorship ground truth with the BCubed F-score [1, 15].

It should be noted that in our experiment we initially set a number of clusters equal to the number of authors. As we mentioned earlier in this paper, in real-life situation the number of authors of anonymous texts could be unknown, but we argue that our approach is viable at least for two reasons. First, in a real-life scenario (especially in forensic settings) two situations are typical, namely when there are small or indefinite set of suspects. In the first case the number of clusters (i.e. possible authors) is known, and the task is to cluster an anonymous text with other texts by a true author rather than not to define the number of the authors. Second, our current goal is to assess the efficiency of a different feature set rather than to define the exact number of authors and then cluster texts over their authorship as it was in previously described PAN competitions.

4 Results and Discussion

4.1 Unmasking Topical Features

First, we have applied recursive feature elimination by iteratively removing the 10 least significant features and evaluating the topic classification performance with the resulting feature set. The topic classification performance for different numbers of the selected features is illustrated in Fig. 1. A very small number of features is needed to achieve a considerably high classification performance. In fact, the best performing number of features is 547 with the classification F1-micro reaching 0.86.

4.2 Author Clustering Performance

The clustering results with sets of topical features iteratively removed are illustrated in Fig. 2. Clustering is evaluated against ground truth authorship with BCubed Precision (P), Recall (R) and F-score (F).

For the full feature set, $P = 0.385$, $R = 0.524$, $F = \mathbf{0.444}$. It is obvious from Fig. 2 that generally all of the selected features are instrumental in author clustering, because clustering performance mostly decreases with feature elimination. However, there is an increase in clustering performance for the set with a short list of eliminated topical features. Indeed, the best clustering performance result is achieved for the dataset with the best 157 topical features removed (ranked from 1 to 16) and 8,340 features left, $P = 0.434$, $R = 0.59$, $F = \mathbf{0.498}$. After that, clustering performance steadily decreases as a result of topical feature elimination.

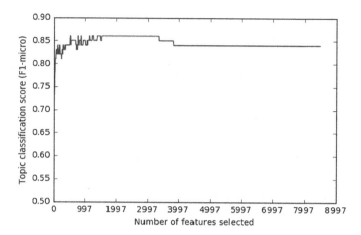

Fig. 1. Topic classification results with the most significant iteratively selected features

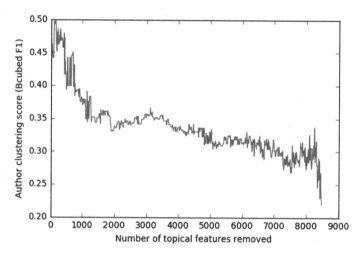

Fig. 2. Author clustering results with the most significant iteratively removed topical features

The clustering results for the full feature set and for the best performing feature set with removed topical features are illustrated in Figs. 3 and 4, respectively. The name of every ground-truth author is written in a specific color; the colors of the 10 sub-trees representing clusters match that of the most frequent author in the given cluster.

The illustrations suggest that there are a few large clusters which are noisy in terms of authorship but mostly representing the topical structure of the dataset. However, the number of large noisy clusters drops from 4 down to 2 as the main topical features are removed from the full feature set.

Fig. 3. Document clustering for the full feature set

Fig. 4. Document clustering with the 157 most significant topical features removed

5 Conclusions and Future Work

We have been able to conduct the analysis of the performance of author clustering after removing significant topical features using a real-world noisy dataset of forum posts in Russian, i.e. we have performed topical feature ranking, removed the most significant topical features iteratively from our dataset and evaluated the resulting document clustering against authorship ground truth.

We have found out that the list of the most significant topical features indeed decreases author clustering performance by introducing more topic-based clusters in the clustering results. By removing the list of topical features we have increased author clustering BCubed F-score by more than 5%. Manual investigation of the clusters reveals that topical feature removal decreases the number of noisy large clusters representing topical information and increases that of actually author-based clusters.

We have concluded that most of the features, including topical ones, are important for author clustering, especially in a dataset where all the documents by one author belong to a single topic. However, for effective authorship attribution even in such a topic-author-imbalanced dataset, it is useful to remove a small number of the highest-ranked topical features during preprocessing.

We expect this effect to be more robust in a dataset balanced by topics and authors, including texts on a range of topics written by each author. It is our intention to construct a topic- and author-balanced corpus in Russian and investigate the influence of the topical features presented here as well as to add more sophisticated semantic and syntactic ones. We will also include a larger number of authors and domains into the dataset while controlling for the mode and genre of texts by each author. Finally, we expect to achieve a list of domain-independent highly stable authorship features in Russian.

Acknowledgment. Authors acknowledge support of this study by the Russian Science Foundation, grant №18-78-10081 "Modelling of the idiolect of a modern Russian speaker in the context of the problem of authorship attribution".

References

1. Amigó, E., Gonzalo, J., Artiles, J., Verdejo, F.: A comparison of extrinsic clustering evaluation metrics based on formal constraints. Inf. Retrieval **12**(4), 461–486 (2009)
2. Chen, H.: Dark web: exploring and mining the dark side of the web. In: European Intelligence and Security Informatics Conference 2011, pp. 1–2. IEEE Computer Society (2011)
3. Darooneh, A.H., Shariati, A.: Metrics for evaluation of the author's writing styles: who is the best?. Chaos: Interdisc. J. Nonlinear Sci. **24**, 033132 (2014)
4. Gómez-Adorno, H., Martín-del-Campo-Rodríguez, C., Sidorov, G., Alemán, Y., Vilariño, D., Pinto, D.: Hierarchical clustering analysis: the best-performing approach at PAN 2017 author clustering task. In: Bellot, P., et al. (eds.) CLEF 2018. LNCS, vol. 11018, pp. 216–223. Springer, Cham (2018). https://doi.org/10.1007/978-3-319-98932-7_20

5. Kestemont, M., Luyckx, K., Daelemans, W., Crombez, T.: Evaluating unmasking for cross-genre authorship verification. In: Meister, J.C. (ed.) Digital Humanities 2012, pp. 249–251. Hamburg University Press (2012)
6. Koppel, M., Schler, J., Bonchek-Dokow, E.: Measuring differentiability: unmasking pseudonymous authors. J. Mach. Learn. Res. **8**, 1261–1276 (2007)
7. Litvinova, T., Litvinova, O., Seredin, P.: Assessing the level of stability of idiolectal features across modes, topics and time of text production. In: 23rd Conference of Open Innovations Association, FRUCT 2018, pp. 223–230. IEEE (2018)
8. Litvinova, T., Panicheva, P., Litvinova, O.: Authorship attribution of Russian forum posts with different types of n-gram features. In: 3rd International Conference on Natural Language Processing and Information Retrieval (NLPIR 2019) Proceedings. ACM (2019, in press)
9. Lui, M., Baldwin, T.: langid.py: an off-the-shelf language identification tool. In: The 50th Annual Meeting of the Association for Computational Linguistics, pp. 25–30. The Association for Computer Linguistics (2012)
10. Pedregosa, F., et al.: Scikit-learn: machine learning in Python. J. Mach. Learn. Res. **12**(Oct), 2825–2830 (2011)
11. Rocha, A., et al.: Authorship attribution for social media forensics. IEEE Trans. Inf. Forensics Secur. **12**(1), 5–33 (2017)
12. Sapkota, U., Bethard, S., Montes-y-Gómez, M., Solorio, T.: Not all character n-grams are created equal: A study in authorship attribution. In: NAACL HLT 2015, pp. 93–102. The Association for Computational Linguistics (2015)
13. Stamatatos, E.: Masking topic-related information to enhance authorship attribution. J. Assoc. Inf. Sci. Technol. **69**, 461–473 (2018). https://doi.org/10.1002/asi.23968
14. Stamatatos, E., et al.: Clustering by authorship within and across documents. In: Working Notes of CLEF 2016, CEUR Workshop Proceedings, vol. 1609, pp. 691–715. CEUR-WS. org (2016)
15. Tschuggnall, M., et al.: Overview of the author identification task at PAN-2017: style breach detection and author clustering. In: Working Notes of CLEF 2017, CEUR Workshop Proceedings, vol. 1866. CEUR-WS.org (2017)

Assessment of Syllable Intelligibility Based on Convolutional Neural Networks for Speech Rehabilitation After Speech Organs Surgical Interventions

Evgeny Kostuchenko[1]([✉]) [iD], Dariya Novokhrestova[1] [iD],
Svetlana Pekarskikh[1], Alexander Shelupanov[1] [iD],
Mikhail Nemirovich-Danchenko[1] [iD], Evgeny Choynzonov[1,2] [iD],
and Lidiya Balatskaya[1,2] [iD]

[1] Tomsk State University of Control Systems and Radioelectronics,
Lenina str. 40, 634050 Tomsk, Russia
key@keva.tusur.ru, nii@oncology.tomsk.ru
[2] Tomsk Cancer Research Institute, Kooperativniy av. 5, 634050 Tomsk, Russia
http://www.tusur.ru, http://www.oncology.tomsk.ru/

Abstract. Head and neck cancer patients often have side effects that make speaking and communicating more difficult. During the speech therapy the approach of perceptual evaluation of voice quality is widely used. First of all, this approach is subjective as it depends on the listener's perception. Secondly, the approach requires the patient to visit a hospital regularly. The present study is aimed to develop the automatic assessment of pathological speech based on convolutional neural networks to give more objective feedback of the speech quality. The structure of the neural network has been selected based on experimental results. The neural network is trained and validated on the dataset of phonemes which are represented as Mel-frequency cepstral coefficients. The neural network is tested on the syllable dataset. Recognition of the phoneme content of the syllable pronounced by a patient allows to evaluate the progress of the rehabilitation. A conclusion about the applicability of this approach and recommendations for the further improvement of its performance were made.

Keywords: Speech rehabilitation · Syllable intelligibility ·
Phoneme recognition · MFCC · CNN

1 Introduction

According to statistics, in Russia, the number of new cases of speech organ cancers has reached 22 thousand in 2016 [1]. Those patients receive a combined treatment that involves a surgical intervention. Hence, the changes in the speech organs occur. After the surgery, most of the patients undergo a speech rehabilitation to learn to pronounce some phonemes again. Currently, the assessment of the speech quality at the rehabilitation is given by several speech therapists for providing more objective results. This procedure is time-consuming for the speech therapists, and requires a patient to come to the hospital. It is not always convenient and possible for a patient. Due to these problems, the idea to automate the rehabilitation process came up. At this moment of time, in Russia, there is no a complete solution of an automated speech quality assessment, however, some approaches are in the process of developing. One of such approaches is based on the application of neural networks.

This work presents a possible option to determine the progress in the speech restoration which uses a CNN model trained on patient's audio recordings made before surgery.

2 Description of the Proposed Approach

The requirements and limitations for the framework are mentioned below.

1. Dependence on the speaker. For each patient a personal model is trained using his audio recordings before surgery. This fact simplifies the training, as well as considers the natural specific characteristics of the speech for each patient.
2. Predefined set of syllables. The audio recordings are defined by the table of 90 syllables in order to make an accent on the problematic phonemes ([k], [s], [t], and their soft implementations).
3. It is known in advance which syllable is pronounced. It means that the phonetic composition of a syllable, recognized by CNN, might be compared with an expected one.

The algorithm of automating the process of rehabilitation includes the following steps.

1. Preprocessing of an audio recording performed by a patient before surgery. This data will be used to train the CNN.
   a. Noise reduction and time-alignment at phoneme level;
   b. Split of the phoneme's periods into a sequence of overlapping frames (frame length is 20 ms, hop length is 1 ms);
   c. Feature extraction as Mel-Frequency Cepstral Coefficient (MFCC) from each of the 20 ms frames (matrix size is 100×44);
2. Defining the structure of Convolutional Neural Network (CNN);
3. Training the CNN, built at the step 2 on the labeled data (phonemes) of the step 1.
4. Building an algorithm of the phoneme detection in an audio recording of a syllable. Each recording of the syllable's set is split into 20 ms frames with 1 ms hop length. Then every frame is labeled by CNN as one of the phonemes learned. When the resulting sequence of labels is obtained, the random phoneme labels are excluded and consecutive phoneme labels are merged. The result is compared with the expected one.

The main idea of this approach was proposed in [2] and has now found an application for working with certain types of speech diseases [3, 4].

3 Data Preprocessing

3.1 Analysis of Phonetic Composition of the Audio Data Given, Splitting Recordings into Frames, and Labeling

There is a set of 90 syllables presented in the Table 1. The table was obtained from the paper [5].

Table 1. Set of 90 syllables used at the speech rehabilitation in Russia.

k'	s'	t'	kʲ	sʲ	Tʲ
k'asʲ Кась	s'osʲ Сось	t'ipʲ Тыпь	kʲæsʲ Кясь	sʲit͡s Сич	tʲʉt Тют
kr'us Крус	sv'um Свум	trʲit Трит	kʲʉj Кюй	sʲosʲ Сёсь	tʲor Тёр
k'up Куп	sʲtʲæl Стял	t'orʲ Торь	kʲæsʲtʲ Кясть	sʲʉt Сюд	tʲipʲ Типь
k'asʲtʲ Касть	s'it͡s Сыч	t'ɛf Тэф	kʲet Кёт	sʲetʲ Седь	tʲʉm Тюм
kr'op Кроп	s'ul Сул	tr'ux Трух	kʲæt Кят	sʲix Сих	tʲænʲ Тянь
rk'ɛt Ркат	fs'ɛn Фсэн	t͡st'ap Чтап	skʲæl Скял	fsʲen Фсен	sʲtʲæl Стял
d'okt Докт	ps'un Псун	ʂt'aj Штай	ʂkʲʉn Шкюн	ksʲet Ксет	ʂtʲæj Штяй
sk'at Скат	ts'al Дсал	st'it͡s Стыч	fkʲen Фкён	psʲʉn Псюн	sʲtʲit͡s Стич
fk'on Фкон	t͡ɕs'ep Чсэб	st'ar Стар	skʲʉn Скюн	ksʲex Гсех	sʲtʲær Стяр
ʂk'un Шкун	rs'at Рсат	t͡st'up Чтуп	ʂkʲet Шкет	tsʲæl Дсял	t͡stʲex Чтех
nʲæk Няк	d'is Дыс	bʲæt Бят	vʲikʲ Викь	plʲisʲ Плись	p'osʲtʲ Пость
j'ek Ёк	g'is Гыс	p'ut Пут	nʲækʲ Някь	n'isʲ Нысь	t͡ɕætʲ Чать
β'ek Фек	zʲdʲes Здес	tʲʉt Тют	β'ekʲ Фекь	s'osʲ Сось	ʂ'etʲ Шеть
vʲik Вик	n'is Ныс	trʲit Трит	pl'akʲ Плакь	ʂ'isʲ Шись	mʲætʲ Мять
pl'ik Плык	g'os Гос	β'et Фёт	f'okʲ Фокь	k'asʲ Кась	mʲitʲ мить

Using open-source audio auditor "Audacity", the positions of all phonemes in each of the 90 syllables of Table 1 were found. The time moments in milliseconds were written into a table.

The analysis of a phoneme content for the 90 syllables showed that this syllable set includes only 35 out of 42 Russian phonemes. Moreover, the occurrence of these phonemes is unevenly distributed.

After splitting the phoneme intervals into 20 ms frames, the distribution of a quantity of examples for each phoneme was obtained (see Fig. 1).

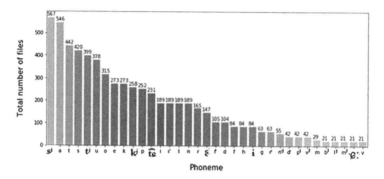

Fig. 1. The distribution of a quantity of examples for each phoneme

Figure 1 shows that the dataset is unbalanced. This fact can cause insufficient results, and should be taken into consideration further.

3.2   Calculating MFCCs of Phoneme Audio Files

The MFCCs describe the energy distribution of a signal in the frequency domain and refers to a perceived frequency. They are widely used as features in automatic speech recognition [6]. To convert a frequency into a mel, the following equation is used:

$$m = 1125 * ln(1 + f/700) \tag{1}$$

To calculate MFCCs for wav audio files, a Python library "librosa" [7] for audio signal processing was applied. An example of a mel-spectrogram representation is shown in Fig. 2.

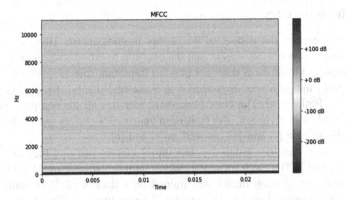

Fig. 2. MFCC spectrogram of 20 ms [k] phoneme.

4 Construction and Training a Neural Network

4.1 Building CNN

For a software realization of the algorithm of the automated speech quality assessment, a high-level programming language Python was chosen. The neural network was coded using Keras library [8] with TensorFlow backend.

The final structure of the chosen CNN is represented in Fig. 3.

Layer (type)	Output Shape	Param #
conv2d_5 (Conv2D)	(None, 96, 40, 32)	832
conv2d_6 (Conv2D)	(None, 93, 37, 48)	24624
max_pooling2d_3 (MaxPooling2	(None, 46, 18, 48)	0
conv2d_7 (Conv2D)	(None, 44, 16, 64)	27712
conv2d_8 (Conv2D)	(None, 43, 15, 120)	30840
max_pooling2d_4 (MaxPooling2	(None, 21, 7, 120)	0
dropout_5 (Dropout)	(None, 21, 7, 120)	0
flatten_2 (Flatten)	(None, 17640)	0
dense_4 (Dense)	(None, 128)	2258048
dropout_6 (Dropout)	(None, 128)	0
dense_5 (Dense)	(None, 64)	8256
dropout_7 (Dropout)	(None, 64)	0
dense_6 (Dense)	(None, 32)	2080
dropout_8 (Dropout)	(None, 32)	0
dense_7 (Dense)	(None, 7)	231

Total params: 2,352,623
Trainable params: 2,352,623
Non-trainable params: 0

Fig. 3. Neural network structure.

4.2   Training the CNN

As mentioned earlier, the dataset of 35 classes is unbalanced. This fact caused law accuracy results. It is for this reason that the decision to group some sounds was taken since the recognition of them does not play an important role.

As a result, the data was regrouped into 9 classes: [k], [s], [t], [kʲ], [sʲ], [tʲ], [ʂ + ɕː+t͡ɕ], [vow], [unknown]. The class [unknown] includes all the rest phonemes which are not a part of other 8 classes. The confusion matrix of 9-classes model showed that it is hard to distinguish [s] and [sʲ], as well as [t] and [tʲ].

The next step was to regroup the data into 7 classes merging the confusing phonemes [s]/[sʲ] and [t]/[tʲ]. Such form of a dataset representation showed the best results.

The 7-class recognition model was trained on a dataset of 1395 audio files (see Fig. 4 left) and validated on the dataset of 422 audio files (see Fig. 4 right).

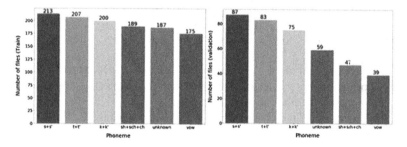

Fig. 4. Distribution of phoneme examples in the 6-classes ([k + kʲ], [s + sʲ], [t + tʲ], [ʂ + ɕː+t͡ɕ], [vow], [unknown]) training dataset (left) and validation dataset (right)

The input shape of data for the model was (1395 × 100 × 44 × 1). The batch size was chosen 100, when number of epochs was 87 in accordance with under-, overfitting balance.

Thus, the training accuracy reached 98%, and the validation accuracy – 91%.

4.3   Phoneme Recognition in the Syllables

The algorithm of the phoneme recognition has the following steps.

1. On the timeline, the interval of a syllable is defined (the process of identifying intervals is supposed to be automated both for syllables, and for phonemes).
2. The entire interval of a syllable is splitted into 20 ms frames with 1 ms hop length.
3. For each of 20 ms frame of a syllable, the label (phoneme's name) is attributed. The result is a list of phoneme labels for one syllable. An example of the resulting output of the recognition for the syllable [kʹasʲ] can be presented as ['k', 'vow', 's'], and shown in Fig. 5.

```
['k', 'k', 'k', 'k', 'k', 'k', 'k', 'k', 'k', 'k', 'k', 'k', 'k',
'unknown', 'unknown', 'k', 'unknown', 'k', 'unknown', 'k', 'vow',
'k', 'unknown', 'vow', 'k', 'vow', 'unknown', 'k', 'unknown', 'vow',
'k', 'vow', 'unknown', 'vow', 'unknown', 'k', 'unknown', 'vow',
'vow', 'vow', 'vow', 'vow', 'vow', 'unknown', 'vow', 'vow', 'vow',
'vow', 'vow', 'vow', 'vow', 'vow', 'vow', 'vow', 'vow', 'vow', 'vow',
'vow', 'vow', 'vow', 'vow', 'vow', 'vow', 'vow', 'unknown', 'vow',
'vow', 'vow', 's', 's', 's', 's', 's', 's', 's', 's', 's', 's', 's',
's', 's', 's', 's', 's', 's', 's', 's', 't', 's', 's', 's', 's', 's',
's', 's', 's', 's', 's', 's', 's', 's', 's', 's', 's', 's', 's', 's',
's', 's', 's']
```

Fig. 5. Full phonetic composition of the syllable [kˈasʲ] as a result of CNN model recognition

4. Occasionally appeared labels are excluded and consecutive labels are merged. The result of this procedure is presented in Fig. 6.

$$['k', 'vow', 's']$$

Fig. 6. Shorten result of phonetic composition of the syllable кась

5. Representation of the syllable shown in Fig. 6 might be further compared with an expected result.

5 Evaluation of the Phoneme Recognition by the CNN

The results of experiments with different number of classes in the dataset gathered in Table 2.

Table 2. Comparative table of results for different number of classes

Number of classes	35	9	6
Set of phonemes	[a], [b], [bʲ], ..., [ch], [sh], [sch], [e]	[k], [s], [t], [kʲ], [sʲ], [tʲ], [ş + ɕ:+t͡ɕ], [vow], [unknown]	[k + kʲ], [s + sʲ], [t + tʲ], [ş + ɕ:+t͡ɕ], [vow], [unknown]
Training dataset size	17 062	2 792	1 395
Validation dataset size	4 267	596	422
Number of epochs	150	20	87
Training accuracy	16%	21%	98%
Validation accuracy	13%	23%	91%

From the consideration of the Table 2, the following conclusions are drawn:

1. To recognize all the phonemes equally, it is necessary to have enough examples and a well-balanced dataset.
2. It might be acceptable to group some phonemes if they are not interesting as problematic phonemes.
3. The problem of [s]/[sʲ], and [t]/[tʲ] confusion might be solved by involving an expert in phonetics who could contribute to create a well-balanced dataset of syllables and to label a training dataset correctly.
4. It is enough to use 200 examples per class for 6-class classification problem. However, if the number of classes increases, it is essential to enlarge the training dataset too.
5. In this paper the time-alignment of phonemes in audio files was performed manually, and it is time-consuming. To make the phoneme recognition process indeed automated, it is also needed to automate the process of performing phoneme time-alignment.

6 Working with Signals After Surgery

In the next stage, the trained model for a 6-class classification was used for classification in syllables that were recorded after surgery (before and after rehabilitation). The diagrams of belonging to six classes before and after the rehabilitation are presented in Figs. 7 and 8 (syllable [kas']). For smoothing, a median filter with a 10 ms window is applied.

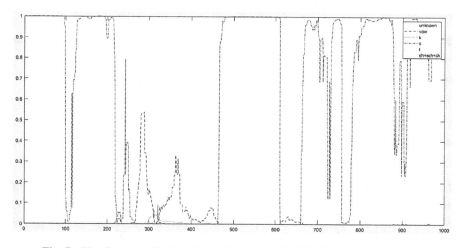

Fig. 7. The diagrams of belonging to six classes [k'asʲ] before the rehabilitation

It can be seen that, before rehabilitation, the syllable is, in fact, classified incorrectly. The phoneme [k] is essentially undefined. In addition, almost all the silence

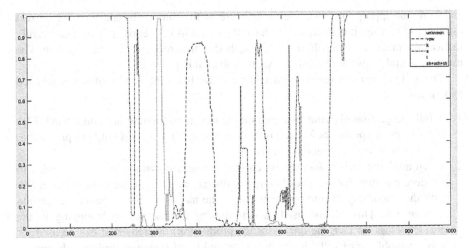

Fig. 8. The diagrams of belonging to six classes [k'asʲ] after rehabilitation

Table 3. The proportion of errors (2-nd type) in the definition of each of the classes before surgery, after surgery and after rehabilitation

	Before surgery	After surgery	After rehabilitation
[unknown]	23%	99%	99%
[vow]	11%	83%	16%
[k + kʲ]	5%	94%	12%
[s + sʲ]	2%	2%	8%
[t + tʲ]	15%	90%	21%
[ş + ɕ:+tɕ]	11%	83%	19%

before and after a syllable is defined as [s], which is associated with changes in the noise environment. After rehabilitation, the measure of belonging is closer to the correct one, with an exception of the problem with silence. The proportion of errors in the definition of each of the classes before surgery, after surgery and after rehabilitation is presented in Table 3.

It can be seen that the quality of recognition decreases after the operation and recovers (although not to the previous level) after rehabilitation.

7   Conclusion

In this paper, the application of speech recognition based on a deep neural network for the problem of estimating syllabic intelligibility according to the method of GOST R 50840-95 "Speech transmission over varies communication channels. Techniques for measurements of speech quality, intelligibility and voice identification" is considered. In the framework of this method, the final deep neural network can act as an auditor and issue an appropriate quantitative estimate at the output. In addition, for correct estimates obtaining, it is necessary to have the opinions of 5 experts. This significantly reduces the practical applicability of the method with direct experts' participation. The use of a neural network instead of experts solves this problem.

The following main conclusions can be made from the results of the conducted experiments.

1. A full recognition of syllables based on the results of training only on the syllables of a particular speaker before the operation (using 90 words) is not very promising, an additional speech material is needed.
2. When applying classes focused on current problematic phonemes, it is possible to get decent results for syllables before the operation. The general error is below 9% with the possibility of improvement due to the use of VAD and better recognition systems [9]. This can be used in determining the metrics of belonging to the problem class (in fact, the quality of the production). Moreover, it can be used for solving problems of syllable segmentation and highlighting of problem phonemes.
3. It is possible to conduct additional research on a similar program, but with prior training on the speech of healthy speakers, additional training on the patient's speech before operation and a subsequent use of the trained neural network to classify phonemes after operation during rehabilitation to assess its quality.

Acknowledgments. The study was performed by a grant from the Russian Science Foundation (project 16-15-00038).

References

1. Kaprina, A., Starinskiy, A., Petrova, G.: Malignant neoplasm in Russia in 2017 (morbidity and mortality). PA Hertsen Moscow Oncology Research Center - Branch of FSBI NMRRCof the Ministry of Health of Russia, Moscow (2018)
2. Nikolaev, A.: Mathematical models and software package for automatic assessment of speech signal quality. Thesis for the degree of candidate of technical sciences in the specialty "Mathematical modeling, numerical methods and program complexes", Russia, Ekateriburg (2002)
3. Kostyuchenko, E., Novokhrestova, D., Balatskaya, L.: Evaluation of syllable intelligibility through recognition in speech rehabilitation of cancer patients. In: Schaerf, M., Mecella, M., Igorevna, D.V., Anatolievich, K.I. (eds.) Proceedings of REMS 2018 – Russian Federation & Europe Multidisciplinary Symposium on Computer Science and ICT, Stavropol, Dombay, Russia, 15–20 October 2018
4. Laaridh, I., Meunier, C., Fredouille, C.: Dysarthric speech evaluation: automatic and perceptual approaches. In: LREC 2018 - 11th International Conference on Language Resources and Evaluation, pp. 1995–2001 (2019)
5. Kostyuchenko, E., Ignatieva, D., Meshcheryakov, R., Pyatkov, A., Choynzonov, E., Balatskaya, L.: Model of system quality assessment pronouncing phonemes. In: Proceedings of 10th Dynamics of Systems, Mechanisms and Machines (Dynamics) Conference, Omsk, Russia, pp. 1–5 (2016)

6. Mel-frequency cepstral coefficients (MFCC) and speech recognition. https://habr.com/post/140828/. Accessed 15 Oct 2018
7. McFee, B., Raffel, C., Liang, D., P.W. Ellis, D., McVicar, M.: librosa: audio and music signal analysis in python. In: Proceedings of 14th Python in Science Conference, pp. 18–24. SciPy, Austin (2015)
8. Documentation of Keras: The Python Deep Learning library. https://keras.io/. Accessed 12 Nov 2018
9. Karpov, A.A.: An automatic multimodal speech recognition system with audio and video information. Autom. Rem. Control **75**(12), 2190–2200 (2014)

Corpus Study of Early Bulgarian Onomatopoeias in the Terms of CHILDES

Velka Popova[(⊠)] and Dimitar Popov

Konstantin Preslavsky University of Shumen,
Universitetska str. 115, 9700 Shumen, Bulgaria
labling@shu.bg

Abstract. The paper focuses on the earliest phases of grammatical ontogenesis. The object of observation and research is child-produced onomatopoeias from the periods of pre-morphology and the transition to proto-morphology, excerpted from the spoken language corpora of two Bulgarian girls (Alexandra and Stefani, marked in the respective longitudes in CHAT-format in the CLAN programme as ALE and TEF respectively).

Keywords: Onomatopoeia · Bulgarian child language corpus · CHILDES

1 Introduction

Onomatopoeias are among the first words in the vocabulary of small children. They represent words based on the imitation of typical sounds produced by animals, machines, people, and objects, and they can be included in the group of iconic signs.

In the present work, an attempt has been made to outline the role of onomatopoeia in establishing the verb as a part of speech in the earliest phases of language acquisition. To this end, the chronological model of natural morphology has been used, according to which the beginning of the ontogenesis is associated with two phases that precede the development of grammar (the morphological phase), and namely – the pre- and proto-morphological phase, when any real system (or even module) of morphological grammar till does not exist, since this still is not necessary for extra-grammatical operations and the few rudimentary precursors to later morphological rules. In the group of pre-morphological means are included the different units, including onomatopoeias, which play the role of ancillary mechanisms in the process of language acquisition [2,5].

The publication of the Paper is funded by the project CLaDA-BG – National Interdisciplinary Research E-Infrastructure for Bulgarian Language and Cultural Heritage Resources and Technologies integrated within European CLARIN and DARIAH infrastructures (Contract Nr. 01-164/ 28.08.2018).

A. A. Salah et al. (Eds.): SPECOM 2019, LNAI 11658, pp. 370–380, 2019.
https://doi.org/10.1007/978-3-030-26061-3_38

The observations and analysis in this research encompass onomatopoeias in child language from the period of pre-morphology and the transition to proto-morphology, excerpted from the speech corpora of two Bulgarian girls, Alexandra and Stefani.

2   The Data

The longitudinal and observational data in the present study are taken from mother-child interactions of two Bulgarian girls, Alexandra (ALE) and Stephani (TEF) (Bulgarian child language corpus[1]). Both children have been observed for a comparatively long period of time (ALE from the age of 1;01-2;04, and TEF - from 1;03-2;05). On average, a 60-min recording has been made monthly in different situations, such as playtime, feeding, reading books. The data consist of 30 h of recordings of the children's spontaneous speech in interactions with their caregivers. ALE has been observed between the ages of 1;1-2;4, and TEF, between 1;3-2;5. The data have been transcribed using CHILDES [4]. For the purposes of the study, each child's files have been grouped to correspond to the pre-morphological, transitional, and proto-morphological phases of their language development (Table 1).

Table 1. Data

Subject		age	
ALE	0;11-1;4	1;05-1;7	1;08-2;4
Total of word tokens: ALE:13 058; Mother, Father, older Sister: 17 970			
TEF	1;1-1;8	1;9-2;1	2;1-2;5...
Total of word tokens: TEF: 11514; Mother, Grandmother, Investigator: 20 498			
	premorphology transitional phase		protomorphology
	phases		

ALE and TEF's data are very suitable for the empirical verification of the acquisition models as these two children have "considerable individual differences" in acquiring the language. Between the two girls there are individual differences in the style of language acquisition [1]. ALE (a very early speaker) is a "reference" child and TEF (a typical average speaker) is an "expressive" child.

3   Onomatopeias in the Early Speech of Two Bulgarian Children

Onomatopoeias are found even in the first recordings of both of the two girls studied, ALE and TEF. They belong in the category of the so-called pre-

---

[1] The research described here is based on empirical material from the Bulgarian child language corpus (and in particular on Corpus A), created by the team at the Laboratory of Applied Linguistics at Shumen University "Konstantin Preslavski." See [6].

morphological means, highlighting their specific role as ancillary mechanisms that they play in the acquisition of certain language phenomena. Before proceeding with a detailed analysis of how onomatopoeia works in the framework of the early stages in the language development of the two children, it is worth outlining in general terms its place among the other pre-morphological means. It will immediately be clear that the two corpora are saturated with examples of extra-grammatical morphological operations, namely:

(a) Reduplications: bau-bau ('dog'), mjau-mjau ('cat'), pa-pa ('duckling'), am-am/am-ma ('eating'/'eat'), vova [:voda] ('water'), nani-nani ('sleep'), lju-lju ('swing'), puf-paf/pu-paf ('train'), Ni-ni (Niki), Ti-ta (Čita), etc.;
(b) Shortenings: boni [:bonboni] ('bonbons'), lad/olad [šokolad] ('chocolate'), kal [:portokal] ('orange'), min [komin] ('chimney');
(c) Truncations/abbreviations of various kinds, e.g. in unpredictable hypocoristics of the type: Stefani→Teti, Teče; Ivelin→Iči, Vin.
(d) Surface analogies such as Pipika (instead of Pipi) by analogy with Anika.
(e) Blends: akapiš (akam + pišam 'poop + pee'), pljunki (pljušeni pantalonki 'fleece pants@diminut'), kakajeja (kaka + lelja 'older sister + aunt'). And interesting example in this regard is introduced by Jean-Paul Sartre in his autobiographical book "Les Mots", namely the blend Karlémami, a combination of Karl + Mamie (Karl et Mamie): "... I adored her: since she was my grandmother. It had been suggested that I call her Mamie and call the head of the household by his Alsatian name, Karl. Karl and Mamie, that sounded better than Romeo and Juliet, than Philemon and Baucis. My mother would repeat to me a hundred times a day, not without a purpose: 'Karlemami are waiting for us; Karlemami will be pleased; Karlemami...', conjuring up, by the intimate union of those four syllables, the perfect harmony of the persons. I was only half taken in, but I managed to seem to be entirely: first of all, to myself. The word cast its shadow on the thing; through Karlemami I could maintain the flawless unity of the family and transfer a good part of Charles' merits to Louise. Suspect and sinful, always on the verge of erring, my grandmother was held back by the arms of angels, by the power of a word" [7].

The extra-grammatical morphological operations shown above, used by the observed children during their pre-morphological phase, are accompanied by many onomatopoeias (bau-bau, myau-myau, lyu-lyu, am-am, bum, etc.), non-prototypical diminutives (pisi – a diminutive of kitten, čiči – a diminutive of čičo 'uncle', Teti – a diminutive of Stefani, babi – a diminutive of baba 'granny', mami – a diminutive of mama 'mummy'), "frozen" forms (rote-learned forms) of the type mina'pass', daj 'give', njama 'don't, won't', la tuka [:ela tuk] 'come here'. The extra-grammatical morphological operations, as well as the non-prototypical rules, however, do not follow the functional evolution of the Bulgarian morphological system and therefore tend to preserve their characteristics of the pregrammatical phase (especially in the early diminutives with their non-prototypical pragmatic meaning). In such a case the only data from the pre-morphological phase, during which one would expect switching on of phases of grammatical-ization, are the rote-learned inflected forms (which are a necessary basis for the metamorphosis of early universal morphological preferences, which lead to the language-specific system adequacy that can only be supported by a grammatical module). In this line of thinking the role of onomatopoeia could more likely be expected in the morphosemantics than in the morphotactics.

The data from the two corpora recording the relative portion of pre-morphological means in the speech of ALE and TEF (presented in Fig. 1) are indicative of the significant place of onomatopoeia among the other precursors of grammar.

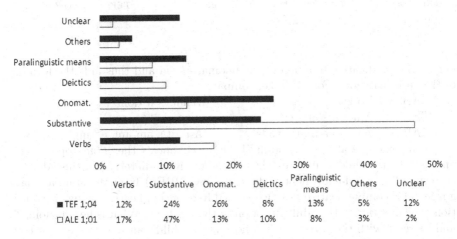

Fig. 1. Percentage of pre-morphological means (ALE and TEF).

From the very beginning of the recording, both children use onomatopoeias, marking by them the situations completely and not – partially. For example, when TEF (1;06) looks at the table as well as at the cake, plates, and the utensils sitting on it, she says: "Am-am." This am-am may refer to practically anything involved in the situation: the cake, the utensils, the participants, the process of eating. The mixed use of the onomatopoeias without any clear referential relation is typical. So, for example, lyu-lyu in the speech of TEF (1;06) can be observed regularly both in the sense of 'cradle' and 'to swing' (Table 2):

From the examples indicated it immediately becomes clear that the parts of speech have not been differentiated yet, though in the child's production there are already formal possibilities for this (cf. the later realizations of the sort Teti lyu-lyu, in which the predicative function of the onomatopoeia is clearly differentiated, versus uses from the sort of Mau-mau papa).

Later, onomatopoeia is used more often particularly for marking the per-ceived subject or event (action). At this stage of the language development (before the verb appears), the question of the adult determines to a certain

Table 2. Bulgarian onomatopoeia lyu-lyu in different contexts

Context 1:	Context 2:	Context 3:
BAB: *Na lyulkata kak praviš, babo?* 'How do you do in the cradle, Granny?' BAB: *Kak se lyuleeš?* 'How do you swing?' TEF: *Lyu-lyu*@onomat.	BAB: *Kăde shte hodim?* 'Where will we go to?' TEF: *Lyu-lyu*@onomat.	BAB: *Kakvo e tova?* 'What is this?' TEF: *Lyu-lyu*@onomat.
BAB: *I kakvo šte pravim tam?* 'And what will we do there?' TEF: *Ulka [:lyulka].* 'Cradle.'	BAB: *Kăde shte hodite s vuyčo?* 'Where will you go with uncle?' TEF: *Ulka [:cradle].* 'Cradle.'	BAB: *Kakvo e tova?* 'What is this?' TEF: *Ulka [:lyulka].* 'Cradle.'

degree the predicative function of the onomatopoeia and thus aids the forming of the verbs category. For example, compare:

*BAB: To kakvo pravi?   'What is it doing?'
*TEF: Am-am@onomat.
*BAB: A-a, to am-am, yade.   'A-a, it's am-am, eating'

In the example above, the adult (BAB) first repeats the onomatopoeia am-am, used by the child to indicate the action, and immediately after this adds the corresponding word-equivalent yade 'eat' (3SG PRES) from the standard language. This communicative practice is used frequently in early language acquisition. The question of the adult (most often the mother) "What is he/she doing?" and its reply with the correct verb following the child's answer create clear conditions to highlight the "place" of the onomatopoeia and the verbs among the remaining classes of words, and it makes it easier for the child to acquire the word itself. The child, following this sort of "training" strategy of the mother, often repeats the corresponding form. At the same time, there are instances of the first attempts of the girls studied to make the connection between the onomatopoeia and the normative lexeme, when they selectively repeat after the adult only the normative equivalent of the onomatopoeia. For example:

*DIM: A kăde e, tati, kokoškata?   'And where is, daddy['s child], the hen?'
*ALE: Ko-ko@onomat.
*VEL: Ko-ko@onomat, kokoška.
*ALE: Koka [:kokoška].   'hen'

The use of the onomatopoeia is an important stage in the acquisition of verb morphology, because it helps the child: (a) to learn how to make difference between events (actions) and subjects; (b) to recognize different kinds of situations (with the help of the interlocutor's explanations) and to mark them initially with onomatopoeias, and then also with the relevant verbs. The adult's strategy to repeat selectively the onomatopoeia with the relevant verbs and nouns can additionally catalyze the process of forming word categories. In this way, a moment is reached in the child's speech production when there has been clearly outlined the tendency towards dissociation of the global system into two fields, namely – that of the noun and that of the verb. Thus, for example, in the longitudinal data of TEF at the age 1;08.0, when there had already been made the first steps in this process, there are observed specific uses of onomatopoeias, in which there has been clearly demonstrated the striving for formal representation of a fragment of the reality once as a complete (limited) essence, i.e. - as a noun, and in another context – as an unlimited essence, i.e. - as a verb. Compare, for example:

| *BAB: | Kakvo e tova, babo? | 'What is this, [grandchild]?' |
| *BAB: | Pile? | 'Chicken?' |

%sit: she shows her a toy chicken

*TEF:	Pi-pi@onomat.	'Pi-pi'
*BAB:	Kakvo pravi pileto?	'What is the chicken doing'
*TEF:	Pi-pi-pi@onomat.	'Pi-pi-pi'
*VEL:	Kakvo ima tam?	'What is this there?'
*TEF:	Pipi [:pile].	'Pipi' [:pile: 'chicken']

Similar onomatopoeic realizations in the speech of TEF are not the only proof for the availability of primary lexical paradigms during the age discussed. Together with them, the aspiration of the child to mark certain lexemes as verbs is shown also in the use of inflected verb forms for naming actions, though very often this is accomplished incorrectly. Thus, in the child's utterances there are inflections for 1P SG, 1P PL; 3P SG (Present); 3P SG (Aorist); 2P SG (imperative); as well as a form for 3P SG (perfective). As an illustration, there will be quoted the verb lemmas (together with the formal types) and the onomatopoeias that marked 'action' in the speech passage analyzed: 14 verb lemmas/62 tokens/17 types versus 11 onomatopoeias/16 tokens (TEF – 1;08.0). See Table 3.

In the given speech fragment, regarding the act of 'feeding', it can be observed how the child "rewrites" the corresponding action from one format to another, namely, how she reformats the onomatopoeia a-am/am-am/am-am-am-am into the verb ama. Alongside this, in the same type of contexts during this recording, multiple uses of the verb papam 'eat' are recorded. The statistical analysis shows that at the age 1;08.0, in the presence of synonymous means for formal marking of a certain verbal concept, TEF demonstrates an apparent preference for the verb forms at the expense of the onomatopoeic ones, which is illustrated in Fig. 2.

In further language development, the tendency towards functional limiting of the onomatopoeias has been observed, and in a certain moment it has even resulted in encountering them only in predicative use (cf. for example TEF – 1;11.04: Granny, pish ('I will pee'); Bebito. Kok-kok ('jumps'); Dus-dus ('I joggle'); Rm-rm-rmy-rmy ('growls'); Botzi ('I stick/prick'); Am ('Eat!')). Some of them change also their phonetic appearance and start looking like verbs (for example – the botzi form instead of the usual so far botz/botz-botz onomatopoeia used), and some of them have already totally lost their onomatopoeic character and are perceived mostly as elements of the relevant verbal paradigm

Table 3. Verbs and onomatopoeias (TEF – 1;08.0)

Verbs – 14 lemmas / 62 tokens / 17 types	Onomatopoeias – 11 lemmas / 16 types
amam 'eat'	1 a-am / 2 am-am / 1 am-am-am-am
ama [:amam] – *3/1P SG PRES	1 a-kha
dam 'give'	2 bum
3 daj – 2P SG IMP	1 kh-kh-kh / 1 khu-khu
dojda 'come'	1 lju-uu
1 ela – 2P SG IMP	1 mush
4 elja [:ela] – 2P SG IMP	1 na
mina 'pass'	1 opa
3 mina – 3P SG AOR	1 piš
molja 'please'	1 skok
1 motja [:molja te] – 1P SG PRES	1 pi-pi-pi
1 motja [:molja te] – 1P SG PRES	
nanjam/njanjam 'sleep'	
9 nani [:nanjam] – *3/1P SG PRES	
1 nani-nani [:nanjam] – *3/1SG PRES	
1 nanja [:nanjam] – *3/1P SG PRES	
nedej 'don't'	
1 dej [:nedej] – 2S IMP	
njama 'won't, there isn't'	
13 njama – 3SG PRES	
placha 'cry'	
1 pači [:plače] – 3SG PRES	
opravja 'fix'	
2 pai [:opravim] – *3SG/1PL PRES	
papam 'eat'	
12 papa – 3SG PRES	
2 papa [:papam] – *3/1P SG PRES	
1 papaj [:papam] – *2SG IMP/1SG PRES	
1 papau [:papal] – *SG PART/PL	
pija 'drink'	
1 pij [:pie] – 3SG PRES	
1 pija – 1SG PRES	
otivam 'go'	
2 tiva [:otivam] – *3/1P SG PRES	
*titam [:slušam] 'listen'– quasiverb	
1 titam [:slušam] – 1P SG PRES	

(for example the chipi form, used in parallel with chipa 'bathe', has been associated with 3P SG PRESENT form and could be explained by the peculiar competition of the language forms at the entry during the process of constituting the miniparadigms).

When both of the children studied were still in the one-word phase, for describing actions consisting of one act, or which appear to be complete and limited in scope, the use of single onomatopoeias (e.g. *muš, štrak, pus/puš, bum,* etc.) is observed, whereas for indicating continuous actions or actions consisting of separate motions of the same type, reduplicated onomatopoeias are observed

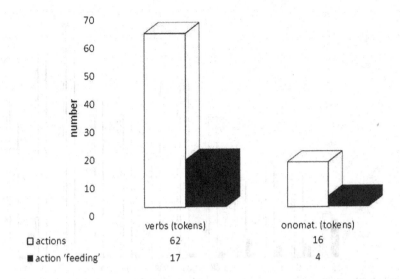

Fig. 2. Quantitative indicators for the designation of actions (TEF, 1;08)

(e.g. *lju-lju, am-am, kok-kok/kok-ko-kop, mjau-mjau-mjau-mjau, tik-tak-tik-tak,* etc.). For indicating duration of action, in some cases lengthened pronunciation of the relevant onomatopoeia (of the type: muuš, aam, naa, etc.) is observed, which accompanies the carrying out of the action itself.

The role of onomatopoeia as "laying the foundation" for the verb appearing is undoubted. In the case of both children, there has been observed a period of accelerated use of onomatopoeias in predicative function. With the appearance of the verb (as well as its contrastive forms), the reverse tendency has been detected – in both children's recordings there has been registered decreased use of onomatopoeias (cf. for example Graph 3, which illustratively represents how even from their origination, the first verb forms become apparently preferred by ALE). Thus, for example, in the case of ALE, the first significant decrease is from 15,4% (during the age of 1;01.29) to 5,3% (during the age of 1;05.06). After an unimportant increase at 1;07 to 7%, later this percent does not exceed 2%. The first decrease in the use of onomatopoeia is observed during the transition from pre- to proto-morphology, when the first proto-morphological signs appear; the second considerable decrease, observed at the age of 1;08, is accompanied by increase of a relative share of the utterances with verbs (more than 50%), which coincides with the beginning of the proto- morphological stage and the appearance of real mini-paradigms. This is illustrated in Fig. 3.

In the case of Stefani, the first significant decrease in the use of onomatopoeias in the predicative function is observed at the age of 1;08, which (as with Alexandra as well) corresponds with the beginning of the transition from pre- to proto-morphology. During this phase, in the following months, onomatopoeias gradually decrease to 0,9%. The stabilized presence of verbs after the age of 2;01 (over 50%) signals the establishment of the proto-morphological phase (see Fig. 4).

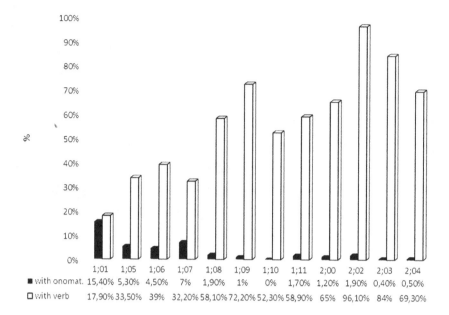

Fig. 3. Percentage of utterances with onomatopoeia (ALE)

	1;01	1;05	1;06	1;07	1;08	1;09	1;10	1;11	2;00	2;02	2;03	2;04
■ with onomat.	15,40%	5,30%	4,50%	7%	1,90%	1%	0%	1,70%	1,20%	1,90%	0,40%	0,50%
☐ with verb	17,90%	33,50%	39%	32,20%	58,10%	72,20%	52,30%	58,90%	65%	96,10%	84%	69,30%

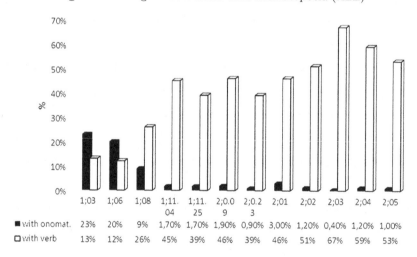

	1;03	1;06	1;08	1;11. 04	1;11. 25	2;0.0 9	2;0.2 3	2;01	2;02	2;03	2;04	2;05
■ with onomat.	23%	20%	9%	1,70%	1,70%	1,90%	0,90%	3,00%	1,20%	0,40%	1,20%	1,00%
☐ with verb	13%	12%	26%	45%	39%	46%	39%	46%	51%	67%	59%	53%

Fig. 4. Percentage of utterances with onomatopoeia (TEF)

From Alexandra's and Stefani's data analyzed, it becomes clear that during
the earliest stages, the predicative functions can be expressed by onomatopoeias
(including onomatopoeic reduplications), i.e. by extra-grammatical means (for
more details cf. [6]). Little children have a rich repertoire of means for expressing
predication, even before they have mastered the correct verb forms. But even

though they have forms of specific verbs expressing a pragmatic or morpho-semantic sense, they may use in the same meaning non-verbs as well (called also predecessors of verbs), together with onomatopoeias (cf. also: dolu 'down' in the meaning of 'put me down!'; opa in the meaning of 'pick me up!'; na in the meaning of 'take!'/'give' (ALE, 1;01.29)); and peculiar fillers, which consti-tute the phonetic structure of the relevant verb being mastered from the sort of tititeni, tititani respectively, in the meaning of 'sit down' and 'stand up' (TEF). During the transitional stage from pre- to proto-morphology, these verb prede-cessors are gradually replaced by the real verb lemmas, whose increase, however, is insignificant. This is evidence of the instability of the verb system, in which pre-morphological and proto-morphological elements cohabit. The appearance of verbs is followed by dramatic changes in the whole grammar system: con-trastive forms – conjugated forms for perfect and imperfect type (in the case of verbs) – appear; there are observed changes in the structure of sentence (sen-tences with subjects and predicates); and children start an intensive movement towards generalization of grammatical rules.

4   Conclusion

In conclusion, the use of onomatopoeias is an important step in the earliest phases of morphology acquisition, because it helps the child: (a) to learn to differentiate events (actions) and subjects; (b) to recognize different types of sit-uations and to designate them first with onomatopoeias and subsequently with the corresponding verbs. In this way, in their capacity as precursors of gram-mar in the phase of pre-morphology, onomatopoeias have a special contribution primarily in a child's morphosyntactic acquisition. At the same time, however, from the observations and analysis it become clear that these language units play a role also as a type of base for the primary testing of different inflectional forms. Thus to a large extent their use is a necessary preliminary step in the awareness of the relationship of form and function, which is realized in the onto-genetic process first in the initial global differentiation of child speech in two areas: the verb and the noun. This initial differentiation of classes of words, which is actually the first proto-grammatical opposition [3,6], gives grounds to assert that onomatopoeias are not simply a component of the early childhood lexicon, but are a type of ancillary mechanism in the mastery of language, which is contained in the language itself. To corroborate this statement, other data with the characteristics of onomatopoeia can be identified (atypical displays of echolalia, late babbling, vocal harmony, and others), some of which are observed not only in the dawn of language ontogenesis, but also through the entire period of childhood. Research on these phenomena, however, is not within the param-eters of this work, but is an open possibility for the future. The work presented here has a more modest goal. With the review of the data presented here from the two Bulgarian girls studied, Alexandra and Stefani, an attempt was made to demonstrate the place and role of onomatopoeia in the earliest phases of lan-guage acquisition. It was demonstrated how with the help of onomatopoeia, the child gradually manages to free herself from the constraints of so-called expressive morphology, based only on general cognitive principles and not subject to inclusion in any specific grammatical module. The copyright of the media files created during experiments can be protected using steganographic methods [8].

References

1. Bates, E., Dale, Ph., Thal, D.: Individual differences and their implications for theories of language development. In: Fletcher, P., MacWhinney, B. (eds.) Handbook of Child Language, pp. 96–151. Basil Blackwell, Oxford (1995)
2. Bittner, D., Dressler, W. U.: Introduction. In: Bitner, D., Dressler, W.U., Kilani-Schock, M. (eds.) ZAS Papers in Linguistics. Volume 18: First Verbs: On the way to Mini-paradigms, Berlin/Wien/Lausanne, pp. 1–6 (2000)
3. Bittner, D.: The emergence of verb inflection in two German-speaking children. In: Bittner, D., Dressler, W.U., Kilani-Schock, M. (eds.) Development of Verb Inflection in First Language Acquisition. From First Form to Miniparadigms. Mouton de Gruyter, Berlin/New York (2003)
4. MacWhinney, B.: The CHILDES Project. Tools for Analyzing Talk, 3rd edn. Lawrence Erlbaum Ass., Mahwah (2000)
5. Popova, V.: Rannata gramatika na detskija ezik. Kognitivni aspekti na glagolnata ontogeneza. Faber, V. Tărnovo (2006). (in Bulgarian)
6. Popov, D., Popova, V.: Multimodal presentation of Bulgarian child language. In: Ronzhin, A., Potapova, R., Fakotakis, N. (eds.) SPECOM 2015. LNCS (LNAI), vol. 9319, pp. 293–300. Springer, Cham (2015). https://doi.org/10.1007/978-3-319-23132-7_36
7. Sartre, J.-P.: Les Mots. Gallimard, Paris (1964)
8. Stoyanov, B.P., Zhelezov, S.K., Kordov, K.M.: Least significant bit image steganography algorithm based on chaotic rotation equations. Comptes rendus de l'Academie Bulgare des Sciences **69**(7), 845–850 (2016)

EEG Investigation of Brain Bioelectrical Activity (Regarding Perception of Multimodal Polycode Internet Discourse)

Rodmonga Potapova[1]([✉]) , Vsevolod Potapov[2] ,
Nataliya Lebedeva[3], Ekaterina Karimova[3] , and Nikolay Bobrov[1]

[1] Institute of Applied and Mathematical Linguistics,
Moscow State Linguistic University, 38 Ostozhenka Street,
Moscow 119034, Russia
RKPotapova@yandex.ru
[2] Centre of New Technologies for Humanities,
Lomonosov Moscow State University, Leninskije Gory 1,
Moscow 119991, Russia
volikpotapov@gmail.com
[3] Institute of Higher Nervous Activity and Neurophysiology of RAS
(IHNA&NPh RAS), 5A Butlerova Street, Moscow 117485, Russia
lebedeva@ihna.ru

Abstract. This paper considers the pilot experiment regarding the perception functioning of various brain areas channels in respect of multimodal polycode Internet discourses. The investigation focuses on three variants of EEG-analysis: solely auditory, exclusively visual and integrative auditory-visual perception. Regarding functional properties, it has been found that brain bioelectrical activity and all brain rhythm power values are dependent on the type of mental modality: visualization, audition and integrative stimuli perception. The experiment included a number of special tests involving perception of polycode Internet discourse, where subjects' brain bioelectrical activity dynamics were evaluated on the basis of EEGs. The frequency spectra were calculated in the special "Typology" program. The primary aim of this experiment was to find out what kind of Internet stimuli (auditory, visual and complex ones) have the greatest influence on all brain rhythm power values. The interpretation of the results may help in studying the influence on the brain areas observed during participation of young users (18–25 years old) in polycode Internet discourses. In the first series of experiments, differences in the brain bioelectrical activity dynamics were studied. The purpose was to evaluate how the brain performs auditory, visual and auditory-visual complex analyses with two indicators – positive and negative ones – of the brain area activity.

Keywords: Brain bioelectrical activity · Polycode internet stimuli ·
Mental multimodality · EEG analysis · Brain area ·
Auditory-visual-complex perception analysis

A. A. Salah et al. (Eds.): SPECOM 2019, LNAI 11658, pp. 381–391, 2019.
https://doi.org/10.1007/978-3-030-26061-3_39

1 Introduction

This project is a longitudinal study aimed to investigate the influence of polycode social-network discourse on the Internet on the brain bioelectrical activity of young Internet users. It is known that speaking and listening to speech are both extremely complex processes. Yet more complex is the process of decoding polycode complex stimuli. Many publications presented results of investigations on the domain of Internet addiction, Internet gaming disorders, pathological Internet use and others. The investigation tasks were combined with each of the following terms: "brain imaging", "resting state", "qualitative EEG". "Internet Gaming Disorder", etc. [1, 5, 7, 16, 23].

The present fundamental cross-disciplinary research project has a valeological focus, namely the influence of aggressive multimodal polycode communicative environment formed under the conditions of social networks upon transformation of psychophysiological and cognitive characteristics of mental and speech activity of young Internet users. Multimodal polycode communication in modern social networks has a number of features causing its negative influence over recipients. The most important of them is the presence of different kinds of polycode stimuli, including acoustic noise (auditory channel, which can be, in particular, affected by background noise) and other types of noise in a broader sense: informational, visual and emotional. In this project we propose to study the influence of different types of polycode stimuli over the functional status of the users' personality by monitoring the changes in psychophysiological and cognitive behavior parameters and the variations of cognitive reactions. The main hypothesis of the research is that the influence of different types of polycode stimuli upon human brain is characterized by the same main regularities as the influence of acoustic noise, which can be described, for example, using Lombard's model. The study of transformation of cognitive processes is based on previous research conducted using special tests (e.g. "Indicators of attention and speed of sensorimotor reactions" after Schulte, Toulouse-Pieron) before and after immersion in conditions typical of social network communication involving visual and auditory perception channels. Cognitive transformation will also be measured using "Numbers repeating", "Semantic verbal fluency" tests [4, 9, 10, 12–14]. The plan involved the development of new special tests oriented to the peculiarities of perception of multimodal polycode stimuli in both element-wise and complex modes, which would be especially interesting to compare with results described in [8].

The main goal of the research is to determine the cause-effect links between transformation of psychophysiological and cognitive characteristics of Internet users (in particular, social network users) and the influence of stressors forming the peculiar aggressive "ecosystem" of the Internet, which will allow to develop a set of valeological recommendations taking into account the social status, age, and gender and other factors related to internet-addiction prevention [15, 17, 18, 23].

The main focus of the research will be placed on the functional status of the subjects based on psychophysiological personality characteristics (excitability, lability, reactivity etc.) and also on cognitive deterioration under the influence of such stressors as different types of polycode stimuli, as well as simultaneous effect of aggressive visual and auditory information in multimodal social network communication [2, 3, 6,

11, 20–22]. An additional factor that needs to be considered in the research is that of influence of **polycode** stimuli in social network communication on the behavior of the recipients. It is expected that the research will help reveal the mechanism of social network addiction development. The object of these investigations is "electronic personality", individual differences and Internet use [3, 16, 17, 23]. Investigations, e.g. those in the domain of Internet Gaming Disorders, indicated that "... negative outcomes affected the covariance between risk level and activation of brain regions related to value estimation (prefrontal cortex), anticipation of rewards (Ventral striatum), and emotional-related learning (hippocampus), which may be one of the underlying neural mechanisms of disadvantageous risky decision-making in adolescents with Internet Gaming Disorders" [22, 24].

2 Method, Results

The aim of this pilot study is to analyze the EEGs indicating the brain bioelectrical activity on the basis of perceptual auditive, visual and complex indicators as relative signs of the brain bioelectrical activity dynamics with due account for fatigue. The experimental material corpus included Internet social-network discourse (polycode fragments) with verbal, paraverbal, non-verbal and extraverbal information (N = 30). The participants of this project (recipients of these stimuli) were university students, both male and female, aged 20–25. During the experiment, a special questionnaire was used, which included a set of questions regarding perception of auditive, visual and complex information. EEG (electroencephalographic) recordings were obtained from native Russian listeners and participants of visual probation experiments [11, 16, 17].

The dynamics of brain bioelectrical activity were evaluated on the basis of electroencephalographic data (EEG) using a technique similar to that described in [19]. EEG recording was performed using a Neurovizor encephalograph-analyzer with 13 electrodes (F3, F4, Fz, C3, C4, Cz, P3, P4, Pz, T3, T4, T5, T6) located according to the EC 10–20 system, in a monopolar way relative to the combined ear electrodes, A1 and A2. For all of these, the sampling frequency was set at 250 Hz, the filtration bands were 0.5–70 Hz, and the impedance was less than 20 kΩ. At the first stage, the EEG recording took place in the "Typology" program. When the electrodes are properly attached to the head, the "Typology" program on a PC connected to the encephalograph will start recording the EEG (if the electrodes are applied incorrectly, the EEG recording will be impossible). At the second stage, for the EEG recording, in the "Typology" program, the frequency spectra were calculated over epochs equal to 1216 Hz or 4.86 s for further processing. As a result of spectral analysis, the amplitudes of the spectral power amplitudes and peak frequencies in the bands of the delta-, theta-, alpha- and beta1-, and beta2- rhythms were obtained for each of the 13 channels. Figure 1 demonstrates the absolute power values of the brain rhythms averaged over all brain areas. *Stimulus 1* was the audio signal without visual information; *stimulus 2* was the video without the audio track; and *stimulus 3* was the video signal together with the same audio track. The duration of each stimulus was 51 s (for the purpose of this pilot study it was decided that the effects of natural fatigue should be avoided). The stimuli were administered by an operator three times each with short (about a minute) intervals of rest. The video stimuli were demonstrated using a large LED monitor (Sony Bravia 52") placed in front of the subject at a distance of about 3 meters. The audio track was played back over a high quality loudspeaker system (Microlab X1/2.1) placed behind the subject at a distance of about 2 m. These conditions were supposed to create maximum immersion effect. It is notable that, when listening only to the audio signal (stimulus 1), the power values of all the brain rhythms decreased compared to the state prior to the listening. At the same time, when perceiving a video and a video with an audio track (stimulus 2 and stimulus 3), on the contrary, an increase of the power values of rhythms was observed in all frequency ranges compared to the state prior to the visual perception. In addition, throughout the study, there is an increased level of beta-rhythm power values compared to other bands, which can be associated, firstly, with the subject's tense posture – since during the study, the subject was sitting without any support for their back, as it was necessary to fill in a questionnaire; secondly, it was necessary to correctly answer the questions on the stimulus material in the question-naire, and the state of readiness to perform the tasks increased the activation of the brain cortex.

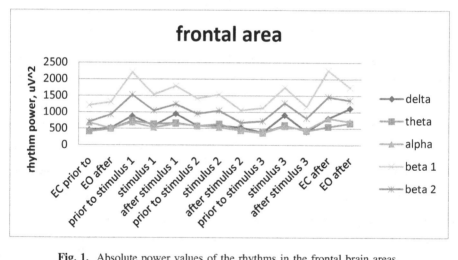

Fig. 1. Absolute power values of the rhythms in the frontal brain areas.

Comparison of the spectral values of the absolute power of the brain rhythms in the frontal, central, temple and parietal areas did not reveal significant differences in the dynamics of the rhythms (Figs. 2, 3 and 4).

The increased delta-activity in the resting state indicates the presence of inhibitory processes in the cerebral cortex, as a result of tiredness. In addition, the relative values of rhythm powers were calculated prior to and immediately after the presentation of each type of stimulus material (Fig. 6). To make it easier to understand the dynamics of the rhythm power values, below are the values of the relative power of the rhythms. Relative values of the power demonstrate changes in the rhythms in the resting state after the presentation of the stimuli. The values of relative power were calculated by the formula: AFTER/PRIOR − 1. Accordingly, values greater than zero indicate an increase in power after presentation of the stimulus material; values less than zero indicate a decrease in power after the stimulation. Background values obtained with closed and open eyes (EC and EO, respectively) that were recorded prior to and after the entire study demonstrate an increase in power over all frequency ranges. After the experiments involving visual and auditory perception of the stimulus material with eyes closed, an increase in delta- and beta- rhythms was observed most obviously; and with eyes open, a significant increase in the delta-rhythm only was observed (Fig. 5). As a result, after the listening to the audio track (stimulus 1), the power values of the delta-rhythm increased, while the power values of the other types of rhythms decreased. But after the visual analysis of the video fragments together with the audio-track, the power values of the alpha-activity increased.

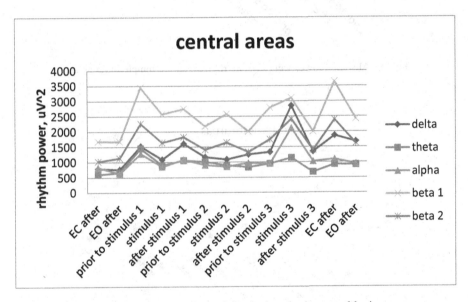

Fig. 2. Absolute power values of the rhythms in the central brain areas.

1. Stimulus 1 – Audio track

In Fig. 7 one can observe a decrease in the activity of all types of rhythms when listening to an audio signal. After the listening experiment, the power values of the rhythms increase, but not to the initial level (except for the delta-rhythm).

2. Stimulus 2 – Video signal

Curiously, during the perception of video material without the audio track, on the contrary, the power values of all rhythms increase compared to the resting state immediately prior to this (Fig. 8). At the same time, after the visual analysis, the power values of all rhythm types decrease even compared to the "prior" resting state. Frequency indicators showed greater stability throughout the study (Fig. 10).

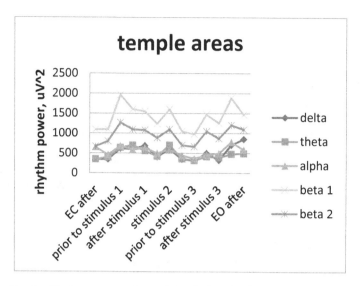

Fig. 3. Absolute power values of the rhythms in the temple brain areas.

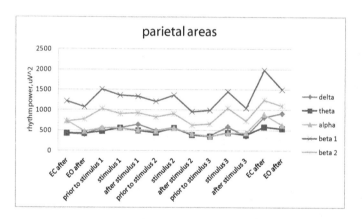

Fig. 4. Absolute power values of the rhythms in the parietal brain areas.

In general, the values of the dominant frequency are a much more stable indicator than the power value of the rhythm. The frequency of the beta2-rhythm did not change in various samples and remained at 32 Hz. The dynamics of other peak frequency values can be observed in Figs. 11, 12. During the perception of the audio signal, the frequencies of theta-, alpha-, and beta1-rhythms increased, while when watching only the video material, the only frequency that increased was that of the theta-rhythm, and when perceiving the video with the audio track, the frequency of the theta-rhythm increased.

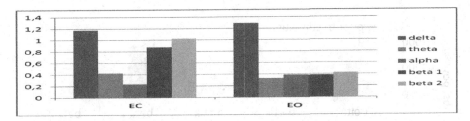

Fig. 5. Relative power values of the rhythms (their dynamics) after the experiments – in the resting state, with closed and open eyes

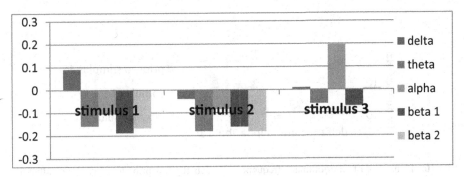

Fig. 6. Relative power values of the rhythms (their dynamics) after presentation of each stimulus.

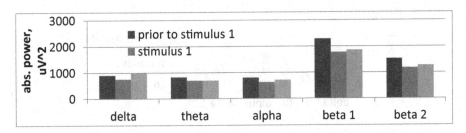

Fig. 7. Absolute power values of the rhythms prior to, during and after the presentation of stimulus 1.

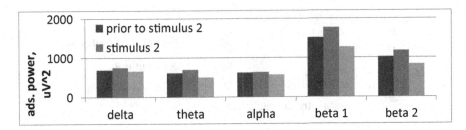

Fig. 8. Absolute power values of the rhythms prior to, during and after the presentation of stimulus 2.

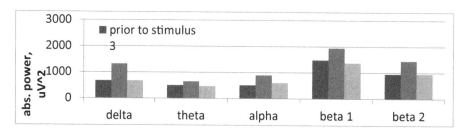

Fig. 9. Absolute power values of the rhythms prior to, during and after the presentation of stimulus 3.

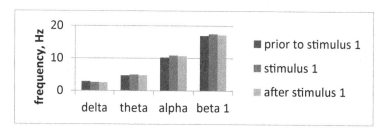

Fig. 10. Dynamics of the dominant frequency of each rhythm prior to, during and after the presentation of stimulus 1.

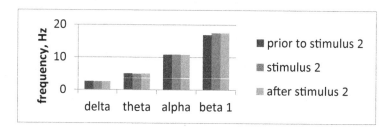

Fig. 11. Dynamics of the dominant frequency of each rhythm prior to, during and after the presentation of stimulus 2.

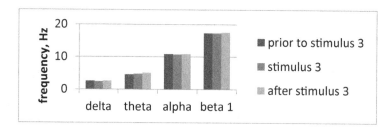

Fig. 12. Dynamics of the dominant frequency of each rhythm prior to, during and after the presentation of stimulus 3.

3. Stimulus 3 – Video with the audio track

After the perception of the video fragment with the audio track, an even greater increase in the power values of all rhythms occurs; after the watching, the power values of all rhythms decrease, but the alpha-activity values remain above those "prior" the stimulation (Fig. 9).

3 Conclusion

In conclusion, it may be said that after the preliminary study, signs of fatigue were revealed regarding all subjects. The power value of the delta-rhythm in all leads increased significantly. The EEG spectral indicators showed various dynamics upon presentation of the stimulus material of various modalities. The first stimulus (audio only) differed the most – while listening to it, the power values of all frequency ranges decreased and the peak frequency of the theta-, alpha-, and beta1-rhythms increased. When analyzing the video fragment without and with the audio track, on the contrary, an increase in the power values of all rhythms was observed, but the frequency value practically did not change. At the same time, an analysis of relative changes in power values after/prior to presentation of the stimuli revealed that after the first and second stimuli (the audio track and the video presented separately), the rhythm power values decreased, and after the presentation of the third stimulus (the video fragment together with the audio track) the power values of the alpha-rhythm increased significantly. The different dynamics of the EEG spectral indicators upon the presentation of the stimuli of various modalities and after each sample indicates that audio and video materials are perceived differently and have a different delayed effect on the state of the cerebral cortex.

The problem of multimodal polycode social network communication and its influence upon psychophysiological and cognitive characteristics of Internet users is of both academic and practical interest. Polycode communication on the Internet is a major trend of the recent years, and the necessity of researching it is determined by the fact that its nature renders the traditional linguistic methods of analysis only partially applicable. This explains the importance of the problem for theoretical linguistics.

Results obtained on the basis of cross-disciplinary approach will help to establish a perspective for development of an ecological model of health, in particular, for student-age population. It is common knowledge that ecological model of health (mental health, in particular) depends on personality-environment interaction. For the young people of today a big part of this environment is the Internet and social networks. Immersion in this environment can influence the transformation of psychophysiological and cognitive personality characteristics. Taking into account the polysemiotic nature of online communication, one can suggest that different semiotic arrays of the same social network can have different effects on the mental activity of the user. Therefore it is very important to address the problem of influence of the multimodal polycode stimulus – reaction mechanism upon psychophysiological and cognitive personality characteristics, taking into account possible variations of this influence depending on social, age and gender factors. It is well known that noise as a type of wave pollution leads to neurological and mental disorders, hearing deterioration etc. Internet users (social network users, in particular) frequently encounter different kinds of noise forming the context of network multimodality. Multimodal polycode texts containing both linguistic and non-linguistic information (images, sounds, videos etc) puts even a bigger load on the psychocognitive system. Given all the above said, the proposed research project is important for linguistics (as it will expand its methods and supply it with new methods to deal with multimodal polycode texts) and other sciences having the ecosystem of human as their object.

Acknowledgments. The research is supported by the Russian Science Foundation, project № 18-18-00477.

References

1. Aboujaoude, E.: Problematic Internet use: an overview. World Psychiatry **9**, 85–90 (2010). https://doi.org/10.1002/j.2051-5545.2010.tb00278.x
2. American Psychiatric Association: Diagnostic and Statistical Manual of Mental Disorders. DSM-5. American Psychiatric Association, Washington (2013). https://doi.org/10.1176/appi.books.9780890425596
3. Cao, J., Zhao, L.: The electrophysiological correlates of internet language processing revealed by N170 elicited by network emoticons. Neuroreport **29**(13), 1055–1060 (2018). https://doi.org/10.1097/wnr.0000000000000954
4. Casserly, E.D., Wang, Y., Celestin, N., Talesnick, L., Pisoni, D.B.: Supra-segmental changes in speech production as a result of spectral feedback degradation: comparison with lombard speech. Lang. Speech **61**(2), 227–245 (2018). https://doi.org/10.1177/0023830917713775
5. Clark, L.: Decision-making during gambling: an integration of cognitive and psychobiological approaches. Philos. Trans. R. Soc. B: Biol. Sci. **365**(1538), 319–330 (2010). https://doi.org/10.1098/rstb.2009.0147
6. Drijvers, L., Oezuerek, A.: Native language status of the listener modulates the neural investigation of speech and iconic gestures in clear and adverse listening conditions. Brain Lang. **7**(17), 177–178 (2018). https://doi.org/10.1016/j.bandl.2018.01.003
7. Kraut, R., Kiesler, S., Boneva, B., et al.: Internet paradox revisited. J. Soc. **58**(1), 49–74 (2002)
8. Martín-Pascual, M., Andreu-Sánchez, C., Delgado-García, J., Gruart, A.: Using electroencephalography measurements and high-quality video recording for analyzing visual perception of media content. J. Vis. Exp. (135) (2018). https://doi.org/10.3791/57321
9. Park, B., Han, D.H., Roh, S.: Neurobiological findings related to Internet use disorders. Psychiatry Clin. Neurosci. **71**(7), 467–478 (2017). https://doi.org/10.1111/pcn.12422
10. Potapov, V.V.: Applied aspects of speech signal investigation (regarding automatic speech recognition and transformation process) (an overview). Domestic and foreign literature. Series 6: Linguistics, vol. 3, pp. 102–106 (2019). (In Russian)
11. Potapov, V.V.: Experimental electrophysiological investigation of brain functioning regarding the speech perception for mono- and polycode regimes. Social sciences and humanities. Domestic and foreign literature. Series 6: Linguistics, vol. 2, pp. 119–123 (2019). (in Russian)
12. Potapov, V.V.: Experimental-phonetic researches of segmental level typology of speech utterances (an overview), Domestic and foreign literature. Series 6: Linguistics, vol. 3, pp. 145–148 (2019)

13. Potapov, V.V.: Prosody as the Background of multi-aimed interdisciplinary researches. Social sciences and humanities (an overview). Domestic and foreign literature. Series 6: Linguistics, vol. 2, pp. 58–63 (2019). (In Russian)

14. Potapova, R., Potapov, V.: Acoustic and perceptual-auditory determinants of transmission of speech and music information (in regard to semiotics). In: Eismont, P., Mitrenina, O., Pereltsvaig, A. (eds.) LMAC 2017. CCIS, vol. 943, pp. 35–46. Springer, Cham (2019). https://doi.org/10.1007/978-3-030-05594-3_3

15. Potapova, R., Potapov, V.: Auditory and visual recognition of emotional behaviour of foreign language subjects (by native and non-native speakers). In: Železný, M., Habernal, I., Ronzhin, A. (eds.) SPECOM 2013. LNCS (LNAI), vol. 8113, pp. 62–69. Springer, Cham (2013). https://doi.org/10.1007/978-3-319-01931-4_9

16. Potapova, R.K., Potapov, V.V.: Fundamentals of multi-versatile voice and speech research of the "electronic personality" on the basis of voice and speech on the information and communication Internet medium. Hum. Being: Image Essence. Humanitarian Aspects **1–2**, 28–29, 87–111 (2017). https://doi.org/10.31249/chel/2018.03.00. (In Russian)

17. Potapova, R.K., Potapov, V.V.: Language, Speech, Personality. Language of Slavic Culture, Moscow (2006). (In Russian)

18. Potapova, R.K., Potapov, V.V., Lebedeva, N.N., Agibalova, T.V.: Interdisciplinarity in the Study of Speech Polyinformativity. Languages of Slavic Culture, Moscow (2015). (In Russian)

19. Poulsen, A., Kamronn, S., Dmochowski, J., Parra, L., Hansen, L.: EEG in the classroom: synchronised neural recordings during video presentation. Sci. Rep. **7**, 43916 (2017). https://doi.org/10.1038/srep43916

20. Weinstein, A., Lejoyeux, M.: New developments on the neurobiological and pharmaco-genetic mechanisms underlying Internet and videogame addiction. Am. J. Addict. **24**(2), 117–125 (2015)

21. Weinstein, A., Livni, A., Weizman, A. New developments in brain research of Internet and gaming disorder. Neurosci. Biobehav. Rev. (2017). https://doi.org/10.1016/j.neubiorev.2017.01.040

22. Weinstein, A.M.: An update overview on brain imaging studies of internet gaming disorder. Fronters Psychiatry **8**, 185 (2017). https://doi.org/10.3389/fpsyt.2017.00185

23. Amichai-Hamburger, Y.: Personality, individual differences and Internet use. In: Joinson, A. N., McKenna, K.Y.A., et al. (eds.) Oxford Handbook of Internet Psychology (2009, 2012). https://doi.org/10.1093/oxfordhb/9780199561803.013.0013

24. Zhang, F., Zhao, L.: The dysfunction of face processing in patients with internet addiction disorders: an event-related potential study. Neuroreport **27**(15), 1153–1158 (2016). https://doi.org/10.1097/wnr.0000000000000670

Some Peculiarities of Internet Multimodal Polycode Corpora Annotation

Rodmonga Potapova[1]([✉]) [iD], Vsevolod Potapov[2] [iD],
Liliya Komalova[1,3] [iD], and Andrey Dzhunkovskiy[1] [iD]

[1] Institute of Applied and Mathematical Linguistics,
Moscow State Linguistic University, Ostozenka Street 38,
119034 Moscow, Russia
{RKPotapova, GenuinePR}@yandex.ru,
Vetinari01@gmail.com
[2] Centre of New Technologies for Humanities,
Lomonosov Moscow State University, Leninskije Gory 1,
119991 Moscow, Russia
volikpotapov@gmail.com
[3] Resource Capability Development Department, Department of Linguistics,
Institute of Scientific Information for Social Sciences of the Russian Academy
of Sciences, Nakhimovsky Prospect 51/21, 117997 Moscow, Russia

Abstract. This paper presents a novel deep parametric annotation method in regard to database items of Russian polycode social network discourse. The database is used as the background for interdisciplinary research in the field of psycho-physiologic and cognitive transformation of young Internet users' personality. The present report focuses on different semiotic sign aspects of human-human communication: verbal, paraverbal, non-verbal, extra-verbal. With respect to the individual personality applications of polycode acts of behavior this paper is relevant for three reasons: polycode Internet information may influence the cognitive peculiarities of Internet discourse corpora perception; sense interpretation of multimodal perception channels, and some types of variability of quantitative and qualitative personality changes. The compatibility of deep parametric corpora annotation data may be important in certain investigations pertaining to material cases.

Keywords: Polycode social-network discourse · Multimodality ·
Deep parametric annotation method · Young Internet users

1 Introduction

This paper is part of a project aimed at a cross-disciplinary study of influence of aggressive Internet environment in multimodal polycode social network communication upon transformation of psychophysiological and cognitive features of Internet user personality (with regard to adolescent and young adult Internet users). According to the research hypothesis, multimodal polycode communication in modern social networks possesses a number of features causing its negative influence over recipients. "The detrimental effects of this environment are compared to the effects of acoustic noise"

© Springer Nature Switzerland AG 2019
A. A. Salah et al. (Eds.): SPECOM 2019, LNAI 11658, pp. 392–400, 2019.
https://doi.org/10.1007/978-3-030-26061-3_40

[9, p. 408]. We focus on the consequences of such noise impact on "the functional status of the subjects based on psychophysiological personality features" [9, p. 409], on the one hand, and "cognitive deterioration under the influence of such stressors as different types of noise" [9, p. 409], on the other hand.

We consider polycodedness as "a result of interaction between codes of different semiotic systems and discourses" [3, p. 129]. A polycode text is at the center of "interaction of different codes, i.e. symbols, systems of symbols, signs and rules of their combinations with each other for the transmission, processing and storage of information in the form most adapted thereto. This term describes the phenomenon of textual heterogeneity at the level of form achieved through a mix of different semiotic systems, such as verbal and visual" [3, p. 130]. The literature argues that "polycode text usage changes categorial realia of communication through information perception management resulting in modification of recipients' value orientation" [12, p. 223].

2   Background and Method

"Multimodality is a concept introduced and developed in the last two decades to account for the different resources used in communication to express meaning. As a phenomenon of communication, multimodality defines the combination of different semiotic resources, or modes, in texts and communicative events, such as still and moving image, speech, writing, layout, gesture, and/or proxemics." [1, p. 114]. "Research has shown that when emotional stimuli are conveyed only in one channel, emotion recognition is more accurate in the visual modality than in the auditory modality [4, p. 194]. "The robustness hypothesis argues that multiple modalities ensure message delivery when one modality is occluded by noise in the environment or noise in the perceptual system of the receiver" [2, p. 441]. "Signallers seeking to transmit complex messages benefit from a multimodal strategy as it both increases the diversity of information flowing to a receiver and increases the robustness of the signal" [2, p. 447].

The method of gathering data that was to be included in the resulting database included a set of instructions for researchers. Prior to the beginning of work on the database, it has been elected to use a cloud-based storage service for the purposes of forming and editing the database.

The criteria for choosing entries into the database included the following:

1. The entries must be written in Russian (with the possible inclusion of foreign language elements);
2. The data must be in open access on the Internet (that includes social networks, personal blogs, microblogs, videoblogs and podcasts);
3. Entries must be exhibit multimodality;

Prior to analyzing the entries, all materials (audio, video, text, images) related to them were to be saved both within the cloud-based structure and on backup hard drive devices.

Prior to research, various aspects of Russian social network discourse were analyzed. These included the effects of deprivation on the final speech product in Internet communication [8, 10], the acmeological aspect of emotional-modal state of Internet users [6], database annotation principles (in connection with the semantic field of "aggression")

[11], personal user trait profiling, etc. [9, p. 411]. The introduced deep parametric annotation creation approach [7, p. 224] encompasses such traditional parameters as message platform, authorship, material type, date of publication, author location, subscription numbers or user friend counts, "like", view, repost and comment counts, as well as information regarding whether Russian is the author's mother tongue. Furthermore, the annotation method includes additional information on types of modality included in the message, playback length for audio and video elements, the type of speech (prepared, unprepared, semi-prepared), the inclusion of foreign language elements, intertextuality, emotionality, temporality, etc. The basis of the deep parametric annotation method model is conceptualized within four dimensions: verbal (linguo-semantic content), paraverbal (intonational-prosodic, timbral components), non-verbal (proxemic-mimic-gesticulation component) and extraverbal (situational-discursive component) [5, pp. 67–72]. Every nomination includes own n-parameters, the number of which can reach 120 and beyond. As such, the deep parametric annotation method encompasses not only the token sphere of annotation, but also demands special knowledge from the linguist.

3   Results and Discussion

The employed deep parametric annotation method encompasses four major clusters of data: metadata, communicant data, fragment data, and additional data (Fig. 1).

At the current stage of the research, the annotated database of Russian polycode social network discourse of young Internet users includes more than 1500 entries and is

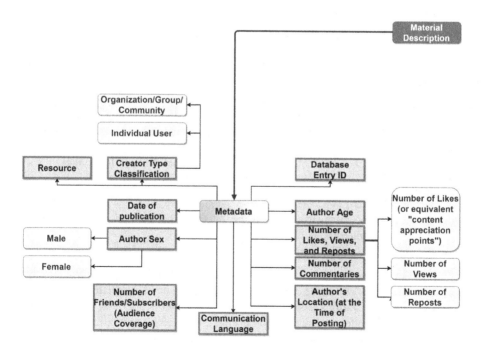

Fig. 1. Metadata analytical cluster

subject to an interdisciplinary approach with linguists, sociologists, psychophysiologists and psychiatrists taking part in its development.

The first analytical cluster, metadata, was used for recording information about the author and about the entries as an object within cyberspace: Database entry ID; Author age (if created by an individual user); Sex of the entry author: (Male; Female); Author's location (at the moment of posting the analyzed content); Date of publication; Creator type classification (By an individual user; By an organization, group or community); Resource (platform) of publication; Number of friends/subscribers within the online resource (Audience Coverage); Number of likes, views and reposts (Number of views; Number of likes (or equivalent "content appreciation points"); Number of reposts); Number of commentaries; Communication language.

The second cluster, communicant data, covers information regarding the number and peculiarities of the communicants (Fig. 2).

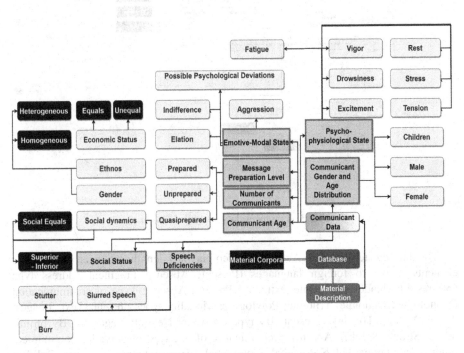

Fig. 2. Communicant data analytical cluster

The second cluster includes: Communicant age; Number of communicants; Message preparation level (Prepared; Unprepared; Quasiprepared); Emotive-modal state of the communicants (Elation; Indifference; Aggression; Possible Psychological Deviations); Psychophysiological state (Fatigue; Vigor; Drowsiness; Excitement; Rest; Stress; Tension); Communicant Gender and Age Distribution (Number of children; Number of male communicants; Number of female communicants); Speech deficiencies (Stutter; Burr; Slurred Speech); Social Status (Social dynamics (Social equals;

Superior – inferior); Gender (Heterogeneous; Homogeneous); Ethnos (Heterogeneous; Homogeneous); Economic status (Equals; Unequals)).

The fragment data cluster includes information regarding the situation of the communication, communication types, types of polycode communication and some other variables (Fig. 3).

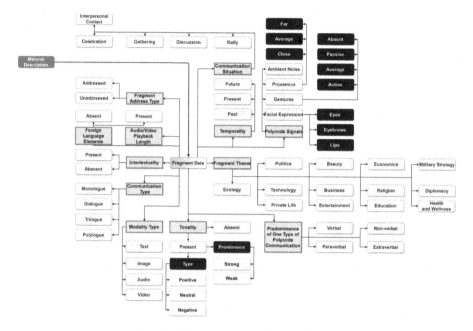

Fig. 3. Fragment data analytical cluster

The third cluster includes: Audio and video playback length; Inclusion of linguistic elements native to foreign languages (Present; Absent); Fragment address type (Addressed; Unaddressed); Intertextuality (Present; Absent); Type of communication (Monologue; Dialogue; Trilogue; Polylogue); Modality types present (Text; Images; Audio; Video); Tonality (Present (By type (Positive; Neutral; Negative); By prominence (Strong; Weak)); Absent); Predominance of one type of polycode communication (Verbal; Paraverbal; Non-verbal; Extraverbal); Fragment theme (Ecology; Politics; Technology; Private life; Beauty; Business; Entertainment; Economics; Religion; Education; Military strategy; Diplomacy; Health and wellness); Temporality (Past; Present; Future); Polycode signals present (Facial expression (Eyes; Eyebrows; Lips); Gestures (Absent; Passive; Average; Active); Proxemics (Far; Average; Close); Ambient noise); Communication situation (Interpersonal contact; Celebration; Gathering; Discussion; Rally).

The final data cluster, additional data, is a technical cluster used for database navigation and database development optimization (Fig. 4).

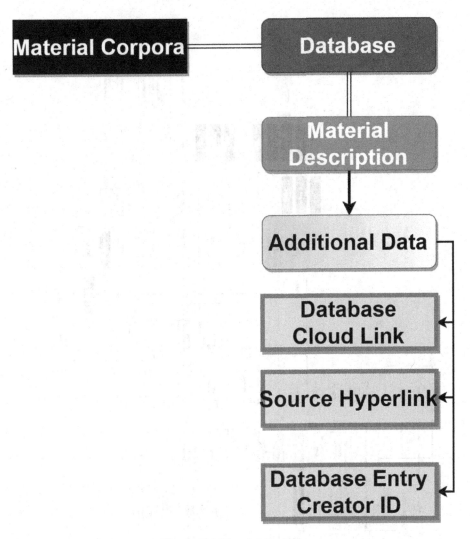

Fig. 4. Additional data cluster

This cluster includes: In-database links to cloud-save data; Data source hyperlinks; Database entry creator IDs.

Hereafter we present a full view of the analysis method (Fig. 5).

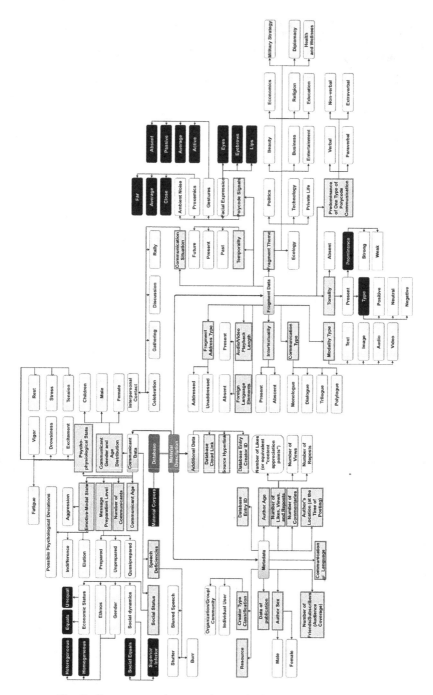

Fig. 5. Deep parametric annotation method visualization overview

4 Conclusion

In summation, the described novel deep parametric annotation method allows for considerable depth when analyzing Internet communication. By separating variables into thematic clusters, a number of goals is accomplished: first and foremost, the method allows for a synthesized approach that encompasses text-as-object analysis, user analysis, communicant psychophysiological and emotive-modal state analysis, communication situation analysis and semantic analysis of the communication situation, etc. Furthermore, the method allows for a large degree of visualization of research findings.

Acknowledgments. This research was supported by the Russian Science Foundation (RSF) according to the research project № 18-18-00477.

References

1. Adami, E.: Multimodality. In: García, O., Flores, N., Spotti, M. (eds.) Oxford Handbook of Language and Society. Oxford University Press, Oxford (2017). https://doi.org/10.1093/oxfordhb/9780190212896.013.23. http://www.oxfordhandbooks.com/view/10.1093/oxfordhb/9780190212896.001.0001/oxfordhb-9780190212896-e-23
2. Ay, N., Flack, J., Krakauer, D.C.: Robustness and complexity co-constructed in multimodal signalling networks. Phil. Trans. R. Soc. B **362**, 441–447 (2007). https://doi.org/10.1098/rstb.2006.1971. http://europepmc.org/backend/ptpmcrender.fcgi?accid=PMC2323562&blobtype=pdf
3. Dmitrichenkova, S.V., Dolzhich, A.E., Popova, T.G.: Cognitive & pragmatic aspects of polycodedness of a scientific text, a case study of the Spanish language. Int. J. Appl. Linguist. Engl. Lit. **6**(1), 128–135 (2017). https://doi.org/10.7575/aiac.ijalel.v.6n.1p.128. https://journals.aiac.org.au/index.php/IJALEL/article/view/2721
4. Paulmann, S., Pell, M.D.: Is there an advantage for recognizing multi-modal emotional stimuli? Motiv. Emot. **35**(2), 192–201 (2011). https://doi.org/10.1007/s11031-011-9206-0. https://link.springer.com/article/10.1007%2Fs11031-011-9206-0
5. Potapova, R., Potapov, V.: Language, Speech, p. 496. Personality. Languages of Slavic Culture, Moscow (2006). (in Russian)
6. Potapova, R., Potapov, V.: Main determinants of the acmeologic personality profiling. In: Karpov, A., Jokisch, O., Potapova, R. (eds.) SPECOM 2018. LNCS (LNAI), vol. 11096, pp. 542–551. Springer, Cham (2018). https://doi.org/10.1007/978-3-319-99579-3_56
7. Potapova, R., Potapov, V.: On deep parametric annotation method with regard to the databases of Russian polycode social network discourse. In: Remneva, M.L., Kukushkina, O.V. (eds.) Russian Language: its Historical Destiny and Present State. The International Congress of Russian Language Researchers. Proceedings and Materials, p. 224. MSU, Moscow (2019). (in Russian)
8. Potapova, R., Potapov, V.: Cognitive entropy in the perceptual-auditory evaluation of emotional modal states of foreign language communication partner. In: Karpov, A., Potapova, R., Mporas, I. (eds.) SPECOM 2017. LNCS (LNAI), vol. 10458, pp. 253–261. Springer, Cham (2017). https://doi.org/10.1007/978-3-319-66429-3_24

9. Potapova, R., Potapov, V.: Human as acmeologic entity in social network discourse (multidimensional approach). In: Karpov, A., Potapova, R., Mporas, I. (eds.) SPECOM 2017. LNCS (LNAI), vol. 10458, pp. 407–416. Springer, Cham (2017). https://doi.org/10.1007/978-3-319-66429-3_40

10. Potapova, R., Potapov, V.: Polybasic attribution of social network discourse. In: Ronzhin, A., Potapova, R., Németh, G. (eds.) SPECOM 2016. LNCS (LNAI), vol. 9811, pp. 539–546. Springer, Cham (2016). https://doi.org/10.1007/978-3-319-43958-7_65

11. Potapova, R., Komalova, L.: Multimodal perception of aggressive behavior. In: Ronzhin, A., Potapova, R., Németh, G. (eds.) SPECOM 2016. LNCS (LNAI), vol. 9811, pp. 499–506. Springer, Cham (2016). https://doi.org/10.1007/978-3-319-43958-7_60

12. Vashunina, I.V., Ryabova, M.E., Egorova, L.A.: Polycode hypertext in polylingual discourse of intercultural communications. XLinguae 11(2), 218–231 (2018). https://doi.org/10.18355/xl.2018.11.02.17. http://www.xlinguae.eu/files/XLinguae2_2018_17.pdf

New Perspectives on Canadian English Digital Identity Based on Word Stress Patterns in Lexicon and Spoken Corpus

Daria Pozdeeva[1]($\boxtimes$), Tatiana Shevchenko[1], and Alexey Abyzov[2]

[1] Moscow State Linguistic University, 38 Ostozhenka St., Moscow 119034,
Russian Federation
{da_pozdeeva, tatashevchenko}@mail.ru
[2] Ivanovo State Polytechnic University, 21 Sheremetev Av., Ivanovo 153000,
Russian Federation
axxel68@mail.ru

Abstract. The study develops our previous research reported in [17] which established the specific Canadian English (CE) lexical stress pattern of secondary stress located after the main stress as more frequent than in British English (BE) and American English (AE). The pattern was recognized and detected in sound speech by native speakers of CE in the set of most frequent words (n = 89). At the present stage of the research we applied the methods of corpus analysis and the overall lexicon analysis in national dictionaries to explore the actual usage of the pattern in CE as compared to BE and AE. The objective data was bound to test the presence of the pattern previously identified through the subjective perceptions of native speakers of CE (n = 40). National dictionaries [9, 20] were the source of word stress patterns codified in the norms (n = 12648); the corpus of spoken CE speech (IDEA) (n = 3352) provided support of the rhythmical lexical stress location. Comparison of Anglophone and Francophone areas of CE speakers' residence gave evidence of the rhythmical tendency being the impact of the French language contact. The right edge prominence known as the effect of French borrowings in the history of English was further supported by the constant language contact on the territory of Canada. Thus the digital identity of CE compared to BE and AE, when based on the overall analysis of lexicon across the three major varieties of English and in CE corpus of spoken speech, was verified.

Keywords: Canadian English · Lexical stress · Identity · Lexicon ·
Sound corpus · Frequency

1 Introduction

The issue of Canadian English (CE) identity in pronunciation is generally perceived as rather complex and elusive not only for foreigners but for Canadians themselves. Being one of the North American varieties of English, CE possesses both American and British features, as well as the impact of language contact with French, First Nations languages and a multitude of emigrant languages which the Government policy

A. A. Salah et al. (Eds.): SPECOM 2019, LNAI 11658, pp. 401–413, 2019.
https://doi.org/10.1007/978-3-030-26061-3_41

encourages to develop. In 2004 Charles Boberg, a prominent Canadian linguist, wrote about the growth of a distinct Canadian identity, reflected in a small set of unique Canadian features, among which the most diagnostic of all is the phonetic process of "Canadian Raising", i.e. the pronunciation of/ai/and/au/with a raised central onset before voiceless, as in *out* and *bite* [1]. Based on our previous research into comparison of lexical stress in BE, AE and CE, another pronunciation feature could be enlisted, which, though not unique in its origin, may be distinctively Canadian for its frequency, in comparison with BE and AE. That was a particular stress pattern with a rhythmical secondary stress (also known as "tertiary") that is normally located after the primary stress. Following the "Primary Stress First" theory proposed by van der Hulst we argue that the occurrence of secondary stress in English has a rhythmic nature. We also agree that no one has proved that the secondary stress after the primary stress is less prominent than the secondary stress which is located before the primary stress. Positional differentiation of the two secondary stresses will be reflected in the terms *pretonic secondary stress* and *post-tonic secondary stress*; both stresses are rhythmical by origin [17, 19].

In our previous research based on three national corpora (BNC, COCA, CCE) we showed the stability of the accentual system of English: lexical stress divergent words are equally rare in the three national varieties, and they are mainly loan words from Romance languages. When we started with a limited number of words with stress patterns different in BE and AE (n = 1400), only a tiny part of them (n = 89) was found to be relatively frequent, at 50 words per million, across all the three major varieties of English. However, the words of medium frequency are known to differentiate the national varieties, and the distinction is an important part of national identity in speech. CE native speakers (n = 30), for instance, in express survey demonstrated that they possess the pattern of post-tonic secondary stress in their mental repertoire when they were asked to select the right patterns for the 89 words. Another set of CE native speakers (n = 10) took part in the perception test, and were able to detect the pattern with accuracy [17]. What remains to be found is how often CE native speakers actually employ the pattern in their speech. A corpus of natural CE speech (IDEA) is bound to show it.

Another distinctive word stress feature might be found in the domain of disyllables. Although the dominant pattern in English is stress on the first syllable (*trochaic rhythm*), it is generally accepted that AE, in contrast to BE, tends to select the pattern with stress on the second syllable (*iambic rhythm*), especially in the words of French origin, e.g. *de'tail, bal'let, buf'fet, de'but, Mo'net*. The right-edge prominence is typical of the French language, but analogy might operate in cases with loan words from other languages, e.g. *sig'nor* (Italian), *dik'tat* (German), *koi'ne* (Greek), *di'nar* (Arabic) [1, 15, 20]. In our data of CE there were cases of both patterns, e.g. in *detail, adult*, and, what is more specific, with two stresses in the same word *'de,tail*, a primary stress followed by a secondary one, i.e. by a post-tonic stress. An overall analysis of the whole lexicon included in the dictionary and realized in CE native speakers' talks might reveal a more realistic landscape of stress patterns distribution.

The French impact on English word stress system may be a historical legacy as well as language contact effect in Canada, which could be particularly evident in the Francophone area of bilingual Quebec. Comparison of word stress characteristics in the speech of Quebec residents, when compared with those of the Anglophone Ontario residents, opens more opportunities to test our observations about the distinctive CE word stress patterns.

The *goal* of the current study is to test the validity of the previous findings on specific word stress pattern in CE based on a wider lexicon represented in IDEA corpus of natural speech.

Our *hypothesis* is:

From the historical, geographical and demographic perspectives language contact with the French language will facilitate the incidence of the rhythmical stress patterns in CE compared to AE and BE, and the residents of bilingual Francophone Quebec will score higher than the residents of the Anglophone Ontario. Right edge prominence characteristic of the French language and the universal final lengthening will provide the conditions for higher frequency of the patterns in the final position of the intonation phrase.

2 Methods

Overall Quantitative and Structural Analysis of the Lexicon: What is the Domain of the Rhythmical Patterns? New perspectives on lexical stress patterns in CE involved looking at the whole lexicon included in the national dictionary, i.e. going over from one specific feature in a limited set of words to the *overall quantitative analysis* of all the polysyllabic words that are supplied with transcriptions, or at least stress marks, in Gage [9]. The new approach gave us a chance of focusing on the structural composition of polysyllabic words and stress patterns distribution in various structures. Comparison of the CE data with BE and AE stress patterns frequencies with rhythmical stresses in Longman Dictionary (LPD) [21] gave evidence of similar patterns distribution across the three major varieties of English. Digital national identity in lexical stress patterns, as any other sort of identity, becomes recognized and established only in relation to others, similar or different, identities [10, 13, 18].

In exploring BE and AE distribution of patterns in LPD we worked with an electronic version of the dictionary. By creating a program to recognize and discriminate primary and secondary stresses we could index the categories as follows: (0) one-syllable words with no stress, (1) secondary stress, (2) primary stress, (1 + 2) pre-tonic stress + primary, (2 + 1) primary + post-tonic. However, the problem of space saving made the publishers leave out the cases in which AE pronunciation pattern was identical with BE, which made the digital statistics for the former less accurate. On the whole, the common tendencies were quite vivid. Nevertheless, to be more statistically certain, in CE the Gage data collection, analysis and calculations were done by hand.

The fact that in Canada there is no pronunciation dictionary, and Gage does not provide transcription for the whole lexicon of 95 000 words, only a limited part of the lexicon was submitted to the overall quantitative analysis (n = 12 648).

Auditory Analysis: Which Patterns do CE Native Speakers Actually Use? Auditory analysis of the discourse in the CE spoken corpus IDEA in which 68 CE speakers from all over Canada talk about their place of residence and memories from childhood [11] yielded 3352 polysyllabic words in 68 tapescripts (total time is 2 h 30 min) which were annotated for the incidence of primary and secondary stresses. In accordance with the goal of the research the latter were grouped into two classes: pre-tonic secondary rhythmical stress (before the primary stress) and post-tonic secondary rhythmical stress (after the primary stress) cases.

In our previous study reported in SPECOM 2017 we compared the level of agreement between CE native speakers (10) and Russian phoneticians, experts in English phonetics (10) on detecting both primary and secondary stresses in CE speech. The 90% agreement testified to the fact that the 10% difference was due to the latter's previous experience in listening only to BE and AE speech.

In the current study four Russian experts listened to a number of identical CE talks with a very high agreement score in stress placement (91.3%), and after that preliminary test the first author did the overall auditory analysis of all the 68 tapescripts.

Comparative Analysis: the Dictionary and the Corpus. At the next step of our analysis we aimed at finding the correlation between the stress patterns recommended in the national dictionary and the actual usage of those in the spoken corpus. All the polysyllabic words (n = 3352) that were realized in speech by 68 speakers of CE in their talks were checked for stress patterns codified in the CE dictionary Gage [9]. The limitations of the present study consisted in the fact that there is no pronunciation dictionary for CE yet, and not all entries in Gage dictionary are supplied with transcription. Stress patterns of words included in Gage dictionary (n = 1634) and supplied with transcription (n = 888) were compared with the stress patterns realized in the same lexicon of the corpus, including repetitions of words with recurrent or varying stress patterns. Correlation was calculated.

Contrastive Analysis: in Search of Regional Identity. For the purpose of testing our hypothesis that most of CE digital identity is due to the French language contact effect we contrasted frequencies of identical patterns in the speech of Ontario residents with the ones in Quebec. The *narrow corpus* of 20 speakers, equally balanced for number, gender and age in the two provinces provided data on Quebec scores which were expected to be higher for the French-affected rhythmical patterns. Given that French is noted for right-edge prominence in separate words pronounced in isolation, as well as in intonation phrases, we looked at the position of words under analysis in the structure of the intonation phrase (IP). All the polysyllabic words (n = 531) that were realized in speech by residents of Ontario and by residents of Quebec (n = 565) were checked for the *initial, medial, final* positions in IPs, with special reference to pre-tonic (40 vs. 67) and post-tonic (43 vs. 44) secondary stresses.

Linguistic and Sociocultural Interpretation: Digital Identity is due to Language Contact. The data in the Discussion accounts for the differences, however small, in the stress patterns inventories across the three major varieties of English and also in the performances of CE speakers in the provinces of Ontario and Quebec. They are determined, the authors argue, by the language contact with French in the history of English over the centuries, the constant contact with French in Canada and the particular close contact in the area of contemporary bilingual Francophone Quebec.

3   Results

3.1   Overall Quantitative and Structural Analysis of the Lexicon

BE and AE data are deduced from working with an electronic version of LPD by Wells [20] with special software which enabled us to discriminate and index cases of: words with no stress (0), words with a secondary stress (1), words with a primary stress (2), words with a pre-tonic secondary stress + primary stress (12), words with a primary + post-tonic secondary stress (21). In fact, apart from these basic types, there were cases which are unlikely to appear in speech: incomplete words or morphemes with one secondary stress only or two pre-tonic stresses with one primary stress only. The results are as follows:

(0) No stress (one-syllable words) 15%
(1) Secondary stress solely 2%
(2) Primary stress solely 66%
(1 + 2) Pre-tonic + Primary 14%
(2 + 1) Primary + Post-tonic 2%
(1 + 1 + 2) Two Pre-tonic + Primary 4%.

Thus we can see that apart from short one-syllable words with no stress at all which were reported to take up to 80% of the total amount of words in the English vocabulary [4, 5], the majority of BE words have one primary stress only (66%), and then comes pre-tonic + primary pattern as most frequent in the compound combinations (14%), with primary + post-tonic pattern to occupy the last place (2%).

The Canadian Gage dictionary provided transcription for only part of the lexicon: 12 648 polysyllabic words out of 95 000 words. The selected transcribed polysyllabic lexicon fell into three basic classes: primary stress only (70%), pre-tonic + primary and primary + post-tonic. See the distribution of patterns with secondary stresses (n = 3813) (Table 1):

Table 1. Pre-tonic and post-tonic stress in CE [9].

Structures	Pre-tonic + Primary	Primary + Post-tonic	%
1. Two-syllable	16 (4,9%)	309 (95,1%)	325 (100%)
2. Three-syllable	382 (24,6%)	1170 (75,4%)	1552 (100%)
3. Four-syllable	678 (55,8%)	537 (44,2%)	1215 (100%)
4. Five-syllable	478 (87,5%)	68 (12,5%)	546 (100%)
5. Six-syllable	122 (94,6%)	7 (5,4%)	129 (100%)
6. Seven-syllable	42 (100%)	–	42 (100%)
7. Eight-syllable	4 (100%)	–	4 (100%)
Total:	1722	2091	3813

Structurally, it is two-syllable and three-syllable words that constitute the basis of Post-tonic secondary rhythmical stress domain. The Post-tonic secondary stress is more frequent than the Pre-tonic one in two-syllable words: Cf. 95.1% vs. 4.9%, e.g. *'mo‚vie, 'bath‚tub, 'cray‚fish,* and also in three-syllable words: 75.4% vs. 24.6%, e.g. *'conse‚quence, 'other‚wise, 'motor‚bike.* The difference is statistically significant: $x^2 = 62.33$, p = 0.01. Longer structures, like four-syllable, five-syllable and six-syllable words form the domain of the Pre-tonic secondary stress, e.g. *‚compe'tition, ‚inte'resting, ‚oppor'tunity, ‚par'ticularly, ‚quarter'final.* Pre-tonics dominate in the above structures (in the order named): 55.8% vs. 44.2%; 87.5 vs. 12.5%; 94.6% vs. 5.4% (Fig. 1), the difference is statistically significant: $x^2 = 219$, p = 0.01.

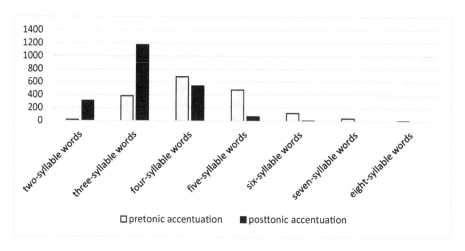

Fig. 1. Pre-tonic and post-tonic stress patterns in CE [9].

3.2 Spoken Corpus and the Dictionary Data Compared

According to the design of the research, auditory analysis of 68 CE speakers' talks, monologue parts of the interviews in which they told a story about themselves, was carried out, and all polysyllabic words were annotated for stress and selected for the stress patterns research. As predicted, in spoken English the highest frequency was registered for monosyllables: 80% frequency of monosyllables previously reported by A. C. Gimson in 1962 and revised by Cruttenden in 2001 [3], was confirmed by Cutler and Carter in 1987 [4]. That percentage was slightly exceeded (by 4%) in the current study of CE corpus, and was estimated at 84%. The list of polysyllabic words selected in the corpus included 4098 items that were checked for pronunciation in Gage dictionary. Part of the words (746) were not transcribed in the dictionary and, therefore, excluded from the analysis. The remaining 3352 words were split into two classes according to their word structures: 2251 two-syllable words, 1101 three-syllable and other polysyllabic words.

In the class of two-syllable words (n = 2251) the following observations were made: 70% of words tend to demonstrate the dominant trochaic rhythm pattern with the primary stress on the initial syllable (1577), while 22% have an iambic pattern with the primary stress on the final one (497) (See Discussion for assessing the specificity of the pattern). Something special was found as well: two adjacent syllables could both carry a stress (8%), (n = 177), which might be taken as a sign of syllable-based rhythm. The patterns recommended by the dictionary did not show much variance: the differences in the order of 2% were common (Table 2).

Table 2. Two-syllable word stress patterns in the dictionary and in the spoken corpus.

Regions	Two-syllable stress patterns						
	Primary on the initial syllable		Primary on the final syllable		Primary and secondary		No transcript in the dictionary
	Dictionary	Speech	Dictionary	Speech	Dictionary	Speech	
British Columbia	14	41	0	7	0	0	9
Manitoba	3	27	2	11	0	4	7
New Brunswick	1	14	0	1	0	1	4
Newfoundland	21	108	12	35	1	21	29
Nova Scotia	21	98	12	28	4	7	25
Alberta	22	53	9	16	0	10	14
Ontario	210	840	54	244	47	80	151
Prince Edward Island	21	65	4	13	0	6	19
Saskatchewan	36	125	17	31	1	7	37
Quebec	34	206	15	111	6	41	17
Total	**383** **68%**	**1577** **70%**	**125** **22%**	**497** **22%**	**59** **10%**	**177** **8%**	**312**

Three-syllable words were grouped together with other polysyllabic words, with a constant drop in frequency associated with a growing number of syllables. 1535 words were spoken altogether, from which amount 434 were not transcribed in the dictionary, which left only 1101 for analysis. Nevertheless, three-syllable words being especially relevant for the rhythmical stress domain, as we noted in Sect. 3.1, it is here that the pre-tonic and post-tonic secondary stresses were most numerous, their frequency in the group estimated at 18% (Table 3).

Table 3. Polysyllabic stress patterns in the dictionary and in the spoken corpus.

Regions	Polysyllabic stress patterns						
	Primary only		Primary and pre-tonic secondary		Primary and post-tonic secondary		No transcript in the
	Dictionary	Speech	Dictionary	Speech	Dictionary	Speech	dictionary
British Columbia	3	8	1	3	0	3	14
Manitoba	3	6	0	1	1	5	8
New Brunswick	1	3	0	2	0	1	6
Newfoundland	16	58	1	10	6	23	38
Nova Scotia	23	49	1	7	6	27	36
Alberta	10	27	3	14	2	13	33
Ontario	105	417	28	53	33	74	210
Prince Edward Island	6	27	1	5	3	10	24
Saskatchewan	22	61	2	7	1	7	43
Quebec	25	110	11	38	7	32	22
Total	**214** **67%**	**766** **70%**	**48** **15%**	**140** **12%**	**59** **18%**	**195** **18%**	**434**

By comparing the data from the spoken corpus and the dictionary pronunciations of the same lexicon we could not find many discrepancies: the differences were in the order of 3% only. Besides, there was no distinction between the frequencies of pre-tonic and post-tonic rhythmical stresses in the corpus: in speech both patterns were estimated at 18%, with the sum of both rhythmical patterns going up to 36%. Statistical analysis confirmed that there is close correlation between the patterns proposed in the dictionary and their actual usage in speech; two-syllable words: Primary stress on the initial syllable ($r = 0.99$), Primary stress on the final syllable ($r = 0.95$), Primary and secondary ($r = 0.92$) (Fig. 2); polysyllabic words: Primary stress only ($r = 0.99$), Primary and pre-tonic secondary stress ($r = 0.95$), Primary and post-tonic secondary

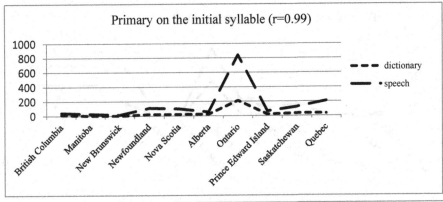

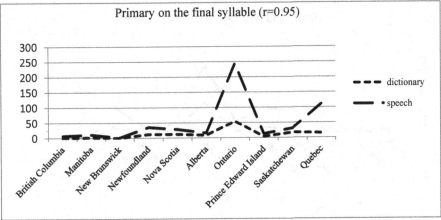

Fig. 2. Correlation of corpus and dictionary data (two-syllable words).

stress (r = 0.97) (Fig. 3). The graph also indicates that the Ontario area has the highest values which corresponds with the density of population, the greatest number of recorded CE speakers and, hence, the largest amount of tokens collected in that area. A more balanced amount of speakers will be represented in 3.3.

The data suggest that lexical stress patterns codified in the dictionary are actually reproduced in the speech of CE speakers and provide the basis for oral speech comprehension. The "sound image" of words, when preserved through recurrent use in running speech, provide for word recognition and, consequently, speech recognition.

However, the digital identity becomes transparent only in relation to other varieties of English, i.e. BE and AE stress patterns occurrence (See Discussion).

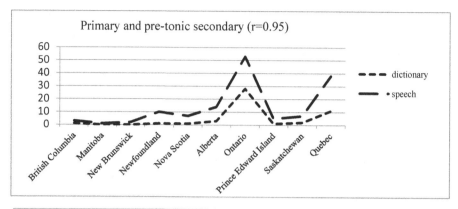

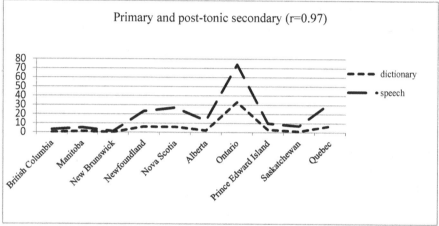

Fig. 3. Correlation of corpus and dictionary data (polysyllabic words).

3.3 Regional Identity in Ontario and Quebec

Although we found remarkable agreement between the spoken corpus and the dictionary data, there were obvious distinctions between the provinces' scores. In this section we will contrast the data from the Anglophone area of Ontario and the Francophone bilingual province of Quebec by balancing the two groups for number, gender and age (n = 20). In two-syllable words the iambic pattern occurs more regularly in Quebec, i.e. one in two words (Table 2), e.g. *ci'ty, ho'tel, to'ward,* while in Ontario it is less common, one in three cases, e.g. *my'self, e'lite.* In three-syllable words we found a higher percentage of both types of rhythmical stresses in Quebec, e.g. *ˌinter'view, ˌMontre'al* and *'everyˌthing, 'water fall, 'uniˌverse.* The latter distinction is not significant: $x^2 = 2.79$, $p = 0.1$.

Another important factor that called for investigation was the impact of word position (*initial, medial, final*) in the intonation phrase (IP) on the rhythmical stress occurrence: there is evidence of all types of rhythmical stresses gravitating towards the final position in IP. Higher values in rhythmical stresses data in Quebec are illustrated (Fig. 4).

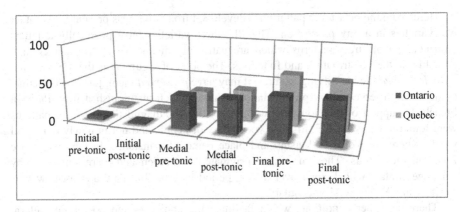

Fig. 4. Positional distribution of stress patterns with rhythmical stress (Ontario and Quebec).

Notable is the fact that the three main tendencies (iambic rhythm, rhythmical stress patterns and the increase of their frequency towards the end of IP) are realized in Quebec speech to a greater extent than in Ontario. Right-edge prominence as a characteristic of French stress suggests itself as the most plausible (and probable) explanation.

4 Discussion and Conclusions

The results of the overall quantitative lexicon and sound corpus analysis of digital identity in CE lexical stress patterns can be assessed in relation to our previous data on BE and AE [15]. Focused on distinctions found between the two major varieties registered in Cambridge Pronouncing Dictionary, the previous data revealed that AE tends to apply an iambic pattern more often than BE. The facts are known to be loan words from Romance and other languages. In the two-syllable domain we can draw the following comparisons:

BE: trochaic 67%; iambic 23%; pre-tonic 10%; post-tonic none.
AE: trochaic 34%; iambic 57%; pre-tonic 8%; post-tonic 1%.
CE: trochaic 68%; iambic 22%; pre-tonic 1%; post-tonic 9%.

Basically, as one can see, CE has preserved the British patterns but it has also introduced and developed the post-tonic pattern, common with AE, which may be interpreted as the effect of language contact with French. Two adjacent syllables bearing stress, we can assume, is a sign of syllable-based rhythm, typical of the French language as a prototypical syllable-timed language.

In the three-syllable domain the comparisons are as follows:

BE: primary only 68%; pre-tonic 30%; post-tonic 2%.
AE: primary only 67%; pre-tonic 26%; post-tonic 7%.
CE: primary only 67%; pre-tonic 15%; post-tonic 18%.

Here again the post-tonic pattern has developed from what was present in the other two varieties in a tiny proportion. Thus the three varieties have practically identical nomenclature of stress patterns which are nationally distinctive in frequencies and, probably, in their distribution and functions. The point of argument is that CE may not have *developed* the identifying features, it may have *preserved* them, just like Canadian French has preserved a few pronunciation features which distinguish it from Parisian French. In support of this argument we can say that the diagnostic post-tonic patterns were found in everyday CE, in basic vocabulary of people and not in newly borrowed words. There are words of kinship and place names, for instance, in the lexicon we found in the corpus. They may have originated in French and were supported by language contact with French over a long period of time, but they are not new borrowings in CE speakers' vocabulary.

There are other conditions which facilitate the choice of the post-tonic pattern, among them the position of the polysyllabic word in the intonation structure of IP. Although we collected earlier in CE native speakers' survey enough data to confirm the cognitive reality of the pattern [17], we acknowledge that there are certain phonetic contexts, widely attested in literature (Cf. overview in [8]) that provoke the prolongation of the last syllable both in the word and in the intonation phrase [16], and facilitate the pronunciation of a long vowel in the right-edge final position. In the CE spoken corpus of IDEA the general tendency for final prolongation was verified and supported by the frequency data on rhythmical stress patterns at the termination of intonation phrases, with special reference to the Francophone area of Quebec.

The general conclusions are as follows:

1. By collecting an impressive amount of data from dictionaries and the spoken corpus of CE lexical stress we have corroborated the theories of English stress which proposed both stability and variance in the matrix of lexical stress patterns shared by the three major varieties [15, 17–20]. Language contact with French resulted in the interplay of two basic tendencies, *recessive*, common with other Germanic languages (stress on the initial syllable) and *rhythmical*, caused by the stress on the final syllable and alternating strong and weak syllables.

2. CE demonstrates digital identity in relation to the other two varieties, BE and AE. The most robust data on national and regional identity of CE speech can be found in the domains of two-syllable and three-syllable stress patterns where the diagnostic feature is the post-tonic rhythmical stress and its frequency.

3. Taking into account the role of lexical stress in word recognition [5, 7, 14], we assume that the stability of the stress patterns system in English across the three major varieties provides for speech intelligibility and listening comprehension in oral discourse, as well as for speech recognition systems. Nevertheless, the digital identity of Canadian English as a distinct autonomous variety of English which, we hope, has been established in the present lexicon and the corpus study, may also become relevant for intercultural communication.

References

1. Berg, T.: Stress Variation in American English. World Englishes **18**(2), 123–143 (1999)
2. Boberg, Ch.: English in Canada: phonology. In: Schneider, E.W., Burridge, K., Kortmann, B., Mesthrie, R., Upton, C. (eds.) A Handbook of Varieties of English: a Multimedia Reference Tool, vol. I: Phonology, pp. 351–365. Mouton de Gruyter, Berlin/New York (2004)
3. Cruttenden, A.: Gimson's Pronunciation of English, 6th edn. Arnold, London (2001)
4. Cutler, A., Carter, D.M.: The predominance of strong initial syllables in the English vocabulary. Comput. Speech Lang. **2**, 133–142 (1987)
5. Cutler, A.: Lexical stress in English pronunciation. In: Reed, M., Levis, J.M. (eds.) The Handbook of English Pronunciation, pp. 106–124. Wiley-Blackwell, Chichester (2015)
6. Durand, J., Laks, B. (eds.): Phonetics, Phonology and Cognition. Oxford University Press, Oxford (2004)
7. Field, J.: Intelligibility and the listener: the role of lexical stress. TESOL Q. **39**(3), 399–424 (2005)
8. Fletcher, J.: The prosody of speech: timing and rhythm. In: Hardcastle, W.J., Laver, J., Gibbon, F.E. (eds.): The Handbook of Phonetic Sciences, 2nd edn. pp. 523–602. Wiley-Blackwell, Chichester, U.K. (2013)
9. Gage Canadian Concise Dictionary: Gage Learning Corporation, Toronto (2003)
10. Gumperz, J.J. (ed.): Language and Social Identity. Cambridge University Press, Cambridge (1982)
11. International Dialects of English Archive. http://www.dialectsarchive.com/canada. Accessed 17 Oct 2015
12. Ladefoged, P.: A Course in Phonetics. Harcourt College Publishers, New York (2001)
13. Llamas, C., Watt, D. (eds.): Language and Identities. Edinburgh University Press, Edinburgh (2010)
14. McQueen, J.M., Cutler, A.: Cognitive processes in speech perception. In: Hardcastle, W.J., Laver, J., Gibbon, F.E. (eds.) The Handbook of Phonetic Sciences, 2nd edn, pp. 489–520. Wiley-Blackwell, Chichester (2013)
15. Postnikova, L.V., Buraya, E.A., Galochkina, I.Y., Shevchenko, T.I.: Typologia Variantov Fonologicheskoy Systemy Angliyskogo Yazyka. (Typology of Varieties in English Phonology System). Tula University Press, Tula (2012). (in Russian), Shevchenko, T.I. (ed.)
16. Potapov, V.V.: Analiz udareniya v mnogoyazychnoy rechi kak osnova dlja formirovaniya ustno-rechevyx baz dannyx dlja slavyanskix yazykov (Analysis of stress in multilingual speech as a basis for creating spoken databases of Slav languages). Vestnik MSLU, № 1 (712), 165–177, Moscow (2015)
17. Shevchenko, T., Pozdeeva, D.: canadian english word stress: a corpora-based study of national identity in a multilingual community. In: Karpov, A., Potapova, R., Mporas, I. (eds.) SPECOM 2017. LNCS (LNAI), vol. 10458, pp. 221–232. Springer, Cham (2017). https://doi.org/10.1007/978-3-319-66429-3_21
18. Shevchenko, T.I.: Sociofonetica: nacionalnaya i socialnaya identichnoct' v angliyskom proiznoshenii (Sociophonetics: National and Social Identity in English Pronunciation), 2nd edn. LENAND, Moscow (2016). (in Russian)
19. van der Hulst, H. (ed.): Word Stress: Theoretical and Typological Issues. Cambridge University Press, Cambridge (2014)
20. Vishnevskaya, G.M., Abyzov, A.A.: Kanadskyi yazykovoy razlom (anglo-francuzskii bilingvism) (Canadian Linguistic Break: English-French Bilingualism). Ivanovo University Press, Ivanovo (2016)
21. Wells, J.C.: Longman Pronunciation Dictionary, 3rd edn. Pearson Longman, Harlow (2008)

Automatic Speech Recognition for Kreol Morisien: A Case Study for the Health Domain

Nuzhah Gooda Sahib-Kaudeer[(✉)], Baby Gobin-Rahimbux,
Bibi Saamiyah Bahsu, and Maryam Farheen Aasiyah Maghoo

Department of Software and Information Systems, Faculty of Information,
Communicatio and Digital Technologies, University of Maurtius,
Reduit, Mauritius
{n.goodasahib,b.gobin}@uom.ac.mu, {bibi.bahsu,
maryam.maghoo}@umail.uom.ac.mu

Abstract. Automatic Speech Recognition (ASR) has revolutionized human-machine interactions as it allows the use of speech as an input modality. Speech is easy, natural and it is a skill that most people possess in their respective languages. Therefore, speech technology contributes to the usability and inclusivity of applications. ASR in languages such as English is extensively developed as there are large amounts of relevant resources available such as audio or transcribed data. For languages which are under-resourced, such as Kreol Morisien, ASR is a monumental task. In this paper, an attempt at developing an ASR system in Kreol Morisien is described. The ASR system was developed for the health domain to enable the automatic recognition of medical symptoms in spoken Kreol. The data collection process included the manual creation of a list of 848 symptoms along with 4000 audio files. Using the created corpus, the acoustic model for Kreol recognition was built and trained. This paper also describes a user evaluation which was conducted in different environments. Findings showed that the accuracy of the acoustic model was mainly affected by the level of noise. The gender of the speaker and the pronunciation style (depending on the region where the speaker originates from) did not cause any significant difference in the performance of the acoustic model.

Keywords: Automatic Speech Recognition · Kreol Morisien · Under-resourced languages

1 Introduction

Automatic Speech Recognition (ASR) has been the subject of research for many decades. However, with the recent popularity of technologies such as Amazon Alexa and Apple Siri, ASR has received a new surge of interest [1]. The worldwide technological advancements in terms of mobile devices such as smartphones and tablets have also highlighted the need for speech-based interactions [2] as speech is the primary means of human communication. Speaking is faster and more natural, therefore increasing the usability of many applications. Speech-based applications are also more inclusive [3] as they provide access to non-standard populations such as the elderly, the low-literacy group or the visually impaired.

© Springer Nature Switzerland AG 2019
A. A. Salah et al. (Eds.): SPECOM 2019, LNAI 11658, pp. 414–422, 2019.
https://doi.org/10.1007/978-3-030-26061-3_42

Creating speech-based applications in well-resourced languages such as English and French is not a big task, since text-to-speech systems are already available for these languages. On the other hand, creating speech-based applications for languages that do not offer the resources for Human Language Technologies (HLT) is a monumental task. ASR in such cases require large amounts of transcribed data for the training process and very often, for these languages, there are no existing corpus of data that can be used. Generating this required transcribed data is an expensive process in terms of both manpower and time [4].

In Mauritius, to the best of our knowledge, there is only one previous research [5] on ASR in Kreol. It is most likely due to the absence of a corpus of text and audio data in the language. Yet, there are many possible applications of ASR in the Mauritian context since Kreol Morisien is spoken by the majority of the population [7]. For example, despite English being the official language, Kreol is used extensively in schools, the workplace and in most public institutions such as hospitals. In this paper, a first attempt at ASR in Kreol Morisien is presented whereby the authors describe their approach to building an acoustic model that is able to recognize spoken medical symptoms being experienced by patients. The health domain has been chosen only because of the authors' previous work in developing smart health applications for Mauritius [6]. The rest of this paper is structured as follows: Sect. 2 provides a literature review on Kreol Morisien and Automatic Speech Recognition. Section 3 describes the implementation of the acoustic model for Kreol recognition. In Sect. 4, the user evaluation process is outlined along with findings and discussions. We conclude the paper in Sect. 5.

2   Literature Review

2.1   Kreol Morisien

According to Ethnologue[1] (Accessed April 2019), the Kreol language, also known as Kreol Morisien, is the de facto language of national identity in Mauritius and is spoken by 1,339,200 around the world. Kreol can be defined as a French-based language including a number of words from English and from the African and South Asian languages spoken in Mauritius [6]. The status of Kreol Morisien has been the subject of an ongoing debate since Mauritius attained independence from the British in 1968. However, it is only in recent times that efforts have been made by the Government to formalize the language: In 2010, Akademi Kreol Morisien (AKM) was created and different committees were set up to define and standardize the spelling, syntax, pronunciation and grammar of the Kreol language. In 2012, the Government of Mauritius introduced the language in the curriculum of primary education.

2.2   Automatic Speech Recognition for Under-Resourced Languages

Automatic Speech Recognition (ASR) is an important technology for the most natural human-computer interaction, given that speech is a skill that the majority of people

---

[1] https://www.ethnologue.com.

have [1]. Speech technology can address barriers in human-human interactions (two people speaking different languages can use ASR to communicate seamlessly) as well as human-machine interactions (applications such as Voice Search [8] and Personal Digital Assistants [9]). ASR has already changed the way people live and work as speech becomes the input modality of human-machine interactions [1]. This is especially true for established languages such as English and French, for which a large amount of resources is available.

However, the same cannot be said for languages from developing countries which have so far received a lot less attention [12]. Yet, the need for speech technology in these languages is high as speech-based interactions are easy and thus accessible to a wider population including the low literate, the elderly and people with certain impairments [3]. The challenge for ASR in such languages is the limited availability of resources which has led to these languages being termed as 'under-resourced'. The concept of under-resourced language was introduced by [10] and [11]. In a survey for ASR in the context of under-resourced languages, [12] summarized the concept as a language with some or all of the following: "lack of a unique writing system or stable orthography, limited presence on the web, lack of linguistic expertise, lack of electronic resources for speech and language processing, such as monolingual corpora, bilingual electronic dictionaries, transcribed speech data, pronunciation dictionaries, vocabulary lists, etc."

In the context of Kreol Morisien, it can be considered as an under-resourced language mostly for the lack of electronic resources required for speech processing. In this paper, a first attempt at developing an ASR system in Kreol Morisien is described. The ASR system, through its acoustic model, aims to recognize spoken symptoms from patients using a health diagnosis tool. Thus, the conversation patients may have with a nursing staff while describing their symptoms is being simulated (A snapshot of such a conversation can be found in Table 1). Since, the focus of this paper is ASR, only the speech recognition part of this work is described, omitting details on health diagnosis.

Table 1. Examples of medical symptoms in Kreol Morisien and English

Kreol Morisien	English
Mo latet p fermal	*I have a headache*
Mo p gagne la fievre	*I have a fever*
Mo p tousser	*I am coughing*

3   Implementation of Acoustic Model

3.1   Data Collection

Since there are no existing corpus for Kreol Morisien, the implementation of the acoustic model included the data collection process during which both text and audio data was manually created.

Text Corpus. Since there are no corpus available for Kreol Morisien, the implementation of the acoustic model included the data collection process. A list of 848 commonly used words to describe symptoms in Kreol was created and based on these words, a list of 2989 sentences was manually created to be used for language modelling.

Audio Recording. The audio for each word and sentence was recorded using Audacity[2] and saved as .wav files. Four different speakers (two males and two female) recorded 1000 audio files each. Therefore, a total of 4000 audio recordings was obtained. The absence of noise was ensured during the recording process as noise would cause interferences during the training of the acoustic model. Presence of noise would cause the amplitude of the audio to increase and therefore, it was ensured that the amplitude remained between −0.5 and 0.5.

3.2 Building of Phonetic Dictionary

A template dictionary of the list of 848 Kreol symptoms was constructed using the Lexicon tool[3] to understand the phonetic representation of each word (known as phoneme). Different pronunciations for the same word were catered for (see Fig. 1) to boost efficiency of the recognition model since the Kreol language is articulated differently by different individuals. The dictionary was built using the French phones since they are closer to Kreol pronunciation than English. For example, 'a' is represented as 'AE' in English phones whereas in French, it is represented as 'aa'.

```
acoz aa kk oo zz
adapter aa dd aa pp tt ei
adolessan aa dd oo ll ai ss an
adult aa dd uu ll tt
adilt aa dd ii ll tt
azitasion aa zz ii tt aa ss yy on
agitasion aa jj ii tt aa ss yy on
azitasian aa zz ii tt aa ss yy an
azitashion aa zz ii tt aa sh yy on
agitashion aa jj ii tt aa sh yy on
```

Fig. 1. Snapshot of Phonetic Dictionary

3.3 Building of Language Model

The Lexicon tool was used to generate the language model in order to calculate the probabilistic occurrence of words. A total of 2989 sentences and 784 words was used to build the language model.

3.4 Preparation of Transcript Files

The transcription files were manually created based on the audio recordings from the data collection process. Both Kreol_train.transcription and Kreol_test.transcription

---

[2] https://www.audacityteam.org/.

[3] www.speech.cs.cmu.edu/tools/lmtool.html.

have been prepared, one for training and one for testing respectively. Each word and sentence in the files were allocated a unique identifier. The transcription files was updated each time new audio recordings became available. This was an effort intensive task that required in depth revisions since mistakes could lead to failure in training.

3.5   Training the Acoustic Model

CMU Sphinx[4] was used to train the acoustic model with 80% of the audio recordings corresponding to 3.2 h of audio data. A phoneset file of all phones in the dictionary was created and a context dependent model was used for training. The details of the final version of the acoustic model are described in Table 1.

4   User Evaluation

A user evaluation was conducted to determine the accuracy of the acoustic model in correctly recognising the symptoms spoken by users in continuous speech. There were two main parts of the user evaluation, referred to as User Study 1 and User Study 2 for the rest of this paper. A set of 50 sentences in Kreol Morisien, that did not occur in the train and the test sets, was created to conduct the user studies. Bothe studies used the same sentences to ensure that while other variables such as level of noise were changing, the complexity of the speech was the same across studies.

4.1   User Study 1

The aim of this study was to determine the accuracy of the acoustic model in varying environments in order to simulate circumstances in which people may be using such an application in real-life settings. The participants and the methodology are described in the following.

Participants. Ten participants were involved in User Study 1 and they were divided into two groups (A and B) such that two different participants were assigned the same group of sentences. Additional demographic information about the participants which was collected through a questionnaire can be found in Table 2.

Table 2. Demographic information of participants in User Study 1.

	Group A	Group B
Age	34.5	21
Gender	Male (3) Female (2)	Male (3) Female (2)
Region	Urban (2) Rural (3)	Urban (2) Rural (3)
Level of Kreol	Native Speaker (5)	Native Speaker (5)

---

[4] https://cmusphinx.github.io.

Methodology. The sentences were split in 5 sets of 10 sentences (S1 to S5) and each participant in Group A and Group B were assigned one set of sentences to speak. For comparison purposes, it was ensured that each set of sentences were assigned to speakers of the same gender from both groups. However, different speakers from each group tested the acoustic model in different environments in terms of noise levels. The participants spoke the sentences using the same hardware and the acoustic model output the transcribed speech for evaluation purposes.

Findings and Discussion. The ability of the acoustic model to recognize speech in Kreol Morisien is evaluated based on Word Error Rate (WER). WER is calculated as the total number of insertions, deletions and substitutions in the output of the acoustic model divided by the total number of words in the reference sentence. For each user study, the Sentence Error Rate (SER) is also provided. SER is the proportion of the sentences which have an error in them. In this paper, all reported WER and SER values have been calculated using the Python module for ASR evaluation[5].

The Word Error Rate for User Study 1 was 17.91%, that is, the overall accuracy of the acoustic model across all participants was 82.09%. In Fig. 2, WER for each participant from both Group A and Group B are displayed. Statistical testing was carried out at $p < 0.05$ using a two-sample t-test for unequal variances. There was no significant difference between Group A and Group B ($p = 0.07$). The regions from which the participants originated (Urban or Rural) and the gender did not cause any significant difference in the performance of the acoustic model ($p = 0.26$ and $p = 0.17$). The SER value was 57% across the sentences spoken by the participants.

In this user study, the authors did not control the environment with respect to noise level. Therefore, it was performed in mixed environments with some speakers inside a room with background noises like a running fan and some in open air with people

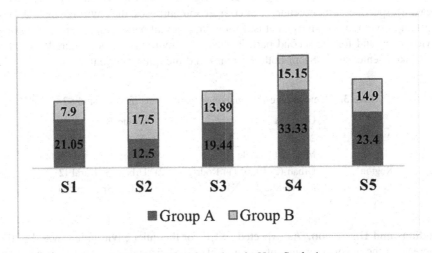

Fig. 2. WER of speakers in User Study 1

---

[5] https://github.com/belambert/asr-evaluation.

talking and moving nearby. The average accuracy is 82.09% for all the sentences across all speakers. The biggest differences in accuracy are between speakers 1A (21.05%) and 1B (7.9%) and speakers 4A (33.33%) and 4B (15.15%), despite each pair speaking the same sentences. This difference may have arisen because as per data gathered in the questionnaire, despite being a native creole speaker, speaker 1A speaks French on a daily basis and thus her accent is different from speaker 1B who speaks Kreol Morisien regularly. Speaker 1A was also in a noisier environment. The difference between speakers 4A and 4B may also have resulted due to the difference in environments.

4.2   User Study 2

Following User Study 1 in mixed environments where the accuracy of the acoustic model in different levels of noises was studied, User Study 2 was conducted with 10 participants in two different environments. The aim of this user evaluation was to study how the acoustic model performed in two different environments: a noisy environment as well as a quiet environment. For the noisy environment, an open corridor with people talking and laughing, sounds of doors opening and closing and people walking loudly was chosen. There was also a car park nearby and thus, there was also vehicle-related noises in the background. The quiet environment was indoors, in a classroom with closed doors.

Participants. Ten participants, who were all students from the University of Mauritius took part in this study. They were divided into two groups (A and B) such that two different participants were assigned the same group of sentences for each environment. Additional demographic information about the participants are given in Table 3.

Methodology. The same set of sentences as in User Study 1 were used whereby each participant in Group A and Group B were assigned one set of sentences (S1 to S5) to speak, irrespective of their gender. For comparison purposes, the environment was kept constant throughout the study, that is, for the first part all participants were in the noisy environment and for the second part, in the quiet environment. For example, speaker 1A spoken sentence set S1 in both the noisy and the quiet environments.

Table 3. Demographic information of participants in User Study 2.

	Group A	Group B
Age	20	20.5
Gender	Male (3) Female (2)	Male (2) Female (3)
Region	Urban (2) Rural (1) Rodrigues (2)	Urban (3) Rural (2)
Level of Kreol	Native Speaker (5)	Native Speaker (5)

Findings and Discussion. As expected, WER for the quiet environment was 13.70% whereas for the noisy environment, it was 37.01%. Statistical testing was carried out at $p < 0.05$ with a paired t-test and the difference between the two environments was statistically significant ($p = 0.000004$). In the noisy environment, insertions and substitutions are more likely given the background noises and this significantly affected the

WER and the overall accuracy of the acoustic model. For the noisy environment, there was no statistically significant difference in the performance of the acoustic model for gender (p = 0.30) and region (p = 0.24). The SER value for the noisy environment was 90% while for the quiet environment it was 42%. Gender and Region did not cause statistically significant differences in the quiet environment (p = 0.46) and (p = 0.12).

For User Study 2, there were two participants (3B and 4B) from Rodrigues. Rodrigues is an autonomous outer island of the Republic of Mauritius and their style of Kreol can be different from people in the main island. Statistical testing was performed between participants from Mauritius and Rodrigues for the same sentences using a paired t-test at p < 0.05. Between participants 3A (from Mauritius, Rural region) and 3B, no statistically significant differences were observed for the ten sentences of S3 in both the noisy (p = 0.11) and the quiet environments (p = 0.63). Similarly, there were no statistically significant differences between participants 4A (from Mauritius) and 4B for the ten sentences of set S4 in the noisy environment (p = 0.18) and the quiet environment (p = 0.94) (Table 4 and Fig. 3).

Table 4. WER for participants in User Study 2

Sentence set	WER			
	Noisy environment		Quiet environment	
	Group A	Group B	Group A	Group B
S1	32.21	34.21	15.79	7.90
S2	30.00	40.00	15.00	17.50
S3	44.44	30.56	13.89	11.11
S4	54.55	42.42	15.15	15.15
S5	29.79	31.92	12.77	12.77

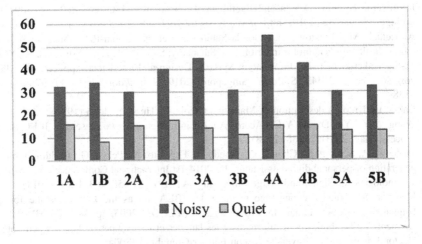

Fig. 3. WER for speakers in User Study 2

5 Conclusion and Future Work

In this paper, an initial investigation regarding Automatic Speech Recognition (ASR) in Kreol Morisien was presented. The context under study was the health domain whereby the aim of the ASR system was to be capture patients' symptoms as described through speech. Given the lack of a corpus in Kreol Morisien, the data collection process included the manual creation of both audio and transcribed data which was then used for training an acoustic model to recognize the language.

Given the widespread use of Kreol in Mauritius, speech technology can undoubtedly have a significant impact. However, given its under-resourced status with regards to the lack of resources for speech processing, the challenge is to investigate potential approaches for generalized ASR in Kreol without having to start from scratch as discussed by [12]. Future work will focus on how existing corpus for English and French can be used as a starting point in order to decrease the extensive efforts required to build a corpus for a new language from scratch.

References

1. Yu, D., Deng, L.: Automatic Speech Recognition. Springer, London (2016)
2. De Vries, N.J., et al.: A smartphone-based ASR data collection tool for under-resourced languages. Speech Commun. **56**, 119–131 (2014)
3. Neerincx, M.A., Cremers, A.H., Kessens, J.M., Van Leeuwen, D.A., Truong, K.P.: Attuning speech-enabled interfaces to user and context for inclusive design: technology, methodology and practice. Univ. Access Inf. Soc. **8**(2), 109–122 (2009)
4. Lamel, L., Gauvain, J.L., Adda, G.: Lightly supervised and unsupervised acoustic model training. Comput. Speech Lang. **16**(1), 115–129 (2002)
5. Noormamode, W., Gobin-Rahimbux, B., Peerboccus, M.: A speech engine for Mauritian Creole. In: Satapathy, S.C., Bhateja, V., Somanah, R., Yang, X.-S., Senkerik, R. (eds.) Information Systems Design and Intelligent Applications. AISC, vol. 863, pp. 389–398. Springer, Singapore (2019). https://doi.org/10.1007/978-981-13-3338-5_36
6. Aubeeluck, M., Bucktowar, U., Gooda Sahib-Kaudeer, N., Gobin-Rahimbux, B.: A smart mobile health application for mauritius. In: Satapathy, S.C., Bhateja, V., Somanah, R., Yang, X.-S., Senkerik, R. (eds.) Information Systems Design and Intelligent Applications. AISC, vol. 863, pp. 333–343. Springer, Singapore (2019). https://doi.org/10.1007/978-981-13-3338-5_31
7. Baker, P.: Kreol: a description of Mauritian Creole. C. Hurst, London (1972)
8. Wang, Y.Y., Yu, D., Ju, Y.C., Acero, A.: An introduction to voice search. IEEE Signal Process. Mag. **25**(3), 28–38 (2008)
9. Milhorat, P., Schlögl, S., Chollet, G., Boudy, J., Esposito, A., Pelosi, G.: Building the next generation of personal digital assistants. In: 2014 1st International Conference on Advanced Technologies for Signal and Image Processing (ATSIP), pp. 458–463. IEEE (2014)
10. Krauwer, S.: The basic language resource kit (BLARK) as the first milestone for the language resources roadmap. In: Proceedings of SPECOM 2003, pp. 8–15 (2003)
11. Berment, V.: Méthodes pour informatiser les langues et les groupes de langues peu dotées. Doctoral dissertation, Université Joseph-Fourier-Grenoble I (2004)
12. Besacier, L., Barnard, E., Karpov, A., Schultz, T.: Automatic speech recognition for under-resourced languages: A survey. Speech Commun. **56**, 85–100 (2014)

Script Selection Using Convolutional Auto-encoder for TTS Speech Corpus

Meysam Shamsi[✉], Damien Lolive, Nelly Barbot, and Jonathan Chevelu

Univ Rennes, CNRS, IRISA, Rennes, France
{meysam.shamsi,damien.lolive,nelly.barbot,jonathan.chevelu}@irisa.fr

Abstract. In this study, we propose an approach for script selection in order to design TTS speech corpora. A Deep Convolutional Neural Network (DCNN) is used to project linguistic information to an embedding space. The embedded representation of the corpus is then fed to a selection process to extract a subset of utterances which offers a good linguistic coverage while tending to limit the linguistic unit repetition. We present two selection processes: a clustering approach based on utterance distance and another method that tends to reach a target distribution of linguistic events. We compare the synthetic signal quality of the proposed methods to state of art methods objectively and subjectively. The subjective measure confirms the performance of the proposed methods in order to design speech corpora with better synthetic speech quality.

Keywords: Corpus design · Deep neural networks ·
Embedding space · Clustering · Text-to-speech synthesis

1 Introduction

Text-to-speech synthesis is widely used in industry nowadays. Nevertheless, some applications still require improvements for further developments, like audiobooks generation.

In practice, the synthetic speech quality is strongly affected by the quality of the corpus used to build the voice. Previous studies [1–3] have shown that a random selection is not efficient to design such speech corpora. This is true especially for unit selection-based speech synthesis but also statistical parametric and hybrid ones. A random or unbalanced corpus contains lots of phonological unit repetitions and, most importantly, does not guarantee a sufficient variety of units for the speech synthesis process.

Moreover, the corpus should be as small as possible in order to minimize the human cost of high quality recording and labeling checking stages. In the case of unit selection and hybrid approaches, a reduced corpus size may also accelerate the synthesis process considering the smaller search space. In that case, removing redundant elements while adding critical ones to the corpus is important. A well-designed corpus combines parsimony and balanced unit coverage in order to gain a satisfactory level of richness with a minimal cost construction. The aim of this

© Springer Nature Switzerland AG 2019
A. A. Salah et al. (Eds.): SPECOM 2019, LNAI 11658, pp. 423–432, 2019.
https://doi.org/10.1007/978-3-030-26061-3_43

study is to design an automatic method to select the best recording script from the book. The selection is done at the utterance level to help the speaker have a well-adapted intonation. The recorded signals form a voice corpus on which is based a text-to-speech synthesis system to vocalize the complementary part of the book.

Several works on automatic TTS corpus design have been carried out since early 2000s (for instance [4–6] for some preliminary ones). The covering of linguistic units under a parsimony constraint is the main idea of script corpus design. In particular, the case of full covering can be formalized as a set-covering problem [6]. Two axes have been mainly studied: which units should be better to cover, and which algorithmic approach is the most adequate to best produce a solution according to the chosen optimization criteria? Many unit types have been considered: allophones [6], "sandwich" units [7], triphones, syllable and morpheme elements [8] for instance. [1] focused on maximum variability of unit features in the selected subset instead of defining a discrete unit set to be covered. The most commonly used algorithmic strategy is the greedy one which provides solutions close to optimal ones [9].

Regardless of set covering, some studies [10,11] investigated the distribution of units in the corpus. [10] suggested to design TTS corpora according to a constraint of minimization of the Kullback-Leibler Divergence (KLD) between their diphoneme and triphoneme distribution and a prior distribution. They then focused on the usage frequencies by the TTS system and the distribution of units in reduced speech corpus [12]. They assumed that the most used units by the synthesis process are the most important to be covered by the reduced corpus. However, the achievements of this method directly depend on the performance of unit selection. Recently, the maximization of an extended entropy of phonetic and prosodic context has been considered in [13] to design corpora and the results have underlined that this contextual information should be taken into account.

Increasing the number of features and samples leads to an exponential growth of the covering size if no feature selection is done. Instead of introducing expert knowledge to select the features, we propose to use a model for that task. Deep neural networks and particularly deep auto-encoders could be used to do so. [14] introduced an approach to build *Paragraph Vectors*, also called *Doc2Vec*. Their model maps variable length pieces of text to a fixed-length vector. This method was introduced to work with words as units. [15] presented a sequence-to-sequence model based on long short-term memories (LSTM). However their proposition was used for translation task, the LSTM hidden states can be used as embedding vectors for utterances when the model has been trained as an auto-encoder. Although the context and application of these studies were different, in both approaches, the linguistic information of each *piece of text* is embedded in a fixed-length vector. In our case, we use a Convolutional Neural Network (CNN) to map utterances to an embedding space. Then, we try to find a tiling of the embedding space, in order to offer a larger linguistic covering, that could improve the speech synthesis quality compared to standard approaches. These selection approaches are compared to the LSTM and the Doc2vec methods as well as a standard set covering one, implemented as the covering of all diphonemes using a greedy strategy [3,9]. The perceptual evaluation shows that the proposed methods are more efficient than the standard one. Moreover, a crucial asset of these embedding-based approaches is that it is not necessary to select features, they adapt automatically to the book to be generated.

Section 2 explains the corpus design procedure in three steps. In Sect. 3, the objective and subjective results are presented. Finally, Sect. 4 discusses the results and future works.

2   Methodology

The main idea of this paper is to derive a vector representation of the linguistic information in order to facilitate the selection of a subset of utterances having a good linguistic variety from a text corpus. The proposed approach relies on convolutional neural networks [16] with the aim of learning a non linear transformation from textual and linguistic data into a new pertinent representations without manual feature extraction/selection. The derived utterance embedding enables to guide and compare some selection algorithms to extract a set of utterances as a subset offering a large linguistic richness. The first algorithm is to cover all clusters of the embedding space stemming from a K-means algorithm. The second one is based on a greedy strategy to design an utterance subset close to a target linguistic distribution.

Figure 1 shows the process of corpus design. The overall process is the following: (1) information extraction from the text corpus, (2) projection of feature vectors into an embedding space, and (3) utterance selection.

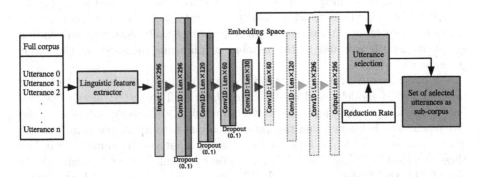

Fig. 1. Corpus design process and CNN auto-encoder architecture. "Len" is the length of the input and output layers.

2.1   Information Extraction

We define a linguistic feature vector, for each phoneme in the text utterance, providing information about the phoneme, e.g., its identity, preceding and following neighbours, its position in the syllable/word/utterance it belongs to, etc.

The linguistic features are automatically extracted [17]. The linguistic vector, of size 296, contains categorical and numerical features. The categorical attributes represent information about quinphonemes, syllables, articulatory features, and POS for the current, previous and following words. These features are converted to a one-hot vector. The numerical features take into account information such as the phoneme position inside the word or utterance. These numerical features are normalized so that all the entries of the linguistic vector are in the range [0, 1]. The linguistic content of an utterance is then represented by the sequence of linguistic feature vectors associated to the phonemes that compose it.

2.2 Embedding Space

From this initial representation of the linguistic content at phoneme and utterance levels, using an embedding space enables to derive a continuous and compressed representation. Importantly, this approach avoids the injection of expert knowledge to drive the selection of the most important features, letting the model reveal what is of interest.

To build up this embedding space, an auto-encoder based on a multi-layer CNN has been implemented, as shown on Fig. 1. To avoid overfitting, a dropout layer is used with a 0.1 drop probability after each layer in the encoder [18]. CNN layers are used with kernel size of 5 and the tanh activation function. The loss function is the Mean Squared Error (MSE).

Two kinds of training sets have been tested to learn the CNN auto-encoder: a set of utterances (*Utt*) with variable length, and a set of chunks provided by a sliding window (*SW*) of size 100 phoneme instances with a step size of 10 phonemes. The best configurations will be selected to be compared perceptually.

After training, the network is used to generate, for each input sequence of linguistic vectors at utterance level, a sequence of unit vectors in embedding space. Its length is equal to the number of phoneme instances in the input utterance.

To compare our proposed method to state of the art models, we have also used an LSTM model based on [15] and *Doc2vec*. The LSTM model has two layers, one for encoding and one for decoding with 30 memory units each. The *Doc2vec* model is learnt using the *gensim* toolbox with an output dimension of 30, a window size of 5 and a minimum count of input vectors equal to two. For these two models, we have searched for the best configuration and an embedding size of 30 with *SW* (resp. *Utt*) for LSTM (resp. *Doc2vec*) gives the best results.

2.3 Utterance Selection

The main idea behind utterance selection is to extract a set of utterances from a book that offers a representative linguistic coverage while limiting the linguistic unit repetitions. In our case, the term unit stands for phonemes in context, based on the linguistic features used. The concrete goal is to provide a large variety of options to the TTS system while minimizing the voice size. We propose two methods for selecting utterances: the first one is based on a clustering approach, the second tends to reach a target distribution of linguistic events.

Clustering. The clustering methods group vectors based on the similarity of their attributes. By selecting one vector per cluster, we assume that it represents the information of other elements of its cluster. In particular, one can consider that the most representative vector is the closest one to the cluster center.

In order to compute a similarity measure between utterances with different lengths, we have built a numerical and fixed dimensional representation of utterances. Let us consider an utterance u composed of m phoneme instances, its ith phoneme instance is represented by the embedded vector $p_i = (x_1^i, \ldots, x_N^i)$, where N corresponds to the embedding dimension. Several aggregation operators could be used to take into account the contributions of phonemes in u, like the sum, and we have chosen the average to avoid the utterance length-dependency: u is then represented by $\hat{u} = (f_1, \ldots, f_N)$ where $f_j = 1/m \sum_{i=1}^m x_j^i$.

The clustering of the full text corpus $\mathcal{F}$ is made based on the K-Means algorithm using the Euclidean distance between utterance vectors $\hat{u}$ as the similarity measure. As mentioned above, the closest vector to the cluster center is selected from each cluster. The length l_S of the set S of selected sentences is given by the sum of the length of its elements (in terms of number of phoneme instances). In order to achieve a target reduction rate τ^* of $\mathcal{F}$, the cluster number is iteratively updated (the selection is then redone): its initial value K_0 is set to $\lfloor \tau^* \times (\text{number of utterances in } \mathcal{F}) \rfloor$; resulting from step i, a selected subset S_i is derived using K_i clusters and K_{i+1} is set to the $\lfloor K_i \times \tau^* \times l_{\mathcal{F}}/l_{S_i} \rfloor$.

KLD Minimization. A greedy strategy to minimize the Kullback-Leibler divergence in the context of corpus design has been proposed in [10]. Although this method was based on the phonological unit distributions, the idea can be transposed to continuous values in embedding space. In our case, the target distribution is the natural one, given by the unit distribution in the full corpus.

Precisely, for each dimension of the embedded phoneme vectors, values are normalized to the range $[0, 1]$ and an histogram h is then computed by binning the values into ten bins ($X = \{[0, 0.1), \ldots, [0.9, 1]\}$). Thus, for each latent feature f_j, its probability distribution can be defined using histogram $h(f_j)$; the KLD between the probability distribution P_S^j of f_j in the selected set of utterances S and the probability distribution P_t^j in the target set of utterances is derived as follows:

$$KLD(P_S^j \parallel P_t^j) = -\sum_{x \in X} P_S^j(x) \log \left(\frac{P_S^j(x)}{P_t^j(x)} \right).$$

To achieve a target sub-corpus size, at each iteration, a greedy process selects the utterance which minimizes the average of KLDs (one KLD per feature) between the target distribution and the distribution computed from the new set of utterances, including the candidate utterance.

3   Experiments and Results

3.1   Experimental Setup

The initial corpus contains 3,339 utterances of a French expressive audio-book spoken by a male speaker. The overall length of the speech corpus is 10h44. More information on the annotation process can be found in [20]. The audio-book has been divided into two parts. A test set T which is randomly selected as a continuous part with 334 utterances (10% of the whole corpus). The rest of the audio book is named the full corpus and is denoted F in the remainder. F is composed of 3,005 utterances and 362,126 phoneme instances. The objective is to extract from F a subset S of a given size. The natural signal samples of S will be used to synthesise the utterances of T by the IRISA TTS system [19]. To derive the embedded representation of utterances of F, 90% of F are used for training the CNN models and 10% are used as a validation set to avoid overfitting.

The conversion of Utt (i.e. F here) into SW generates 36206 samples with an average length of 100 phoneme instances. Several embedding sizes have been tested ($N = 240, 120, 60, 30, 15$). As $N = 30$ gives the best reconstruction error for the CNN models (0.00021 for SW and 0.00067 for Utt), we keep that embedding size for the experiments. For comparison, the reconstruction error for the LSTM model is 0.056 for SW with $N = 30$.

3.2   Best Configuration Selection

In order to compare the performance of the selection methods and evaluate the impact of the selection size on the synthesised speech quality, several sub-corpus sizes of F have been tested: 50%, 40%, 30%, 20%, and 10%. The selection methods under comparison are the following:

- *Random*: the baseline method is a random selection of utterances. To have representative results, 10 random selections have been built for each reduction size, and for the evaluation, the average values are considered.
- *SC*: this system is based on a greedy strategy to solve a Set Covering problem [9]. The utterances are selected so as the solution under construction covers at least η times each linguistic feature. Starting from 1, η is incremented until the target sub-corpus size is reached.
- *GreedyKLD*: a greedy algorithm is used to minimize the KLD between the diphoneme distribution of the selected subset S and F as done in [10].
- *Doc2Vec/LSTM/CNN_KMeans*: as detailed in Sects. 2.2 and 2.3, the selection strategy is K-Means algorithm which clusters the embedding space. This embedding is derived by Doc2Vec model or LSTM auto-encoder, which are presented in Sect. 1, or a CNN auto-encoder.
- *CNN_KLD*: it is a variant of *GreedyKLD*. The considered distributions are those associated to the embedded vectorial representation as explained in Sect. 2.3.

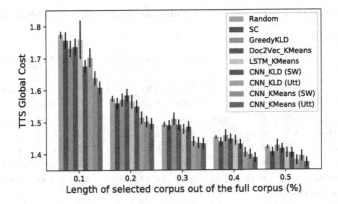

Fig. 2. TTS global cost for the different systems.

For each selection method and reduction size, the obtained voice is used to synthesize the utterances of $\mathcal{T}$. Figure 2 displays the associated average TTS global cost (the average concatenation and target costs are not detailed here since they indicate the same trends). We can observe that the reduced set provided by *CNN_KMeans* achieves the best performance. We have also compared the proposed CNN embedding to the Doc2Vec and LSTM models. The results show, on TTS global cost, that the CNN based approach performs better.

Considering TTS global cost results, we keep the two following approaches, relying on different selection strategies, for further evaluations: *CNN_KMeans* (using *Utt* as training set) and *CNN_KLD* (with *SW*).

3.3   Coverage Rate and KLD Evaluation

As for the assessment of the phonological richness of a selected subset $\mathcal{S}$ of $\mathcal{F}$, its associated *diphoneme* (resp. *triphoneme*) *coverage rate*, i.e. the rate of distinct diphonemes (resp. triphonemes) of $\mathcal{F}$ present in $\mathcal{S}$, is computed. Futhermore, the KLD between diphoneme (resp. triphoneme) distributions of $\mathcal{S}$ and $\mathcal{F}$ is also calculated in order to evaluate the closeness of both distributions, or, in other words, the naturalness of unit distribution in $\mathcal{S}$. Table 1 details these statistics for each selection method and several sub-corpus sizes.

For both criteria, when the sub-corpus size increases, all the methods get obviously better. Globally, with a sub-corpus size of 50%, all the methods have very close results in terms of coverage rate and KLD.

More precisely, although the reduced subsets resulting from *SC* naturally offer the best diphoneme coverages, *CNN_KMeans* provides better diphoneme and triphoneme coverage rates than the other approaches. Concerning KLD, the *GreedyKLD* method yields the best results for diphonemes, as expected. However, the *CNN_KMeans* method achieves a lower KLD of triphonemes in comparison with *GreedyKLD* method. Globally, the *CNN_Kmeans* methods has very good results on both criteria.

Table 1. The coverage rate and KLD for diphonemes (Diph) and triphonemes (Triph)

SubCorpus Size	10%		20%		30%		40%		50%	
Method	Diph	Triph	Diph	Triph	Diph	Triph	Diph	Triph	Diph	Triph
Coverage rate										
Random	0.84	0.52	0.90	0.66	0.93	0.74	0.95	0.80	0.96	0.85
SC	1	0.56	1	0.69	1	0.78	1	0.86	1	0.89
GreedyKLD	0.86	0.52	0.92	0.66	0.95	0.74	0.96	0.80	**0.99**	0.85
Doc2Vec_KMeans	0.82	0.50	0.91	0.66	0.93	0.74	0.96	0.81	0.97	0.86
LSTM_KMeans	0.83	0.51	0.90	0.65	0.93	0.74	0.95	0.80	0.97	0.85
CNN_KLD	0.86	0.54	0.91	0.67	0.94	0.76	0.95	0.82	0.97	0.86
CNN_KMeans	**0.88**	**0.61**	**0.93**	**0.75**	**0.97**	**0.83**	**0.97**	**0.88**	0.98	**0.91**
Kullback Leibler Divergence										
Random	0.012	0.153	0.006	0.077	0.003	0.048	0.002	0.032	0.001	0.022
SC	0.015	0.163	0.006	0.079	0.003	0.048	0.003	0.033	0.002	0.022
GreedyKLD	**0.002**	0.133	**0.000**	0.067	**0.000**	0.042	**0.000**	0.028	**0.000**	0.019
Doc2Vec_KMeans	0.013	0.153	0.006	0.078	0.003	0.047	0.002	0.032	0.001	0.022
LSTM_KMeans	0.013	0.150	0.006	0.079	0.004	0.049	0.002	0.032	0.001	0.022
CNN_KLD	0.011	0.139	0.005	0.071	0.003	0.043	0.002	0.028	0.001	0.019
CNN_KMeans	**0.008**	**0.099**	**0.003**	**0.044**	**0.002**	**0.026**	**0.001**	**0.016**	**0.000**	**0.011**

While the average length of utterances in the whole book is about 120 phonemes, this value for the selected sub-corpus of 10% by *CNN_KMeans* is 104 (this value varies from 115 to 155 for other systems). In fact, among all the considered methods and for each reduction size, *CNN_KMeans* selects significantly shorter utterances on average.

3.4   Subjective Evaluation

Based on objective measures, three methods have been chosen to be compared perceptually: *SC*, *CNN_KMeans* (using *Utt*) and *CNN_KLD* (using *SW*). The utterances of the test section have been synthesized using 10% of $\mathcal{F}$ selected by each of these methods. Three AB preference tests have been conducted to compare the following pairs of systems:

1. *CNN_KLD* and *SC*, 19 listeners
2. *CNN_KMeans* and *SC*, 17 listeners
3. *CNN_KMeans* and *CNN_KLD*, 13 listeners.

Each test is composed of the 100 samples with the highest DTW on MCep features from test set [21]. The samples are shorter than 7 s. The listeners were asked to compare 30 pairs in terms of overall quality. The results are reported on Fig. 3.

Synthetic signals provided by *CNN_KMeans* and *CNN_KLD* are judged to be of better quality than the ones from *SC*, which confirms the ranking between these methods provided by the objective measures. Moreover, listeners have a small preference for the *CNN_KMeans* method rather than the *CNN_KLD* one but this trend is not really significant.

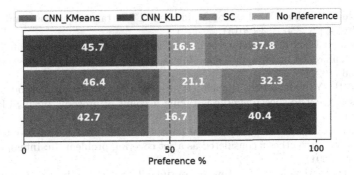

Fig. 3. Listening test results

4   Conclusion

In this paper, we presented a method for sentence selection. In the framework of TTS corpus design, we showed that a CNN auto-encoder can be used successfully to extract linguistic information. The K-Means clustering and the KLD methods work properly using embedded representations achieving better results than random, or even than the best state-of-the-art methods such as greedy based set covering algorithm. We have also compared the proposed CNN embedding approach to *Doc2Vec*, and it proves to work better in the particular context of corpus design. The subjective evaluation confirmed this result showing a preference for the proposed approaches.

As for future works, first, the embedded phoneme representations should be used for hybrid TTS as well. Second, in these experiments, the model corresponds to a linguistic auto-encoder and it could be beneficial to use a general encoder-decoder from linguistic information to acoustic information for corpus design. Third, in order to generate a whole audio-book as a mix of natural and synthetic signal, the selection method should take into account the utterances which are not selected as the target of synthesizing. First results obtained here tend to show that trying to minimize KLD between selected utterances and T achieves better results than minimizing KLD with a global distribution like F.

Acknowledgements. This study has been realized under the ANR (French National Research Agency) project SynPaFlex ANR-15-CE23-0015 and also funded by the Région Bretagne and the Conseil Départmental des Côtes d'armor.

References

1. Bozkurt, B., Ozturk, O., Dutoit, T.: Text design for TTS speech corpus building using a modified greedy selection. In: 8th European Conference on Speech Communication and Technology, pp. 277–280 (2003)
2. Isogai, M., Mizuno, H.: Speech database reduction method for corpus-based TTS system. In: 11th Annual Conference of the International Speech Communication Association, pp. 158–161 (2010)

3. Chevelu, J., Lolive, D.: Do not build your TTS training corpus randomly. In: EUSIPCO, pp. 350–354 (2015)
4. van Santen, J.P.H., Buchsbaum, A.L.: Methods for optimal text selection. In: European Conference on Speech Communication and Technology (Eurospeech), pp. 553–556 (1997)
5. Kawai, H., Yamamoto, S., Higuchi, N., Shimizu, T.: A design method of speech corpus for text-to-speech synthesis taking account of prosody. In: ICSLP, vol. 3, pp. 420–425 (2000)
6. François, H., Boëffard, O.: Design of an optimal continuous speech database for text-to-speech synthesis considered as a set covering problem. In: Interspeech, pp. 829–832 (2001)
7. Cadic, D., D'Alessandro, C.: Towards optimal TTS corpora. In: LREC, pp. 99–104 (2010)
8. Isogai, M., Mizuno, H., Mano, K.: Recording script design for corpus-based TTS system based on coverage of various phonetic elements. In: ICASSP, pp. 301–304 (2005)
9. Barbot, N., Boëffard, O., Chevelu, J., Delhay, A.: Large linguistic corpus reduction with SCP algorithms. Comput. Linguist. **41**(3), 355–383 (2015)
10. Krul, A., Damnati, G., Yvon, F., Moudenc, T.: Corpus design based on the Kullback-Leibler divergence for text-to-speech synthesis application. In: ICSLP, pp. 2030–2033 (2006)
11. Shinohara, Y.: A submodular optimization approach to sentence set selection. In: ICASSP, pp. 4112–4115 (2014)
12. Krul, A., Damnati, G., Yvon, F., Boidin, C., Moudenc, T.: Approaches for adaptive database reduction for text-to-speech synthesis. In: Interspeech, pp. 2881–2884 (2007)
13. Nose, T., Arao, Y., Kobayashi, T., Sugiura, K., Shiga, Y.: Sentence selection based on extended entropy using phonetic and prosodic contexts for statistical parametric speech synthesis. IEEE/ACM Trans. Audio Speech Lang. Process. **25**(5), 1107–1116 (2017)
14. Le, Q., Mikolov, T.: Distributed representations of sentences and documents. In: International Conference on Machine Learning, pp. 1188–1196 (2014)
15. Sutskever, I., Vinyals, O., Le, Q.: Sequence to sequence learning with neural networks. Advances in Neural Information Processing Systems, pp. 3104–3112 (2014)
16. LeCun, Y., Bengio, Y.: Convolutional Networks For Images, Speech, and Time Series. The Handbook of Brain Theory and Neural Networks. MIT Press, Cambridge (1995)
17. Perquin, A., Lecorvé, G., Lolive, D., Amsaleg, L.: Phone-level embeddings for unit selection speech synthesis. In: Dutoit, T., Martín-Vide, C., Pironkov, G. (eds.) SLSP 2018. LNCS (LNAI), vol. 11171, pp. 21–31. Springer, Cham (2018). https://doi.org/10.1007/978-3-030-00810-9_3
18. Srivastava, N., Hinton, G., Krizhevsky, A., Sutskever, I., Salakhutdinov, R.: Dropout: a simple way to prevent neural networks from overfitting. J. Mach. Learn. Res. **15**(1), 1929–1958 (2014)
19. Alain, P., Barbot, N., Chevelu, J., Lecorvé G., Simon, C., Tahon, M.: The IRISA Text-To-Speech System for the Blizzard Challenge 2017. In: Blizzard Challenge workshop (2017)
20. Boeffard, O., Charonnat, L., Le Maguer, S., Lolive, D., Vidal, G.: Towards Fully Automatic Annotation of Audio Books for TTS. In LREC, pp. 975–980 (2012)
21. Chevelu, J., Lolive, D., Le Maguer, S., Guennec, D.: How to compare TTS systems: a new subjective evaluation methodology focused on differences. In Interspeech (2015)

Pragmatic Markers Distribution in Russian Everyday Speech: Frequency Lists and Other Statistics for Discourse Modeling

Natalia Bogdanova-Beglarian[1] ⓘ, Tatiana Sherstinova[1,2(✉)] ⓘ, Olga Blinova[1] ⓘ, and Gregory Martynenko[1] ⓘ

[1] Saint Petersburg State University, 7/9 Universitetskaya nab., St. Petersburg 199034, Russia
{n.bogdanova, t.sherstinova, o.blinova, g.martynenko}@spbu.ru
[2] National Research University Higher School of Economics, 190068 St. Petersburg, Russia
tsherstinova@hse.ru

Abstract. Pragmatic markers (PMs) are discourse units (words and multiword expressions) with a weakened referential meaning, which perform a variety of pragmatic tasks. For example, in English the common PMs are "well", "you know", "I think", and many others. PMs are integral elements of spoken discourse in every language. According to the results obtained from the ORD corpus of everyday Russian, their share can reach up to 6% of the total number of words in speech of individual speakers. More than that, in some speech fragments, PMs may even exceed the share of significant units (i.e., standard words). However, despite their frequency and usualness, PMs are still poorly understood. Current NLP and discourse modeling systems lack information on PMs distribution and usage, this fact leads to noticeable shortcomings in work of these systems when they face spontaneous speech of everyday spoken discourse. In this paper we present top frequency lists of PMs for Russian dialogue and monologue spoken speech in general, and also for separate sociological groups of informants (by gender and by age). Our current list of PMs for Russian contains 450 units which are the variants of 50 main structural types. Besides, we consider the most frequent functions of PMs in spoken Russian. The presented quantitative data may be used for improvement of NPL and discourse modeling systems.

Keywords: Spoken Russian · Everyday discourse · Pragmatics · Pragmatic markers · Spoken dialogue · Spoken monologue · Speech corpus · Statistics · Frequency lists · Sociolinguistics · NLP

1 Introduction

Pragmatic markers (PMs) are discourse units (words and multiword expressions) with a weakened referential meaning, which perform a variety of pragmatic tasks [1]. They are used to express speaker's attitude to speech content, help to introduce new topics and to structure the discourse as the whole, provide the speaker time to find the proper word,

A. A. Salah et al. (Eds.): SPECOM 2019, LNAI 11658, pp. 433–443, 2019.
https://doi.org/10.1007/978-3-030-26061-3_44

etc. [2]. In earlier papers on spoken discourse, PM were considered within a wider class of *discourse particles* or *discourse markers* [3–7, etc.]. In this paper we adhere to understanding PM as it was proposed in [8], and the distinction between pragmatic markers (PMs) and discourse markers (DMs) is presented in [9].

It can be assumed that PMs may be observed in every natural spoken language. And more than that, they are integral elements of every spoken discourse. For example, in English the common PMs are "well", "you know", "I don't know", and many others, and in Russian the similar PMs are "tak" ("well"), "znaesh" ("you know"), "ne znaju" ("I don't know"), etc.

According to the results obtained from the ORD corpus of everyday Russian [10, 11], their share can reach up to 6% of the total number of words in speech of individual speakers. More than that, in some speech fragments, PMs may even exceed the share of significant units (i.e., standard words). However, despite their frequency and usualness, PMs are still poorly understood. Current NLP and discourse modeling systems lack information on PMs distribution and usage, this fact leads to noticeable shortcomings in work of these systems when they face spontaneous speech of everyday spoken discourse [9].

In this paper we present frequency lists of PMs for Russian dialogue and monologue spoken speech in general, and also for separate sociological groups of informants. Besides, we consider the most frequent functions of PMs in spoken Russian.

2   Research Data

2.1   Dialogue Everyday Speech

For the analysis of dialogue everyday speech, 149 macroepisodes of everyday communication [12] were selected from the ORD corpus, obtained from 98 volunteer participants. The total sample size is 308905 words. To form a balanced subcorpus, the representatives of different gender, age and professional groups were included in the sample, and the information from participants' psychological tests concerning their psycho type and temperament was used as well. Moreover, when forming the sample, different conditions of everyday communication (locus, participants, type of communication) were taken into account.

As a result, the research subcorpus contains speech samples from participants of different professional groups—service workers, IT-specialists, representatives of engineering specialties, "office" workers, representatives of power structures, university professors, etc. The presented communicative settings relate to both formal and informal communication (with colleagues at work, with classmates, friends or parents, and communication in the family). Among the sample participants are 45 women (46%) and 53 men (54%). Speakers' age varies in a wide range (from 17 to 83 years).

2.2   Monologue Speech

For the study of monologue speech, texts of various types, obtained from 34 informants, were selected from the SAT corpus, known as "Balanced Annotated Text

Library" [13]. The sample consists of 50128 words. When selecting spoken texts for a balanced subcorpus, we tried to balance texts reflecting different scenarios of mono-logue speech generation, as well as speech samples from participants belonging to different gender, age and professional groups.

The outcome subcorpus contains monologues of 5 communicative scenarios types: retelling of both narrative and non-narrative texts, description of both narrative and non-narrative images, and a free story on some definite topic. The sample contains 34 texts of each type, so the sample is balanced, first of all, according to the types of monologue texts included in it.

The subcorpus presents the monologue speech of informants belonging to two professional groups—lawyers and doctors (JUR and MED subcorpora), in total there are 170 monologue texts in the sample. Women predominate among participants, since the "medical speech" of MED subcorpus was recorded only from women. The sample of lawyers-participants is gender-balanced: it includes monologues from 8 women and 9 men. In the SAT sample, the age of speakers ranges from 23 to 49 years. The majority of speakers (22 informants) have a high level of speech competence, 12 informants belong to groups with an average and low level of speech competence.

2.3   Data Annotation

The both subsamples were annotated in ELAN [14] using the scheme described in [9]. Thus, the annotators had to fill in four additional levels: (1) PM, (2) PM function, (3) speaker's code, and (4) comments.

For PM annotation the list of Russian PMs containing 450 units being the variants of 50 main structural types was used. This current list of PMs main structural types is given in Table 1.

For each PM, its main function was assigned. The list of these functions is the following [9]:

(1)   A—marker-approximator ("tipa", "kak by", etc.);
(2)   G—boundary marker, including *starting, final,* and *navigational* markers ("vot", "koroche", etc.);
(3)   D—deictic marker ("vot etot vot", "vot takoj vot", etc.);
(4)   Z—replacement marker referring to some whole set or its part ("i tak dalee", "i vs'o takoe", "to-sio"), as well as for imitating someone else's speech ("bla-bla-bla");
(5)   K—"xeno" marker that introduces someone's speech ("tipa", "govorit", etc.);
(6)   M—meta-communicative marker that refers to "communication about commu-nication" ("znaesh", "vidish");
(7)   F—"reflexive" marker that expresses reflection on what is said ("tak skazat'");
(8)   R—rhythm-forming marker ("vot", "tam", etc.);
(9)   C—marker of self-correction ("v smysle", "vernej", etc.);
(10) H—hesitation markers ("eto", "vot", "tam", etc.) [9].

Apart from the "pure" types, the "mixed" (or polyfunctional) functions could be registered (e.g., AG, AGH, GRH, AF, etc.), reflecting the overall polyfunctionality of PMs, which is very typical in oral speech [6].

Table 1. The main structural types of PM in spoken Russian with the number of correspondent variants

Structural type	The number of variants	Structural type	The number of variants
vot takoj vot	109	*tak*	5
pyatoe desyatoe	30	*tam*	5
eto	30	*znachit*	4
vsyo takoe	25	*i to i drugoe*	4
eto samoe	18	*predstav'*	4
znaesh'	17	*ne znayu*	4
takoj	13	*da*	4
to syo	11	*minutu*	3
vrode	10	*i tak dalee*	3
slushaj	9	*ili kak ego/eto*	6
dumayu	9	*sekundu*	3
tipa	8	*na samom dele*	2
smotri	8	*i vse dela*	2
tak i tak	8	*prikin'*	2
ponimaesh'	8	*zaceni*	2
predstavlyaesh'	8	*glyan'*	2
boyus' chto	8	*voobshche*	2
chto eshchyo	8	*zamet'*	2
skazhem	7	*vot*	2
vidish'	6	*kak by*	2
vsyo	6	*ili chto*	2
ili eshchyo chto-to takoe	6	*kak ego*	2
govorit	6	*koroche*	1
kak eto	6	*sobstvenno*	1
to to	5	*kak ih*	1

Processing the results of PMs annotation based on corpus material allowed us to obtain data on the frequency of occurrence of individual pragmatic markers and their functions, as well as on the dependence of PMs use on speaker's characteristics. Below are some of the data obtained.

3   Frequency Lists of Pragmatic Markers in Monologue and Dialogue Speech

Two top frequency lists of PMs are presented in Tables 2 and 3, which include: the ranks, the frequency of PMs in absolute numbers, the share of specific PMs from all the PMs in the sample (in %), and the share of specific PMs from all words in the sample (ipm). The data presented here were calculated on the subsample of 60000 words for dialogue speech, and on that of 15000 words for monologue speech.

It is seen from the Tables 2 and 3, that the most commonly used PM in the both types of Russian speech turned out to be "vot", which is usually used as a "boundary marker" (G), a hesitation (H) and rhythm-forming (R) marker. Besides, among the frequent PMs of both types are "tak", "tam", "kak by", and "nu vot".

Table 2. The most frequent PMs in Russian dialogue speech

Rank	PM	Abs. number	The share (%) of PM among the other PMs	IPM (to the total number of tokens)
1	*vot*	149	14.06	2483
2	*tam*	117	11.04	1950
3	*da*	82	7.74	1367
4	*govorit*	70	6.60	1167
5	*kak by*	60	5.66	1000
6	*eto*	44	4.15	733
7	*eto samoe*	43	4.06	717
8	*znaesh'*	41	3.87	683
9	*koroche*	38	3.58	633
10	*tak*	36	3.40	600
11	*ne znayu*	25	2.36	417
12	*slushaj*	23	2.17	383
13	*znachit*	21	1.98	350
14	*nu vot*	21	1.98	350
15	*tipa*	21	1.98	350
16	*ponimaesh'*	19	1.79	317
17	*takoj*	17	1.60	283
18	*vidish'*	11	1.04	183
19	*takie*	11	1.04	183
20	*na samom dele*	10	0.94	167
21	*etot*	9	0.85	150
22	*vot takoj vot*	7	0.66	117
23	*govoryu*	7	0.66	117
24	*vot eti vot*	6	0.57	100
25	*dumaju*	5	0.49	83

Table 3. The most frequent PMs in Russian monologue speech

Rank	PM	Abs. number	The share of PM am. the other PMs (%)	IPM (to the total number of tokens)
1	*vot*	139	51.48	9232
2	*znachit*	15	5.56	996
3	*tak*	15	5.56	996
4	*tam*	13	4.81	863
5	*kak by*	12	4.44	797

(*continued*)

Table 3. (*continued*)

Rank	PM	Abs. number	The share of PM am. the other PMs (%)	IPM (to the total number of tokens)
6	*nu vot*	12	4.44	797
7	*vsyo*	4	1.48	266
8	*i tak dalee*	4	1.48	266
9	*vot tak vot*	3	1.11	199
10	*nu tak*	3	1.11	199
11	*takaya*	3	1.11	199
12	*takie*	3	1.11	199
13	*vot eta vot*	2	0.74	133
14	*da*	2	0.74	133
15	*kak eto nazyvaetsya*	2	0.74	133
16	*ya dumayu chto*	2	0.74	133
17	*v eti*	1	0.37	66
18	*vot sejchas by vot*	1	0.37	66
19	*vot takaya vot*	1	0.37	66
20	*vot takoe vot*	1	0.37	66
21	*vot eti vot*	1	0.37	66
22	*vot eto vot*	1	0.37	66
23	*vot etot vot*	1	0.37	66
24	*vrode*	1	0.37	66
25	*vrode by*	1	0.37	66

In the top zone of the frequency list for dialogue speech we can also see meta-communications (M) —"da", "znaesh", "ponimaesh", "vidish", hesitation markers (H) "eto", "eto samoje", "koroche tak", the xeno-indicator marker (K) "govorit" (which is often reduced), and many others. In the monologue speech subsample, the upper zone of PM frequency list contains mainly different types of boundary markers (G), which mark the beginning or end of the monologue or are serving as discourse navigators—"vot"/"nu vot", "znachit tak", "vsyo". We should mention the high frequency of the deictic marker (D) "vot tak vot" as well.

Table 4 presents the lists of most typical PMs for Russian dialogue and monologue speech types measured in difference of correspondent IPM values. It could be seen from this table, that the maximum difference is observed for PM "vot", which occurs much more often in monologues then in dialogue.

Table 4. The most obvious differences in PMs usage between dialogue and monologue speech

"Dialogue" PMs			"Monologue" PMs		
Rank	PM	IPM difference	Rank	PM	IPM difference
1	*da*	−951	1	*vot*	7262
2	*govorit*	−926	2	*znachit*	718
3	*tam*	−684	3	*tak*	520

(*continued*)

Table 4. (*continued*)

"Dialogue" PMs			"Monologue" PMs		
Rank	PM	IPM difference	Rank	PM	IPM difference
4	*eto samoe*	−569	4	*nu vot*	519
5	*znaesh'*	−542	5	*i tak dalee*	266
6	*eto*	−516	6	*nu tak*	186
7	*koroche*	−503	7	*takaya*	159
8	*slushaj*	−304	8	*vot tak vot*	146
9	*tipa*	−278	9	*kak eto nazyvaetsya*	120
10	*ne znayu*	−265	10	*ya dumayu chto*	120

The research presented in [15] has shown that the differences in the use of PMs between dialogue and monologue types of speech according to the Mann-Whitney test can be considered statistically significant.

4 The Functions of Pragmatic Markers in Monologue and Dialogue Speech

Table 5 presents the top frequency lists of PMs functions in dialogue and monologue Russian speech (the meanings of the codes were listed above in Sect. 2.3), and in Table 6 one may see the comparison of PMs functions frequency in these two types of spoken Russian.

Table 5. The top frequency lists of PMs functions in dialogue and monologue Russian speech

"Dialogue" PMs			"Monologue" PMs		
Rank	PM function	IPM	Rank	PM function	IPM
1	H	5283	1	GH	6110
2	M	3317	2	H	4251
3	GH	2417	3	AH	2125
4	K	1717	4	RH	1528
5	RH	1167	5	G	1129
6	AH	867	6	D	332
7	G	550	7	DH	332
8	A	500	8	Z	332
9	N/A	383	9	N/A	266
10	D	333	10	GM	199

Table 6. The difference in distribution of PMs functions in dialogue and monologue speech

"Dialogue" PMs			"Monologue" PMs		
Rank	PM function	IPM difference	Rank	PM function	IPM difference
1	M	3184	1	GH	−3693
2	K	1650	2	AH	−1259
3	H	1033	3	G	−579
4	A	367	4	RH	−361
5	N/A	118	5	DH	−282
6	ARH	50	6	FH	−199
7	GR	50	7	Z	−149
8	GRH	50	8	AF	−133
9	AR	34	9	GDM	−133
10	KR	33	10	R	−99

It is seen from Table 5, that in both speech types, PMs of hesitation (H), boundary markers (G), and deictic markers (D), as well as bifunctional GH, AH, and RH are rather frequent. In general, it turned out that monofunctional use of PMs in dialogue speech is significantly higher (68.7%) than in monologue speech (37.4%).

According to Table 6, the most frequent "dialogue" functions are the following: (1) meta-communicative marker (M), (2) "xeno" marker (K), (3) hesitation marker (H), and (4) approximator (A). Among the polyfunctional PMs the rhythm-forming function is a typical component. It should be mentioned that in dialogue speech there occurred more cases when the experts could not attribute the PM function (N/A).

As for monologue speech, there are comparatively more boundary markers (G), replacement (Z), and rhythm-forming markers (R) here. Among the polyfunctional PMs the hesitation function prevails, probably because of the difference in communication scenarios of the SAT corpus [13].

5 Top Frequency Lists of Russian PMs for Speakers of Different Gender and Age Groups

This section reflects peculiarities of PMs usage in Russian everyday dialogue speech by different groups of speakers. Thus, Table 7 presents the top lists of PMs in male and female speech. In this table, as well as in the following one (Table 8), the numbers refer to the share of PMs in the correspondent social group.

Table 7. The top frequency lists of PMs in female and male Russian speech

Female speech			Male speech		
Rank	PM	%	Rank	PM	%
1	*vot*	15.92	1	*tam*	19.24
2	*govorit*	8.80	2	*vot*	10.20
3	*da*	7.40	3	*da*	8.45

(continued)

Table 7. (*continued*)

Female speech			Male speech		
Rank	PM	%	Rank	PM	%
4	*tam*	7.12	4	*koroche*	6.12
5	*kak by*	6.28	5	*tak*	4.37
6	*eto*	5.03	6	*kak by*	4.37
7	*eto samoe*	4.75	7	*tipa*	3.21
8	*znaesh'*	4.47	8	*eto samoe*	2.62
9	*tak*	2.93	9	*znaesh'*	2.62
10	*koroche*	2.37	10	*takie*	2.33

Table 8. The top frequency lists of PMs in Russian speech of different age groups

	Youth group		Middle-age group		Senior group	
Rank	PM	%	PM	%	PM	%
1	*vot*	12.06	*tam*	15.90	*vot*	21.77
2	*tam*	11.36	*vot*	10.88	*eto samoe*	8.87
3	*da*	8.22	*govorit*	10.04	*govorit*	6.85
4	*kak by*	6.99	*da*	7.53	*da*	6.85
5	*koroche*	5.59	*kak by*	6.69	*tam*	5.65
6	*govorit*	5.07	*znachit*	5.02	*eto*	5.65
7	*znaesh'*	4.02	*eto samoe*	5.02	*znaesh'*	5.24
8	*eto*	3.67	*tak*	4.18	*tak*	4.84
9	*ne znayu*	3.32	*eto*	3.35	*ponimaesh'*	2.82
10	*tipa*	3.15	*koroche*	2.51	*nu vot*	2.42

The limited volume of this article does not give us the opportunity to consider in detail all the differences observed in speech of different social groups, even for the top zone of frequency lists. However, we should mention high frequency of "tam" and "koroche" in male speech, whereas "govorit" and "kak by" are more peculiar to female speech. These results largely coincide with those obtained earlier [16–18]. As for age variation, "eto samoe" and "ponimaesh'" are mainly used by seniors, whereas "koroche" and "tipa" are more frequent in speech of youth group.

6 Conclusion

This study showed that PMs are indeed the integral elements of Russian spoken discourse. In speech of individual speakers, their share can reach up to 6.6% of the total number of words, and in individual speech fragments it can even exceed the share of significant units. The most common PM in almost all frequency lists is "vot", and in monologue speech, the high frequency of occurrence has shown PM "znachit".

PMs frequency lists analysis showed that we can confidently talk about statistically significant differences in use of PMs in dialogue and monologue. The most frequent PMs functions in speech of all groups of informants are metacommunicative, boundary-marking, and xeno-indicator. Pragmatic markers of these classes are often multifunctional and implement a number of additional functions.

Finally, the pilot annotation of the corpus data showed the qualitative heterogeneity of PMs, which manifests itself both in terms of the diversity of functions performed by them, and in terms of uniqueness of their identification and classification. The presented quantitative data may be used for improvement of NPL and discourse modeling systems.

Acknowledgements. The presented research was supported by the Russian Science Foundation, project #18-18-00242 "Pragmatic Markers in Russian Everyday Speech".

References

1. Fraser, B.: Pragmatic markers. Pragmatics **6**(2), 167–190 (1996)
2. Bogdanova-Beglarian, N., Sherstinova, T., Blinova, O., Martynenko, G., Baeva, E.: Towards a description of pragmatic markers in Russian everyday speech. In: Karpov, A., Jokisch, O., Potapova, R. (eds.) SPECOM 2018. LNCS (LNAI), vol. 11096, pp. 42–48. Springer, Cham (2018). https://doi.org/10.1007/978-3-319-99579-3_5
3. Schiffrin, D.: Discourse Markers. Cambridge University Press, Cambridge (1987)
4. Fraser, B.: An approach to discourse markers. J. Pragmat. **14**, 383–395 (1990)
5. Fischer, K., Drescher, M.: Methods for the description of discourse particles: contrastive analysis. Lang. Sci. **18**(3–4), 853–861 (1996)
6. Scheler, G., Fischer, K.: The many functions of discourse particles: a computational model of pragmatic interpretation. In: Proceedings of CogSci 1997 (1997)
7. Shourup, L.: Discourse markers. Lingua **107**, 227–265 (1999)
8. Bogdanova-Beglarian, N.V.: Pragmatems in Spoken Everyday Speech: Definition and General Typology [Pragmatemy v ustnoj povsednevnoj rechi: opredelenie pon'atia i obshchaja tipologia]. In: Perm University Herald. Russian and Foreign Philology [Vestnik Permskogo universiteta. Rossijskaja i zarubezhnaja filologia], issue no. 3(27), pp. 7–20 (2014)
9. Bogdanova-Beglarian, N., Blinova, O., Martynenko, G., Sherstinova, T., Zaides, K.: Pragmatic markers in Russian spoken speech: an experience of systematization and annotation for the improvement of NLP tasks. In: Balandin, S., et al. (eds.) Proceedings of the FRUCT'23, Bologna, Italy, 13–16 November 2018, pp. 69–77. FRUCT Oy, Finland (2018b). https://doi.org/10.23919/FRUCT.2018.8588101
10. Asinovsky, A., Bogdanova, N., Rusakova, M., Ryko, A., Stepanova, S., Sherstinova, T.: The ORD speech corpus of Russian everyday communication "One Speaker's Day": creation principles and annotation. In: Matoušek, V., Mautner, P. (eds.) TSD 2009. LNCS (LNAI), vol. 5729, pp. 250–257. Springer, Heidelberg (2009). https://doi.org/10.1007/978-3-642-04208-9_36
11. Bogdanova-Beglarian, N., et al.: Sociolinguistic extension of the ORD corpus of Russian Everyday speech. In: Ronzhin, A., Potapova, R., Németh, G. (eds.) SPECOM 2016. LNCS (LNAI), vol. 9811, pp. 659–666. Springer, Cham (2016). https://doi.org/10.1007/978-3-319-43958-7_80

12. Sherstinova, T.: Macro episodes of Russian everyday oral communication: towards pragmatic annotation of the ORD speech corpus. In: Ronzhin, A., Potapova, R., Fakotakis, N. (eds.) SPECOM 2015. LNCS (LNAI), vol. 9319, pp. 268–276. Springer, Cham (2015). https://doi.org/10.1007/978-3-319-23132-7_33

13. Bogdanova-Beglarian, N., Sherstinova, T., Zajdes, K.: Corpus "Balanced Annotated Text Library": methodology of multi-level analysis of the Russian monological speech [Korpus "Sbalansirovannaja Annotirovannaja Tekstoteka": metodika mnogourovnevogo analiza russkoj monologicheskoj rechi]. In: Analysis of Spoken Russian (AR3-2017). Proceedings of the 17th International Seminar, St. Petersburg, pp. 8–13 (2017)

14. Web: ELAN (Version 5.2) [Computer software]. Max Planck Institute for Psycholinguistics, Nijmegen. https://tla.mpi.nl/tools/tla-tools/elan/. Accessed 04 Apr 2019

15. Bogdanova-Beglarian, N., Blinova, O., Sherstinova, T., Martynenko, G.: Pragmatic markers annotation in Russian speech corpus: research problem, approaches and results. In: Komp'juternaja Lingvistika i Intellektual'nye Tehnologii, 2019 International Conference on Computational Linguistics and Intellectual Technologies, Dialogue 2019, Moscow, Russian Federation, vol. 2019-May, issue no. 18, pp. 72–85 (2019)

16. Sherstinova, T.: The most frequent words in everyday spoken Russian (in the Gender Dimension and Depending on Communication Settings). In: Komp'juternaja Lingvistika i Intellektual'nye Tehnologii, 2016 International Conference on Computational Linguistics and Intellectual Technologies, Dialogue 2016, Moscow, Russian Federation, 30 May 2018–2 June 2018, Moscow, RGGU, vol. 2016, issue no. 15(22), pp. 616–631 (2016)

17. Potapova, R.K., Potapov, V.V.: Language, Speech, Personality [Yazyk, rech', lichnost']. Yazyki slavyanskoj kul'tury, Moscow (2006)

18. Romaine S.: Corpus Linguistics and Sociolinguistics, Corpus Linguistics: An International Handbook, Mouton de Gruyter, Berlin, vol. 1, pp. 96–111 (2008)

Curriculum Learning in Sentiment Analysis

Jakub Sido[(⊠)] and Miloslav Konopík

NTIS – New Technologies for the Information Society, Faculty of Applied Sciences,
University of West Bohemia, Technická 8, 306 14 Plzeň, Czech Republic
{sidoj,konopik}@kiv.zcu.cz
http://nlp.fav.zcu.cz

Abstract. This work deals with curriculum learning for deep learning models for the sentiment analysis task. We design a new way of curriculum learning for text data. We reorder the training dataset to introduce the simpler examples first. We estimate the difficulty of the examples by measuring the length of the sentences. The simple examples are supposed to be shorter. We also experiment with measuring the frequency of the words, which is a technique designed by earlier researchers. We attempt to evaluate changes in the overall accuracy of the models using both curriculum learning techniques. Our experiments do not show an increase in accuracy for any of the methods. Nevertheless, we reach a new state of the art in the sentiment analysis for Czech as a by-product of our effort.

Keywords: Sentiment analysis · Curriculum learning ·
Transfer learning

1 Introduction

With an increasing trend of using deep learning techniques for their superior results in many different applications, the lack of training stability showed up. We often observe lots of runs stuck in different local optima [3]. There are many historically described techniques for supporting stability training and performance of deep neural network systems. In this work, we decided to examine the effect of various attitudes in the curriculum learning on a specific task in the text domain - the sentiment analysis.

2 Related Work

An interesting idea of curriculum learning was introduced in 2009 [1]. Authors discovered better results on several tasks with using a specific order of samples during training. Curriculum learning can be seen as a sequence of training criteria starting with an easy-to-optimise objective and moving to the actual objective.

© Springer Nature Switzerland AG 2019
A. A. Salah et al. (Eds.): SPECOM 2019, LNAI 11658, pp. 444–450, 2019.
https://doi.org/10.1007/978-3-030-26061-3_45

On image classification task they used samples with high contrast first. After a part of the training, they extend training set for samples with some noise and deformation.

In the case of language modelling, they suggest using increasing vocabulary size during a time. Texts with unknown words are discarded in each epoch given the actual vocabulary size.

3 Experiment Setup

Our goal is to explore how **curriculum learning** can improve sentiment classification task. In this case, we use two different neural network architectures: one is based on convolutional neural networks and the other one on recurrent neural networks.

3.1 Curriculum Epochs Design

For a particular task like sentiment analysis, we can tailor the construction of training data according to our knowledge of the task.

We try two different approaches to curriculum learning epoch designing. Firstly, repeat epochs until over-fitting is noticeable and then we expand the data. Secondly, we extend the data set with hard samples before over-fitting is observed. The right time for changing epochs is set experimentally.

Text Length. Our intuition to use text lengths as meta information for estimating difficulty of the examples is that the authors of the reviews must express themselves in a more straightforward fashion in shorter texts than in longer texts. The details of our settings are shown in Table 2.

Size of Word Vocabulary. Authors of [1] showed benefit of curriculum learning in the language modelling task. We expect an increase of accuracy (in terms of Macro-F_1 score) in our models as well. We split data set into several epochs. Firstly, we use only sentences containing words in a small vocabulary of the most frequent words. We try more different setups. In every iteration, we used only samples containing more than 80% of top X known words. Last epoch was not limited in any way (Table 1).

Table 1. Vocabulary size experiments

	Vocabulary setup	Amount of samples	Repetition of epochs
voc1	[2000, 5000, −]	[29700, 42581, 82244]	[3, 3, −]
voc2	[2000, 5000, −]	[29700, 42581, 82244]	[10, 10, −]

Table 2. Text length experiments

	Max. sentence length	Amount of samples	Repetition of epochs
len1	[10, 20, 50, –]	[6546, 19629, 47382, 82244]	[2, 2, 1, –]
len2	[10, 20, 50, –]	[6546, 19629, 47382, 82244]	[5, 5, 5, –]

3.2 Architecture

LSTM. In our LSTM [5] architecture (see Fig. 1), we first transform words into their vector representations using an embedding layer. We use pre-trained vectors from the FastText tool [2] to set the weights for the embedding layer.

After the embedding layer, we attach two stacked bi-directional LSTM layers and one fully connected softmax layer. We use the maximum length of sequences set to 150 words, and the dimension of hidden states is set to 128.

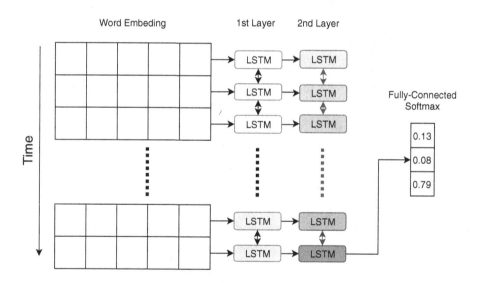

Fig. 1. LSTM architecture.

CNN. In our architecture, we use the same embedding layer as in the LSTM architecture and add only one convolution layer followed by max pooling. This approach is quite standard for text processing. We use 2D convolution kernels where one dimension is set to the embedding dimension, and the other one is set to 2, 3 and 4 respectively. This way the network looks for patterns in 2, 3 and 4 following words. We apply 32 2-word kernels, 32 3-word kernels and 16 4-word kernels.

In the end, we connect two fully connected layers, one with Sigmoid activation, the other one with soft-max (see Fig. 2).

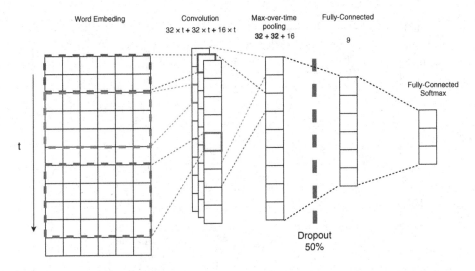

Fig. 2. CNN architecture. Where t is time.

3.3   The Data Set

The CSFD dataset consists of 91,381 movie reviews written in Czech from the Czech Movie Database[1]. The reviews are split into three categories according to their star rating (0–1 stars as negative, 2–3 stars as neutral, 4–5 stars as positive). The dataset contains 30,897 positive, 30,768 neutral, and 29,716 negative reviews. 82,244 reviews are used for training and 9,137 for testing. More details about the dataset can be found in [4].

4   Experiments Results

The Figs. 3, 4, 5 and 6 show the process of training and evaluation. The baseline is the same model we used in curriculum strategy, only the data set is randomly shuffled. We can identify the various training epochs by looking at the accuracy jump for *len1/len2* and *voc1/voc2* datasets. Every experiment was measured five times, and results are mean of all runs.

We can look at the process of the curriculum learning like on a specific case of a transfer learning [6] from an easier task to a harder one.

Using different maximum lengths for different epochs turn out to be not helping either.

We observed similar results on the RNN architecture (see Fig. 6). Any significant result improvement was not reached.

The RNN model achieved the best results. We reach **80.5%** ±0.155 on 95% confidence interval what is a new state of the art on this data set [4]. The CNN model achieved **78.7%** ±0.245 on 95%. These results are obtained on the test part of the original dataset by running a fixed number of epochs (in our case 3) and be averaging scores from 10 runs.

---

[1] https://www.csfd.cz/.

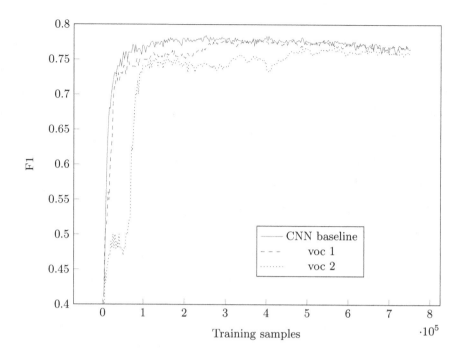

Fig. 3. Curriculum experiments with CNN architecture and vocabulary size

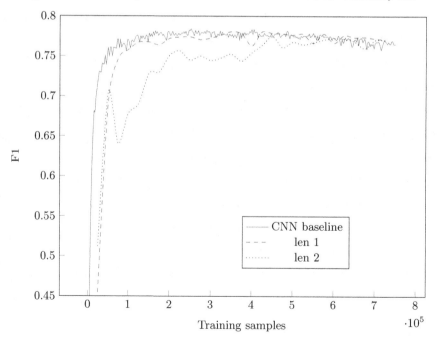

Fig. 4. Curriculum experiments with CNN architecture and length of texts

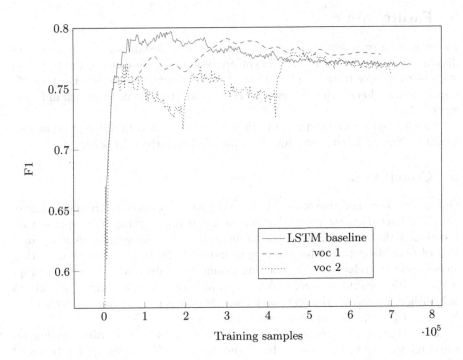

Fig. 5. Curriculum experiments with RNN architecture and vocabulary size

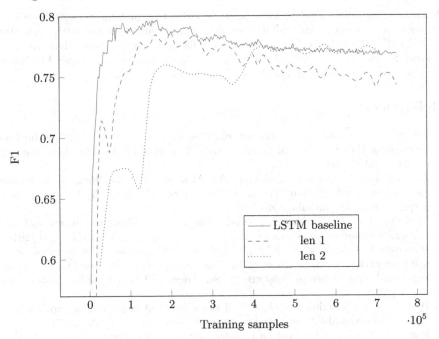

Fig. 6. Curriculum experiments with RNN architecture and sentence length

5   Future Work

There is a clear room for improvements. We can design other approaches of dividing the dataset for the sentiment analysis task. We can use the rating in stars (for example from 1 to 5) and start with the extreme cases - i.e. 1 and 5. Later, we would add other reviews (2–4). We want to try this approach in future work.

Another option for the future work is to experiment with different tasks - for example, Named Entity recognition, Semantic Similarity and others.

6   Conclusion

Our models were not able to benefit from any of the proposed curriculum strategies. This fact does not prove that our design is not working. We suppose that the reason that we were not able to measure any improvement may lay in a lack of training data. Although, it may indeed indicate that our premise that short sentences relate to easy training examples is incorrect. However, manipulation with vocabulary size, which works in language modelling task, did not help either. So maybe, the sentiment analysis task is not suitable for curriculum learning. Clearly, some more investigation is needed.

Even though we were not able to increase the accuracy using curriculum learning, we reached a new state of the art of 80.5% accuracy (in terms of Macro-F_1 score) for the sentiment analysis in Czech.

Acknowledgement. This work has been supported by Grant No. SGS-2019-018 Processing of heterogeneous data and its specialized applications, and was partly supported from ERDF "Research and Development of Intelligent Components of Advanced Technologies for the Pilsen Metropolitan Area (InteCom)" and by the project LO1506 of the Czech Ministry of Education, Youth and Sports.

References

1. Bengio, Y., Louradour, J., Collobert, R., Weston, J.: Curriculum learning. In: Proceedings of the 26th Annual International Conference on Machine Learning, pp. 41–48. ACM (2009)
2. Bojanowski, P., Grave, E., Joulin, A., Mikolov, T.: Enriching word vectors with subword information. Trans. Assoc. Comput. Linguist. **5**, 135–146 (2017). http://aclweb.org/anthology/Q17-1010
3. Cirik, V., Hovy, E., Morency, L.P.: Visualizing and understanding curriculum learning for long short-term memory networks. arXiv preprint arXiv:1611.06204 (2016)
4. Habernal, I., Ptáček, T., Steinberger, J.: Sentiment analysis in Czech social media using supervised machine learning. In: Proceedings of the 4th Workshop on Computational Approaches to Subjectivity, Sentiment and Social Media Analysis, pp. 65–74 (2013)
5. Hochreiter, S., Schmidhuber, J.: LSTM can solve hard long time lag problems. In: Advances in Neural Information Processing Systems, pp. 473–479 (1997)
6. Pan, S.J., Yang, Q.: A survey on transfer learning. IEEE Trans. Knowl. Data Eng. **22**(10), 1345–1359 (2010)

First Minute Timing in American Telephone Talks: A Cognitive Approach

Tatiana Shevchenko and Tatiana Sokoreva$^{(\boxtimes)}$

Moscow State Linguistic University,
38 Ostozhenka Street, 119034 Moscow, Russian Federation
tatashevchenko@mail.ru, jey-t@yandex.ru

Abstract. Cognitive perspective gives insight into the temporal organization of speech production based on acoustic cues of articulation rate, mean pause duration, total pause time, mean length of pause-free run, phonaton:pause ratio elicited from the first minutes of 30 American speakers' telephone talks. We assume that by balancing the number of speakers in three age groups (young, middle-aged, old) and two gender groups we found age effects and gender differences in the acoustic data which was revealing as regards overall speaking rates and fluency, as well as suggested interpretation in terms of the speed of online processing and working memory capacity of the speakers. Basic findings are concerned with the following: positive correlation between articulation rate and mean length of run; negative correlation between silent pause duration and mean length of run; positive correlation between phonation/pause ratio and mean length of run; negative correlation between silent pause duration and phonation/pause ratio. Cognitively significant is the evidence that men spend more time in thinking but articulate faster than women. Women spend less time in pauses. However, young women are still the fastest talkers in the six sub-groups. Age-related changes are most characteristic for the transition from young age to middle age when middle-aged speakers tend to shorten both their pauses and pause free runs. Mean length of run measured in number of syllables increases in old age compared to the middle age. The interplay of biological and social factors appears to account for the new facts found in middle-aged and old-aged groups of American speakers on the phone.

Keywords: American English · Timing · Cognitive perspective · Age · Gender

1 Introduction

In the era of modern technologies information based on 'big data' may not be available when we have to deal with a limited amount of sound samples. In real life situations we need to identify the voice of the speaker or at least place one geographically and socially, as well as make judgments about the personality of the speaker and the purpose of the call within the first minute. The objective of the present study is to look at the sound image of the speaker in the cognitive perspective by analyzing the constituents of timing: articulation rate, average pause duration, length of run between pauses, total pause time and phonation/pause ratio elicited from the first minute of telephone talks. By comparing the durations of the timing units in three age groups and

© Springer Nature Switzerland AG 2019
A. A. Salah et al. (Eds.): SPECOM 2019, LNAI 11658, pp. 451–458, 2019.
https://doi.org/10.1007/978-3-030-26061-3_46

specifying the gender differences we can evaluate fluency, working memory capacity and the speed of online processing according to the individual image projected by each speaker.

The following parameters of temporal speech organization indicative of cognitive processes became the subject of interdisciplinary research in psychology [7], cognitive phonology [4, 10, 19], forensic phonetics [11], sociophonetics [14, 17], pedagogical sciences [16, 18] and automatic speech recognition and speech synthesis [8, 12]. To begin with, *pauses*, both silent and filled, were found to perform at least three functions:

- physical, necessary for breathing, i.e. for respiration;
- cognitive, to show the time of online information processing, including perception time, the search for words and their retrieval from memory, lexico-grammatical coordination through collocation and colligation, parsing into meaningful units, etc.;
- social, to signal the interaction with the interlocutor according to the conventions of turn-taking, as well as for rhetorical purposes to show anticipation of an important word in focus, and, finally, to project an image of a person with a particular social status, a certain social role suitable for age and gender in a certain community.

Pauses, therefore, were reported to participate in style-shifting, and thus be distinctive for prepared reading, on the one hand, and spontaneous speech, on the other [6]. The proportion of time taken by pauses, relative to the time of phonation, was estimated for monologue at 30%, vs. 70%, or, in case filled pauses were also counted as phonation, at 20% vs. 80% [13]. In our data, however, based on mass media performances in weather forecasts and radio news on American TV, these proportions were utterly destroyed in favor of the phonation share on account of lack of time on the air [14]. See also a detailed review of cross-linguistic data on pauses, speech rate and rhythm in [5].

Cognitive research into the mechanisms of speech production and perception is also concerned with *overall speaking rate* (together with pauses) which is distinguished from *articulation rate* measured in the number of speech units (words or syllables) per second or per minute; alternatively, it was assessed as mean syllable duration (in msec or seconds). As regards the aged-related changes in articulation rate, the general assumption about the slowing down of tempo in old age is documented in comparison with the young generation, and is reflected in longer pauses, greater hesitancy, lower articulation rate and shorter phrases [1, 5, 9]. However, our previous research in which we introduced data on middle-aged group, gave evidence of a more complex way of prosody development with age, at least as far as accentuation is concerned [15]. In the current study we set ourselves the task of testing the hypothesis about a particular age effect in articulation rate/pause correlation for middle-aged people. Gender differences are also expected to emerge and to either support the stereotype of fast-talking, cooperative and friendly women in telephone conversations who spend less time in thinking than men, or refute it.

Of particular interest for the present study is the duration of speech unit between the two pauses, an *uninterrupted run of phonation* which is also called *intonation phrase (ip)* [6]. The time of the speech run from pause to pause and the amount of words or syllables it holds may have certain implications for evaluating one's working memory capacity.

By way of summarizing the parameters of the current research aimed at cognitive assessment of speech production in three groups of men and women, balanced for gender, we can name again pauses, articulation rate, uninterrupted run between pauses, phonation/pause ratio. In our methodology we propose a wholistic approach of considering the whole cluster of prosodic parameters simultaneously, as they occur in natural speech, to maximally correlate their co-occurrence and to reveal their actual interdependence. The cognitive processes which might transpire are bound to be connected with biological and social factors determining human speech production.

The *goal* of the present study is to find how the elements of timing correlated for the cognitive task of starting a telephone conversation by speakers at three stages of life, with special reference to gender.

2 Methodology

2.1 Data

The material under analysis is based on Switchboard Corpus of American English telephone conversations, recorded by LDC [3]. Sound sample type is 2-channel ulaw at 8000 Hz sample rate. The recording conditions implied that each time the informant was speaking to a different interlocutor on a different topic. All participants consented to being recorded providing information about their age, education and regional affiliation.

For the present research we selected one-minute fraction of telephone conversation data from 30 interlocutors counting from five up to sixteen phrases from the beginning of the dialogues that totals to 30 min of recorded speech. The informants are balanced for gender (15 male and 15 female speakers) and age: ten young (20–39), ten middle-aged (40–59) and ten old (60–69) speakers.

All the dialogue remarks were analyzed by means of computer program PRAAT [2] when pause and phonation durations were calculated and manually corrected. Such disfluencies as coughing and laughing were excluded from the analysis while filled pauses (e.g. 'um', 'uh' and the like) and partial words containing an initial consonant and a vowel remained. The total numbers of IPs and SPs analyzed are 812 and 499 respectively.

2.2 Measurements

Speech rate measures comprise the following variables:

Silent pause duration (SPD) – the time attributed to silent pauses of 100 ms length and above. The separate silent pauses were identified together with total time of silence in each phrase.

'Phonation: Pause' ratio (PPR) – the percentage of time spent speaking (including filled pauses) relative to the time attributed to silent pauses.

Articulation rate (AR) – the average number of fluent syllables produced per second over the total amount of time talking (excluding silent pauses, but including filled pauses and partial words containing an initial consonant and a vowel).

Mean length of run (MLR) – the mean number of syllables in utterances between silent pauses of 100 ms and above.

Statistical processing included one-way analysis of variance (ANOVA) that was conducted to test the difference in the above-mentioned speech rate parameters between three age groups and two gender groups of speakers. Furthermore, the correlation analysis (Spearman correlation coefficient) was run to test the relationship between the four extracted measures. Statistical procedures were performed in STATISTICA program (PAWS Statistics).

3   Results

According to ANOVA results the values of SPD significantly vary in three age groups with the most dramatic changes occurring in the middle-aged participants' speech as compared to the young speakers (F = 2.969, p = .052).

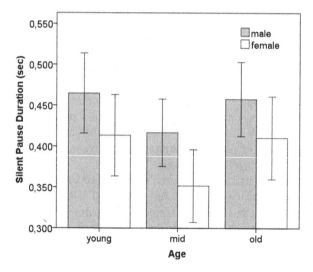

Fig. 1. Mean duration of silent pauses across three age groups of men and women (n = 30).

As is seen in Fig. 1 the time spent for silent pauses first decreases and then increases with age. ANOVA results also reveal gender-related difference in mean silent pause duration manifested in shorter pauses in female speech in comparison with the male one (F = 7.436, p < .01).

'Phonation:pause' time ratio values differ significantly only in two gender groups as revealed by ANOVA (F = 10.220, p < .01). Female speakers appear to spend much less time on pauses compared to men (Table 1) supporting the previous finding of gender-related SPD changes.

Table 1. Mean values of speech rate parameters across three age groups of men and women.

	Male			Female		
	Young	Mid	Old	Young	Mid	Old
SPD (ms)	0,465	0,417	0,458	0,413	0,352	0,410
PPR	6,6	6,7	7,4	8,3	13,8	9,5
AR (syll/sec)	4,8	5,1	5,2	5,4	4,1	4,2
MLR (syll)	7,3	8,6	10,1	12,1	8,4	10,5

Articulation rate unsurprisingly also varies across three age groups of speakers (Fig. 2) with the most noticeable distinction between young and middle-aged informants as provided by ANOVA (F = 4.797, p < .01) as well as it proves to be different in men's and women's speech (F = 14.829, p < .001). The results point that young women possess the fastest speech while men's speech is characterized by a smooth grow in AR with age.

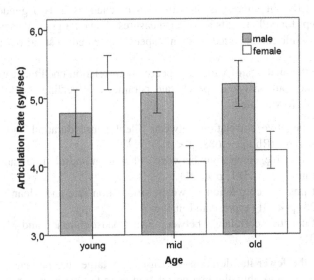

Fig. 2. Articulation rate of speakers across three age groups of men and women.

ANOVA scores for MLR parameter testify to significant age - (F = 3.001, p = .051) and gender-related changes (F = 7.491, p < .01) where male figures rise with increasing age and female values fall in the middle age and rise in the old age with young numbers being the highest (Fig. 3).

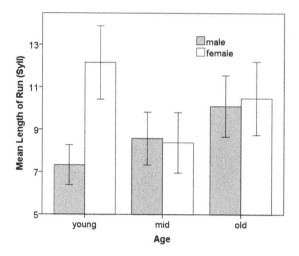

Fig. 3. Number of syllables between silent pauses across three age groups of men and women.

It is worth mentioning that all the four speech rate parameters proved to have gender differences while age-related changes were validated only in three of them (SPD, AR, MLR). Of interest is the direction of changes in two gender groups of speakers: except for SPD results all other measures showed a gradual increase in male speech values while middle-aged women's speech appeared to stand out against other age groups.

Alongside the analyses of variance Spearman correlation coefficient was found for each pair of the four analyzed speech rate parameters revealing the following relationships that were validated:

- Significant negative correlation between Silent pause duration and 'Phonation:-pause' time ratio (Rho = −.688, p < .01)
- Significant positive correlation between 'Phonation:pause' time ratio and Mean length of run (Rho = .581, p < .01)
- Significant positive correlation between Articulation rate and Mean length of run (Rho = .528, p < .01) represented in Fig. 4
- Significant negative correlation between Silent pause duration and Mean length of run (p < .01).

Obviously the fewer the duration of pauses, the larger the phonation time in the 'Phonation:Pause' ratio, thus the first correlation from the list is apparent. The second correlation result reveals that the larger the phonation duration, the bigger the quantity of syllables in IP. The positive correlation between AR and MLR indicates that the faster the rate of articulation, the more syllables are there in IP (Fig. 3). And negative correlation between SPD and MLR reflects the tendency that the more syllables are there in IP the fewer the duration of silent pauses in it.

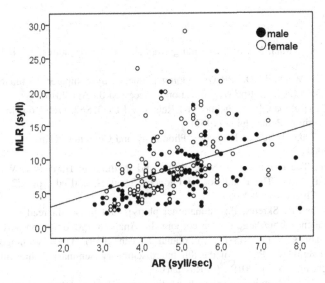

Fig. 4. Scatterplot of AR and MLR (n = 289).

4   Discussion and Conclusions

The data obtained by means of acoustical and statistical analyses has given evidence of speaker-dependent variance in the chosen parameters of temporal speech organization for the cognitive task of starting a telephone conversation on a predetermined topic. The first minute of the talk, we assume, gave a well of information about the speaker's ability to monitor and balance speaking time and pause time, articulation rate and length of pause-free run according to one's social practice and biological condition.

Cognitively significant are the facts that American men spend more time in thinking, i.e. online information processing, which is reflected in their total amount of pause time. At the same time men's articulation rates are higher than the corresponding values in American women's speech. However, young women are exceptionally fast speakers, as their scores on articulation rates suggest.

Age-related changes, it transpired, are most dramatic between young and middle age. By cutting down on the length of pauses and pause-free runs middle-aged people opt to produce the effect of businesslike, energetic manner of talking (sometimes called 'ping-pong' style of talk). As middle-aged people normally have the advantage of both higher social statuses than the young and better physical condition than the old, their timing might symbolize a most successful, by American standards, balance of speech and silence. The young and the old American speakers demonstrated comparable scores in silent pause durations and in length of pause-free runs, which could be informative about their working memory capacity.

The limitations of the present study consist in focusing on one particular communicative situation at the beginning of the telephone talk. Nevertheless, the communicative strategies of the speakers were found to have impact on the temporal organization of their speech and on the sound image they tend to project.

References

1. Amerman, J., Parnel, M.: Speech timing strategies in elderly adults. J. Phon. **20**, 65–76 (1992)
2. Boersma, P., Weenink, D.: PRAAT: doing phonetics by computer [Computer program]. Version 5.3.80 (2015). http://www.praat.org/. Accessed 05 Apr 2015
3. Godfrey, J., Holliman, E.: Switchboard-1 Release 2 LDC97S62. Web Download. Linguistic Data Consortium, Philadelphia (1993)
4. Durand, J., Laks, B. (eds.): Phonetics, Phonology and Cognition. Oxford University Press, Oxford (2004)
5. Fletcher, J.: The prosody of speech: timing and rhythm. In: Hardcastle, W.J., Laver, J., Gibbon, F.E. (eds.) The Handbook of Phonetic Sciences, 2nd edn, pp. 523–602. Wiley-Blackwell, Chichester (2013)
6. Kachkovskaia, T., Skrelin, P.: Intonational phrases and pauses in read and spontaneous speech: evidence from large speech corpora. In: Analyz razgovornoy russkoy rechi (AR^3-2019) (Analysis of the Russian Colloquial Speech 2019). Trudy vosmogo mezhdisciplinarnogo seminara (Papers of the 8th Interdisciplinary Seminar). Politechnika-Print, St. Petersburgh, pp. 46–54 (2019). (in Russian)
7. Kess, J.F.: Psycholinguistics: psychology, linguistics, and the study of natural language. John Benjamins Publishing Company, Amsterdam/Philadelphia (1992)
8. Krivnova, O.F.: Speech tempo control in automatic speech synthesis. SPECOM, pp. 277–281. MSLU, Moscow (2007)
9. Linville, S.E.: Vocal Aging. Singular Publishing Group, San Diego (2001)
10. Nathan, G.S.: Phonology: A Cognitive Grammar Introduction. John Benjamin Publishing Company, Amsterdam (2008)
11. Potapova, R.K., Potapov, V.V.: Yazyk, Rech, Lichnost' (Language, Speech, Personality). Yazyki Slavyanskoy Kultury, Moscow (2006). (in Russian)
12. Potapova, R.K., Potapov, V.V.: Rechevaya Kommunikaciya: otzvuka k vyskazyvaniyu (Speech Communication: from sound to utterance). Yazyki Slavyanskix Kultur, Moscow (2012). (in Russian)
13. Ratnikova, Ye.I.: Temporalnaya organizaciya ustnoporozhdayemogo monologicheskogo vyskazyvaniya: sootnosheniye dlitelnosty fonacii I pauzy (Temporal organization of the oral monological utterance: relation between duration of the voice set and pause). Int. Res. J. **07**(61), 130–135 (2017). (in Russian). V. 1
14. Shevchenko, T.I.: Sociofonetika: nacionalnaya I socialnaya identichnost' v anglijskom proiznoshenii (Sociophonetics: national and social identity in English pronunciation), 2nd edn. URSS, Moscow (2016). (in Russian)
15. Shevchenko, T., Sokoreva, T.: Corpus data on adult life-long trajectory of prosody development in American English, with special reference to middle age. In: Karpov, A., Jokisch, O., Potapova, R. (eds.) SPECOM 2018. LNCS (LNAI), vol. 11096, pp. 606–614. Springer, Cham (2018). https://doi.org/10.1007/978-3-319-99579-3_62
16. Skehan, P.: A Cognitive Approach to Language Learning. Oxford University Press, Oxford (2008)
17. Thomas, E.R.: Sociophonetics: An Introduction. Palgrave Macmillan, London (2011)
18. Thomson, R.I.: Fluency. In: Reed, M., Levis, J.M. (eds.): The Handbook of English Pronunciation, Wiley Blackwell, Chichester, pp. 209–226 (2015)
19. Valimaa-Blum, R.: Cognitive Phonology in Construction Grammar: analytic tools for students of English. Mouton de Gruyter, Berlin (2005)

Syntactic Segmentation of Spontaneous Speech: Psychological and Cognitive Aspects

Anton Stepikhov[1,2](✉), Anastassia Loukina[3], and Natella Stepikhova[1,2,3]

[1] The Russian Language Department,
St. Petersburg State University,
7/9 Universitetskaya emb., St. Petersburg 199034, Russia
a.stepikhov@spbu.ru

[2] Research Institute for Applied Russian Studies, Herzen University,
48 Moika emb., St. Petersburg 191186, Russia

[3] Educational Testing Service, 660 Rosedale Rd, Princeton, NJ 08541, USA
aloukina@ets.org

Abstract. The paper examines the properties of expert manual annotation of Russian spontaneous speech. While it is well known that experts exhibit variability in the ways they mark transcripted speech, our aim is to arrive at the reasons behind such variability. In this study we focus on the annotator's psychological profile (personality traits, working memory capacity, processing speed and lateral asymmetry). Our focus is to determine whether there is a relationship between the annotated sentence length and the psychological and cognitive characteristics of the annotator. We also study inter-annotator agreement in different text types. The participants ($n = 80$) detected sentence boundaries in the transcripts of Russian spontaneous speech and performed several test tasks. Personality traits were measured using the Five Factor Personality Inventory. Working memory capacity was measured through reading span and operation span tasks. To compute processing speed we used Letter Comparison and Pattern Comparison tasks. A dominant hemisphere for speech processing was established based on a dichotic listening task. The data analysis did not reveal any relationship between annotators individual characteristics and segmentation results. However, we found that annotators do tend to mark sentence length in a way that is individual to them and that such practices remain relatively stable regardless of text type or even language.

Keywords: Personality · Working memory capacity ·
Lateral asymmetry · Dominant hemisphere · Annotation ·
Segmentation · Sentence boundary detection · Spontaneous speech ·
Russian

1 Introduction

The problem of ambiguity of expert annotation of speech is well-known and was reported in a number of studies (see cf. [1–3]). Variability of expert segmentation

© Springer Nature Switzerland AG 2019
A. A. Salah et al. (Eds.): SPECOM 2019, LNAI 11658, pp. 459–470, 2019.
https://doi.org/10.1007/978-3-030-26061-3_47

may result in placing boundaries in different positions as well as giving different lengths to annotated sentences. Nevertheless, this type of syntactic annotation has been considered the gold standard to establish sentence boundaries in spontaneous discourse and to model them in automatic algorithms. The annotations of several experts are generalised into the overall inter-annotator agreement. Understanding the reasons behind variability among experts is important and would help improve automatic sentence boundary detection – a significant challenge in natural language processing [4].

Our previous studies have shown that differing boundary placements may be determined by differing factors: language-specific features (relatively free word order in Russian or asyndetic connection between clauses), the speaker's gender and profession, or the type of text [5]. Moreover, pilot experiments on the relationship between segmentation and experts' psychological traits revealed association between personality measured by the Five-Factor Personality Inventory and the length of annotated sentences. For example, for German we found that neuroticism has a significant effect on segmentation; i.e. more emotional people had a tendency to divide speech into shorter sentences [6]. For Russian, we showed that highly emotional and highly extroverted people are more likely to mark unique boundaries (marked by only one annotator from the expert group) [7].

Since "the language is the vehicle of personality" [8] and a personal profile is not limited by personality traits, but also includes other individual characteristics, we designed a psycholinguistic experiment involving both psychological and cognitive characteristics such as working memory capacity, processing speed and a dominant hemisphere in speech processing (lateral preference) to examine a possible effect of an expert's psychological profile on annotation.

Within this set of individual characteristics, working memory capacity is the most important parameter since it plays a prominent role in sentence comprehension and speech planning and production. For example, [9,10] revealed the association between higher working memory capacity and a large scope of speech planning. Moreover, as [11] argues the role of working memory cannot be reduced to that of simple storage. It allows speakers to be more efficient in utterance planning. Finally, the results of syntactic parsing are 'bounded by the limits of working memory capacity' [11], i. e. higher working memory allows for assembling larger packages of information for later parsing decisions. Thus, we hypothesised that when transcripts were annotated by sentence boundaries, higher working memory capacity would lead to longer sentences.

The experiment was conducted on German and Russian language material to enable us to compare the results obtained in different languages and to reveal common or language-specific features of sentence boundary detection.

The analysis of the first stage of the experiment performed in German was reported in [6]. In this paper we report the results of the second stage of the experiment performed on the Russian language material.

2   Data and Experimental Design

2.1   Participants

The participants of the experiment were Russian native monolinguals with a minimum one year experience in linguistic research or studies. In total 80 participants took part in the experiment—70 females and 10 males. Their age was between 18 to 57 years, with the median age of 21. Experts' linguistic experience varied from 1 to 40 years, with the median experience of 3.5 years.

The experimental session lasted 70–75 min on average.

2.2   Experimental Stimuli

The experiment consisted of two parts – text task and tests. For the text task, five different types of texts were extracted from the Corpus of Russian spontaneous monologues described in [5]. In our previous research we found that type of text had an effect on segmentation [5], therefore all text types from the corpus were included into the text task. These were: descriptive text retelling (Text 1), story retelling (Text 2), free comment on one of two themes: "My leisure time" or "My way of life" (Text 3), description of a cartoon series (Text 4) and picture description (Text 5).

The author of these text was a man of 40 years old with higher non-linguistic education (Speaker 1). The pilot experiment conducted earlier on the German material showed that the character of speech segmentation is affected by syntactic cohesion in the transcript: asyndetic connection between clauses led to longer annotated sentences [6]. To check whether this trend is also common for Russian we complemented the text part of experimental stimuli by two monologues recorded from another speaker who preferred asyndetic connection between clauses. These monologues were a picture description and a description of a cartoon series.

The information about text size is summarised in Table 1.

Table 1. Summary statistics of the text stimuli (words).

	Text 1	Text 2	Text 3	Text 4	Text 5
Speaker 1	162	225	266	244	312
Speaker 2	–	–	–	269	223

For the experiment, the recordings were transcribed without punctuation and capitalisation (except for proper names). They did not contain any signs of prosodic segmentation such as speakers' hesitation (*eh*, *uhm*) or non-verbal behaviour (e.g. *laughter*).

The task for the experts was to annotate sentence boundaries using "/". In the instruction, it was also stated that a sentence might consist of several clauses, for example, the main clause and the subordinate clause. For other decisions the experts could rely on their intuition of what a sentence is. The annotators were only provided with transcriptions of the recordings and did not have access to the audio since according to [12] the influence of the semantic factor on the segmentation of Russian spontaneous speech outweighs that of the tone factor. The annotators did not have any time limits for this task.

A control text was also included in the set of text stimuli to make sure that the participants understood the task correctly. For this control task we selected a short story (371 words) with relatively simple syntax and short sentences. This text was processed in the same way as other monologues to remove punctuation and capitalisation and presented along with other texts. The control text was given first.

2.3   Personality Inventory

Experts' personality traits were measured by Five Factor Personality Questionnaire (Big Five Inventory) [13] adopted and validated for Russian by [14]. The inventory consists of 75 items with five-level Likert scale (from -2 to 2 including 0). Each item has two opposite statements, and a respondent has to choose the closest score on the scale to one or another statement. The results of FFPQ are interpreted along five scales corresponding to five super-trait factors to describe personality: (1) introversion vs. extraversion, (2) separateness vs. attachment, (3) naturality vs. controlling, (4) unemotionality vs. emotionality, and (5) practicality vs. playfulness[1]. Each scale ranges from 15 to 75. The questionnaire was administered on paper.

2.4   Measuring Working Memory Capacity

According to the recommendations suggested in [15] the working memory capacity of the experts was measured by two working memory span tasks – reading span and operation span, and then the average of the two tasks was used as the measure of ex-pert's working memory capacity. The result was computed according to the partial unit score approach [15]. The completion of each task took about 10 min.

Working memory span tasks were computer-administered. They were developed by [16] for German based on the above mentioned approach [15] and adopted for Russian by the experimenter for the purposes of the described research.

The task for reading span was to read elements (sentences) aloud from the screen one by one, evaluate whether they have sense, memorise the words after each element and then recall the words. The number of sentences varied from 2 to 5, each sequence repeated three times (i.e. 2×3, 3×3, 4×3 and 5×3) in the randomised order. In total, reading span task consisted of 12 series of sentences.

The operation span task was similar except for the expert had to check the validity of simple math equations and memorise the letters that appear after each element. The size of the task was the same.

---

[1] We follow [13] for factor names since this version of the Big Five was used as the basis for the Russian version.

2.5   Processing Speed Tasks

As supplementary tasks we used speed processing tasks—Letter Comparison (Fig. 1) and Pattern Comparison (Fig. 2) [17]. The tests measure perceptual speed, with Letter Comparison additionally measuring memory abilities, and Pattern Comparison—spatial abilities. The task was to define whether two sequences of letters or two line patterns are the same or not. The participant had to give as many correct answers as possible for one minute. The number of correct answers constituted the total score.

ЖСХ _____ ЖМХ

НТЯВДР _____ НТЯВДР

ЛНДПРСКЧВ _____ ЛНДПРСЙЧВ

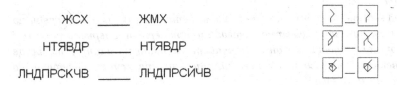

Fig. 1. The sample of Letter Comparison.   **Fig. 2.** The sample of Pattern Comparison.

2.6   Dichotic Listening

To define a dominant hemisphere for speech processing we used a test for dichotic listening [18]. Each expert had to listen to 30 pairs of words simultaneously through headphones (one word was given into the right ear, and the other word into the left) and repeat the words. The pairs were combined into the sequence with the interval of three seconds between them. After that we computed the coefficient of lateral preference (CLP) using the following formula:

$$CLP = \frac{N_{right} - N_{left}}{N_{right} + N_{left}}$$

where N_{right} is the number of words given into the right ear and repeated first, N_{left} is the number of words given into the left ear and repeated first. Based on the CLP we then defined the dominant hemisphere for speech processing:

- $-0.1 \leqslant CLP \leqslant 0.1$: no preference (no dominant hemisphere)
- $CLP < -0.1$: left-sided preference (the right hemisphere is dominant)
- $CLP > 0.1$: right-sided preference (the left hemisphere is dominant).

3   Data Analysis

Initial data processing revealed that two annotators did not follow instruction guidelines and segmented transcripts into clauses rather than sentences. The third annotator segmented the speech transcripts into longer stretches of text that were more likely to correspond to paragraphs than to sentences, with the maximum "sentence" size of 243 words (the control text though was segmented correctly—the average sentence size was 15.46 words). Thus, the data obtained from those experts was not used for further analysis.

An example of three various annotations of the same text fragment is given below.[2]

a. Three sentences: *серия картинок называется «Шляпа» / на первой из них мужчина показан в шляпном магазине примеряет в зеркало шляпы / очевидно она ему подошла он ее покупает выходит на улицу на улице сильный ветер он срывает с него шляпу шляпа летит долетает до водоема плавает в воде /* [2]

b. Seven sentences: *серия картинок называется «Шляпа» / на первой из них мужчина показан в шляпном магазине примеряет в зеркало шляпы / очевидно она ему подошла / он ее покупает выходит на улицу / на улице сильный ветер / он срывает с него шляпу / шляпа летит долетает до водоема плавает в воде /*

c. Nine sentences: *серия картинок называется «Шляпа» / на первой из них мужчина показан в шляпном магазине примеряет в зеркало шляпы / очевидно она ему подошла он ее покупает / выходит на улицу / на улице сильный ветер / он срывает с него шляпу / шляпа летит / долетает до водоема / плавает в воде /*

3.1   Descriptive Analysis of the Data

Summary statistics of the data is shown in Tables 2, 3, 4, 5, 6 and in Fig. 3.

Table 2. Average sentence length (words) in different texts across speakers (S).

	Median	SD	Min	Max
S. 1, text 1	19.75	3.26	13.17	26.33
S. 1, text 2	16.07	2.91	9.00	25.00
S. 1, text 3	17.28	3.86	10.03	28.27
S. 1, text 4	15.25	2.77	10.17	24.40
S. 1, text 5	22.17	5.14	12.09	44.33
S. 2, text 4	10.62	3.35	5.72	27.88
S. 2, text 5	12.18	3.30	6.87	20.62

---

[2] *'the series of pictures is called "The Hat" /a, b, c/ in the first of them a man is shown in a hat shop is trying on hats in the mirror /a, b, c/ obviously it suits him /b/ he buys it /c/ goes out into the street /b, c/ in the street there is strong wind /b, c/ it blows the hat off him /b, c / the hat is flying /c/ is reaching a pool /c/ is floating on the water /a, b, c/'.*

Table 3. Personality scores.

Scale	Median	SD	Min	Max
Neuroticism	59.50	10.36	37	75
Extraversion	47.50	10.99	22	69
Openness	59.00	7.15	37	71
Agreeableness	54.00	8.46	34	73
Conscientiousness	53.00	9.73	31	74

Table 4. Working memory capacity (WMC) scores.

	Median	SD	Min	Max
Reading span	0.79	0.12	0.45	0.98
Operation span	0.75	0.13	0.38	0.95
WMC	0.77	0.11	0.41	0.94

Table 5. Scores of processing speed tasks.

	Median	SD	Min	Max
Pattern comparison	42.00	7.50	24	57
Letter comparison	25.00	5.59	15	37

Table 6. Dominant hemisphere.

Hemisphere	Left	Neutral	Right
Total	38	17	22

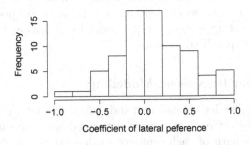

Fig. 3. Histogram of the coefficient of lateral preference.

The analysis of sentence length revealed statistically significant correlations of average sentence length across different texts for the same annotator in all compared pairs of text types (see Table 7). This result corresponds to that obtained earlier for German [6], which may indicate that an annotator has a tendency to use an individual strategy of speech segmentation.

Table 7. Correlations (Spearman's r) of average sentence length for each annotator across text types. Sentence length is compared pairwise within all annotated texts except control text. Statistical significance: * for $p < 0.05$, ** for $p < 0.01$, *** for $p < 0.001$.

	S. 1, text 2	S. 1, text 3	S. 1, text 4	S. 1, text 5	S. 2, text 4	S. 2, text 5
S. 1, text 1	.32**	.29*	.33**	.26*	.24*	.32***
S. 1, text 2		.63***	.56***	.39***	.39***	.42***
S. 1, text 3			.62***	.44***	.51***	.51***
S. 1, text 4				.44***	.51***	.56***
S. 1, text 5					.39***	.56***
S. 2, text 4						.66***

The comparison of average annotated sentence length across two speakers based on the texts 4 and 5 showed statistically significant difference ($p < 0.001$). This fact demonstrates that the strategy of an annotator is rather flexible and varies depending on a speaker's style.

3.2 Inter-annotator Agreement

For all annotated text we computed inter-annotator agreement. The agreement was estimated using Fleiss' κ. This measure was computed twice: first, for all inter-word positions in analysed texts and, second, only for those positions where at least one annotator marked a sentence boundary. For each place where a boundary was marked, we assigned 1 to each annotator who marked a boundary at this location, and 0 to those annotators who did not mark the boundary.

We found moderate inter-annotator agreement, with the highest agreement in the control text for all inter-word positions (see Table 8). For positions annotated by at least one expert agreement for the control text was comparable with the results obtained for speech transcripts.

3.3 Mixed Linear Regression Modelling

To study the possible effect of different individual characteristics on the length of sentence annotated by each expert we performed mixed linear regression analysis. We used the length of each sentence as dependent variable, speaker, text and annotator as random factors and the individual annotators' characteristics as fixed factors. There were 10 fixed factors: 5 personality scores, working

Table 8. Inter-annotator agreement

Speaker and text	Fleiss κ	
	All inter-word positions	Only positions annotated by at least one expert
S. 1 text 1	0.589	0.598
S. 1 text 2	0.577	0.543
S. 1 text 3	0.482	0.446
S. 1 text 4	0.611	0.518
S. 1 text 5	0.503	0.496
S. 2 text 4	0.616	0.52
S. 2 text 5	0.482	0.436
Control text	0.728	0.599

memory capacity, two scores for processing speed tasks, the coefficient of lateral preference, and a dominant hemisphere. The model was fitted in R using lmerTest package [19].

In contrast to the results obtained earlier for German [6] the model did not show any statistical significance.

4 Discussion and Conclusions

Our study was focused on syntactic segmentation of Russian spontaneous speech which is characterised by the various length of annotated sentences. The aim of the study was to reveal a potential relationship between the sentence length and an ex-pert's psychological profile. We performed a psycholinguistic experiment to verify the hypothesis that the results of annotation may be affected by speaker's psychological, cognitive and physiological characteristics such as personality traits, working memory capacity, processing speed or dominant hemisphere in speech processing. In particular, we assumed that sentence length positively correlates with working memory capacity. Since this experiment continues our work started earlier on the German language we also intended to compare the obtained results to reveal possible common trends of expert sentence boundary detection between different languages.

The analysis revealed moderate inter-annotator agreement in transcript-based speech segmentation. Quite unexpectedly, inter-annotator agreement for Russian spontaneous speech was significantly higher than that for German. Probably such difference is partly determined by the much smaller number of the participants of the experiment conducted in German. Nevertheless, the data shows that both Russian and German experts face similar difficulties while performing segmentation. This fact may be explained by the very nature of spontaneous speech and probably by the means by which it is represented. A speech transcript is the "meeting point" for written and oral speech, and therefore it may be the site of an indeterminate interaction between strategies for processing two different language forms and thus result in variability.

The most important conclusion concerning sentence length is that annotators differ regarding the sentence length they prefer. An expert's decision in favour of shorter or longer sentences does not depend on text type and usually demonstrates a steady trend between texts. We observed moderate correlation between average sentence length across different texts for the same annotator in Russian (in German the correlation was significantly higher and achieved $r = 0.88$, which may be explained by less flexible word order). Thus, sentence length may be considered the individual characteristic of an annotator which remains relatively stable regardless a text type or a language.

At the same time, sentence length may be affected by a speaker's style. We found that annotators changed their strategy when the syntax of the annotated texts changed. The typical strategy was to segment texts with dominating asyndetic connection between clauses (texts by Speaker 2) into shorter sentences. These changes were usually observed across all annotators (see Fig. 4).

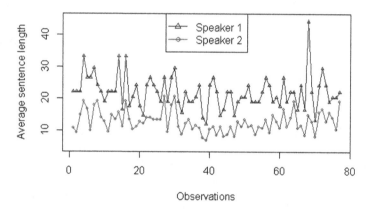

Fig. 4. Average sentence length for two speakers (y-axis) across experts (x-axis) (Text 4).

Mixed linear modelling of sentence length based on psychological and cognitive characteristics of annotators did not reveal statistically significant association between a speaker's psychological profile and annotation results. In contrast to the initial hypothesis working memory capacity of annotators was not related to the length of an-notated sentences, which we had earlier also observed for German. This result, however, may be determined by the fact of high density of the range between the first and the third quartiles of WMC data (0.136 out of 1, see Fig. 5) as well as by the absence of time limits for performing the annotation.

Surprisingly, the result of the present research contradicts that described in [20] where we reported an association between sentence length and two personality traits measured by the Big Five – emotionality and practicality (they

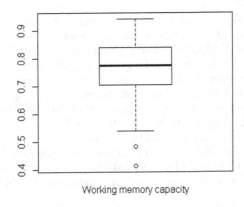

Fig. 5. The boxplot of working memory capacity.

accounted for 18% of the variance in sentence length). This fact may be explained by the 20% higher inter-annotator agreement observed for the sample of the present research. Since higher agreement suggests the lower extent of individual differences of annotators, we may assume that, with regard to individuality, the present sample was more uniform, which did not let annotators' personality traits measured by the Big Five manifest themselves in segmentation.

In future we plan to examine individual differences in annotations based on both textual and prosodic information. This type of task suggests a greater role for working memory and other parameters of an expert's psychological profile in syntactic segmentation since it is performed with time restrictions.

Acknowledgments. This study was supported by the Russian Foundation for Basic Research, project No. 15-04—00165. We also thank three anonymous reviewers for their valuable comments and suggestions.

References

1. Guaïtella, I.: Rhythm in speech: what rhythmic organizations reveal about cognitive processes in spontaneous speech production versus reading aloud. J. Pragmatics **31**, 509–523 (1999)
2. Lee, A., Glass, J.: Sentence detection using multiple annotations. In: Proceedings of Interspeech 2012, pp. 1848–1851 (2012)
3. Stepikhov, A.: Resolving ambiguities in sentence boundary detection in Russian spontaneous speech. In: Habernal, I., Matoušek, V. (eds.) TSD 2013. LNCS (LNAI), vol. 8082, pp. 426–433. Springer, Heidelberg (2013). https://doi.org/10.1007/978-3-642-40585-3_54
4. Shriberg, E.: How people really talk and why engineers should care. In: Proceedings Interspeech 2005, pp. 1791–1794 (2005)
5. Stepikhov, A.: Analysis of expert manual annotation of the Russian spontaneous monologue: evidence from sentence boundary detection. In: Železný, M., Habernal, I., Ronzhin, A. (eds.) SPECOM 2013. LNCS (LNAI), vol. 8113, pp. 33–40. Springer, Cham (2013). https://doi.org/10.1007/978-3-319-01931-4_5

6. Stepikhov, A., Loukina, A.: Personality, working memory capacity and expert manual annotation of German spontaneous speech. In: Karpov, A., Jokisch, O., Potapova, R. (eds.) SPECOM 2018. LNCS (LNAI), vol. 11096, pp. 656–666. Springer, Cham (2018). https://doi.org/10.1007/978-3-319-99579-3_67
7. Stepikhov, A., Loukina, A.: Low inter-annotator agreement in sentence boundary detection and annotator personality. In: Ronzhin, A., Potapova, R., Németh, G. (eds.) SPECOM 2016. LNCS (LNAI), vol. 9811, pp. 461–468. Springer, Cham (2016). https://doi.org/10.1007/978-3-319-43958-7_55
8. Sanford, F.H.: Speech and personality. Psychol. Bull. **39**(10), 811–845 (1942)
9. Petrone, C., Fuchs, S., Krivokapić, J.: Consequences of working memory differences and phrasal length on pause duration and fundamental frequency. In: Proceedings of the 9th International Seminar on Speech Production (ISSP), Montreal, pp. 393–400 (2011)
10. Swets, B., Jakovina, M.E., Gerrig, R.J.: Individual differences in the scope of speech planning: evidence from eye-movements. Lang. Cogn. **6**, 12–44 (2014)
11. Swets, B.: Psycholinguistics and planning: a focus on individual differences. In: Fuchs, S., Pape, D., Petrone, C., Perrier, P. (eds.) Individual Differences in Speech Production and Perception. (Speech Production and Perception, vol. 3), pp. 89–121 (2015)
12. Vannikov, Yu., Abdalyan, I.: Eksperimentalnoe issledovanie chleneniya razgovornoj rechi na diskretnye intonacionno-smyslovye edinicy (frazy) (Experimental research of segmentation of spontaneous speech into intonational and semantic units (phrases). In: Sirotinina, O.B., Barannikova, L.I., Serdobintsev, L.Ja. (eds.) Russkaya razgovornaya rech, Saratov, pp. 40–46 (1973). (in Russian)
13. Tsuji, H., et al.: Five-factor model of personality: concept, structure, and measurement of personality traits. Jpn. Psychol. Rev. **40**(2), 239–259 (1997)
14. Khromov, A.B.: Pyatifactornyj oprosnik lichnosti: Uchebno-metodicheskoe posobie (Five-factor personality inventory: Textbook). Izd-vo Kurganskogo gosudarstvennogo universiteta, Kurgan (2000). (in Russian)
15. Conway, A.R.A., Kane, M.J., Bunting, M.F., Hambrick, D.Z., Wilhelm, O., Engle, R.W.: Working memory span tasks: a methodological review and user's guide. Psychon. Bull. Rev. **12**(5), 769–786 (2005)
16. von der Malsburg, T.: Py-Span-Task - a software for testing working memory span (2015). https://doi.org/10.5281/zenodo.18238
17. Salthouse, T.A.: The processing-speed theory of adult age differences in cognition. Psychol. Rev. **103**(3), 403–428 (1996)
18. Lyakso, E.E., Ogorodnikova, E.A., Alexeev, N.P.: Psikhofiziologiya slukhovogo vospriyatia (Psychophysiology of auditory comprehension). St. Petersburg (2013). (in Russian)
19. Kuznetsova, A., Brockhoff, P.B., Christensen, R.H.B.: lmerTest: tests in linear mixed effects models. R package version 2.0-20. http://CRAN.R-project.org/package=lmerTest
20. Stepikhov, A., Loukina, A.: Annotation and personality: individual differences in sentence boundary detection. In: Ronzhin, A., Potapova, R., Delic, V. (eds.) SPECOM 2014. LNCS (LNAI), vol. 8773, pp. 105–112. Springer, Cham (2014). https://doi.org/10.1007/978-3-319-11581-8_13

Dual-Microphone Speech Enhancement System Attenuating both Coherent and Diffuse Background Noise

Mikhail Stolbov$^{(\boxtimes)}$ and Quan Trong The$^{(\boxtimes)}$

University ITMO, St. Petersburg, Russia
stolbov@mail.ifmo.ru, quantrongthe@itmo.ru

Abstract. In this paper, we present an adaptive dual-microphone array to suppress coherent as well as diffuse noise in disturbed speech signals. This system consists of a dual microphone array and an algorithm for processing their signals. The algorithm for target speech enhancement consists of two main algorithmic steps: segmentation and enhancement. The segmentation is realized using GCC-PHAT signal processing algorithm. This algorithm allows to detect the target speaker's speech and extract it in a noisy environment. Further the target speaker's speech is enhanced using an adaptive Minimum Variance Distortionless Response (MVDR) filter implemented in the frequency domain. This paper proposes a practical improvement of MVDR filter which allows better save speech of the target speaker. Experiments with real recordings demonstrate the reduction of both coherent and diffuse background noise. The main advantage of the proposed technique is simplicity of its use in a wide range of practical situations.

Keywords: Dual-microphone array · Speech activity detection ·
Adaptive MVDR beamformer · Coherent · Diffuse noise · Cross-talk

1 Introduction

The task of recognizing keywords in speech is important for many applications (1). The effective method of Extraction of Desired Speech Signals in Multiple-Speaker Reverberant Noisy Environments is using of microphone arrays (MA) [1,2].

To recognize the operator's keywords in the office, we proposed a simple dual-microphone (MA2) system [3,4]. The advantage of this solution is the simplicity and compactness of the system. The drawback is the lack of effective suppression of nonstationary ambient noise. The goal is to improve the performance of the MP2.

A possible solution to the problem may be the use of adaptive signal processing algorithms, allowing suppress environmental noise (coherent and diffuse noise) more efficiently. The comparison of various adaptive noise reduction

© Springer Nature Switzerland AG 2019
A. A. Salah et al. (Eds.): SPECOM 2019, LNAI 11658, pp. 471–480, 2019.
https://doi.org/10.1007/978-3-030-26061-3_48

algorithms for MA2 was made in [5,6], and the conclusion was drawn that the MVDR algorithm is more efficient. The possibility of additional noise suppression of diffuse noise using dual-microphone superdirective beamforming, which can be considered as a modification of the MVDR algorithm is shown in [7]. The equivalence of the adaptive MVDR algorithm to the adaptive null steering algorithm in the direction of the coherent interference source is shown in [8]. Thus, we assume that the adaptive MVDR algorithm will make it possible to more effectively suppress nonstationary environmental noises.

A number of articles are devoted to the problem of joint suppression of both coherent and incoherent noise [9–13]. In this paper, we investigate the use of an adaptive MVDR algorithm to suppress nonstationary coherent and diffuse noise.

2   Dual Microphone System

A microphone array consists of two closely spaced omnidirectional microphones. The microphone array is placed in the workplace of the target speaker. The signal processing scheme in a dual-microphone system is shown in Fig. 1.

The algorithm for target speaker's speech enhancement consists of two main steps: signal segmentation and speech enhancement. The purpose of segmentation is to allocate the operator's speech, the goal of enhancement is to attenuate the background noise on these segments.

The acoustic environment is characterized by the following features:

- An office with many employees (operators) whose speech can reach the work place of the target speaker.
- Location of the interfering operators, whose positions are not known be fore-hand and can change.
- A customer (speaker 2) located on the opposite side relative to the operator (speaker 1).
- The target speaker (operator) is located in his or her workplace and can insignificantly change position and turn his or her head relative to the microphone.
- The noise level in an office can be high.

Consider the general algorithm for processing MA2 signals in the frequency domain. In the representation of the short-term Fourier transform, the signal $S(f, k)$ of the target speaker from the direction θ_s (angle from the axis of MA2) and additive noise $V(f, k)$ on the microphones form a vector of signals:

$$X(f, k) = S(f, k)D(f, \theta_s) + V(f, k) \tag{1}$$

where f, k are the indexes of frequency and frame number respectively.

$D(f, \theta_s) = D_s(f) = [e^{+j\phi_s}, e^{-j\phi_s}]^T$ is a vector of phase shifts of microphone signals relative to the center point between microphones, $()^T$ denotes transpose of a vector or matrix and $\phi_s(f)$ are phase shifts:

$$\phi_s(f) = \pi d cos(\theta_s)/\lambda = \pi f \tau_0 cos(\theta_s) \tag{2}$$

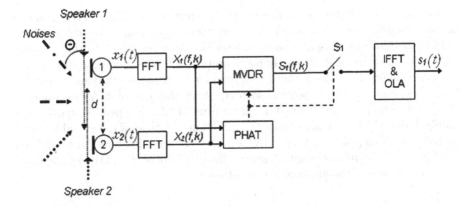

Fig. 1. The scheme of the system.

where $S(f, k)$ is the target, $\tau_0 = d/c$ is the sound delay between the microphones, d is the distance between the microphones, c is the sound speed $(340\,\text{m/s})$, θ_s - the angle of the direction of arrival of the signal relative to the axis MA2.

The evaluation of the signal of the target speaker $\hat{S}(f, k)$ in the k-th frame at the output of MA2 is formed by weighing the input signals with complex weights:

$$\hat{S}(f, k) = \boldsymbol{W}^H \boldsymbol{X}(f, k) \tag{3}$$

where $\boldsymbol{W}(f)$ is the vector of the coefficients, $()^H$ is the symbol of Hermitian conjugation.

The final processing step is the transition from the frequency domain to the time domain. This is done using the inverse Fourier transform and the overlap-and-add (OLA) algorithm.

The purpose of processing is to extract the signal of the target speaker. This is achieved by highlighting the target speaker's speech intervals and suppressing noise. Consider these steps in detail.

3   The Separation of Sounds Using Dual-Microphone Array

The first problem with the use of the adaptive MVDR algorithm is to tune the coherent signal of the operator's speech. The solution is to detect operator activity intervals and termination at these MVDR tuning intervals.

The operator's activity detection algorithm uses (relies on) the following script features: first, the operator changes its position in a known limited range of angles. Secondly, as a rule, only one of the speakers is in turn. Thirdly, the speech of the operator is usually significantly louder than the sounds of the environment (apart from the speech of the customer).

These circumstances make it possible to detect the activity of an operator by determining the direction of arrival of the sound of a coherent source and comparing this direction with the range of directions of the possible position of the operator. The generalized cross-correlation with phase transform (GCC-PHAT) method was chosen as an algorithm for estimating the direction of sound arrival. We used the algorithmic implementation of the method described in [14].

The results of applying the algorithm can be demonstrated using the following experiment. Two speakers located along the axis of MA2 on opposite sides at a distance of approximately 70 cm from MA2. The speakers spoke alternately. Using the PHAT algorithm, the direction of arrival of the sound was estimated at various points in time. MA2 signals were recorded under the condition $d = 4.25$ cm, $Fs = 16$ kHz. Figure 2 shows the waveform of one of the microphones and an estimate of the angle of arrival of sound.

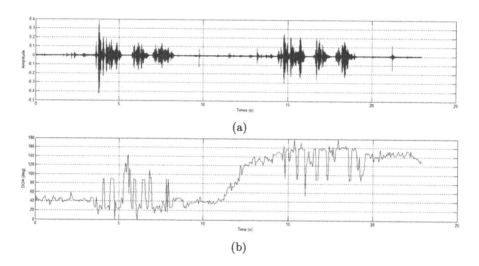

(a)

(b)

Fig. 2. (a) Microphone waveform, (b) An estimate of direction of arrival.

The results of the experiment prove the possibility of estimating the speech intervals of the target speaker.

4   Speech Enhancement Using Adaptive MVDR

The MVDR algorithm is based on the condition of undistorted signal reception from the target direction θ_s and minimization of the total noise power at the MA2 output [6]. The solution of the optimization problem leads to the following relation for the vector of optimal weights under assumption a homogeneous noise field [1]:

$$W_0(f,k) = \frac{\boldsymbol{\Gamma}^{-1}(f,k)\boldsymbol{D}_s(f)}{\boldsymbol{D}_s^H(f)\boldsymbol{\Gamma}^{-1}(f,k)\boldsymbol{D}_s(f)} \tag{4}$$

where $\boldsymbol{\Gamma}$ is a coherence matrix, which is calculating as follows:

$$\Gamma_{ij}(f,k) = \frac{P_{ij}(f,k)}{\sqrt{P_{ii}(f,k)P_{jj}(f,k)}} \tag{5}$$

where $P_{ij}(f,k)$ are the smoothed cross-spectra:

$$P_{ij}(f,k) = \beta P_{ij}(f,k-1) + (1-\beta)X_i^*(f,k)X_j(f,k) \tag{6}$$

where β is the averaging factor.

The adaptive algorithm allows the update the coherence matrix in varying noise environment and adjusts the filter coefficients for noise suppression. In this case, the speech signal of the target speaker is partially distorted. In the case when the spectral components of the speech of the target speaker are far superior to the components of the noise, it is advisable to turn off its suppression and form the look direction in the direction of the target speaker. This can be achieved by the following modification of the coherence matrix:

$$\boldsymbol{\Gamma}(f,k) = \begin{bmatrix} \Gamma_{00} & \Gamma_{12} * F(f,k) \\ \Gamma_{21} * F(f,k) & \Gamma_{00} \end{bmatrix} \tag{7}$$

where

$$F(f,k) = \frac{1}{1+SNR(f,k)} = min(1, \frac{P_{vv}(f,k)}{|(X(f,k)|^2}) \tag{8}$$

$$SNR(f,k) = \frac{P_{ss}(f,k)}{P_{vv}(f,k)} \tag{9}$$

where $P_{ss}(f,k), P_{vv}(f,k)$ are spectral power density of target speech and noise respectively. In the case of $SNR(f,k) \gg 1, \Gamma = I, W_0(f,k) = \frac{1}{2}\boldsymbol{D}_s$. MA2 forms a beam in look direction using the DAS algorithm and. In the case of $SNR(f,k) \approx 1$, MA2 tends to suppress noise.

Experiments have confirmed the effectiveness of the proposed solution in a number of cases. However, this solution requires further investigation.

5   Experiments and Results

The purpose of the experiments was to test the possibility of suppressing both coherent and diffuse noise using the adaptive MVDR algorithm, as well as comparing it with other speech enhancement algorithms for MA2. All experiments were performed with the following parameters: sampling rate $Fs = 16\,\mathrm{kHz}$, $NFFT = 512$, Hamming window, 50% overlap of frames averaging factor $\beta = 0.5$.

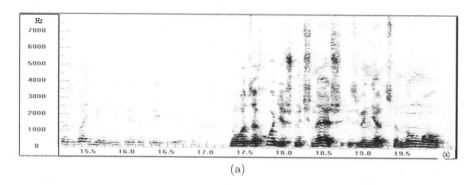

(a)

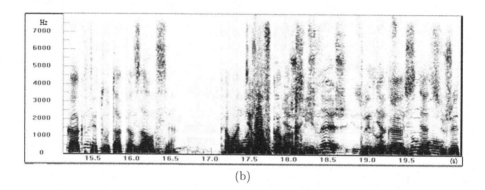

(b)

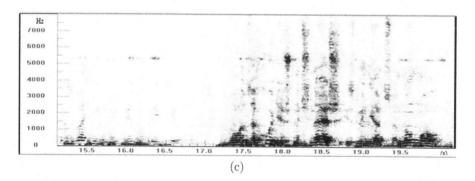

(c)

Fig. 3. The spectrograms of the signals: (a) - a fragment of the speech of the target speaker, (b) - a fragment of the mixture of the speech of the target and the interfering speaker, (c) - a fragment of the mixture after processing.

5.1   Experiments with Artificial Mixture

The purpose of the model experiment was to check the possibility of distinguishing the operator's speech (target speaker) against the background of the speech of an outside speaker.

The following scenario was simulated. The speech of the target announcer is synchronous in both channels, which corresponded to the angle of arrival (relative to the MA2 normal 0°, the speech of the interfering announcer enters the channels with a time shift of 2 times, which corresponds (provided $d = 5$ cm, $Fs = 16$ kHz) to the angle of arrival 60°. The signal-to-noise ratio ranged from 0 dB to −12 dB.

The MVDR algorithm, in the absence of the speech of the target speaker, was tuned to suppress the third-party speaker. At the site of simultaneous speech of the target and third-party announcer, the MVDR algorithm continued to adaptively adjust the coefficients. The spectrograms of the signals at the corresponding intervals are presented in Fig. 3.

The results of the experiment prove the possibility of effectively distinguishing the speech of the target speaker of the operator against the background of the speech of the disturbing speaker using the MVDR algorithm. A similar result was obtained for the broadband interference scenario.

5.2   Experiment in Anechoic Chamber

The purpose of the experiment was to test the MVDR algorithm on real signals and to assess the possibilities of adaptation to changes in the direction of noise arrival. The scheme of the experiment is shown in Fig. 4.

The target direction was set in the direction of the speaker ($\phi_v = -30°$), the distance between the microphones $d = 5$ cm.

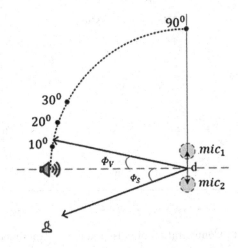

Fig. 4. The scheme of the experiment in anechoic chamber.

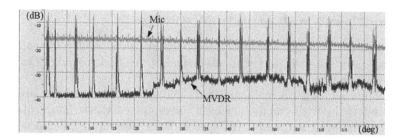

Fig. 5. RMS of microphone signal and MVDR output signal ($\phi_v = 0°...60°$).

Experimental results prove the ability of the algorithm to suppress non-stationary interference while maintaining the speech signal of the target speaker. The noise reduction was about 18 dB (Fig. 5).

5.3   Experiments in Reverberant Room

The purpose of the experiment was to compare the effectiveness of the suppression of diffuse noise in the room by various algorithms. The scheme of the experiment is shown in Fig. 6.

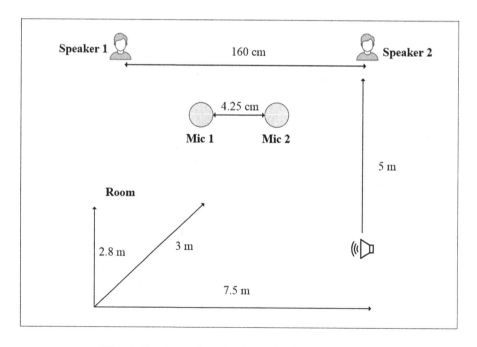

Fig. 6. Configuration of noise reduction experiment.

The experiment was conducted in an office space, $T_{60} = 320\,\text{ms}$. Noise was generated through the speaker at a distance about $5\,\text{m}$ from the microphone array. We tested six frequency domain algorithms as noise reduction frontiers: broadside Delay and Sum beamformer (DAS), Generalized Sidelobe Canceller (GSC), Differential microphone arrays (Cardioid and Hypercardioid), MVDR (broadside and end-fire configuration). Table 1 presents the obtained results.

Table 1. Noise suppression rate (dB) for various microphone arrays.

DAS	GSC	Hypercardioid	Cardioid	MVDR broadside	MVDR end-fire
1.5	3.5	5.5	6.5	9.5	7.5

It follows from the table that MVDR has an advantage over the considered algorithms by the criterion of the degree of suppression of diffuse noise and provides 3...4 dB more suppression of diffuse noise.

6   Conclusions

In this paper we investigated a dual-microphone noise reduction system for suppression of coherent and diffuse noise in disturbed speech signals which is based on adaptive MVDR beamformer. The experimental results demonstrated that the proposed system works well for a large range of noisy conditions. We have shown that adaptive MVDR beamformer is a good algorithm to suppress both coherent and diffuse background noise which allows to reduce speech recognition errors for the target speaker. The MVDR algorithm has the ability to suppress coherent noise coming from different directions, while preserving the speech of the target speaker. This experiment also showed that the MVDR algorithm provides 3...4 dB more suppression of diffuse noise compared to the other considered algorithms. Proposed algorithm could be used as a pre-processor and enhancement unit for speech recognition and communication systems.

References

1. Brandstein, M., Ward, D. (eds.): Microphone Arrays: Signal Processing Techniques and Applications. Springer, Heidelberg (2001). https://doi.org/10.1007/978-3-662-04619-7
2. Herbordt, W.: Sound Capture for Human/Machine Interfaces: Practical Aspects of Microphone Array Signal Processing. Springer, Heidelberg (2005). https://doi.org/10.1007/b99807
3. Stolbov, M., Tatarnikova, M.: Speech and crosstalk detection for robust speech recognition using a dual microphone system. In: Železný, M., Habernal, I., Ronzhin, A. (eds.) SPECOM 2013. LNCS (LNAI), vol. 8113, pp. 310–318. Springer, Cham (2013). https://doi.org/10.1007/978-3-319-01931-4_41

4. Stolbov, M., Tatarnikova, M., The, Q.T.: Using dual-element microphone arrays for automatic keyword recognition. In: Karpov, A., Jokisch, O., Potapova, R. (eds.) SPECOM 2018. LNCS (LNAI), vol. 11096, pp. 667–675. Springer, Cham (2018). https://doi.org/10.1007/978-3-319-99579-3_68

5. Lockwood, M., et al.: Performance of time- and frequency-domain binaural beamformers based on recorded signals from real rooms. J. Acoust. Soc. Am. **115**(1), 379–391 (2004)

6. Bitzer, J., Simmer, K., Kammeyer, K.: Multi-microphone noise reduction techniques for hands-free speech recognition - a comparative study. In: Proceedings of Robust Methods for Speech Recognition in Adverse Conditions (ROBUST 1999), Tampere, Finland, pp. 171–174 (1999)

7. Bitzer, J., Kammeyer, K., Simmer, K.: An alternative implementation of the superdirective beampormer. In: Proceedings of 1999 IEEE Workshop on Applications of Signal Processing to Audio and Acoustics, pp. W99-1–W99-4 (1999)

8. Stolbov, M., The, Q.: Study of MVDR dual-microphone algorithm for speech enhancement in coherent noise presence. Sci. Tech. J. Inf. Technol. Mech. Opt. **19**(1), 180–183 (2019). https://doi.org/10.17586/2226-1494-2019-19-1-180-183. (in Russian)

9. Fischer, S., Simmer, K.: An adaptive microphone array for hands-free communication. In: Proceedings of IWAENC 1995, Norway, pp. 1–4 (1995)

10. Buck, M., et al.: A compact microphone array system with spatial post-filtering for automotive applications. In: Proceedings of ICASSP 2009, pp. 221–224 (2009)

11. Habets, E., Benesty, J.: Coherent and incoherent interference reduction using a using a subband tradeoff beamformer. In: Proceedings of 19th European Signal Processing Conference (EUSIPCO 2011), pp. 481–485 (2011)

12. Park, J., et al.: Two-microphone GSC with post-filter based speech enhancement in composite noise. ETRI J. **38**(2), 366–375 (2016)

13. Wang, Z., Lu, J.: Dual-channel speech enhancement system attenuating both background noise and interfering speech. In: Proceedings of Inter-Noise 2017, (BSS), pp. 3061–3068 (2017)

14. Blandin, C., Ozerov, A., Vincent, E.: Multi-source TDOA estimation in reverberant audio using angular spectra and clustering. Sig. Process. **92**, 1950–1960 (2012)

Reducing the Inter-speaker Variance of CNN Acoustic Models Using Unsupervised Adversarial Multi-task Training

László Tóth[1]([⊠]) and Gábor Gosztolya[2]

[1] Institute of Informatics, University of Szeged, Szeged, Hungary
tothl@inf.u-szeged.hu
[2] MTA-SZTE Research Group on Artificial Intelligence, Szeged, Hungary
ggabor@inf.u-szeged.hu

Abstract. Although the Deep Neural Network (DNN) technology has brought significant improvements in automatic speech recognition, the technology is still vulnerable to changing environmental conditions. The adversarial multi-task training method was recently proposed to increase the domain and noise robustness of DNN acoustic models. Here, we apply this method to reduce the inter-speaker variance of a convolutional neural network-based speech recognition system. One drawback of the baseline method is that it requires speaker labels for the training dataset. Hence, we propose two modifications which allow the application of the method in the unsupervised scenarios; that is, when speaker annotation is not available. Our approach applies unsupervised speaker clustering, which is based on a standard feature set in the first case, while in the second case we modify the network structure to perform speaker discrimination in the manner of a Siamese DNN. In the supervised scenario we report a relative error rate reduction of 4%. The two unsupervised approaches achieve smaller, but consistent improvements of about 3% on average.

Keywords: Convolutional neural network · Siamese neural network · Multi-task · Adversarial training · Unsupervised training

1 Introduction

Since the introduction of Deep Neural Network-based technologies, the error rate of speech recognition systems has decreased significantly [8]. However, improving the robustness of the recognizers is still an active area of research, as even these DNN-based systems are sensitive to various adversarial environmental conditions such as background noise, reverberant environments, and different speaker accents. The sensitivity to these factors can partly be explained by the fact that neural networks are inclined to overfit the actual training data, and generalize poorly to cases that were not seen during training. Among other options, regularization methods are routinely applied to tackle this overfitting phenomenon [6].

© Springer Nature Switzerland AG 2019
A. A. Salah et al. (Eds.): SPECOM 2019, LNAI 11658, pp. 481–490, 2019.
https://doi.org/10.1007/978-3-030-26061-3_49

For example, it is known that presenting multiple tasks to the network at the same time – known as multi-task training [3] – also has a regularization effect. That is, having to solve two (or more) similar, but slightly different tasks at the same time forces the network to find a more general and more robust inner representation. Multi-task training has been shown to reduce the speech recognition error rate in several studies [2,14].

While multi-task training seeks to minimize the error of both tasks, there is a newer variant of the method known as adversarial multi-task training [5]. Here, we maximize the error of the secondary task. With this modification, we expect the network to prefer inner representations that are *invariant* with respect to the secondary task. In speech technology, adversarial multi-task training has mostly been applied to enhance the domain independence (i.e. noise robustness) of DNN acoustic models [4,15]. But we also found examples where it is used to make the system less sensitive to other factors like the accent of the user [16]. In this study, we seek to apply the adversarial multi-task training method to alleviate the sensitivity of speech recognizers to the identity of the actual speaker. Our starting point will be the recent study of Meng et al. [12]. The approach they described requires a training data set that contains speaker annotation. However, most of the current large training databases contain only transcripts of the text spoken without any speaker labels, which renders the method of Meng et al. inapplicable in practice. Here, we experiment with two possible extensions that do not require speaker annotation, and hence these methods are unsupervised in terms of the speakers. For the experimental evaluation we use the TIMIT database, which contains brief samples from significantly more speakers than the corpus used by Meng et al, so the task is presumably more difficult. Moreover, as TIMIT contains a speaker identifier for each file, we can directly compare the supervised approach with the proposed unsupervised methods.

2   Multi-task and Adversarial Multi-task Training

The typical Y-shaped architecture of a multi-task deep neural network is shown schematically in Fig. 1. The network has a dedicated output layer for both tasks (addressing more tasks is also possible, but here we shall assume there are just two tasks). Typically, the uppermost hidden layers are also arranged into task-specific counterparts. Both output layers have a corresponding error function, which are denoted in the figure by L_{CD} and L_S, while the corresponding parameters (weights) are denoted by θ_{CD} and θ_S. Although the network has two output layers, it has only one input layer, and the lower layers are also shared between the two tasks. This forces the network to find a hidden representation in these shared layers which is useful for both tasks. During error backpropagation, the errors coming from the two branches are combined by a simple linear combination. We can perform this using equal weights, but typically the accuracy of one of the tasks is more important for us than that of the other. We can express this importance using a λ weight in the combination formula (see Fig. 1). In our case, the more important main task will be speech recognition (the recognition of the

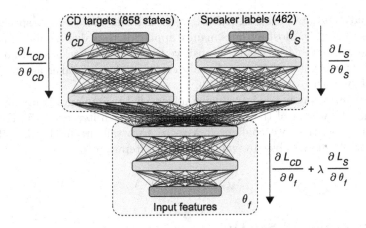

Fig. 1. Schematic structure of an (adversarial) multi-task neural network.

Hidden Markov Model states), while the secondary task will be the recognition of the actual speaker. Note that the secondary task is added only during training, as we expect it to help learn the main task. However, the actual accuracy score attained by this branch of the net is used only for verification purposes, and this branch is discarded in the evaluation phase.

Besides λ, another parameter of the model is the depth where the two branches should join. Intuitively, more different tasks require more task-specific and fewer shared layers (see, e.g. [18]), but the optimal configuration can be found only experimentally. Likewise, it is impossible to tell in advance whether a certain secondary task will help learn a given main task, but intuitively, the secondary task should be related, but slightly different from the main task.

To our knowledge, multi-task training was first applied in speech recognition in a study by Lu et al., where the secondary task was to clean the noisy speech features [11]. In the deep learning framework it was first applied by Seltzer and Droppo, who used the recognition of the phonetic context as a secondary task along with the main phone recognition task [14]. A similar solution was implemented by Bell and Renals, who combined the tasks of context-dependent and context-independent modeling [2].

Multi task-learning has a variant called *adversarial* multi-task learning [5]. Instead of preferring a hidden representation that helps handle both tasks, adversarial multi-task learning seeks to find a hidden representation that is invariant with respect to the secondary task, meaning that it contains no information that would allow the identification of the secondary targets. In adversarial training the Y-shaped network structure is the same as that for the standard multi-task model. However, we will try to *maximize* the error of the secondary task instead of minimizing it. Technically, it is realized by still minimizing the secondary error, but using a *negative* value for λ. This way, the task-specific secondary branch tries to solve the secondary task, but the shared layers will seek a representation that works against this (performing a sort of 'min-max' optimization [16]).

The adversarial multi-task training approach was first used in speech technology in 2016 [15]. Most authors mainly applied it to make the neural network 'domain-invariant' ([4]); that is, insensitive to the actual background noise, but we know of examples where the domain corresponds to speaker accent [16], or the identity of the actual speaker [12].

Shinohara recommends introducing adversarial training gradually, by slowly increasing the weight of the adversarial branch in each iteration [15]. Following his recommendation, we configured λ so as to attain its final value after 10 iterations, setting its absolute value in the kth iteration to

$$\lambda_k = min(\frac{k}{10}, 1) \cdot \lambda.$$

3   Experimental Set-Up

We used the English TIMIT speech dataset for our experiments. Though this dataset is now considered tiny for speech recognition purposes, we chose it because it also contains speaker annotations. Moreover, it is ideal in the sense that is contains samples from a lot of speakers in a uniform distribution. The train set consists of 8 sentences from 462 speakers, while the core test set comprises 24 other (independent) speakers. As the development set, we randomly separated 44 speakers from the train set, and we evaluated the models on the core test set.

For the recognition, we applied a standard Hidden Markov Model - Deep Neural Network (HMM/DNN) hybrid [8]. The neural network component was trained on a mel-spectrogram, and it contained convolutional neurons in its lowest layer (performing frequency-domain convolution) [1]. The convolutional layer was followed by two additional fully connected layers, which together formed the shared part of the network. The task-specific parts of the network consisted of 1-1 hidden layers, as this was found optimal in preliminary experiments. All the hidden layers contained 2000 rectified (ReLU) neurons. In the speech recognition (or main) branch, the output layer consisted of 858 softmax neurons, corresponding to the states of the HMM. In the speaker recognition (or secondary) branch, the 462 softmax neurons had to identify the speakers of the database. The network was trained using standard backpropagation, applying the frame-level cross-entropy function as the loss function for both output layers.

4   Results with Supervised Adversarial Training

In the first adversarial training experiment we trained the network in a supervised manner; that is, using the original speaker labels as training targets for the secondary task. To find the optimal value of λ, we varied it between -0.05 and -0.25 with a step size of 0.05. Table 1 shows the frame-level error rates got for both branches. It should be mentioned that for the secondary task we have scores only for the train set, and we listed these scores only to verify the behavior

Table 1. The frame-level and phone-level error rates obtained for various values of λ, using supervised training.

Parameter	Frame error rate		Phone error rate	
λ	(train, sec. task)	(dev, main task)	(dev. set)	(test set)
0 (baseline)	24.7%	35.4%	16.6%	18.8%
−0.05	70.8%	34.7%	16.3%	18.4%
−0.10	77.2%	34.8%	**16.0%**	**18.0%**
−0.15	86.4%	34.9%	16.2%	18.1%
−0.20	89.3%	35.1%	16.3%	18.2%

of the network, as this branch of the network is not used by the final recognition system. For the main task we listed the results on the independent development set, as this tells us more about the generalization ability of the model. The rightmost columns of the table show the phone recognition error rates on the development and test sets, obtained after performing HMM decoding using the state-level probabilities produced by the main branch of the network. The first row contains the baseline result, which is obtained with $\lambda = 0$. We will call this the 'passive' configuration, as in this case the secondary branch is allowed to learn, but it cannot influence the shared hidden representation. The table shows that by decreasing λ, the frame error rate of the secondary task rose consistently, just as one would expect. The frame error rate of the main task decreased in parallel until it reached its optimum point, then it started to rise again when λ became smaller. The phone recognition error rate attained its optimum both for the development and test sets at $\lambda = -0.1$, but the scores are consistently lower than those for the baseline system for all parameter values tested. In the best case the relative error rate reduction was 4.2% on the test set. As for Meng et al., they reported an error rate reduction of 5% [12].

It is well known that adding a small disturbance to either the weights or the input of the neural network can reduce overfitting, and bring a slight improvement in the scores [6]. We wanted to verify that the improvement was not simply due to this effect. Hence, we calculated the variance of the recognition scores with respect to the speakers, and we found that it decreased by about 10%, compared to the baseline model. This confirms that the adversarial training method indeed makes the model less speaker-sensitive – although the model is still far from being 'speaker-invariant'. Meng et al. themselves reported additional improvements by applying speaker adaptation after adversarial training [12]. We found earlier that the application of CNNs instead of fully connected DNNs reduces the inter-speaker variance by about 5.7% [17]. As we used CNNs here, the reduction of 10% was obtained in addition to this previously reported improvement.

Table 2. The error rates obtained using the conventional speaker clustering method.

No. of clusters	Parameter λ	Frame error rate (dev)	Phone error rate (dev)	Phone error rate (test)
–	0 (baseline)	35.4%	16.6%	18.8%
50	−0.10	34.8%	16.4%	18.6%
100	−0.15	34.6%	**16.0%**	**18.0%**
150	−0.10	34.8%	**16.0%**	18.3%
200	−0.10	34.8%	16.2%	18.4%
250	−0.10	34.6%	**16.0%**	18.3%

5   Unsupervised Training Without Speaker Labels

The approach we presented in the previous section has a big drawback, namely that it requires the annotation of the speakers. Though this is available in the case of the TIMIT dataset, nowadays we train our systems on much larger corpora, which are usually recorded under more natural conditions. For these databases a precise speaker-level segmentation and labelling is typically not available, which means that our adversarial training method cannot be directly applied. Here, we propose two approaches to overcome this limitation. These methods do not require speaker annotation, but they create the training targets for the speaker classifier branch of the network in an unsupervised manner. The only assumption is that there is no speaker change within a file, so each file belongs to exactly one speaker. This is a much weaker constraint in general than that of the availability of a speaker annotation.

5.1   Conventional Speaker Clustering

Not having speaker labels, we can apply a clustering method to group the files into clusters, according to the similarity of the speakers' voices. Many conventional algorithms exist for this, and we chose a hierarchical clustering method that was accessible to us. The original algorithm applies a bottom-up, agglomerative hierarchical cluster method, which merges clusters based on the generalized likelihood ratio of Gaussian models fit on standard acoustic features like mel-frequency cepstral coefficients (MFCCs) [7]. Various modifications of the algorithm were later suggested by Wang et al. [19] and Kaya et al. [9].

When using the clustering algorithm, the number of clusters becomes an additional parameter. We tried to vary this value between 50 and 250 with a step size of 50. We applied the adversarial training method just as before, but the speaker labels were replaced by the automatically found cluster identifiers. Table 2 lists the recognition results obtained in this case. For each cluster size we report only the λ value that gave the best score on the development set. On the development set we attained the same error rate (16.0%) as that with the supervised approach for several cluster sizes. However, the improvement did

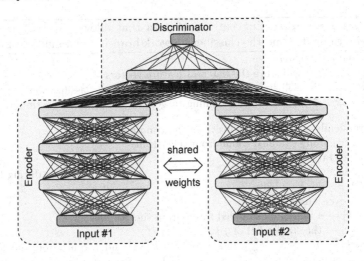

Fig. 2. Illustration of the architecture of a Siamese neural network.

not carry over to the test set, where the best supervised score (18.0%) was achieved only in one configuration. Disregarding the cluster size of 50 (which gave an inferior performance), the average score on the test set was 18.25%, which corresponds to a 3% relative error rate reduction over the baseline.

5.2 Clustering Using a Siamese Multi-task Network

The conventional speaker clustering method we applied is built on MFCCs and Gaussian modelling, but our acoustic model is a CNN that uses mel-frequency energy features. This means that we calculate two types of features and two types of models, which is a waste of resources. We could do better if we adjusted our network (more precisely, its speaker classifier branch) to the unsupervised task. The approach we applied is based on the method outlined by Ravanelli and Bengio [13], but it is also closely related to the concept of Siamese neural networks [20]. Siamese networks are usually applied to decide whether two images depict the same object or not, and they consist of two main parts (see Fig. 2). The upper, discriminator part is trained to discriminate *a pair* of input vectors. In our case, the discriminator consists of one hidden layer and an output layer of just two neurons, which try to decide whether two input speech frames belong to the same speaker or not. The lower, encoder part seeks to find the optimal representation for this discrimination. As we try to discriminate a pair of inputs, the encoder is present in two copies in the network, but these are practically identical (technically, this can be solved by weight sharing, for example).

In the case of our multi-task network, the lower, shared part will serve as the encoder, and the network branch corresponding to the speaker classification task has to be replaced by the discriminator. We had to solve two problems to achieve this. First, the discriminator required two input vectors instead of just one. Second, we had to create pairs that came from the same file (negative examples),

Algorithm 1. Constructing batches of data that allows the training of the speaker discriminator and the classifier network branches in a multi-task fashion

---

Let N denote the batch size
$f[k]$ ($k = 1, ..., N$) will store the batch of feature vectors
$l_c[k]$ ($k = 1, ..., N$) will store the training targets for state classification
$l_s[k]$ ($k = 2, ..., N$) will store the training targets for the speaker discriminator

$j \leftarrow$ a randomly selected file index from the training file list
$f[1] \leftarrow$ a randomly sampled frame from the jth file
$l_c[1] \leftarrow$ the state label of $f[1]$
$l_s[1] \leftarrow$ undefined   ▷ Not used during training
for (k=2; $k \leq N$; k++) **do**
    if k is even **then**
        $f[k] \leftarrow$ a randomly sampled frame from the jth file
        $l_c[k] \leftarrow$ the state label of $f[k]$
        $l_s[k] \leftarrow 0$ ▷ $f[k-1]$ and $f[k]$ are from the *same* file
    if k is odd **then**
        $j \leftarrow$ a randomly selected new file index, different from the previous value of j
        $f[k] \leftarrow$ a randomly sampled frame from the jth file
        $l_c[k] \leftarrow$ the state label of $f[k]$
        $l_s[k] \leftarrow 1$ ▷ $f[k-1]$ and $f[k]$ are from *different* files

Train the main network branch using $f[k]$ and $l_c[k]$ ($k = 1, ..., N$)
Train the secondary branch using the $< f[k-1], f[k] >$ pairs and $l_s[k]$ ($k = 2, ..., N$)

---

and pairs that came from different files (positive examples) in turn. We created an algorithm that constructs the data batches in such a way that it allows one to train the speech recognition and the speaker discriminator branches in parallel, in a multi-task fashion (see Algorithm 1). That is, the N data vectors returned by the algorithm can be used to train the speaker recognition branch directly, while the $N-1$ pairs of neighboring vectors are alternating positive and negative examples for the 2-class speaker discriminator branch. We should add that while we want to discriminate the speakers, our implementation approximates this by discriminating the *files*, as we have no access to speaker labels. However, as long as the train set consists of many speakers, the chance of mislabelling a pair is actually quite low (in this case, 8 files out of 418 belong to the same speaker).

In our preliminary tests the Siamese speaker discriminator branch of the network attained an error rate of 18% in passive training mode. In multi-task mode the error decreased to about 2%, which is similar to that reported by Ravanelli and Bengio [13]. However, both in multi-task and in adversarial multi-task training the discriminator branch had only a negligible influence on the accuracy of the other branch. We think that deciding whether the speaker is the same or different is a much weaker constraint on the hidden representation than actually identifying the speakers.

As we were unable to apply adversarial training using the Siamese branch directly, we opted for a two-stage approach. After training the network, we performed a clustering on the training files, using the discriminator output as the

Table 3. The error rates obtained using the Siamese network-based clustering method.

No. of clusters	Parameter λ	Frame error rate (dev)	Phone error rate	
			(dev)	(test)
—	0 (baseline)	35.4%	16.6%	18.8%
50	−0.10	34.9%	16.4%	18.4%
100	−0.35	34.8%	**16.0%**	**18.3%**
150	−0.30	34.6%	16.1%	18.4%
200	−0.50	34.7%	16.3%	18.3%
250	−0.55	34.8%	16.2%	18.2%

distance function. We applied complete-linkage agglomerative hierarchical clustering [10], where the distance between two files was estimated in the following way. The speaker discriminator branch outputs posterior estimates (scores between 0 and 1) of whether two frames belong to the same file or not. We defined the distance between any two files as the average of these posterior values over ten randomly selected frame pairs. After we had performed the clustering, we repeated the training of the adversarial multi-task network using the cluster labels as training targets for the secondary branch.

The recognition error rates obtained with this clustering method are shown in Table 3. Similar to the standard clustering method, the score obtained with 50 clusters is just slightly better than the baseline score. For larger cluster sizes, on the development set the results are typically slightly worse than those got with the standard clustering method. However, on the test set the average improvement is not significantly different, corresponding to a relative error rate reduction of about 3% relative to the baseline.

6   Summary

Here, we examined the applicability of adversarial multi-task training to reduce the inter-speaker variance of CNN acoustic models. First, we investigated supervised training that requires speaker annotation, and then we proposed two unsupervised solutions to generate training targets when speaker labels are not available. In the supervised case we reported relative phone error rate reductions of 4%, and both unsupervised approaches performed slightly worse, giving an error rate reduction of about 3%. Currently both proposed methods require a clustering step, but in the future we intend to modify the Siamese network-based approach so that it can work in one training pass, without the need for clustering and re-training.

Acknowledgments. This research was supported by the Ministry of Human Capacities, Hungary by grant number TUDFO/47138-1/2019-ITM. László Tóth was supported by the Janos Bolyai Research Scholarship of the Hungarian Academy of Sciences. The GPU card used for the computations was donated by the NVIDIA Corporation.

References

1. Abdel-Hamid, O., Mohamed, A., Jiang, H., Penn, G.: Applying convolutional neural network concepts to hybrid NN-HMM model for speech recognition. In: Proceedings of ICASSP, pp. 4277–4280 (2012)
2. Bell, P., Renals, S.: Regularization of deep neural networks with context-independent multi-task training. In: Proceedings of ICASSP, pp. 4290–4294 (2015)
3. Caruana, R.: Multitask learning. J. Mach. Learn. Res. **17**(1), 41–75 (1997)
4. Denisov, P., Vu, N., Font, F.: Unsupervised domain adaptation by adversarial learning for robust speech recognition. In: Proceedings of ITG Conference of Speech Communication (2018)
5. Ganin, Y., et al.: Domain-adversarial training of neural networks. J. Mach. Learn. Res. **17**(59), 1–35 (2016)
6. Goodfellow, I., Bengio, Y., Courville, A.: Deep Learning. MIT Press, Cambridge (2016)
7. Han, K.J., Kim, S., Narayanan, S.S.: Strategies to improve the robustness of Agglomerative Hierarchical Clustering under data source variation for speaker diarization. IEEE Trans. Audio Speech Lang. Process. **16**(8), 1590–1601 (2008)
8. Hinton, G., Deng, L., Yu, D., Dahl, G., Mohamed, A., Jaitly, N., et al.: Deep neural networks for acoustic modeling in speech recognition: the shared views of four research groups. IEEE Sig. Process. Mag. **29**(6), 82–97 (2012)
9. Kaya, H., Karpov, A., Salah, A.: Fisher vectors with cascaded normalization for paralinguistic analysis. In: Proceedings of Interspeech, pp. 909–913 (2015)
10. Krznaric, D., Levcopoulos, C.: Fast algorithms for complete linkage clustering. Discrete Comput. Geom. **19**(1), 131–145 (1998)
11. Lu, Y., et al.: Multitask learning in connectionist speech recognition. In: Proceedings of Australian International Conference on Speech Science and Technology (2004)
12. Meng, Z., et al.: Speaker-invariant training via adversarial learning. In: Proceedings of ICASSP, pp. 5969–5973 (2018)
13. Ravanelli, M., Bengio, Y.: Learning speaker representation with mutual information. Interspeech (2019). https://arxiv.org/abs/1812.00271
14. Seltzer, M., Droppo, J.: Multi-task learning in deep neural networks for improved phoneme recognition. In: Proceedings of ICASSP, pp. 6965–6969 (2013)
15. Shinohara, Y.: Adversarial multi-task learning of deep neural networks for robust speech recognition. In: Proceedings of Interspeech, pp. 2369–2372 (2016)
16. Sun, S., Yeh, C., Hwang, M., Ostendorf, M., Xie, L.: Domain-adversarial training for accented speech recognition. In: Proceedings of ICASSP, pp. 4854–4858 (2018)
17. Tóth, L.: Phone recognition with hierarchical convolutional deep maxout networks. EURASIP J. Audio Speech Music Process. 25 (2015)
18. Tóth, L., Grósz, T., Markó, A., Csapó, T.: Multi-task learning of speech recognition and speech synthesis parameters for ultrasound-based silent speech interfaces. In: Proceedings of Interspeech, pp. 3172–3176 (2018)
19. Wang, W., Lu, P., Yan, Y.: An improved hierarchical speaker clustering. Acta Acustica **33**(1), 9–14 (2008)
20. Zagoruyko, S., Komodakis, N.: Learning to compare image patches via convolutional neural networks. In: The IEEE Conference on Computer Vision and Pattern Recognition (CVPR), June 2015

Estimates of Transmission Characteristics Related to Perception of Bone-Conducted Speech Using Real Utterances and Transcutaneous Vibration on Larynx

Teruki Toya[1](✉), Peter Birkholz[2], and Masashi Unoki[1]

[1] Japan Advanced Institute of Science and Technology,
Asahidai 1-1, Nomi, Ishikawa 923-1292, Japan
{yattin_yatson,unoki}@jaist.ac.jp
[2] Technische Universität Dresden, 01062 Dresden, Germany
peter.birkholz@tu-dresen.de

Abstract. Beacause transmission characteristics of bone-conducted (BC) speech from the larynx to auditory systems have not yet been clarified, this paper investigates the transmission characteristics related to the BC speech perception focusing on temporal bone (TB) vibration signals and ear canal (EC) radiated speech signals. First, long-term average spectra (LTAS) of the normally produced speech signals recorded at the lips, TB and EC were analyzed. It was found that the frequency components above 2 kHz were relatively decreased in the TB vibration and those below 1 kHz and above 3 kHz were relatively decreased in the EC-radiated speech. Second, transfer functions from the larynx to the observation positions (the lip, TB, and EC) were measured using transcutaneous excitation at the larynx. It was found that the larynx-to-TB transfer functions partially emphasized the frequency region below 1 kHz and the larynx-to-EC transfer functions attenuated the frequency components below 1 kHz and above 3 kHz. These results indicate that the lower frequency components of BC speech are transmitted through TB vibration and the higher frequency components are transmitted through EC-radiated speech.

Keywords: Auditory feedback · Bone-conduction ·
Spectral characteristics · Transmission characteristics

1 Introduction

In human speech communication, speakers perceive their own voices to control their speech production systems [1]. This mechanism is referred to as auditory feedback. If speakers perceive the delayed speech of their own by Delayed Auditory Feedback (DAF), stutter-like speaking is observed [2]. This phenomenon suggests that human auditory systems and speech production systems are strongly connected.

© Springer Nature Switzerland AG 2019
A. A. Salah et al. (Eds.): SPECOM 2019, LNAI 11658, pp. 491–500, 2019.
https://doi.org/10.1007/978-3-030-26061-3_50

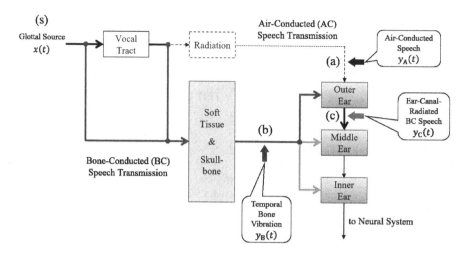

Fig. 1. Transmission pathways of air- and bone-conducted speech

While speaking, people perceive their own voices through both air-conduction (AC) and bone-conduction (BC). The authors previously found that the DAF presented as not only AC but also BC speech affects one's speech production [3]. Additionally, several subjective investigations have gradually clarified the whole amplitude characteristics of BC speech [4,5]. However, acoustical features and transmission pathways of BC speech related to auditory feedback have not yet been clarified.

Stenfelt assumed that the BC sound is transmitted to the outer, middle and inner ear part through multiple pathways from a physiological study [6]. In his study, the BC sound source was located on the skull. On the other hand, while hearing one's own voices through BC, the sound source should be a vocal organ, especially the larynx. In this paper, the transmission pathways of AC and BC speech are assumed to be as shown in Fig. 1.

Our motivation is to understand how the BC speech is transmitted from the larynx (glottal source) to the outer, middle and inner ear. To do this, this paper investigates the transmission characteristics of BC speech, focusing on observable transmission pathways (temporal bone (TB) vibration and ear canal (EC) radiated speech). First, spectra of the TB vibration and the EC-radiated speech are analyzed using real utterances. Second, transfer functions from the larynx to the TB and the EC are measured using a transcutaneous excitation signal.

2   Analysis of the Long-Term Average Spectrum

To analyze universal spectral characteristics independent of vocal tract shapes, long-term average spectra (LTAS) of the AC speech, the TB vibration and the EC-radiated speech were analyzed.

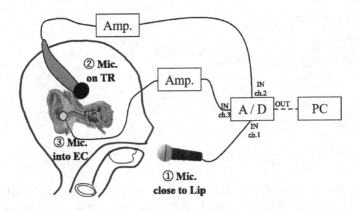

Fig. 2. Schematic diagram of the recording system

2.1 Speakers

Seven students (five males and two females, aged 22 to 26) participated in the production tasks for vocal recording. All speakers had normal hearing, and none had a speaking disorder. None was a native English speaker, but they all had enough experiences of speaking English in daily life.

2.2 Apparatus and Procedure

Figure 2 shows a schematic diagram of the recording system. The production tasks were conducted in a soundproof room. Speakers' AC and BC voices were simultaneously recorded close to their lips, on their TBs, and in their ECs through an AC microphone (audio-technica AT845Ra), a BC microphone (TEMCO HG70), and a probe microphone (Etymotic Research ER-10C), respectively. The distance between the speakers' lips and the AC microphone was 20 cm. These recorded signals were routed through amplifiers and an A/D converter (MOTU 828mk3) to a PC (Windows 10 with Adobe Audition). The sampling frequency was 10 kHz and the number of quantizing bits was 16.

The speakers were asked to utter a 31-word English sentence with as constant vocal intensity as possible. Each utterance duration was around 10 sec.

2.3 Analysis

LTAS of the voiced parts in the recorded signals were calculated and analyzed. The LTAS were obtained in the frequency range from 0.2 to 5 kHz as the average of short-term spectra derived from the frames in the voiced parts. In the short-term spectrum analysis, a Hanning window with a 10 ms frame length was used. The shifting length was 2.5 ms. The extracted LTAS were normalized with the maximum power as 0 dB.

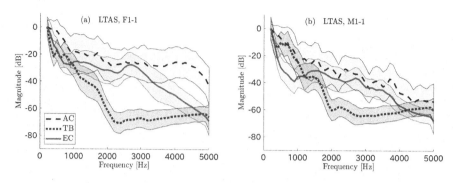

Fig. 3. LTAS of AC speech, TB vibration and EC-radiated speech: (a) Female speaker F1-1 and (b) male speaker M1-1. Each light-colored area represents the standard deviation. (Color figure online)

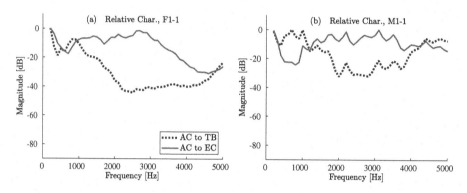

Fig. 4. Relative characteristics from AC speech to TB vibration and EC-radiated speech: (a) Female speaker F1-1 and (b) male speaker M1-1

The spectral characteristics of the TB vibration signals were obtained as acceleration responses since the BC microphone was a kind of acceleration sensor. To compare these characteristics to the others obtained as displacement responses, the absolute displacement responses $|D(f)|$ was calculated as $|A(f)|/f^2$, where $A(f)$ was the obtained acceleration responses. Additionally, frequency characteristics of the BC microphone itself were compensated with the same procedure as in the authors' previous investigation [7].

When the EC-radiated speech signals were recorded through a probe microphone, the speakers' ECs were occluded. To estimate the spectral characteristics of the EC-radiated speech with their ECs opened, the occlusion-effect characteristics of ECs [8] were compensated.

2.4   Results and Discussions

Figure 3 shows LTAS derived from AC speech, TB vibration and EC-radiated speech. Figure 3(a) and (b) show the results for female speaker F1-1 and male speaker M1-1. The dashed, dotted and solid lines represent LTAS of AC speech, TB vibration and EC-radiated speech. Each light-colored area represents the standard deviation of each LTAS.

The relative power of the AC speech decreased gradually as the frequency increased. The relative power of the TB vibration decreased suddenly as the frequency exceeded 2 kHz. Then the spectral shape was almost flat in the frequency range above 2 kHz. The relative power of EC-radiated speech decreased steeply as the frequency increased in the frequency range below 1 kHz, and little increase/decrease of the power was found in the frequency range between 1 to 3 kHz. Then the power decreased gradually as the frequency increased in the frequency range above 3 kHz. These trends were observed among almost all speakers.

To estimate the transmission characteristics of the TB vibration and the EC-radiated speech, relative characteristics from the AC speech to the TB vibration and EC-radiated speech were derived as in Fig. 4. Figure 4(a) and (b) show the results for female speaker F1-1 and male speaker M1-1. For TB vibration, the frequency components above 2 kHz were reduced by 30 to 40 dB compared with the AC speech. For EC-radiated speech, the frequency components below 1 kHz and above 3 kHz were reduced by 10 to 30 dB compared with the AC speech.

These results indicated that TB vibration has relatively low-pass (below 2 kHz) characteristics compared with AC speech signals, wheras EC-radiated speech has relatively band-pass (from 1 to 3 kHz) characteristics.

3   Transfer Function Measurement for BC Speech Transmission

To investigate the transmission characteristics related to the BC speech perception, transfer functions from the larynx to the observable positions (TB and EC) were measured.

3.1   Participants

Seven students (five males and two females, aged 24 to 32) participated in the measurement. Besides one male and one female participants (M-1 and F-1), all participants were different from the speakers of the previous vocal recording stated in Sect. 2.1. All speakers had normal hearing, and none had a speaking disorder. None was a native English speaker, but they all had enough experiences of English in daily life.

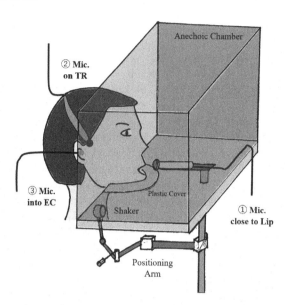

Fig. 5. Schematic illustration of the apparatus for transfer function measurements

3.2   Apparatus

Figure 5 schematically illustrate the apparatus. The measurements were conducted in a soundproof room. Transcutaneous excitation signals to participants' necks were presented through a shaker (Adafruit 1785). The position of the shaker could be adjusted by a positioning arm. The observation signals were simultaneously recorded close to their lips, on their TRs and in their ECs. The same microphones as the previous recording stated in Sect. 2.2 were used. A small anechoic chamber was used to prevent noise leaking from the shaker to the AC microphone. The sampling frequency was 44.1 kHz and the number of quantizing bits was 16.

3.3   Procedure

Before the measurement, participants were asked to silently articulate five vowels (/a/, /e/, /i/, /o/, and /u/) one by one while a white noise was emitted by the shaker. At that time, they were asked to adjust the shaker to a suitable position to cleanly hear the vowel sounds. During the measurement, they were asked to maintain each vowel articulation and shaker position while an excitation signal was emitted by the shaker. A logarithmic sweep-tone signal lasting 7 s was used for excitation. The frequency band was from 0.2 to 5 kHz. The signal was presented 10 times for each vowel articulation. The total number of measurement trials was 50.

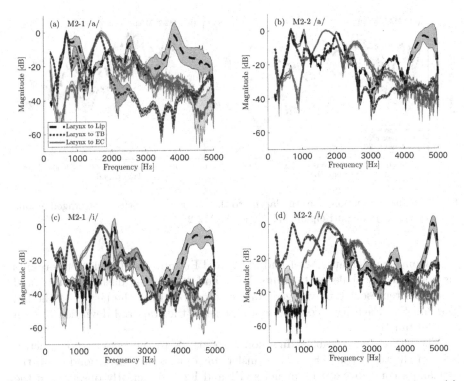

Fig. 6. Measured transfer function from the larynx to the observation positions: (a) Male participant M2-1 with vowel /a/, (b) M2-2 with vowel /a/, (c) M2-1 with vowel /i/ and (d) M2-2 with vowel /i/. Each light-colored area represents the standard deviation. (Color figure online)

3.4   Analysis

Here, the logarithmic sweep-tone signal is $x(t)$, and the recorded signal at three observation positions ((a), (b), and (c)) is $y_O(t)$ (O = {A, B, and C}) as in Fig. 1. The impulse responses of the transmission paths from the larynx to the observation positions ($h_O(t)$) was calculated as $h_O(t) = y_O(t) * x_{inv}(t)$, where $x_{inv}(t)$ is a time-mirrored and amplitude-modified signal of $x(t)$. The transfer function from the larynx to the observation positions ($H_O(f)$) was calculated as $H_O(f) = \text{FFT}\,[h_O(t)]$. The amplitude characteristics $|H_O(f)|$ were averaged among 10 measurement trials in each vowel articulation and used for evaluation. The frequency characteristics of the apparatus were compensated in the same way as stated in Sect. 2.3.

3.5   Results and Discussion

Figure 6 shows the measured transfer functions from the larynx (s) to the observation positions ((a), (b), or (c)). Figure 6(a) and (b) show the results for vowel

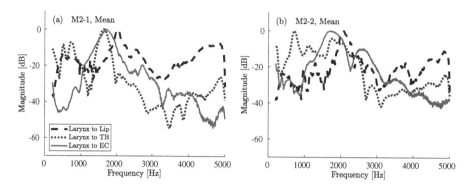

Fig. 7. Transfer function from the larynx to the observation positions averaged among five vowels: (a) male participant M2-1 and (b) M2-2

/a/ by male participants M2-1 and M2-2, and Fig. 6(c) and (d) show the results for vowel /i/ by male participants M2-1 and M2-2. The dashed, dotted and solid lines represent the averaged transfer functions from the larynx to the lip, TB, and EC. Each light-colored area represents the standard deviation of each transfer function.

The larynx-to-lip transfer function corresponds to the resonance characteristics of the vocal tract. For this transfer function, peaks corresponding to the first and second formant frequencies (F1 and F2) were clearly observed in the results of almost all vowels by some participants (e.g. Fig. 6(b)).

With regard to the larynx-to-TB transfer function, peaks corresponding to F1 were observed in the results for almost all vowels by some participants (e.g. Fig. 6(a)). Additionally, there was a common trend that the frequency components above 2 kHz were relatively decreased compared with those below 2 kHz in all participants and vowels.

With regard to the larynx-to-EC transfer function, there were no peaks corresponding to F1 or F2 in the results of almost all vowels and participants. On the other hand, there was a common trend that the frequency components from 2 to 3 kHz were more emphasized than those in the other frequency regions.

To investigate the universal transmission characteristics independent of vowels, the obtained transfer functions were averaged among five vowels. Figure 7 shows the vowel-averaged transfer functions from the larynx to the observation positions. Figures 7(a) and (b) are the results from male participants M2-1 and M2-2.

With regard to all vowel-averaged transfer functions, there was a common trend that the frequency components around 2 kHz were more emphasized than those in the other frequency regions. However, only in the larynx-to-TB transfer functions was the frequency region below 1 kHz partially emphasized. Moreover, only in the larynx-to-EC transfer functions were the frequency components below 1 kHz and above 3 kHz reduced by more than 20 dB compared with those in the other frequency regions.

These results indicated that the BC speech transmission from larynx to TB has relatively low-pass characteristics (below 1 kHz) and that from larynx to EC has band-pass characteristics (around 1 to 3 kHz).

4   General Discussions

Results of the spectral analysis (Sect. 2) and the transfer function measurement (Sect. 3) are summarized as follows:

- With regard to the TB vibration, the frequency components above 2 kHz were relatively attenuated.
- With regard to the EC-radiated speech, the frequency components below 1 kHz and above 3 kHz were relatively attenuated.
- In many cases, the lower formant frequencies such as F1 were observed in the larynx-to-TB transfer function.

From these results, it is assumed that relatively lower frequency components of speech sounds are transmitted through TB vibration and relatively higher frequency components of speech sounds are transmitted through EC-radiated speech. Previous perceptual investigation related to BC speech [4,5] indicated that BC speech perception dominates in the frequency region around 0.7 to 2 kHz while perceiving one's own voice. Considering this point, it could also be assumed that the EC (outer ear) part of BC speech transmission is only a main contributor to the perception of higher (e.g. around 2 kHz) frequency components, while middle/inner ear parts contribute to the perception of lower (e.g. below 2 kHz) frequency components in BC speech.

In this paper, spectral characteristics of the TB vibration signals are assumed to represent of the soft-tissues or skullbones transmission characteristics, as shown in Fig. 1. Under this assumption, the low-pass characteristics of the TB vibration signals might be derived mainly from the soft-tissue transmission characteristics. In addition, the characteristics of the EC-radiated speech are assumed to contain the resonance characteristics of EC itself (around 3 kHz). Stenfelt et al. reported the vibration characteristics of the middle/inner ear organs related to BC hearing from their previous physiological measurements [9,10]. By combining the findings in this paper and the characteristics of middle/inner ear organ [9,10], BC speech transmission is expected to be further understood.

5   Conclusion

This paper estimated transmission characteristics related to the bone-conducted (BC) speech perception focusing on temporal bone (TB) vibration signals and ear canal (EC)-radiated speech signals.

First, long-term average spectra (LTAS) of the normally produced speech signals from the lip, TB and EC were analyzed. It was found that the frequency components above 2 kHz were relatively decreased in the TB vibration, and those below 1 kHz and above 3 kHz were relatively decreased in the EC-radiated speech.

Second, transfer functions from the larynx to the observation positions (lip, TB and EC) were measured using transcutaneous vibration at the larynx. It was found that the larynx-to-TB transfer functions partially emphasized the frequency region below 1 kHz and the larynx-to-EC transfer functions attenuated the frequency components below 1 kHz and above 3 kHz.

These results indicate that the lower frequency components of BC speech are transmitted through TB vibration and the higher frequency components are transmitted through EC-radiated speech.

Acknowledgment. This work was supported by JSPS KAKENHI Grant No. 16H01669, No. 17J03679 and No. 18H05004. The authors are grateful to Prof. Hirahara, T. for providing us with the equipment and knowhow for the measurement of BC microphone response. We are also grateful to all participants in the vocal recording and transfer function measurements.

References

1. Denes, P.B., Pinson, E.N.: The Speech Chain, 2nd edn. W. H. Freeman and Co., New York (1993)
2. Lee, B.S.: Effects of delayed speech feedback. J. Acoust. Soc. Am. **22**(6), 824–826 (1950)
3. Toya, T., Ishikawa, D., Miyauchi, R., Nishimoto, K., Unoki, M.: Study on effects of speech production during delayed auditory feedback for air-conducted and bone-conducted speech. J. Sig. Process. **20**(4), 197–200 (2016)
4. Reinfeldt, S., Östli, P., Håkansson, B., Stenfelt, S.: Hearing one's own voice during phoneme vocalization - transmission by air and bone conduction. J. Acoust. Soc. Am. **128**(2), 751–762 (2010)
5. Pörschmann, C.: Influences of bone conduction and air conduction on the sound of one's own soice. Acta Acust. United Acust. **86**(6), 1038–1045 (2000)
6. Stenfelt, S.: Acoustic and physiological aspects of bone conduction hearing. Adv. Oto-Rhino-Laryngol. **71**, 10–21 (2011)
7. Toya, T., Unoki, M.: Study on acoustical characteristics of bone-conducted speech perceived by speakers. In: Proceedings ASJ Autumn Meeting (Japan), 3-P-10 (2017)
8. Stenfelt, S., Wild, T., Hato, N., Goode, R.L.: Factors contributing to bone conduction: the outer ear. J. Acoust. Soc. Am. **113**(2), 902–913 (2003)
9. Stenfelt, S., Hato, N., Goode, R.L.: Factors contributing to bone conduction: the middle ear. J. Acoust. Soc. Am. **111**(2), 947–959 (2002)
10. Stenfelt, S., Goode, R.L.: Bone-conducted sound: physiological and clinical aspects. Otol. Neurotol. **26**(6), 1245–1261 (2005)

Singing Voice Database

Liliya Tsirulnik[1]([✉]) and Shlomo Dubnov[2]([✉])

[1] NTENT, San Diego, USA
liliya.tsirulnik@gmail.com
[2] University of California in San Diego, San Diego, USA
sdubnov@ucsd.edu

Abstract. The first publicly available singing voice database, which was first released in 2012, is presented in this paper. This database contains recordings of professional singers including one Grammy Award winner. The database includes so-called plain singing as well as singing with nine different singing expressions. For all the material there are both vocal and glottal voice recordings, where glottal recordings were made by placing the microphone on the neck of the singer near the glottis. Part of the database is annotated on the phoneme and pitch level, which makes it much easier to do automated analyses of different singing voice phenomena. Such varied content of the singing voice database makes it possible to use different types of singing voice for research, including interconnection of vocal and glottal singing voice signals, acoustic phenomena which take place in singing voice, different acoustic phenomena and effects of different expressions in singing voice, as well as comparing singing voice phenomena and acoustic effects of different singers. This database can also be used for simplified singing voice synthesis.

Keywords: Singing voice synthesis · Singing voice database · Speech Synthesis

1 Introduction

Singing Voice Synthesis Systems, as well as Speech Synthesis Systems, have been developed over several decades. Though the general approaches to Singing Voice Synthesis and Speech Synthesis are similar, singing voice is very different from spoken voice in terms of its production and perception by a human. Intelligibility of phonemic message in speech is very important, while in singing it is often secondary to the intonation and musical qualities of the voice. During singing voice synthesis it is important to convey singing voice phenomena, such as vibrato, jitter, drift, presence of singer's formant, and others.

Singing Voice Synthesis systems utilize different approaches, as presented in Sect. 2, using different amounts and different representations of voice units. But until recently, there was no publicly available singing voice database which would allow research on singing voice phenomena and formulate necessary and sufficient content of Singer's database for high quality singing voice synthesis. The present work describes the first (to the best of the authors' knowledge) annotated singing voice database, which was initially released in 2012. This database will allow the study of how various voice

© Springer Nature Switzerland AG 2019
A. A. Salah et al. (Eds.): SPECOM 2019, LNAI 11658, pp. 501–509, 2019.
https://doi.org/10.1007/978-3-030-26061-3_51

phenomena and effects are represented by spectral, temporal, and amplitude characteristics, as well as to create a simplified singing voice synthesis system.

The rest of the paper describes the database (Sects. 3 to 5), ending with our conclusions and possible uses of this database in Sect. 6.

2 Previous Work

Approaches to Singing Voice Synthesis systems include an articulatory approach [1], a
formant synthesis [2, 3], and a concatenative and corpus-based synthesis [4–6]. In
contrast to TTS-synthesis systems, where the input is a text and the output is a speech
signal, for Singing Voice Synthesis systems the input is usually a musical score with
lyrics, and the output is a synthesized singing voice signal.

The articulatory singing voice synthesis system SPASM [1] maps physical characteristics of the vocal tract to singing voice characteristics and produces a voice signal.
The input to this system is not musical notes but the vocal tract characteristics. The
system requires the user to have a knowledge of music and musical acoustics. For each
note the user should specify seven parameters, including vocal tract shape (radius of
each tract section), tract turbulence (noise spectrum and localization), performance
features (random and periodic pitch), and others. The system takes into account singing
voice phenomena, but the singing voice does not sound realistic.

The formant singing voice synthesizer CHANT [2] works with the English language. It is based on rules derived from signal and psychoacoustic analyses, such as the
automatic determination of the formant relative amplitudes or bandwidths, or their
evolutions depending on the variation of other external or internal parameters. CHANT
uses an excitation resonance model to compose a singing voice signal. For each resonance, a basic response is generated using Formant Wave Functions, then these
signals are summed to produce the resulting signal. The system's synthesis results are
impressive in some cases, although it is said that this require tedious manual tuning of
parameters.

Another formant singing voice synthesizer Virtual Singer [3] supports several
languages, including French, English, Spanish, Italian, German, Japanese, and others.
Virtual singer is an opera-like singing synthesizer. Its main attributes are the wide
amount of languages that the synthesizer supports, the sound-shaping control (timbre
and intonation), and the RealSinger function, which allows defining a Virtual Singer
voice out of recordings of the user's own voice. The singer's database of Virtual Singer
includes the set of phonemes with additional first parts of the diphthongs, represented
as spectral envelopes. It assumes that only three to six formants are sufficient to
generate a phoneme with acceptable quality. The advantage of this method is that only
a small amount of data is required to generate a phoneme, and it is far easier to modify
these data slightly to produce another voice timbre. However, the result is generally
less realistic than with recorded speech elements.

The MaxMBROLA [4] is a concatenative synthesis system. It supports 30 languages and has 70 voice databases. MaxMBROLA is a real-time singing synthesizer
based on the MBROLA speech synthesizer. It uses the standard MBROLA acoustic

base which includes diphones and conveys singing voice phenomena by modifying the voice signal.

Another concatenative singing voice synthesis system – Flinger [5] – supports the English language. The singer's database of Flinger includes 500 segments of the consonant-vowel-consonant (CVC) structure: 250 on low pitch and 250 on high pitch, which is about 10 min of singing voice signal. The units are represented using Harmonic Plus Noise model. The system supports the following singing voice effects: vibrato, vocal effort, and variation of spectral tilt with loudness (crescendo of the voice is accompanied by a leveling of the usual downward tilt of the source spectrum).

Vocaloid [6] is currently considered as the best singing voice synthesizer for popular music. It supports the English and Japanese languages. It's a corpus-based system with possible pitch and duration changing with signal generation from the sinusoidal model. Singer's database includes natural speech segments. It should contain all the diphones (pairs of CV, VC, VV for English, where C is a consonant, V is a vowel) and can contain polyphones as well. The size of singer's base is 2000 units per one pitch.

3 Singing Voice Database Content

The main goal of creating the database was to represent different singing voice phenomena rather than a full set of phonemes for a particular language. That's why the a-priori database cannot be used for a full-fledged singing voice synthesis (where the input is a musical score and lyrics), rather for a simplified singing voice synthesis, where the input is a musical score.

The Singing Voice Database (SVDB) includes two parts: (1) Singing musical scale recordings and (2) Singing song recordings. The first part includes:

1.1. The scale (musical notes) performed using "ah" vowel ("ah-ah-ah" recordings)
1.2. The transitions between notes performed using "ah" vowel
1.3. The scale (musical notes) performed using "la" syllable ("la-la-la" recordings)
1.4. The transitions between notes performed using "la" syllable.

The second part includes just the song "Twinkle, twinkle, little star" [7].

Both parts contain plain recordings and recordings with special singing expressions described in Table 1. The database contains vocal recordings and also the so-called "glottal" recordings, which are made by placing the second microphone on a neck of the singer near the glottis.

4 Singing Voice Database Recording

All the recordings were performed in a studio by professional singers. For both the musical scale and the song one female and one male voice were recorded. For the musical scale the voices of Bonnie Lander [8] and Philip Larson [9] were recorded. For the song the voices of Grammy Award winner Susan Narucki [10] and Philip Larson were recorded. The singers' voice characteristics are given in Table 2.

Both vocal and glottal recordings were made simultaneously. The air microphone was used for vocal recordings and a contact microphone was used for glottal recordings.

The recordings are in WAVE PCM format with the following characteristics: 44100 Hz; 16 bit; 1 channel (mono).

Table 1. Singing expressions.

Expression #	Expression name	Description
1	Bounce	Increased articulation on consonants (slight increase of weight on initial consonants) followed by decrease of weight on adjacent vowels. More rhythmic vitality of a regular sort
2	Hollow	Less articulation of consonants. Modification of vowels to minimize their differences with the addition of "air" in the tone (as opposed to focused tone)
3	Light	Minimal initial articulation and weight. Modification of vowels to emphasize "brightness" upper partials
4	Soft	Modification of vowels; some air added, low volume. Consonants are present, but not sharply defined
5	Sweet	Extreme legato. Pure vowels. Consonants present but without extra articulated weight
6	Flat	Affectless. Consonants and vowels with same weight. Minimizing melodic contour
7	Mature	Emphasis on heavier vibrato in sound, (irregular) emphasis on lower partials of vowels (dark rather than bright)
8	Sharp	Emphasis on forward placement of vowel, cutting off lower partials. Aggressive articulation of consonants
9	Husky	Irregular rhythmic inflection in phrasing. Irregular pronunciation of consonants and vowels, additional throat grab noises and air to vowel mix
10	Clear	Purity of vowels and consonants. Emphasis on regularity of pronunciation. Sincere effect

Table 2. Singers voice characteristics.

Type of recordings	Singer	Gender	Voice	Musical notes range
Musical scale	Singer 1	F	Soprano	C4 to H5
Musical scale	Singer 2	M	Bass-baritone	C3 to H4
Song	Singer 3	F	Soprano	
Song	Singer 4	M	Bass-baritone	

5 Singing Voice Database Processing

The musical scale recordings were processed in the following way:

- pauses between recordings (unvoiced fragments) were automatically identified and marked,
- pitch annotation of voiced fragments was made.

For voiced/unvoiced fragments identification the following algorithm was used:

1. For each 5 ms audio frame with a step of 1 ms:
   1.1 The zero-crossing rate was calculated using the formula:

$$Z_n = \sum_{m=0}^{N-1} \frac{|sgn[(x(n-m+1)] - sgn[x(n-m)]|}{2N} \tag{1}$$

where N – frame size,
$x(n)$ – signal at the n-th sample,

$$sgn[x(n)] = \left\{ \begin{array}{l} 1, x(n) \geq 0 \\ -1, x(n) < 0 \end{array} \right\}$$

1.2. The energy was calculated as a root-mean-square level:

$$E_n = \sqrt{\frac{1}{N} \sum_{m=0}^{N-1} |x(n-m)|^2} \tag{2}$$

To calculate energy on each frame the Hamming window was used.

2. To smooth out the result the median value with the window size equal to 7 was calculated for each Energy and Zero-crossing rate.
3. The frame is considered to be voiced if

$$Z_n < Z_{th} \text{ and } E_n > E_{th} \tag{3}$$

where Z_{th} is a zero-crossing threshold and E_{th} is an energy threshold. The values for threshold were chosen experimentally $Z_{th} = 40$ and $E_{th} = 0.06$

Pitch annotation algorithm was based on the fact that the recordings contain consequently sung notes. For example, the consequence of notes C4, D4, E4, F4 corresponds to the fundamental frequencies 261.63 Hz, 293.66 Hz, 329,63 Hz, 349,23 Hz. It means that the length of pitch period changes gradually. For automatic pitch annotation software the initial fundamental frequency (F_0) was specified manually. The software then finds and marks as a pitch period border the nearest zero crossing point in a singing voice signal, taking into account the length of the previous pitch period and voiced/unvoiced parts of the signal. The results were manually verified and corrected when needed.

For the second part of the recordings – song recordings – phoneme boundaries were semi-automatically found and all the vowel phonemes were annotated.

All the annotations were made in the TIMIT database files format [11]. For phonetic transcription the ARPABET code [12] was used. The phonetic transcription of the whole song as well as all the vowel phonemes marked in recordings are presented in Table 3.

Table 3. The lyrics and phonetic transcription of a song "Twinkle, twinkle, little star".

#	Word	Transcription	Vowel phonemes	#	Word	Transcription	Vowel phonemes
1	Twinkle	'T, W, IX, NG, K, L	IX	35	Blazing	'B, L, EY, Z, IX, NG	EY, IX
2	Twinkle	'T, W, IX, NG, K, L	IX	36	Sun	S, AH, N	AH
3	Little	'L, IX, T, L	IX	37	Is	IX, Z	IX
4	Star	S, T, AA	AA	38	Gone	G, AH, N	AH
5	How	H, AW	AW	39	When	W, EH, N	EH
6	I	AY	AY	40	There's	DH, AXR, Z	AXR
7	Wonder	'W, AH, N, D, AX	AH, AX	41	Nothing	'N, AH, TH, IX, NG	AH, IX
8	What	W, AH, T	AH	42	He	H, EE	EE
9	You	J, UX	UX	43	Shines	SH, AY, N, Z	AY
10	Are	AA	AA	44	Upon	AX, 'P, AH, N	AX, AH
11	Up	AH,P	AH	45	Then	DH, EH, N	EH
12	Above	AX, 'B, AH, V	AX, AH	46	You	J, UX	UX
13	The	DH, AX	AX	47	Show	SH, OW	OW
14	World	W, ER, L, D	ER	48	Your	J, AO	AO
15	So	S, OW	OW	49	Little	'L, IX, T, L	IX
16	High	H, AY	AY	50	Light	L, AY, T	AY
17	Like	L, AY, K	AY	51	Twinkle	'T, W, IX, NG, K, L	IX
18	A	AX	AX	52	Twinkle	'T, W, IX, NG, K, L	IX
19	Diamond	'D, AY, M, AX, N, D	AY, AX	53	Through	TH, R, UX	UX
20	In	IX, N	IX	54	The	DH, AX	AX
21	The	DH, AX	AX	55	Night	N, AY, T	AY
22	Sky	S, K, AY	AY	56	Twinkle	'T, W, IX, NG, K, L	IX
23	Twinkle	'T, W, IX, NG, K, L	IX	57	Twinkle	'T, W, IX, NG, K, L	IX

(*continued*)

Table 3. (*continued*)

#	Word	Transcription	Vowel phonemes	#	Word	Transcription	Vowel phonemes
24	Twinkle	'T, W, IX, NG, K, L	IX	58	Little	'L, IX, T, L	IX
25	Little	'L, IX, T, L	IX	59	Star	S, T, AA	AA
26	Star	S, T, AA	AA	60	How	H, AW	AW
27	How	H, AW	AW	61	I	AY	AY
28	I	AY	AY	62	Wonder	'W, AH, N, D, AX	AH, AX
29	Wonder	'W, AH, N, D, AX	AH, AX	63	What	W, AH, T	AH
30	What	W, AH, T	AH	64	You	J, UX	UX
31	You	J, UX	UX	65	Are	AA	AA
32	Are	AA	AA	66	In	IX, N	IX
33	When	W, EH, N	EH	67	The	DH, AX	AX
34	The	DH, AX	AX	68	Dark	D, AA, K	AA
69	Blue	B, L, UX	UX	85	The	DH, AX	AX
70	Sky	S, K, AY	AY	86	Morning	'M, AO, N, IX, NG	IX
71	So	S, OW	OW	87	Sun	S, AH, N	AH
72	Deep	D, EE, P	EE	88	Does	D, AH, Z	AH
73	Through	TH, R, UX	UX	89	Rise	R, AY, Z	AY
74	My	M, AY	AY	90	Twinkle	'T, W, IX, NG, K, L	IX
75	Curtains	'K, ER, T, N, Z	ER	91	Twinkle	'T, W, IX, NG, K, L	IX
76	Often	'AH, F, N	AH	92	Little	'L, IX, T, L	IX
77	Peep	P, EE, P	EE	93	Star	S, T, AA	AA
78	For	F, AO	AO	94	How	H, AW	AW
79	You	J, UX	UX	95	I	AY	AY
80	Never	'N, EH, V, AX	EH, AX	96	Wonder	'W, AH, N, D, AX	AH, AX
81	Close	K, L, OW, Z	OW	97	What	W, AH, T	AH
82	Your	J, AO	AO	98	You	J, UX	UX
83	Eyes	AY, Z	AY	99	Are	AA	AA
84	Till	T, IX, L	IX				

The resulting singing voice database has the following characteristics:

Part 1—"Ah-ah" and "La-la" recording of a male and a female voice. The overall length of the male voice recordings is 23 min and the female voice recordings is 33 min.

Part 2—song recordings of male and female voices. The overall length of the male voice recordings is 13 min and the female voice recordings is 15 min.

6 Conclusions

The singing voice database described here is publicly available from [13] and [14]. The database was first released in 2012 and is quite popular for research groups in Europe and America.

The advantage of the database created is that it includes not only so-called "plain" singing, but also singing with different expressions. It has both vocal and glottal recordings made simultaneously. It is partly annotated on pitch and phoneme levels. All these characteristics make it possible to use the database for different types of research, as well as for simplified singing voice synthesis.

Indeed, this database can be used to research different singing voice effects, including, but not limited to:

- interconnection of vocal and glottal singing voice signals,
- acoustic phenomena which take place in singing voice,
- different acoustic phenomena and effects of different expressions in singing voice, and
- comparison of singing voice phenomena and acoustic effects for different singers.

The first part of a database can be used for a singing voice synthesis as well. However, because it includes just "Ah-ah" and "La-la" sounds, it cannot be used for a full-fledged singing voice synthesis, as was mentioned before. But it can be successfully used for singing voice synthesis where the input is just musical notes (without lyrics).

References

1. Cook, P.R.: Singing Synthesis System. http://www.cs.princeton.edu/∼prc/SingingSynth. html
2. Rodet, X., Potard, Y., Barrière, J.-B.: The CHANT project: from the synthesis of the singing voice to synthesis in general. Comput. Music J. **8**(3), 15–31 (1984)
3. Virtual Singer. http://www.myriad-online.com/en/products/virtualsinger.htm
4. MaxMBROLA. http://tcts.fpms.ac.be/synthesis/maxmbrola/description.php
5. Macon, M.W., Jensen-Link, L., Oliverio, J., Clements, M.A., George, E.B.: A singing voice synthesis system based on sinusoidal modeling. In: 1997 IEEE International Conference on Acoustics, Speech, and Signal Processing, Munich, Germany, pp. 348–352. IEEE Computer Society Press (1997)
6. Kenmochi, H., Ohshima, H.: Vocaloid - commercial singing synthesizer based on sample concatenation. In: 8th Annual Conference of the International Speech Communication Association, ISCA, Antwerp, Belgium, pp. 87–88 (2007)
7. "Twinkle, twinkle, little star" song. https://en.wikipedia.org/wiki/Twinkle,_Twinkle,_Little_ Star
8. Lander, B.: http://www.bonnielander.com/p/about.html

9. Larson, P.: https://music-cms.ucsd.edu/people/faculty/regular_faculty/philip-larson/index.html
10. Narucki, S.: http://www.susannarucki.net/home
11. TIMIT. https://catalog.ldc.upenn.edu/LDC93S1
12. ARPABET. https://en.wikipedia.org/wiki/ARPABET
13. Singing Voice Database. https://liliyatsirulnik.wixsite.com/svdb
14. Singing Voice Database. http://crel.calit2.net/projects/databases/svdb

How Dysarthric Prosody Impacts Naïve Listeners' Recognition

Vass Verkhodanova[1,2(✉)], Sanne Timmermans[3], Matt Coler[1], Roel Jonkers[4], Bauke de Jong[2,3], and Wander Lowie[2,4]

[1] Campus Fryslân, University of Groningen, Groningen, The Netherlands
{v.verkhodanova,m.coler}@rug.nl
[2] Research School of Behavioural and Cognitive Neurosciences,
University of Groningen, Groningen, The Netherlands
w.m.lowie@rug.nl
[3] University Medical Center Groningen, Groningen, The Netherlands
{s.h.timmermans,b.m.de.jong}@umcg.nl
[4] Center for Language and Cognition Groningen, University of Groningen,
Groningen, The Netherlands
r.jonkers@rug.nl

Abstract. The class of speech disorders known as dysarthria arise from disturbances in muscular control over the speech mechanism caused by damage of the central or peripheral nervous system. Dysarthria is typically classified into one of six classes, each corresponding to a different neurological disorder with distinct prosodic cues [3]. The assumption in this classification is that dysarthric speech can be classified implicit on the basis of perception. In this study, we investigate how accurately naïve listeners can recognize stress and intonation in dysarthric speech, and if different neurological disorders impact the ability to convey meaning with these same two cues. To those ends, we collected speech data from Dutch speakers diagnosed with cerebellar lesions (ataxic dysarthria), Parkinson's Disease (hypokinetic dysarthria), Multiple Sclerosis (mixed classes of dysarthria) and from a healthy control group. Thirteen naïve Dutch listeners participated in the perceptual experiment which targeted recognition of intended realization of four prosodic functions: lexical stress, sentence type, boundary marking and focus. We analyzed recognition accuracy for different groups and performed acoustic analyses to check for fundamental frequency trajectories. Results attest to different accuracy recognition results for different disease groups. The sentence type recognition task was the most sensitive of all tasks for differentiating different diseases both on perceptual and acoustic levels of analysis.

Keywords: Dysarthria · Prosody · Parkinson's disease ·
Multiple sclerosis · Spinocerebellar ataxia · Speech perception ·
Speech recognition

© Springer Nature Switzerland AG 2019
A. A. Salah et al. (Eds.): SPECOM 2019, LNAI 11658, pp. 510–519, 2019.
https://doi.org/10.1007/978-3-030-26061-3_52

1   Introduction

Dysarthria is a condition which is caused both by weakness of muscles used in speech and by difficulties in the control over them. The most common and simple description of this speech disorder is "slow speech that can be difficult to understand" [1]. Common causes of dysarthria arise from cerebral dysfunction at the level of brainstem nuclei, supra nuclear brain dysfunction or neuromuscular impairment. Neurological conditions that may lead to dysarthria include Parkinson's Disease (PD), Amyotrophic Lateral Sclerosis (ALS), Multiple Sclerosis (MS), head injury, Spinocerebellar Ataxia (SCA) and a number of others. Since dysarthria causes communication difficulties, it may lead to social deprivation and depression [1].

The seminal contribution to understanding dysarthria was made by Darley et al. [2,3], who introduced the classification system of dysarthrias. Since then the system (hereafter, the *Mayo System*) has been widely used for research and clinical purposes. The Mayo System links brain pathology based on the lesion site and perceptual speech characteristics, united in clusters of deviant speech dimensions. Despite the wide use of the system, there are doubts in its suitability for clinical purposes. For example, two independent studies tested the classification accuracy for neurologists and neurology trainees [4], and for neurologists, residents in neurology, and speech therapists [5]. Both had reported accuracy of correct classification to be from about 35% to 40%, concluding that perceptual judgement alone is not reliable, and other sources of information should be taken into consideration by clinicians.

Since then, researchers have tried to classify dysarthrias using acoustic cues to support the Mayo System. In the study by Guerra et al. [6], authors matched the acoustic measurements to the perceptual cues used by clinicians, and compared performance of two different classifiers to the clinicians' judgements on the speech corpus of different dysarthrias linked to eight neurological disorders in their corpus. The combined feature set of perceptual judgments and objective measurements provided more accurate information about the speech disturbances, while the best classifier proved to be self-organising maps (SOM), which improved the accuracy of clinicians' judgements by nearly 20% [6]. These findings indicate the value of acoustic analysis as an additional tool for clinical purposes.

There has been research dedicated to purely acoustic metrics to reliably differentiate dysarthrias. In the study by Liss et al. [12] the rhythm metrics are assessed, addressing dimension of prosody on the corpus of five different dysarthrias with different prosodic profiles. The results showed the ability of rhythm metrics to distinguish healthy speech from moderate and severe dysarthric speech as well as to discriminate dysarthria subtypes with accuracy up to 80%. The follow up study [11] investigated whether speech envelope modulation spectra, which quantifies the rhythmicity of speech within specified frequency bands, could be used for automatic analysis. Discriminant function analysis showed 84%–100% accuracy for different dysarthrias compared to all others, with hypokinetic dysarthria scoring at 100% [12].

Another study by Lansford and Liss [10] explored the dimension of articulation, focusing on the vowel metrics. They investigated whether such metrics could be used to distinguish healthy from dysarthric speech and among three different classes of dysarthria (ataxic, hypokinetic dysarthria, hyperkinetic and mixed flaccid-spastic dysarthria). All explored vowel metrics, particularly metrics that capture vowel distinctiveness, showed significant differences between dysarthric and healthy control speakers to be more sensitive and specific predictors of dysarthria. However, only the slope of the second formant (F2) demonstrated between-group differences across the dysarthrias. The second study by Lansford and Liss [9] investigated whether vowel metrics reflect the human perceptual performance, namely judging intelligibility of dysarthric speech, showing the correlation between classification by disordered vowels metrics and intelligibility judgements.

The study by Kim et al. [8] explored both dimensions of articulation and prosody simultaneously, using eight acoustic features as predictors for classification of different classes of dysarthria occurring from PD, stroke, multiple system atrophy or traumatic brain injury. Interestingly, the reported results have shown that classification accuracy by dysarthria type was typically worse than by disease type or severity, while the best classification was achieved when disease type was the grouping variable. Regarding intelligibility, F2 slope showed significance for each disease group, serving as the universal predictor. Articulation rate however was not a significant predictor of speech intelligibility for speakers with Parkinson's Disease, while it showed significance in the pooled analysis [8].

In this study, we further investigate the perceptual side of dysarthria classes. We explore if different dysarthias affect the ability of speakers to convey intended prosody. We have collected recordings of three groups of diseases - Parkinson's Disease (PD), SpinoCerebellar Ataxia group (SCA) and Multiple Sclerosis (MS) that are frequent causes of different dysarthrias, namely hypokinetic dysarthria, ataxic dysarthria and either spatic, flaccid or mixed dysarthria. Many studies have indicated that such dysarthrias have different prosodic deficit profiles [2,11,15], which, among other cues, is reflected by different disturbances of fundamental frequency (f_0).

To determine if naïve listeners could recognise intended intonation and stress patterns produced by speakers of different disease groups, we approached the question from two perspectives: first related to prosody recognition and second related to acoustics. For the former we hypothesized, that if there is a correlation between disease groups and accuracy of recognition, PD would be most prominent. For the latter, we hypothesised that f_0 would hinder the listeners' accuracy of recognition at least for PD group. To test these hypotheses we collected data (Sect. 2.1), designed a perception experiment (Sects. 2.2–2.4), and performed an acoustic and recognition accuracy analyses (Sect. 2.5).

2   Methods

2.1   Data Collection

Speech recordings were collected from 32 Dutch native speakers, 24 patients (eight per disease group) and eight control speakers. The demographics can be seen in Table 1.

Table 1. Participants demographics. Age and duration of disease are given in years

Group name	Mean age	Gender (F:M)	Diagnoses	Disease duration mean, range
PD	53.9	4:4	Idiopathic PD	mean: 11.5, range: 20
SCA	55.3	5:3	Spinocerebellar ataxia, adult form of Alexander disease, idiopathic late onset cerebellar ataxia, multiple system atrophy with cerebellar ataxia	mean:6, range: 10
MS	51.9	4:4	Primary progressive MS, secondary progressive MS, relapsing-remitting MS	mean: 13.5, range: 21
HC	56.2	4:4	–	–

Every participant except for the healthy control speakers (HC) exhibited dysarthric symptoms due to neurological disorder according to the neurologist. Speakers reported (corrected-to) normal vision and hearing and signed informed consent. Exclusion criteria for patients were cognitive problems assessed by Minimal Mental State Examination (MMSE < 26), brain damage caused by stroke that inflicted aphasia and/or apraxia of speech, and language and/or (motor) speech disorders other than dysarthria. Exclusion criteria for healthy controls were cognitive problems (MMSE < 26), brain damage, language and/or (motor) speech disorders. The recording sessions took place in quiet rooms at the University Medical Centre Groningen or at participants' homes with the TASCAM-DR100 recorder and an external Senheiser e865 microphone placed at around a 40 cm distance from a participant.

The collection and analysis of the material was approved by the Medical Ethics Committee of the University Medical Center Groningen.

2.2   Participants for Perceptual Experiment

Thirteen native Dutch listeners participated in the prosody recognition experiment (mean age 29). All 13 were "naïve" listeners with no prior experience with speech disorders. All participants reported normal hearing.

2.3   Stimuli

Stimuli for this study were created from a prosody task, that included exercises on four Dutch prosody functions: lexical stress, sentence type, boundary marking, and focus intonation [13]. Table 3 summarizes Dutch prosody functions and their perceptual correlates based on [13, 18].

Table 2. Prosodic functions and their perceptual correlates based on [13, 18]. Perceptually prominent correlates according to Rietveld and Heuven [18] are marked bold.

Function name	Description	Perceptual correlates (for undisturbed speech)	Name used in the current study
Lexical function	Discriminates between words	f_0 **change**, (vowel) duration, intensity	Lexical stress
Phrasing function	Segments the speech stream in information units	**preboundary lengthening pauses**, f_0 change	Boundary Marking
Attentional marking	Highlights the most important elements in a unit	f_0 **change**, (vowel) duration, intensity	Focus
Intentional marking	Nuances meaning	f_0 change	–
Sentence type	Discriminates between questions and statements	**general f_0 rise (question)**, high initial f_0 (question)	Sentence Typing
Emotional prosody	Discriminates between different emotional states	**general f_0, f_0 span, speech rate**	–

Four exercises included sentence completion (to elicit lexical stress and boundary intonation), repetition (boundary intonation) and the production of negative/affirmative questions and statements (sentence type). As the result, from these exercises we had created pairs of stimuli for every prosody function:

- Words segmented from the completed sentences that differ by stress placement: first or second syllable (e.g., *dóórlopen* - 'continue' and *doorlópen* - 'complete');
- Phrases syntactically identical but different in question or statement intonation (e.g. *de toets gehaald?* - '<he> passed the test?' and *de toets gehaald.* - '<he> passed the test');
- Phrases syntactically identical but different in complete/statement or incomplete/iteration intonation (e.g., *Andre houdt van honden, <...>* - 'Andre likes dogs, <...>' and *Andre houdt van honden.* - 'Andre likes dogs');

– Phrases syntactically identical but different in prosodically emphasised words
- focus intonation (e.g., *ik ken haar van **dansles**.* - 'I know her from the
dancing class.' (as opposed to another class) and *ik ken haar van dansles.*
- 'I know her from the dancing class.'.

The total amount of stimuli was 1233, 320 for the stress and for sentence
type, and 310 and 283 for boundary marking and focus. Fewer stimuli for two
latter functions was due to patients quitting during the last part of the protocol
and due to their incorrect execution of exercise parts.

2.4   Procedure

Participants of the recognition experiment completed a recognition task in which
they listened to the stimuli in four blocks corresponding to four prosody functions. Participants were told that they would hear words and phrases that were
different either in stress or intonation and were asked to answer a simple question
by picking one option from a list (e.g., "was the phrase question or statement?"
– "(1) question, (2) statement, (3) impossible to decide"), there were always
three options with one being "impossible to decide". The experiment was built
within the OpenSesame program [14]. For every block, procedure consisted of a
short practice session and a main part. In the practice session, to get participants
acquainted with the task, they were asked to assess two stimuli of two different
voices. For the main part there were 192 stimuli randomly pooled from the set
representing current prosody function in such a way, that there would be six
stimuli per speaker in each block. The speech samples were intensity normalized
and presented over headphones (Koss Pro4S). Participants could listen to each
sample only once.

2.5   Analysis

To analyse listeners' accuracy of dysarthric prosody recognition we calculated
percentage of correct, incorrect and unspecified ("impossible to decide") answers
along with the confidence interval (CI) estimation for the particular answers
using Normal Approximation Method of the Binomial Confidence Interval.

To analyse pitch trajectories of different disease groups and healthy speakers,
we assessed f_0 slopes within each stimulus. To do so, we divided each stimulus
recording in two parts (the ratio between parts was 1:1 for stimuli of the lexical
stress function, for other stimuli it was 7:3). For each part we calculated f_0 average derivative and calculated the difference between the parts of the recording.
Pitch tracking was performed with the Talkin's RAPT algorithm [19] implemented in the SPTK toolkit for Python [17]. The RAPT algorithm identifies
pitch candidates with the cross-correlation function and then attempts to select
the "best fit" at each frame by dynamic programming [16,19]. RAPT results
have been shown to be informative for Dutch dysarthric speech [20].

3 Results

General accuracy calculation for different disease groups did not show any striking differences, though predictably the HC group were recognized best of all, and the PD group performed worst with the highest percentage of unspecified answers. The percentage of unspecified answers was also very small for the HC group compared to other groups (see Table 3).

Table 3. Recognition accuracy for different disease groups and healthy speakers

Disease group	Percentage of correct answers with CI	Percentage of incorrect answers with CI	Percentage of unspecified answers with CI
HC	67 ± 1.8	27 ± 1.8	4 ± 0.8
MS	60 ± 2.0	28 ± 1.8	11 ± 1.3
SCA	56 ± 2.0	28 ± 1.8	14 ± 1.4
PD	55 ± 2.0	25 ± 1.7	18 ± 1.5

When assessing the differences for listeners' performance depending on the target prosodic function, disease groups yielded different accuracy results. Overall, boundary and focus tasks were the most difficult prosodic functions for listeners to recognise intended prosody, especially the focus where the percentage of the unspecified answers was the highest (up to 23 ± 3.4), but even those functions showed difference between healthy and dysarthric speech. Lexical stress was relatively successful for HC and MS, while SCA and PD showed lower accuracy results. Sentence type was the best recognised function for every disease group, with the smallest numbers of unspecified answers. It was also the only function where PD group did not score the worst.

Further analysis of accuracy targetted specific prosody patterns, that is first or second syllables for the lexical stress, question or statement for the sentence type, finished or unfinished intonation for boundary marking, presence or absence of focus intonation for the focus. Except for the focus, the difference between accuracy for two specific prosody patterns was very clear within each group. Questions were better recognised than statements, stressed first syllable - better than the stressed second syllable, finished intonation - better than unfinished.

To determine, if f_0 trajectories would reflect perceptual aspect, we conducted Kruskal-Wallis rank sum tests for non-parametric data to determine f_0 trajectory differences across the data. We compared differences between the f_0 derivatives for stimuli pairs. For all but one stimuli pair, significant results were found in sentence type task for two disease groups: HC and PD. Other prosodic functions did not exhibit any stable significant results within any disease group. The box plot of f_0 trajectories for sentence type function in different diseases is shown on Fig. 1.

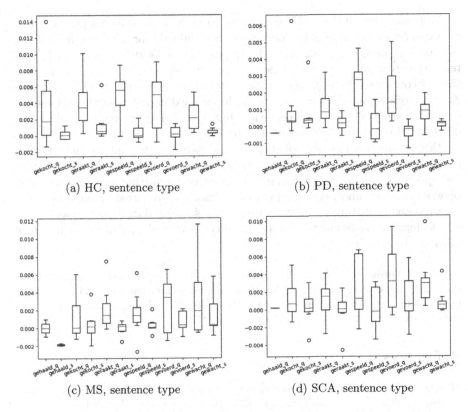

Fig. 1. HC and PD f_0 derivative differences in sentence typing. Difference between derivatives are placed on the y-axis, stimuli tags are placed on the x-axis: 'q' after each word means question, 's' - statement.

We also checked if there was a correlation between accuracy of listeners' recognition and speakers' disease duration, and found that there was none.

4   Discussion

In this study we explored the abilities of naïve listeners to recognitize intonation and stress patterns produced by speakers of different disease groups. We indeed found that different diagnoses, that cause different dysarthria types, affect the intelligibility of prosodic patterns differently. HC group was always distinguishable from any dysarthria groups based on the listeners' recognition accuracy. As we hypothesised, listeners performed poorest on stimuli produced by PD group (three out of four prosody function tasks). Sentence type was the function that listeners were more successful at recognising in the PD group than in the SCA group. This might be because the SCA speaker's tendency towards equalized vowel/syllable durations within utterances and unusually large f_0 range across utterances [7] interfered with their ability to mark sentence types.

Moreover, not all the tasks were found to be reliable to assess prosody deficiency. The focus recognition task was very difficult for listeners in general, causing high numbers of unspecified ("impossible to decide") answers. The sentence type recognition proved to be the clearest task, and was the only one that showed correlation with f_0 trajectories estimation. However, it is obvious that f_0 trajectories cannot act as a single predictor for different dysarthria classes or for the accuracy of listeners recognition, but it is obviously a meaningful cue for differentiating healthy and dysarthric speech.

Despite the small number of speakers and participants, and the lack of information about severity of dysarthria, we showed that assessing the naïve listeners' speech perception is potentially informative for further exploring the link between acoustic and perceptual cues for classifying different dysarthrias. Further research will target other acoustic cues such as duration, temporal cues and formant measurements that might affect listeners' prosody recognition of different dysarthric speech.

Acknowledgements. We thank Lea Busweiler, the student research assistant, for the help in the data collection and Vladimir Shapranov for assistance and advice with Python scripting. We also thank all the participants who volunteered to participate in our experiment.

References

1. Mayo Clinic: dysarthria overview. https://www.mayoclinic.org/diseases-conditions/dysarthria/symptoms-causes/syc-20371994. Accessed 10 Apr 2019
2. Darley, F.L., Aronson, A.E., Brown, J.R.: Clusters of deviant speech dimensions in the dysarthrias. J. Speech Lang. Hear. Res. **12**(3), 462–496 (1969)
3. Darley, F.L., Aronson, A.E., Brown, J.R.: Differential diagnostic patterns of dysarthria. J. Speech Lang. Hear. Res. **12**(2), 246–269 (1969)
4. Fonville, S., Van Der Worp, H., Maat, P., Aldenhoven, M., Algra, A., Van Gijn, J.: Accuracy and inter-observer variation in the classification of dysarthria from speech recordings. J. Neurol. **255**(10), 1545–1548 (2008)
5. Van der Graaff, M., et al.: Clinical identification of dysarthria types among neurologists, residents in neurology and speech therapists. Eur. Neurol. **61**(5), 295–300 (2009)
6. Guerra, E.C., Lovey, D.F.: A modern approach to dysarthria classification. In: Proceedings of the 25th Annual International Conference of the IEEE Engineering in Medicine and Biology Society (IEEE Cat. No. 03CH37439), vol. 3, pp. 2257–2260. IEEE (2003)
7. Kent, R.D., Kent, J.F., Duffy, J.R., Thomas, J.E., Weismer, G., Stuntebeck, S.: Ataxic dysarthria. J. Speech Lang. Hear. Res. **43**(5), 1275–1289 (2000)
8. Kim, Y., Kent, R.D., Weismer, G.: An acoustic study of the relationships among neurologic disease, dysarthria type, and severity of dysarthria. J. Speech Lang. Hear. Res. 417–429 (2011)
9. Lansford, K.L., Liss, J.M.: Vowel acoustics in dysarthria: mapping to perception. J. Speech Lang. Hear. Res. 68–80 (2014)
10. Lansford, K.L., Liss, J.M.: Vowel acoustics in dysarthria: speech disorder diagnosis and classification. J. Speech Lang. Hear. Res. 57–67 (2014)

11. Liss, J.M., LeGendre, S., Lotto, A.J.: Discriminating dysarthria type from envelope modulation spectra. J. Speech Lang. Hear. Res. 1246–1255 (2010)
12. Liss, J.M., et al.: Quantifying speech rhythm abnormalities in the dysarthrias. J. Speech Lang. Hear. Res. 1334–1352 (2009)
13. Martens, H., Van Nuffelen, G., Cras, P., Pickut, B., De Letter, M., De Bodt, M.: Assessment of prosodic communicative efficiency in Parkinson's disease as judged by professional listeners. Parkinson's Dis. **2011** (2011). https://doi.org/10.4061/2011/129310
14. Mathôt, S., Schreij, D., Theeuwes, J.: OpenSesame: an open-source, graphical experiment builder for the social sciences. Behav. Res. Methods **44**(2), 314–324 (2012)
15. Miller, P.H.: Dysarthria in multiple sclerosis: clinical bulletin, information for health professionals. Accessed 29 Mar 2019
16. Morrison, D., Wang, R., De Silva, L.C.: Ensemble methods for spoken emotion recognition in call-centres. Speech Commun. **49**(2), 98–112 (2007)
17. Research Group of Professor Satoshi Imai, Kobayashi, P.T.: SPTK: the speech signal processing toolkit (version 3.11). http://sp-tk.sourceforge.net/
18. Rietveld, T., Van Heuven, V.J.: Algemene Fonetiek (3e geheel herziene druk). Coutinho, Bussum (2009)
19. Talkin, D.: A robust algorithm for pitch tracking (RAPT). In: Speech Coding and Synthesis, pp. 495–518 (1995)
20. Verkhodanova, V., Coler, M.: Prosodic and segmental correlates of spontaneous dutch speech in patients with Parkinson's disease: a pilot study. In: Speech Prosody 9th International Conference, pp. 163–166 (2018)

Light CNN Architecture Enhancement for Different Types Spoofing Attack Detection

Marina Volkova[1]([✉]), Tseren Andzhukaev[1], Galina Lavrentyeva[2], Sergey Novoselov[1,2], and Alexander Kozlov[1]

[1] STC-innovations Ltd., St. Petersburg, Russia
{volkova,andzhukaev,novoselov,kozlov-a}@speechpro.com
[2] ITMO University, St. Petersburg, Russia
lavrentyeva@speechpro.com

Abstract. The widely acknowledged vulnerability of automatic speaker verification systems (ASV) to various spoofing attacks requires the development of countermeasures robust to unforeseen spoofing trials. In this paper we consider deep learning approach based on Light CNN architecture and its modification for replay attack detection on the base of ASVspoof2017 V2. The efficiency of Light CNN based approaches for replay attacks detection has already been confirmed during ASVspoof2017 (for ASVspoof V1 corpora) and ASVspoof2019 Challenges. We enhanced Light CNN architecture previously considered by the authors via applying angular margin based softmax activation for training robust deep Light CNN classifier. The proposed system achieved Equal Error Rate of 5.5% on the evaluation part of ASVspoof2017 V2. In addition, we also investigated the possibility of unified LCNN-based approach to detect not only replay spoofing attacks but also attacks of logical level, specifically speech synthesis and voice conversion. The experiment results were obtained for microphone part of PHONESPOOF database.

Keywords: Spoofing · Anti-spoofing · Speaker recognition · Replay attack detection · ASVspoof · PHONESPOOF

1 Introduction

At the present time, the popularity of using authentication systems based on individual biometric characteristics of a person's voice is growing. Such authentication systems are being introduced in various call-centers to confirm the identity of users for example of the credit institutions or banks. As well voice biometrics is used in forensic investigations and other areas of law enforcement.

Along with the increasing quality of voice biometric techniques, there is a continuous improvement of their hacking techniques, so-called spoofing attacks. According to the [1] ASV spoofing attacks can be classified pursuant to the stage they are applied to. In this paper we focus on the direct attacks aimed to

A. A. Salah et al. (Eds.): SPECOM 2019, LNAI 11658, pp. 520–529, 2019.
https://doi.org/10.1007/978-3-030-26061-3_53

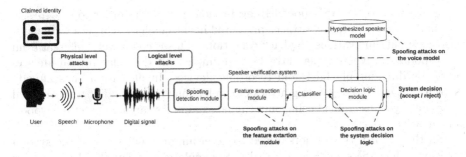

Fig. 1. ASV system with possible points of attacks.

substitute the input data on the physical (input signal recording) or logical level (transmission), see Fig. 1. Since speaker verification is mostly used in automatic systems without face-to-face contact, these attacks are more likely to be used by the criminals.

Spoofing attacks can also be divided into 3 main classes according to the technologies these attacks were generated with [2]: speech synthesis, voice conversion and replay attacks. For replay attack fraudster uses speech sample of the target speaker preliminary recorded via any recording device or smartphone. From the practical point of view replay attacks are much easier to implement than other types and, consequently, are currently the main threat to voice biometric systems.

In order to encourage the design of anti-spoofing systems and assess the current state of spoofing detection technologies, the ASVspoof initiative was organized [3]. ASVspoof Challenge was held three times: in 2015 [3], 2017 [4] and in 2019 [5]. It spurred the significant interest of the research community to the problem of generalised countermeasures development robust to unforeseen spoofing attacks. Also, the corpora, collected by the organizers, in some sense have become a common standard for evaluating various anti-spoofing systems.

ASVspoof2015 focused on the attacks of speech synthesis and voice conversion. The results obtained during the competition showed the ability of modern at that time systems to detect attacks of speech synthesis and voice conversion. ASVspoof2017 switched focus to the replay attacks which are easy to implement but difficult to detect. ASVspoof2019 combined these types of attacks into two separate scenarios: a scenario with logical access to the system (speech synthesis and voice conversion) and physical access (replay attacks).

During the ASVspoof2017 Challenge, the authors of the article presented a system based on the LightCNN architecture [6], which showed the best quality of replay attacks detection on the evaluation set. During ASVspoof2019 Challenge, the presented architecture was improved [7]. In particular, the angular based softmax activation function (a-softmax) of the last layer instead of a well-known softmax was used for training LightCNN-based spoofing detector in both scenarios. Additionally, we enlarged the number of network parameters and added batch normalization layers.

According to the ASVspoof2019 evaluation plan [8], in order to control the evaluation setup all replay-attacks presented in the challenge corpora were modeled by simulating various playback conditions. This is completely different from ASVspoof2017, where replay attacks were implemented similar to real life scenario by different playback and recording devices. In [9] authors has already shown that emulated spoofing attacks for telephone channel differ from the real cases and systems trained using only emulated samples can not detect real spoofing attacks.

In this regard, the authors aimed to determine the efficiency of the system developed for ASVspoof2019 for real (non-simulated) replay attacks using the corpora ASVspoof2017 V2.

This paper considers several modifications of the LightCNN-based spoofing detection system. The systems were trained and tested on the ASVspoof2017 V2 corpora database to create a generalized anti-spoofing solution able to detect real replay attacks in different acoustic environments. Experiment results for ASVspoof2017 V2 and microphone part of the PHONESPOOF corpora confirm the generalizing ability of the proposed architecture.

2   Deep Learning Approach

2.1   Light CNN Classifier

Light CNN architecture (LCNN) was used by the authors for replay-attack detection in ASVspoof2017 and showed good results for such type of tasks [6]. Light CNN architecture is based on Max-Feature-Map activation (MFM) which can be considered as alternative of Rectified Linear Unit (ReLU) and extension of Max-Out activation function [10]. The main motivation of MFM is to separate informative and noisy signals via a feature selection between pairs of feature maps. Each LCNN block includes a combination of two independent sets of feature maps, computed on the input data of a layer (Fig. 2). The MFM activation function calculates elementwise maximum for each pair of feature maps. Such feature extraction allows to significantly reduce the number of network parameters. Unlike ReLu which learns to suppress low-activation neurons by the threshold, MFM resorts to max function to implement a competitive relationship between feature maps and does not depend on parameters or threshold. That allows MFM-based CNN models to achieve better generalization even for different data distributions.

Compared to Maxout activation, Max-Feature-Map activation does not use hidden nodes, so the scale of MFM-networks is smaller than Maxout-networks.

MFM function is defined as

$$y_{ij}^k = max(x_{ij}^k, x_{ij}^{k+\frac{N}{2}}),$$
$$\forall i = \overline{1,H}, j = \overline{1,W}, k = \overline{1,N/2}$$

where x is the input tensor of size $H \times W \times N$, y is the output tensor of size $H \times W \times \frac{N}{2}$. Here i, j indicate the frequency and time domains and k is the channel index. Figure 2 illustrates MFM for a convolutional layer. MFM usage allowed us to reduce CNN architecture. That is why such CNN architecture is called Light CNN (LCNN) [10].

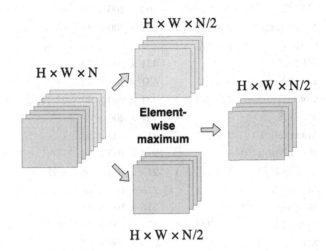

Fig. 2. MFM for convolutional layer

2.2   LCNN System Modifications

LCNN based architecture used in ASVspoof2017 consisted of 5 convolution layers, 10 Max-Feature-Map layers, 4 max-pooling layers and 2 fully connected layers.

For ASVspoof2019 competition we developed an enhanced modification of that LCNN [7]. New architecture has two times larger number of parameters, uses angular margin based softmax (A-softmax) loss and includes batch normalization layers after MFM and MaxPooling layers in order to increase stability and speed convergence during the training process.

Besides, in ASVspoof2019 we used this LCNN modification for final score estimation without GMM scoring backend, because it did not give a gain in quality.

The detailed architecture for feature size 863×400 is described in Table 1.

2.3   Angular Margin Based Softmax Activation

The key difference of the novel $LCNN_{wide}^{asx}$ system is angular margin based softmax (A-softmax) loss used for training the described architecture.

A-softmax was introduced in [11] and demonstrated an elegant way to obtain well-regularized loss function by forcing learned features to be discriminative on a hypersphere manifold. Thus angular margin based softmax loss can be described as:

Table 1. $LCNN_{wide}^{asx}$ architecture

Type	Filter/Stride	Output	Params
Conv_1	$5 \times 5/1 \times 1$	$863 \times 400 \times 64$	1.6K
MFM_2	–	$864 \times 400 \times 32$	–
MaxPool_3	$2 \times 2/2 \times 2$	$431 \times 200 \times 32$	–
Conv_4	$1 \times 1/1 \times 1$	$431 \times 200 \times 64$	2.1K
MFM_5	–	$431 \times 200 \times 32$	–
BatchNorm_6	–	$431 \times 200 \times 32$	–
Conv_7	$3 \times 3/1 \times 1$	$431 \times 200 \times 96$	27.7K
MFM_8	–	$431 \times 200 \times 48$	-
MaxPool_9	$2 \times 2/2 \times 2$	$215 \times 100 \times 48$	–
BatchNorm_10	–	$215 \times 100 \times 48$	–
Conv_11	$1 \times 1/1 \times 1$	$215 \times 100 \times 96$	4.7K
MFM_12	–	$215 \times 100 \times 48$	–
BatchNorm_13	–	$215 \times 100 \times 48$	–
Conv_14	$3 \times 3/1 \times 1$	$215 \times 100 \times 128$	55.4K
MFM_15	–	$215 \times 100 \times 64$	–
MaxPool_16	$2 \times 2/2 \times 2$	$107 \times 50 \times 64$	–
Conv_17	$1 \times 1/1 \times 1$	$107 \times 50 \times 128$	8.3K
MFM_18	–	$107 \times 75 \times 64$	–
BatchNorm_19	–	$107 \times 50 \times 64$	–
Conv_20	$3 \times 3/1 \times 1$	$107 \times 50 \times 64$	36.9K
MFM_21	–	$107 \times 50 \times 32$	–
BatchNorm_22	–	$107 \times 50 \times 32$	–
Conv_23	$1 \times 1/1 \times 1$	$107 \times 50 \times 64$	2.1K
MFM_24	–	$107 \times 50 \times 32$	–
BatchNorm_25	–	$107 \times 50 \times 32$	–
Conv_26	$3 \times 3/1 \times 1$	$107 \times 50 \times 64$	18.5K
MFM_27	–	$107 \times 50 \times 32$	–
MaxPool_28	$2 \times 2/2 \times 2$	$53 \times 25 \times 32$	–
FC_29	–	160	10.2 MM
MFM_30	–	80	–
BatchNorm_31	–	80	–
FC_32	–	2	64
Total	–	–	6.9MM

$$L_{\text{ang}} = \frac{1}{N} \sum_i - \log \left(\frac{e^{\|x_i\| \cos(m\theta_{i,y_i})}}{e^{\|x_i\| \cos(m\theta_{i,y_i})} + \sum_{i \neq y_i} e^{\|x_i\| \cos(m\theta_{i,y_i})}} \right) \quad (1)$$

where N is the number of training samples $\{x_i\}_{i=1}^N$ and their labels $\{y_i\}_{i=1}^N$, θ_{i,y_i} is the angle between x_i and the corresponding column y_i of the fully connected classification layer weights W, and m is an integer that controls the size of an angular margin between classes.

This approach has been already used in [12] for high-level speaker embedding extractor. The learned features are constrained to a unit hypersphere. Such regularization technique also addresses the problem of overfitting by separating classes in cosine similarity metric.

2.4   Front-End

Several papers [6,13] presented the successful experience of using time-frequency signal representations as input features for spoofing detection task. This approach allows to detect local spectral artifacts presented in spoofing attacks that distinguish it from genuine speech.

Our previous LCNN based system for replay attack detection from [6] used normalized log power magnitude spectrum obtained via Fast Fourier Transform (FFT) in the form of images.

During ASVspoof2019 we abandoned the quantized image representation of spectrum and used source spectrum without normalization.

According to our experience in ASVspoof2017 features normalization plays a crucial role in real scenarios. Due to this in the current investigation we used mean and variance normalization for log-power spectrum extracted via FFT. Here we also considered a special technique for obtaining a unified time-frequency (T-F) shape of features. It implies truncation of the spectrum along the time axis with a fixed size. During this procedure short files are extended by repeating their contents if necessary to match the required length.

During the experiments we considered FFT-spectrograms of two shapes as input features: 863×400 - similar to as it was used in ASVspoof2017 system and 512×512 in order to increase processing speed.

3   Experimental Setup

3.1   Datasets

In this research we conduct experiments on the ASVspoof2017 Version 2.0 database [14]. Our interest in this database is dictated by the fact that it contains actual recorded replay attacks in contradistinction to ASVspoof2019 where it were simulated.

ASVspoof2017 Version 2.0 corpora was presented by the organizers after the competition and became a fixed version of the original ASVspoof2017 base [14]. The second version of the database excludes data anomalies (like zero-valued segments) presented in the original version. These anomalies can impact on the assessment of replay detection performance according to the post-evaluation experiments [14].

The ASVspoof2017 V2 corpora include three parts: training, development and evaluation. Each LCNN model described in this paper was trained on both training and development data and evaluation part was used only for the experiments.

3.2   Experiments

In this paper we compared 4 LCNN systems. We investigated the impact of the amount of network parameters on the replay attack detection quality and considered original $LCNN$ from [6] and its wider version $LCNN_{wide}$. Furthermore, we explored the efficiency of applying A-softmax activation function for training mentioned above architectures. These systems are referred further with asx index.

- $LCNN^{asx}$ is similar to original LCNN architecture from [6] but includes additional batch normalization layers. The key difference is A-softmax activation function used instead of softmax. We trained two systems based on this architectures. The first system used normalized FFT spectra with size 863×400. The second one used 512×512 size features and due to this was computationally lighter.
- $LCNN_{wide}$ is the extended version of LCNN from [6]. In contrast to that network it has double amount of feature maps in each layer. As in the original article, it uses conventional softmax activation function on the last layer. As input features the normalized FFT spectra with size 863×400 were used.
- $LCNN_{wide}^{asx}$ is the combination of two previously described systems. It is based on wide LCNN architecture with additional batch normalization layers and utilize A-softmax activation function for training.
  As input features the normalized FFT spectra with size 863×400 were used.

As can be seen on Fig. 3, angular margin based softmax loss allows not only to improve system quality but also to stabilize the training process.

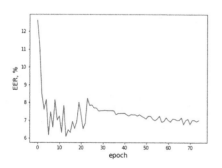 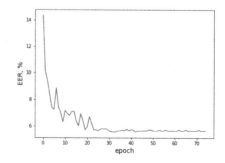

Fig. 3. EER during training process for $LCNN_{wide}$ (left) and $LCNN_{wide}^{asx}$ (right)

4   Results and Discussion

The experimental results for all described systems on the evaluation part of ASVspoof2017 V2 corpora are presented in Table 2.

Table 2. Experimental results for different LCNN systems obtained on the evaluation part of ASVspoof2017 V2 (EER%)

System	Feature size	EER
$LCNN_{wide}$	863×400	6.09
$LCNN_{wide}^{asx}$	863×400	5.5
$LCNN^{asx}$	863×400	6.78
$LCNN^{asx}$	512×512	8.17

This results in first two rows of Table 2 demonstrates the efficiency of usage A-softmax loss which gives an advantage almost in 0.6 % EER. This confirms our findings during ASVspoof2019 [7] about the expediency of usage A-softmax loss in LCNN for spoofing detection task.

Besides, we can conclude that extended architecture $LCNN_{wide}^{asx}$ demonstrates higher spoofing detection quality than $LCNN^{asx}$ but it has much more computational complexity (with computational cost of 5.6 GFLOPs versus 1.5 GFLOPs for $LCNN^{asx}$).

The final experiment was aimed to check the most computationally light system $LCNN^{asx}$ with 512×512 feature size. As expected, this system shows the worst quality among considered systems, but due to its relative simplicity and satisfying performance it can be used if high processing speed is under demand. The average computational cost of this system was 1.2 GFLOPs.

Inspired by the impressive results of the described systems we were aimed to design the generalized LCNN-based system for both logical and physical access spoofing attacks. In order to do this we trained $LCNN^{asx}$ on the combination of ASVspoof2015, ASVspoof2017 V2 training and development parts and the microphone channel of PHONESPOOF dataset described in [9]. This system was trained to distinguish between spoofing and genuine classes, which means that it did not use any information about attack type during training. The training data was balanced across the types of attacks and varieties of TTS. As input features normalized FFT-spectra with 512×512 size were used. The obtained system was evaluated on the ASVspoof2015 and ASVspoof2017 V2 accordingly. In addition we assess its ability to detect different types of known and unknown types of open source TTS. The experiment results are presented in the Table 3.

Table 3. Experiment results for generalized spoofing detection system, EER (%).

Spoofing attacks type	Test dataset	EER (%)
Replay	ASVspoof2017 eval	15.31
TTS	Google	0.03
	Yandex	0.12
	IBM	0.19
	STC	0.55
	Lyrebird	2.64
TTS + VC	ASVspoof2015	0.24

Obtained results confirm the generalization ability of the proposed architecture. Detection quality of voice conversion and speech synthesis from ASVspoof2015 outperform many published results obtained for this data set including systems performed during the Challenge and after that [3, 15–17]. This significant improvement can be explained by the variability of the training set, that included training and development parts of ASVspoof2015 as well a substantial amount of TTS samples from different open sources, such as Google, Yandex.

It is worth mentioning that the general system demonstrate lower detection quality for replay attacks from ASVspoof2017 evaluation part than an individual system which can be explained by not sufficient amount of learning network parameters for the generalized task.

5 Conclusion

In this paper we considered several modifications of LCNN for spoofing attack detection. Performed experiments show that solutions proposed during ASVspoof2019 Challenge for solving spoofing detection task in modeled conditions provide high spoofing detection quality even for non-simulated data from ASVspoof V2. These approaches include the extension of previous LCNN architecture with additional batch normalization layers and usage of the (A-softmax) softmax loss for training this architecture. $LCNN_{wide}^{asx}$ system showed the best replay attack detection with 5.5% of EER. It was shown that input feature size reduction can be used in order to increase the processing speed of the ASVspoof system. However, this leads to system performance degradation. Presented investigations show that the unified LCNN based system can be effectively trained for both logical and physical access spoofing attacks detection simultaneously. Such system demonstrates reliable performance for both antispoofing attacks scenarios.

Acknowledgments. This research was partially financially supported by the Government of the Russian Federation (Grant 08-08).

References

1. Faundez-Zanuy, M., Hagmüller, M., Kubin, G.: Speaker verification security improvement by means of speech watermarking. Speech Commun. **48**(12), 1608–1619 (2006)
2. Wu, Z., Evans, N., Kinnunen, T., Yamagishi, J., Alegre, F., Li, H.: Spoofing and countermeasures for speaker verification: a survey. Speech Commun. **66**, 130–153 (2015)
3. Wu, Z., et al.: ASVspoof 2015: the first automatic speaker verification spoofing and countermeasures challenge. In: INTERSPEECH (2015)
4. Kinnunen, T., et al.: The ASVspoof 2017 challenge: assessing the limits of replay spoofing attack detection. In: INTERSPEECH (2017)
5. Todisco, M., et al.: ASVspoof 2019: future horizons in spoofed and fake audio detection (2019)
6. Lavrentyeva, G., Novoselov, S., Malykh, E., Kozlov, A., Kudashev, O., Shchemelinin, V.: Audio replay attack detection with deep learning frameworks. In: Proceedings of the INTERSPEECH 2017, pp. 82–86 (2017)
7. Lavrentyeva, G., Novoselov, S., Tseren, A., Volkova, M., Gorlanov, A., Kozlov, A.: STC antispoofing systems for the ASVspoof2019 challenge (2019)
8. ASVspoof 2019: Automatic speaker verification spoofing and countermeasures challenge evaluation plan (2019)
9. Lavrentyeva, G., Novoselov, S., Volkova, M., Matveev, Y., De Marsico, M.: Phonespoof: a new dataset for spoofing attack detection in telephone channel. In: Proceedings of the ICASSP 2018 (2018)
10. Wu, X., He, R., Sun, Z.: A lightened CNN for deep face representation. CoRR, vol. abs/1511.02683 (2015)
11. Liu, W., Wen, Y., Yu, Z., Li, M., Raj, B., Song, L.: SphereFace: deep hypersphere embedding for face recognition. In: The IEEE Conference on Computer Vision and Pattern Recognition (CVPR), vol. 1 (2017)
12. Novoselov, S., Shulipa, A., Kremnev, I., Kozlov, A., Shchemelinin, V.: On deep speaker embeddings for text-independent speaker recognition, pp. 378–385 (2018)
13. Tian, X., Xiao, X., Siong, C.E., Li, H.: Spoofing speech detection using temporal convolutional neural network. In: 2016 Asia-Pacific Signal and Information Processing Association Annual Summit and Conference (APSIPA) (2016)
14. Delgado, H., et al.: ASVspoof 2017 version 2.0: meta-data analysis and baseline enhancements (2018)
15. Patel, T.B., Patil, H.A.: Combining evidences from mel cepstral, cochlear filter cepstral and instantaneous frequency features for detection of natural vs. spoofed speech. In: INTERSPEECH (2015)
16. Novoselov, S., Kozlov, A., Lavrentyeva, G., Simonchik, K., Shchemelinin, V.: STC anti-spoofing systems for the ASVspoof 2015 challenge. In: 2016 IEEE International Conference on Acoustics, Speech and Signal Processing (ICASSP), pp. 5475–5479 (2016)
17. Alam, M.J., Kenny, P., Gupta, V., Stafylakis, T.: Spoofing detection on the ASVspoof 2015 challenge corpus employing deep neural networks (2016)

Deep Neural Network Quantizers Outperforming Continuous Speech Recognition Systems

Tobias Watzel[(✉)] [ID], Lujun Li[ID], Ludwig Kürzinger[ID], and Gerhard Rigoll[ID]

Institute for Human-Machine Communication,
Technical University of Munich, Munich, Germany
{tobias.watzel,lujun.li,ludwig.kuerzinger,rigoll}@tum.de

Abstract. In Automatic Speech Recognition (ASR), the acoustic model (AM) is modeled by a Deep Neural Network (DNN). The DNN learns a posterior probability in a supervised fashion utilizing input features and ground-truth labels. Current approaches combine a DNN with a Hidden Markov Model (HMM) in a hybrid approach, which achieved good results in the last years. Similar approaches using a discrete version, hence a Discrete Hidden Markov Model (DHMM), have been disregarded in recent past. Our approach revisits the idea of a discrete system, more precisely the so-called Deep Neural Network Quantizer (DNNQ), demonstrating how a DNNQ is created and trained. We introduce a novel approach to train a DNNQ in a supervised fashion with an arbitrary output layer size even though suitable target values are not available. The proposed method provides a mapping function exploiting fixed ground-truth labels. Consequently, we are able to apply a frame-based cross entropy (CE) training. Our experiments demonstrate that the DNNQ reduces the Word Error Rate (WER) by 17.6 % on monophones and by 2.2 % on triphones, respectively, compared to a continuous HMM-Gaussian Mixture Model (GMM) system.

Keywords: Deep Neural Network Quantizer ·
Discrete speech recognition · Mini-batch sampling

1 Introduction

In recent years, Automatic Speech Recognition (ASR) systems have reduced their Word Error Rate (WER) progressively. The recognition rates increased even on challenging tasks like the AMI [3] corpus. Recently, Xiong et al. [19] reached a new milestone. They achieved a human-like recognition rate by combining several models and training on a large dataset. However, the training of these models is not feasible without sufficient computational power. In fields where only limited resources are available or the amount of training data is restricted, different approaches need to be considered. Therefore, HMM-GMM systems and hybrid systems, which combine a HMM with a single DNN, are still

© Springer Nature Switzerland AG 2019
A. A. Salah et al. (Eds.): SPECOM 2019, LNAI 11658, pp. 530–539, 2019.
https://doi.org/10.1007/978-3-030-26061-3_54

popular and in use with slight adjustments in their architectures [5,10]. Usually, these approaches determine the AM of the ASR by a continuous posterior distribution $p(y|x)$ given the input features x. The time-variant model component is modeled by an HMM [2].

Besides continuous models like GMMs or DNNs, another system category was popular but has been disregarded in recent past: ASR systems consisting of a discrete AM, hence, a DHMM. However, discrete ASR systems are usually performing worse due the loss of information during discretization. Regardless of this disadvantage, several approaches tried to compete in a discrete fashion. In the beginning, the well-known and fast k-means algorithm was used as a baseline to cluster the training data yielding a predefined number of cluster centroids. With the help of these centriods, a Vector Quantizer (VQ) is used to assign a feature vector to the nearest cluster. The AM is trained with the created label stream.

In an alternative approach [13], Neukirchen and Rigoll introduced the Neural Network Vector Quantizer (NNVQ). The NNVQ is a shallow neural network and acts as a VQ, which labels the data. The model is trained with the mutual information criterion. The index of the neuron in the output layer with the highest activation returns the label for the training sample, thus, performs the quantization to assign the input feature to a specific cluster. Furthermore, the input features were split into four separated streams. For each feature stream, a single shallow NNVQ was trained. During the NNVQ training, applying a quantization is not feasible since it is impossible to compute a derivative (note, quantization corresponds to $argmax$ of the output layer). To tackle this problem, the authors used a scaled version of the $softmax$ function to approximate the $argmax$ operation. The $softmax$ function is fully derivable, which is necessary to calculate the gradients for training the NNVQ. In the end, their model was able to slightly outperform a k-means system and nearly equalized continuous systems. However, the evaluation was done on the Resource Management database [11], which only provides a limited amount of training samples.

The same NNVQ architecture was also used in [14] for a large-vocabulary speech recognition task on the Wall Street Journal database [8]. The NNVQ was able to achieve better performance compared to a k-means system but could not reach the performance of continuous systems. Besides using triphones, they added context by splicing adjacent frames. However, they were not able to obtain comparable results to continuous systems in [7].

In this work, we revisit discrete ASR investigating the limits of such systems. We consider recent state-of-the-art developments and enhance the ideas of the aforementioned approaches [13,14]. Our work makes the following contributions:

- We demonstrate how to build up a DNNQ for discrete ASR.
- We propose a novel training algorithm for DNNQs with arbitrary output layer size.
- In contrast to [14], we illustrate how a DNNQ is able to outperform continuous GMM systems.

2   Proposed Method

2.1   Deep Neural Network Quantizer Training

Let $\mathcal{D} = \{(\boldsymbol{x}_i, \hat{y}_i)\}_{i=1}^{N}$ be a dataset of size N consisting of features $\boldsymbol{x}_i \in \mathbb{R}^D$ with their corresponding ground-truth labels $\hat{y}_i \in \mathbb{N}_1$ (note that $\mathbb{N}_1 = \mathbb{N} \setminus \{0\}$). We want to find a function $f : \boldsymbol{x}_i \mapsto \hat{y}_i$ mapping all input features onto their ground-truth labels. In our approach, we use a DNNQ to approximate f with $g_\theta : \boldsymbol{x}_i \mapsto \hat{m}_i$, where θ represent the weights of the network and $\hat{m}_i \in \mathbb{N}_1$ defines the index of the maximum value in the DNNQ output layer $\boldsymbol{m}_i \in \mathbb{R}^{N_{\text{clu}}}$ as follows

$$\hat{m}_i = \arg \max_{1 \leq j \leq N_{\text{clu}}} m_i^j. \tag{1}$$

The size of the output layer is represented by N_{clu} and the index j describes the j-th neuron in the layer. In order to approximate the *argmax* operation, we apply a scaled version of the *softmax*

$$m_i^j = \frac{\exp(a_i^j T_{\text{sca}})}{\sum\limits_{l=1}^{N_{\text{clu}}} \exp(a_i^l T_{\text{sca}})} \quad \forall 1 \leq j \leq N_{\text{clu}}, \tag{2}$$

produce a single spiking output. Depending on the value of T_{sca}, the activations a_i^j of the previous layer are getting higher or lower scaled, consequently the output of the DNNQ is spikier or smoother. By applying the *softmax*, we are still able to take the derivative of the output $\boldsymbol{m}_i$ which is a requirement to train the DNNQ. Depending on size N_{clu} the emitting labels $\hat{m}_i$ are in the range $[1, N_{\text{clu}}] = \{\hat{m}_i \in \mathbb{N}_1 \mid 1 \leq \hat{m}_i \leq N_{\text{clu}}\}$. The ground-truth labels are in the range $[1, N_K] = \{\hat{y}_i \in \mathbb{N}_1 \mid 1 \leq \hat{y}_i \leq N_K\}$, where N_K represents the dimension of the label space.

In classic deep learning training, the well-known cross entropy loss $\mathcal{L}_{CE}$ is utilized in every mini-batch containing N_b examples to optimize the weights, i.e.,

$$\mathcal{L}_{\text{CE}} = -\frac{1}{N_b} \sum_{i=1}^{N_b} \sum_{k=1}^{N_K} \delta(\hat{y}_i, k) \log m_i^k, \tag{3}$$

where $\delta(\cdot)$ represents the Kronecker delta. Usually, the dimension of the output layer and the ground-truth label space are equal, thus, $N_{\text{clu}} = N_K$. However, it does not apply for our DNNQ. Before we take a closer look as to why, we define the discrete random variables M and Y with their probability mass functions

$$P(M = \hat{m}^j) = \frac{1}{N} \sum_{i=1}^{N} \delta(\hat{m}_i, j) \quad \forall 1 \leq j \leq N_{\text{clu}} \tag{4}$$

and

$$P(Y = \hat{y}^k) = \frac{1}{N} \sum_{i=1}^{N} \delta(\hat{y}_i, k) \quad \forall 1 \leq k \leq N_K. \tag{5}$$

The probability mass functions are created by counting the number of occurrence $\hat{m}^j$ and $\hat{y}^k$ based on all the samples $\hat{m}_i$ and $\hat{y}_i$. Thereby, we are able to define the mutual information $I(Y; M)$ by

$$I(Y; M) = H(Y) - H(Y|M). \tag{6}$$

$H(Y)$ represents the entropy of Y and $H(Y|M)$ is the entropy of Y conditioned on M. Note that the entropy $H(Y)$ is fixed during training as we are not able to adjust the ground-truth labels $\hat{y}_i$ in Eq. 5. Hence, we can only minimize $H(Y|M)$ by altering the output of the DNNQ to maximize $I(Y; M)$. In our approach, we implicitly maximize $I(Y; M)$ by minimizing $\mathcal{L}_{CE}$ [18] instead of minimizing $H(Y|M)$ directly like in [13]. Since $I(Y; M)$ is strongly dependent on the size of m_i, we need to increase the variety of emitted labels $\hat{m}_i$, thus raising N_{clu}. However, $\mathcal{L}_{CE}$ requires identical dimensions and if we vary N_{clu}, we no longer have suitable target values available for training the DNNQ.

In order to use $\hat{y}_i$ for a variable output layer size m_i, i.e. $N_K \neq N_{clu}$, we introduce a novel training method: First, we create the joint probability $P_b(Y, M)$ of the ground-truth labels $\hat{y}_i$ and the DNNQ outputs m_i employing the input features x_i in every mini-batch. Then, we condition on the DNNQ output

$$P_b(Y|M) = P(\hat{y}_{b,k}|m_{b,j}) \approx \frac{\varepsilon + \sum_{i=1}^{N_b} \delta(\hat{y}_i, k)m_i^j}{\varepsilon N_{clu} + \sum_{i=1}^{N_b} m_i^j} \quad \forall 1 \leq j \leq N_{clu}, \forall 1 \leq k \leq N_K, \tag{7}$$

where ε is a small constant and $P_b(Y|M) \in \mathbb{R}^{N_K \times N_{clu}}$. Note that dimensions can be unequal, thus, $N_K \neq N_{clu}$. The aforementioned theory has similarities to [13]. However, instead of creating $P(Y|M)$ by using the entire dataset, we take mini-batches with a sufficient batch size to approximate $P_b(Y|M) \approx P(Y|M)$. Then, we use $P_b(Y|M)$ and the output m_i of the DNNQ to obtain

$$m_{tra,i} = P_b(Y|M)m_i \quad \forall 1 \leq i \leq N_b, \tag{8}$$

with $m_{tra,i}$ denoting the transformed outputs which are mapped from dimension N_{clu} to dimension N_K. Now, we are able to calculate $\mathcal{L}_{CE}(m_{tra,i}; \hat{y}_i)$ for each sample ensuring equal dimensions. In that way, we can train a DNNQ with arbitrary output layer size N_{clu} using fixed ground-truth labels y_i.

During training, the DNNQ reduces $\mathcal{L}_{CE}(m_{tra,i}; \hat{y}_i)$ progressively. Since $P_b(Y|M)$ only maps the output $m_i \in \mathbb{R}^{N_{clu}}$ to $m_{tra,i} \in \mathbb{R}^{N_K}$, we are actually reducing the cross entropy between m_i and $\hat{y}_i$ on frame-level. By doing so, we implicitly maximizing the mutual information $I(Y; M)$ by minimize $\mathcal{L}_{CE}(m_{tra,i}; \hat{y}_i)$.

2.2 Discrete Hidden Markov Model Training

For the time-variant model component we apply a DHMM. The main difference between a normal HMM and a DHMM is the the emission probability b_{s_k}

$$b_{s_k} = P(x|s_k), \tag{9}$$

where s_k represents a state in a DHMM/HMM and $p(\boldsymbol{x}|s_k)$ is the posterior modeled by a GMM or DNN. In our approach, the emission probability $b_{s_k}(\hat{m}_j)$ is a histogram, which is learned during Viterbi training of the DHMM. The histograms for every state s_k are created via maximum likelihood (ML)

$$b_{s_k}(\hat{m}_j)^{\text{ML}} = \frac{\sum_{i=1}^{N} \delta(\widetilde{s}_i, s_k)\delta(\hat{m}_i, j)}{\sum_{i=1}^{N} \delta(\widetilde{s}_i, s_k)} \quad \forall\, 1 \le k \le N_K, \forall\, 1 \le j \le N_{\text{clu}}. \tag{10}$$

Here, $\widetilde{s}_i$ is the state sequence created by a Viterbi alignment. Depending on the number of states N_K in the DHMM we receive N_K histograms with N_{clu} bins corresponding to the occurring labels. These labels are created by the aforementioned DNNQ.

3   Experimental Setup

All our experiments are based on the public TEDLIUMv2 [15] dataset. The dataset is split into three subsets: train, test and dev, with the train set containing 207 h of audio data. Besides training the DNNQ in tensorflow [1], we use kaldi [9] to prepare the dataset and decode the final model for the evaluation.

First, we extract 12-dimensional MFCCs and the log-energy for every 25 ms signal frame, applying a cepstral mean normalization and adding delta and delta-delta features. Then, we train a HMM-GMM by maximum likelihood to receive basic state alignments for every utterance in the dataset. Next, we cluster the states to form a triphone model. We take the resulting model and perform a forced-alignment on the entire dataset to retrieve state-based labels for the DNNQ training. Next, we create our network architecture as depicted in Fig. 1. The network consists of four fully-connected layers with 512 neurons and ReLU activations followed by a batch normalization [4] layer, respectively. After the fourth batch normalization layer we add a dropout [16] layer for regularization. Besides dropout, we regularize all the weights of the network with L2-Regularization scaled with 10^{-8}. The latter regularization reduces network complexity and improves overall generalization. An subsequent fully-connected layer with *sigmoid* activations and a scaling layer form the output layer. The output layer consists of N_{clu} neurons representing the number of clusters N_{clu}. The scaling layer as mentioned in Eq. 2 forces the DNNQ to produce spiky outputs, which are then fed into the *softmax* function. By adjusting the T_{sca} the networks produce smoother or spikier outputs. We received prime results without numerical instabilities with $T_{\text{sca}} = 15.0$. In summary, the network consists of 1.4 M trainable parameters. We optimize the DNNQ with the Adam optimizer [6]. We begin the training with a learning rate of 0.01. Depending on the experiment, we lower the learning rate after N_{epo} epochs if there is no performance gain on validation set indicating that the mutual information is not increasing further.

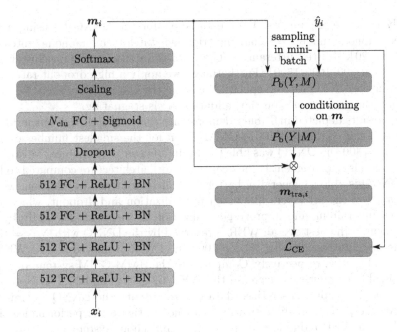

Fig. 1. The architecture of the DNNQ with fully-connected (FC) and batch normalization (BN) layers. We sample $P_b(Y|M)$ in the current mini-batch and transform the output m_i to $m_{b,\text{tra}}$ for calculating the $\mathcal{L}_{\text{CE}}$.

During our frame-wise cross entropy training, we sample $P_b(Y|M)$ in each mini-batch and create $P_b(Y|M)$ with $\varepsilon = 0.01$ by applying Eq. 7. In order to obtain a representative statistic $P_b(Y|M)$ we set the mini-batch size to $N_b = 15\,000$ which works well in all our experiments. Then, we perform the label mapping using Eq. 8. Instead of applying one-hot-encoded labels, we take smoothed labels [17] with a smoothing factor of 0.1 providing a faster and more stable training.

After training the DNNQ, we decode on the test set. For creating the lattices of the test data, we take a lattice beam size of 6.0 and an acoustic scale of 0.25. The beam decoder applies a beam size of 13.0 to find the ideal sequence through the decoding graph. We use the small version of the 4-gram language model, which is already provided for the dataset.

4   Results

4.1   Number of Clusters

We evaluate our approach in two different experiments. Firstly, we train a HMM-GMM on monophone states. Instead of using the entire training set, we take the 20 k shortest utterances in the training set. Short utterances contain only a few words and by performing a maximum likelihood training, we obtain already accurate alignments. We create labels for the DNNQ by using a pre-trained triphone model. We map the triphone states to monophone states and select the 20 k shorted utterances. Then, we train the DNNQ on cluster sizes $N_{clu} \in \{400, 700, 1000, 1500\}$. Furthermore, we apply a high dropout rate of 0.5 and train the DNNQ for 100 epochs. We halve the learning rate every $N_{epo} = 6$ epochs if the performance on the validation set is stagnating.

The results depicted in Table 1 demonstrate that our approach outperformes a conventional continuous HMM-GMM. Even for the smallest number of clusters $N_{clu} = 400$ the DNNQ was able to obtain a better performance. Mostly, the reason for this improvement is the deeper network architecture compared to [14]. The DNNQ is able to generalize better using deeper layers. In addition, we are using state-of-the-art layers like batch normalization and dropout, which help to speed up training and improve generalization as we could also verify by our experiments. The best overall WER is returned by the DNNQ with $N_{clu} = 1000$. On the dev and test sets for $N_{clu} = 1000$ the DNNQ achieved a final WER of 44.5 % and 45.1 %, respectively. Compared to the HMM-GMM system, our approach is able to relatively decrease the WER by 17.9 % and 17.6 %. Note that even though we apply discretized data generated with the DNNQ to train the DHMM, the process of discretization does not mitigate the performance since we achieve a WER reduction compared to a continuous system.

4.2   Number of Spliced Frames

The second experiment examines the effect of splicing. We vary different numbers of neighboring frames. By setting $N_{spl} = 0$, we only use a single frame, thus a 39-dimensional input for the DNNQ. In other cases, we take a 117-dimensional (left and right frame) and 195-dimensional (2 left and 2 right frames) input, respectively. All splicing options are evaluated on triphone states. We train the continuous GMM and the discrete DNNQ system on the entire train set. Due to the small size of our DNNQ and the huge amount of training data, satisfying generalization performance can be achieved even without dropout. Moreover, we train for 50 epochs and halve the learning rate every $N_{epo} = 10$.

We observe similar results as in the first experiment. As illustrated in Table 3, the DNNQ returned a better WER, however, only for $N_{spl} = 1$ and $N_{spl} = 2$ we notice a slightly improvement compared to the HMM-GMM. The continuous model reached a WER of 28.2 % on the dev set and a WER of 27.7 % on the test set. In accordance with [12], our experiments support the increase in WER for higher N_{spl} in continuous systems as illustrated in Table 3. The parameter estimation of the GMMs becomes problematic since the dimension of the input feature is increased causing a significant growth of the parameters.

The DNNQ with $N_{spl} = 2$ achieves the best results with a WER of 27.1 % on the dev and 27.1 % on the test set. This corresponds to a relative decrease of 3.9 % and 2.2 % respectively. Despite the huge improvement of the DNNQ for monophone states, the performance gain is not directly transferable to triphone states. A reason for this could be the added context in the features itself since we

Table 1. WERs (%) for different number of cluster $N_{clu} \in \{400, 700, 1000, 1500\}$ taking the 20k shortest training set utterances.

Monophone states					GMM
	DNNQ				
N_{clu}	400	700	1000	1500	-
dev	52.0	45.8	**44.5**	45.8	54.2
test	52.2	46.9	**45.1**	47.0	54.7

Table 2. WERs (%) for $N_{clu} = 1000$ and $N_{spl} \in \{0, 1, 2\}$ taking the entire training set.

Monophone states		
DNNQ		
N_{spl} 0	1	2
dev 43.7	37.5	**36.2**
test 45.1	38.9	**37.2**

Table 3. WERs (%) for $N_{spl} \in \{0, 1, 2\}$ and $N_{clu} = 1000$ using the entire training set.

Triphone states						
	DNNQ			GMM		
N_{spl}	0	1	2	0	1	2
dev	30.5	**27.1**	**27.1**	28.2	35.2	45.9
test	31.7	28.1	**27.1**	27.7	36.3	48.0

splice adjacent frames together to a bigger more context-based frame. By doing so, the DNNQ is able to use context to improve the ability to assign an input feature to a specific cluster. Our assumption is supported by taking a closer look at the performance of the monophone states with spliced features in Table 2, in which we present the WER for varying N_{spl}. It is clear that the performance already improved by splicing adjacent frames as we added context information to the features. Hence, the expected gain by using context-dependent triphone states should be lower, which is affirmed by Table 3.

5   Conclusion

We revisited the idea of discrete ASR using a DNNQ and revealed that despite the loss of information due to discretization we can achieve a smaller WER compared to a continuous model. The novel way of training the DNNQ, more precisely training it with an arbitrary output layer size exploiting fixed ground-truth labels, allows us to easily scale the size of the DNNQ. Furthermore, we are able to integrate our model into future approaches. We are planning to investigate whether the DNNQ is able to support a classical vanilla DNN for ASR. We believe that the output of the DNNQ contains information which could be combined with the output of a classical vanilla DNN into a model fusing approach.

References

1. Abadi, M., et al.: Tensorflow: a system for large-scale machine learning. OSDI **16**, 265–283 (2016)
2. Bourlard, H.A., Morgan, N.: Connectionist Speech Recognition: A Hybrid Approach, vol. 247. Springer, New York (2012)
3. Carletta, J., et al.: The AMI meeting corpus: a pre-announcement. In: International Workshop on Machine Learning for Multimodal Interaction, pp. 28–39. Springer (2005). https://doi.org/10.1007/11677482_3
4. Ioffe, S., Szegedy, C.: Batch normalization: accelerating deep network training by reducing internal covariate shift. arXiv preprint arXiv:1502.03167 (2015)
5. Kanda, N., Fujita, Y., Nagamatsu, K.: Lattice-free state-level minimum Bayes risk training of acoustic models. In: Proceedings of the INTERSPEECH (2018)
6. Kingma, D.P., Ba, J.: Adam: a method for stochastic optimization. arXiv preprint arXiv:1412.6980 (2014)
7. Neukirchen, C., Rigoll, G.: Advanced training methods and new network topologies for hybrid MMI-connectionist/HMM speech recognition systems. In: 1997 IEEE International Conference on Acoustics, Speech, and Signal Processing, vol. 4, pp. 3257–3260. IEEE (1997)
8. Paul, D.B., Baker, J.M.: The design for the wall street journal-based CSR corpus. In: Proceedings of the Workshop on Speech and Natural Language, pp. 357–362. Association for Computational Linguistics (1992)
9. Povey, D., et al.: The Kaldi speech recognition toolkit. In: IEEE 2011 Workshop on Automatic Speech Recognition and Understanding. No. EPFL-CONF-192584. IEEE Signal Processing Society (2011)
10. Povey, D., et al.: Purely sequence-trained neural networks for ASR based on lattice-free MMI. In: INTERSPEECH, pp. 2751–2755 (2016)
11. Price, P., Fisher, W.M., Bernstein, J., Pallett, D.S.: The DARPA 1000-word resource management database for continuous speech recognition. In: 1988 International Conference on Acoustics, Speech, and Signal Processing, pp. 651–654. IEEE (1988)
12. Rath, S.P., Povey, D., Veselý, K., Cernocký, J.: Improved feature processing for deep neural networks. In: INTERSPEECH, pp. 109–113 (2013)
13. Rigoll, G., Neukirchen, C., Rottland, J.: A new hybrid system based on MMI-neural networks for the RM speech recognition task. In: 1996 IEEE International Conference on Acoustics, Speech, and Signal Processing, vol. 2, pp. 865–868. IEEE (1996)
14. Rottland, J., Neukirchen, C., Willett, D., Rigoll, G.: Large vocabulary speech recognition with context dependent MMI-connectionist/HMM systems using the WSJ database. In: Fifth European Conference on Speech Communication and Technology (1997)
15. Rousseau, A., Deléglise, P., Esteve, Y.: Enhancing the TED-LIUM corpus with selected data for language modeling and more TED talks. In: LREC, pp. 3935–3939 (2014)
16. Srivastava, N., Hinton, G., Krizhevsky, A., Sutskever, I., Salakhutdinov, R.: Dropout: a simple way to prevent neural networks from overfitting. J. Mach. Learn. Res. **15**(1), 1929–1958 (2014)

17. Szegedy, C., Vanhoucke, V., Ioffe, S., Shlens, J., Wojna, Z.: Rethinking the inception architecture for computer vision. In: Proceedings of the IEEE Conference on Computer Vision and Pattern Recognition, pp. 2818–2826 (2016)
18. Veselý, K., Ghoshal, A., Burget, L., Povey, D.: Sequence-discriminative training of deep neural networks. In: INTERSPEECH, pp. 2345–2349 (2013)
19. Xiong, W., et al.: Achieving human parity in conversational speech recognition. arXiv preprint arXiv:1610.05256 (2016)

Speaking Style Based Apparent Personality Recognition

Jianguo Yu[1](✉) ⓘ, Konstantin Markov[1](✉) ⓘ, and Alexey Karpov[2](✉) ⓘ

[1] The University of Aizu, Fukushima, Japan
{d8182103,markov}@u-aizu.ac.jp
[2] SPIIRAS, St. Petersburg, Russia
karpov@iias.spb.su

Abstract. In this study, we investigate the problem of apparent personality recognition using person's voice, or more precisely, the way he or she speaks. Based on the style transfer idea in deep neural net image processing, we developed a system capable of speaking style extraction from recorded speech utterances, which then uses this information to estimate the so called Big-Five personality traits. The latent speaking style space is represented by the Gram matrix of convoluted acoustic features. We used a database with labels of personality traits perceived by other people (first impression). The experimental results showed that the proposed system achieves state of the art results for the task of audio based apparent personality recognition.

Keywords: Automatic Apparent Personality Recognition ·
First impression prediction · Speaking style representation ·
Computational Paralinguistics

1 Introduction and Related Works

The interest for Automatic Personality Recognition (APR) has rapidly risen in recent years as it has many important applications [28], such as products, jobs, or services recommendation [8,23], mental health diagnosis [6], computer-assisted tutoring systems [29], social network analysis [2], etc. But since it is very difficult to infer a person's true personality, many researchers started to pay attention to a less complex problem instead: Automatic Apparent Personality Recognition (AAPR), which is the personality perceived by other people (first impression). AAPR also has many practical applications since people constantly estimate other persons personality. For example, if the interviewer's first impression on the job candidate is bad, he has lower chance to get the job; The audiences' first impression on a YouTuber's voice also influences whether they continue watching or close the video.

1.1 The Big-Five Model

The personality, as well as apparent personality, are formally described by five dimensions known as the Big-Five personality traits [19]:

© Springer Nature Switzerland AG 2019
A. A. Salah et al. (Eds.): SPECOM 2019, LNAI 11658, pp. 540–548, 2019.
https://doi.org/10.1007/978-3-030-26061-3_55

- **EXT**raversion vs. Introversion (sociable, assertive, playful vs. aloof, reserved, shy).
- **NEU**roticism vs. Emotional stability (calm, unemotional vs. insecure, anxious).
- **AGR**eeableness vs. Disagreeable (friendly, cooperative vs. antagonistic, fault-finding).
- **CON**scientiousness vs. Unconscientious (self-disciplined, organized vs. inefficient, care-less).
- **OPE**ness to experience (intellectual, insightful vs. shallow, unimaginative).

For personality recognition, the true labels are usually obtained by self-assessment questionnaire [7], where people rate their own behavior with Likert scales [1]. While for the apparent personality recognition, the labels are obtained by other people's first impression [9].

1.2 Audio Based AAPR

The personality traits can be inferred based on many types of observations, such as text [17,18,30], audio [20,24], video [22,31], or any combination of them, each of which has its own applications, depending on the availability of observations in different situations. For example, the audio based AAPR is very useful for the producers who make education or explainer videos since the audiences' first impression on their voices can largely affect the trustiness and attractiveness of the videos.

The conventional methods of AAPR from audio typically use a large pool of potentially prosody features (e.g. Mel Frequency Cepstral Coefficients, pitch, energy, and their 1st/2nd order temporal derivatives) and "Interspeech 2012 Speaker Trait Challenge" [26] is the first, rigorous comparison of different approaches over the same data and using the same experimental protocol for audio based AAPR, where the performances of most approaches depend heavily on careful feature selection [3,13,21,25]. Many of those features are included in the open-source openSMILE tool [10] and can serve as baseline for audio based AAPR. For example, the winner in the ChaLearn 2017 Job Candidate Screening Competition also used the openSMILE feature configuration that served as challenge baseline in the INTERSPEECH 2013 Computational Paralinguistics Challenge, which is 6373-dimensional feature set and was found to be the most effective acoustic feature set among others for personality trait recognition [12]. In order to learn useful features automatically, deep learning based methods have also been proposed for audio based AAPR. The audio model baseline provided by the organizer is a variant of the original ResNet18 model [9], which was trained on random 3s crops of the audio data and tested on the entire audio data. However, since the general network architecture is not specifically designed for AAPR, it doesn't appear to clearly outperform the conventional methods.

1.3 Neural Style Transfer

The neural style transfer became popular after the paper [11], where the style representation of an image is described as the correlation between different filter responses given by the Gram matrix. The basic idea was developed to classify image style in work [4], where the VGG-19 network [27] trained on the ImageNet dataset was used to obtain filter responses at different layers whose Gram matrix is calculated and transformed into a style vector, which is then classified by an SVM (support vector machine) classifier.

But the characteristics of audio signals are different from those of the images, e.g. speech is a sequential signal while the image is a 3D-tensor, and the duration varies for different utterances. Moreover, the Gram matrix representing styles is usually calculated from pre-trained networks and might not hold the best features for the desired task. In this work, we propose a system that automatically captures speaking styles for apparent personality recognition.

2 System Description

The proposed system evaluates a speech signal and returns 6 scores for the 5 personality traits and an interview variable (whether a candidate will be invited for a job interview).

In our neural network, the Gram matrix is not calculated from any pre-trained networks. Everything is jointly learned from scratch. The overall architecture is illustrated in Fig. 1.

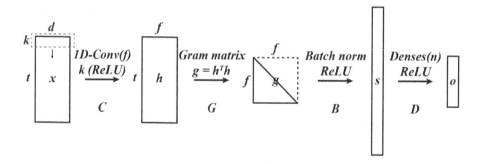

Fig. 1. Neural network architecture used in our system.

- **Input:** the input $x \in R^{t \times d}$ to our network contains d-dimensional speech features obtained at t timesteps.
- **Target:** the learning target $t \in R^6$ is a 6-dimensional vector (representing five traits and the interview variable), whose range is [0,1].
- **Convolutional layer:** the input x is first fed to a convolutional layer with f number of filters, $k \times d$ kernel size, 1 stride, and "same" zero padding, resulting in a feature map $h \in R^{t \times f}$. This is intended to automatically filter

out the silence and extract useful features for computing the speaking styles. A Rectified Linear Unit (ReLU) activation function is then applied to introduce non-linearity.

- **Gram layer:** Gram matrix g is then calculated from the feature map h, where $g = h^T h$. The lower (or upper) triangular matrix and diagonal are flattened into a vector $g* \in R^{(f+1)*f/2}$ for the next layer. A Gram layer actually represents the speaking styles as the correlations between different channels of the feature maps from the previous convolutional layer.
- **Batch norm layer:** since the norms of values in $g*$ are very big, a batch normalization layer with a ReLU activation function is added to solve this issue, resulting in a vector s that represents the speaking styles.
- **Fully connected layers:** the style vector s is then fed to one or more fully connected layers (dense layers) with ReLU activation function that further transforms s to higher level features.
- **Output layer:** finally, an output layer without activation function follows the dense layer(s) to produce an output o with 6 dimensions.
- **Loss function:** We tackle this task as a regression problem, so the mean squared error (MSE) is used as loss function.

3 Experiments and Results

3.1 Dataset

The dataset used in our experiments was the first impressions data set (CVPR 2017) [9], which comprises of 10,000 clips (with an average duration of 15s) extracted from more than 3,000 different YouTube high-definition (HD) videos of people facing a camera and speaking in English. People in videos have different gender, age, nationality, and ethnicity. Each clip is labeled for the Big Five personality traits scores along with an interview variable score that recommends whether a job candidate should be invited for an interview or not.

The train/val/test split used by the CVPR 2017 workshop participants is 6000/2000/2000 and we followed the same protocol (The numbers in parenthesis are the actual number of examples used in our experiments due to data corruption): train the networks on the trainset (5992), tune the networks using validation set (2000) to find the best hyper-parameters, with which the networks are retrained on both train and validation sets (7992), and finally test on the testset (1997).

For each of the five traits and the interview variable, the performance was evaluated by the Mean Absolute Error (MAE) subtracted from 1, which is formulated as follows:

$$E = 1 - \frac{\sum_{i=1}^{N} |target_i - predicted_i|}{N} \tag{1}$$

The score varies between 0 (worst case) and 1 (best case).

3.2   Low Level Feature Extraction

16kHz audio signals are extracted from the video clips and 13 dimensional Mel frequency cepstral coefficients (MFCCs) are computed every 10 ms over a 25 ms window, along with their first and second derivatives and used for our acoustic feature vector $x \in R^{1528 \times 39}$, where 1528 is the number of timesteps.

3.3   Overall Settings

In all the networks to be trained, every hidden dense layer has 512 nodes and is followed by a dropout layer with a drop rate of 40%. The kernel size of every convolutional layer is 3. Each network was trained by 300 epochs using Adam [16] update method with a learning rate of 1e-4 and a batch size of 16. We chose 300 epochs because the networks after 300 epochs perform fairly well on the validation set. The L2 regularization with a rate of 1e-4 is also added to the final loss, which is $10^{-4} \sum (\|\theta\|^2)/2$ and θ is the weights vector of a layer.

3.4   Our Baseline

In order to verify whether the performance improvement is provided by the speaking styles captured by the Gram matrix, we also trained networks without it. We tried recurrent networks with GRU (Gated Recurrent Unit) cell [5] and found they are not as good as convolutional networks for this task. The networks with max pooling layer or more than one convolutional layers didn't show improvement either. We found the best network architecture without Gram layer is the network with one 1D-convolutional layer, one average pooling layer over all timesteps, one dense layer, and the output layer.

3.5   Results and Discussion

The experimental results of testset in terms of 1-MAE are summarized in Table 1. The column "System" denotes different DNN configurations. Thus, C(32) stands for a convolutional layer with 32 filters, P - an average pooling layer over all timesteps, B - a batch normalization layer with ReLU activation and D - a dense layer (2D means 2 consecutive dense layers).

Because it is hard to keep the numbers of parameters in the baseline and proposed architectures the same, we tried many hyper-parameter combinations and found that C(32)+P+2D was the best one among architectures without speaking styles. From the results, we can see that batch normalization layer didn't show any improvement in these cases and could not outperform the ResNet18. However, when the Gram layer along with a batch normalization layer is used, all configurations shows significant performance increase with the C(128)+G+B+2D achieving the best audio based AAPR results.

Table 2 shows the Big-Five traits and the interview score classification results. The ground truth labels and the system predictions were binarized based on the training set mean scores. If a given score is above the corresponding mean, the label or the prediction is considered positive, otherwise - negative. The accuracy results also show that our proposed architecture brings significant improvements for both the personality traits and interview variable.

We also noticed that the Gram layer cannot be jointly trained without a batch normalization layer (e.g. C(32)+G+D didn't converge). The reason might be that the values of the Gram matrix are changing dramatically for each batch when the Gram matrix is not calculated from the pre-trained (fixed) convolutional layer, but from a convolutional layer that is also being trained.

Table 1. 1 − *MAE* results. OPE: openness to experience. CON: conscientiousness. EXT: extroversion. AGR: agreeableness. NEU: (non-)neuroticism. Inter: interview invite variable. Ave: the average score of 5 traits (interview variable is not included).

System	Ave	OPE	CON	EXT	AGR	NEU	Inter
Published Results							
ResNet18 [9]	0.9004	0.9024	0.8966	0.8994	0.9034	0.9000	0.9032
OS_IS13 [14]	0.8996	0.9022	0.8919	0.8980	0.9065	0.8991	0.8999
Models without Speaking Style							
C(256)+B+P+D	0.8996	0.9017	0.8981	0.8980	0.9034	0.8968	0.9013
C(32)+B+P+2D	0.8999	0.9021	0.8970	0.8984	0.9038	0.8981	0.9017
C(32)+P+2D	0.9004	0.9023	0.8964	0.9005	0.9047	0.8983	0.9020
C(128)+P+2D	0.8993	0.9027	0.8948	0.8983	0.9040	0.8967	0.9013
C(256)+P+2D	0.9001	0.9022	0.8967	0.8994	0.9043	0.8979	0.9022
Models with Speaking Style							
C(32)+G+B+D	0.9013	0.9025	0.9008	0.9004	0.9035	0.8993	0.9044
C(128)+G+B+D	0.9050	0.9055	0.9054	0.9040	0.9063	0.9038	0.9083
C(256)+G+B+D	0.9053	0.9058	0.9055	0.9049	0.9068	0.9037	0.9078
C(128)+G+B+2D	**0.9061**	0.9062	0.9072	0.9049	0.9073	0.9049	**0.9101**

Table 2. Big five traits and interview variable F1 score results for different systems.

System	Ave	OPE	CON	EXT	AGR	NEU	Inter
Published Results							
OS_IS13 [15]	67.93	-	-	-	-	-	69.25
Models without Speaking Style							
C(32)+P+2D	68.35	70.15	69.90	68.50	64.79	68.40	69.30
Models with Speaking Style							
C(128)+G+B+2D	**70.92**	70.45	74.16	70.50	66.44	73.05	**72.20**

4   Conclusion and Future Work

In this work, we developed a convolutional neural network with the Gram matrix that is intended to capture the speaking styles for audio based AAPR.

The proposed architecture can learn to capture the speaking styles end-to-end and the experimental results showed that the idea of style capturing also works in the audio domain. The correlation between different dimensions of a speech signal can help to infer the personality traits and interview variable and our proposed system C(128)+G+B+2D achieves the state of the art results for audio based AAPR: the average score of five traits is 0.9061 and the interview variable score is 0.9101.

In future work, we plan to apply this technique on other modalities (e.g. text, video) and merge it with generative adversarial networks (GANs) to generate the voice with particular personality traits scores.

References

1. Boyle, G., Helmes, E.: Methods of personality assessment. In: The Cambridge Handbook of Personality Psychology, p. 110. Cambridge University Press, Cambridge (2009)
2. Celli, F., Rossi, L.: The role of emotional stability in twitter conversations. In: Proceedings of the Workshop on Semantic Analysis in Social Media, pp. 10–17. Association for Computational Linguistics (2012)
3. Chastagnol, C., Devillers, L.: Personality traits detection using a parallelized modified SFFS algorithm. In: Thirteenth Annual Conference of the International Speech Communication Association (2012)
4. Chu, W.T., Wu, Y.L.: Image style classification based on learnt deep correlation features. IEEE Trans. Multimed. **20**(9), 2491–2502 (2018)
5. Chung, J., Gulcehre, C., Cho, K., Bengio, Y.: Empirical evaluation of gated recurrent neural networks on sequence modeling. arXiv preprint arXiv:1412.3555 (2014)
6. Cohen, A.S., Elvevåg, B.: Automated computerized analysis of speech in psychiatric disorders. Curr. Opin. Psychiatry **27**(3), 203 (2014)
7. Costa Jr., P.T., McCrae, R.R.: Domains and facets: hierarchical personality assessment using the revised NEO personality inventory. J. Pers. Assess. **64**(1), 21–50 (1995)
8. Denscombe, M.: The Good Research Guide: For Small-Scale Social Research Projects. McGraw-Hill Education, London (2014)
9. Escalante, H.J., et al.: Explaining first impressions: modeling, recognizing, and explaining apparent personality from videos. arXiv preprint arXiv:1802.00745 (2018)
10. Eyben, F., Wöllmer, M., Schuller, B.: Opensmile: the munich versatile and fast open-source audio feature extractor. In: Proceedings of the 18th ACM International Conference on Multimedia, pp. 1459–1462. ACM (2010)
11. Gatys, L.A., Ecker, A.S., Bethge, M.: A neural algorithm of artistic style. arXiv preprint arXiv:1508.06576 (2015)

12. Gürpinar, F., Kaya, H., Salah, A.A.: Multimodal fusion of audio, scene, and face features for first impression estimation. In: 2016 23rd International Conference on Pattern Recognition (ICPR), pp. 43–48. IEEE (2016)

13. Ivanov, A., Chen, X.: Modulation spectrum analysis for speaker personality trait recognition. In: Thirteenth Annual Conference of the International Speech Communication Association (2012)

14. Kaya, H., Gürpınar, F., Salah, A.A.: Multi-modal score fusion and decision trees for explainable automatic job candidate screening from video CVs. In: Proceedings of the IEEE Conference on Computer Vision and Pattern Recognition Workshops, pp. 1–9 (2017)

15. Kaya, H., Salah, A.A.: Multimodal personality trait analysis for explainable modeling of job interview decisions. In: Explainable and Interpretable Models in Computer Vision and Machine Learning, pp. 255–275. Springer, Cham (2018). https://doi.org/10.1007/978-3-319-98131-4

16. Kingma, D., Ba, J.: Adam: a method for stochastic optimization. arXiv preprint arXiv:1412.6980 (2014)

17. Mairesse, F., Walker, M.A., Mehl, M.R., Moore, R.K.: Using linguistic cues for the automatic recognition of personality in conversation and text. J. Artif. Intell. Res. 30, 457–500 (2007)

18. Majumder, N., Poria, S., Gelbukh, A., Cambria, E.: Deep learning-based document modeling for personality detection from text. IEEE Intell. Syst. 32(2), 74–79 (2017)

19. Matthews, G., Deary, I.J., Whiteman, M.C.: Personality Traits. Cambridge University Press, New York (2003)

20. Mohammadi, G., Vinciarelli, A.: Automatic personality perception: prediction of trait attribution based on prosodic features. IEEE Trans. Affect. Comput. 3(3), 273–284 (2012)

21. Montacié, C., Caraty, M.J.: Pitch and intonation contribution to speakers' traits classification. In: Thirteenth Annual Conference of the International Speech Communication Association (2012)

22. Pianesi, F., Mana, N., Cappelletti, A., Lepri, B., Zancanaro, M.: Multimodal recognition of personality traits in social interactions. In: Proceedings of the 10th International Conference on Multimodal Interfaces, pp. 53–60. ACM (2008)

23. Piwek, L., Ellis, D.A., Andrews, S., Joinson, A.: The rise of consumer health wearables: promises and barriers. PLoS Med. 13(2), e1001953 (2016)

24. Polzehl, T., Moller, S., Metze, F.: Automatically assessing personality from speech. In: 2010 IEEE Fourth International Conference on Semantic Computing, pp. 134–140. IEEE (2010)

25. Sanchez, M.H., Lawson, A., Vergyri, D., Bratt, H.: Multi-system fusion of extended context prosodic and cepstral features for paralinguistic speaker trait classification. In: Thirteenth Annual Conference of the International Speech Communication Association (2012)

26. Schuller, B., et al.: The interspeech 2012 speaker trait challenge. In: Thirteenth Annual Conference of the International Speech Communication Association (2012)

27. Simonyan, K., Zisserman, A.: Very deep convolutional networks for large-scale image recognition. arXiv preprint arXiv:1409.1556 (2014)

28. Vinciarelli, A., Mohammadi, G.: A survey of personality computing. IEEE Trans. Affect. Comput. 5(3), 273–291 (2014)

29. Vinciarelli, A., et al.: Bridging the gap between social animal and unsocial machine: a survey of social signal processing. IEEE Trans. Affect. Comput. **3**(1), 69–87 (2012)
30. Yu, J., Markov, K.: Deep learning based personality recognition from facebook status updates. In: 2017 IEEE 8th International Conference on Awareness Science and Technology (iCAST), pp. 383–387. IEEE (2017)
31. Zhang, C.L., Zhang, H., Wei, X.S., Wu, J.: Deep bimodal regression for apparent personality analysis. In: European Conference on Computer Vision, pp. 311–324. Springer (2016). https://doi.org/10.1007/978-3-319-49409-8_25

Diarization of the Language Consulting Center Telephone Calls

Zbyněk Zajíc(✉) , Josef V. Psutka , Lucie Zajícová , Luděk Müller ,
and Petr Salajka

Faculty of Applied Sciences, NTIS - New Technologies for the Information Society
and Department of Cybernetics, University of West Bohemia, Univerzitní 8,
306 14 Pilsen, Czech Republic
{zzajic,psutka_j,lskorkov,muller,salajka}@ntis.zcu.cz

Abstract. In this paper, we describe a diarization of the archive
data from the project "Access to a Linguistically Structured Database
of Enquiries from the Language Consulting Center". This project is
attempting to provide improved access to the large archives of the Czech
language of mainly telephone conversations collected continuously by
The Language Consulting Center. One part of this archives contains
mono recordings, where the data of the client and the language counsellor are mixed in one channel. In our proposed approach to a diarization,
we used the information about the identity of the language counsellor
acquired from the text transcription on the beginning of the conversation.
For the initial stage of the diarization, our system based on clustering
the x-vectors was adopted. The resegmentation step is used for refining
the boundaries of speaker changes by the pre-trained Gaussian mixture
model of the counsellor. Because of the uniqueness of our data, we compared our results with the Kaldi diarization as the baseline system.

Keywords: Diarization · x-vector · Automatic speech recognition ·
GMM

1 Introduction

The Language Consulting Center (LCC) of the Czech Language Institute of the
Academy of Sciences of the Czech Republic provides a unique language consul-
tancy service in the matters of the Czech language via a telephone line open to
public calls. These telephone recordings contain completely new language material which is the only source of advice for new language problems. The main goal
of the project "Access to a Linguistically Structured Database of Enquiries from
the Language Consulting Center" is to publish these unique data in the newly
created database. For this purpose, the Automatic Speech Recognizer (ASR)
and the language processing methods (like topic detection, keyword spotting,
etc.) are being designed to describe the speech data to allow their better accessi-
bility. These problems and the proposed solution was presented in our previous
paper [25].

© Springer Nature Switzerland AG 2019
A. A. Salah et al. (Eds.): SPECOM 2019, LNAI 11658, pp. 549–558, 2019.
https://doi.org/10.1007/978-3-030-26061-3_56

The telephone calls from the LCC are considered to be the primary source for the database. Before this project, the LCC has been recording data only on the analogue telephone line (8 kHz, μ-law resolution) stored only in mono - counsellor and client mixed in one channel. These data, almost 8k recordings, are very challenging for the automatic recognition and subsequent categorization because of their bad quality and containing the question and the answer mixed in one source. The diarization of these data can improve the ASR results using an adaptation of the acoustic and language model, also the topic identification (the previous paper [25] has shown the differences in using only an answer instead of all of the recording data to categorize the topic in the recordings). Recently, the new recording system was applied to store the queries called to LCC with better quality (8 kHz, 16 bit resolution) and with the separated channels. Nevertheless, the amount of the data and the uniqueness of the information in these archived mono recordings is not negligible. Therefore, we applied our method for the speaker diarization (SD) to separate the question of the LCC's client from the answer of the language counsellor.

The most common approach to the SD consists of the segmentation of an input signal, followed by the merging of the segments into the clusters corresponding to individual speakers [9,13,15]. Alternatively, the segmentation and the clustering step can be combined into a single iterative process [8,17]. In this paper, we investigate the state-of-the-art off-line SD approach based on the x-vector representation of the speech segments [3,14,19]. As our initial stage, we used our SD system [24,26] applied for the First and Second DIHARD Challenge [12]. Additionally, we are exploiting the known information about the identity of the language counsellor for the last stage of the diarization process - the resegmentation stage - by a similar way as in work [1,5].

2   Archive Data Description

The part of the LCC's audio archive contains the recorded data (2013–2016) only on the analogue telephone line (8 kHz, μ-law resolution) stored in one channel. For the purpose of the ASR and the topic detection, around 10% of mono data were manually transcribed by annotators. They have been instructed to focus on the precise transcription of the spoken words but not to be so punctual on the precise position of words in the case of overlapped speech, which incorporates some errors in the diarization point of view. Additionally, the role of the speaker (client vs. counsellor) was annotated, and the gender of each client was added to the transcription.

We have used these data for our domain trigram language model in our ASR. During the project, the stereo data with better audio quality were obtained and the ASR were trained primarily for these data. The results of our ASR can be found in [25].

These manually transcribed mono data were then force-aligned to find the precise time where the word or phone has been spoken and also which part of the data belongs to each speaker. These data were used for training the individual model of each counsellor and for testing of our diarization system.

The number of the recordings belonging to each counsellor is very unsettled: $\#rec = \{13, 14, 24, 24, 37, 52, 61, 243, 247\}$, two counsellors are dominating the whole archive. The histograms of the length of the individual telephone conversation and the length of constant speaker segments can be seen in Fig. 1 (note that the speaker change can occur also between speech and silence segments). The majority of the phone calls has only 200 s and less which is an extremely small amount of data. Contrariwise, the average length of the segments is a bit longer than in another telephone database CallHome [2] used for the diarization evaluation.

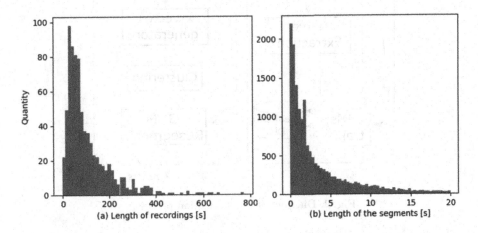

(a) Length of recordings [s]   (b) Length of the segments [s]

Fig. 1. The histograms of the length of the recording and the speaker segment.

3 Speaker Diarization

Our initial system for SD [23] is based on clustering the speech segments represented by x-vectors [18]. As the segmentation step, only the constant window segmentation instead of the segmentation based on the Speaker Change Detection (SCD) [6,21,22] was applied, mainly because of the advantage of x-vectors' ability to represent short segments and the application of the resegmentation step after the initial segmentation. The main contribution to our problem is the knowledge of the identity of one part of the conversation, the language counsellor. In contrast with the identity of the client (where there are potentially infinite number of the speakers), the list of the language counsellors answering the language queries is limited and known. A diagram of our proposed diarization system is shown in Fig. 2.

This section provides the description of the main steps of the diarization process. The speaker identification and the modified resegmentation are described in Sects. 4 and 5.

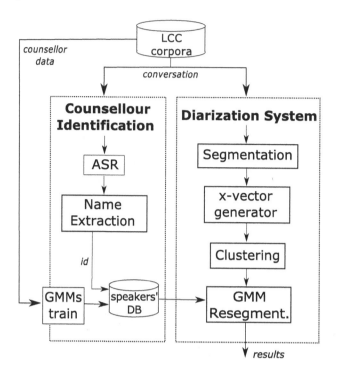

Fig. 2. Diagram of the diarization process.

3.1   Segmentation

As a feature vector, we used Linear Frequency Cepstral Coefficients (LFCCs), Hamming window of length 25 ms with 10 ms shift. There are 40 triangular filter banks linearly spread across the frequency spectrum, and 25 LFCCs are extracted. The resulted 50-dimensional feature vector also included delta coefficients. Cepstral Mean Normalization (CMN) was applied to compensate for channel variations.

The segmentation provides chunks of speech between important non-speech events. To exploit the ability of x-vectors to represent small amounts of data and to minimize the presence of more than one speaker in a segment and subsequently divide these segments into sub-segments, longer segments were split into intervals of max. 1.5 s, with 0.75 s overlaps.

3.2   Segment Description

The x-vectors were obtained using a Kaldi recipe[1] [14] for a diarization. A Time Delay Neural Network (TDNN) was used as an x-vector extractor, and x-vectors were extracted from the affine component of the second-to-last layer with dimension 128. As the whitening transformation, we used a conversation-dependent

---

[1] https://github.com/kaldi-asr/kaldi/tree/master/egs/callhome_diarization/v2.

Principal Component Analysis (PCA) [16] computed on the data in the current conversation to reduce the dimension of the x-vectors into 9.

3.3   Clustering

The telephone recordings generally contain only two parties, mainly two speakers. For the LCC's recordings, this applies almost without exceptions. For this reason, we have limited our clustering part only to the k-means method with the known number of clusters. As a distance measure, the cosine distance between two x-vectors was applied. We have also investigated the use of a Probabilistic Linear Discriminant Analysis (PLDA) model [7] for calculating the similarity of two x-vectors, but it did not bring any improvements in the final result.

3.4   Resegmentation

The final decision about the speaker boundaries in the conversation was refined via the resegmentation step. The previous decision had been based on the constant length segments, therefore the speaker's boundaries were not precisely selected. Also, the overlap of the windows can bring a situation where two consecutive x-vectors were assigned to different clusters, and the overlapped part was associated with two identities.

We trained the Gaussian Mixture Model (GMMs) over the feature vectors in the actual recording, one GMM for each speaker cluster. Then the whole conversation is redistributed frame by frame according to the likelihoods of the GMMs, filtered by a Gaussian window (length 75 ms with shift 50 ms) to smooth the peaks in the likelihoods. The number of GMM components depended on the amount of data in each cluster and ranged between 1 and 64 depending on the cluster data size.

4   Speaker Identification

The identity of the counsellor in the recording was obtained from the transcription (done by the annotators for sake of this paper). The whole list of counsellors employed by the LCC was known and they were instructed to introduce themselves to the phone with their name and organization (LCC). For this reason, the identification task was reduced to find one name from the list appearing at the beginning of the transcription. Then the relevant speaker model was selected to represent this counsellor and used for the modified resegmentation step.

4.1   Training the Speakers GMMs

For each counsellor, the general GMM (UBM - Univeral Background Model) with 1028 components was adapted on his/her data obtained from manually transcribed and force-aligned mono recordings. These recordings were divided into the counsellor and client data according to the transcription also. For the other side in the conversation, the LCC's client, we adapted the same general model into female and male client GMM. As we mentioned above, these transcriptions were not flawless, especially in the case of the overlapped speech (see Sect. 2).

5 Modified Resegmentation Step

Instead of creating the speaker model for the resegmentation only from the limited amount of the cluster data, we decided to use the known identity of the counsellor and the gender of the client to initialize the speaker models. From the initial step of the diarization, we got two clusters of the conversation data. At first, the counsellor GMM (known from the transcription) was assigned to the cluster according to the maximum likelihood criteria. The second cluster was considered as the client. The gender of this cluster was detected via maximum likelihood for two gender client GMMs. After this process, we got for each cluster its most appropriate model from the database. Both of these models were then adapted on the assigned cluster's data to receive the best representation of the speaker in this cluster using the actual and the archive data of him. The adaptation step on the end was there to compensate the time span of the recordings (the difference of the test and train data conditions for the individual counsellor and client) and to exploit the relatively precise initial step of the diarization.

6 Kaldi Diarization System

Because of the uniqueness of the data from the LCC, we have decided to use the Kaldi recipe for the diarization [14] as our baseline system for the comparison of the results. The input features are the same LFCCs as in our system, so is the segmentation and the x-vectors generation step (see in Sects. 3.1 and 3.2). The PLDA model to compute the similarity between the segments is used with the between-class dimension equal to the feature dimension. The x-vectors are whitened before the PLDA estimation by subtracting the mean and transforming by an Linear Discriminant Analysis (LDA) matrix. As a clustering method, the AHC with the stopping threshold set for two clusters is used.

7 Experiments

This section describes our experiments on 715 recordings, a small part of the mono data from the LCC which contains a manual transcription.

7.1 Training Data

The following LDC corpora were used as training data for general GMM, TDNN and PLDA: NIST 2004,05,06 (LDC2006S44, LDC2011S01, LDC2011S04, LDC2011S09, LDC2011S10, LDC2012S01, LDC2011S05, LDC2011S08),

SWBD2 Phase2,3 (LDC99S79, LDC2002S06) and SWBD Cellular1,2 (LDC2001S13, LDC2004S07). Additionally, data augmentation (additive noise, music, babble and reverberation) was applied to this data.

The list of counsellors consisted of 9 speakers (3 males and 6 females). For testing the influence of the modified segmentation step we used 4 or 10 first recordings for each counsellor, marked as a set A and B. Because of the small number of recordings for half of the counsellors, in the set B only 5 counsellors (2 males and 3 females) was left with enough recordings for training the speaker GMM. The rest of the available data was used for training the counsellor's identity GMM. The amount of the training data for the counsellors varies from 9 to 243 recordings in the set A and from 27 to 237 recordings in the set B respectively. The reason for creating two sets for testing was the inconsistent amount of available data for the individual counsellor - in the case A, one of the counsellor has only 9 recordings (cca 9 minutes) for training his speaker model. In the B set, there are only counsellors containing sufficiently enough data for training their GMM model (min. cca 25 minutes).

The second side of this train telephone data was used for representing the male and female client model (210 males and 505 females).

The hyper-parameters for the diarization process (length of the segmentation window, the components of the GMMs etc.) were tuned on a related task (CallHome corpus [2], DIHARD coprus [10,11]), so development set was not needed.

7.2   Results

The Table 1 presents the results in terms of Diarization Error Rate (DER) [4] on all archived mono recordings with the available transcription for our speaker diarization system with the classical resegmentation step (SD resegm.) compared to the baseline Kaldi system. These results are there for the overall comparison of our resegmentation approach on the bigger amount of data.

Table 1. DER [%] for our systems with resegmentation step (SD resegm.) and for Kaldi approach on all available data.

Set	Kaldi system	SD resegment.
All transcribed data	11.11	**10.09**

These results confirm expected differences (described in Sect. 2) in comparison with the results on the similar evaluation phone-call database Callhome [20]. Also, the gain of the resegmentation step is expected [23].

The Table 2 presents a comparison of our system for the speaker diarization with the classical resegmentation based on the data only from the actual conversation (SD resegment.) and our system with modified resegmentation step based on the identified counsellor and the client model (SD resegment. ID) on the test set A and B. For the comparison of the efficiency of our system, the Kaldi result is also presented in the Table 2.

Table 2. DER [%] for our systems (SD) and for Kaldi approach on different test set.

Set	Kaldi system	SD resegment.	SD resegment. ID
Test-set-A	8.92	8.26	**7.99**
Test-set-B	12.44	11.63	**11.33**

Our proposed approach for the modified resegmentation step improved the results of our baseline system for both of the test sets. The benefits of our approach on both test sets is comparable, the small amount of train data for some of the counsellors in test set A did not effect the result.

8   Discussion

The task of this paper was to propose a new method for the diarization with the known identity of one speaker in the two-party conversation. The discussion of the influence of the resegmentation step in the telephone conversation can be seen in the paper [23] and it is obvious from the significant amount of the speaker segments (see Fig. 1) less then 1.5 s set for proper representation of x-vector.

The character of the data and their imprecise transcription, the small average length of the recordings, as well as the time span where the counsellors data were recorded, allows us only a limited improvement of the standard approach with the resegmentation step using only the available data from the actual recording. As our future work, our plan is to use the additional data in a different way for making the information about the counsellor more precise. One possibility is the initialization of one of the k-means' cluster by the average x-vector from the archived counsellor's data to refine the clustering step of the diarization. Another possible approach can focus on the selection of the appropriate data from the database of the language counsellors instead of using all his/her data in the form of the pre-trained GMM model. This solution can solve the problem with a big variance in the data from one counsellor.

9   Conclusion

In this paper, we outlined the problem of the mono data stored in the archive of The Language Consulting Center and the need for their automatic process-ing. We presented the results for the diarization of these data. Because of the limited list of counsellors appearing as one party in the recordings, we proposed a new approach for the resegmentation step of the diarization initialized by the clustering of the segments in recordings. For the comparison, we applied a Kaldi recipe for the diarization. At addition, we discussed another exploitation of the data from the known identity of the language counsellor.

Acknowledgements. This research was supported by the Ministry of Culture Czech Republic, project No. DG16P02B009. Access to computing and storage facilities owned by parties and projects contributing to the National Grid Infrastructure MetaCentrum, provided under the programme "Projects of Large Research, Development, and Innovations Infrastructures" (CESNET LM2015042), is greatly appreciated.

References

1. Campr, P., Kunešová, M., Vaněk, J., Čech, J., Psutka, J.: Audio-video speaker diarization for unsupervised speaker and face model creation. In: Sojka, P., Horák, A., Kopeček, I., Pala, K. (eds.) TSD 2014. LNCS (LNAI), vol. 8655, pp. 465–472. Springer, Cham (2014). https://doi.org/10.1007/978-3-319-10816-2_56
2. Canavan, A., Graff, D., Zipperlen, G.: CALLHOME American English speech, LDC97S42. In: LDC Catalog. Linguistic Data Consortium, Philadelphia (1997)
3. Diez, M., et al.: BUT system for DIHARD speech diarization challenge 2018. In: Intespeech, Hyderabad, pp. 2798–2802 (2018)
4. Fiscus, J.G., Radde, N., Garofolo, J.S., Le, A., Ajot, J., Laprun, C.: The rich transcription 2006 spring meeting recognition evaluation. Mach. Learn. Multimodal Interact. **4299**, 309–322 (2006)
5. Geiger, J.T., Wallhoff, F., Rigoll, G.: {GMM}-{UBM} based open-setonline speaker diarization. In: Interspeech, Makuhari, pp. 2330–2333 (2010)
6. Hrúz, M., Zajíc, Z.: Convolutional neural network for speaker change detection in telephone speaker diarization system. In: ICASSP, pp. 4945–4949. IEEE, New Orleans (2017)
7. Ioffe, S.: Probabilistic linear discriminant analysis. Lect. Notes Comput. Sci. **3954**, 531–542 (2006)
8. Kenny, P., Reynolds, D., Castaldo, F.: Diarization of telephone conversations using factor analysis. IEEE J. Sel. Top. Sign. Proces. 4(6), 1059–1070 (2010)
9. Rouvier, M., Dupuy, G., Gay, P., Khoury, E., Merlin, T., Meignier, S.: An open-source state-of-the-art toolbox for broadcast news diarization. In: Interspeech, Lyon, pp. 1477–1481 (2013)
10. Ryant, N., et al.: DIHARD Corpus. Technical report, LDC (2018)
11. Ryant, N., Church, K., Cieri, C., Cristia, A., Du, J., Ganapathy, S., Liberman, M.: DIHARD Corpus. Technical report, LDC (2019)
12. Ryant, N., et al.: The second DIHARD diarization challenge: dataset, task, and baselines. In: INTERSPEECH, Gratz (2019)
13. Sell, G., Garcia-Romero, D.: Speaker diarization with PLDA I-vector scoring and unsupervised calibration. In: IEEE Spoken Language Technology Workshop, South Lake Tahoe, pp. 413–417 (2014)
14. Sell, G., et al.: Diarization is hard: some experiences and lessons learned for the JHU team in the inaugural DIHARD challenge. In: Interspeech, Hyderabad, pp. 2808–2812 (2018)
15. Senoussaoui, M., Kenny, P., Stafylakis, T., Dumouchel, P.: A study of the cosine distance-based mean shift for telephone speech diarization. Audio Speech Lang. Proces. **22**, 217–227 (2014)

16. Shum, S., Dehak, N., Chuangsuwanich, E., Reynolds, D., Glass, J.: Exploiting intra-conversation variability for speaker diarization. In: Interspeech, pp. 945–948. Florence (2011)
17. Shum, S.H., Dehak, N., Dehak, R., Glass, J.R.: Unsupervised methods for speaker diarization: an integrated and iterative approach. Audio Speech Lang. Proces. **21**(10), 2015–2028 (2013)
18. Snyder, D., Garcia-Romero, D., Sell, G., Povey, D., Khudanpur, S.: X-Vectors: robust DNN embeddings for speaker recognition. In: ICASSP, pp. 5329–5333 (2018)
19. Sun, L., et al.: Speaker diarization with enhancing speech for the first DIHARD challenge. In: Interspeech, pp. 2793–2797 (2018)
20. Wang, Q., Downey, C., Wan, L., Mansfield, P.A., Moreno, I.L.: Speaker diarization with LSTM. In: ICASSP, Calgary, pp. 5239–5243 (2017)
21. Wang, R., Gu, M., Li, L., Xu, M., Zheng, T.F.: Speaker segmentation using deep speaker vectors for fast speaker change scenarios. In: ICASSP, pp. 5420–5424. IEEE, New Orleans (2017)
22. Zajíc, Z., Hrúz, M., Müller, L.: Speaker diarization using convolutional neural network for statistics accumulation refinement. In: Interpeech, Stockholm, pp. 3562–3566 (2017)
23. Zajíc, Z., Kunešová, M., Radová, V.: Investigation of segmentation in i-vector based speaker diarization of telephone speech. In: Ronzhin, A., Potapova, R., Németh, G. (eds.) SPECOM 2016. LNCS (LNAI), vol. 9811, pp. 411–418. Springer, Cham (2016). https://doi.org/10.1007/978-3-319-43958-7_49
24. Zajíc, Z., Kunešová, M., Zelinka, J., Hrúz, M.: ZCU-NTIS speaker diarization system for the DIHARD 2018 challenge. In: Interspeech, Hyderabad, pp. 2788–2792 (2018)
25. Zajíc, Z., et al.: First insight into the processing of the language consulting center data. In: Karpov, A., Jokisch, O., Potapova, R. (eds.) SPECOM 2018. LNCS (LNAI), vol. 11096, pp. 778–787. Springer, Cham (2018). https://doi.org/10.1007/978-3-319-99579-3_79
26. Zajíc, Z., Kunešová, M., Hrúz, M., Vaněk, J.: UWB-NTIS speaker diarization system for the DIHARD II 2019 challenge. In: Submitted to Interspeech 2019. Gratz (2019). https://arxiv.org/abs/1905.11276

NN-Based Czech Sign Language Synthesis

Jan Zelinka[✉], Jakub Kanis, and Petr Salajka

Faculty of Applied Sciences, New Technologies for the Information Society, University of West Bohemia, Univerzitní 8, 306 14 Pilsen, Czech Republic
{zelinka,jkanis,salajka}@kky.zcu.cz

Abstract. This paper describes our Czech sign language synthesis that converts a Czech text into a series of skeletal poses. Our main goal is to avoid demanding handcrafted annotations of videos and to avoid a manual mapping between sign language glosses and skeletal poses. Thus, instead of solving these task separately, we join a model of an implicit neural-network-based translator and a model of the mapping between sign language glosses and we train both models together. For this purpose, we propose a simple differentiable operation that decomposes input symbols and it allows to produce a required series without any recurrent mechanism. We used The OpenPose toolbox to automatically extract skeletal poses and we designed a gradient-descend-based algorithm that converts a 2D skeleton model to a 3D skeleton model in order to fix misplaced and missing joints. Weather forecast parts of The daily news in Czech sign language were used to obtain our training and testing data. Our experiments demonstrate the benefit of the implicit translator and an ability of the designed sign language synthesis system to produce naturally formed skeletal poses.

Keywords: Sign language synthesis · 3D skeleton reconstruction · Implicit translation

1 Introduction

Our research and applications [7–10] that are focused on Czech sign language (CSE) lead us to design a CSE synthesis system converting a text form of spoken language into a series of skeletal poses. CSE differs from spoken Czech not only on a lexical level but Sign Language (SL) has also a radical different grammatical structure. An SL annotation of a video is a very expensive, slow and inaccurate process. Especially when some complex notation system such as Hamburg notation system is used. Furthermore, building a corpus of parallel texts in SL is an

This work was supported by the European Regional Development Fund under the project AI&Reasoning (reg. no. CZ.02.1.01/0.0/0.0/15 003/0000466). Access to computing and storage facilities owned by parties and projects contributing to the National Grid Infrastructure MetaCentrum provided under the programme "Projects of Large Research, Development, and Innovations Infrastructures" (CESNET LM2015042), is greatly appreciated.

© Springer Nature Switzerland AG 2019
A. A. Salah et al. (Eds.): SPECOM 2019, LNAI 11658, pp. 559–568, 2019.
https://doi.org/10.1007/978-3-030-26061-3_57

extensive complication when big data such as daily broadcasting is processed. Hence, we designed a method that does not rely on any explicit annotation of spoken language into SL.

We utilized a third party framework OpenPose for skeletal poses extraction. We extract not only arms but also hands because fingers positions are crucial in SL. Despite the fact that we used this state-of-the-art (sota) method, some errors occurred. Misplaced joints bring some noise to our ground true and missing joints make using of a skeletal pose even impossible. Thus, we designed a method that converts our 2D skeleton model into a 3D skeleton model and that takes advantage of some invariances such as bone lengths. These invariances allow interpolating all missing joints and giving more precision to obtained joints.

Even though we do not train any explicit translator, we use bidirectional GRU to provide an implicit translation. Besides the translation, a special transformation was designed to incorporate a repository-of-signs making into our training process. This transformation allows assigning a short series of skeletal poses to each input symbol. We see the main contribution of our work in our end-to-end synthesizer that consists of the implicit translator and the linear differentiable transformation and that utilizes Dynamic Time Warping (DTW) as a part of our loss function. The end-to-end synthesizer contains sequence-to-sequence model and translates a text form of spoken language into a geometric form of SL whilst only the text form and the geometric form is necessary for a training process.

In our experiments, we used weather forecast parts of Czech TV daily news in CSE. This TV news is available online in high definition quality and a performer occupies a substantial part of a picture.

2   Related Work

An SL synthesis is usually performed by a virtual avatar [1,11]. An approach described in [12] deals with the translation of the spoken language to the glosses by employing the sota sequence-to-sequence (seq2seq) Neural Machine Translation (NMT) approach based on an RNN with an attention mechanism. Subsequent direct generation of a video from the given glosses (constituted by skeletal poses extracted from training data using OpenPose framework) and basic speaker's pose using a method of direct image generation based on a convolutional image encoder are followed by a generative adversarial network. The main difference between our approach to SL synthesis and the approach presented in [12] lies in omitting all explicit SL translation or video annotation and we also did not split the SL synthesis into two sub-tasks solved separately. Furthermore, we add the finger joints that are not considered in [12].

Other work [2] covers the opposite direction of the translation from SL to the words. A video of SL is converted to spatial embeddings and then translated by the sota seq2seq NMT method to words either using glosses as an intermediate representation or without any intermediate representation. From [2] we differ in an investigation of the opposite direction of the translation between SL and spoken language and usage of skeletal poses instead of spatial embeddings for SL representation.

We used DTW in our loss function. Although DTW is differentiable, a gradient does not try to change the optimal path directly which can be seen as a disadvantage. There is another approach called soft-DTW that tries to remove this disadvantage [3].

We applied backpropagation to a 3D skeleton model directly. Another approach uses a special generative model which is uniform in the space of anatomically plausible 3D poses [5]. A complex deformation model application could lead to more accurate pose estimation [6] but these techniques are not primarily designed for missing parts interpolation and errors correction.

3   Skeleton Model Restoration

Examples of OpenPoses's results are shown in Fig. 1. Despite the fact that the OpenPoses framework extracts 2D skeleton model with high accuracy, some errors occur. Technically, misplaced joints can be used as a ground true but missing joints cannot. The missing joints must be found or the whole skeleton with a missing joint must be omitted. Because we do not want to cut our videos, we design an interpolation that finds the missing joints.

Fig. 1. Examples of OpenPose's outputs (bet in colors). In spite of high quality, some joints are missing or they are misplaced due to rapid movements or covered hands. (Color figure online)

An interpolation which uses a whole time-series usually finds some invariances to interpolate missing data and to correct obtained data. It is not easy to find such useful invariances in a 2D skeleton model but there are fortunately some obvious invariances in a 3D skeleton model such as bone lengths. Thus, we construct a 3D skeleton model with constant bone lengths from whole videos by means of fitting its 2D projection with 2D skeleton model. A role of a perspective is minimal in our video. Our 2D projection is simple omitting third coordinates.

Our technique creates a 3D skeleton model for each picture of a video and it is an iterative process. An initialization that we used works as follows: All missing joints are linearly interpolated from its neighborhood (in time). Because the maximal bone length in 2D space is a suitable bone length estimation for 3D space only when no errors occur, we estimate bone length as an average of the 2D lengths. When a bone lengths and 2D projection are known and MSE is a criterion of optimality, finding the optimal joint position in 3D space is a relatively simple task that could be solved analytically. The only problem is to choose between two possible solutions when a bone is too long. We chose the solution that corresponds to a more probable position (e.g. arms are situated in front of a torso etc.)

Naturally, the resultant 3D skeleton is only a suboptimal solution. Moreover, the bone lengths are only a heuristic estimation. Thus, we apply a backpropagation mechanism to correct bone lengths and joint positions in the initialization. We use two L2 regularizations. The first regularization minimizes trajectory lengths. The second regularization minimizes bone lengths. The first regularization makes movements more smooth and both regularizations prevent absurd bone lengths that unregularized MSE criterion produces.

The 3D skeletons extraction is designed only for missing joints interpolation and noised position correction and it is not ready to produce skeletons suitable for an avatar. Hence, we used only the 2D projections of the resultant 3D skeletons as our ground-true skeletons.

Because the speakers' heights are different and speakers do not always stay on the same spot, we scaled coordinates in the following way: We trained a positive weight for each video. A loss function was a distance between a coordinates variance along the time axis in a video and a global variance of coordinates computed from all videos.

4   Sign Language Synthesis

We used only a text form of the spoken language obtained from a spoken commentary. We do not have any parallel SL representation in any form except a video in the form of a series of 2D skeletal poses. These videos are not segmented, i.e. no sign and even no sentences boundaries are labeled. This is the reason why it is not possible to apply some standard or modern methods for translation. But some methods still could be used if cross-entropy or another criterion suitable for translation is replaced with MSE loss.

We computed that one word in a spoken commentary including Beginning of a Sentence (BoS) and end of a sentence (EoS) symbols corresponds on average to $N = 14$ skeletal poses. We designed a method that generates a series that is exactly N times longer than an input text. We chose MSE as our loss function. Naturally, generated series and a target series usually have different length and they are probably not synchronized even if they have the same length. That is the reason why we incorporated DTW-based synchronization into our loss function. The loss is computed in the following way:

$$loss(y, tar) = \frac{1}{n_{DTW}} \sum_{k=1}^{n_{DTW}} \|y(i_1(k)) - tar(i_2(k))\|^2, \tag{1}$$

where $i_1(k)$ and $i_2(k)$ are the first and the second coordinates of the optimal path obtained applying DTW and n_{DTW} is a length of the path. The used distance in DTW was the same Euclidean distance used in our loss. This loss is differentiable and it could be used in gradient propagation.

Our 2D skeleton model has 50 joints. We do not train our SL synthesis to produce 100 coordinates of the joints because accurate mutual positions of limbs are much more important than accurate absolute positions. We, therefore, train the synthesis to produce vectors that represent the 49 limbs. The output of the synthesis has 98 elements. Figure 4 shows that these vectors produce a naturally looking skeleton model.

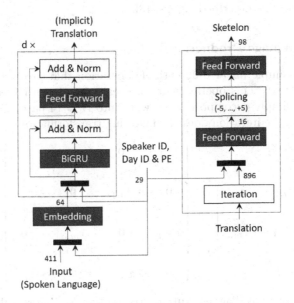

Fig. 2. A structure of the proposed implicit translator (left) and a structure of the designed SL production model (right).

4.1 Implicit Sign Language Translation

We do not explicitly train a complex translator but we train a system with a simplified structure that provides an implicit translation. The simplification lies in omitting the usual encoder-decoder passage and translating directly into a sentence with the same length. An SL differs from a spoken language not only on the lexical level but it has also different grammatical structure. Hence, a word-by-word translation is unusable. Our system translates words with their contexts using usual bidirectional GRU layers.

We add a speaker ID to each word because not only skeleton proportions and signs but also speaking manners and even grammar could be idiosyncratic. There is usually used the word "tomorrow" in a spoken commentary and there is a name of a day such as "on Monday" in CSE. Thus we add a day ID as well. The last added information is a positional encoding (PE) that helps distinguish between the same words on different positions.

After a usual embedding layer, several blocks are applied. Each block consists of one usual bidirectional GRU layer [4] with skip connection and layer normalization and one feed-forward network with skip connection and layer normalization. The feed-forward networks consist of one hidden layer with ReLU activation function and a dropout layer and one linear output layer. The speaker ID, the day ID and the PE are concatenated with an input of each block. The described model structure is shown on the left side of Fig. 2. The structure is similar to a structure described e.g. in [13].

4.2   Sign Language Production

We designed a simple linear differentiable operation that produces a sequence from an input text. This operation iterates each input word (vector x_i) in a special way. It simply decomposes each word into $N = 14$ parts and joins these parts. Formally, the iteration does the following transformation:

$$
\begin{bmatrix} x_{1,1} & \cdots & x_{1,n} \\ \vdots & \ddots & \vdots \\ x_{m,1} & \cdots & x_{m,n} \end{bmatrix} \mapsto \begin{bmatrix} x_{1,1} & \cdots & 0 & x_{1,n} & \cdots & 0 \\ \vdots & \ddots & \vdots & \cdots & \vdots & \ddots & \vdots \\ 0 & \cdots & x_{1,1} & 0 & \cdots & x_{1,n} \\ \vdots & & \vdots & & \ddots & & \vdots \\ x_{m,1} & \cdots & 0 & x_{m,n} & \cdots & 0 \\ \vdots & \ddots & \vdots & \cdots & \vdots & \ddots & \vdots \\ 0 & \cdots & x_{m,1} & 0 & \cdots & x_{m,n} \end{bmatrix}, \tag{2}
$$

where the size of each diagonal sub-matrix is $N \times N$. Figure 3 illustrates the role of this operation. In a case of classical one-hot coding and a trainable linear transformation following the iteration, this model is a trainable building of an SL repository. This transformation avoids any recurrent mechanism and this facilitates the usual training process.

The obvious disadvantage of this approach are fixed and equal sign lengths. But the implicit translation can split a longer sign into two or more symbols if it is properly trained. Another disadvantage is that a skeleton might not respect its context. To prevent unpleasant cuts in a resultant skeleton series, we add splicing operation and one additional linear transform. Because heights of speakers were not normalized completely, speakers have different proportion and signs are always a little bit distinctive, we add the speaker ID and another statistic as well as in the case of the embedding layer and the implicit translation. The complete structure of the described model is shown on the right side of Fig. 2.

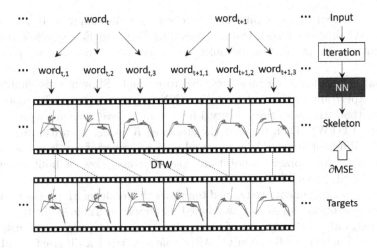

Fig. 3. An illustration of the iterating input words for $N = 3$ (we used $N = 14$).

5   Experiments and Results

We utilized an internet archive of The Czech TV daily news in CSE[1]. We focused only on weather forecasts. Our corpus consists of 947 videos (from September 2015 to July 2018) of forecast in CSE performed by five different CSE speakers. Videos contain 569,089 frames and the spoken commentaries contain 40,877 words. Due to a very small dataset, we tested ten different training sets (875 videos), development sets (36 videos), and test sets (36 videos). We transcribed days of the week of broadcasting and speaker's IDs manually from credits.

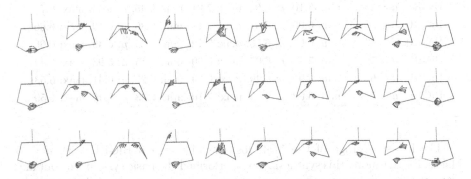

Fig. 4. Examples of generated skeletal poses: the first line contains target skeletons, the second Text Only synthesizer ($d = 0$), the third the best synthesizer with BiGRU-based implicit translator ($d = 5$).

---

[1] https://www.ceskatelevize.cz/ivysilani.

All Czech texts were lemmatized to decrease redundancy. Our vocabulary contains 411 different Czech lemmas including BoS and EoS symbols that are important for SL production because they correspond to a resting pose (see Fig. 4).

In our experiments, we measure MSE to evaluate SL synthesis quality. We have no expert annotation but we train a NN to produce "oracle" annotations. In our method, the NN selects every 14th vector on average (not equidistantly due to used DTW). Then we used the standard K-means algorithm to make a number of different selected vectors equal to the number of words in the spoken commentary. These oracle annotations give us some view of limits that this approach to SL production has.

In the first experiment, we trained ten times the model of SL production from the oracle annotations (see a row labeled as Oracle in Table 1). In the second experiment, only the text form of the spoken commentary was used instead of the oracle annotation (Text Only). After that, we tried a different number of blocks of the implicit translator (see BiGRU from $d = 1$ to $d = 7$). Statistics of resultant MSEs are presented in Table 1. We also computed how many times a system was outperformed by another system on the same test sets. These numbers are in Table 2. Figure 4 shows examples of resultant skeletal poses.

Table 1. MSEs for investigated SL synthesis systems. Minimal (min), average (μ) and maximal (max) achieved MSE are recorded in the table.

Model	MSE - development test set	MSE - test set
Oracle	min: 4.66, μ: 5.06, max: 5.51	min: 4.89, μ: 5.05, max: 5.26
Text Only ($d = 0$)	min: 6.93, μ: 7.39, max: 8.01	min: 7.13, μ: 7.32, max: 7.53
BiGRU, $d = 1$	min: 6.17, μ: 6.69, max: 7.28	min: 6.54, μ: 6.63, max: 6.83
BiGRU, $d = 2$	min: 6.10, μ: 6.62, max: 7.21	min: 6.45, μ: 6.54, max: 6.73
BiGRU, $d = 3$	min: 6.05, μ: 6.57, max: 7.11	min: 6.36, μ: 6.49, max: 6.66
BiGRU, $d = 4$	min: 6.04, μ: 6.56, max: 7.12	min: 6.39, μ: 6.49, max: 6.66
BiGRU, $d = 5$	min: 5.83, μ: 6.07, max: 6.60	min: 5.75, μ: 5.93, max: 6.44
BiGRU, $d = 6$	min: 5.99, μ: 6.49, max: 6.99	min: 6.25, μ: 6.41, max: 6.53
BiGRU, $d = 7$	min: 6.02, μ: 6.55, max: 7.10	min: 6.33, μ: 6.46, max: 6.59

The lowest average of the MSE loss has the system BiGRU with $d = 5$ blocks. Furthermore, this synthesizer outperformed the basic system without any translator and even any other translator every single time naturally except the Oracle. The results show that the usage of the implicit translator is significantly beneficial, i.e. on average it reduces an error obtained without any translator to its 81% whilst usage of the Oracle reduces it to 69%. In our case, it is not beneficial to use a translator with more than five blocks. Because errors on training sets are still decreasing ($\mu = 5.52$ for $d = 5$, $\mu = 5.41$ for $d = 6$ and $\mu = 5.37$ for $d = 7$) we see the reason why more blocks (layers) is not beneficial in overfitting. Using some much larger corpus will probably allow much deeper and powerful models.

Table 2. This table contains numbers how many times a SL synthesis system S_2 was outperformed by a system S_1. Bidirectional GRUs were used as the implicit translator. The sums represent the overall evaluations (lower is better) of investigated synthesizers.

S_1 vs. S_2	$d = 0$	$d = 1$	$d = 2$	$d = 3$	$d = 4$	$d = 5$	$d = 6$	$d = 7$
$d = 0$	0	0	0	0	0	0	0	0
$d = 1$	10	0	0	0	0	0	0	0
$d = 2$	10	10	0	0	0	0	0	0
$d = 3$	10	10	10	0	2	0	0	0
$d = 4$	10	10	10	8	0	0	0	2
$d = 5$	10	10	10	10	10	0	10	10
$d = 6$	10	10	10	10	10	0	0	10
$d = 7$	10	10	10	10	8	0	0	0
Σ	70	60	50	38	30	0	10	22

6   Conclusion

This paper deals with CSE synthesis. We designed an SL synthesis that converts a text form of an utterance in spoken language into a series of 2D skeletal poses. We avoid manual annotations of videos containing SL because these annotations are too expensive and slow to potentially capitalize on big data such as daily news in SL or some daily shows with SL commentary. We designed a mapping between glosses and short sequences of skeletal poses and we incorporated this mapping into our training process instead of constructing or training this mapping separately. We also trained an implicit translator that together with the designed mapping allows accomplishing our main goal, i.e. to construct end-to-end SL synthesis system. We employed a third-party framework that extracts 2D skeletal poses and we designed a gradient-descend-based algorithm that converts a 2D skeleton model to a 3D skeleton model in order to fix misplaced or missing joints. Our corpus contains online available weather forecast in CSE. These forecasts were recorded between the years 2015 and 2018. Our experiments show the benefit of the implicit translator. Moreover, the experiments show the designed SL synthesis system ability to produce naturally formed skeletal poses.

References

1. Almeida, I., Coheur, L., Candeias, S.: Coupling natural language processing and animation synthesis in Portuguese sign language translation. In: Proceedings of the Fourth Workshop on Vision and Language, pp. 94–103. Association for Computational Linguistics, Lisbon (2015)
2. Camgoz, N.C., Hadfield, S., Koller, O., Ney, H., Bowden, R.: Neural sign language translation. In: IEEE Conference on Computer Vision and Pattern Recognition (CVPR) (2018)
3. Cuturi, M., Blondel, M.: Soft-DTW: a differentiable loss function for time-series. In: ICML (2017)
4. Dey, R., Salemt, F.M.: Gate-variants of gated recurrent unit (GRU) neural networks. In: 2017 IEEE 60th International Midwest Symposium on Circuits and Systems (MWSCAS), pp. 1597–1600 (2017)
5. Jahangiri, E., Yuille, A.L.: Generating multiple diverse hypotheses for human 3D pose consistent with 2D joint detections. In: 2017 IEEE International Conference on Computer Vision Workshops (ICCVW), pp. 805–814 (2017)
6. Joo, H., Simon, T., Sheikh, Y.: Total capture: a 3d deformation model for tracking faces, hands, and bodies. CoRR abs/1801.01615 (2018)
7. Kanis, J., Müller, L.: Advances in Czech - signed speech translation. In: 12th International Conference on Text, Speech and Dialogue, September 2009, pp. 48–55 (2009)
8. Kanis, J., Zahradil, J., Jurčíček, F., Müller, L.: Czech-sign speech corpus for semantic based machine translation. In: 9th International Conference on Text, Speech and Dialogue, Brno, September 2006, pp. 613–620 (2006)
9. Krňoul, Z., Kanis, J., Železný, M., Müller, L.: Czech text-to-sign speech synthesizer. In: 4th International Workshop on Machine Learning for Multimodal Interaction, Brno, June 2007, pp. 180–191 (2008)
10. Krňoul, Z., Železný, M., Müller, L., Kanis, J.: Training of coarticulation models using dominance functions and visual unit selection methods for audio-visual speech synthesis. In: 9th International Conference on Spoken Language Processing/INTERSPEECH 2006, Pittsburgh, PA, pp. 585–588. International Speech and Communication Association (2006)
11. Naert, L., Larboulette, C., Gibet, S.: Coarticulation analysis for sign language synthesis. In: Antona, M., Stephanidis, C. (eds.) Universal Access in Human-Computer Interaction. Designing Novel Interactions. pp. 55–75, Springer, Cham (2017)
12. Stoll, S., Camgöz, N.C., Hadfield, S., Bowden, R.: Sign language production using neural machine translation and generative adversarial networks. In: BMVC (2018)
13. Vaswani, A., et al.: Attention is all you need. In: Guyon, I., et al. (eds.) Advances in Neural Information Processing Systems 30, pp. 5998–6008. Curran Associates, Inc. (2017)

Re-evaluation of Words Used in Speech Audiometry

Aleksandar Živanović[1], Vlado Delić[2(✉)], Siniša Suzić[2],
Ivana Sokolovac[3], and Maja Marković[1]

[1] Faculty of Philosophy, University of Novi Sad, Novi Sad, Serbia
{aleksandar.zivanovic,majamarkovic}@ff.uns.ac.rs
[2] Faculty of Technical Sciences, University of Novi Sad, Novi Sad, Serbia
{vlado.delic,sinisa.suzic}@uns.ac.rs
[3] Faculty of Medicine, University of Novi Sad, Novi Sad, Serbia
ivana.sokolovac@mf.uns.ac.rs

Abstract. The aim of this paper is to identify the words which significantly increase or decrease recognition accuracy in speech audiometry at the Clinic for Ear, Throat and Nose Diseases in Novi Sad, Serbia. The subjects of this research were 66 patients diagnosed with multiple sclerosis, most of whom are hearing unimpaired. Words with the highest and the lowest percentage of recognition are explained from a linguistic point of view, taking into consideration their occurrence, existence of similar words, phonetic characteristics of sounds and phonological makeup of the words. The analysis suggests that minimal pairs are more likely to cause incorrect repetitions than words which do not have minimal pair neighbours (plosives are especially difficult in this respect, due to the feature of voicing and formant transitions of the following vowel). Our results also show that longer and more frequent words are easier for identification, as well as the words with rising accents.

Keywords: Speech perception · Speech audiometry · Linguistics · Serbian

1   Introduction

SPEECH audiometry is a fundamental tool of hearing ability assessment, i.e. of the ability of patients to perceive speech. The standardized tests for Serbian and related languages contain 16 groups of 10 pre-recorded words, uttered by a male speaker and reproduced at a specific intensity level. The subjects are first presented with a 10 word group at low intensity levels. With healthy (hearing unimpaired) subjects, the initial intensity levels are at 10 to 20 dB, while in the hearing impaired subjects the level depends on the thresholds obtained in the prior liminar tonal audiometric tests. The subsequent 10 word groups are tested at intensity levels increased by 5 dB, up to the level required for a 100% recognition score for a specific subject. One measurement with a 10 word group is expected to reveal recognition accuracy percentage at the given intensity level, and should not depend on the specific words used in the testing procedure.

© Springer Nature Switzerland AG 2019
A. A. Salah et al. (Eds.): SPECOM 2019, LNAI 11658, pp. 569–577, 2019.
https://doi.org/10.1007/978-3-030-26061-3_58

The goal of this study is to identify the words which significantly deviate from the average recognition measurements at a given intensity level, based on a number of speech audiometric tests conducted. Such words would make the testing procedure word-dependent at a certain intensity level, and should therefore be replaced by different words. In order to do so, such words need to be subject to perceptual analysis from the linguistic, acoustic and medical point of view. The ultimate objective of the research presented in this paper is to re-evaluate the testing corpus consisting of 16 groups of 10 words commonly used in speech audiometry tests in Serbia, and to propose a somewhat modified corpus.

This paper is organized in the following sections: Sect. 2 describes the methodology employed in the research; Sect. 3 deals with the identification of potentially inadequate testing words; Sect. 4 accounts for the observed difficulties related to the choice of words from the linguistic point of view. The concluding section sums up the findings and points to the lines of further research.

2 Methodology

2.1 Hypotheses

1. Some of the words used in speech audiometry in the standardized test for the Serbian language are more frequently incorrectly recognized by subjects regardless of their hearing ability at all intensity levels (difficult words). In contrast, some words are easier for recognition by all subjects at all intensity levels (easy words).
2. Both difficult and easy words can be explained from the linguistic point of view, taking into consideration their occurrence, existence of similar words, phonetic characteristics of sounds and phonological makeup of the words.

2.2 The Testing Tool

Words used for audiometric speech testing need to constitute balanced sets in terms of frequency, intensity and speech tempo. The sets of words used in speech audiometry at the Clinic for Ear, Throat and Nose Diseases (ENT Clinic) are the first four out of the eight sets proposed in [1]. They were subject to several modifications mainly due to the dialectal differences between the original ijekavian (Croatian) and the target ekavian dialect (Serbian). For example, the word *ljeto* was replaced by *leto*, *plaća* by *plata*, etc. The sets are grouped into columns A, B, C and D (while column E is not used at the ENT Clinic), each of which comprises 10 words. Each column contains 9 disyllabic and 1 monosyllabic words, as well as 9 words with consonantal beginning and 1 beginning in a vowel. The total number of words analyzed in this study is 160. The words were pre-recorded and read by a professional male reader according to the standards of speech audiometry.

2.3 Subjects

The subjects of this research were 66 patients (41 women and 25 men) diagnosed with multiple sclerosis, most of whom are hearing unimpaired. The age of the patients ranges from 20 to 57, with the mean age 39.1, st. dev. 9.4. The other results in the database of the ENT Clinic in Novi Sad were not taken into consideration for the purpose of this study, since they are related to the research of hearing impaired patients.

2.4 Procedure

The testing procedure involved three different contexts – the stimuli were presented through headphones to the left ear, to the right ear, and to both ears in free field. The total duration of the testing was 15–20 min. The subjects were asked to repeat the word they heard and their answers were noted as correct or incorrect by the examiner. The results were subsequently turned into binary data (correct answer – 1, incorrect answer – 0) and entered into Microsoft Excel. We then selected the words which were the most frequently incorrectly recognized at the intensity levels ranging from 25 to 40 dB and subjected them to the linguistic analysis. These levels were taken into consideration because persons with normal hearing are deemed to have high percentage of recognized words, i.e. to hear without any difficulty. The results of recognition at the lowest and the highest levels of intensity were excluded from the analysis, but were reported in [2].

3 Results

In this section, we report the results indicating which words have the highest and the lowest percentage of recognition within each group from A-I to D-IV across four different intensity levels (25–40 dB). The graph (Fig. 1) includes the words which have the highest and the lowest mean accuracy scores for the entire range. The former are represented in green and the latter in red; the length represents the extent to which these values increase or decrease the mean of each group.

As regards words which are perceived better than others, the most frequently occurring one in A-I is *gavran* ('raven'; 85%). On the other hand, the words with the lowest recognition accuracy in this group are *vi* ('you'; 13% – on average near 50% below the mean in A-I group) and *kosti* ('bones'; 41%).

In A-II *mirno* ('peacefully') and *lokva* ('pool') have high percentage of identification accuracy – 93%. The word *ide* ('goes'; 72%) has the lowest score in this group.

The word *lutka* ('doll') in the group A-III has 97% of correct responses and the word *pismo* ('letter') received 94% of recognition accuracy. There are two words which are identified less correctly than other words in this group: *plata* ('salary'; 69%) and *mi* ('we'; 72%).

The only word which is recognized by all the participants in A-IV is *seka* ('kid sister'). Another word which is recognized well in this group is *kriva* ('guilty'; 93%). The following words can be said to decrease the average percentage of recognition: *teta* ('auntie'; 43%) and *čelo* ('forehead'; 50%).

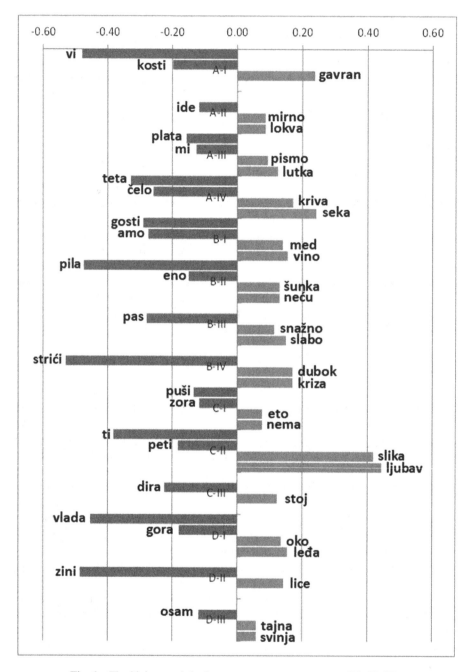

Fig. 1. The highest and the lowest mean accuracy scores (25–40 dB).

In B-I there are many words which were repeated çorrectly many times. The ones that we would like to single out are *vino* ('wine'; 98%) and *med* ('honey'; 97%). Words with the lowest scores are *gosti* ('guests'; 54%) and *amo* ('here'; 56%).

Words with the highest percent of recognition accuracy in B-II are: *neću* ('I don't want to'; 93%) and *šunka* ('ham'; 88%). The word *pila* ('drank'; 28%) has the lowest percent of recognition accuracy in this group. It is followed by *eno* ('there!'; 60%).

The most successfully recognized words in B-III are: *slabo* ('weakly'; 96%) and *snažno* ('strongly'; 93%). As regards poor recognition accuracy, *pas* ('pass'; 54%) differs from other words.

There are two words in B-IV which have 100% of correct repetitions – *dubok* ('deep') and *kriza* ('crisis'). The word *strići* ('shear'; 30%) has the lowest recognition accuracy – on average more than 50% below the mean in B-IV group.

In C-I *eto* ('look!') and *nema* ('doesn't have') have the highest number of correct responses - 91%. The patients made the largest number of errors while pronouncing *puši* ('smokes'; 70%) and *zora* ('dawn'; 72%).

Ljubav ('love'; 98%) and *slika* ('picture'; 95%) are the words which are most frequently correctly identified in C-II – on average more than 40% above the mean in this group. The two words have much lower scores than the other words: *ti* ('you'; 15%) and *peti* ('fifth'; 35%).

In C-III *stoj* ('halt!') is the only word with 100% of correct repetitions at all intensity levels. Based on the results, the word *dira* ('touches'; 65%) can be assessed as more difficult than the rest.

There are four words in C-IV which have 100% of correct repetitions - *medo* ('teddy bear'), *iskra* ('spark'), *toči!* ('pour!') and *nosi* ('carries'). In this group there is no word which stands out as more difficult for identification.

The words with the highest percent of recognition accuracy in D-I are *leđa* ('back'; 96%) and *oko* ('eye'; 94%). The words *vlada* ('government'; 35%) and *gora* ('mountain'; 63%) brought about the highest number of incorrect repetitions.

The word *lice* ('face'; 97%) can be assessed as the easiest word for recognition in D-II. The word *zini* ('gape!'; 34%) has a significantly lower number of correct identifications than the rest of the group.

In D-III there are two words with 100% of recognition accuracy at all intensity levels: *tajna* ('secret') and *svinja* ('pig'). The word with slightly worse recognition in this group is *osam* ('eight'; 82%).

There are many words with 100% of correct repetions in D-IV (and only two instances of incorrect identifications), but a sample is rather small – only five patients in total. For this reason, no word can be claimed to differentiate from others in this group.

4   Discussion

When examining the words with the lowest recognition rates, we analyzed them from various linguistic perspectives, taking into consideration the existence of similar words familiar to the subjects (minimal pairs) and the phonetic and phonological makeup of words.

Judging from the results, we presume that words which form minimal pairs are more likely to cause errors in speech audiometry than the stimuli which do not share so many simlarities with other words. This assumption is justified by the results of previous studies which show that similar words are recognized less accurately [3, 4]. In our research, the words *pila, gosti, teta, dira*, which would form potential minimal pairs with *bila, kosti, peta, bira* exhibit low recognition accuracy. Both the words in our corpus and their minimal pair neighbours belong to the register of everyday, familiar and highly frequent words. On the other hand, words which do not have minimal pair neighbours, such as *gavran, dućan, ptica* are recognized correctly by the majority of patients, which is why we can employ this concept as one of the explanations for different percentage of recognition accuracy.

The presence of a number of alternatives raises the question of the difference between hearing and intelligibility. As indicated by Padovan [1], some patients may produce a higher number of correct responses in speech audiometry despite unsatisfactory pure tone audiometry results (and vice versa). Lyregaard [5] highlights the importance of the purpose for which the test is constructed, the relevant distinction being between assessment of communication ability and diagnosis. For instance, if a person is not able to successfully discriminate between the fricatives /s/ and /ʃ/, an appropriate diagnostic test would include a large number of fricatives, whereas the one containing more phonemically balanced words would not prove useful for this purpose. Since some of the words used in speech audiometry at the ENT Clinic in Novi Sad may offer a wider choice of possible responses and thus be more difficult for recognition (from the viewpoint of assessment of communication ability), their use should be re-examined. In other words, in recognizing those words, the subjects may rely more heavily on their general linguistic knowledge than on the auditory input, and as a result, their responses may be random guesses based on equal probabilities, rather than reliable indicators of their hearing ability.

Upon a closer look at these words, it can be seen that all of them contain plosives, but the members of the first two potential minimal pairs (*pila*: *bila*; *kosti*: *gosti*), differ in voicing, whereas the second two differ in the place of articulation (*peta*: *teta*, *dira*: *bira*). In this section we analyze why these particulars features may be problematic in the recognition of word initial plosive sounds.

Firstly, the feature of voicing appears to be problematic for recognition with initial plosives, but not with fricatives. In contrast to words beginning with plosives, the word *seka* ('kid sister', A-IV) had 100% correct responses at all intensity levels observed, despite the existence of the potential minimal pair neighbour *zeka* ('bunny'). We presume that the feature of voicing in fricatives /s/ and /z/ is accompanied by other acoustic cues in Serbian, including the difference in mean noise segment duration [6]. With initial plosives, voicing feature is achieved by the difference in Voice Onset Time (VOT) alone, which, judging from our results, appears to be a much less salient auditory cue. However, no systematic research on the acoustics of word initial voiced and voiceless consonants and the impact of voicing on speech perception has been conducted for the Serbian language, so our findings may raise the importance of such studies.

As for the recognition of the place features in plosives, it is known that besides the energy distribution in the burst, one of the most important cues is the transition in the second formant (F2) of the following vowel [6]. The stylized spectrograms of F1 and F2 transitions in plosives with all places of articulation and before different vowels are represented in Fig. 2.

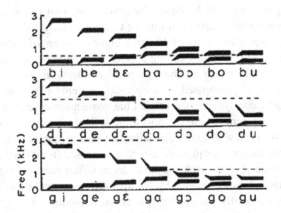

Fig. 2. F1 and F2 transitions with plosives, adapted from [7].

The patterns of F1–F2 transitions are the most similar between the bilabial and alveolar plosives when they are followed by the high front vowel /i/ and the closed front vowel /e/. This may well be the reason why our subjects had difficulty recognizing the words *peta* and *bira*, since without a context they are acoustically rather similar to equally probable words *teta* and *dira*.

With all this in mind, we conclude that the words like the ones described in the preceding section should be replaced by different words in future audiometric tests, with the goal of increasing the reliability and accuracy of the results in relation to the subjects' hearing ability.

Except for the phonemic content of the words tested, it is known that word length has an effect on the perception of words. Longer words are deemed to be easier for identification, probably due to a larger number of acoustic redundant cues [8]. Words with higher percentage of recognition accuracy in the corpus that we analyze are slightly longer (4.56 phonemes) than words with lower percentage of recognition accuracy (3.82 phonemes). Even though there is not a large difference in length between them, our results are in accordance with this tendency. This explanation can also be related to the concept of phonological neighbours – longer words are less likely to have more neighbours than shorter words. Length seems to be one of the main reasons for the poor recognition of monosyllables in the corpus, such as *vi*, *ti*, and *mi*. As personal pronouns, these words are certainly among the words with the highest frequency and degree of familiarity. However, all of them have potential minimal pair neighbours with a consonant in the final position (e.g. *vir*, *vid*, *mir*, *mit*, *tih*). Since the coda consonant in monosyllables is generally less acoustically salient, we presume that listeners do not rely on this position in word perception, but make choices based on probability instead.

Another phonological factor that has to be taken in consideration in audiometric studies for the Serbian language, is the fact that Serbian is a language with four pitch accents: long falling, long rising, short falling and short rising. In falling accents, F0 reaches its maximum on the tonic syllable, while in rising accents, the maximum is on the post-tonic syllable [9]. The results reported above allow us to hypothesize that the words with rising accents will be easier for perception than is the case with falling accents. Our results speak in favour of this idea. Namely, long rising accents are more numerous in the group of words which have the highest percent of recognition accuracy in the entire corpus (11) than long falling accents (6). On the other hand, long falling accents more frequently occur in the group of words with the lowest percent of recognition accuracy (7) compared to long rising accents (4). Due to the acoustic saliency of the post-tonic syllable, the listener has more auditory cues to rely on than in words with a falling accent, where the post-tonic syllable is rather weak. Our findings here are in contrast to [1], who found that falling accents generally increase the saliency of the initial consonants or consonant groups in the stressed (tonic) syllable. We believe that this difference may be the results of the dialectal differences in the pronunciation of words with falling and rising accents by the speakers who read them in our research. Standard Serbian, especially the variety spoken in Vojvodina, where the experiments were conducted, is peculiar for the acoustic saliency of the post-tonic syllable(s) in words with rising accents, which therefore may more strongly facilitate word recognition than the strength of the initial segment(s) in the tonic syllable. This finding should also be tested in future studies.

One last suggestion for the revision of sets of words used for audiometric studies is concerned with the overall familiarity with the words used in the test setup. Words which are archaic or less frequently used in everyday speech, such as *strići*, *amo*, *pâs*, are more difficult for identification than words whose meaning is familiar to all the participants. Having in mind that the corpus of words this research deals with was compiled in the 1950s, it is not surprising that some of them are unknown to the patients. The word *strići* is especially difficult in this respect and it may even be considered a pseudoword. The results presented in [10] and [11] suggest that low-frequency words are less intelligible than high-frequency words. In order to test subjects hearing ability, rather than their knowledge of vocabulary, words such as these should be avoided in future studies.

5   Conclusions

The aim of this study was to present and analyze the results of speech audiometry tests from a linguistic point of view. Both hypotheses are confirmed: there are words which have a significant impact on the results – some of them can be assessed as much easier for identification, others as much more difficult; both difficult and easy words can be explained from a linguistic perspective.

The most important characteristic of difficult words is the existence of phonologically similar words. Such words are prototypically used in the diagnostic test. On the other hand, the purpose of the test which the ENT Clinic employs is to assess patients' communication ability, which is why we propose that the words in question should be substituted with words which do not form minimal pairs.

The drawback of this research was the fact that the responses were noted only as correct or incorrect – the examiners did not write down the words which the patients pronounced. In order to be able to provide a more complete linguistic analysis, we would need to be acquainted with the nature of incorrect repetitions, which is something that we will bear in mind for future research.

Acknowledgements. The research was financed by the Serbian Ministry of Education, Science and Technological Development within the project Development of Dialogue Systems for Serbian and Other South Slavic Languages (TR32035) and by the Provincial Secretariat for Science and Technological Development of Vojvodina (114-451-2570/2016-01) within the project Central Audio Library of the University of Novi Sad.

References

1. Padovan, I.: Temelji kliničke audiometrije. Školska knjiga, Zagreb (1957)
2. Živanović, A., Suzić, S., Sokolovac, I., Delić, V.: Analiza grešaka u govornoj audiometriji. In: Proceedings of 26th TELFOR 2018, Belgrade, Serbia, pp. 643–646 (2018)
3. Luce, P.A., Pisoni, D.B.: Recognizing spoken words: the neighborhood activation model. Ear Hear. **19**(1), 1–36 (1998)
4. Ziegler, J.C., Muneaux, M., Grainger, J.: Neighborhood effects in auditory word recognition: phonological competition and orthographic facilitation. J. Mem. Lang. **48**(4), 779–793 (2003)
5. Lyregaard, P.: Chapter 2: towards a theory of speech audiometry tests. In: Martin, M. (ed.) Speech Audiometry, pp. 33–61. Whurr, London (1997)
6. Kent, R.D., Read, C.: The Acoustic Analysis of Speech. Singular Publisher Group, San Diego (1992)
7. Delattre, P.C., Liberman, A.M., Cooper, F.S.: Acoustic loci and transitional cues for consonants. J. Acoust. Soc. Am. **27**(4), 769–773 (1955)
8. Miller, G.A., Wiener, F.M., Stevens, S.S.: Transmission and reception of sounds under combat conditions. Summary Technical Report of Division 17, vol. 3. National Defense Research Council, Washington (1946)
9. Lehiste, I., Ivić, P.: Word and Sentence Prosody in Serbocroatian. MIT Press, Cambridge (1986)
10. Savin, H.B.: Word-frequency effect and errors in the perception of speech. J. Acoust. Soc. Am. **35**(2), 200–206 (1963)
11. Bell, T.S., Wilson, R.H.: Sentence recognition materials based on frequency of word use and lexical confusability. J. Am. Acad. Audiol. **12**(10), 514–522 (2001)

Author Index

Printed in the United States
By Bookmasters